Urban Economics

This textbook offers a rigorous, calculus-based presentation of the complexities of urban economics, which is suitable for students who are new to the subject. It focuses on structural details and explains the elements that make cities such highly productive entities, and also explores the mechanisms of labor productivity enhancement that are unique to cities.

Written with a focus on location theory, key topics include:

- how cities are arranged;
- housing prices;
- urban transportation;
- why some cities grow rapidly while others decline;
- how local cost of living adjusts to local wages;
- how suburbs function in relationship to the urban core;
- public finance.

This book will be essential reading for Urban Economics courses at both undergraduate and postgraduate levels.

John M. Hartwick is Professor of Economics at Queen's University, Canada.

Urban Economics

John M. Hartwick

Routledge
Taylor & Francis Group
LONDON AND NEW YORK

First published 2015
by Routledge
2 Park Square, Milton Park, Abingdon, Oxon OX14 4RN

and by Routledge
711 Third Avenue, New York, NY 10017

Routledge is an imprint of the Taylor & Francis Group, an informa business

British Library Cataloguing in Publication Data
A catalogue record for this book is available from the British Library

Library of Congress Cataloging in Publication Data
Hartwick, John M. Urban economics / John M. Hartwick.
pages cm
Includes bibliographical references and index.
1. Urban economics. I. Title.
HT321.H367 2015
330.9173'2–dc23 2014042053

ISBN: 978-0-7656-4617-0 (hbk)
ISBN: 978-1-138-88564-6 (pbk)
ISBN: 978-1-315-71809-5 (ebk)

Typeset in Times New Roman
by Sunrise Setting Ltd, Paignton, UK

Contents

Figures

Tables

Preface: economics and cities

In reflecting on persistent poverty in small, isolated communities in Kentucky, Lowrey (2014) observes: "Density means more workers to choose from, more potential customers, more spillover knowledge from nearby companies. As such cities punch above their weight, economically speaking. The 10 largest metro regions produced more than a third of the country's entire economic output in 2012." Urban economics strives to fill in details of these remarks. Why exactly are cities such productive "vehicles" for combining workers and capital? The analogy of the city as a vessel containing firms and households is helpful. Think of x firms and y households spread out somewhat randomly over the state of Texas. We would have an economy and we would have measurable outputs. Then consider the same x firms and y households within the confines of a city. Typically the firms and households yield more product when confined within "a city." Partly this is because transportation costs of inputs, products and labor are economized on by the "city form" but typically the capital and labor in the x firms and y households are simply more productive—there is more product per unit input when the inputs are placed in a city, in a dense efficient framework, than when they are spread out in low density arrangements. The city can be viewed as a valuable vessel for putting in the ingredients, firms and households, and getting extra "product."

In this book we pursue details of various mechanisms of labor productivity enhancement associated with cities. First, consider each person as a Ricardian "nation," with specific skills and engaged in trade with other individuals. This trading set-up will be more productive the less friction there is in trade as with, for example, trade across distance. Hence when individuals as traders are located close to one another there are more gains from trade and specialization (Chapter 6). Of course when individuals are close to one another, we are talking about villages, towns and cities: lower transportation costs, more gains from specialization and trade. Another process we dwell on involves gains to an individual with highly specialized skills being in a large community where her skills can be fully engaged rather than being in a small community where her skills are only partly engaged. A brain surgeon will have a steady flow of patients when she is practicing in a city and an intermittent flow when she is practicing in a small town. The well-known Helsley–Strange model captures this efficiency advantage of community largeness (Chapter 4). A different gain associated with a large city can accrue to an individual who faces uncertain spells of unemployment. When this person resides in a larger community rather than a smaller one, her chances of being taken up by another firm that is hiring when she faces a lay-off are higher in a larger city. We explore the details of this law of large numbers payoff to a worker in a larger community (Chapter 4). These are three processes of a worker's efficiency being higher when she is located in a larger community. We explore each of these arguments in detail in various chapters.

A different argument we emphasize is the tendency of activities with scale economies to head to larger communities where market size tends to be larger and thus more supportive of a larger scale of operation (Chapter 6). Related to this general argument is the argument that intermediate goods producers tend to locate near their buyers in order to be able to serve the buyers better and also to cut down on transportation costs. Larger places will then have more intermediate goods producers located within their borders than will smaller communities. The latter will tend to have their necessary intermediate goods produced "abroad" and transported in to the demander's local production place. We explore this scale-economy argument in detail. Why do the populations of cities continue to grow relative to the number of rural folk, the world over? For many centuries, informed observers would argue that cities were parasitical social appendages, essentially living off the farming sectors of nations. Today cities are seen as the engines of economic growth of nations. This thought drives our narrative and analysis in this book. Of course we recognize that cities can be excessively crowded and tend to be places where crime, noise and smog persist. We will reflect on these costs of urban living as well. Ludwig Mies van de Rohe's famous dictum "God is in the details" incorporated too much artistic license. Most architects consider themselves artists rather than engineers. The real thought is that when the details of an argument are right, the argument achieves a certain closure in our minds, an "ah-ha moment." This is the crux of academic activity. Fill in the details correctly and the general argument shines brightly. We also fill in details of the housing sector of an economy (Chapter 8), the transportation sector (Chapter 7) and local government finance and provision of services (Chapter 9).

If a person could put a group of economic models of households together with a group of economic models of firms, with the firms manned by persons from the households, plus say retail firms servicing the households, all appropriately linked together over space with transportation costs of some sort, the result would be an economic model of a city. There are some such models in the economics literature and we report on a few in this book but it is fair to say that to date there is no standard model out there. In contrast, economic models of a nation have been worked on for decades and we can make the case that there are a few standard versions. Cities are difficult to model in part because most of economics has been developed without the inclusion of space or geography. The famous Ricardian model of Portugal trading wine for English cloth takes no account of geography or even transportation costs. The trading nations must have area if grapes are being grown but are really treated as points, presumably with no distance separating them! When transportation costs are introduced into the basic Ricardian model, new interesting patterns of trade can emerge but textbook writers seldom investigate these matters. It would be nice to build up from standard models of households and firms and end up with a benchmark model of a city. We could then carry out policy simulations with the model—perturb tax rates, say, or the efficiency of labor—and attempt to discern ways to make actual cities better. "Cities better" is itself something of a loaded term. The world is full of politicians, planners and assorted experts focusing, generally full-time, on "making cities better." What criteria are they using? Who benefits from the implementation of policy x? There is urban economics and there is urban policy development and implementation. In an ideal world these subjects would overlap a good deal, but it is fair to say that in fact communication between planners in cities and economists interested in urban issues has been slight. Cities are complicated economic entities and the absence of a standard model has made dialogue between planners, professionals trained to think about urban issues and economists particularly difficult.

My teacher, Edwin S. Mills, could get animated, almost angry, in discussing the ways experts not trained in economics could set out policy prescriptions for improving a particular situation in a city. They were confident of their prescriptions. What is the criterion for improvement, he would ask? There is welfare economics and there are cost–benefit methods and procedures seldom appealed to in policy design or evaluation. He wanted policy design to be more systematic and the criteria of success or failure of a policy intervention to be clearer. He was asking a great deal because a city is a complicated economy. In 1967 Mills pushed forward with important new details of a monocentric city model. There is some validity to the claim that Mills was setting down the first complete model of an urban economy, a version of which we take up in Chapters 2 and 3. This is "the monocentric city" model, one in which all production activity occurs in the center of a disc, a point surrounded by households who commute each day to the production point. This may be a pretty complete and economically sound model of a city and Mills inserted some numbers to create a Baltimore on paper, but it is of course a "textbook" city, not close to a real pulsating Tokyo or Denver. There are important variants of his basic model, on which we also report in Chapters 3, 4 and 9. Mills followed up with a linear programming version of his model of a complete city and we report on this in Chapter 5. These studies of urban economics are important because decisions about the development of cities are being made every day and these decisions often have large impacts on the lives of residents of cities.

Roughly speaking, we set out an economics model of a city or an important aspect of a city in each of our first nine chapters. Sometimes we set out more than one model of certain phenomena. Our idea is to get at economics issues that connect with urban structure and functioning. We do not press forward to develop some sort of textbook model of a city, although this is a good goal to keep in mind while studying "urban economics." Nor do we end up with a checklist that will guide a policy-maker in making important decisions about improving matters in a city or aiding in its development. But this goal also is good to keep in mind. A keen student could do well to arrive at the end of an urban economics course with a checklist that could guide a policy-maker in, say, the planning department of a city.

One reason that urban economics is complicated economics is that there are ubiquitous tricky scale issues to keep track of. For example, similar types of workers typically register higher productivity in larger cities. Larger city-size or scale yields a productivity premium that is tricky to pin down. Larger cities typically have more expensive housing, by which we really mean higher average site rents per house. Average per unit land rent for a single-family home is higher in larger cities. The average commuting distance per household will be larger for a resident of a larger city. There are diverse scale economies in the public sector serving a larger city. Much consolidation of small municipalities into larger units with one new local government is generally motivated by this desire to take advantage of scale economies in, say, the delivery of fire protection services, garbage collection services or policing services. Government administration itself or public goods such as fire protection can be "shared" over many more rate-payers when the goods are being provided to a large city. Local government "bureaucracies" can often administer matters such as tax collection and infrastructure redevelopment at about the same cost for a large city as for a small one. On the other hand, many residents live with high costs of getting out into the country on a weekend when their home is part of a large city. Congestion and crowding are part of the average person's life when that person is living in a larger urban area. There are so-called disamenities, such as noise and vehicle exhaust, associated with life in a big city. We will try to shed light on many of these issues of scale.

The analysis of economies of scale is something of an orphan in standard textbook economics. We know they pop up in many situations but they are hard to analyze. Paul Krugman was awarded the Nobel Prize in economics for his fairly systematic treatment of how scale economies can yield agglomerated economic activity. A large city represents a large market with low distribution costs. Customers are clustered, so to speak, in a large city. A firm that is producing here can move down its average cost curve and in a sense keep outside competitors from selling into its local market. A large production run represents an opportunity for suppliers to our large firm to locate nearby and thus add to the cost advantage of our firm in a large market. There is a sense then in which the gains are cumulative as outside firms get attracted to places with large local markets. Krugman's work on aspects of this is reported on in Chapter 6. When time is moving forward in an economy with scale economies, it is easy to see "path dependency" emerging. The history of one city's land use can be very different from that of another simply because one city grew up rapidly in a different "era," decades apart. For example, each city could have a quite different type of road structure. Working with benefit–cost analysis when path dependency is a central issue becomes extremely complicated.

To a first approximation a city is just an economy in which households and firms are economizing on transportation costs. One can imagine a magician waving a wand over any city and moving all buildings slightly farther from each other, with all roads, bridges and mass transit still functioning in the same way. The city would become a higher-cost economy because all activity would stay the same but each tiny activity in the economy will occur with more resources being used up in movement or transportation. What about our magician moving all buildings a tiny bit closer to each other? Our mind naturally contemplates more crowding, congestion and new instances of gridlock. (The Hartwick–Hartwick model reported on in Chapter 5 can almost accommodate these sorts of experiments for a pretty detailed model of a city.) But once we accept this clustering or agglomerating argument for the existence of a city, there remain many issues in transportation development, residential area layout and organization of firms, schools, shopping centers, etc. to consider. We may understand what kind of an economy a city is at a high level of abstraction, but many of the interesting economic questions involve the details of a city's structure. In this book we attempt to deal with those details.

Acknowledgements

Thanks to Edwin Mills for introducing me to urban economics many years ago; to many students who experienced the development of this material in various courses; to Emma Kotzer, Aviner Hartwick and Erin Forward for research assistance and to the Huguette and W. Bentley McLeod Fund for the support of research assistants.

1 The city as a trading entity

A city with a minimal internal structure trading as a "nation" in a system of cities (other "nations"). Equilibrium size of the city. Effects of local climatic amenities. Recent data on trade among cities in the United States.

Introduction

One way to think of one's own city is as a point on the globe engaged in trade with many other places in one's own country and often beyond. This is how we start our inquiry into urban economics or the economic analysis of cities. Often when people think of their city, they think of the downtown and their neighborhood and perhaps the airport and the local stadium. This involves thinking about the internal structure of a city, a standard perspective in urban economics. A third perspective might be the fiscal health of one's city—how much concern is being expressed about high property taxes, and difficulties about councillors balancing the city's budget. We will of course get to the economics of the internal structure of a city as well as issues in city budgeting and revenue generation. First, however, we deal with a city as a trading entity living off exports, so to speak. Early urban economists spoke of a city's basic activity (exporting key commodities) and its non-basic activity (local retail and government, and production for the local market). Our model of a city as trader, below, will comprise the city's export activity, its residential activity, its government activity and its production of a local or non-traded good.

First, we look at some recent information on US cities as trading entities, information compiled by the Brookings Institution in Washington, DC (Tomer *et al.* 2013). The new data come in 12 categories (five commodities associated with "advanced industries" and seven associated with "non-advanced industries"). The typical observation is aggregate flow in dollars of a commodity into and out of a city. The Brookings–JP Morgan "Global Cities Initiative" has established that:

> the 100 largest American metropolitan areas trade the greatest volume of and the most valuable goods. Products leaving these areas are worth more than the products entering them… every metro area has trade surpluses in at least one commodity and almost all in more than one.
>
> (Tomer *et al.* 2013; p. 1)

The Brookings study also established that:

- the 100 most active trading cities trade commodities with an average value of US$1563 per ton, about 40 percent above the average value of all traded goods in the United States, while non-metropolitan regions trade commodities worth US$680 per ton (Tomer *et al.* 2013; p. 7); and

- the 100 large-trade cities dominate American international trade as well (some 63 percent of total foreign trade). Goods traded internationally tend to be in the high value per ton category (precision instruments, electronics, machinery/tools and transportation equipment). New York, Houston and San Jose are in the top five of cities doing international trade, by weight. Jackson, MS, Honolulu and Tulsa are not huge trading cities *per se*, but their trade is oriented to international markets (Tomer *et al.* 2013; p. 12).

We focus here on the top 25 cities by trade value. This set is not quite the same as the top 25 cities by value of production (local gross domestic product (GDP)), but there is much overlap (the top 25 commodity traders have local GDPs that sum to 49 percent of the national GDP for 2010). Drawing on tables in the Brookings report, we link large-trade flows by commodity type to these top trading cities. We observe a pattern. The largest traders are fairly diversified across commodity types in their trade but tend to be large traders in advanced industrial activities. The medium-sized large trading cities are also quite diversified but tend not to exhibit concentrations in particular commodities. The smaller large traders tend to be specialized in certain non-advanced commodities. See Table 1.1 for details. The Brookings study has not developed trade flows for services such as government, advertising, legal work and medicine. Almost all cities have a market area for such services and certain key large cities have large market areas.

Tomer *et al.* offer further insight into trade deficits and a service-based economy:

> How do metropolitan areas offset trade deficits in particular commodities? Some metro areas use their surpluses in other traded goods to pay for these products, but they also use tradable services. These include a range of occupations, from financiers and product designers to hotel managers and professional athletes. When service firms and workers sell their products to outside markets, they bring new income to a metropolitan area. The United States already runs an international surplus in tradable services—primarily driven by services exported from the 100 largest metropolitan areas—and there is every reason to believe the same is occurring on the domestic side. These services help fund inflows and in some places may be enough to offset local goods deficits. Unfortunately there are no metro measures for services trade.
>
> (Tomer *et al.* 2013; p. 17)

> Washington's service-based economy depends on global goods trade to operate, even though it primarily functions as a consumer rather than a producer. In stark contrast to industrial hubs like Houston and Portland, Washington does not have many surplus goods to distribute beyond its borders, except waste. However, that deficit should not diminish the metro area's importance in global value chains, as it adds value in ways beyond physical production through its many service activities.
>
> (Tomer *et al.* 2013; p. 19)

Thus the portrait of cities as traders and specialists in Table 1.1 is somewhat partial but still tells an important story. Cities tend to be very large traders when measured against their aggregate annual product and the largest traders are the largest cities (only six had a commodity trade value lower than the value of their GDP for 2010). They are quite diversified in their commodity types but tend to dominate the trade in advanced commodities.

(Glaeser and Kohlhase 2004; p. 219) suggest that we view population distribution in the United States in terms of eight "great centers": the Boston–Washington corridor, the Los Angeles area, the San Francisco Bay area, the Portland–Seattle corridor, Chicago, Atlanta, Miami and southeastern Texas. To a first approximation we expect trade within each of these "conurbations" to be large-scale relative to trade between any two of them.

Commodity trade of large cities in the United States

Table 1.1 lists the 25 largest trading cities by value of total commodity flows in plus flows out, in descending order. Across the top are first five "advanced" commodities followed by seven "non-advanced" commodities. Entries in the table are total trade flow values per commodity and city. The flow values entered are taken from two tables based on large flows by commodity, with city noted. One table was for the five advanced commodities and the other table was for the seven non-advanced commodities. Before scrutinizing the entries, we might ponder what we might expect to see in the tables.

First, since larger cities are overall larger traders, the larger cities will likely have more entries for large trades in various commodities. This is what we observe. Larger traders have more entries for more commodity groups, with a tilt in favor of large trades in the five "advanced" commodities. Second, cities further down the large-trade list will by definition be doing less trade and hence typically register smaller entries. Third, the largest overall traders are generally the largest cities by population and GDP and we hypothesize they will be most diversified in industrial structure. This we observe. A city higher up on the list is typically registering large trades in "many" commodities. And Miami, San Francisco, Riverside and Washington are sufficiently diversified that they exhibit no concentration in trade in a commodity. These are middle-weight traders. We want to qualify this here. Three of these cities are relatively large providers of services (legal services, advertising services, government services, etc.) to a region and their exports of these services are not counted in the commodity categories. Nevertheless, for Miami, San Francisco and Riverside we can infer that they are quite diversified in their trading. Fourth, when we get to the smaller "large traders" further down our list, we observe a quite regular pattern of "large trade" in a single commodity, often a less advanced one. We infer that these cities are less diversified in their trade and less diversified in their industrial structures and are also not large providers of service outputs. Smaller "large traders" are relatively specialized in their industrial structures. This is an idea of long standing and we can see it in the data from the Brookings study. Observe that the large "large traders" and the small "large traders" tend to have a concentration in "mixed freight," essentially warehousing, logistics and transshipment activity. They are types of trading hubs for commodity flows.

We also presumed that large entries would occur in the top left-hand corner (large traders have large flows associated with advanced commodities). And roughly speaking, this is what we observe. Cities that are "large traders" tend to do more of their trade in advanced (high value to weight) commodities. This leaves of course the lesser "large traders," say the bottom 12 cities, to have smaller entries on average and be less "specialized" in advanced commodities. This pattern is there in our table and it would be clearer if we excised a few outliers (outlying data points) from the top right and lower left parts of Table 1.1.

Column-wise, only Memphis and Cleveland are "large traders" with a specialization in their own particular commodity (agricultural products for Memphis and wood products for Cleveland). An anomaly is that Houston has no entry for energy. New Orleans and Tulsa are major energy products traders but are not in the list of 25 "large traders."

Table 1.1 Large-trade US cities and large flows of selected commodities traded (2010 US$billion)

	Chm[a]	*Tran*	*Elec*	*Mach*	*Pr-in*	*Enr*	*Tex*	*MxF*	*Met*	*Agr*	*Furn*	*Wd*
New York City	28.0				6.4		13.5					
Los Angeles	3.9	22.6	18.4	15.6	10.6		13.5	13.4			2.8	
Chicago	31.4	5.7	4.2	6.7				5.4	12.1			
Houston	33.8	4.4		5.4								
Dallas	6.8			6.9				7.1			2.1	
Philadelphia	6.0			4.5				3.7				
Atlanta									2.8			
Detroit		30.2										
San Francisco												
Boston			4.5		7.1							
Minneapolis				8.6	13.4							
San Jose			11.8		7.8							
Phoenix	6.0		4.7					2.4				
St Loius		4.8				2.7						
Seattle		9.5										
Memphis	32.2			3.3	6.4			3.9		2.0		
Columbus	7.5	4.5										
Cincinnati		4.2		10.2				5.7				
Miami												
Washington												
Riverside												
Baltimore								3.0				
Kansas City							3.3	3.6				
Indianapolis								3.8				2.2
Cleveland				7.8					2.7			

Note

a Chm (chemicals/plastics); Tran (transportation equipment); Elec (electronics); Mach (machinery/tools); Pr-in (precision instruments); Enr (energy products); Tex (textiles); MxF (mixed freight); Met (metals); Agr (agricultural products); Furn (furniture); Wd (wood products).

Source: Based on data from Tomer *et al.* (2013), a Brookings Institution (Washington, DC) study.

The accounts for a "small" open city

We turn now to some basic economics in characterizing a city "living off" exporting a key commodity. In the simplest case, a city can be viewed as a factory producing flows of output q_X per year and importing flows, say of a consumption good, food, as $p_C q_C$ per year, where q_C is quantity and p_C is "world price." The price of the exports in the world is unity. The inputs to production, capital, labor and land are assumed to "reside" in the city. It is reasonable to infer that the city is in a value balance relationship for the long run, in which case

$$q_X = p_C q_C.$$

Hence the city is neither growing nor shrinking: q_X has "world price," unity.

Also in the interest of keeping matters simple, assign constant returns to scale in production. We have production function $f(K_X, N_X, L_X)$ for the city's export activity, where K_X is produced capital as with, for example, buildings, machines, roads and sewers, N_X is labor (a worker is also a household here) and L_X is land. Hence, given the assumption of constant returns to scale in production, we have

$$\begin{aligned} q_X &= f(K_X, N_X, L_X) \\ &= K_X f_{K_X} + N_X f_{N_X} + L_X f_{L_X} \\ &= K_X r + N_X w + L_X p_A, \end{aligned}$$

where r is the rental rate (price for use of a ton per year) for capital, w is the wage and p_A is the rental price per unit of land (price for use of a hectare per year). (Note that f_{K_X}, f_{N_X} and f_{L_X} are first derivatives of $f(.)$ or are marginal products.) It is reasonable to consider our city as being part of a large system of cities or a price taker. Then r, w and p_A are fixed for our small, open city. For the time being, think of the land rent, p_A as the rent per hectare paid by farmers. The city is then in a sense "taking" land from farming at the going price and using the land for its factory and yard.

So far we have a pretty complete city, an export "machine" living on imports of a consumption good. Workers can be living in lofts above the factory. Hence we abstract from the housing sector. Local land owners and capital owners are assumed to live somewhere in the city (say above the workers in the factory). Hence total income in the city is $K_X r + N_X w + L_X v$ and is all spent on the importation of the consumption good.[1] We have then a city-wide budget constraint:

$$p_C q_C = K_X r + N_X w + L_X p_A.$$

Matters become simpler if we assume that the workers also own all the local capital and land in equal amounts. Then income per capita is $[K_X r + N_X w + L_X p_A]/N_X$.

A local goods sector added on

There is actually a lengthy tradition in urban economics of viewing a city as two dominant sectors, the basic or goods producing export sector and the non-basic or local goods sector (perhaps doing retail activity inside the city). Let us go down this road and examine a two-good city and its accounts. We have local good, q_H, produced under constant returns to scale and consumed entirely inside the city. The production function is $g(K_H, N_H, L_H)$ and we can proceed with

$$\begin{aligned} q_H &= g(K_H, N_H, L_H) \\ &= K_H g_{K_H} + N_H g_{N_H} + L_H g_{L_H} \\ &= \{K_H r + N_H w + L_H p_A\}/p_H, \end{aligned}$$

where g_{K_H}, g_{N_H} and g_{L_H} are first derivatives. Production efficiency involves $g_{K_H} p_H = r$, $g_{N_H} p_H = w$ and $g_{L_H} p_H = p_A$.

Let us continue to have workers live above their factory and shop premises and own all the land and capital in use in equal shares. A resident is now consuming two goods, $\frac{q_C}{N}$ of the consumption good being imported and $\frac{q_H}{N}$ of the local good being produced, with $N = N_X + N_H$. Our city has the "national account" expressed in an accounting matrix in Table 1.2. A sum of entries across a row is registered in an entry in the right hand column. A sum of entries for a column shows up in an entry in the bottom row. Under constant returns

Table 1.2 Accounts matrix

	Capital	*Labor*	*Land*	*Row sums*
Export good	rK_X	wN_X	$L_X p_A$	$q_X = p_C q_C$
Local good	rK_H	wN_H	$L_H p_A$	$p_H q_H$
Column sums	$r[K_X + K_H]$	$w[N_X + N_H]$	$p_A[L_X + L_H]$	

to scale the value of the column entries summed equals the value of the row entries summed. The column sum is net domestic product[2] and the row sum is net income for the economy. Placing the entries correctly in the matrix provides a discipline to keeping one's accounting correct. The matrix is also a snapshot of the economy under study.

Our city's account is working as a national account so far, except that our consumption good q_C is completely imported, rather than produced locally. This departure from a "nation's" account is made trivial because we assume that our export good precisely funds the import of q_C. Hence our sum of final column entries will equal the sum of the final row entries, and such value balance results from our assumption of constant returns to scale in the production of q_X and q_H.

We have then a fairly complete model of a city in a system of cities, living off exporting a good q_X, with local residents consuming equal amounts of the import good, q_C and a local good, q_H, this latter being, say, retail activity. One can think of a basic goods sector employing certain workers and a non-basic sector employing different workers. Some urban economists look at a particular city and sort workers by activity into basic (employed in export activity) and non-basic (employed in within-city activities). To this point, we have no explicitly defined movement of people or goods within our city. Within-city movement of goods and people has been swept under the carpet, so to speak.

We have not addressed the relative size of the local goods sector. A good way to tie up this loose end is to assume that each resident is the same and has a utility function defined over her q_C/N and q_H/N as in $u(q_C/N, q_H/N)$, where $N = N_X + N_H$. Then, given the budget constraint per household, the price p_H becomes defined inside the model and we can obtain an equilibrium ratio for q_C/q_H. The size of our city is actually still not nailed down since it faces a fixed export price and can in principle export as much as it wants, simply by a proportional expansion of inputs, each at its own fixed price.

A local housing sector added on

We can extend our simple basic/non-basic goods city to one with explicit housing produced. Since housing is a private good, the addition of housing closely follows the steps gone through in the addition of the non-basic good in the previous section. We are going to identify housing closely with its site; hence the subscript L for housing (a house is defined by the area of its site, here). We have a constant returns-to-scale production function $q_L = h(K_L, L_L)$ with only capital and land as inputs for this good. The expression q_L is housing services per year and thus inputs K_L and L_L are services of capital and land in housing per year. It is as if a resident does not purchase her home, rather she is a perpetual renter and her annual rent $p_L q_L/N$ covers the service flow per year from capital or structure and land or site. A resident's budget constraint contains an annual flow-disbursement for housing rather than the outright purchase price of a house at a single date.[3] We abstract from the annual disbursement to account for some labor input in our annual cost of a resident's housing.

Table 1.3 Accounts matrix with housing

	Capital	*Labor*	*Land*	*Row sums*
Export good	rK_X	wN_X	$L_X p_A$	$q_X = p_C q_C$
Local good	rK_H	wN_H	$L_H p_A$	$p_H q_H$
Housing	rK_L	0	$L_L p_A$	$p_L q_L$
Column sums	$r[K_X + K_H + K_L]$	$w[N_X + N_H]$	$p_A[L_X + L_H + L_L]$	

Following the analysis in the previous section, we have

$$\begin{aligned} q_L &= h(K_L, L_L) \\ &= K_L h_{K_L} + L_L h_{L_L} \\ &= \{K_L r + L_L p_A\}/p_L. \end{aligned}$$

We carry this housing sector account into our city-wide accounting matrix in Table 1.3.

Recall that the sum of entries in the right-hand column is aggregate production in dollars and the sum of entries in the bottom row is aggregate income in dollars for our city. We continue to assume that each resident household-worker owns an equal amount of local capital and land in use. Each household is then the same and has the same income. A household's welfare would be defined by her utility level in $u(q_C/N, q_H/N, q_L/N)$. We fill in details of the level of utility and the prices of goods below.

A local public sector

The local government goods sector will be treated differently because we will draw on the theory of public goods. We will posit a local government producing a government good, q_G, under constant returns to scale with inputs K_G, N_G and L_G, i.e. $q_G = m(K_G, N_G, L_G)$. So far matters are the same as we had them above. We depart, however, by assuming that q_G is consumed in this amount q_G by each resident, i.e. q_G is a local public good. Payment per household follows the public goods tradition, with each resident paying p_G/N for her consumption flow q_G. It is not out of line to say that the theory of public goods is about, first off, an unusual way that output gets paid for. However, it is also true that the assumption on how output is distributed over households is novel and central to the theory of public goods.

As above then we have

$$\begin{aligned} q_G &= m(K_G, N_G, L_G) \\ &= K_G m_{K_G} + N_G m_{N_G} + L_G m_{L_G} \\ &= \{K_G r + N_G w + L_G p_A\}/p_G. \end{aligned}$$

And including this sector in our accounting matrix, Table 1.4, makes the accounts look quite "symmetric" with what has gone before.

We have for $K = [K_X + K_H + K_L + K_G]$, $N = [N_X + N_H + N_G]$, and $L = [L_X + L_H + L_L + L_G]$. Different, however, is our inclusion of the per person payment $[q_G \times p_G/N]$ and sectorial revenue $[q_G \times p_G/N] \times N$ with the value of government product in the right-hand column.

Table 1.4 Accounts matrix with a government good produced

	Capital	*Labor*	*Land*	*Row sums*
Export good	rK_X	wN_X	L_Xp_A	$q_X = p_Cq_C$
Local good	rK_H	wN_H	L_Hp_A	p_Hq_H
Housing	rK_L	0	L_Lp_A	p_Lq_L
Public good	rK_G	wN_G	L_Gp_A	$p_Gq_G = [q_G \times p_G/N] \times N$
Column sums	rK	wN	p_AL	

Table 1.4 captures an urban economy, living on exports, with residents importing a consumer good and producing three other consumer goods locally, namely housing, the non-basic good (retail activity) and the local government product. The typical resident will have utility level, $u(q_C/N, q_H/N, q_L/N, q_G)$, with N equal to $N_X + N_H + N_G$ and income $\{r[K_X + K_H + K_L + K_G] + w[N_X + N_H + N_G] + p_A[L_X + L_H + L_L + L_G]\}/N$.

For a well-defined city economy, we must first complete "consumer equilibrium" for a representative consumer. This involves purchases by a consumer conforming to the conditions of tangency of the indifference curve to the budget constraint. The consequent "tangency conditions" are

$$\frac{u_{[q_C/N]}}{u_{[q_H/N]}} = \frac{p_C}{p_H}; \quad \frac{u_{[q_C/N]}}{u_{[q_L/N]}} = \frac{p_C}{p_L}$$

and

$$\frac{u_{[q_C/N]}}{u_{q_G}} = \frac{p_C}{[p_G/N]},$$

and we also require that each consumer satisfies her budget constraint. Expenditure per person is $p_Cq_C/N + p_Hq_H/N + p_Lq_L/N + q_Gp_G/N$.

We have a complete economy now, identified as a city living off export activity and also doing local production activity. However, the scale or size of our city, N, remains typically undefined at this point. This is clear when for example the utility function is of the Cobb–Douglas form: $[q_C/N]^{\alpha}[q_H/N]^{\beta}[q_L/N]^{\gamma}[q_G]^{1-\alpha-\beta-\gamma}$ with α, β and γ each between zero and unity. Our exogenously given input prices mean that each sector is operating as if it had fixed coefficients. With any value of N, we have a perfectly well defined city given satisfaction of the basic equilibrium conditions above. And for any exogenously given size N, there will be an area $L(N)$ occupied by the city. There is in a sense perfect sprawl working here since the area will grow proportionately with population N. For area to grow more slowly than N, we need some sort of force of agglomeration.

There are two new conditions that essentially transform the above largely flat economy, without a specific scale of size, into a more distinctly urban economy. First, one introduces a required or necessary movement of people for, say, reasons of commuting. Typically commuting costs more for an average household when it takes place in a larger city. A simple alternative mechanism of agglomeration is explored by Lucas and Rossi-Handsberg (2002). They introduce external payoffs to each firm being close to another firm. This leads to firms clustering in various places and roughly speaking tends to force worker-residents to live away from their place of employment. Workers are assumed to not live in or above their places of work. A household that lives close to its place of employment pays more for its standard "home" than one that ends up living farther from its place of employment. This approach implies agglomeration of firms and compulsory movement of workers to jobs and back to residences. Land is least valuable when the accessibility associated with a site is poorest. This is a fairly parsimonious way to introduce agglomeration into an otherwise non-agglomerating model. We buy into an abstract version of this narrative. We simply say that our urban economy has each household incurring some cost of movement within the city, the per worker cost rising with the area occupied by the city. We gloss over explicitly linking household i to firm z. Each household pays for its cost of movement or commuting by receiving an income inclusive of a share of the high local land rent in the city and in turn pays a base or low rent for land (the agricultural rent value) for its residence. It is as if every household has a site with equally poor accessibility, while market rent within the city is defined by the balance of demand and supply of sites. When we simulate the model in the next section, we simplify further by assuming that a home is simply a site or piece of land and that non-housing production activity in the city uses no land. This implies that within-city land rent is simply the agricultural land rent p_A plus the endogenous cost of movement per household.

Second, one posits an exogenous utility value for each identical resident or household in our city. The idea here is that our city is one of many in a system of cities and free migration between cities, for a relocating household responding to higher utility levels "away", leads to our city being in migration equilibrium when the utility level of a representative household is the same as that prevailing for such households "out" in the large system of cities. This way of looking at things is referred to as "the open-city assumption." Following our first amendment to the model, the land rent in our city becomes endogenous. Larger cities end up with higher average land rents per unit land. Following our second adjustment to the model, we make the wage rate in our city endogenous, given the utility level is exogenous. Typically, larger cities exhibit a higher wage for a representative worker-resident. And indeed it is true that cities of different sizes have significantly different wages for essentially identical workers. Equilibrium follows when utility levels, not the wage, become equalized per worker-resident over diverse cities. Our model above becomes distinctly urban when we can solve it with a particular size or scale and this becomes possible when we add our two assumptions: (a) internal movement of people in our city implies that average land rent is higher for larger cities; and (b) the open-city assumption prevails and thus the utility level for a household in our city is given exogenously to our city.

Simulating our small open city

We turn to simulation of our model of a small, open city exporting q_X at world prices and importing q_c in return, and we report on the city's response to an improvement in labor efficiency in the export sector. The higher wage associated with the efficiency improvement typically applies to a city that is larger and more densely settled (the law of urban growth; more detail later in this section). We observe this for a city with a sector producing housing, an additional non-traded good (haircuts) and a local public good (a government sector that we require to be small as defined below[4]). Equilibrium size for our city turns on within-city mobility costs incurred by a household, costs that rise for each household with city size. A household moving into our city faces a locally fixed level of utility (the so-called open-city assumption). What is distinctly urban about our small, open economy is labor supply turning on the local utility level facing a household rather than the local wage and the within-city mobility costs a representative household cannot avoid.

Empirical work has established that larger cities in many places, including the United States, have a higher productivity for labor, controlling for a worker's education and experience, as well as higher wages and average housing prices (Ciccone and Hall 1996; Glaeser and Mare 2001; Van Nieuwerburgh and Weill 2010). Settlement density is higher in the larger cities as well. Ciccone and Hall estimated labor productivity in various counties in the United States as a function of the density of local residents. They controlled for worker education and local infrastructure abundance. They observed strong gains in worker productivity with increased local density. Glaeser (2010; Introduction) estimated the per capita payoff to the resident of a city in the United States for an increase in the density of the resident's city. He observed a "strong relationship between area density and per capita gross metropolitan product" (Figure 1; p. 3). Glaeser estimates that per capita gross metropolitan product rose by 0.005 for each unit increase in the log of population density for the year 2000 in the United States. New York City, Philadelphia, Chicago and Boston are pretty much on his estimated (regression) line at the top end. However, above his fitted line are the many dynamic cities in the United States (e.g. San Francisco, Denver, Houston, Atlanta, Portland and Phoenix) while below the line are the many slow-growth places such as Buffalo, Rochester, Pittsburgh, New Orleans, Syracuse and Springfield. The tricky issue of whether density actually causes a productivity premium in a worker to appear or whether productive places attract "extra" in-migrants is investigated for France by Combes *et al.* (2010). They observe that skilled workers are especially attracted to cities (dense places) in France and that the same dense places today were also dense centers more than 170 years ago.

Glaeser and Mare (2001) present the standard evidence for "the law of urban growth": a positive coefficient on city size in estimations of Mincer equations. The basic Mincer equation "explains" a worker's wage as a weighted combination of her education and experience. In addition, higher wages correlate positively with city size, even when worker education and experience are controlled for.[5] Van Nieuwerburgh and Weill (2010) estimate a model of a many-city labor market that includes the local cost of housing. They have worker heterogeneity, housing heterogeneity within a city and city-specific heterogeneity of the industrial structure. They conclude:

> House price differentials between metropolitan areas compensate for the income differential of the marginal, lowest ability household in the location, making that household indifferent between staying and moving to the next best metropolitan area. Households also live in smaller and more expensive quarters if they choose to work in higher-income metropolitan areas. Lastly, higher-income metropolitan areas have on average a larger housing stock and a larger workforce.
>
> (Van Nieuwerburgh and Weill 2010; p. 1568)

Part of the positive correlation of city wage and size has obviously to do with (a) larger cities exhibiting higher proportions of better educated residents and (b) the high average wage in a large city discouraging firms in certain "low-wage" industries from operating in a particular city.[6] There are then these tricky labor force and industry composition effects at work in the larger city–higher wage relationship. Our abstract city is homogeneous, unburdened by composition effects. Our worker-households are homogeneous. We adhere to the idea that the extra productivity a worker exhibits in a larger city is due to some complicated urbanness factor, such as easier and more productive networking with fellow workers, when a worker is employed in a higher density arrangement. We remain open-minded on the source of the extra productivity a worker gains from being in a larger city. We simply take the extra productivity as real and explore its implications in a model of a small, open city.

Our model also allows us to work through a boost in the climate amenity enjoyed by citizens of our city. Where our public sector is small or non-existent we observe that the "free utility" from the boost shows up by making our city larger and more densely settled. Where our public sector is large, the boost to the amenity makes our city smaller and less densely settled. We also note that the introduction of a local, non-traded goods sector (e.g. haircuts) does not change our results. We turn now to the details of our model of a small, open city.

The basic model

Our city imports consumption goods q_C at "world" price p_C and exports a good q_X at "world" price p_X. Capital K in the city is available in unlimited quantities at rent r and labor enters into or exists in the city when a worker's utility is lower or higher than $\overline{u}$. The export good is produced with labor and capital in fixed proportions:[7]

$$q_X \times an = N, \tag{1.1}$$

$$q_X \times ak = K. \tag{1.2}$$

We assume that the production of this good requires no land. The value of imports equals the value of exports:

$$q_C = q_X \times [p_X/q_C].$$

The local wage will be $w = p_X \times (1/an)$. A resident-worker in our city will have her utility $u(q_C/N, L/N)$ equal to $\overline{u}$ in[8]

$$u\left(\frac{q_C}{N}, \frac{L}{N}\right) = \overline{u}, \tag{1.3}$$

with q_C/N per capita consumption good and L/N per capita housing (a house is simply a land area[9]). A resident's income–expenditure equality is

$$w + \frac{rK}{N} + \frac{L \times p_L}{N} - t(L) = \frac{q_C p_C}{N} + \frac{L \times p_A}{N}$$

where p_L is the local land rent and p_A is the land rent at the edge of the occupied area (land rent for agricultural activity). Total land rent is returned to households as a per capita, lump-sum grant and a household pays out $(L \times p_A)/N$ to land owners "abroad." A resident is assumed to own K/N and get rental income from this holding.[10] The expression $t(L)$ represents a geographic friction cost incurred by a household, largely a commuting cost for getting to one's place of work. This per capita cost increases with city area.[11] Each household desires more space for a residence and low-cost access to, on average, all other places in the city. This spatial friction cost prevents our city from having an indeterminant number of residents. If each resident lived above her workplace and did no commuting or shopping or visiting then the city would have an indeterminant size.[12]

Table 1.5 Solutions to the four-equation system

	q_X	N	L	p_L	w	N/L
$an = 0.1$	6.4391	0.6439	2.3016	1.4921	16.00	0.2798
$an = 0.09$	10.3572	0.9321	2.4290	2.2741	17.78	0.3837

Since $wN + rK = p_X q_X = p_C q_C$, our income–expenditure relationship reduces to

$$\frac{L \times p_L}{N} - t(L) = \frac{L \times p_A}{N}. \tag{1.4}$$

"High" land rent reflects "large" costs for a resident to move about the city. A household is assumed to take p_L as the cost of a marginal unit of residential land (a household does not connect its per capita land rent "dividend" as related to its "purchase" of land (housing)). Hence

$$\frac{u_{q_C/N}}{u_{L/N}} = \frac{p_C}{p_L}. \tag{1.5}$$

We can set $p_C = 1$ and eliminate q_C with $q_C = q_X \times [p_X/q_C]$. K can be solved for after q_X has been obtained. Hence we have a four-equation system to solve for q_X, N, L and p_L. (See Appendix 1.1 for details of the Matlab program for solving this set of equations.)

We select the utility function to be Cobb–Douglas in $[q_C/N]^a[L/N]^{(1-a)}$ and can solve our system. For $a = 0.75$, $an = 0.1$, $p_X = 1.6$, $p_A = 0.01$, $\overline{u} = 11$ (and $w = (1/an) \times p_X$), we can solve to get the results shown in line 1 of Table 1.5.

We improve the productivity of labor (an to 0.09 from 0.10) and solve our system again, getting the results shown in line 2 of Table 1.5. The changes characterize "the law of urban growth": output, q_X and the wage all rise. Area occupied, population and the density of settlement in the city all increase.

The addition of a local public sector

We take the local government as Samuelsonian in the sense that it supplies a local public good in a non-varying quantity to each household and charges in accord with marginal benefits, here simply p_G/N. We proceed, then, with our above model but with q_G produced with its own Cobb–Douglas production function,

$$q_G = [K - K_X]^{ag}[N - N_X]^{(1-ag)}.$$

Efficient use of inputs involves

$$\frac{ag \times (1/[K - K_X])}{(1 - ag) \times (1/[N - N_X])} = \frac{r}{w},$$

and zero profits requires

$$p_G q_G = r \times [K - K_X] + w \times [N - N_X].$$

Table 1.6 Solutions to the seven-equation system

	q_X	N	K	L	p_L	q_G	p_G	p_G/N	w	N/L
$an=0.1$	16,859	3,203	5,901	4	11,384	1,431	19	0.0059	16.00	800.75
$an=0.09$	14,094	2,410	4,933	4	9,029	1,088	21	0.0087	17.78	602.50

These are three new equations for our economy with a local public good. In addition, utility per household is now

$$u\left(\frac{q_C}{N}, \frac{L}{N}, q_G\right)=\overline{u},$$

and we require the additional marginal condition on consuming the public good to be satisfied:

$$\frac{u_{q_C/N}}{u_{q_G}}=\frac{p_C}{p_G/N}.$$

Our budget constraint is unchanged since income from the production of the public good accrues to households and this income equals the expenditure by a household. Hence our new system is seven equations in q_X, N, K, L, p_L, q_G and p_G. We make use of $K_X=ak\times q_X$ and $N_X=an\times q_X$ in solving the seven-equation system.

The utility function is now $[q_C/N]^a[L/N]^b[q_G]^{1-a-b}$, with $a=0.4$ and $b=0.2$. For the production function for the government good, we take $ag=0.1$. For the production of q_X we have $K_X=ak\times q_X$ and $N_X=an\times q_X$ for $ak=0.3$ and $an=0.1$. In addition we have $p_C=1$; $p_X=1.6$; $\overline{u}=11$; $r_A=0.01$; and $r=3.2$. The results we obtain from solving this set of equations are in Table 1.6.

With an improvement in labor productivity in the export sector (an to 0.09 from 0.1) we get the results shown in line 2. Output, population, density and government output *decline*. We refer to such scenarios as violations of the law of urban growth. The cost of the public good has risen because the wage in the economy has risen. Each household sees its charge per unit of q_G (namely p_G/N) rise considerably and there is a general contraction in q_G being supplied by the government. To maintain a "reasonable level" of q_G, resources get drawn out of the export sector, including labor and essentially the city contracts, including its area occupied. Recall that Baumol (1967) argued that improvements in labor productivity in the non-government sector would lead to wage increases in a city and to a rise in costs for operating a city's public sector. We are seeing a variant of this Baumol phenomenon ("unbalanced growth") here. Our public sector, however, is always in budget balance.

It is not surprising and perhaps reassuring to see that when the government good figures "small" in the utility function of the household that the law of urban growth "returns." For example, when we switch a from 0.4 to 0.79 in the utility function (b remains at 0.2 and the exponent on q_G becomes 0.05) and solve the model, we observe that an improvement in labor productivity in the export sector leads to an expansion in output, q_X, population and density of settlement. Table 1.7 reports on solving the model for this experiment with a "small" coefficient for q_G. Line 1 in Table 1.7 shows the base case and line 2 shows the outputs when labor productivity improves in the export sector.

Table 1.7 Solutions to the seven-equation system with "small" coefficient for the government good

	q_X	N	K	L	p_L	q_G	p_G	p_G/N	w	N/L
$an = 0.1$	5.2790	0.5339	1.5870	2.0413	1.0999	0.0057	18.8541	35.31	16.00	0.2615
$an = 0.09$	9.6332	0.8769	2.8961	2.1559	1.9004	0.0094	20.7294	23.64	17.78	0.4067

Observe that q_G has increased as charge per unit p_G/N has declined. Also, although the rent per unit of land has almost doubled, consumption of land per household has increased, albeit by a small amount. This scenario with productivity improvement and "small government" yields a reverse-Baumol phenomenon. The wage increase goes along with an increase in q_G and a decline in charge per unit, namely p_G/N. We observe a tension between (a) scenarios that conform to the law of urban growth and (b) scenarios that exhibit the Baumol phenomenon of "high cost" local government. Our take on this issue is that scenarios that exhibit "the law of urban growth" are the empirically plausible cases. The scenarios that "violate" the law of urban growth are doing so because our public sector has been set up as Samuelsonian and the Samuelson public goods approach is not the one that we can link to Baumol's argument. Baumol was working with stylized facts taken from real-world local public sectors and real-world public sectors appear to be quite different from what the Samuelson formulation, which we are relying on, dictates. In short we get good simulations of actual cities when our public sector "counts small" in the utility function of a household and we get theoretical curiosities when our public sector "counts large" in the utility function of a household. Our model does well at capturing the law of urban growth, given the government good "counting small" in the representative household's utility function, but poorly at capturing Baumol's "cost disease" at the municipal government level.

A local non-traded good (haircuts)

Now we restructure our basic model to be without a government sector and introduce a locally produced, non-traded consumption good. This is important because, as Moretti (2012) explains:

> the vast majority of jobs in a modern society are in local services... This sector exits only to serve the needs of a region's residents and is largely insulated from national and international competition.
>
> (p. 56)

and

> most jobs in innovative industries belong to the traded sector... productivity growth is different in the two sectors... in many parts of the non-traded sector, labor productivity does not grow very much.
>
> (p. 57)

One can interpret what we are doing here as changing the government good in the previous section into a local, non-traded private good. (The government sector is re-introduced in the next section.) Relative to our basic model at the outset (four equations in four unknowns) we add three equations related to the production of the non-traded good:

$$q_H = [K - K_X]^{ah}[N - N_X]^{(1-ah)}.$$

Efficient use of inputs involves

$$\frac{ah \times (1/[K - K_X])}{(1-ah) \times (1/[N - N_X])} = \frac{r}{w},$$

and zero profits requires

$$p_N q_N = r \times [K - K_X] + w \times [N - N_X].$$

These are three new equations for our economy with a local non-traded good. In addition, utility per household is now[13]

$$u\left(\frac{q_C}{N}, \frac{L}{N}, \frac{q_H}{N}\right) = \bar{u},$$

and we require the additional marginal condition on consuming the non-traded good to be satisfied:

$$\frac{u_{q_C/N}}{u_{q_H/N}} = \frac{p_C}{p_H}.$$

Our budget constraint is unchanged since income from the production of the non-traded good accrues to households and this income equals the expenditure by a household. Hence our new system is seven equations in q_X, N, K, L, p_L, q_H and p_H. We make use of $K_X = ak \times q_X$ and $N_X = an \times q_X$ in solving the seven-equation system. The utility function is now $[q_C/N]^a[L/N]^b[q_H/N]^{1-a-b}$, with $a = 0.3$, $b = 0.4$. For the production function for the non-traded good, we take $ah = 0.2$. For the production of q_X we have $K_X = ak \times q_X$ and $N_X = an \times q_X$ for $ak = 0.3$ and $an = 0.1$. In addition we have $p_C = 1$; $p_X = 1.6$; $\bar{u} = 11$; $r_A = 0.01$; and $r = 3.2$. We solve with Matlab and obtain the results shown in Table 1.8.

We observe in Table 1.8 that the improvement in labor efficiency in the export sector leads to increases in q_X, N, L, q_H, N/L and the wage. The law of urban growth is being displayed in this "experiment." The price of the non-traded good has increased somewhat while the aggregate quantity consumed has increased marginally. Similarly the rent per unit of land has increased somewhat, as has the aggregate quantity consumed.

Table 1.8 Solutions to the seven-equation system with non-traded good replacing public good

	q_X	N	K	L	p_L	q_H	p_H	w	N/L
$an = 0.1$	0.1298	0.0234	0.0519	3.2353	0.0856	0.0109	19.127	16.00	0.00723
$an = 0.09$	0.1691	0.0274	0.0676	3.4509	0.1045	0.0130	20.8091	17.78	0.00794

The basic model with a non-traded and a government good

We now add a Samuelsonian government sector to the model in the previous section. Each household consumes q_G, the current production of the government good, and pays p_G/N per unit, where p_G is the current cost of producing q_G. Hence to the model above we add three equations pertaining to the production of q_G:

We add the Cobb–Douglas production function,

$$q_G = [K_G]^{ag}[N_G]^{(1-ag)}.$$

Efficient use of inputs in producing q_G involves

$$\frac{ag \times (1/[K_G])}{(1-ag) \times (1/[N_G])} = \frac{r}{w},$$

and zero profits requires

$$p_G q_G = r \times [K_G] + w \times [N_G].$$

These are three new equations for our economy with a local public good. In addition, utility per household is now

$$u\left(\frac{q_C}{N}, \frac{L}{N}, \frac{q_H}{N}, q_G\right) = \overline{u},$$

and we require the additional marginal condition on consuming the public good to be satisfied:

$$\frac{u_{q_C/N}}{u_{q_G}} = \frac{p_C}{p_G/N}.$$

Our reduced budget constraint is unchanged since income from the production of the public good accrues to households and this income equals the expenditure by a household. Hence our new system is 11 equations in q_X, N, K, L, p_L, q_H, p_H, q_G, p_G, K_G and N_G. We make use of $K_X = ak \times q_X$ and $N_X = an \times q_X$ in solving the 11-equation system. The utility function is now $[q_C/N]^a[L/N]^b[q_H/N]^c[q_G]^{1-a-b-c}$, with $a = 0.3$, $b = 0.4$, $c = 0.25$. For the production function for the government good, we take $ag = 0.3$. For the production of q_N, we have $ah = 0.2$. For the production of q_X we have $K_X = ak \times q_X$ and $N_X = an \times q_X$ for $ak = 0.3$ and $an = 0.1$. In addition we have $p_C = 1$; $p_X = 1.6$; $\overline{u} = 10.48$; $r_A = 0.01$; and $r = 3.2$. Note that the exponent on q_G in the utility function is small for this solving, namely at 0.05. The results we obtain from solving this set of equations are shown in Table 1.9.

When we introduce an exogenous improvement in labor productivity in the export sector, we observe the results shown in line 2 of Table 1.9. The law of urban growth is being displayed in the data. Observe that the charge per unit of q_G, namely p_G/N, has declined while the quantity consumed per household has risen.

We turn to solving this set of equations with the exponent on q_G in the utility function being relatively large. In the utility function we now have $a = 0.1$, $b = 0.2$ and $c = 0.05$. Other parameters are unchanged.[14] The results obtained are shown in Table 1.10.

Table 1.9 Solutions to the 11-equation system

	q_X	N	K	L	p_L	q_H	p_H
$an = 0.1$	0.0561	0.0100	0.0229	2.9945	0.0399	0.0039	19.1270
$an = 0.09$	0.0767	0.0123	0.0313	3.2620	0.0501	0.0049	20.8091
	p_G	p_G/N	q_G	K_G	N_G	w	N/L
$an = 0.1$	18.1854	1818.54	0.0008	0.0014	0.0007	16.00	0.0033
$an = 0.09$	19.5774	1591.66	0.0010	0.0019	0.0008	17.78	0.0038

Table 1.10 Solutions to the 11-equation system with relatively "large" household consumption of government services

	q_X	N	K	L	p_L	q_H	p_H
$an = 0.1$	244.20	145.30	323.57	2.32	336.97	10.21	19.13
$an = 0.09$	246.79	132.16	326.99	2.44	323.06	9.49	20.81
	p_G	p_G/N	q_G	K_G	N_G	w	N/L
$an = 0.1$	18.19	0.125	139.66	238.10	111.11	16.00	62.63
$an = 0.09$	19.58	0.148	131.10	240.62	101.06	17.78	54.16

We can see that q_X and L rise with the improvement in labor productivity in the export sector, while q_H and q_G decline. The charge per unit of q_G, namely p_G/N, has increased while the quantity q_G consumed per household has declined. The decline in N and in density conforms to our earlier notion of a violation of the law of urban growth.

We can summarize our model in a national account framework, as shown in Table 1.11. The top row and left side have labels. Net "national" product is the sum of the entries in the right-hand column and "national" income is the sum of entries in the final row of the table. Entries inside the table for a column (row) sum to the entry on the bottom (right side).

We could have housing produced with both land and capital. We introduce a constant returns to scale production function with inputs K_R and L for the production of q_R. We then have a zero profit condition $\overline{p_R} \times q_R = rK_R + p_A L$, and an efficiency condition for the use of inputs (three new equations in K_R, q_R and $\overline{p_R}$). Since land rent is at the agricultural value, p_A, we expect the capital to land ratio to not be large. In place of our earlier budget constraint we now have

$$\frac{p_R q_R}{N} - t(L) = \frac{\overline{p_R} \times q_R}{N},$$

with new variable p_R (replacing variable p_L from the formulation of a plot of land as a house). The value of capital here will cancel from each side, leaving the consumer rent for land above the production rent by the cost per household for mobility, $t(N)$. Alternatively, the $L - otpt$ row in Table 1.11 can be replaced by $rK_R + p_A L = \overline{p_R} \times q_R = p_R q_R - [t(L) \times N]$. Again, if each household were to live on marginally less land, each household could access the rest of the city at lower cost (i.e. $t(L)$ would decline for each household).

Table 1.11 Accounts matrix based on 11-equation framework

	$K - inpt$	$N - inpt$	$L - inpt$	NNP
$q_X - otpt$	rK_X	wN_X	0	$= q_X p_X = p_C q_C$
$q_H - otpt$	rK_H	wN_H	0	$= p_H q_H$
$q_G - otpt$	rK_G	wN_G	0	$= p_G q_G = [\frac{p_G}{N}][Nq_G]$
$L - otpt$	0	0	$p_A L$	$= p_L L - [t(L) \times N]$
NNI	$= rK$	$= wN$	$= p_A L$	

Table 1.12 Solutions to the 11-equation system including a climate premium

	q_X	N	K	L	p_L	q_H	p_H
$A = 1$	244.20	145.30	323.57	2.32	336.97	10.21	19.13
$A = 1.05$	219.29	130.48	290.56	2.32	302.59	9.17	19.13
	p_G	p_G/N	q_G	K_G	N_G	w	N/L
$A = 1$	18.19	0.125	139.66	238.10	111.11	16.00	62.63
$A = 1.05$	18.19	0.139	125.41	213.80	99.78	17.78	56.24

Sunnier cities

We turn to consider the incidence of a climate premium for a city, say more temperate and sunny days per year for one city relative to another. Such amenities are generally priced indirectly into a household's equilibrium bundle and possibly wage. There are no agency charges at the entrance to a city for a household relocating to a particular city with a better climate. Formally, then, a household will have a different amenity value A in the utility function when living in different cities; that is, we have $\overline{u} = u(\frac{q_C}{N}, \frac{q_H}{N}, \frac{L}{N}, q_G, A)$.[15] Our interest is in the incidence of, say, an increase in the value of A, or in the indirect pricing of "more A." We take up this issue by solving our complete model city in the previous section with different values of A (the wage remains unchanged[16]). Formally, we choose a simple channel for a local amenity premium to be registered, namely $\overline{u} = A \times u(\frac{q_C}{N}, \frac{q_H}{N}, \frac{L}{N}, q_G)$, for $u(.)$ our base Cobb–Douglas utility function. More local amenities correspond to a larger value for A.

We take our base case from the first line in Table 1.10 (the case of q_G registering large in the utility function of a household). We have $a = 0.1$, $b = 0.2$, $c = 0.05$ and $an = 0.1$. Other parameters are unchanged. Our equilibrium city is defined by results shown in the first line of Table 1.12. Parameter $A = 1$. We change the value of A to 1.05 and re-solve. The results are shown in line 2 of Table 1.12.

The city experiences a large contraction in population and production activity. The area occupied is unchanged and hence density declines. Our "sunnier city" is less populous and more spread out. Each agent is consuming less government services, q_G, at a higher charge per unit. To a first approximation, we say that the price of more sunshine to an agent is having to live with relatively less government good. Since the city actually contracts in population and density, a second-order effect would be a decline in worker productivity and a shift down in the average wage in the city. We take this second-order effect as small and ignore it here. Recall that the basic city in this analysis has q_G "counting" relatively large in a household's utility function. We turn to the case of q_G "counting" relatively small.

The first line of Table 1.9 is our base case now. The results are reproduced as line 1 in Table 1.13 below. The utility function now has $a = 0.3, b = 0.4, c = 0.25$. The exponent on q_G in the utility function is 0.05. The results we obtain from solving the model are shown in the second row of numbers in Table 1.13.

The city with the amenity increase is reported in line 2 of Table 1.13. Population, city area and density have increased. The outputs of q_X, q_H and q_G have all increased. The rent on land has increased while the charge per unit of q_G has decreased. Roughly speaking, we would say that the amenity premium is being charged for to a household by an increase in "rationing" of residential land per household. Each household ends up with a smaller lot size or more generally with less "housing" per family. The price that a household pays for enjoying more sunshine is that it lives with less housing in the sunnier city. Since the city has a larger, more densely arranged population, labor productivity and the wage should rise somewhat. This would be a second-order force causing the city to expand, but we abstract this force here.

We see two very different scenarios of the capitalization of amenity improvement for a city, one with the public sector "counting large" in utility and the other with the public sector "counting small." In the second case the city is larger, more populous and denser. This case conforms to our prior expectations on the effect of a climate premium for city i. This case is in a sense the companion scenario to the law of urban growth, a scenario with solid empirical support. Hence we infer that the presence of a relatively large local government sector causes the capitalization of a local amenity premium for city i to "go the wrong way," as we argued above, for the case of an exogenous boost in labor productivity in the export sector. However, these thoughts remain speculations. Careful empirical work is called for.

We noted above that (Moretti 2012; p. 169) somewhat casually remarks that a typical household in the United States spends about 40 percent of its income on housing each year. This is more likely to be true for residents of large, dynamic cities. Some lenders refuse mortgages to households that will be spending such a high fraction of their incomes on housing. We note in Chapter 8 that some observers consider there to be an affordability crisis with regard to housing in the United States. Again, these observers are probably taking costs in the large, dynamic cities as the benchmark. In any case it is interesting to contemplate the notion of "high housing costs" in the United States. An economist would say supply has not been keeping up with demand and this is why prices have become "high." This leads one to consider developers as being slow to build new houses. In some cities there can be land shortages (e.g. Vancouver, British Columbia) while in other places it is more likely to be slowness on the part of municipal authorities to authorize new tract development at the edge of cities or in some places new condominium development in the centers of cities. In our

Table 1.13 Solutions to the 11-equation system including a climate premium, with "small" consumption of government services

	q_X	N	K	L	p_L	q_H	p_H
$A = 1.0$	0.0561	0.0100	0.0229	2.9945	0.0399	0.0039	19.1270
$A = 1.05$	0.0660	0.0118	0.0269	3.0598	0.0460	0.0046	19.1270

	p_G	p_G/N	q_G	K_G	N_G	w	N/L
$A = 1.0$	18.1854	1818.54	0.0008	0.0014	0.0007	16.00	0.0033
$A = 1.05$	18.1854	1541.14	0.0010	0.0016	0.0008	17.78	0.0039

model above, the supply of housing is endogenous and prices can rise when, for example, the cost of the imported consumer good declines. Thus "high" housing costs will emerge in the model relative to other goods a household is currently purchasing. This is something of a general equilibrium version of "high" housing prices.

Adaptive equilibria

An adaptive equilibrium is an equilibrium in which households and firms take the population of a place and its distribution over the local land area, and its built environment, as given and optimize or adjust margins to these constraints. In our case, the population size affects the local cost of movement for households directly and the local cost of housing somewhat indirectly. Agents are optimizing in the face of—or adapting to—a local population constraint. A standard economic model has a household adjust its purchases to current prices and its income, which may well depend of the price of labor. Quantities get "spoken for" and prices are assumed to respond or adjust to current "excess supply" or "excess demand." An equilibrium has market prices "settle down" to stationary values, while households "become content" with their "final" quantities chosen. In equilibrium, prices are stationary and each household is in a "choice equilibrium" with respect to its quantities chosen at the equilibrium prices. In an adaptive equilibrium, the built environment and local population distribution must be reacted to as the decision-maker chooses her favored bundle of commodities to consume. In addition the agent has a time allocation problem to solve each day as well as a movement distribution problem. A household must adjust more than just its quantity margins as it optimizes repeatedly over a typical day. Its "margins" involve time allocation over, say, a day (see, for example, Becker 1965) and "movement distribution" between home, work and, say, the supermarket. In an adaptive equilibrium each household optimizes its purchases with respect to prices and its income, and in addition optimizes with respect to its time and movement allocation. The main point is that the built environment and the local population distribution are to a first approximation given for each household, and an allocation in the city becomes an equilibrium when households get all their margins "right," including traditional quantities in their "consumption baskets."

An adaptive equilibrium for a city is considerably more complicated than is a familiar, micro-theory economic equilibrium. Schweizer *et al.* (1976) observed that the standard Arrow–Debreu model of general equilibrium implicitly has each agent consuming in multiple locations, essentially simultaneously. They addressed this issue in a reformulation which cast one agent to one location. Then the distribution of households over space shows up in densities that become central to defining an equilibrium, rather than following the traditional route of accounting for each household individually. Roughly speaking this connected the Arrow–Debreu model to familiar methods in urban economics. However, establishing when an adaptive equilibrium is, say, a Pareto optimum is very complicated. Firms within a city will be adjusting their margins simultaneously with households. The built environment reacts to current household choices: government planners build new roads and bridges and retailers build new outlets, for example.

Our discussion of an adaptive equilibrium is not simply a theoretical excursion. In actual cities residents optimize against the built environment. The built environment can be "clunky" and residents adapt to the environment and create an adaptive equilibrium. In a sense a city will always be a second-best system with agents optimizing within the constraints created by the built environment and the local population distribution. Each agent may be optimizing "against" the choices of others as well as the built environment, but it is difficult to conceive of the local economy supporting an optimum when it is in equilibrium.

In particular, with a large city we associate a larger population size with a higher level of labor efficiency, averaged over many workers. Firms must adjust their "margins" in a complete adaptive equilibrium. More population or higher density probably affects a household negatively (e.g. with more congestion), while it affects firms positively. This may be the deep trade-off that is at work determining city sizes and large-scale population distribution. Many margins get adjusted by firms and households to the city size, the local population distribution and the infrastructure or the built environment more generally. Such equilibria we call "adaptive equilibria."

Summary

We defined our city as a place in a spatial setting, living off export activity, so to speak. We explored the law of urban growth and the law of capitalization of an amenity premium. Our models without a local public good yield results compatible with these laws. Our models with a local public good yield violations of the two laws when the public good registers strongly in the utility of a resident. Our point of departure for this work was the development of an "international trade" framework for a city, a framework that would have the law of urban growth baked in from the outset. We took for granted that our framework would have an endogenous local public good. It was a surprise that the law of urban growth turned out to be sensitive to the way we introduced a local public good into our model. We are not claiming that our avenue to the violation of the law of urban growth is unique. There are many parameters in our model to experiment with. However, the particular violation which we came upon and which we report on is, we believe, worthy of much reflection.

We have drawn together diverse strands of urban economics literature into a unified framework, one that is a particular instance of the classic model of a small, open economy. When the trading economy in question is a city rather than a nation, one must amend the basic trade model in certain ways in order to accommodate "standard assumptions" about cities. Of particular interest is utility-level "taking" by a worker free to select her place of work and residence. Utility-level "taking" becomes a key part in the determination of equilibrium size for a city. In our view the complementary part is the fact that local land rent rises with city size. We are able to proceed largely as if neither explicit scale economies in production, nor externalities between close-by firms are central to the question of equilibrium size for our city. We end up with a simple framework for exploring city size and local wage levels, a subject of considerable current exploration. Our framework also allows for an easy look at the question of city size and local climate amenities. And certainly novel in a small, open economy model is our introduction of the production of a local pure public good. From the perspective of n equations in n unknowns, our models are fairly complicated but have the merit of being numerically solvable with Matlab software.

We took our land-supply function as exogenous: more land available to our city at a higher price (land rent; rent is charged per year). One might argue that this is a loose end that needs tying up and this is correct. To generate a land-rent function, we need to develop an internal structure for our city and the standard one derives from the so-called monocentric city. The monocentric city, which is focused on in Chapters 2 and 3, posits that all jobs are in a center and all residences surround the center and are land-using. The central employment area may or may not use land in a first-pass formulation. We take the central employment area as a point in space. The central economics idea in the monocentric city model is that a typical resident— and they are all taken as very similar at first—wants a home with some space around it while at the same time wanting to be close to her place of work, in the center. In the end, a typical household that resides close to the center incurs less commuting costs and gets less land per residence and pays more per unit of land for its residence; one farther from the center incurs more commuting costs but gets somewhat more land for its residence at a lower price per unit. This trading off of more space for more commuting expenditure allows us to tease out an equilibrium land-rent function that leaves each very similar household on the same indifference curve, regardless of their relative distance from their place of employment. Deriving such land-rent functions and the household equilibrium that is part of an equilibrium rent function is the subject of Chapter 2. Chapter 3 can be viewed as a series of important extensions (footnotes) to the basic model of Chapter 2. In Chapter 4 there is a section with details about a climate amenity premium and the monocentric city model and in Chapter 9 there are sections with details about government goods and finance for the monocentric city model.

Main points of Chapter 1

1 A city typically exports its "basic good" and imports essential consumption goods, such as foodstuffs. We assume that the value of exports equals the value of imports for our abstract city.
2 The open-city assumption indicates that two identical households must end up on the same indifference curve, no matter which city they end up living in. (Very low costs of relocating are being assumed.)
3 With land for housing available in our city at a constant price per acre (hectare) and costs of internal movement per household at zero, our city has no equilibrium size. (Constant returns to scale in producing the export good matter.)
4 When land for a residence is higher in a larger city, our city has an equilibrium size.
5 A public or government-produced good, such as "security on the streets," is assumed to be consumed in equal amounts by each household. Each household's payment, with similar households, becomes a tax defined by the total cost of producing the public good divided by the number of households in the city.
6 Technical progress for a city can be viewed as the labor content of the export good becoming less intense. This usually goes hand-in-hand with the wage in our city rising, given technical progress. (This is the law of urban growth: labor is more productive in larger cities and average wages are higher in larger cities.)
7 We observed an exception to the law of urban growth. The condition for the exception was that each household was a heavy consumer of the government good produced in the city.
8 The hedonic wage equation allows one to break a worker's wage into contributing components, principally years of education and years of experience.
9 An urban amenity, such as more days of sunshine per year for a city, is like a public good for a particular city that no one is charging for. Hence the amenity is charged for indirectly, for example through "higher average housing costs" per household in a sunnier city.

Questions and problems

1 (Moretti 2012; p. 169) sets out this estimate of a representative American household's expenditure pattern: 14 percent of her income on food and beverages, 17 percent on transportation and 40 percent on housing.

a. Suppose an average household in your city is three people with an annual family income of US$90,000. Using Moretti's expenditure pattern as a guide, estimate annual dollar imports of key commodities to your city.
b. List the activities in your city that might have a large component of exports out to other places.
c. Does the annual value of exports approximately equal the annual value of imports to your city? Sketch some evidence for your view.
d. Given a "misalignment" of the value of commodity exports and imports to your city, per year, how is some sort of balance in trade value achieved?

2. a. The total value of stuff produced in a city in a year is that city's gross domestic product (GDP). A fraction of this value is "local services of government." Estimate the ratio of dollars of local government services to local GDP for your city. Would larger cities have a higher or lower ratio?
   b. Is your local government a heavy or light user of imports to your city?
3. The "law of urban growth" connects increases in labor productivity (and "parallel" average wage increases) to larger city size. Does the larger population cause the productivity increase or does a labor productivity increase lead to growth in the city? Trace the steps of labor productivity increase to population increase. (Keep the open-city assumption in mind here.)
4. Higher income cities have proportionately more workers with more education and thus more workers with high-end wages. Is this the root of the law of urban growth or is there more economics going on?

Appendix 1.1: example of Matlab program: simplest city

```
4 equations in qx, N, La, pL....
  function f = urm(x)
  % hello
  a = 0.75; an = 0.09; pc = 1; px = 1.6; uB = 11; rA = 0.01;
  qx = x(1);
  % qc = qx*px/pc;
  N = x(2);
  % K = x(3);
  La = x(3);
  pL = x(4);
  w = (1/an)*px;
  % equations
  f(1) = uB - ((qx*px/pc)/N)^a*(La/N)^(1 - a);
  f(2) = a*(pL)*La - (1 - a)*pc*(qx*px/pc);
  f(3) = N - qx*an;
  % friction factor per resident is 1*[La]^2...
  % income equals expend reduces to... land rent paid and returned to resident
  % except for ag land rent (goes abroad)
```

$f(4) = (pL^*La/N - (1.0^*(La)\text{^}2)) - (rA^*(La/N));$
% $an = 0.1,\ a = 0.75$
% 6.4391 $N = 0.6439$ $La = 2.3016$ 1.4921, $dens = .2798$
% $an = 0.09\ldots$ law established
% 10.3572 0.9321 2.4290 2.2741, $dens = .3837$

Notes

1 As is standard in this sort of accounting analysis, the factory brings "air" in at one end and produces q_X out of the end door, using machines and workers in the process of getting q_X. The factory sits on a site of area L_X.
2 Gross national product (GNP) is defined for a nation as the dollar value of Aggregate Consumption + Government Expenditures + Investments + Exports + Foreign Production by US Companies—Domestic Production by Foreign Companies. Net National Product (NNP) subtracts the dollar value of "capital consumption" or "depreciation" for the year. Gross domestic product (GDP) measures the value of product produced *within* the borders of a nation over a year. Income earned locally from production abroad is excluded from GNP when defining GDP.
3 Working out the annual flow-cost of living in a house one owns or has purchased is an important exercise that we take up in Chapter 8.
4 With a "large" government sector producing a local public good, we observe a quite general violation of the law of urban growth (we see a smaller, less dense city; one with the size of the public sector shrinking with the wage increase). The scenario with the public sector shrinking as the city-wide wage increases echoes somewhat Baumol's (1967) argument that technical progress in the private sector of a city raises the local wage thereby increasing local government costs, which in turn makes budget balance for the local government difficult to achieve. In our framework with local government always in budget balance, the higher wage induces a contraction in the quantity of the local government good produced and a compensating rise in the quantity of housing consumed by each household.
5 Glaeser and Gyourko (2005) note that there is a lag in the productivity improvement exhibited by an in-migrant to a large city.
6 Duranton and Puga (2001) provide evidence that firms doing innovative activity tend to be located in larger centers and firms doing more routine activity in smaller, lower-cost places. Moretti (2012; Map 2, p. 91) emphasizes that a worker in a city with more residents with college degrees will earn more than her counterpart in a city with residents who lack as many college degrees.
7 We employ a fixed coefficient technology here because it makes the introduction of technical progress in the export sector easy.
8 This "the open-city assumption." A better approach would be to have migration determined by a response to lifetime welfare attainable in various places (see, for example, Eaton and Eckstein (1997) and Lucas (2004)). The better approach would complicate our analysis greatly. In a somewhat stationary world, current utility for a person is a reasonable proxy for lifetime utility.
9 We take up the possibility of a house comprising some capital as well as land below.
10 Capital income is mutualized. An entrant to the city is assumed to acquire an ownership share in total K.
11 The consumer price of a home comprises land-input cost plus a city-wide accessibility "charge." As an alternative to the accessibility charge based on city area, one might consider a charge based on city density. We do not distinguish diverse accessibility costs based on different locations in, say, a disc-shaped city. See, for example, Lucas and Rossi-Hansberg (2002). The internal movement of people from home to workplace typically generates a particular pattern of demand for land in a city, a so-called rent function.
12 Lucas and Rossi-Hansberg (2002) allow for the possibility of a household having no motion in the city, and they build in productivity gains to a firm locating near another firm.
13 "The average American spends only 14 percent of her income on food and beverages and 17 percent on transportation... By far the largest item in the budget is housing, which accounts for 40 percent of spending" (Moretti 2012; p. 169).

14 Note that we have made the exponent in the utility function for the non-traded good small. We did this to achieve "solvability" of our system with Matlab's simultaneous equation solver. Matlab requires an initial guess at the solution values. Solving successfully was difficult and to achieve a solution we ended up making the non-traded good count small. Hence this current specification of the problem numerically resembles our simple model with a government sector fairly closely.

15 Haurin (1980) allows for firms to respond directly to a climate amenity. We only have worker-households responding directly. Firms are assumed not to be climate sensitive.

16 Rosen's pioneering 1979 study of the pricing of amenities and disamenities in various cities (a sample of 19) assumed that the local wage reflected the indirect pricing of the amenities. Roback (1982) allowed for local "cost of living" differences (largely land prices) to register part of the indirect pricing of amenity premia. Here we leave local wages unchanged and let other variables register the indirect pricing of, say, a better local climate.

2 Land use for the simplified city

Basics of land-use analysis: von Thunen and efficient allocation of activities to sites. The simple monocentric city with uniform density. Declining density when households can substitute between housing and other consumption goods. Wage increments and capitalization in land rent shifts. Commuting cost decrements and capitalization in land rent shifts. Suburbanization of residential activity (sprawl).

Land allocation

The monocentric city, a basic model, has all jobs in the center, say where the export good is being produced, and residences of workers in an annulus, a sort of donut shape, surrounding the center. Each worker-household commutes back and forth each day from her residence and pays a cost per unit distance. With very similar worker-households, the wage is the same for each but commuting costs differ, depending on the distance a residence is from the center. Roughly speaking a worker with a longer (more expensive) commute gets a site for her residence that has lower-cost land. In a fairly complete model, the farther out worker-household ends up with more land per residence, with land at lower unit cost and more expenditure on commuting. When we work out when each household is in equilibrium we obtain the equilibrium land rent (price per unit per year) schedule. In other words the equilibrium land rent schedule is the schedule that allows each worker-household to be in equilibrium or be content with her "consumer choices," including her place of residence. This view of a simple city, a disc of residences with production activity in the center, descends fairly directly from the classical analysis of land use (crop distribution) in a large farm-estate, first set out in 1849 by von Thunen, a wealthy farm-estate owner in northern Germany.

We take up first the basic land-use model set out by von Thunen and then "leap" to land use in a simple city.[1] Von Thunen (1826) took up the question of which crops should be grown at which potential sites on a large rural estate. Harvested crops were to be delivered to a center. The urban version has residences "grown" on land surrounding a central point to which workers commute each day, where they earn a market wage. Since commuting costs money there is a central trade-off between increased spending on commuting by a worker and decreased cost of land for a residence marginally farther from the center. This trading off by many very similar households, each in a utility-maximizing equilibrium, generates an equilibrium land-rent function, one with the price of land declining with distance from the center.

The news here is that basic consumer theory, when combined with a von Thunen land-use model, ends up "implying" a fairly realistic looking city. It is rather like taking simple LEGO blocks and ending up with a large, interesting structure. There are shortcomings of our first-pass model in this chapter and we take some of them up in the next chapter. In addition to being able to generate a fairly good city with "minimal" ingredients, our model is able to exhibit an important trade-off when inserted into a system of similar abstract cities. Under the so-called "open-city" assumption, similar workers (almost the same education, training, experience and family structure) will migrate from city A to city B when the utility level of a similar worker in city B is above that for the worker in city A. Similar workers will be getting the same utility wherever they reside in an equilibrium, given of course more than one city under consideration. This is a form of spatial arbitrage—the elimination of utility differences by costless "migration." What about an equilibrium wage for similar workers in different places? Our model accommodates an equilibrium for two or more cities with the utilities of similar workers the same while the equilibrium wages remain different. Urban economics has a theory of equilibrium wage differences for very similar workers. The wage gap for two workers in different cities is "closed" by a housing cost gap (local land rent differences). Two similar workers, one in small city A and the other in large city B, can be on the same indifference curve even though the one in A is receiving a wage lower than her counterpart in B. This is possible because the "cost of living" in A is lower than that in B, where "cost of living" reflects mostly average land rents in the city in question. Average land rents are in general higher in a larger city and wages for similar workers are also in general higher in a larger city. Basic land-use theory for cities provides a straightforward explanation for this empirical relationship. We ask readers to resist inferring that wages are high in large cities because it is expensive to live in relatively large cities. Instead, we ask you to buy into the simple notion that a worker's wage reflects her productivity to her employer. Then one makes the inference that high-wage cities are typically those that are expensive to live in (have high land rents) and not the reverse. A person has no trouble living in an expensive city when wages there are on average high. A high wage is presumed to reflect high relative productivity of a worker. We take this up below in this chapter, in addition to basic land-use theory.

The classic statement of land allocation (von Thunen)

Von Thunen owned a large estate in the northern part of Germany in the mid-nineteenth century. He also had an academic interest in what we today call economic questions. He pondered the matter of using his land in some sort of optimal fashion. He reflected on how to divide his terrain up into different parcels devoted to different activities (different crops) in some optimal fashion. Naturally the problem should be posed as one of profit maximization on the estate, given the land as a central input into the production of crops to be harvested and sold. He simplified matters by postulating that crop i required a_i units of land per unit output and b_i units of labor per unit output. A unit of output had to be transported to a marketplace or loading place at cost t_i per unit distance.

Suppose the destination is a small port on the estate and the land will be used in semi-circular discs around the port. At the port, a unit of crop i, matured and harvested, commands price p_i. An equilibrium with a positive amount of crop i grown at distance x from the port must satisfy

$$p_i - t_i x = w b_i + a_i r_i(x).$$

This is the zero profit condition for activity i at distance x, and similarly for a crop j grown say at distance y from the port, i.e. $p_j - t_j y = w b_j + a_j r_j(y)$ where w is the wage of a worker. The $r_i(x)$ and $r_j(y)$ are referred to as land rent, an annual payment to the owner of the land for the use of a unit of land at x and y, respectively, for one year. (The owner could be the farmer himself and then the land rent is implicitly being paid to the owner.) The rent can also be interpreted as the profit per year or a residual income which a landowner gets from doing the crop-raising and paying off his other expenses (transportation cost and labor cost).

Getting the right activities (crops) to the right locations reduces to determining that, given a hypothetical allocation of crops to sites, no "other crop" can be introduced at any site and yield a higher land rent. Hence, roughly speaking, the correct allocation of activities to sites is "land rent maximizing."

We illustrate this model in Figure 2.1.

Observe that we have at correct boundary x_B

$$r_1(x_B) = r_2(x_B)$$

and at correct boundary x_E, we have

$$r_2(x_E) = r_3(x_E)$$

and at the edge, where land rent had declined to zero, we have

$$r_3(x_H) = 0.$$

For the correct allocation there is a complete rent function which is a convex outer envelope with a series of facets. We can see that the wrong crop to a site is "bidding" less at that site than the correct crop is "bidding." Rent functions are sometimes referred to as "bid-rent" schedules. The equilibrium boundary between competing activities is defined by the bids for land on either side of the boundary being the same. No new bid for a site will result in a new equilibrium boundary. Hence the boundary has no tendency to shift, given the correct allocation of crops to sites. For the boundary to be "stable," rent in competing activities on

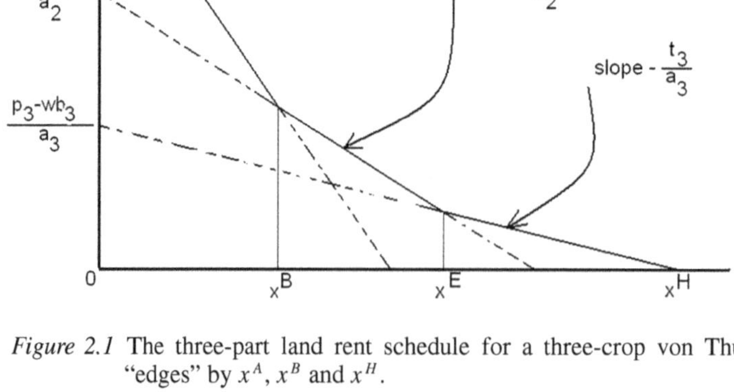

Figure 2.1 The three-part land rent schedule for a three-crop von Thunen model. Land use "edges" by x^A, x^B and x^H.

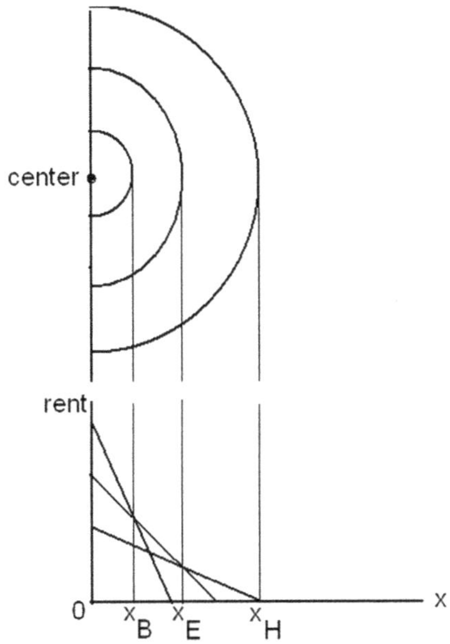

Figure 2.2 Three distinct activities on land (top) and "bid-rents" for the land sub-areas (bottom). Outputs travel from place produced to market at the center.

either side of the boundary must be the same. This characterization of an efficient land-use allocation is the one we will make use of frequently below.

In Figure 2.2 we have land use illustrated with the rent function and a bird's eye view of the land allocation.

A simple monocentric model of a city with constant residential density

The simplest model city has each resident with L-shaped "parallel" indifference curves (based on Leontief utility functions). An equilibrium has each resident (household here equated with a worker) living on the same indifference curve (obtaining the same utility level). Hence the consumption bundle (c, h) for "other consumption" and housing (here simply a site) is the same for every resident. Every worker is employed in the center[2] and receives wage w which is allocated to her round-trip commute, costing tx for distance x from the center, her "other consumption," costing $1 \times c$ dollars, and her housing costing $r(x) \times h$ dollars. Her budget constraint is then

$$w - tx = c + hr(x), \text{ for a resident at distance } x.$$

The center might be a transportation node such as a deep water port and all residents could be employed at the port. In this case our city would be a half disc. Toronto fits the half disc description as it grew up around a port on Lake Ontario. Alternatively the center might be dominated by jobs in a financial industry and workers gather each day to carry out face-to-face transactions. The city would then be exporting financial services to a market, say a territory surrounding it with smaller towns and farms. More on such cities below. Our maintained assumption is that a firm employing workers in the center has its profit, for the most part, unaffected by local climate or "bright lights" amenities. Our typical firm simply needs a workforce, first off. We do not deny that a firm's position relative to its input and output markets matters or that it might be seeking a location with scale advantages, in the future. These considerations are being held in abeyance for the moment. We are focusing primarily in this chapter and the next on workers moving between cities in response to prospective utility gain from a move.

It follows from the budget constraint for a representative resident that the land-rent function is linear in x in

$$r(x) = \frac{w-c}{h} - \frac{t}{h}x.$$

Here $\frac{w-c}{h}$ is the intercept of the rent function and $\frac{-t}{h}$ is the slope. The outer most resident pays r_A per unit land for her housing at the edge, $\overline{x}$, where r_A is the unit cost of land in farming or agriculture at the edge of the city. Hence $w - t\overline{x} = c + hr_A$, which implies that

$$\overline{x} = \frac{w-c}{t} - \frac{hr_A}{t}.$$

We have then a pretty complete portrait of a simple monocentric city. The farther out a resident lives, the cheaper is land rent and thus her so-called housing. This trade-off is calibrated in the model by the particular rent function that leaves each resident on the same indifference curve (here with the same "Liontief" bundle (c, h)). The rent function summarizes the "calibration" or the trade-off between consuming more commuting by moving farther out and being compensated with a cheaper house. From our rent function, the trade-off can be written as

$$h\frac{dr(x)}{dx} = -t.$$

Note that $\frac{dr(x)}{dx}$ is negative. This Mills equation turns out to remain valid for versions of the monocentric city in which a household has smooth, curved indifference curves (substitutability between c and h), and appears in a number of textbooks. The basic implication is that similar households cannot increase their utility by shifting their location a small amount. They may get a cheaper house by moving a bit farther from the center but they will be incurring somewhat more in commuting costs. These two "forces" balance to keep any household from increasing its utility by shifting its current location. We will come back to this Mills condition again.

Our economic analysis of the consumer differs from the standard consumer problem because we start from the assumption that many individuals are attaining the same utility level and then we solve for a price schedule (the rent function) that yields a uniform utility level for similar households.

Area of a city

Consider an example. Suppose our city were shaped like a semi-circle around a port at the "center" and was 10 miles in radius. (A mile is 5,280 feet.) Then this city would

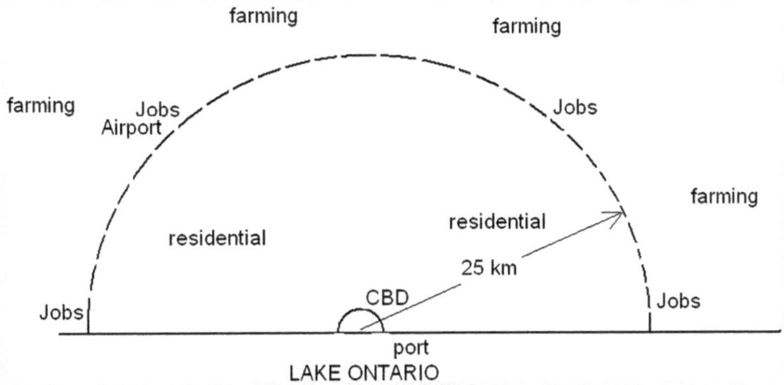

Figure 2.3 Toronto as half-disc on Lake Ontario.

comprise $\frac{1}{2}[2\pi \times (10 \times 5{,}280)^2]$ square feet of area. Say 40 percent of land were used up in roads, parks, schools, industrial and retail activity (Mills and Hamilton 1994; p. 136). Then land available for residences would be $0.60 \times \frac{1}{2}[2\pi \times (10 \times 5{,}280)^2]$. If each resident had a lot of 40×80 square feet ("small" because we want an average size that includes apartments and multi-family units), then the number of "houses" in our city would be

$$\frac{0.60 \times \frac{1}{2}[2\pi \times (10 \times 5{,}280)^2]}{40 \times 80} = 1{,}641{,}340.8$$

If each residence had 2.58 people[3] living in it, then our city's population would be 4,234,659.26. This is a quite populous city compared with, say, Toronto, which is semi-circular and is fairly built up ten miles out from its center on Lake Ontario, see Figure 2.3. Mills and Hamilton (p. 133) indicate that a typical circular city in the United States with a 15 mile radius has a population of about 2 million people. This implies that the number of square feet per residence is

$$\frac{[0.6 \times 2\pi \times (15 \times 5{,}280)^2]}{2{,}000{,}000/3.7} = 43{,}725.3,$$

which is almost 14 times our figure of 3,200 square feet per residence.[4] It seems that a city with a 15 mile radius would in fact have many large open spaces that are not being taken account of by Mills and Hamilton. Our "Toronto" is (a) only ten miles in radius and is (b) taken as a semi-circle and is still far more populous than the actual City of Toronto.

In Figure 2.4, we have a picture of Toronto as "Census Metropolitan Area" (CMA) from above. The "cells" in the map are "census tracts." Toronto's CMA contains about 5.58 million people and comprises 1,003 "Census Tracts" or about 5,563 people per census tract. However, there are census tracts with 25,000 people near the downtown. Data on neighborhoods are collected by a government agency on the basis of census

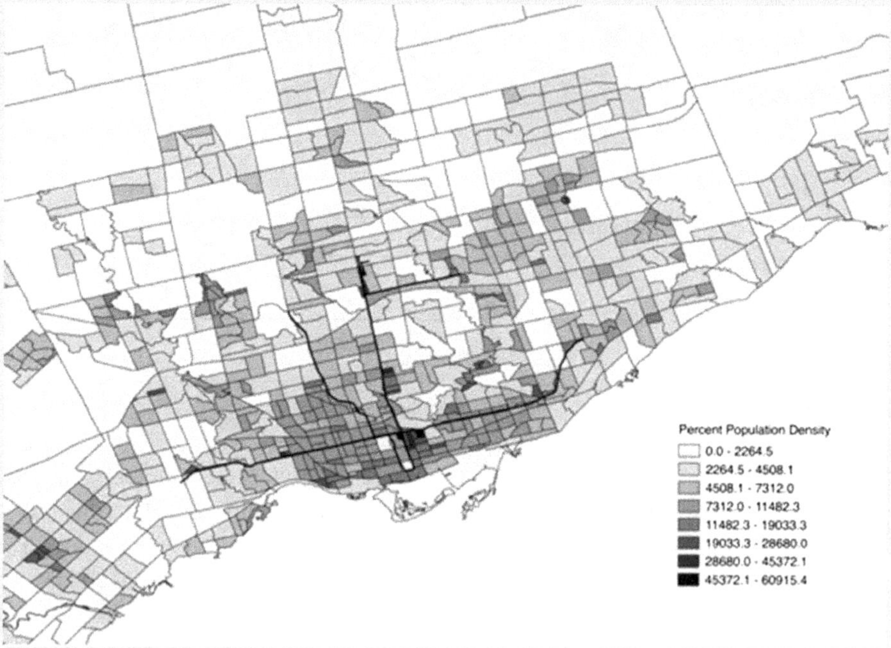

Figure 2.4 Population per census tract (Toronto).
Source: Based on Census Tract data.

tracts, a specific area within a city. The "Dissemination Area" is smaller than a census tract and data are often collected and recorded for each of these units of area. Very many pieces of data are collected for a census tract, such as number of home owners, number of home renters, number of commuters by public transit and so on. A somewhat larger version of "Toronto" is the GTA (Greater Toronto Area) with 6.05 million people. The GTA is defined by boundaries of municipalities near the city of Toronto[5]. Its area is 2,646 square miles (7,124 km^2). The City of Toronto contained 2.79 million people in 2011 and covered an area of 234 square miles. Figure 2.4 illustrates the numbers of people per census tract. Census tracts are not equal in area and hence Figure 2.4 does not capture true density. There turn out nonetheless to be more people residing per tract close to the central business district (CBD). See Figure 2.4, bottom center, near Lake Ontario.

Just as there are three concepts of Toronto (essentially three different definitions of its geographic reach), there are multiple concepts of Boston or Detroit or many other cities. This issue in defining the city under consideration makes empirical research in urban economics very difficult. Detroit, for example, is a city with large budget problems and a large population loss since about 1955. However, the huge county surrounding Detroit, Oakland County, comprises many towns and suburbs that have been doing very well economically.[6] They have experienced much population growth

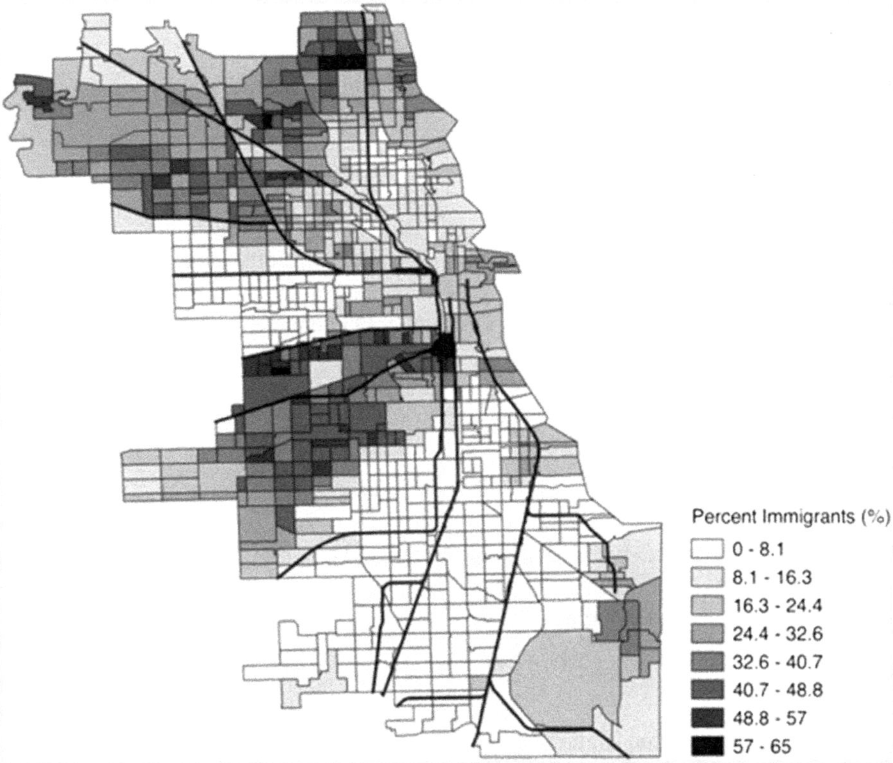

Figure 2.5 Census tracts in Chicago (2011) with most recent immigrants.
Source: Based on Census Tract data.

and a considerable inflow of large and small businesses. Thus when we say "Detroit has been an extremely troubled city in recent decades," we are talking about Detroit as "central city" rather than Detroit as "extensive urban area." Boston also is legally a mid-size city but is surrounded by many other legally defined towns such as Cambridge and Newton. Some researchers ignore legal boundaries when they do urban economics and define their cities as geographic areas with relatively dense residential and business activity (e.g. Holmes and Lee 2010). Figure 2.5 maps Chicago,[7] sketching areas with most residents who are recent immigrants. Lake Michigan is on the right-hand side.

The black lines are mass transit links, which converge on the CBD near the shoreline. Most immigrants are located along mass transit lines tending northwest and southeast.

Population in our equal-density abstract city (stylized Toronto) in the example above is

$$N(\overline{x}) = \int_0^{\overline{x}} \frac{2\pi x}{h} dx = \frac{\pi \overline{x}^2}{h}, \text{ for } h \text{ land per worker.}$$

Total land rent can be calculated or summed over a series of very thin circles, the one at distance x with rent $2\pi x r(x)dx$. Total rent in this abstract city is

$$R(\overline{x}) = \int_0^{\overline{x}} 2\pi x r(x)dx = 2\pi \left\{ \frac{w-c}{h}\frac{x^2}{2} - \frac{t}{h}\frac{x^3}{3} \right\} \Big|_0^{\overline{x}}$$

$$= 2\pi \left\{ \frac{w-c}{h}\frac{\overline{x}^2}{2} - \frac{t}{h}\frac{\overline{x}^3}{3} \right\} \text{ for } \overline{x} = \left[\frac{w-c}{t} - \frac{hr_A}{t} \right].$$

This cumbersome expression for total land rent in our abstract city becomes interesting when we ask: what change in total land rent occurs when the wage, w, in the city rises, as with a dose of technical progress for example? This land rent change is

$$\frac{dR(\overline{x})}{dw} = \frac{2\pi\overline{x}}{t}\left\{ \frac{w-c}{t} - \frac{t\overline{x}}{h} \right\} + \frac{\pi\overline{x}^2}{h}$$

$$= 2\pi\overline{x}r_A\frac{d\overline{x}}{dw} + N(\overline{x}),$$

where $\frac{1}{t} = \frac{d\overline{x}}{dw}$. Note that $\pi\overline{x}^2 r_A$ is total agricultural land rent that forms the base of total land rent associated with the city. Thus $2\pi\overline{x}r_A d\overline{x}$ is land rent in a thick "circle" at $\overline{x}$, where the thickness of the circle is defined by $d\overline{x}$. Now

$$R(\overline{x}) - \pi\overline{x}^2 r_A$$

is referred to as "differential land rent." We will use the equivalent term "net land rent" often. Thus our expression above for change of total land rent can be written as

$$\frac{dR(\overline{x})}{dw} - 2\pi\overline{x}r_A\frac{d\overline{x}}{dw} = N(\overline{x})$$

or as

$$\Delta R_n = N(\overline{x})\Delta w,$$

for

$$\Delta R_n \ (= dR(\overline{x}) - 2\pi\overline{x}r_A d\overline{x}),$$

change in net land rent, and $N(\overline{x})\Delta w$ is the total wage change associated with the $N(\overline{x})$ worker-residents in the city. The left side is the change in differential land rent, now. In words, we have: change in differential land rent equals city-wide wage increase. An alternative verbalization is: city-wide wage changes are precisely capitalized in change in net land rent. We have net land rent change induced by an exogenous wage increase for the city equal to the number of workers multiplied by the wage increase. See Figure 2.6.

Thus if we consider that $N(\overline{x})\Delta w$ represents the total impact of technical progress on this city, then this impact is being measured by the net land rent increase. We might label this: measurement of technical progress by land rent increase. Formally the wage increase is simply pushing the original linear land rent schedule outwards, and keeping the new one parallel to the original schedule. And the shift in the rent schedule involves

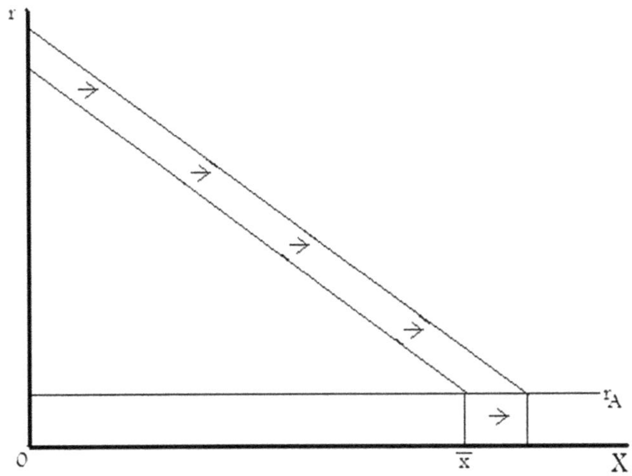

Figure 2.6 The rent function shifts out as w increases.

a small adjustment term for rent at the edge of the city as the edge moves out with the wage increase.

Measuring technical change with land rent change

Suppose we have a system of cities, each with identical worker-households, but each with different wages. This can be an equilibrium because we are assuming that every worker is on the same indifference curve (indifference curve for her (c, h) bundle) both within each city and across cities. Costless relocation of very similar worker-households should equalize utilities for very similar workers within and between cities, even those with different equilibrium wages for the very similar workers. Consider two such cities, with different populations and different wages for very similar workers. By our analysis, the one with the higher wage will be larger in both spatial footprint and population. Given the higher wage, we infer that a worker there must be more productive in the center-city activity (basic activity[8]) than is a worker in the smaller city. To a first approximation the wage difference, summed over workers, is showing up precisely in the total land rent difference between the two cities. We have then a simple measure of the technical superiority of the big city: its premium of total rent.

For two workers, one more productive than the other, a wage difference seems obvious but unravelling the source of superior productivity is not straightforward. The Mincer equation in labor economics asks the researcher to attribute a worker's higher wage to more education, training or experience. We on the other hand are considering two nominally similar workers. In a Mincer world, these two workers should be getting the same wage. However, the data on wages, worker characteristics and different cities indicate that there is a city size effect that shows up in wages. This takes the analysis beyond the basic Mincer theory of wage differences. Two similar workers will end up with different wages, the higher wage for the worker in the larger city. We also say that the worker in the larger city is more productive, this productivity premium being what "supports" the higher wage. City size can be said to be imparting a productivity premium to the workers in the city.

Glaeser (1998; p. 148) has found that

> individuals who come to cities do not immediately receive the urban wage premium… instead, their wages grow at a somewhat faster rate over the next five years. Individuals who leave cities do not experience major wage declines … [and] the urban wage premium is much higher for older urban workers, who have presumably had a greater time period to learn in cities.

This city size effect in the wage is at first glance mysterious but we accept its presence and return to discussing it later. For now, we take this city size effect as unambiguous. However, once one accepts that city size is itself embodied in local wages, one is obliged to reflect on how firms react to paying more for very similar workers in larger cities. The easiest way to address this is to assume that firms in larger cities will be specialized in different lines of productive activity compared with smaller cities. For example, New York City has a financial services sector that no other city in the United States has, though we of course acknowledge that other cities do offer generic financial services. Once we accept that larger cities have workers very similar on paper to those in smaller cities and the former are receiving higher wages, we are forced to consider that the higher-wage cities have firms that are most likely specialized in distinct activities. It is reasonable to infer that there is an industrial structure dimension (a city composition effect) to the wage premium associated with city largeness. This is emphasized by Moretti (2012).

Firms can benefit from a favorable geography effect, for instance when they locate near a good shipping node such as a good deep water port. Firms with cheaper transportation may end up offering higher wages to workers, though it seems more likely that the transportation cost premium would show up in a site rent premium. Until further notice, however, one should think about the higher wage attached to a worker in a larger city being the result of a large-city productivity effect. Glaeser (1998; pp. 142–43) remarks:

> Given standard neoclassical assumptions, higher wages for the same workers in cities must reflect a higher marginal productivity of labor for workers. This remains true even though the higher wages in cities are completely offset, from the workers' point of view, by the higher cost of living in cities…. Since the urban wage premium appears to be a centuries-old phenomenon, we must assume that over the long run, firms are quite willing to pay these higher wages. In fact the wage premium may underestimate the (productivity) benefits created by agglomeration, because agglomerative forces can also create non-work related benefits…. Lower distances between people may create a more active social environment.

In Table 2.1 in Glaeser's article, with results based on a sample of 50 large US cities in 1980, we observe that a one percent rise in annual earnings correlates with a 10 percent rise in city size; a one percent rise in the local cost of living correlates with a 16 percent rise in city size; and a one percent rise in housing costs correlates with a 19 percent rise in city size. Boustan *et al.* (2013) have investigated the urban wage premium for a group of US cities as far back as the early nineteenth century. The premium rose with the industrialization of the economy up to 1880 and then declined to 1940. Part of the wage premium they attribute to a worker productivity premium and part to a compensation for more ill health per resident in cities. The decline in the premium to 1940 they attribute mostly to the improvement in public health infrastructure in US cities. They also document the recent rise in the urban wage premium in US cities. They attribute this to the rise in the skill-based technology "bias." In 2003, Mayor Bloomberg of New York City was quoted as saying:

> If New York City is a business, it isn't Wal-Mart—it isn't trying to be the lowest-priced product in the market. It's a high-end product, maybe even a luxury product. New York offers tremendous value, but only for those companies able to capitalize on it.

And in support of the high cost of living in New York City, we note that in 2010 a monthly parking space in Manhattan was US$550, a nanny was US$600 per week, a dog-walker was US$10,000 per year and breakfast for four at the corner diner was US$40.[9]

The open-city assumption

For our two-city situation described immediately above, a worker in the smaller city might say: "I am going to relocate to the larger city where the wage is higher for workers very similar to me." However, we defined our equilibrium system of cities with every homogeneous worker[10] on the same indifference curve. This assumption refers to the fact that costless mobility by very similar households must result in each household being on the same indifference curve in equilibrium. Hence the wage facing a worker might be higher in a larger city, but her attainable utility level is the same everywhere. If she is foolish enough to go for the higher wage in the larger city, she will find that the extra income she gets from the higher wage is precisely eaten up by higher costs of housing and accompanying commuting. We see that a wage premium in a higher wage place is precisely capitalized ("reflected") in the higher land rents of the larger city. It makes no economic sense for our potential mover to relocate to the higher wage place.

Though the no-gain to relocation is correct for our abstract system of cities set-up, it retains much validity in less cut-and-dried set-ups. Free migration of very similar households will equalize the utility levels of the relevant units, say the bread-winners or head of household. This is an important zero "profit" spatial arbitrage phenomenon: costless migration will equalize utility levels for very similar households.[11] Hence wage differences between different places represent an illusory incentive to relocate. A wage gain from a move will in general be offset by a higher cost of living, usually a higher land rent cost. A 2007 survey of house prices for different cities in the United States noted that similar homes in Long Beach, California and in Detroit were priced at about US$1.6 million and US$0.076 million, respectively. A superficial examination suggests that the wage for similar workers would be much higher in California as well. We will have more to say about the no-gain to relocation theorem in Chapter 3.

The so-called open-city assumption in urban economics is the statement that utility levels of very similar workers cannot be different in different cities. Of course the cost of moving a family from city to city can be expensive but we abstract away from this friction. The United States has a reputation for much relocation activity by families per year. Between 1995 and 2000 fully one half of households relocated and half of these movers relocated within their counties (Hofmeister 2005). And there were large flows of immigrants setting up new homes in the United States at the same time. Job changes would be at the root of many of the relocations. Demographers have noticed a gradual decline in the internal "migration" of households in the United States in the past 60 years. Since 1950, the tendency for a family to move in a year has declined from 20 percent of households to 12 percent. A typical household now lives in their home for 8.6 years rather than the 5 years they did in the 1950s. Even younger working people have reduced their relocation by about 40 percent since the 1980s. Oddly enough, rates of relocation are no different for renting families compared with home-owning families. Current rates of household movement are similar to those in Denmark or Finland. One provocative explanation is that jobs are becoming more homogeneous so that position x in Phoenix is little different from position y for the same worker in Salt Lake City. One is not inclined to relocate in order to fit one's skills better to an alternative position. Evidence for this being the root explanation of the slowdown in relocation is not compelling, however. The data support the curious phenomenon of households actually tending to move to places with low-priced housing rather than high-wage jobs.[12] It is difficult to think of the United States being in essentially a household locational equilibrium with only a small number of relocators active at any one time, but this is the benchmark case from which we should start. It seems best to gloss over the frictions households face in relocating as well as the churning (turnover) that is part of any labor market. It is fair to say that in economic analysis one has to have the nature of the equilibrium set-up well understood before one can move on to the analysis of a related disequilibrium. Part of the open-city assumption is the view that the system we are analyzing is in or is very close to an equilibrium.

Rent change from a transportation improvement

A reduction in commuting cost t per unit distance changes a city's land rent in a way analogous to a change in the wage in the city. We perturb unit travel cost t and examine the impact on total land rent in the city. For this case, population, $N(\overline{x})$, is replaced by total miles of commuting by all residents, namely $M(\overline{x}) = \int_0^{\overline{x}} \frac{2\pi x}{h} x dx$, where $\frac{2\pi x}{h} dx$ is the number of people living in a very thin annulus at x and $\frac{2\pi x}{h} x dx$ is total miles of commuting of these people living at distance x from the center. One obtains

$$\frac{dR(\overline{x})}{dt} - 2\pi \overline{x} r_A \frac{d\overline{x}}{dt} = -M(\overline{x}),$$

or

$$\Delta R(\overline{x}) - 2\pi \overline{x} r_A \Delta \overline{x} = -M(\overline{x}) \Delta t.$$

Here the increase in t shrinks the city so that $\frac{dR(\overline{x})}{dt} < 0$ and $\frac{d\overline{x}}{dt} < 0$ and $\frac{dR(\overline{x})}{dt} - 2\pi \overline{x} r_A \frac{d\overline{x}}{dt}$ is the net rent change induced by the small increase in t. For the shrunken city, the total savings on commuting costs is $-M(\overline{x})\Delta t$. Hence the shrinkage in differential rent matches the increase in aggregate commuting cost for the shrunken city.

If dt were negative, as with some transportation improvement in the city that benefitted every commuter, then the city would expand at the edge and there would be more aggregate commuting travel ($-M(\overline{x})\Delta t$ would be positive) and the differential rent change would also be positive. The value of this commuting cost improvement is exactly captured by the city-wide rent increase. See Figure 2.7.

The idea of transportation improvements showing up in local rent increases goes back many decades. For example, some municipalities (e.g. Hong Kong) consider paying for part of the cost of a new subway line by charging higher taxes to businesses along the route, those whose site values have increased because of the improved access provided by the new subway. Here the idea emerges fairly precisely in an abstract model of a complete city.

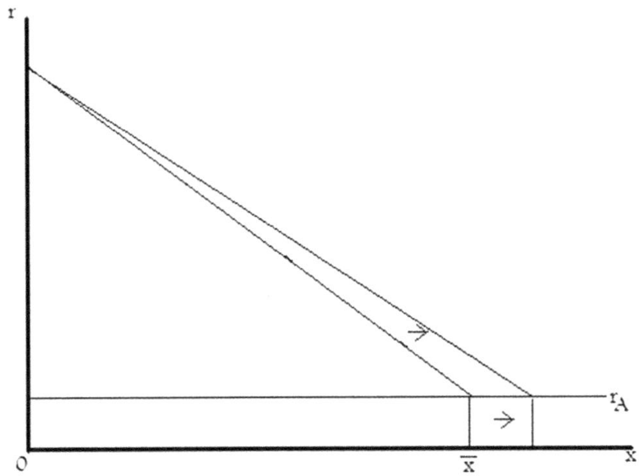

Figure 2.7 The rent function rotates out as t declines.

Cobb–Douglas utility functions

We now make our households more realistic by introducing the possibility of purchasing more "housing" (land) when land price is lower. All workers migrate to the center and receive wage w which they spend back at the site of their residences, as given by

$$w - tx = c(x) + r(x)h(x).$$

Housing here is simply some amount of bare land (the tent city), $h(x)$, and $r(x)$, land rent, is outlay per year per unit of land; $c(x)$ is consumption of "other goods" and has price unity, and t is commuting cost per unit distance, round-trip. Identical households with identical income w implies

$$\frac{dw}{dx} = t + \frac{dc}{dx} + r(x)\frac{dh}{dx} + h(x)\frac{dr}{dx} = 0.$$

Households are taken to be identical (same skill and experience per worker and same demographics per household) and they are assumed to end up with the same utility, $\overline{U} = U(c, h)$. Hence

$$\frac{dU}{dx} = U_c\frac{dc}{dx} + U_h\frac{dh}{dx} = 0.$$

Efficiency in consumption implies the ratio of marginal utilities equal to the price ratio or

$$\frac{U_c}{U_h} = \frac{1}{r(x)}.$$

Hence

$$\frac{dc}{dx} = -\frac{U_h}{U_c}\frac{dh}{dx} = -r(x)\frac{dh}{dx}.$$

This can be inserted in the $\frac{dw}{dx}$ relation to get

$$h(x)\frac{dr}{dx}+t=0,$$

which as we observed above (the Mills equation) is the expression that reflects very well each household being on the same indifference curve in our city. Though it is the same expression it is now holding more generally since households are able now to substitute $h(x)$ for $c(x)$ if they were to relocate.

For our Cobb–Douglas case, we have $\overline{U}=c(x)^{\alpha}h(x)^{1-\alpha}$ and efficiency in consumption is

$$\frac{\alpha h}{(1-\alpha)c}=\frac{1}{r(x)}.$$

In Appendix 2.1 we obtain

$$h(x)=\frac{Z}{r(x)^{\alpha}}\text{ for }Z=\overline{U}\left(\frac{1-\alpha}{\alpha}\right)^{\alpha},$$

and

$$c(x)=\left(\frac{\alpha}{1-\alpha}\right)Zr(x)^{1-\alpha}.$$

Placing these in the budget constraint and solving for $r(x)$ results in

$$r(x)=\left(\frac{1-\alpha}{Z}\right)^{1/(1-\alpha)}\times(w-tx)^{1/(1-\alpha)}.$$

Since $w-tx$ gets smaller as x increases, we have our rent function declining with distance. See Figure 2.8.

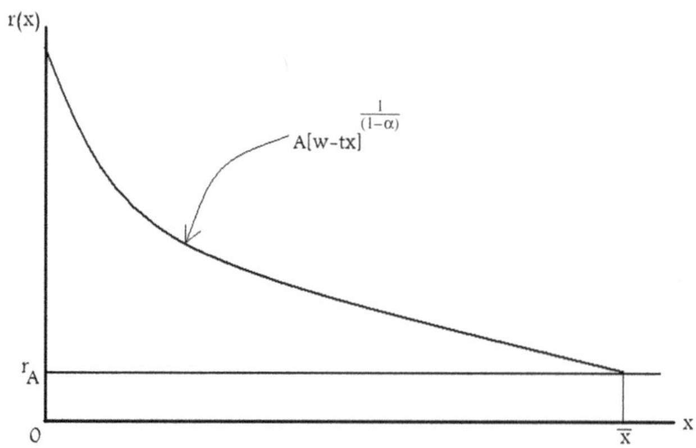

Figure 2.8 The rent function, given the Cobb–Douglas utility function; A is a constant and α is between zero and unity.

The slope of the rent function is

$$\frac{-t}{1-\alpha}\left(\frac{1-\alpha}{Z}\right)^{1/(1-\alpha)} \times (w-tx)^{\alpha/(1-\alpha)}$$

and the second derivative is positive, indicating the expected convex shape (declining faster near the center). The percentage decline of

$$\frac{dr(x)/dx}{r(x)} = \frac{-t}{(1-\alpha)(w-tx)}$$

turns out to be somewhat larger in absolute value farther from the center. The decline is slightly "more linear" than exponential. Recall that in the case of the utility function in the Leontief form, the rent function was precisely linear in distance from the CBD.

The shape of the rent function

For 1990, Mills and Hamilton (1994) take w to be US$20,000, $1-\alpha$ to be 0.2 (20 percent of income is spent on "housing") and $\frac{dr(x)/dx}{r(x)} = -0.04$. If we insert these figures into our formula for $x=0$, we obtain $t=$ US$160 per year for an average worker (US$160 is cost per mile round trip). This is in fact the figure that Mills and Hamilton make use of. At 10 miles from the center, we have $w - tx = 20{,}000 - 1{,}600 =$ US$18,400. This implies that $\frac{dr(x)/dx}{r(x)} = -0.043$. The land-rent function would be exponentially declining if the percentage change were unchanging with distance from the CBD (favored by Mills and Hamilton) but for our case (Cobb–Douglas utility function) the percentage decline varies with distance from the CBD. Our rent function is somewhat "more linear" than the comparable exponential case.[13]

Suppose that in 2010 the average resident has a wage of US$70,000 per year. We can of course make use of the Mills–Hamilton values of $1-\alpha = 0.2$ and $\frac{dr(x)/dx}{r(x)} = -.04$ and insert a w of US$70,000 per year. This implies that t must rise by 3.5 to US$560 per year per mile. It remains true in our Cobb–Douglas world that $\frac{dr(x)/dx}{r(x)}$ must be greater than $-.04$ in absolute value when distance x is positive. Fairly early in his extensive empirical work on land-rent functions, Mills elected to deal with rents that were exponentially declining from the center, as with $r(x) = Ae^{-\delta tx}$. For this rent function, $\frac{dr(x)/dx}{r(x)} = -\delta t$. This compares with our case of $\frac{dr(x)/dx}{r(x)} = \frac{-t}{(1-\alpha)(w-tx)}$. Hence for tx relatively small compared with w, our $\frac{dr(x)/dx}{r(x)}$ will be approximately constant or largely independent of distance—approximately exponentially declining and analogous to Mills's $\frac{dr(x)/dx}{r(x)}$. But we have a weighting factor $\frac{1}{(1-\alpha)(w-tx)}$, which makes the pace of decline approximately exponential and different in value from that in Mills. Nevertheless, one might say that the Cobb–Douglas utility function is compatible with an almost exponentially declining land-rent function given that our 0.04 and 0.043 are pretty close and the two households in question are ten miles apart.

Suppose parking in 2010 costs about US$1,200 per year at work (a low estimate) and a 10 mile round trip per day costs US$3,600 in fuel. (The household is five miles from the center.) Suppose further that the automobile used for commuting costs US$5,000 in depreciation, repairs and insurance per year. This is approximately US$10,000 per year or US$2,000 per mile round trip per year. That is, t is US$2,000. Given $(1-\alpha)=0.2$ and the rent function declining at 4 percent per mile, one needs an annual income of about $\frac{2,000}{160} \times 20,000 =$ US$250,000 per year to balance the equation. This income level seems high for an average big-city resident in Canada or the United States. It comes out high in our Mills–Hamilton approach because we started with an estimate for t and then proceeded to our estimate for w. Mills and Hamilton worked from w to a value for t.

General capitalization in rent change

Let us now consider a general model with identical households with utility defined in $U(c(x), h(x))$. Everyone is employed in the center and gets wage w and attains utility level $\overline{U}$. A household's budget constraint is

$$w - tx = c(x) + r(x)h(x),$$

and consumption efficiency obtains in

$$\frac{U_h}{U_c} = r(x)$$

for each household. We also have the fixed edge rent r_A.

We analyze capitalization of, say, wage increase for our city, given U unchanging. Keep in mind that part of the response by a resident to the wage change is the adjustment in the amount of land that her home is built on. Consider the two total derivatives

$$dU = U_c dc + U_h dh = 0$$

and

$$\begin{aligned} dw &= tdx + dc + rdh + hdr \\ &= tdx + hdr \end{aligned}$$

since

$$dc = -\frac{U_h}{U_c} dh = -rdh.$$

Hence we have $\frac{dr}{dw} = \frac{1}{h} - \frac{t}{h}\frac{dx}{dw}$. This can be inserted in the expression for net land-rent change (see Appendix 2.2) and we obtain

$$\Delta R_n(\overline{x}) = N(\overline{x})dw - \Delta T(\overline{x})dw.$$

This expression includes the "extra" term[14] $\Delta T(\overline{x})dw$ which we refer to as the city-wide adjustment cost. In words we might refer to our result as: net rent changes capitalize city-side wages increments directly and include an indirect adjustment term. The adjustment cost reflects the fact that when the wage w is increased for all residents, each resident re-optimizes for their best consumption bundle and ends up with a slightly different location as well as a chosen bundle (c, h). Thus in re-optimizing with a new larger w, each household is adjusting its location and best bundle. The sum of these individual adjustment costs turns out to be captured in our term ΔT, which is in fact a term representing the sum of each household's changed commuting costs. Hence the total adjustment cost (restructuring the city) is captured in an aggregate commuting cost adjustment. Each resident will shift location marginally farther from the center and thus $\Delta T dw$ will be positive. Hence net land-rent change underestimates the total wage change by what we take to be a small amount.

Our capitalization result for commuting cost change will also hold quite generally. That is, for an improvement in transportation ($dt < 0$) we could derive

$$\Delta R_n = -M(\overline{x})dt + \Delta T dt,$$

where $-\Delta T dt$ is the city-wide adjustment cost. If, however, commuting cost were not linear in distance from the center, the capitalization result for changes in commuting cost would end up being more complicated. The assumption that commuting cost per unit distance does not vary with the distance a residence is from the center is clearly unsatisfactory as a "stylized fact"; but arriving at a good commuting cost function is an open topic.

Our results above for the case of a Cobb–Douglas utility function become illustrations of our general results in this section. It is easy to make the case that the increase in family incomes and the lowering of costs of commuting to work since, say, 1900 have contributed centrally to the suburbanization of residential activity in the United States and elsewhere. As Mills (1999; p. 1) stated: "In US metropolitan areas, some 57% of population and 70% of employment were located in central cities in 1950; by the mid-1990s the figures were 30–35% and 40–45%," and also "High income residents demand large quantities of housing, and cheap land for large houses is available away from central cities."[15] See also Brueckner and Fansler (1983). Mills (1999; p. 3) was exasperated with people who see low density residential development as a negative outcome:

> It is unfortunate that today's anti-suburbanization literature is hardly ever written in the context of modern welfare economics.... I have presumed ... that any suburban land misallocation is the result of mispricing of resources. This mispricing, in turn, results from the ineffective regulation of externalities, or from other failed government policies.

A "mis-price" that some anti-sprawl observers note is when the developer of a new tract of houses at the edge of a city is not assessed for the full cost of installing sewers, streets, street lights, etc. The buyers of the new homes can get them marginally below full cost and the taxpayers in the "old part" of the city end up subsidizing the owners of the new homes at the city's edge. Developers can sell new homes more easily when the price is slightly lower. The "mis-charging" for the development of a new suburb can lead to more development at the edge of a city. The way to reduce sprawl is of course to make land expensive for new suburbs. Developers will then tend to lay out projects with marginally smaller lot sizes in an effort to keep the price of new homes accessible to new buyers. Brueckner (2000) links sprawl to excessive commuting and excessive congestion in cities. He proposes the creation of congestion taxes to assist in restraining sprawl. Brueckner restates his earlier position, namely that population growth, household income growth and declining commuting costs are the basic drivers of low-density development at the edge of cities.

We define sprawl as residential development at the edge of a city with much land per home.[16] Burchfield *et al.* (2006) use detailed satellite data of the United States for two dates ten years apart and conclude that the amount of land per home at the edge of cities has not been increasing. Hence they infer an absence of sprawl for the United States for recent years. Angel (2011) discovered, using satellite data, that in a sample of 120 cities from around the world, population was growing at about 1.6 percent per year and land area was expanding at about 3.7 percent per year between 1990 and 2000. This hints at something like a law of urban sprawl. However, densities for these same cities, that is people per built-up hectare, varied considerably. Cities in Angel's sample in developed areas had densities about twice those in Europe and Japan and cities in Europe and Japan had densities about three times those in the United States, Canada and Australia, a set of "land-rich" high-income nations. Dhaka, the capital of Bangladesh, and Hong Kong had the highest densities in Angel's sample while Tacoma, Washington had the lowest. Higher income does lead to lower density settlement in cities (double the income and density declines by 40 percent), and population increase is positively related to density increase (double the population and density rises by about 19 percent). Higher levels of income inequality were associated with lower densities. Angel recommends that city leaders do not pursue policies of "containment" to counter the trend to lower density development in cities around the world. People who oppose sprawl are really asking for development at the edge of cities with relatively small amounts of land per residence, though they might not articulate their position this way. A trend of increased sprawl is then new developments, as time passes, with more land per new residence. Glaeser and Kahn (2004) view sprawl as "the inexorable product of car-based living," as well, we add, of truck-based transportation. They express concern that urban folk who cannot afford the cost of owning and operating an automobile are effectively denied access to important job centers. Relative to an unsatisfactory policy of "containment," they are willing to entertain the notion of subsidizing access to cars for low-income residents.

Houston is our quintessential example of a car-based city. Its population of 2.162 million people in 2013 is spread over 600 square miles, leaving a density of only 3,600 people per square mile. The metropolitan area, Houston–the Woodlands–Sugarland contains about six million people, about the population of New York's five boroughs. New York City has a density of about 27,778/sq mile while Manhattan comes in at 70,825/sq mile. In 1940 Houston occupied Harris County alone and its population was about 385,000, making the city twenty-first in size for the United States. About 220,000 residents were added by 1950. By 1960, Houston ranked seventh in population for the United States at 938,000 residents. In 1990 it moved up to fourth place with a population of about 1.63 million people. Currently about half the residents are white with about half of those being Hispanic. About a quarter of the residents are African American. About 400,000 illegal aliens are estimated to be residing in Houston. The city is attached to the Gulf of Mexico, making it a very active port. It is a cosmopolitan, multi-cultural city and is second in the United States for number of headquarters of Fortune 500 companies. The topography is flat and the abundant land and the light-handed land-use regulation has made suburban housing low-priced. In remarking on the high cost of a new condominium in New York City, Glaeser (2011; p. 151) observes: "That's a lot more than the US$200,000 that it costs of putting up a nice 2,500 square foot home in Houston." It makes sense to see low-cost residences as an attraction for many kinds of economic activity. We should presume then that the profile of jobs in Houston will be quite different from those in New York City, since New York is, on average, expensive to live in.

Table 2.1 Labor force percentages, 2013

Category	*Houston*	*New York*
Mining, logging and construction	10	3
Manufacturing	10	3
Trade, transportation and utilities	20	17
Information	1	4
Financial activities	5	10
Professional and business services	15	16
Education and health	12	20
Leisure and hospitality	10	9.4
Other	3.5	4.4
Government	13	14

Source: US Department of Labor, Bureau of Labor Statistics.

The US Bureau of Labor Statistics breaks non-farm employment (2,788,400 and 5,514,900 for Houston and New York City, respectively, for 2013) into ten categories. We record in Table 2.1 the percentages of workers in each category for Houston and New York City (this latter the metropolitan area defined by New York, White Plains, Wayne, NY-NJ).

Table 2.1 indicates that Houston has about three times more workers than New York in the first two categories (Mining, logging and construction, and Manufacturing). New York has about half its labor force in Information, Financial Activities, Professional and business services, and Education and health, while Houston has about 33 percent working in these employment categories. New York City appears to have more high-wage jobs and of course is a more expensive place to get accommodation. We are seeing a clear composition effect: the labor profiles of Houston and New York are different and the average wages and cost of living between the places are different. We are seeing something of a deviation of the trend of average wages with city size here. We should probably attribute the deviation to the distinct geographies of Houston versus New York. Manhattan is densely settled with residents and businesses in part because it is an island, a place with accessibility issues for suburban residents. Houston has developed on a flat plain, with light-handed land-use regulation. This has resulted in a low-density form for the city and has endowed the place with relatively low-cost housing. This in turn has attracted certain types of economic activity, those involving somewhat lower wages than those in New York City. Geography and land-use regulation have yielded somewhat idiosyncratic forms for Houston and New York City. Houston's harbor is different from the one in Chicago or Toronto. In shape, Houston has developed more as a circle rather than as a half circle. There are 263.1 people per square kilometer for Houston and 488.3 people per square kilometer for Chicago.

Sprawl can show up in part as workers commute longer distances to city centers. This has been documented recently for England and Wales. In the 1980s a long commute in England and Wales was about 10 km. The figure was 13.04 on average in 2001 and had moved up to 15 km by 2011. Though most workers commute by automobile, commuting by rail went up by 37 percent between 2001 and 2011. Women in their 30s commuted farthest with about 35 percent clocking more than 10 km each day in 2011. Greater London's population increased by 12 percent between 2001 and 2011. Strict zoning bylaws limit new housing developments directly at the edge of the city. House prices in London jumped 18 percent over 2013 compared with a 9 percent increase country-wide. The centers of cities in Britain are doing better, perhaps in response to the rise in the length of the commutes, with a significant expansion of jobs in Manchester and Birmingham. For London there has been a noticeable decline in jobs in some suburbs.[17]

We can conceive of a system of Cobb–Douglas cities of different sizes (and productivities) and distinct wage rates. If, in addition, households were heterogeneous (Chapter 3 contains some detail on this), we would have a complicated system of cities, not too different from, say, that of the United States. Such a system has recently been modelled and probed with econometrics by Van Nieuwerburgh and Weill (2010). What they say about their analysis helps place our analysis above in their broader context.

> The [Van Nieuwerburgh–Weill] equilibrium provides the endogenous joint dynamics of cross-sectional house prices, construction, labor income and employment. In particular, more able households sort into more productive regions. House price differentials between metropolitan areas compensate for the income differential of the marginal, lowest ability household in the location, making that household indifferent between staying and moving to the next best metropolitan area. Households also live in smaller and more expensive quarters if they choose to work in higher-income metropolitan areas. Lastly, higher-income metropolitan areas have on average a larger housing stock and a larger workforce ... The model features larger increases in wages at the top of the regional wage distribution. Second, it produces a large increase in the ratio of housing price to construction cost, consistent with the findings of Glaeser *et al.* (2007) and Davis and Heathcote (2007) that the non-structure component of house prices has become more important in the last 30 years. Third, it generates an increasing concentration of people in highly productive regions; the fraction of people working in the highest wage quintile increases by 8.2 percentage points in the model and data. Fourth, it is consistent with the observations that, in repeated cross-sectional regressions of house prices on wages, the coefficient on wages increased over the 1975–2007 period. ... a one dollar wage differential became compensated by a larger and larger price differential.
>
> (Van Nieuwerburgh and Weill 2010; pp. 1568–69)

Our city with identical households and Cobb–Douglas utility functions can be considered a component of the more comprehensive, multi-city, heterogeneous household model of Stijn Van Nieuwerburgh and Pierre-Olivier Weill.

Moretti (2012) is particularly interested in cities with workers with different skills, often simply those with college degrees and those without. He developed an indicator of local cost of living (a basket of commodities that an ordinary family consumes) for 288 US cities. The appropriate weights on various commodities which Moretti arrived at for the average family were 14 percent of income on food, 17 percent on transportation, 3 percent on clothing, 6 percent on medical care, 5 percent on recreation and 6 percent on education and communication. Housing came in at 40 percent (p. 169). The 20 most costly places ranked are in column 1 of Table 2.2. The 18 least costly places to live in the United States are in column 2 and are ranked from least costly down. Moretti (2012; p. 168) said that "Most of the differences in the cost of living among metropolitan areas reflect differences in the cost of housing, which in turn mostly reflect differences in the cost of land."

Moretti concludes that the lowest cost places have the weakest "strength of the labor market." Certainly cities with a profile that includes high-tech activity are in the list of expensive places to live. "When the labor market in a city strengthens, both workers' earnings and the cost of housing tend to increase." (p. 170). Moretti (2012) worked out hourly wage values for

Table 2.2 US cities ranked by cost of living

CITY (costly)	*CITY (low-cost)*
San Jose	Johnstown
Stamford, CT	Anniston
San Francisco area	Gadsden
Santa Cruz	Danville
Santa Barbara area	McAllen area
Ventura area	Alexandria, LA
Boston	Altoona
Honolulu	Johnson City area
Santa Rosa area	Duluth area
Salinas area	Brownsville area
New York city area	Joplin
Washington, DC area	Williamsport
Los Angeles area	Lynchburg
San Diego	St. Joseph
Seattle area	Sharon
Trenton	Terre Haute
Bridgeport, CT	Lima
Fort Lauderdale area	Youngstown area
Austin	
Anchorage	

Source: Moretti (2012).

each of his 288 cities. Of the ten highest-wage cities for workers with just High School education, only one, Monmouth-Ocean, NJ, is not among the highest cost places to live (Table 2.2), i.e. there is the strong inference that high wages and high cost-of-living go together. This is also true for workers with college education. Danbury, CT and Monmouth-Ocean, NJ are the only two high-wage cities that are not among the high-cost-of-living cities.

Somewhat different, however, is the situation with the low-wage places. Only three low-wage cities for both workers with only high school and workers with college are among the lowest 18 cost-of-living cities. That is, a low-cost-of-living city is not typically a lowest wage city, though of course the average wage for a low-cost-of-living city can be pretty low. Moretti is inclined to link high average wages for a city to the industrial composition of a city: those with dynamic or high-tech sectors need highly educated and highly trained workers and such workers command high wages. He sees substantial spillovers resulting from the clustering of high-wage workers in certain cities. These well-paid workers demand good hairdressers, dog-walkers, coffee shops, gyms, etc., and the wages of workers in these ancillary activities get pulled up. We have been linking local high cost-of-living to local high wages which in turn we attribute to the high productivity of workers in larger, denser cities. This is not too different from Moretti's line of thought. He wants to distinguish dynamic high-wage places with an abundance of educated workers from sluggish or stagnant large cities that lack leading high-tech sectors employing mostly highly educated workers. Detroit and Cleveland may be large cities but they also have relatively low cost-of-living and lack the abundance of highly educated workers that one finds in Seattle and San Francisco. Moretti asks us to refine our thinking on the strength of the link between city size and average worker productivity. He asks for a city industry composition effect to be kept front and center when we inquire about high average wages in city X.

Summary

Basic land-use theory (Von Thunen theory) is about allocating competing activities to sites. In the absence of externalities, site boundaries for the competing activities shift until an allocation is compatible with a rent function that has no jumps at the spatial boundary. In addition one can envisage competing activities as competing at every site for the space in question: the highest bidder wins and this outcome is part of the definition of an efficient use of the sites. These ideas come out of the classical von Thunen model of allocating crops to areas for an efficient use of land.

Urban economics borrowed from the von Thunen model and developed a model of a city with all jobs at the center and the residences of workers in an area surrounding the center. At the spatial edge, agricultural activity and residential activity compete for sites in a Thunen-like fashion. The generation of an equilibrium land-rent function becomes a central focus. The rent or annual charge on land becomes a sort of puzzle piece that when inserted in a household's utility maximization problem leaves the household in a utility maximizing equilibrium. When we bring the correct land-rent function to each resident of our city, each household maximizes its utility "correctly" and similar households are on the same indifference curve. Or one might think of the equilibrium of many similar households becoming "closed" by the presence of the appropriate land-rent function. Thus a characterization of land-use economics is finding the appropriate rent function. Central to the locational equilibrium of a household is the "cost" of an equilibrium shift in location: a small shift in the location of the household farther from the center involves a cheaper home (land rent declines with distance from the center) but a marginally more costly commute. And the bottom line is: von Thunen analysis plus basic textbook consumer theory allows us to create fairly plausible-looking cities, on paper. We have left open the question of why so many jobs in cities are clustered in a central area (a central business district). This question has no simple unique answer. We will return to this matter of the clustering of jobs many times in this book.

The "open-city" assumption involves very similar worker-households ending up with the same utility in different cities. And two cities of different sizes under the open-city assumption will in general have similar workers with different wages—an odd outcome, at first glance, but one supported by much empirical evidence. The larger city will generally have similar workers earning higher wages but these better paid workers will be facing, on average, higher housing prices in the larger city. This trade-off of higher wages versus higher residential costs allows similar workers to end up on the same indifference curve in two different cities, one large and one small.

A wage increase for one city in a group of cities translates into in-migration from neighboring cities and a restoration of utility-indifference across locations for a household. The restoration mechanism is the shift in land rent upwards, a shift caused by the inflow of new residents. There turns out to be simple and instructive expressions for the land rent shifts caused by the initial wage increases. These are valuable "capitalization results." The wage shift shows up in or is capitalized in a neat package "beyond" the labor market *per se*. Exogenous changes in the cost of commuting operate in a similar fashion. The cost shift gets capitalized in a land rent change that takes on a simple and instructive form.

The urban model above has a single center (the CBD or central business district) where all the jobs in the city are. Two questions arise: why do jobs or firms offering jobs concentrate or agglomerate in a central place, and why do we not see job centers dispersed throughout the area of a modern city? The first question is at the core of urban economics: why geographic concentration of economic activity? Some tentative answers are: workers with special skills fit job vacancies better in larger rather than smaller places; a worker facing irregular spells of employment will get more work on average in a larger city; a producer of widgets finds intermediate input suppliers nearer by in a larger place; and workers involved in invention and innovation find supporting folk more easily in a larger city. The last of these answers is a species of so-called face-to-face activity: it can be interpreted as an exogenous benefit to a "face-to-face" activity firm getting a free spin-off or externality that is larger in a city with a more populous center. If my firm can interact with more workers in a face-to-face setting then my specialized firm will do better than when it must deal with key workers who are widely dispersed. We clearly have to delve into these issues in some depth before we come to the end of urban economics. The second matter, employment center decentralization, can actually be addressed quite easily in a straightforward extension of the monocentric city model. This is done in the next chapter.

Another extension involves the incorporation of different types of workers in a single city. Suppose there are both high- and lower-wage workers employed at the center. We must place these different workers in an equilibrium residential area. We take this up in the next chapter. And we also take up there the matter of tall buildings appearing where land rent is relatively high and fewer tall buildings appearing where land rent is relatively low. The capital to land ratio changes systematically with the local changes in land rent. We incorporate these differences in capital to land ratios in an equilibrium land-use model.

Main points of Chapter 2

1 The simple monocentric city has one type of worker-household with residences spread around on an annulus or "donut," with all jobs in the center. Each household gets the same wage, paid at its workplace in the center. Each household's "at home" wage is net of costs of commuting to and from the workplace in the center.

2 For all similar households to be in equilibrium, each ends up on the same indifference curve. This involves generating a land rent schedule that has land costing less per unit the farther the unit is from the center. A worker with a longer commute can obtain land priced lower per unit for her home.

3 An equilibrium land rent schedule for the monocentric city declines with distance from the center because a lower price for land for a residence compensates a worker-household for incurring more outlay in her budget for commuting.

4 When a worker can substitute housing for other things consumed, she will end up with more housing (a larger home site) the farther from the center she locates her residence.

5 When the wage a worker-household receives in our city is raised, the city expands in area (its footprint, some say) and population. The land rent schedule shifts out and up and the "extra" land value in the city is closely related to the "extra" wage bill going to worker-households.

6 A higher wage paid to a worker is generally associated with the worker being more productive at her task. More productive labor forces for a city tend to be higher-wage labor forces and such cities are typically larger in area and population (the law of urban growth).

7 Lower commuting costs per unit distance result in shifts to the city structure and land rent somewhat analogous to those we observe under a wage increase. Lower commuting cost cities are larger and the rent schedule for the city shifts up and out when unit distance costs decline (Figure 2.6).

8 Sprawl, more land per home at the edge of a city, can be attributed to higher income per household in our monocentric city or lower unit distance costs for commuting.

Questions and problems

1 Consider your city as an area that is approximately a circle ($\pi\overline{x}^2$) or a half circle ($\frac{1}{2}\pi\overline{x}^2$). Recall that $\pi \approx 3.14$. and 1 mile = 5,280 feet. Find the radius $\overline{x}$ of your city.

- a If the average household (three people) occupies about 50 by 30 square feet, what fraction of land in your city is being used for residences?
- b Estimate how much of the remaining area is taken up by roads; by schools, hospitals, government offices, parks and churches; by retail activity; by other commercial and business activity.
- c Estimate cost per square foot of land near the center (CBD) of your city, and the cost per square foot of land in the suburban edge of your city. Multiply each value by the current interest rate (say 4 percent). The line joining these two values over distance from the city center is an approximate land rent schedule.

2 Houston is a dynamic city with low density of residential activity. Is low density a positive contributing factor to Houston's good economic performance or a problem that needs the attention of local and state government?

Appendix 2.1: The Cobb–Douglas utility function for households

All workers migrate to the center and receive wage w which they spend back at the site of their residences in

$$w - tx = c(x) + r(x)h(x).$$

Housing here is simply a patch of land, $h(x)$, and land rent, $r(x)$, is outlay per year per unit of land; $c(x)$ is consumption of "other goods" and has price unity; t is commuting cost per unit distance, round-trip.

Households are taken to be identical (same skill and experience per worker and same demographics per household) and they end up with the same utility, $\overline{U} = U(c, h)$. Efficiency in consumption implies the ratio of marginal utilities equal to the price ratio or

$$\frac{U_c}{U_h} = \frac{1}{r(x)}.$$

For our Cobb–Douglas case, we have $\overline{U} = c(x)^{\alpha}h(x)^{1-\alpha}$ and efficiency is represented by

$$\frac{\alpha h}{(1-\alpha)c} = \frac{1}{r(x)}.$$

Hence $c = \frac{\overline{U}^{1/\alpha}}{h^{(1-\alpha)/\alpha}}$ and the efficiency condition becomes

$$\frac{\alpha h}{(1-\alpha)\frac{\overline{U}^{1/\alpha}}{h^{(1-\alpha)/\alpha}}} = \frac{1}{r},$$

giving us

$$h(x) = \left(\frac{1-\alpha}{\alpha}\right)^{\alpha} \frac{\overline{U}}{r(x)^{\alpha}} = \frac{Z}{r(x)^{\alpha}} \text{ for } Z = \overline{U}\left(\frac{1-\alpha}{\alpha}\right)^{\alpha}.$$

Then

$$c(x) = \left(\frac{\alpha}{1-\alpha}\right) Zr(x)^{1-\alpha}.$$

Residential density is $1/h(x) = r(x)^{\alpha}/Z$ and density moves down from the center somewhat as land rent moves down from the center. A resident farther from the center occupies more land because land is cheaper there.

We now put $h(x)$ and $c(x)$ into the budget constraint and obtain

$$w - tx = \left\{\frac{1}{1-\alpha}\right\} Zr(x)^{1-\alpha}.$$

Thus

$$r(x) = \left(\frac{1-\alpha}{Z}\right)^{1/(1-\alpha)} \times (w - tx)^{1/(1-\alpha)}.$$

It follows that the percentage rent decline from the center is

$$\frac{dr(x)/dx}{r(x)} = \frac{-t}{(1-\alpha)(w-tx)},$$

which gets smaller as x approaches the edge, $\overline{x}$.

Observe that

$$\begin{aligned}
\frac{dr(x)}{dw} &= \frac{1}{1-\alpha}\left(\frac{1-\alpha}{Z}\right)^{1/(1-\alpha)} \frac{(w-tx)^{1/(1-\alpha)}}{(w-tx)} \\
&= \frac{1}{Z}\frac{r(x)}{(w-tx)\left(\frac{1-\alpha}{Z}\right)} \\
&= \frac{1}{Z} r(x)^{\alpha},
\end{aligned}$$

which is $1/h(x)$ (see the expression for $h(x)$ above).

Thus for total rent, $R(\overline{x}) = \int_0^{\overline{x}} r(x) 2\pi x dx$, we have the comparative static result

$$\begin{aligned}
\frac{dR(\overline{x})}{dw} &= \int_0^{\overline{x}} \frac{dr(x)}{dw} 2\pi x dx + 2\pi \overline{x} r_A \frac{d\overline{x}}{dw} \\
&= \int_0^{\overline{x}} \frac{1}{h(x)} 2\pi x dx + 2\pi \overline{x} r_A \frac{d\overline{x}}{dw} \\
&= N(\overline{x}) + 2\pi \overline{x} r_A \frac{d\overline{x}}{dw},
\end{aligned}$$

for r_A equal to edge land rent and $N(\overline{x})$ the total population before the increase in the wage rate. This is our wage increase capitalization result. Analogous steps yield our capitalization result for a commuting cost increase in

$$\frac{dR(\overline{x})}{dt} = -M(\overline{x}) + 2\pi\overline{x}r_A\frac{d\overline{x}}{dt}$$

for $M(\overline{x})$ total miles of commuting in the city, before the commuting cost increase.

Appendix 2.2: General dw and dt incidence

Let us consider a general model with identical households with utility defined by $U(c(x), h(x))$. Everyone is employed in the center and earns wage w and attains utility level $\overline{U}$. A household's budget constraint is

$$w - tx = c(x) + r(x)h(x)$$

and consumption efficiency obtains as in

$$\frac{U_h}{U_c} = r(x)$$

for each household. We also have the fixed edge rent r_A. Hence $\overline{x}$ is defined by $r(\overline{x}) = r_A$.

To analyze capitalization of, say, an increase in w, given U unchanging, we consider the two total derivatives:

$$dU = U_c dc + U_h dh = 0$$

and

$$\begin{aligned} dw &= tdx + dc + rdh + hdr \\ &= tdx + hdr \end{aligned}$$

since

$$dc = -\frac{U_h}{U_c}dh = -rdh.$$

Hence we have $\frac{dr}{dw} = \frac{1}{h} - \frac{t}{h}\frac{dx}{dw}$. This can be inserted in the expression for net land rent change, namely $\frac{dR}{dw} - 2\pi\overline{x}r_A\frac{d\overline{x}}{dw} = \int_0^{\overline{x}} \frac{dr}{dw} 2\pi x dx$, and we obtain

$$\frac{dR}{dw} - 2\pi\overline{x}r_A\frac{d\overline{x}}{dw} = \int_0^{\overline{x}} \left[\frac{1}{h} - \frac{t}{h}\frac{dx}{dw}\right] 2\pi x dx.$$

We can write this more compactly as

$$\Delta R_n(\overline{x}) = N(\overline{x})dw - \Delta T(\overline{x})dw,$$

where $\Delta T(\overline{x}) = \int_0^{\overline{x}} [\frac{t}{h}\frac{dx}{dw}] 2\pi x dx$ is a new term which we have not seen before. We refer to this new term as the city-wide adjustment cost. The adjustment cost reflects the fact that when the wage w is increased for all residents, each resident re-optimizes for their best consumption bundle and ends up with a slightly different location as well a chosen bundle (c, h). Thus in re-optimizing with a new larger w, each household is adjusting its location and best bundle. The sum of these individual adjustment costs turns out to be captured in our term ΔT, which is in fact a term representing the sum of each household's changed commuting costs. Hence the total adjustment cost (restructuring the city) is captured in an aggregate commuting cost adjustment.

Notes

1 William Alonso (1960) developed a simple model of a circular city with jobs in the center and residential activity surrounding the central activity.

2 The assumption that all production activity takes place at the center is fairly standard but there is a literature that allows for the location of production to be endogenous. See, for example, Robert E. Lucas Jr and Esteban Rossi–Hansberg (2002). Pisarski (2006) notes that as of 2001, urban residents in the US segment into 30 percent residing in central cities, 20 percent in non-metro areas and the remaining 50 percent in suburbs. Some 34 million commuters work outside their home counties, an 85 percent increase since 1980 and 3.5 times the number for 1960. For cities under 100,000 half of commuting flows are back and forth from the center: the equivalent is only 24 percent for the largest metro areas. Central cities have 134 jobs for every 100 resident workers and suburbs have 85 jobs per 100.

3 This is the figure of household size for the United States in 2001. See the *2001 National Household Travel Survey*, Federal Highway Administration, US Department of Transportation, 2004.

4 New York City (not the metro area) has about 80 residents per hectare or 1,345 square feet per person. Multiplying by 3.7 persons per household gives 4,976.5 square feet per household which is about 1,800 square feet more than our guesstimate for our "Toronto." Barcelona has some 171 residents per hectare or 629 square feet per person (2,327.3 square feet per household). Paris has about 88 persons per hectare. The dense part of Tokyo (46 percent of its area) has 5,791.5 persons per square kilometer or 579.2 per hectare.

5 The GTA has seven Regional Municipalities: Durham, Halton, Peel, York, Dufferin, Simcoe and the central municipality of Toronto, which itself has 2.5 million people.

6 As of the 2010 census, Oakland County's population was 1,202,362. The county seat is Pontiac.

7 Our map comprises the municipalities of Cook, DeKalb, DuPage, Grundy, Kane, Kendall, Lake, McHenry and Will. Cook County dominates the region.

8 The export activity of a city has been referred to over the decades as the city's basic activity whereas the other activities (retail, municipal services, schools, etc.) are referred to as non-basic. We will make use of this terminology. However, the export activity (making cars, for example) can sustain a tire industry in the city. Is the tire industry basic or non-basic? We will refer to it as an intermediate goods activity.

9 *Globe and Mail*, December 14, 2010, p. L7.

10 Of households in the United States in 2001, 26 percent are single person and yet the 4 percent of households with six or more persons represent a larger population. Working women comprise about 46 percent of the workforce, a fairly stable figure (Alan E. Pisarski 2006).

11 One should think in terms of lifetime utility in different places to be precise. Hence instantaneous utility is here a proxy for lifetime utility. Equalizing lifetime utilities is technically demanding. See, for example, Eaton and Eckstein (1997) and Lucas (2004).

12 David Brooks, *New York Times*, February 10, 2014.

13 In Chapter 8, we report on a study of house prices for a small city in Norway that turned up a land rent decline of about 10 percent instead of 4 percent.

14 This term $\Delta T d\omega$ is in detail $[\int_0^{\overline{x}} \frac{t[dx/dw]}{h} 2\pi x dx]dw$. See Appendix 2.2 for more details.

15 Wheaton (1977) presents evidence that the income elasticity of the demand for space is not as large as conventional wisdom has suggested.

16 An alternative definition of sprawl is, roughly speaking, the extent of leap-frog development at the edge of a city. Large open spaces are left for many years before being developed for residential use.

17 *The Economist*, April 5, 2014, p. 51.

3 Distinct income classes and suburban employment

Different income classes in a monocentric city. Suburban employment ring. Substitution of large structures for land when land prices are high. Geographic amenities and city choice. Government (public) goods in the utility function of each resident.

Introduction

We next add realism to the basic monocentric city model set out in Chapter 2. Here we allow a monocentric city to have both high-income and low-income workers who all commute to their jobs in the city center. The rent functions intersect at the distance from the center at which the settlement switches from lower income to higher income. It turns out to be quite straightforward to have high-wage households and lower-wage households arranged in an orderly way in a land-use equilibrium. A related analysis allows us to lay out a city with a suburban ring of employment places. We develop conditions for similar workers to be indifferent between living "far-out" and commuting to suburban jobs, and living closer-in and commuting to jobs in the center. Again key rent functions intersect at the distance of the ring of suburban jobs from the center. We require an assumption about differences in productivities for suburban workers and central city workers in our analysis of suburban employment. We invoke the law of urban growth and argue that the lower density of workers in the suburban jobs makes them slightly less productive than the workers in the center of the city. We finally sketch how a worker-resident could be "consuming" extra amenities in a particular city and/or how such a household could be consuming a public or government good produced for the monocentric city.

We observe that sunnier cities are more expensive to live in (are larger and with higher land rents) than are their less sunny counterparts. This means that the amenity premium shows up in higher "housing" costs rather than being concentrated in a wage difference. This interesting question is pursued in Chapter 4. With regard to a household consuming a government or public good, we observe that under property taxation, residents at different distances from the center will find that their tax payment is in a different proportion to their dollar valuations of G, the quantity of the government good they consume. This topic is developed more completely in Chapter 9 on cities and municipal government services.

Different income classes in the monocentric city

A general condition (Mills equation from Chapter 2) for our "tent city" model is

$$h(x)\frac{dr(x)}{dx} = -t.$$

This captures the central idea that a marginal move farther out for a household will result in a cheaper house ($h(x)\frac{dr(x)}{dx}$ is negative) but a marginally more costly commute (the $-t$ term).[1] This condition allows us to demonstrate that when all else is the same except incomes w^H and w^L (with $w^H > w^L$), households in the higher-income group will live farther from the center. There will be two broad annuluses, the one close to the center with lower-income households and the one farther out, with the higher-income households. Each lower-income household will be obtaining the same utility as every other lower-income household and each higher-income household will be obtaining the same utility as every other higher-income household. Everyone has the same utility function that is homogenous of degree unity (i.e. indifference curves are "parallel").

Consider then the location equilibrium condition at switch point, $\widetilde{x}$, one condition applying to a household in each of the two income groups:

$$h^L(\widetilde{x})\frac{dr(\widetilde{x})}{dx} = -t$$

$$\text{and } h^H(\widetilde{x})\frac{dr(\widetilde{x})}{dx} = -t.$$

Here $\widetilde{x}$ is the radial distance at which the two rent functions for the two distinct groups cross. See Figure 3.1.

Think about one household from each income group at $\widetilde{x}$ but on either side of the switch point. Each is facing essentially the same ratio of consumer goods prices, namely $(1, r(\widetilde{x}))$ but one household has more income (higher w). The higher-income household will be consuming more of both c and h. That is, $h^H(\widetilde{x}) > h^L(\widetilde{x})$. (We still do not know which household is closer to the center, the two households straddling $\widetilde{x}$.) Take our inference on the higher-income household with the larger h^H to our equations above. It must be that slope $\frac{dr(\widetilde{x})}{dx}$ is smaller in absolute value for the higher-income household.

Given the way our two rent pieces of rent function intersect in our diagram, it must be that the higher-income households are in the annulus of households farther from the center.

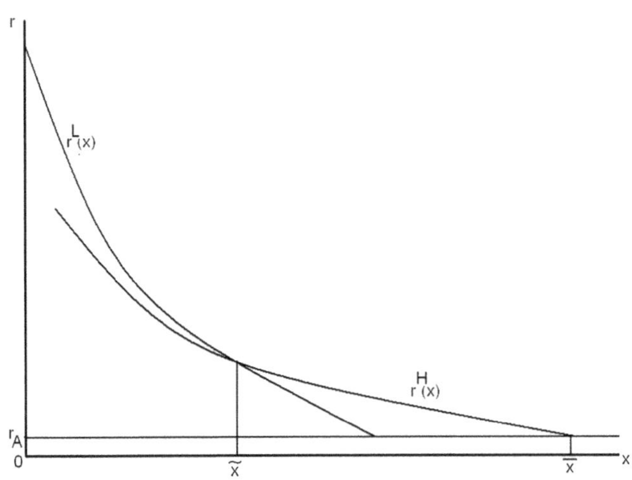

Figure 3.1 The low-wage group outbids the high-wage group for sites close to the CBD.

This is an interesting property of the simple model of a monocentric city. Mills (1999; p. 2) remarks: “The correlation between family income and the home’s distance from the CBD is strong within most US metropolitan areas.” But of course many cities have high-income people living in enclaves close to the center. The real world must be more complicated than the model in some essential way. An obvious shortcoming of the model we have been dealing with is that commuting is represented very simply. More realistic would be commuting cost per mile that rises closer to the center. Near the center is where congestion is usually the most severe. Our model has commuting cost per mile the same whether travel is close to the center or far from the center. In addition we have no time cost or disutility of commuting. Higher-income people often value their marginal hour of leisure more highly than do lower-income people. It is a fact that the fraction of lower-income people using mass transit is significantly higher than that of higher-income people. Of course this is not a simple question of taste. It is also a question of affordability. However, once we depart from our simple formulation of commuting cost, we can well envisage a mechanism (strong dislike for time given up to commuting) that will lead to an equilibrium with some higher-income households ending up living relatively close to the center. In fact there have been research papers published that have taken up such more complicated models and have developed equilibria with some high income households living close to the center.

In addition to commuting cost, there is as well the matter of a taste for big-city activity. Certain people wish to live near the center where they can avail themselves more easily of opera, exciting bars and famous restaurants. This taste for excitement is of course not taken account of in our simple model.

Toronto has no area that one would identify as a slum. Hulchanski (2007) reports striking changes in the distribution of households over the period 1970 to 2005. For each census in this period he obtains the average income in a census tract for Toronto (the city, with a population of 2.79 million) and compares this value to the value for his complete Toronto (about 500 census tracts in total). In 2006 a census tract listed on average 4,700 people. Hulchanski identified a tract with an average income at or below 20 percent under the city average as part of City 3, and a tract with an average income at or above 20 percent above the city average as part of City 1. The remaining or middle income tracts comprise City 2. Thus he has an uncomplicated definition of high-, middle- and low-income areas of the city of Toronto—his Cities 1, 2 and 3—as particular areas classified by average income. In 2011 Toronto turns out to have more than one million residents living in low-income neighborhoods (places with an average income 20 percent or more below the city-wide average.[2] Very high-income neighborhoods (average income 40 percent or more above the city-wide average) rose from 9 percent to 16 percent of all Toronto neighborhoods between 1970 and 2010. The seemingly middle-class district, Scarborough, now has 83 percent of its neighborhoods classified as poor or very poor, up from about 2 percent in 1970. Figure 3.2 is a map of Toronto for 1981, with darker areas indicating places with low incomes.

Figure 3.3 shows the low-income areas of Toronto for 2011. The dark lines are subway lines.

The two maps are very similar: little change is showing up. Areas of low income for 1981 are still the areas of low income for 2011.

Hulchanski’s approach to distinguishing his high-, medium- and low-income “cities” is not free of problems. If a few high-income census tracts had their average incomes rise considerably between 1970 and 2005, then the number of middle income neighborhoods could decline. An extreme case could of course be the existence of only two Hulchanski cities: one

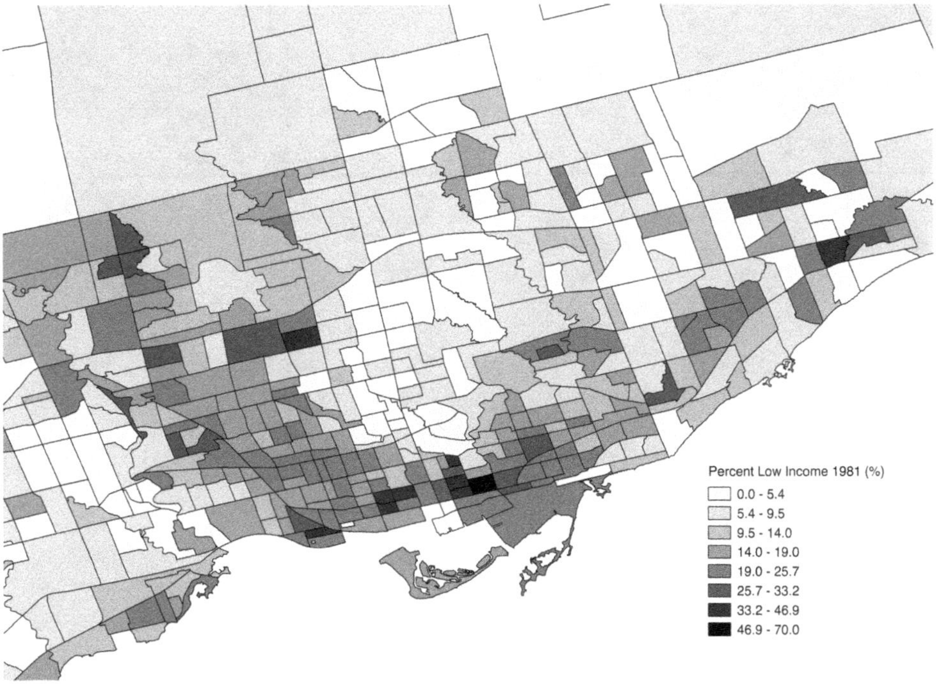

Figure 3.2 Low-income areas of Toronto, 1981.

Source: Based on Census Tract data.

with very high incomes which would make the average income in the city quite high and one with lower incomes, with nevertheless a wide variety of incomes. Hence Hulchanski could be simply observing, in a roundabout way, that the skewness of incomes in many higher-income countries has become considerably greater in recent decades. However, in addition Canada like the United States has seen immigration flows grow in the 1990s. Immigrants tend to move first to larger, more dynamic cities such as New York. Toronto and Vancouver are places of choice by many immigrants to Canada. Since immigrants have on average lower incomes than longer-term residents, Hulchanski's dramatic shrinkage in the number of middle income census tracts in Toronto could be a reflection of a very large inflow of lower-income households. Basic arithmetic again indicates that a large increase in low-income households to Toronto could in itself result in many fewer middle income census tracts in 2005. Hulchanski finds in fact that recent immigrants comprise about 11 percent of each of his three cities within Toronto. But visible minority residents comprise 54 percent of residents of the low-income city (City 3) and about 30 percent of the middle city. For the high-income city, the figure is 16 percent. Hence although immigrants and recent immigrants are not over-represented in any one of the three cities, the high-income city has significantly more white households and significantly fewer households classified as "visible minorities." The flow of immigrants to City 3 has been steady over recent decades. The proportion of residents of City 1 "having a university degree" was almost double the equivalent proportion in City 2 or City 3.

Toronto does have a reputation as a city with a high proportion of immigrant residents already settled, as well as being a place to which immigrants choose to move when they

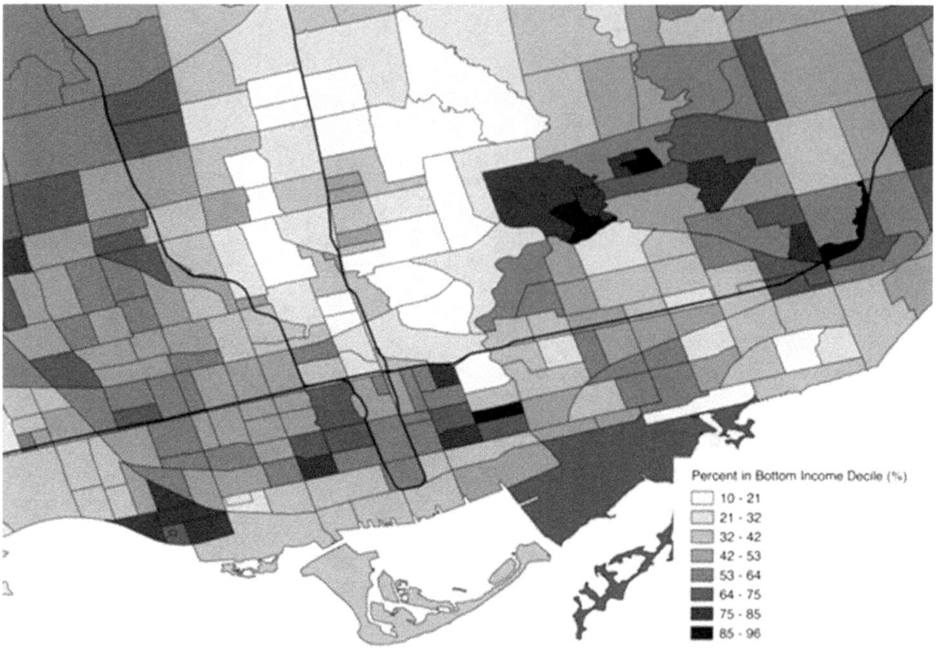

Figure 3.3 Low-income areas of Toronto, 2011.

Source: Based on Census Tract data.

arrive in Canada. Figure 3.5 maps the distribution of recent immigrants by area for the City of Toronto. (Figure 3.4 is the same map for the year 1981. For Chicago the map of recent immigrants is Figure 3.6.) In 1962 Canada's immigration regulations became non-discriminatory. Since then, the rules have become more transparent and there has been a steady flow of between 100,000 and 250,000 in-migrants per year (Murdie 2008). The rules emphasize that a non-refugee must have certain skills to qualify for entry but in addition migrants can bring family members with them. Hence the average skill level of the total immigrant flow each year is probably not high. And of course Canada, like the United States, has been experiencing significant de-industrialization since the 1950s. We have then three factors that might account for the dramatic rise in the number of low-income households in suburban Toronto: (1) immigrants settle in the suburbs of Toronto disproportionately (see Maps 1 and 2 in Murdie (2008)) (2) immigrants on average remain as low-income residents for some years after arrival and (3) the traditional "good" jobs that might have fit the skills of immigrants have been disappearing. So-called blue collar jobs declined from 28 percent to 17 percent in Toronto in the period 1971 to 2005 (Hulchanski 2007; p. 12). Immigrants are finding fewer job possibilities outside of the service sector.[3] Is there something pathological about the phenomenon of Toronto becoming a city with a majority of low-income households? Surely most of the immigrant families will have children who will rise into the middle class after a generation? There remains the possibility that the Canadian economy might stagnate over the next decades and more communities, besides Toronto, could become heavily populated by low-income households. A "generous" immigration policy seems to make little sense for an economy that is not exhibiting steady job-growth. Figure 3.4 indicates heaviest settlement of immigrants just east of Toronto's CBD in 1981. In addition there are significant concentrations in the suburban northwest and north east.

We have moved up to 2011 in Figure 3.5. There turns out to have been a suburbanization of immigrant neighborhoods since 1981. Central city communities are in lower densities and the high density areas are in "remote" suburbs, not well connected with the subway lines.

By contrast, immigrants in Chicago are concentrated in two areas (see Figure 3.6). The south area has its mass transit access to the Loop (Chicago's CBD). The northern area is somewhat less concentrated around the mass transit lines.

People in Toronto could well expect the taxpayers from the rest of Canada to assist in financing the settlement costs required for new immigrants if Toronto remains the place where most immigrants settle. Vancouver and Montreal are also popular places for immigrants to settle and these municipalities too should receive financial assistance for helping with the settlement process. New York City is famous for being a destination favored by immigrants, rich and poor. In recent years both Toronto and New York City have about 50 percent of their residents foreign-born. Toronto could do well to try to learn how immigrant adjustment has evolved in New York City and whether certain policies have worked especially well there. New York City is large, has been persistently prosperous and appears to be a favored place for immigrants to first settle when they move to the United States. A superficial take would be that immigrants seek out vibrant, high-wage cities to settle in. It is interesting to invert this thinking and say, where the immigrants are is where the prosperity is.

As a first pass, if one were to explain the distribution of immigrants by city, one might say: rank the cities by an indicator of current prosperity and the proportion of immigrants in

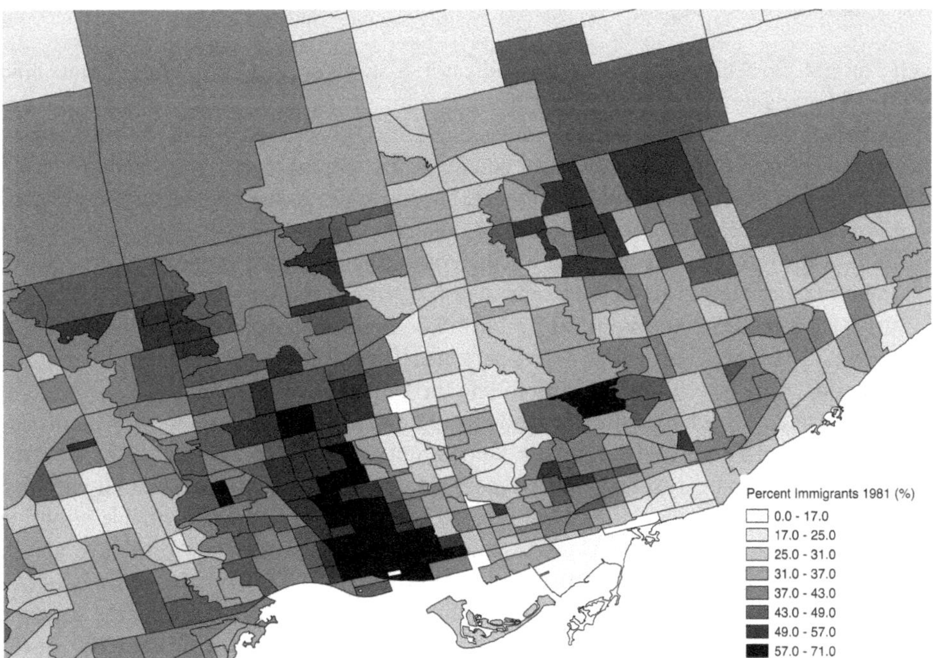

Figure 3.4 Concentrations of immigrants in Toronto, 1981.

Source: Based on Census Tract data.

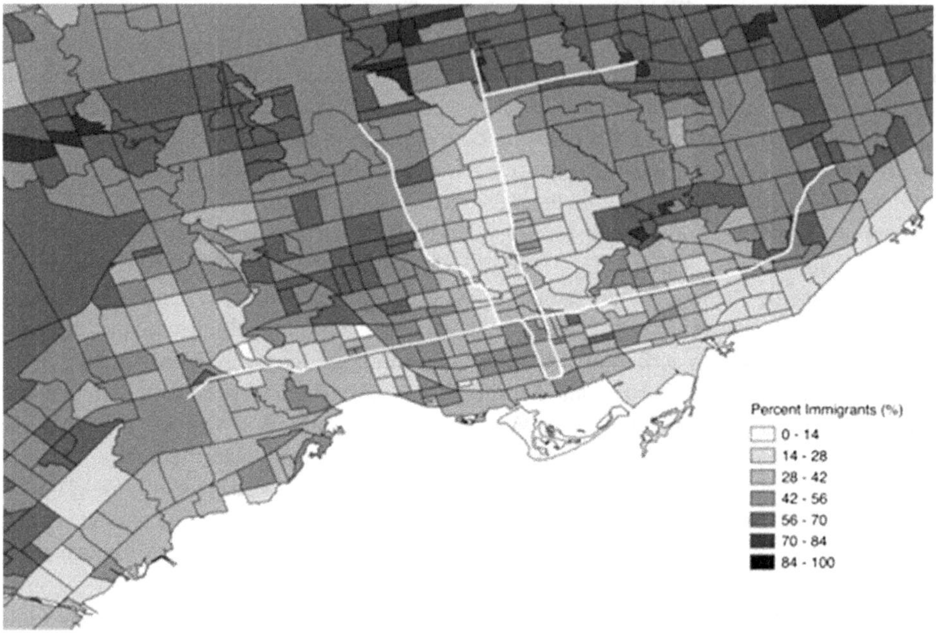

Figure 3.5 Distribution of areas with most immigrants in Toronto, 2011.

Source: Based on Census Tract data.

a city should correlate strongly with this indicator. A stronger predictor of immigrant choice of place is probably the current size of the community using their native language and their native customs. But such own-communities could still be correlated with the current prosperity of the place. Immigrants head for economically vibrant places that also have sizable communities of their native kind. For the ten poorest states in the United States, a naturalized immigrant earns one dollar for the 0.84 dollars earned by a comparable native. (South Carolina is the only low-income state on the coast: the other nine in the set are interior to the country.) For the ten highest income states, a naturalized immigrant earns one dollar for the 0.97 dollars earned by the native-born. Foreign-born have considerably lower rates of divorce (3 percent compared with 24 percent). These figures from Census Bureau data provide some evidence of foreign-born folk in the United States bringing their hussle to the American Dream of a better life. As previously noted, of the 51 large metropolitan areas (more than one million residents) in the United States in 2010, only three (Boston, Providence and Oklahoma City) experienced more growth in their centers compared with their suburban areas. The composition of the suburbs has tilted from 5 percent visible minorities in 1970 to 27 percent in 2010.[4] One presumes that the relative size of the suburbs and the skill composition of its residents reflects in part the demand for workers in the suburbs.

Chicago's high-income areas (dark shaded in the map in Figure 3.7) are for the most part around the city center and north.[5] There are some high-income areas far from the CBD as well.

There is contrast between the distribution of high-income households in Chicago and Houston (Houston[6] is mapped in Figure 3.8). Houston's high-income households are noticeably suburbanized. We might generalize and say that Chicago has become something of a condominium city, with many high-income residents living in and near the downtown while

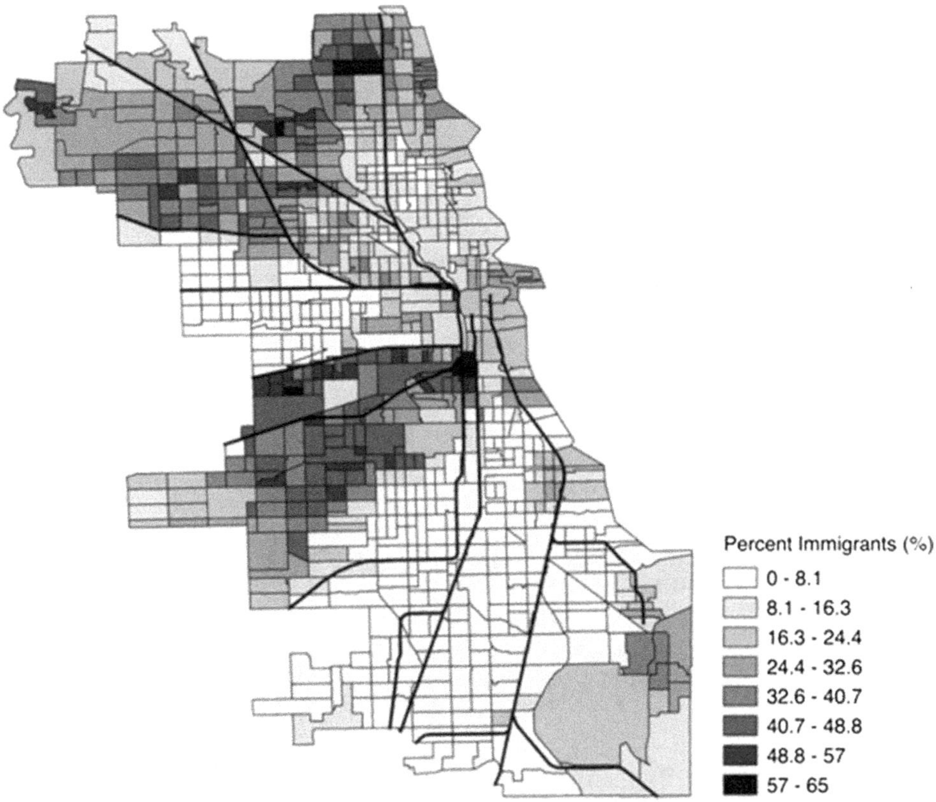

Figure 3.6 Distribution of areas with most immigrants in Chicago, 2011.

Source: Based on Census Tract data.

Houston has evolved as a much more suburban city, with most high-income residents living away from the downtown. We might also label Houston as a largely "post World War II" city while Chicago experienced much of its growth before World War II. Houston grew up in the age of households with automobiles while Chicago developed somewhat before the age of almost every household with at least one automobile.

A suburban ring of jobs

Many cities in North America appear to have evolved from having most jobs in a center to having just a high fraction of jobs in the center, and with many jobs out in the suburbs. The forces contributing to employment suburbanization include the rise of large, efficient trucks as substitutes for trains and barges, congestion in the center and the high cost of parking for workers in city centers, a changed technology of factories toward spread-out, single-storey structures, and the general improvement of suburban highways, making it easier for residents of suburbs to access suburban job places.[7] On this latter point, we should take account of a general rise in the income of the average household, an increase that makes automobile ownership much more widespread across families and even within families. It is not an exaggeration to say that in North America, commuting to work by automobile is the

Figure 3.7 Chicago's high-income census tracts, 2011.

Source: Based on Census Tract data.

norm today. A small fraction of commutes show up as trips by mass transit.[8] In the United States in 2001 about 17 percent of work trips were from suburbs to central cities, 41 percent were between suburbs and 25 percent were within metropolitan areas. These figures provide us with a different snapshot of the trend toward the suburbanizing of jobs in US cities.[9] For very large places (New York, Los Angeles, Chicago), "people who are far from the city center are not commuting downtown at all" (Kahn 2010; p. 12).

How much job decentralization?

Glaeser *et al.* (2001) observed that for the 100 largest cities in the United States, in 2001, about one half of jobs lay more than 11.2 km from the center. (In fact less than 20 percent of all employment in the United States is in city centers: see Glaeser and Kahn 2004.) The comparable distance for the ten largest Canadian cities is 10.8 km. Larger cities have a higher fraction of their jobs outside the central core area. Hence there is a general trend of job decentralization as a city grows. This seems intuitively plausible given the revealed preference of residents farther from the center to be not employed in the central area. One other statistical regularity for Canadian cities is that about one half the residents of larger cities are classified as workers. This leaves about half the people in larger cities as dependants of various sorts.

Although Toronto is notable for long times of commuting by workers, there has been a large accumulation of office building in its suburbs. The downtown core can claim only about 20 percent of office space in the Greater Toronto Area. Outer suburbs (so-called 905 areas) have more square feet of office space than Calgary and Edmonton combined (66 million square feet in Toronto's suburbs). An estimated 325,000 people work in suburban offices and most of these workers commute by car. An estimated 108 million square feet of office space is located away from mass transit stops. There has, however, been a jump in office space in the core, with about 4.5 million square feet of new space arriving on the market between 2007 and 2010. Some attribute this expansion downtown to a recent balancing of commercial and residential real estate taxes. There has also been something of a condominium boom in downtown Toronto, an expansion that may have preceded the recent jump in new office space availability.[10] With the exception of downtown Toronto and North York Centre, new office space has located in areas that are not served by higher-order transit. Highway access has been the basic determinant of new office location. The two major concentrations of office floor space that have emerged since 1990 are at Pearson Airport and the nexus of Highways 404, 7 and 407—both essentially suburban and not connected to the major transit grid. Meadowvale and, to some extent, the QEW corridor in Oakville illustrate the linking of office development to the commuter rail system (the GO rail system). A 2005 study (Canadian Urban Institute at the University of Toronto) indicates that between 1993 and 2005, 62 percent of new office floor space was constructed in non-transit-supportive office parks. Buildings of over 10,000 m^2 of floor space account for half of all office buildings and 80 percent of all floor space constructed since 1990.

In this section we construct a suburban ring of jobs for a simple monocentric city and base our construction on two stylized facts: (1) residents who live on average farther from the CBD are observed to commute in lower numbers to jobs in the CBD compared with residents who reside closer to the CBD and (2) workers who work in places of a high density of fellow workers are more productive than similar workers who work in places of lower density (Ciccone and Hall 1996). We will introduce a ring of suburban jobs, have workers in those jobs live radially beyond them and assume that the wage they receive is lower than similar workers who commute to and work in the CBD. We will proceed under the assumption that workers who work in the CBD reside within the ring of suburban jobs. We are positing a strong separation between two "cities" within one large city—a suburban city with its own jobs and its distinct far-out residential area and a central city with its own jobs and its residential area relatively close to the center. The lower density, we posit for suburban workers, implies slightly lower productivity and a lower wage. This approach allows us to have all workers in the city end up with the same utility level. "Outer folk" end up with larger lot sizes, on average.

As we did above with two income groups, we consider two households at the circumference of suburban jobs, one household within the circumference and commuting to the CBD (hence

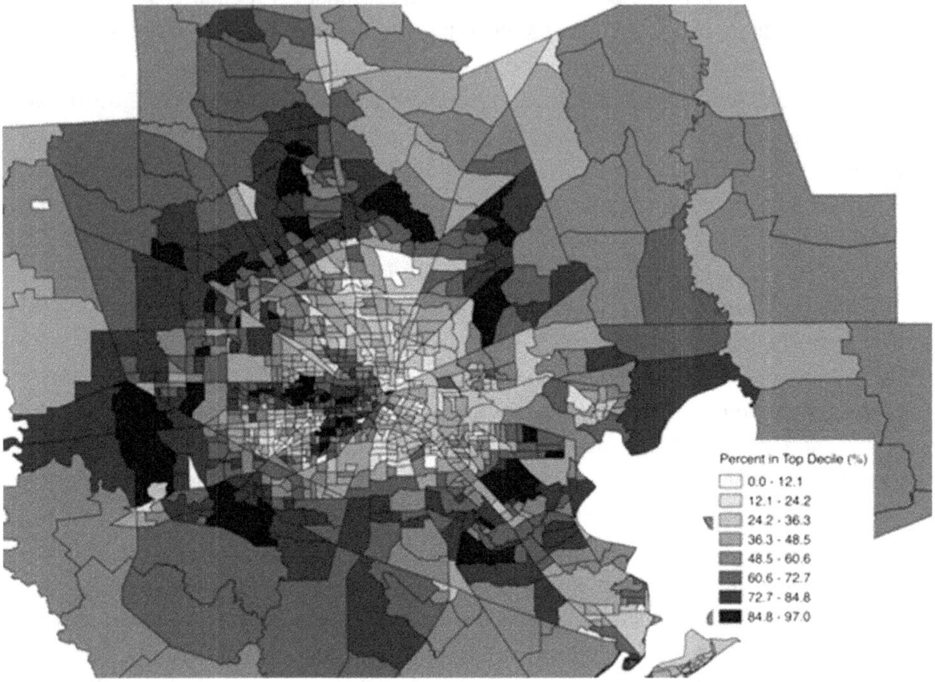

Figure 3.8 Houston's high-income census tracts, 2011.

Source: Based on Census Tract data.

$w^H - t\tilde{x} = c(\tilde{x}) + r(\tilde{x})h(\tilde{x}))$ and one just outside this circumference and residing at the suburban job ring (hence $w^L = c(\tilde{x}) + r(\tilde{x})h(\tilde{x})$). Just inside of $\tilde{x}$, a high-wage resident's wage net of commuting cost equals the wage of a resident living just outside of $\tilde{x}$. We assume that these workers are very similar and hence they must each be on the same indifference curve. They face the same prices for c and h at $\tilde{x}$. See Figure 3.9. (The rent function for "outside" residents intersects the rent function for "inside" residents at $\tilde{x}$. See Figure 3.10.)

To be on the same indifference curve at $\tilde{x}$, w^L must be less than w^H by exactly the commuting cost that the inside household is incurring while living at $\tilde{x}$. We justify this lower wage for all outside households with the inference that outside workers in suburban jobs work in a lower density of jobs and hence achieve a lower productivity than the same inside workers who all work in the center (the CBD). Every household, both inside and outside $\tilde{x}$, will achieve the same utility but every household living beyond $\tilde{x}$ will receive the lower wage, w^L, at the job circle at $\tilde{x}$. All inside households will receive wage w^H at the center.

The precise location of the suburban ring of jobs, here at $\tilde{x}$, will, under our assumptions, reflect an a priori productivity gap, a gap between an inside and outside worker, associated with the particular density of jobs at the center compared with the density of jobs in the suburban ring. Hence the value of $\tilde{x}$ should be taken as endogenous. Though our theory of suburban job ring formation is parsimonious and is based on known empirical regularities of differences in worker productivities, we are the first to invoke these productivity gaps in the construction of a suburban job ring for a classic monocentric city model.

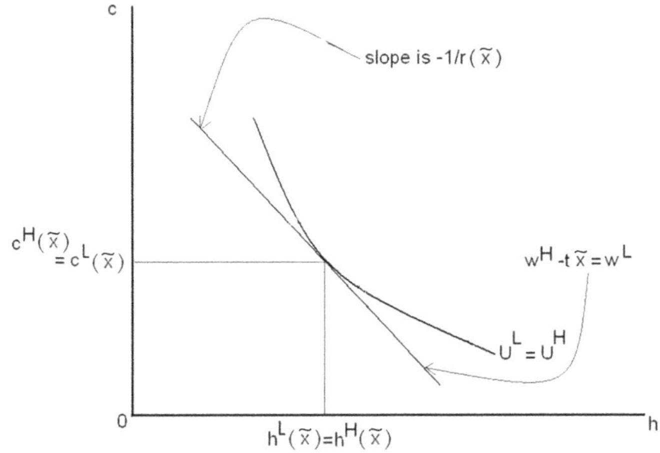

Figure 3.9 Edge equilibrium. At $(\tilde{x})$ residents who commute to the center (from inside $(\tilde{x})$) spend on (c, h) $w^H - t\tilde{x}$ whereas residents who commute to jobs from beyond $(\tilde{x})$ have wage W^L at $(\tilde{x})$.

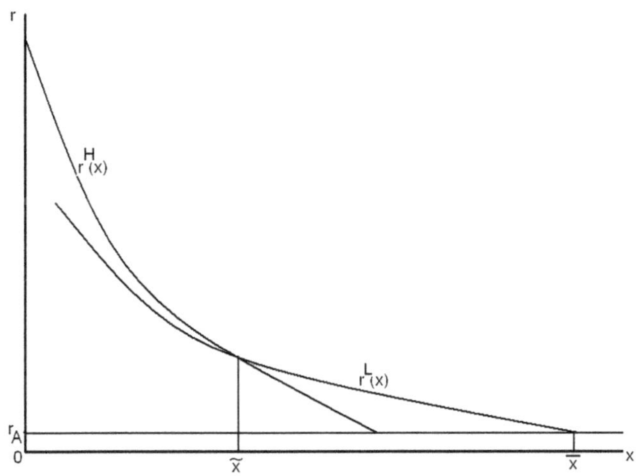

Figure 3.10 Switch point. Lower-wage workers commute from outside $\tilde{x}$ to jobs at $\tilde{x}$. Higher-wage workers commute from inside $\tilde{x}$ to jobs at the center.

One might argue that the suburbanization of residential activity over many decades that Mills emphasized could induce a suburbanization of certain kinds of employment activity. For the United States, the 2010 census indicates that for large cities (more than one million residents), only 8.6 percent of the aggregate population growth over the previous decade ended up in the centers of these places. This figure compares with 15.1 percent for the previous decade. Of the 51 large metropolitan areas (more than one million residents) in the United States, only three (Boston, Providence and Oklahoma City) experienced more growth in their centers compared with their suburban areas.[11] Many European cities had their centers laid out in the days before automobiles existed and the streets in the historic centers are narrow. This makes it natural for modern economic activities to develop away from the centers. Residential activity moves out, along with the employment magnets. "Just like Detroit and St. Louis, the central city of Milan, Italy has lost hundreds of thousands of people, many of whom have moved to more car-intensive suburbs" (Glaeser 2011; p. 179). Glaeser speculates that higher prices for gasoline "are more likely to reduce sprawl in the developing world, where infrastructure isn't yet in place and poorer people will be more responsive to higher costs" (Glaeser 2011; p. 179).

Durable structures in a monocentric city

Modern cities typically have tall buildings in and near the CBD and fewer tall buildings farther from the center. In 1990 North America had 80 percent of the 100 tallest buildings in the world. In 2012, this figure was just 18 percent, and 34 were in China, many in cities with names that we are not familiar with. Chinese cities are re-organizing their CBDs to accommodate new management-type activities related to their many goods-producing entities. We identify a tall building with a high capital to land ratio. We are interested in the phenomenon of this ratio declining with distance from the CBD. Capital here means durable inputs like cement, steel, glass, etc. We can observe that where land is expensive, it is economized on by placing much capital on it and where land is less expensive, economization is not pursued as aggressively. Land is used freely far from the CBD and land is used sparingly in and near the CBD. This substitution of capital for land where land is relatively expensive is the same phenomenon we discuss in introductory economics: the ratio of input prices drives the entrepreneur's selection of her ratio of physical inputs. Capital in our case will have the same rental price (annual charge for a unit) everywhere, but land will exhibit high rent in and near the CBD.

Tall apartment buildings and condominium towers have filled the centers of many cities in the United States in recent years. As Dougherty (2014) puts it:

> The growth in new rental towers which are usually woven into downtown office centers is being driven largely by young professionals starting their careers along with empty nesters who are in some cases downsizing from bigger homes in the suburbs. Together they are helping downtowns evolve from places centered mostly on working and entertainment to more complete neighborhoods, with grocery stores, community centers and community services.

A high rise is defined as 15 storeys or higher and the number of projects underway to build them has doubled since the peak in 2008. Over the past two decades, Vancouver has experienced this sort of tip, from a business-centered CBD to a center with many residential towers. At one point office buildings were being converted to condominiums. The Yale Town area has many condominium high rises as well as good schools and supermarkets. Toronto has been somewhat of an outlier in North America with its many tall apartment buildings, many in the suburbs. In recent years the area between the CBD and the lakefront has been the focus of the construction of many tall rental buildings and condominiums. Austin, Houston and Minneapolis are all experiencing spikes in the construction of tall apartment buildings downtown. "Overall, the growth has been largest in denser and pricier markets like San Francisco and Chicago. But in percentage terms, the increase has been most dramatic in smaller cities like Minneapolis" (Dougherty 2014). Some refer to this development as the Manhattanization of America. This trend runs counter to the trend toward ubiquitous city sprawl—very low density residential development—that many observers have focused on in recent years.

We resume consideration of the household's utility maximization problem. Our derivation of the land-rent function will involve capital being used relatively more where land is expensive. We start with the assumption that a house $h(x)$ is a combination of some land $L(x)$ and some structure $K(x)$. A house then can be thought of as being produced at a date using land and capital, these last rented at prices $r(x)$ per unit and i per unit, respectively. Central to the analysis is the substitution of marginally more land for capital when the rental on land is marginally lower, as it is farther from the center. We employ first the Cobb–Douglas specification, $h(x) = l(x)^{\gamma} K(x)^{1-\gamma}$.

A household continues to purchase housing, $h(x)$ and other consumption goods, $c(x)$, reaping utility in $U = c(x)^{\alpha} h(x)^{1-\alpha}$. Free migration implies the same utility level for each household. Each worker-household earns w for work at the center and commutes tx to distance x from the center. Hence a worker-household budget constraint is represented by

$$w - tx = c(x) + q(x)h(x),$$

where $q(x)$ is the price per unit of $h(x)$. This price will be an annual rental. For the Cobb–Douglas production function, textbooks indicate that we have unit cost

$$q(x) = \Omega r(x)^{\gamma} i^{1-\gamma}, \text{ for } \Omega = \gamma^{-\gamma}(1-\gamma)^{-(1-\gamma)}.$$

We assume that unit price, $q(x)$, is equal to the unit cost of a house. (The general properties of these unit cost functions include $h\frac{\partial q}{\partial r} = l$ and $h\frac{\partial q}{\partial i} = K$.)

Production efficiency (ratio of marginal products equal to price ratio) here is

$$\frac{\gamma K(x)}{(1-\gamma)l(x)} = \frac{r(x)}{i}$$

and we can substitute into the production function to obtain

$$h = \left[\frac{(1-\gamma)r}{\gamma i}\right]^{1-\gamma} l.$$

This result, plus the utility function and constant utility gives us

$$c = \frac{\overline{U}^{1/\alpha}}{\left\{L\left[\frac{(1-\gamma)r}{\gamma i}\right]^{1-\gamma}\right\}^{(1-\alpha)/\alpha}}.$$

Consumption efficiency is

$$\frac{\alpha h}{(1-\alpha)c} = \frac{1}{q}$$

or

$$\frac{\alpha L^{1/\alpha}\left[\frac{(1-\gamma)r}{\gamma i}\right]^{(1-\gamma)/\alpha}}{(1-\alpha)\overline{U}^{1/\alpha}} = \frac{1}{\Omega r(x)^{\gamma} i^{1-\gamma}}.$$

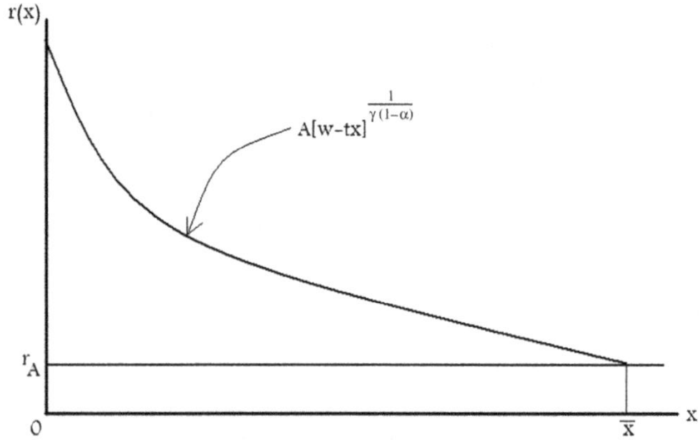

Figure 3.11 The rent function, given the Cobb–Douglas utility function; A is a constant and α and γ are between zero and unity.

This gives us

$$l = \frac{(1-\alpha)^{\alpha}\overline{U}}{[\alpha\Omega r(x)^{\gamma} i^{1-\gamma}]^{\alpha}\left[\frac{(1-\gamma)r}{\gamma i}\right]^{1-\gamma}}.$$

Given $l(x)$, we can solve for $h(x)$ and $c(x)$ in terms of $r(x)$. We substitute these expressions for h and c in the budget constraint and solve for the rent function (see Appendix 3.1). It turns out to be

$$r(x) = \left[\frac{1}{\frac{\overline{U}}{1-\alpha}\left(\frac{1-\alpha}{\alpha}\right)^{\alpha}(\Omega i^{1-\gamma})^{1-\alpha}}\right]^{1/(\gamma(1-\alpha))}(w-tx)^{1/(\gamma(1-\alpha))}.$$

See Figure 3.11 for a graphical representation of the rent function given the Cobb–Douglas utility function.

This rent function is very similar to the one we derived for the case of no structures on land. There is now the production function parameter γ multiplying $(1-\alpha)$ in the exponent of $w - tx$. Since γ is positive and less than unity, the exponent will be larger than it was for the case of no structures. Hence, formally, there is little change from what we observed when we made no allowance for capital/land substitutability toward the center. However, our abstract, back-of-envelope city is now more realistic. It will have tall buildings (apartment buildings) at its center and ranch-style homes in the suburbs.

Observe that $\frac{dr}{dx} < 0$ and $\frac{d^2r}{dx^2} > 0$. We have a rent function declining from the center and convex to the origin. Also

$$\frac{dr}{dx}\frac{1}{r(x)} = \frac{-t}{\gamma(1-\alpha)} \times \frac{1}{w-tx},$$

and this percentage decline will rise, not rapidly, in absolute value with distance x. We observed this same phenomenon for our rent function for the model without structures and argued that the decline was approximately exponential (when tx is a small fraction of w). The same holds here.

Tall buildings

Historically, the key elements in allowing tall buildings to appear were (a) reasonably priced structural steel and (b) motor-powered elevators. For thousands of years buildings were supported directly by their walls. Hence so-called tall structures had thick stone walls. Cathedrals proliferated in Europe after about 1100 and competition ensued for relatively thin walls and large stained-glass windows. To deal with this change, flying buttresses were introduced—exterior supports, almost second walls. Then the abundance of wood in the United States in the nineteenth century led to "balloon construction"—structures with solid wooden skeletons and thin skins to keep the weather out. This idea inspired builders of tall buildings decades later when it became relatively cheap to construct skeletons with steel beams. Chicago and New York were the two places that had the first tall buildings, some eight to ten storeys in height. The Equitable Life Assurance Building in New York city was erected in 1870 and it had a separate steel skeleton. Popular history has identified the Home Insurance Building built in Chicago, Illinois in 1885, as the first "skyscraper." As with balloon construction, the exterior walls were not load-bearing but constituted a skin to keep the weather out. And about the time that structural steel became available at a reasonable price, fairly reliable elevators with electric motors arrived on the market. Otis addressed the issue of preventing an elevator from going into free-fall if its cable gave way and Werner von Siemens built the first elevator with an electric motor for lift in 1880. Tall building construction technology had arrived, and where a site was valuable (high land rent) the sites were usually "intensively utilized," most often covered with large (tall) structures.

Hong Kong has at least 393 skyscrapers, the most of any city in the world. It has 7.2 million people on 1104 km^2. Its Kwun Tong District has 56,000 people per square kilometer compared with London's 5,285. The Burj Khalifa in Dubai is currently the world's tallest building at 2717 feet (828 m). It has 163 floors. A taller edifice is under construction in the Middle East currently (May, 2014).

General utility and production functions and capitalization

Recall that in Chapter 2 we were able to establish wage and commuting cost capitalization in rent without an explicit functional form for the utility functions. Conditions for utility maximization were sufficient. The good news is that we are able to get our capitalization results for our model with structures, again without relying on specific function forms, here for both utility and production functions. We proceed as we did earlier. Instead of a house just being a plot of land we have a house comprising some capital $K(x)$ and land $l(x)$, being produced with a constant returns to scale production function, $h = h(l(x), K(x))$. The price of a house is $q(x)$ and it must of course cover the costs of land and capital embodied in the house. We have $r(x)$ as the rental for a unit of land at x and i the rental for a unit of capital.

We treat i as constant (determined in the larger economy). Production efficiency in housing implies

$$\frac{h_l(x)}{h_K(x)} = \frac{r(x)}{i}.$$

There is a price function $q = g(r, i)$ with the property $\frac{\partial q}{\partial r} = a_{lh}$ where a_{lh} is land per unit of housing.

Given utility constant, we have $U_c dc + U_h dh = 0$ or $dc = -\frac{U_h}{U_c} dh = -q dh$ since $\frac{U_h}{U_c} = r$. And each resident has her budget constraint in $w - tx = c(x) + q(x)h(x)$. The edge of the city is defined by $r(\overline{x}) = r_A$. We turn to how net rent $R_n(\overline{x})$ is impacted by $dw > 0$.

We have then

$$\frac{dR(\overline{x})}{dw} - 2\pi\overline{x}r_A\frac{d\overline{x}}{dw} = \int_0^{\overline{x}} \frac{dr(x)}{dw} 2\pi x dx$$

which after substitution (see Appendix 3.2) gives us

$$\Delta R_n(\overline{x}) = N(\overline{x})dw - \Delta T(\overline{x})dw,$$

where $\Delta R_n(\overline{x})$ is net land rent change caused by the increase in w and $\Delta T(\overline{x})dw$ is the city-side adjustment term. This capitalization expression looks the same as that from Chapter 1 when housing was simply a plot of land. Hence the addition of structures to the model gives us more realistic cities but leaves us with the same formal expression for the capitalization of wage change in land rent. And there is an analogous capitalization expression for a change in the cost of commuting:

$$\Delta R_n(\overline{x}) = -M(\overline{x})dt - \Delta T(\overline{x})dt.$$

Geographic amenity differences between cities

We can extend our analysis to the presence of a geographic amenity in each household's (worker's) utility function as in $U = U(c, h, A)$ with A representing, say, hours of sunshine per year at a particular location.[12] Under the open-city assumption, workers with similar skills, experience and family structure will migrate until the utility level achieved by two such workers in different locations is the same. It is interesting then to examine where an amenity advantage shows up in the analysis. Let us start then with two identical cities which contain workers of the same type.

Suppose that the amenity indicator in one city takes a jump up (more hours of sunshine have arrived suddenly). First, there will be jump up in utility for each resident of the city B, the one with more hours of sunshine. This will induce in-migration from the other city, city A. The in-migration implies that city B has become larger and we will see its rent function shift out, implying that it has become a higher cost place to live relative to city A. (The out-migration from city A will result in its rent function shifting down, implying that it has become a lower cost place to live.) Ultimately migration will continue until the utility levels in each place are the same. But now city B is larger and has a higher average land rent. To a first approximation there should be no change in the wage in either city. The higher land rent will imply, with substitutability, a higher density of settlement in the residential area in city B. Thus there has been, roughly speaking, a substitution of less housing per household (higher density of neighborhoods) for more sunshine per year. The absence of a significant change in the wage between the cities implies that the amenity premium in city B has become capitalized in higher land rents in city B.[13] And we can speak of a resident of city A also experiencing a utility boost, one resulting from the out-migration and the lowering of average land rents in the city. A resident of city A has indirectly substituted more housing for "less sunshine" (in fact the less sunshine is only relative to the new amount for city B).

We can extend our model of a city by introducing a public (government) good into each resident's utility function.[14] This does not work like a geographic amenity because the resident is obliged to pay for the government good. We will assume, quite reasonably, that the sum of the payments from each resident will equal the cost to the government of providing the public good to the city in question. A public good is one which has the government produce it in quantity, G, and this G becomes the quantity consumed by each household in the local economy. Note that although everyone consumes the same G, the value they assign to this quantity can be quite different, depending on their tastes and possibly incomes. It follows that under property taxation for revenue raising, each resident will in general be making a dollar outlay different from the dollar value which the resident assigns to the amount of G supplied. This gap might be interpreted as a dollar wedge which a resident will attempt to close by relocation. However, we construct our city under the assumption that each similar worker-household is on the same indifference curve, with G included in her utility function. Hence two households at different distances from the center will be getting the same G but each will be paying a different tax for it. And each household will be "reaping" the same utility.

Hence these fiscal gaps which appear to provide a motivation for a household to relocate do not constitute a legitimate reason for relocating. If a household did respond with a relocation (personal benefits from G being larger than tax payments at the new site), she would be responding to an illusion. (Our city has been constructed with every household getting the same utility.) This is the same type of illusion we have discussed for the case of a household relocating between cities, in an equilibrium system of cities, in order to "reap" a higher wage. In that case, though the wage elsewhere was higher, so too was the cost of housing and in fact the mover would end up on the same indifference curve if she moved. We infer then that fiscal gaps (dollar benefits from the current quantity, G, different from dollar outlays in property taxes) will be a persistent and significant presence in an equilibrium system of cities framework. Somewhat distinct from this analysis is that of so-called "tax competition," the setting of local taxes by a local government, designed to attract firms that might otherwise locate in another urban place (Wilson 1999).

There is a "tax system" for an urban area which has dollar charges tailored precisely to each resident's dollar benefits from the current output, G. We discussed this in Chapter 1. This system, taxation in accord with marginal benefits, was set out by Samuelson (1954) and can be viewed as a benchmark system against which outcomes under the property tax system can be compared. Such a comparison is developed in detail for two abstract cities in Chapter 9.

Measuring the attractiveness of a city (quality of life indicators)

From an economics perspective, a quality of life indicator for a place is the level of utility, translated generally into dollars, that an individual attains in a particular place. The open-city assumption has each individual in equilibrium at the location where she or he attains the highest utility level. One must somehow aggregate individual utility levels into a level for the household since that is the unit that moves about in search of a best location to work and to "consume." Like most observers, we gloss over the tricky aggregation issue in moving from the utility level of person i to the utility level of person i's household. We treat them as the same thing.

For a household to achieve a particular utility level, we generally take net income, $w - t \times x$, and solve for the utility level $U(c(x), h(x), G, A)$ that the household attains at location x in a particular city, where $h(x)$ is the house and lot at distance x from the city center, $c(x)$ is other private consumption, G is government or public goods, and A is an amenity level. We assume that w is what a firm is willing to pay an individual who possesses a certain level of education and experience. The worker is being paid her value of marginal product to her firm, where she is employed. We assume that similar workers achieve the same level of utility in a city so that radial distance x is not an issue. When a worker is comparing cities to live in, she must decide what level of c, h and G she will achieve with her local wage w and local prices for c, h and G, given local amenity level, A. It is fairly standard to reduce this choice for a household as the trade-off of the local wage w with the local amenity level A. Implicit is the translation of the wage, w, into a bundle (c, h, G). Then one is assuming that a "market bundle" is being traded off with an amenity bundle. We argue that a good first pass way of viewing this choice is: more local A implies higher local housing costs (land rent costs), other things being the same, and typically this translates into the household trading off less housing for living locally with more amenities, A.

This line of thinking is referred to as analysing the local quality of life (QOL), for a household in a particular location. Matters become complicated, however, when one gets down to doing careful calculations. For example, A is typically a vector, comprising items such a annual rainfall, annual hours of sunshine, inches of snow, local crime rate, etc. Government or public goods G is also appropriately viewed as a vector, comprising items such a quality of local schools, level of security in one's neighborhood, quality of municipal street maintenance, etc. Further, h is also a vector of attributes of one's house, lot and nearby homes. Kahn (1993) discusses the process of getting numerical estimates of a QOL indicator for cities in the United States. Roback (1982) is a seminal paper in the large literature on this topic.

Our typical "outcome" is that for two similar workers in two cities with quite different climates, the amount of housing becomes the "compensating factor." The better climate is represented by "free sunshine" in one worker's utility function and to make utility the same across different cities, the extra sunshine (large amenity) is offset somewhat by less housing on more expensive land. However, a voluminous literature on cities has developed around the notion of wage "compensation" offered in cities with relatively poor climates (Rosen 1979). Wage adjustment for a disamenity dates from Adam Smith's discussion of noxious jobs. He introduced the notion of trash collectors being paid more than other unskilled workers because they were obliged to deal with unpleasant odours and sights all day. Wage adjustment is not the only way to compensate a worker for a relatively distasteful job. For example, miners in remote areas with unpleasant climates not only earn high wages but often their terms of employment involve frequent fly-outs from the mine-site for rest and recuperation in a more pleasant place. This is compensation by an adjustment to "intensity of work" rather than to the wage directly. Given the utility function of a worker, a disamenity can be compensated for by, for example, subsidizing standard consumption items such as beverages or steak dinners. Technically we can distinguish between an income adjustment for compensation for a disamenity or a price adjustment for a standard consumption item.

Once we assume that firms in a place are amenity neutral, we end up with wages based on the process productivity of a worker. The wage is largely independent of whether the firm is located in a sunny city or a less attractive place. Compensation for the climate amenity ends up taking place "by price," largely higher "cost of living" (higher average land rents) for a sunnier place. Workers end up paying on average more for a home in a sunnier city and generally consume less "home" (smaller lot sizes, for example). Another price adjustment can take place in the local payment for public services. A worker could end up paying more for local public schools in a sunnier city and this "tax premium" could be viewed as a price for living with more local climate amenity. The bottom line in our framework is that similar workers must end up with the same level of utility in equilibrium and thus the "more sun" amenity for one city must have an offset in a worker's utility function such that two workers in distinct cities end up with the same level of utility.

Albouy (2008) takes issue with the fact that large cities with expensive houses and lots were not being ranked high among places with superior QOL in the United States. If many persons are willing to pay a high price to live in community j, one assumes that community j must have some sort of premium to offer, in addition to a high wage. Big cities are renowned for their "bright lights" and bustle, fine restaurants, quality theatres, galleries, musical presentations and opera, and so on. Albouy adjusts local wages for a household's tax liability given progressivity of the income tax and finds that net wages are not so much larger for residents of large cities. Hence such a resident must be consuming more of the local amenities. He also adjusts for the "extra" expenditure on housing in a large city and this removes a bias against cities with a high cost of living. Finally he makes one more plausible adjustment to the household wage. His new ranking of communities has Honolulu, Santa Barbara, Monterey, San Francisco, San Luis Obispo, Santa Fe, non-metro Hawaii, Cape Cod, San Diego and rural Colorado on top while among states he has West Virginia, Mississippi, Michigan and Texas with the lowest QOL valuations. Albouy's approach ends up with climate amenity and an ocean coast counting large in a QOL measure. Vancouver, British Columbia, has mild winters and nearby snow-capped mountains and high prices for homes. If it were included in Albouy's set of places to consider, it would no doubt have ranked near the top. Portland, Oregon is renowned for its high quality of life and highly educated residents. Yet its increase in per capita personal income has been below that of 42 other US cities between 2000 and 2012.[15] Researchers have worked up happiness indicators for many US cities and they find that even those with poor scores continue to attract new residents. Glaeser *et al.* (2014) argue that affordable housing and good wages can fully compensate for low happiness of the average resident. We return to the issue of a household's choice of city in which to locate in Chapter 4.

One might also ask whether firms respond to the pull of a location with a good climate, as well as workers. Gabriel and Rosenthal (2004)developed quality of location estimates for firms and concluded that on average a firm would locate where workers were available at relatively low wages. They also found that retired people tended to prefer locations with lower local costs, which were the same places as those with relatively low wages. We discuss location choice for firms in more detail in Chapters 4, 5 and 6.

One's local neighborhood can be congenial or bland. Attractive neighborhoods will command higher prices for residences. In a large city, one's apartment rent can vary with access to grocery stores, restaurants, clubs and subway stops. Lower quality access should correlate with somewhat lower rents for apartments. Clearly of central importance is security on the streets in one's neighborhood. The case of a well-known restaurant moving away from one's neighborhood should in the first instance lower one's utility because one is now obliged to walk or drive farther to get to a "good restaurant." This inconvenience is different from the case of losing utility because one's neighborhood is losing "atmosphere." Restaurant operators apparently live in perpetual fear of future rent increases. A new apartment building has been put up on the site of WD-50, a well-known restaurant on the Lower East Side of New York. The developer of the new apartment building has bid the site away from use by the restaurant. If the site were zoned for a restaurant then the apartment developer could not take the site over. This is one of the functions of zoning, namely to prevent a higher bid for the site from being made. If highest bidding activities always prevailed only one kind of activity would emerge in many places. Zoning is in part an instrument for creating a diversity of land uses, when only one kind of activity would prevail under a free market regime. Glaeser has expressed concern that certain kinds of zoning lead to the preservation of "neighborhood atmosphere" when it might make more sense to sacrifice some "atmosphere" in order to get more apartments and condominiums into a neighborhood, simply to assist the new supply to keep rents and prices for homes from rising excessively. Local residents would be biased in favor of the preservation of a local restaurant while newcomers would be most interested in obtaining accommodation at manageable prices. Another example of this kind of thing is on the upper East Side of Manhattan, where a well-patronized diner, "Soup Burg," closed to make way for the branch of a bank. Many Londoners are upset about the loss of distinctive neighborhood "atmospheres" in enclaves in the West End. Around 180,000 m^2 of office floor space has been turned into residential activity since 2003.[16] Paris also has been experiencing rapid gentrification in its center in recent years.

The rent that a restaurant can afford to pay for using a site depends on how much profit it makes, which in turn depends on how large a customer "market area" it can command. Part of demand for the services of a restaurant comes from the option demands of local residents. Many households may not use the restaurant regularly but they value the option or possibility of eating out there occasionally. Option demand takes the form of a payment that would be willingly made for having the restaurant "available" in the neighborhood. The capacity of a restaurant to pay its rent for its site emerges in a somewhat different process of rent generation from that we took up in von Thunen's model. There rent was a residual "profit" per unit of agricultural product on a unit of land. There are in fact many firms which specialize in analysing the quality of sites for new retail activity. Finding profitable sites for new shopping centers is an indirect process of quantifying the rent that a site could afford to pay.

Summary

In this chapter we have replied to critics who feel that the textbook model of the monocentric city captures cities only from an earlier era. The urban economist can adapt the classic monocentric city model to capture modern phenomena such as the decentralization of employment in large cities. We have been able to capture worker heterogeneity (different incomes for different residents) quite directly; similarly for a suburban ring of employment centers; and similarly also for a city with tall buildings in places where land rent is relatively high. We found that the equilibrium rent function provided a useful tool for carrying out our analysis. We indicated that capitalization of wage increases in local land rents is a proposition that holds for quite general function forms of the utility function and the production function for structures.

We carried out two conceptual experiments with our model of a city and a city in a system of cities. We observed that geographic amenities can be seen to show up in local "cost of living" (land rents) in a beneficiary city relative to another city with less of the amenity.

Free migration of like worker-households results in the capitalization of an amenity premium in the local land rent. And we delved into the presence of government goods (public goods) in a resident's utility function. Tricky here is the combination of the public nature of a local government good and payment with a resident's property tax. In general a resident's tax bill will be different from the dollar valuation by the resident of her consumption flow of the government good. Both capitalization of geographic amenities and the production and consumption of public goods are subjects we will return to. Each deserves a full exploration.

The CBD has been something of a black box to this point. The Lucas–Rossi-Hansberg (2002) model starts with the basic monocentric city and introduces explicit land-using firms as the employers. The firms benefit from being close to each other. In a Lucas–Rossi-Hansberg city, the more the firms agglomerate, the farther on average the workers must commute and the less on average workers are obliged to commute the more costs firms incur in being relatively distant from one another. Hence different values of commuting cost per unit distance can generate quite different distributions of residences and firms over space. One wants to think carefully about the kinds of firms that favor a location in the center and those that can do business quite comfortably in the suburbs. We will return to this topic numerous times. We return to the Lucas–Rossi-Hansberg model in Chapter 4. A related trade-off involves most firms desiring to be adjacent to a good port and leaving workers to arrange their residences in the face of this constraint. In recent decades, many firms cluster around airports in order to economize on the costs of shipping outputs and inputs into and out of the city in question. Some places embark on the development of a large airport in order to attract new firms, often with high-wage jobs. August Losch, working in the 1930's, developed the trade-off of better or more scale of production against demanders incurring more transportation costs for purchasing the product. Thus if a huge plant serves a large surrounding market, four smaller plants might serve the market at a smaller scale of production but at considerably lower costs of distribution of the output to the purchasers. One can think about optimal scale of production in such a framework, one not too different from the one that Krugman (1991a) analyzed in depth.

Main points of Chapter 3

1 When the monocentric city has distinct numbers of high-wage and low-wage workers employed in the center, there is a tendency for the high-wage residents to live in an annulus, farther from the center. The distinct rent schedules associated with each group intersect at the boundary, the circle, defining each area.
2 We can postulate a ring of "suburban jobs" at a fixed distance from the center. With similar worker-households, the suburbanized residents will commute to jobs in the suburban ring and the workers living on the inner annulus will work in the center. The similar households all end up with the same utility level, but the suburbanized workers receive a slightly lower wage because their productivity is slightly lower.
3 The lower productivity of suburban workers can be attributed to the fact that they work in suburban jobs arranged in lower densities (the law of urban growth is being called upon here).
4 The utility function of a resident of the monocentric city can include a local amenity such as more hours of sunshine per year. See Chapter 4 for more detail.
5 The utility function of a resident of the monocentric city can include a local public or government good. See Chapter 9 for more detail.

Questions and problems

1 Consider your city as an area that is approximately a circle ($\pi\overline{x}^2$) or a half circle ($\frac{1}{2}\pi\overline{x}^2$). Recall that $\pi \approx 3.14$. and 1 mile is 5,280 feet. Find the radius $\overline{x}$ of your city. Can you estimate the radius of your city for 1960? Explain "sprawl" associated with your city.

2 "The rise of reverse commuting, from within cities out to the edges, may be the most striking consequence of successful consumer cities" (Glaeser 2011; p. 11). What is a "consumer city"? Why would many residents take up reverse commuting? Can you think of a city that has significant reverse commuting taking place?

3 "If commuting into a city is a lengthly torment, then companies will head for the suburbs, no matter how many cool museums the city has" (Glaeser 2011; p. 260). How much has commuting hassle for workers contributed to the suburbanization of firms?

4 The persistent churning of the population of the United States will settle down to a good distribution of people and city sizes. Evaluate this contention.

5 "As of 2008, 36 percent of New Yorkers were foreign-born, and 48 percent spoke a language other than English at home" (Glaeser 2011; p. 78). Is the percentage of immigrants in a city positively correlated with that city's current level of relative prosperity?

Appendix 3.1: Cobb–Douglas utilities and production functions for structures

Consider a house $h(x)$ that combines some land $l(x)$ and structure $K(x)$. A house then can be thought of as being produced at a date using land and capital, these last rented at prices $r(x)$ per unit and i per unit, respectively. Central to the analysis is the substitution of marginally more land for capital when the rental on land is marginally lower, as with farther from the center. Hence we will observe land close to the center with a high capital to land ratio and farther from the center with a lower capital to land ratio. We employ first the Cobb–Douglas specification, $h(x) = l(x)^{\gamma} K(x)^{1-\gamma}$.

A household continues to purchase housing, $h(x)$, and other consumption goods, $c(x)$, reaping utility in $U = c(x)^{\alpha} h(x)^{1-\alpha}$. Free migration implies the same utility level for each household. Each worker-household earns w for work at the center and commutes tx to distance x from the center. Hence a worker-household budget constraint is represented by

$$w - tx = c(x) + q(x)h(x),$$

where $q(x)$ is the price per unit of $h(x)$. This price will be an annual rental. For the Cobb–Douglas production function, we have unit cost

$$\psi(x) = \Omega r(x)^{\gamma} i^{1-\gamma}, \text{ for } \Omega = \gamma^{-\gamma}(1-\gamma)^{-(1-\gamma)},$$

which we will assume equals unit price, $q(x)$. (The general properties of these unit cost functions include $h\frac{\partial \Psi}{\partial r} = l$ and $h\frac{\partial \Psi}{\partial i} = K$.)

Production efficiency (ratio of marginal products equal to price ratio) here is

$$\frac{\gamma K(x)}{(1-\gamma)l(x)} = \frac{r(x)}{i}$$

and we can substitute into the production function to obtain

$$h = \left[\frac{(1-\gamma)r}{\gamma i}\right]^{1-\gamma} l.$$

This result, plus the utility function and constant utility gives us

$$c = \frac{\overline{U}^{1/\alpha}}{\left\{l\left[\frac{(1-\gamma)r}{\gamma i}\right]^{1-\gamma}\right\}^{(1-\alpha)/\alpha}}.$$

Consumption efficiency is

$$\frac{\alpha h}{(1-\alpha)c} = \frac{1}{q}$$

or

$$\frac{\alpha l^{1/\alpha}\left[\frac{(1-\gamma)r}{\gamma i}\right]^{(1-\gamma)/\alpha}}{(1-\alpha)\overline{U}^{1/\alpha}} = \frac{1}{\Omega r(x)^{\gamma} i^{1-\gamma}}.$$

This gives us

$$l = \frac{(1-\alpha)^{\alpha}\overline{U}}{[\alpha\Omega r(x)^{\gamma} i^{1-\gamma}]^{\alpha}\left[\frac{(1-\gamma)r}{\gamma i}\right]^{1-\gamma}}.$$

Then

$$h = \frac{(1-\alpha)^{\alpha}\overline{U}}{[\alpha\Omega r(x)^{\gamma} i^{1-\gamma}]^{\alpha}}$$

and

$$\begin{aligned} c &= \frac{\alpha q h}{(1-\alpha)} \\ &= \frac{\alpha\overline{U}}{(1-\alpha)}\left(\frac{1-\alpha}{\alpha}\right)^{\alpha}(\Omega r(x)^{\gamma} i^{1-\gamma})^{1-\alpha}. \end{aligned}$$

Hence

$$\begin{aligned} w - tx &= c + qh \\ &= \frac{c}{\alpha} \\ &= \frac{\overline{U}}{(1-\alpha)}\left(\frac{1-\alpha}{\alpha}\right)^{\alpha}(\Omega i^{1-\gamma})^{1-\alpha} r(x)^{\gamma(1-\alpha)} \end{aligned}$$

from which our rent function, $r(x)$, emerges.

We digress for a moment to observe that

$$dw = \gamma\overline{U}\left(\frac{1-\alpha}{\alpha}\right)^{\alpha}(\Omega i^{1-\gamma})^{1-\alpha}r(x)^{\gamma(1-\alpha)-1}dr,$$

which gives $\frac{dw}{dr} = l$ after some manipulations of the expression for l above. Hence for $\overline{x}$ in $r(\overline{x}) = r_A$ and $R(\overline{x}) = \int_0^{\overline{x}} r(x)2\pi x dx$ and $N(\overline{x}) = \int_0^{\overline{x}} \frac{1}{l(x)}2\pi x dx$, we have

$$\begin{aligned}\frac{dR(\overline{x})}{dw} &= \int_0^{\overline{x}} \frac{dr(x)}{dw}2\pi x dx + 2\pi\overline{x}r_A\frac{d\overline{x}}{dw}\\ &= N(\overline{x}) + 2\pi\overline{x}r_A\frac{d\overline{x}}{dw}.\end{aligned}$$

This is the basic capitalization of a wage increment in local land rent which we have observed in our simpler models in Chapter 1. Our capitalization of commuting cost increments can also be obtained analogously. That is,

$$\begin{aligned}\frac{dR(\overline{x})}{dt} &= -\int_0^{\overline{x}} \frac{dr(x)}{dt}2\pi x dx + 2\pi\overline{x}r_A\frac{d\overline{x}}{dt}\\ &= -M(\overline{x}) + 2\pi\overline{x}r_A\frac{d\overline{x}}{dt},\end{aligned}$$

for $M(\overline{x}) = \int_0^{\overline{x}} \frac{x}{L(x)}2\pi x dx$, total miles commuting in the city before the marginal change in commuting cost, t. We return to our rent function. That is,

$$r(x) = \left[\frac{1}{\frac{\overline{U}}{1-\alpha}\left(\frac{1-\alpha}{\alpha}\right)^{\alpha}(\Omega i^{1-\gamma})^{1-\alpha}}\right]^{1/(\gamma(1-\alpha))}(w - tx)^{1/(\gamma(1-\alpha))}.$$

This rent function is very similar to the one we derived for the case of no structures on land. Observe that $\frac{dr}{dx} < 0$ and $\frac{d^2r}{dx^2} > 0$. We have a rent function declining from the center and convex to the origin. Also

$$\frac{dr}{dx}\frac{1}{r(x)} = \frac{-t}{\gamma(1-\alpha)} \times \frac{1}{w - tx},$$

and this percentage decline will be rising, not rapidly, in absolute value with distance x. We observed this same phenomenon for our rent function for the model without structures.

Appendix 3.2: Capitalization of dw and dt shifts with structures

We proceed as we have done in Chapter 1. The open-city assumption implies that utility is unchanging under our changes in w and t. Hence

$$dU = U_c dc + U_h dh = 0.$$

This implies $dc = -\frac{U_h}{U_c}dh = -qdh$ for $q(x)$, the price of a unit of housing at x. From the budget constraint, we have

$$\begin{aligned} dw &= tdx + dc + qdh + hdq \\ &= tdx + hdq \end{aligned}$$

since

$$dc = -qdh.$$

Now housing is produced with land $l(x)$ and capital $K(x)$ in a constant returns to scale production function, $h = h(l, K)$, and the rental rate for a unit of K is constant i. Hence

$$\frac{h_l}{h_K} = \frac{r}{i}.$$

We also have price function, $q = g(r, i)$ with the property that $\frac{\partial q(x)}{\partial r(x)} = a_{lh}(x)$, this latter being land per unit of housing. We have $dq = a_{lh}dr$. (Recall that i is a constant.) Hence we have

$$dw = tdx + ha_{lh}dr,$$

which gives us $\frac{dr}{dw} = \frac{1}{ha_{lh}} - \frac{t}{ha_{lh}}\frac{dx}{dw}$.

We are interested in how the wage shift shows up in land rent (our capitalization exercise). We have

$$\begin{aligned} \frac{dR(\overline{x})}{dw} - 2\pi\overline{x}r_A\frac{d\overline{x}}{dw} &= \int_0^{\overline{x}} \frac{dr(x)}{dw}2\pi x dx \\ &= \int_0^{\overline{x}} \frac{1}{ha_{lh}}2\pi x dx - t\int_0^{\overline{x}} \frac{dx}{dw}\frac{1}{ha_{lh}}2\pi x dx. \end{aligned}$$

Since h is housing (floor space) per resident and a_{lh} is land per house, it follows that $\frac{1}{ha_{lh}}$ is resident per unit land. Hence $\int_0^{\overline{x}} \frac{1}{ha_{lh}}2\pi x dx$ is population, $N(\overline{x})$. We can write the capitalization expression as

$$\Delta R_n(\overline{x}) = N(\overline{x})dw - \Delta T(\overline{x})dw,$$

where $\Delta R_n(\overline{x})$ is net land rent change caused by the increase in w and $\Delta T(\overline{x})dw$ is the city-side adjustment term. This latter is present because each household re-optimizes its choice of location and bundle (c, h) when its w is increased. The sum of all these re-optimization costs is $\Delta T(\overline{x})dw$.

Of interest then is how the presence of structures is completely "internalized" in our expression for the capitalization of the wage increment. Our expression above is the same as that from Chapter 1, where we had no structures.

And the same steps will yield the analogous expression for the capitalization of a change in commuting costs, namely a change in t. We will have then

$$\Delta R_n(\overline{x}) = -M(\overline{x})dt - \Delta T(\overline{x})dt$$

for $M(\overline{x})$ total miles commuted each period for the city as a whole.

Notes

1 One might express this condition intuitively as $hdr = -tdx$.
2 *Toronto Vital Signs Report 2013*.
3 See Gilmore, Jason (2009) for a snapshot of recent changes in the unemployment rate for immigrants, male and female separately, and notes on the sectors in which job-finding was most successful.
4 Peter Applebome, *New York Times*, Sunday, June 12, 2011, p. WK 2.
5 Our definition of Chicago comprises nine contiguous counties (census tracts for the year 2011), with a total population of 8.4 million people and an area of 17,200 km^2. Cook County is the largest county in this definition of "Chicago," with a population of 5.2 million in 2011.
6 Houston in our map comprises eight counties (Brazoria, Chambers, Fort Bend, Galveston, Harris, Liberty, Montgomery, Waller) with Harris the largest with 4.1 million people in 2011. There are 895 census tracts and 5.9 million people in total. The area of this Houston is 22,500 km^2. This is 262 people per square kilometer. Chicago above is 488.3 people per kilometer.
7 See Lucas and Rossi–Hansberg (2002) on a general equilibrium model that has commuting "consume" some of a worker-commuter's labor endowment. Each worker is more productive the more other workers there are working near his place of work. For some parameter values all work is in a CBD whereas for other parameter values work places are dispersed. Relatively low commuting costs makes for production activity concentrated in the center.
8 New York City is an outlier with about 30 percent of commutes made by mass transit. Next in the United States come Washington, DC, San Francisco, Boston and Chicago each with less than 15 percent of commutes made by mass transit. In Canada, Montreal, Toronto and Ottawa each have about 20 percent of commutes made by mass transit. (Fifty-seven percent of all trips in Tokyo are made by public transport and commuter rail carries 2/3 of all commuting trips (1,800 miles of line with 1,200 stations). The commuter rail lines are privately owned and receive no subsidies for operating or capital budgets.)
9 National Household Travel Survey (2001), Department of Transportation, Government of the United States. See Pisarski (2006).
10 Marcus Gee, *The Globe and Mail*, Tuesday, April 12, 2011, p. A13.
11 Peter Applebome, *New York Times*, Sunday, June 12, 2011, p. WK 2.
12 Recall that we did in fact carry out this type of analysis in Chapter 1 for our "trading city" without a detailed land-use structure.
13 As we argued in Chapter 1, the increase in size of the city should cause some presumably small increase in average wages. But to a first approximation, it makes sense to assume the wage change is too small to incorporate into the analysis.
14 Recall also that in Chapter 1 we introduced a government good and benefit charges for it in our model. That model had a vaguely defined land-use structure.
15 *New York Times*, September 21, 2014, p. 22.
16 *The Economist*, January 3, 2015, p. 43.

4 Wages, agglomeration and migration

Mechanics of wages rising with city size: lower unemployment in larger cities, higher firm's profits in larger cities and better fit of worker skills to specialized vacancies. Sizes of basic and non-basic sectors feed into local wage formation. Wages rising with population and density. Intercity migration and city sizes. Climate amenities and relative city sizes. Shifts in the edge of the city and the question of sprawl. Rural-urban migration in Third World cities (Harris–Todaro model).

Introduction

Humans have always lived in collectives or villages. Humans are social beings. It was the development of agriculture that drew families away from rudimentary villages in order to work a simple farm. Clearly village-living allowed humans to exploit division of labor in a way that economized on resources used in transportation (there is more on this topic in Chapter 6, dealing with the growth of a community). And of course, collectives of individuals could fend off attackers better than single persons could. Anthropologists have faced the question of the efficient size of these villages in the long period before farming on a private plot was invented. Many take 150 people as the size of a typical "village" in the days before the development of agriculture. Farming provided surpluses that could be traded, typically for town goods and such trade provided for the development of towns, places with more complicated divisions of labor and more complicated social hierarchies. Some groups of individuals organized themselves into rudimentary "firms," collectives with bosses and underlings. And trading arrangements became more complicated with rural folk showing up regularly to sell their produce to townsfolk. What constrained the size of these early "cities"?

Towns were constrained in their growth by the availability of food and because the acquisition of food from farms involved transportation costs. A town's size would be largely constrained by the size of its base of farms with surpluses. This latter notion is tricky since food (grains for example) can be transported by boats and can be stored in granaries. One cannot simply draw a circle around an ancient town and say that the arable area is the one that defines the food constraint for the town in question. Sir William Petty (1686) pursued the farms-constraint approach in his analysis of the maximum population that London could be expected to attain in the long run. He came up with a maximum population of 96,000 for London in 1682 and opined that it could eventually attain seven times that population, given the availability of food in accessible hinterland. (He also arrived at an estimate of ten billion for the maximum which world population could attain.)

We have touched on three sorts of structural changes that coincided with the arrival of farming some 10,000 to 12,000 years ago. First, a new form of large-scale trade developed, namely between the food-producers (farmers) and consumers in towns. Second, a new hierarchy of governors and religious leaders emerged with the increase in size of settlements. And third, division of labor was deepened simply because specialization was taking place with more and more diverse individuals.[1] The division between bosses and underlings would have become more common as community size increased. We can summarize these changes as variants of scale effects. Farming made for larger villages. Larger settlements led to more trade and a finer division of labor. New social roles such as boss and underling and leader and party emerged. Social hierarchies became more evident. The smallest of hunter-gatherer communities would have had some stratification of senior and junior members, if only by age, but larger communities would take on more active and intricate stratifications. The notion of a pecking order is found in almost every community of birds, animals and reptiles, and it was soon apparent in human communities too.

Scale economies

Internal economies of scale refer to a firm being able to produce at a lower unit cost when its output is increased. External economies of scale refer to the cost reduction that accrues to a firm in a group of firms as the group's output is increased. Thus when we say that a city's growth allows a firm in that place to take advantage of scale economies, we could be referring to somewhat distinct phenomena. An "urbanization economy" is a term used to describe the scale economies that can be reaped by a firm in a city as that city grows. This could then be either an internal or external economy of scale that is being exploited by a firm. However a "localization economy" refers to the lower unit cost for a firm with increased production as its own industry increases in size. Thus Silicon Valley south of San Francisco has a high concentration of computer firms (mostly software and development activity rather than hardware production) and its expansion would involve localization economies. In a study with Japanese data, reported on in Rosenthal and Strange (2007), Nakamura finds that a doubling of industry size for certain industries induces a rise in worker productivity of about 4.5 percent. Hence the scale economy, superior worker productivity, will show up partly in higher wages and partly as more profit for a firm. For a doubling of a city population on the other hand, Nakamura finds a productivity increase of about 3.4 percent.

Urbanization economies are related to the diversity of activities in a large city. A firm may well operate at a lower unit cost for a given level of output in a large city rather than in a smaller place, because its inputs are available closer by in the larger and presumably more diversified place. Jane Jacobs (1961) was attracted to this explanation for the success of large American cities. But what forces lead to many firms in the same industry locating relatively close together? Alfred Marshall (1920; pp. 271–274) had two compelling explanations. First, if the industry requires workers with special skills, as with software engineers for example, a new firm does well to locate where such workers can be readily hired. This is an instance of his labor "sharing" argument. In Marshall's words: "Employers are apt to resort to any place where they are likely to find a good choice of workers with the special skill which they require." Note that it also makes sense for new software engineers to settle where demand for their skills is known to be robust. Labor sharing tends to smooth out wage variation in a locality: when some local firms are suffering from a demand slump, their workers can often find work with local firms experiencing a demand upturn. Labor pooling of local firms requires then that the positive and negative shocks to demands of various local firms be uncorrelated. One does not want all local firms experiencing positive or negative shocks at the same time. Edwin Mills (1972a) referred to this stochastic phenomenon, somewhat analogous to pooling health risks of many individuals, as "the most important agglomeration economy" in the many editions of his textbook. More on details of labor pooling below. Second, when the technology of production is special, as with producing computers, important information is "in the air" and it will be to a firm's advantage to be located where the important information is easily plucked from "the air."

Marshall's third idea about the clustering of certain firms is that when a large market is available and a number of suppliers are needed to serve that market, it often pays a firm to locate close to the demanders, to keep its transportation costs low. When inputs are costly to transport, a clustering of like firms can also be found at key supply points. A good natural port is of course a place of low transportation costs and as such can become a node for firms to locate. Different economies of agglomeration can "switch on" as firms agglomerate around a transportation node. Low-cost electricity, where hydro power is abundant, can make certain places especially attractive for certain sorts of smelting of ores. Aluminum production is usually pursued in places where the costs of electricity at industrial scales is relatively cheap. Kolko (2010) finds that firms in service activities tend to locate near customers or near suppliers.

Arzaghi and Henderson (2008) documented productivity advantages to an advertising firm locating close to other such firms in New York City. There is an interesting complicating factor here. The agglomeration of such firms is likely at a sub-optimal scale since when a firm enters the cluster it only takes account of how its own productivity will develop. It does not incorporate the advantages it yields to other such firms in the cluster in its calculation of enter or not-enter. Arzaghi and Henderson observed that in the advertising agencies the productivity advantage to a firm in the cluster is capitalized in location rent rather than in a wage premium for workers. Hence an incumbent advertising firm could close down and sell its office building to an entering advertising firm at a premium. It could monetize the site rent of its operation.

Ellison *et al.* (2010) have investigated co-location of distinct activities in the manufacturing sector in the United States. The clustering they are interested in differs from that associated with, for example, computer firms in Silicon Valley. They were interested in clusters of distinct manufacturing activities, not particularly firms in the same industry. They examined 7,381 pairs of manufacturing activities for 1987, each pair with some index of geographic distance. They regressed this distance index on four explanatory variables (proxied by index numbers): one for flows of goods between pairs, one for similarity in employee characteristics, one for interdependence with information flow and one for dependence on a natural location advantage such as a port. The first three explanatory variables derive from the thinking of Alfred Marshall on forces contributing to agglomeration. The last explanatory variable we referred to earlier in this section.

Among the most co-agglomerated industry pairs were textile and apparel industries. These activities are concentrated in North Carolina, South Carolina and Georgia. But the geographic concentration measures were higher for some within industry agglomerations. The lowest pairwise closeness index was for "guided missiles and space vehicles" and "railway equipment."

Ellison *et al.* (2010; p. 1106) conclude:

> We estimate that shared natural advantages[2] are more important than any single Marshallian factor, but not as important as the cumulative effect of the three Marshallian factors. Among the Marshallian factors, customer-supplier relationships have the strongest effect. These input-output linkages are closely followed by similar labor

> needs. Our proxies for intellectual spillovers are weaker than the other factors but still economically and statistically important.

Shout out for Alfred Marshall, a Cambridge professor whose large *Principles* volume first appeared in 1890.

City size, labor pooling and local unemployment

Early in his classic textbook Edwin Mills (1972a; p. 17) claims the

> most important [of] agglomeration economies [is] statistical in nature and is an application of the law of large numbers. Sales of outputs and purchases of inputs fluctuate in many firms and industries for random, seasonal, cyclical, and secular reasons. To the extent that fluctuations are imperfectly correlated among employers, an urban area with many employers can provide more nearly full employment of its labor force than can an urban area with few employers.[3]

In this claim, city largeness appears to be insuring a representative worker against being "caught" in a lengthy spell of unemployment. Once laid off, the labor pooling argument says that a worker is more likely to be hired quickly by another nearby firm when the worker is in a large city rather than a small city. We turn to a simple statistical model of an abstract city in which larger size is associated with fewer spells of unemployment for a representative worker. We also observe a complementary process: city size provides some insurance to a representative firm in the larger city against a shortfall in labor supply for the firm when the latter is faced with a jump in demand for its product.

Probability of a laid-off worker remaining unemployed

We focus attention on a single period. Each of n identical firms, each in operation in our abstract city with zero profits, tosses a fair coin at the opening of the period. K firms turn up heads and each needs an additional worker and $n - K$ firms turn up tails and each lets a worker go. We are imagining that each firm in our city is being hit by a demand shock in the current period. Hence the shedding of or hiring of a worker. With probability $1/2$ a firm in the current state lays off a worker because its current demand is down and with probability $1/2$ another firm takes on an extra worker because its current demand is up. Each firm letting a worker go can be thought of as experiencing negative profits and vice versa for a firm taking on an extra worker.

The superficial take is that a city with n firms will enjoy zero unemployment, period after period, and each firm will be on average in a zero profit position over many periods. However, in a complete analysis of our single period, one must "disaggregate" the state of the city because it is only on average that half the firms will be hiring and the other half will be laying off a worker. For example in a four-firm city, there are 16 states which the city can be in, in our representative period, with just 6 states in which exactly two firms are hiring and two firms are laying off. In 5 of the other 10 states which the city can be in, there will be excess demand for workers (more firms in an up state than in a down state) and in the other 5 states, there will be excess supply of workers (more firms in a down state than in an up state). Our interest is in the incidence of unemployment for a representative worker who shows up at the edge of a city, hoping to be hired by one of the firms in the city. We will assume that the prevailing wage reflects the zero unemployment state and thus that the wage is not moving up or down in response to the current excess demand or supply of labor.[4]

Suppose then we have an unemployed person standing at the edge of a city and hoping to get a job. We have first the case of exactly four firms in the city, each subject to an independent shock in each period: with probability $1/2$ a firm needs one more worker (the u state) and with probability $1/2$ a firm is obliged to lay off one worker (a firm's d state). This implies one of 16 states will emerge in the next period and our outsider is hoping to be taken on by a firm in the u state.

There are zero jobs available if all firms are in the d state. Hence the outsider remains unemployed when all firms are in the d state. This "all d" state occurs with $1/16$ probability. Hence we have

$$1/16 \times 1$$

as the probability that our outsider remains unemployed, given a particular state of 16 possible current states.

Consider now the case of one firm in the u state and three in the d state. There is then one job available and four persons hoping to get the job (three from the d state firms plus our outsider). Our outsider gets the job with probability $1/4$ and such a state occurs in four different ways. That is, there is a $4/16$ probability that such a one job state occurs and if one such state does occur, our outsider gets the job with probability $1/4$. Hence our outsider remains unemployed with probability

$$4/16 \times 3/4$$

when only one firm of the four is in the up state.

Consider now the case of two firms in the u state and two in the d state. This can arise in six different ways. There will be two jobs available in one such state and three persons hoping to get a job. Hence our outsider gets a job with probability $2/3$ and remains unemployed with probability $1/3$. One of these states arises with probability $6/16$. Hence our outsider remains unemployed with probability

$$6/16 \times 1/3.$$

We move on. Consider the case of one firm in the d state and three in the u state. This can arise in four different ways. There will be three jobs being offered for two applicants. Our outsider will get a job with probability 1 and remain unemployed with probability 0. Hence over these states our outsider remains unemployed with probability

$$4/16 \times 0.$$

Finally there is one realization with all four firms in the u state. There are four jobs being offered and one applicant, namely our outsider. She gets a job with certainty and remains unemployed with probability 0. Hence we have our outsider remaining unemployed in

$$1/16 \times 0.$$

Over all 16 possible outcomes per period, our outsider will remain unemployed with probability

$$1/16 \times 1 + 4/16 \times 3/4 + 6/16 \times 1/3 + 5/16 \times 0 = 0.375$$

This value tends to zero as the number of firms goes from 6 to 8 to 10 and so on to infinity. Hence the central result of labor pooling: it is in the interest of a worker looking for a job to go to a large city rather than a small city. He or she has a smaller probability of remaining unemployed when she attaches herself to a larger city, given the uncertainties in demand hitting our firms in the city.

See Table 4.1 for the case of 4, 6 and 8 firms. Here $b(x; n)$, the binomial coefficient, is the number of distinct arrangements of x firms in the u state out of a total of n firms, $x \leq n$. The case of $n = 4$ we reported on in detail above. The cases of $n = 6$ and $n = 8$, two larger cities, are simply set out in Table 4.1.

We observe that the probability of our outsider remaining unemployed declines as the number of firms defining our city, n, rises. The limiting value is in fact approximately zero, for n very large. Hence the inference: when an unemployed person attaches herself to a larger city, her probability of remaining unemployed in the next period is less than when she attaches herself to a smaller city.

We have done our analysis for a representative laid-off worker in a single "representative" period. If we turned to the evolution of a city of many firms as time moves forward, a firm could be experiencing consecutive periods without a needed worker or consecutive periods of worker shedding. Firm size would be changing over periods. A complete analysis would require details of the evolution of the profits of a firm. The large complication

Table 4.1 Probabilities of remaining unemployed

d	$n = 4$	$n = 6$	$n = 8$
8			$(1 - \frac{0}{9})\frac{b(8;8)}{2^8}$ 0.004
7			$(1 - \frac{1}{8})\frac{b(7;8)}{2^8}$ 0.0274
6		$(1 - \frac{0}{7})\frac{b(6;6)}{2^6}$ 0.016	$(1 - \frac{2}{7})\frac{b(6;8)}{2^8}$ 0.0781
5		$(1 - \frac{1}{6})\frac{b(5;6)}{2^6}$ 0.0783	$(1 - \frac{3}{6})\frac{b(5;8)}{2^8}$ 0.1095
4	$(1 - \frac{0}{5})\frac{b(4;4)}{2^4}$ 0.063	$(1 - \frac{2}{5})\frac{b(4;6)}{2^6}$ 0.1404	$(1 - \frac{4}{5})\frac{b(4;8)}{2^8}$ 0.00564
3	$(1 - \frac{1}{4})\frac{b(3;4)}{2^4}$ 0.1875	$(1 - \frac{3}{4})\frac{b(3;6)}{2^6}$ 0.0783	0 0
2	$(1 - \frac{2}{3})\frac{b(2;4)}{2^4}$ 0.125	0 0	0 0
Sum	$= 0.3755$	$= 0.3130$	$= 0.2738$

would be dealing with a firm which dies (hits a boundary) over many periods. A many period model would take us well beyond a basic analysis of Mills's "most important agglomeration economy."

Evidence for lower rates of unemployment in larger cities

Clearly our formal analysis of labor pooling turns on workers being indistinguishable to firms and firms being indistinguishable to workers. A bit of reflection suggests that unemployment rates are actually quite different for workers with different characteristics, including age, health status, education and experience. Hence the amount of insurance against unemployment that a larger real-world city affords a worker will most plausibly differ considerably by worker type, though it can still remain true that city bigness provides some insurance against unemployment in the current period to each worker, just a different amount, depending on the cohort that the worker belongs to. Helsley and Strange (1990) give a "statistical" model in which a hiring firm is striving to acquire distinctly different workers for distinctly different tasks in the firm in question. Workers are heterogeneous and Helsley and Strange created a clever and tractable index number or indicator for such heterogeneity in their abstract framework. However, there is no possibility of unemployment in their model. We take up their model in the next section. Gan and Zhang (2006) carried out one of the rare econometric analyses of unemployment in cities in the United States and concluded that "an increase of two standard deviations in city size lowers the unemployment rate by 0.7 percentage points." This is empirical support for Mills's inference, based on armchair theorizing. Overman and Puga (2010, Chapter 4) set out a model of labor pooling, a model descending from Krugman (1991a), and test the idea of labor pooling with data for the United States. They calculate the fluctuations in employment of individual establishments relative to their sector. They find "that sectors whose establishments experience more idiosyncratic volatility are more spatially concentrated, even after controlling for a range of other industry characteristics" (p. 150). Unanticipated shocks to demands of "establishments" induces establishments to cluster. Firms are exploiting an economy of being near each other. One might say that a firm is better off coping with uncertain demands for its product when it can hire and shed workers at a low cost and this low cost is easiest to realize when the firm is near other firms each of which is coping with its own uncertain demands each period. Shoag and Veuger (2014) find evidence that at the state level in the United States "preexisting local institutions that heightened uncertainty also increased unemployment" during the 2007–08 recession. Their emphasis is on a link between policy uncertainty facing firms and the reluctance of firms to commit resources to operating in a business-as-usual mode.

Fitting workers with distinct skills to vacancies with distinct requirements

It often takes a big city to support individuals with narrowly specialized skills. For example a neurosurgeon to be well employed needs a steady stream of patients with serious medical problems with their brains. Thus a highly skilled neurosurgeon would be more productive in a place with the required stream of patients. Such a stream is usually associated with a larger community. This fitting of workers with highly specialized skills to tasks "tightly" holds for many kinds of work, besides neurosurgery. We can say that very specialized workers generally need a large place to exercise their skills most productively. There are seldom appropriate slots in smaller places to accommodate individuals with specialized skills in a fully productive fashion. This is of course a compelling reason for a young person with highly specialized skills to locate in a large place when entering the job market. This idea—that specialized skills can be exercised most productively in larger places—has been around for decades, and it was formalized in a convenient way by Helsley and Strange (1990).

Helsley and Strange ask us to measure the fit of skill to task by a simple distance notion. They ask us to place n workers in equal density on a circle with a unit circumference. These n workers will constitute the labor force for a city. They ask us to imagine m firms located on this same circle in equal density with $m < n$. See Figure 4.1.

These m firms will be the employers in a city. We will construct the equilibrium city in a moment but for now one must take this circle (labor market) construction as a visual aid, a purely mental construction that will allow us to measure the quality of the current fit of workers to tasks. Each firm is surrounded on two sides on the circle by its labor force. Each worker is assumed to work at the closest firm on the circle.

There are m arcs on the circle, each arc representing a particular firm's labor force. Each arc is $\frac{1}{m}$ units long. The firm in the center of each arc is employing its own $\frac{n}{m}$ workers, workers located on the circle on either side of the firm, this firm in the center of its arc.

Consider a firm in the center of its arc, with two equal bits of arc on either side. A firm's arc is for the moment in four equal pieces. A moment's reflection will suffice to show that the average distance a worker is from her firm on the unit circle is $\frac{1}{4m}$.[5] A worker a tiny bit farther than $\frac{1}{4m}$ from his firm is fitting less well into his employment niche in his firm. It follows that the shorter the distance on this "imaginary" circle of a worker from her nearest firm, the higher the productivity of that worker. Hence we can think of $\frac{1}{4m}$ as measuring the quality or productiveness of an average worker for a firm in a city with n workers and m firms.

A firm will pay a higher wage for a more productive worker, one at location $\frac{1}{4m} - \varepsilon$, for ε a small distance on the circle. We can use $1/\left[\frac{1}{4m} - \varepsilon\right]$ as measuring productivity of the worker; a closer worker having a higher productivity indicator. Hence the wage for an average worker should reflect $1/\left[\frac{1}{4m}\right] = 4m$. We proceed to define the wage equal to $a[4m]^b$ for a and b positive and $0 < b < 1$ for an average worker in the city.

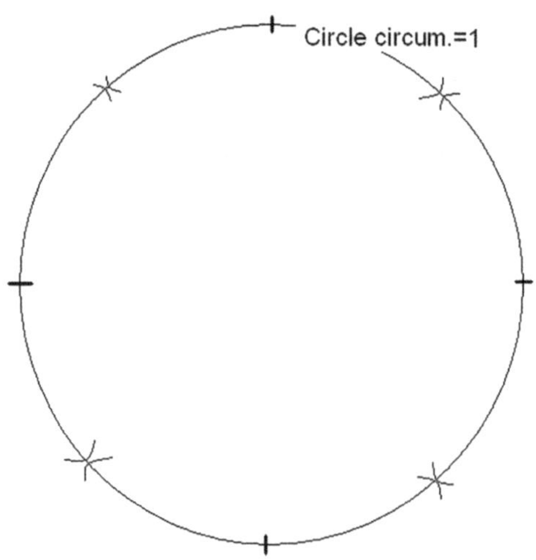

Figure 4.1 A Helsley–Strange unit circle. Here is a case of $m = 4$ firms on the unit circle. Each firm has its own $n/4$ workers. The n workers are also in equal density on the unit circle. The average distance a worker is from her firm is $1/(4m)$ or here $1/16$, and n is considerably larger than m.

Given the labor market and this market connected to firms, we now proceed to construct a simple city. This model is quite different in detail from that in Helsley and Strange (1990). An equilibrium city will be a pair of values, (n, m) that have firms and residents in equilibrium. Then, given an equilibrium city (an (n, m) pair), we wish to verify that $\frac{1}{4m}$ is smaller when our equilibrium city is larger or the city exhibits a tighter fit of workers to tasks in firms. We turn now to a simple monocentric city with m firms and n workers.

For our abstract planned city, we place workers in residences spread out about a central place of employment. Residential density is uniform at $\frac{1}{h}$. Hence each worker's housing is simply h units of land. Each worker has round-trip commuting cost, tx, for x radial distance from the center. The center of the monocentric city is then where the m firms are physically located (at a point). (In an abstract "elsewhere," the m firms are located in equal density on the labor market circle, as well.) There is land available at rent r_A with which to lay out our residential area. We measure the welfare of the average resident by her consumption and this consumption in represented by income net of expenses in

$$\Omega = a[4m]^b - hr(x) - tx - \tau + \frac{R(\overline{x})}{n(\overline{x})},$$

where $hr(x)$ is expenditure on housing, tx is expenditure on commuting to work in the center, τ is a tax which we discuss below and $\frac{R(\overline{x})}{n(\overline{x})}$ is a dividend paid to each resident, derived from the rent on land in the city. $R(\overline{x})$ is total land rent in the city, and $n(\overline{x})$ is the population (number of workers) in the city.

The rent function is $r(x) = r_A + \frac{t}{h}[\overline{x} - x]$. The entry of each of m firms is subsidized, with each resident paying $\frac{mC}{n(\overline{x})}$ each year for support of the subsidies which have been incurred to initially attract m firms. Thus the tax τ above is $\frac{mC}{n(\overline{x})}$. Our planner selects m and n to maximize per capita welfare, residual consumption, Ω above. The optimal values m^* and n^* will be an equilibrium Helsley–Strange city. The key Helsley–Strange proposition is that $\frac{1}{4m}$ is smaller in larger cities. That is, the average fit of a worker to a task (in a nearby firm on the imaginary circle) is better in a larger city, with "larger" here being measured by n being larger.

Consider solving for n^* and m^*. Since h is fixed, we require that consumption, Ω, be the same for each resident. That is, we require $\frac{d\Omega}{dx} = 0$. This is satisfied by $\frac{dr}{dt} = -\frac{t}{h}$, which we have assumed. We in fact maximize Ω by choice of $\overline{x}$ and m. First, we observe that

$$n(\overline{x}) = \frac{\pi\overline{x}^2}{h}$$

and

$$R(\overline{x}) = \int_0^{\overline{x}} \left\{ r_A + \frac{t}{h}[\overline{x} - x] \right\} 2\pi x dx = \pi r_A \overline{x}^2 + \frac{1}{3}\frac{t}{h}\pi\overline{x}^3.$$

Hence $\frac{d\Omega}{d\overline{x}} = 0$ implies

$$\frac{mC - R(\overline{x})}{n(\overline{x})} = \left[tn(\overline{x}) - \frac{dR(\overline{x})}{d\overline{x}} \right] \bigg/ \frac{dn(\overline{x})}{d\overline{x}}$$

or

$$\frac{mC - [R(\overline{x}) - \pi\overline{x}^2 r_A]}{n(\overline{x})} = 0,$$

since $[tn(\overline{x}) - \frac{d[\frac{1}{3}\frac{t}{h}\pi\overline{x}^3]}{d\overline{x}}] = 0$. The term $[R(\overline{x}) - \pi\overline{x}^2 r_A]$ is referred to as "differential rent," namely total rent above value $\pi\overline{x}^2 r_A$. Hence the central result here is that differential rent equals the annual cost, mC.

For the special case of the exogenous edge rent, $r_A = 0$, we observe that $[tn(\overline{x}) - \frac{dR(\overline{x})}{d\overline{x}}] = 0$ and thus we have: land rent equals the annual cost of subsidies to the existing m firms in the economy.[6] Each resident's land rent "dividend" pays for her tax obligation, which is supporting the presence of firms (employers) in the urban economy.

Now $\frac{d\Omega}{dm} = 0$ implies

$$ba[4m]^b = \frac{mC}{n(\overline{x})}.$$

This indicates that fraction b of a resident's wage covers the cost of her annual "tax." Hence

$$\begin{aligned}[1-b]a[4m]^b + \frac{R(\overline{x}) - r_A\pi\overline{x}^2}{n(\overline{x})} &= hr(x) + tx + \Omega \\ &= hr_A + t\overline{x} + \Omega.\end{aligned}$$

This establishes that Ω has the same value for all residents, as we require. Each resident consumes the same h and Ω, this latter being "other consumer goods."

From above we have

$$\begin{aligned}m &= \frac{R(\overline{x}) - r_A\pi\overline{x}^2}{C} \\ &= \left[\frac{t\pi}{3Ch}\right]\overline{x}^3.\end{aligned}$$

Now $ba[4m]^b = \frac{mC}{n(\overline{x})} = \frac{R(\overline{x}) - r_A\pi\overline{x}^2}{n(\overline{x})}$ implies that

$$m = \frac{1}{4}\left[\frac{t\overline{x}}{3ab}\right]^{1/b}.$$

For the special case of $b = \frac{1}{2}$ this becomes $m = \frac{1}{4}\left[\frac{2t\overline{x}}{3a}\right]^2$. We substitute for m to get

$$\overline{x} = \frac{Cht}{3\pi a^2}$$

and substituting into the above gives

$$m = \left[\frac{t^2Ch}{9\pi a^3}\right]^2.$$

It follows that when either t, h or C increase, both $\overline{x}$ and m increase. Also an increase in a decreases both $\overline{x}$ and m. These results are in agreement with the idea that a larger city (larger value for $\overline{x}$ and population) "is compatible with" a better fit of a worker's skill to her task or firm (smaller value for $\frac{1}{4m}$). An average worker is more productive in a larger city.

Face to face activity

New York City has been for many decades the benchmark for a modern large city. It has remained the most populous of cities in the United States since the first census in 1792. For a long time it was a supremely productive place because it possessed a very good port[7] and in addition it was the early gateway to the interior of the United States, the head of the route up the Hudson River and over to Lake Erie via the Erie Canal. More recently its dominance is linked to it being a world financial center, and it also has a concentration of advertising agencies and specialized law firms.

Financial, advertising and legal activities are generally characterized as "face-to-face." Thus for financial firms, the output is financial services, the buying and selling of stocks and bonds, for example on behalf of firms producing manufactured goods and services. Firms need funds for investment and for meeting payroll and other regular expenses. Financial firms are turned to when firms, governments and households need to raise funds. The input to a financial firm is chiefly highly trained people meeting each other to do deals and process documents. The meetings may be scheduled gatherings of people in committees in the same firm or of people from different firms, or the meetings may be informal as "over lunch." Business gets carried out in these face-to-face encounters or somewhat differently via telephone calls or emails before and after the face-to-face meetings. Face-to-face activity involves two or more people being present at the same place. There is a clustering of persons at a point.

At its simplest, face-to-face activity involves two individuals doing business that involves some element of trust. Trust is a complicated human quality that allows people to interact in a lopsided transaction on one day in anticipation that a reciprocal transaction will occur on a future day. Given trust on both sides, anticipations are met. For example, I might deliver \$50,000 of my product to your company one day and expect to be paid within 60 days. I deliver and trust you to pay up at a future date. Of course, legal remedies are available at a cost if my trust that you will pay on time is violated by you. But because legal remedies are costly to resort to in both direct resource outlays as well as time, I will prefer to do most of my business with people who I trust to pay me on time. Deals in financial markets often involve large sums of money and short time horizons. I deliver the bonds you requested worth \$200,000 to your office in anticipation of being paid within 48 hours. Financial people substitute trust for the alternative of going to the courts to force payment. Trust is often built up in the process of repeated face-to-face contact. Trust can often be built up faster when two individuals share similar backgrounds, including religious affiliation and ethnicity. Landa (1981) drew attention to this phenomenon and emphasized how trust, when successful, makes redundant the legal costs that would be incurred when a transaction goes awry. A certain class of transactions can then be carried out most efficiently only in a face-to-face setting. Transactions in a face-to-face setting get carried out; recourse to the courts is avoided; and more trust is fostered. Glaeser (1998; pp. 149–150) argues that new technologies such as Skype will not significantly reduce the need for many workers in cities to be in face-to-face settings in the future. In fact in many cultures, such as the Chinese, face-to-face interaction is insisted upon in many situations.

There are other dimensions of face-to-face activity. Imagine dealing with one's architect only over the telephone. It is difficult to envisage a successful "transaction" in such a setting. There are many transactions, such as the development of a design, that can only be carried out efficiently in a face-to-face setting. The development of an advertisement is like the development of a design with an architect. This is client and contractor in a face to face setting. But why do advertising firms cluster in New York city? Here Alfred Marshall's view seems valid: in a cluster of firms with a similar product, "the mysteries of the trade become no mysteries; but are as it were in the air" (Marshall 1920; p. 271). To be a successful advertising firm, the key personnel must be up to date with the current thinking about the product that is "in the air."[8] Modern communication devices mean that a person can follow fashion relevant for doing business in advertising from a distance. We might expect there to be a trend to de-clustering of advertising firms in New York City because of the availability of new means of keeping up with trends. Marshall's labor-sharing argument may be relevant here, however. A person interested in working in advertising should network with those already in the business and pools of like-minded people build up most likely around the most successful advertising firms. Glaeser and Ponzetto (2010) contend that cities such as New York, Boston, San Franciso, Minneapolis and Chicago were able to bounce back from large losses in manufacturing jobs up to 1980 by gaining "idea-intensive industries like finance, professional services, and new technology." These idea-intensive industries needed large numbers of skilled workers interacting in nodes or centers in networks. Scale economies have been central to success.

Devine (2004) set out to project demand for office space in New York City in 2003. She linked future needs for office space to projections of numbers of "office jobs." An office job was assumed to require 225 square feet. Under the SIC (standard industrial classification) definitions she defined office employment to comprise publishing activity, communications, finance, insurance and real estate (FIRE), legal services, business services, membership organizations, engineering, and management services not classified elsewhere. Under the new North American Industry Classification System (NAICS), office employment comprises information activities, financial services and professional and business services. Devine excluded employment in health care, education, and social services because she considered that these activities tend to take place in non-office type settings. She also excluded jobs in government from "office jobs." She argued that any increase in government activity will involve private contractors and thus be captured in the other categories. She found that the different definitions of "office jobs" track each other closely over 1990 to 2000, with the number under the NAICS marginally larger at each date. The number of office jobs peaks at 1.15 million in 1988 and at 1.25 million in 2001. She indicates that in 2003, about one third of jobs in New York City were "office jobs," up from about one quarter in 1975. Of particular interest to Devine was the possibility of a glut of office space, given three large projects planned or under way: the World Trade Center, the Hudson Yards on the West Side of Manhattan and the Downtown Brooklyn development (42.5 million square feet supplied in total by the three projects—equivalent to the total office space in Houston in 2003). Other projects will have added about 12.3 million square feet by 2014. Assuming that office jobs grow at 0.6 percent per year, Devine foresees a possible shortfall of office space in New York City in 2035.

Given Devine's definition of "an office worker" (defined by #51–56 and #81 of NAICS), we can investigate the locations of residences of such workers. Our results are reported in maps of Chicago in 2010 (Figure 4.2) and Houston in 2010 (Figure 4.3). There is a striking contrast between the two maps. So-called office workers in Houston live in highest

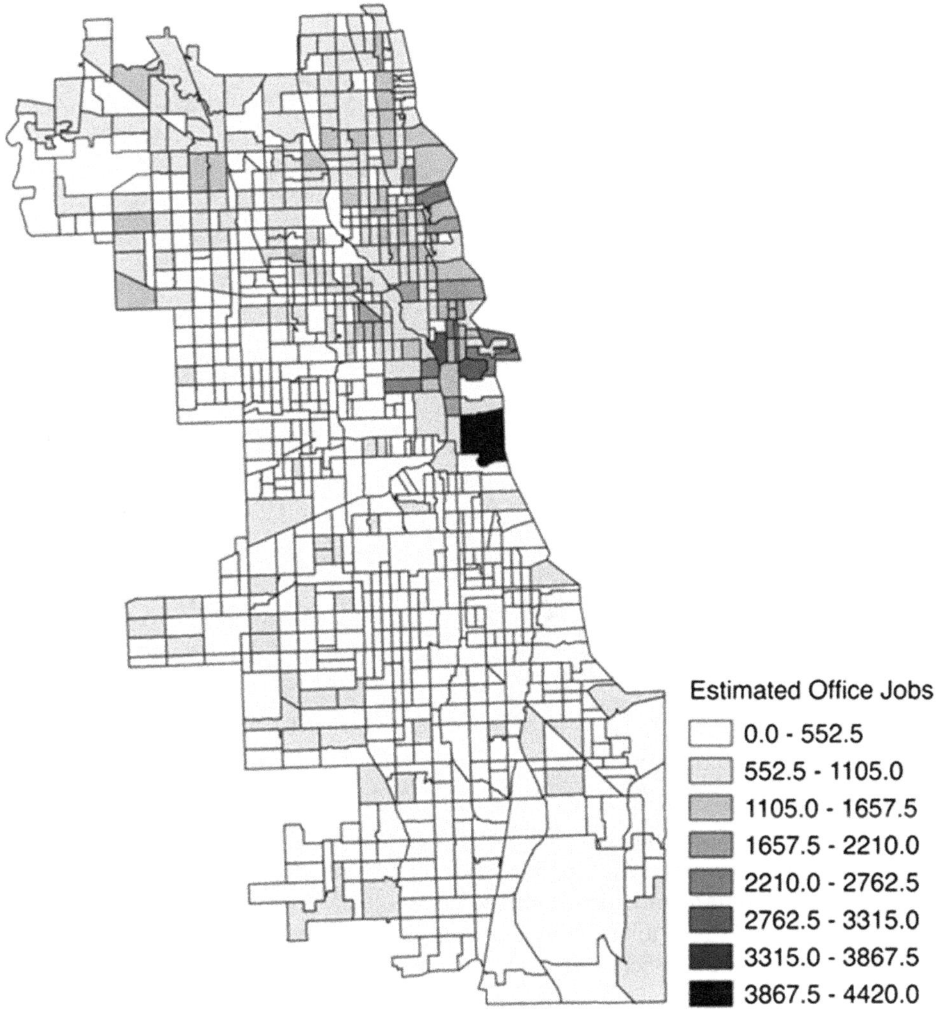

Figure 4.2 Concentration of residents doing "office jobs," Chicago (2010).

Source: Based on Census Tract data.

concentrations in fairly far-out suburbs while those in Chicago live in the center of the city, for the most part, presumably in condominiums and apartments. The inference is that residential living is considerably more decentralized in Houston. We of course expected a trend of this sort but the data suggest a somewhat extreme form of residential decentralization for Houston.

We can conceive then of the output of an abstract New York-like city as financial services and accept the presence of a demand schedule for this output. Let us take this as the only activity for this city and have it all occur in a central place (a CBD). We can conceive of a collection of competitive firms in the CBD, each with a production function in

$$q_i = k_i^{\alpha} l_i^{\beta} \left\{[AN]n_i\right\}^{1-\alpha-\beta}, \quad i = 1, \dots, J,$$

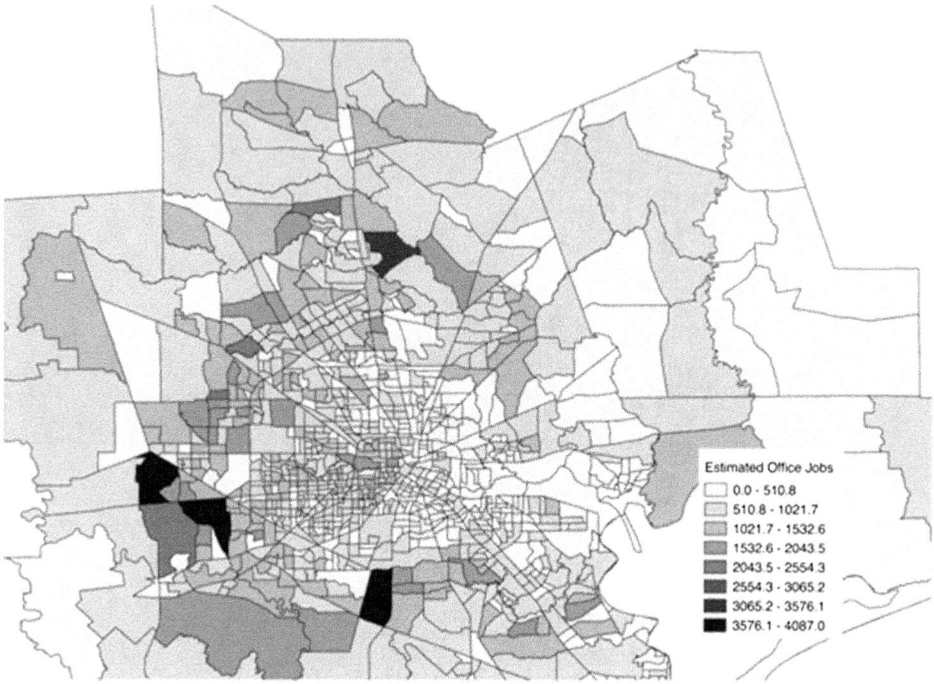

Figure 4.3 Concentration of residents doing “office jobs,” Houston (2010).

Source: Based on Census Tract data.

where k_i is capital, l_i is land, n_i is labor and N is total labor for all $J - 1$ other firms in the center. A is a parameter reflecting the productivity of the N workers. We have appealed to a Cobb–Douglas form only for specificity. We would draw on a quite general production function for a firm. Central to one’s thinking here is that the productiveness of the n_i workers for firm i turns on the number of workers in the CBD. There is then an externality here—more workers in the CBD makes each firm’s workers more productive than they would be with fewer workers in the CBD. This is a key dimension of face-to-face activity and urbanness. We assume that each firm is small and remains ignorant of the details of the externality. Each firm simply hires workers and accepts their productivity. A planner, however, would devise mechanisms, presumably a subsidy of some sort, to induce the entry of firms to a level above that which the free market yields.

This line of thinking, a scale economy that goes unexploited in the absence of the intervention by a planner, is very common in urban economics. Cities are indirectly defined by economic activity taking place in dense arrangements and high density usually goes with high site rent. Firms must get a production advantage from being located in high density because they have the option of moving away from a cluster of firms and avoiding high site rents. Many do not exercise this move-away option. Once we accept that a dense arrangement of firms is a productive configuration, we must sort out the question of an optimal density and this almost always takes us into issues of pro- or anti-productivity externalities. To say that there are scale economies from dense arrangements of firms is really a shorthand way of saying that each firm enjoys a productive externality from being in a cluster of firms. Office space rentals provide some evidence of the value of getting workers into high-density settings each day. Rio de Janeiro recently registered somewhat more expensive rates for prime office rentals than Manhattan (US$120 versus US$115 per square foot). Hong Kong was highest in the world at US$241; London's West End was at US$233 and Tokyo was at US$166.[9] One can reflect about the gap between these rates and those for office space in the suburbs of each of these cities. Firms are willing to pay the high rates in order to have their workers in geographic arrangements that are most conducive to fostering a high productivity per worker.

The simple monocentric city can be interpreted as a situation in which all residents gather each day at a point and engage in face-to-face activity, this latter yielding an export from the city, say financial services. The Lucas–Rossi-Hansberg model, taken up below, adds the assumption that production, say face-to-face activity, is also land-using. This assumption makes the competition for sites between residential activity and production activity a central focus. Beckmann (1976) and others inquired about a "meetings" arrangement for residents of a city that was different from the one in which all residents gather at a point each day. He held to the assumption of obligatory meetings for every pair of worker-residents but allowed for meetings that could occur on a one-to-one basis in distinct or non-central places. He thus ended up with a dispersed city, one without a single location dedicated to meetings or interactions of workers. (See also Bazhanov and Hartwick 2006.) That land-using by firms, those that benefit from proximity to neighboring firms as in Lucas and Rossi-Hansberg, can lead to a dispersed or non-monocentric city is probably a more empirically relevant parable than the line of thought pursued by Beckmann and others. In Lucas and Rossi-Hansberg the separation of residential activity and production activity emerges as one of a multiplicity of land-use equilibria.

The clustering of firms often creates congestion for shippers and commuters. There may be noise pollution as well. Thus clustering can be associated with significant negative externalities. The presence of externalities makes policy design for "the good city" difficult. Policies with respect to transportation infrastructure become especially important.[10]

Positive externalities between neighboring firms

A city is thought to be replete with externalities: congestion on roads, noise spillovers and agglomeration payoffs to certain types of workers and to certain types of firms. The unpriced payoff to a firm from locating near other firms can lead to an area concentrated with firms, a CBD. Hence the naturalness of dense clusters of firms in cities. With one large cluster, we have a monocentric city. The more clustered the firms, however, the more dispersed are the residences of workers, workers who demand some space with their homes. The more dispersed the residences, the higher will be average per capita commuting costs. Hence a tricky trade-off exists between extra efficiency for firms when more clustered and an extra transportation cost burden for workers in those firms in a city. The simple prediction from this line of thought is that when commuting cost per unit distance is sufficiently high, welfare per household could be improved by the creation of sub-clusters of firms in place of one large cluster. Hence the monocentric city emerges as a special case of a larger collection of land-use patterns. Fujita and Ogawa (1982) developed this idea formally, namely the laying out of different efficient land-use arrangements for a city, under different specifications of the parameters governing such things as per unit distance commuting costs (see also Lucas and Rossi-Hansberg 2002).[11] They made many simplifying assumptions (fixed coefficient production technology for firms, fixed land-use per residence for workers, a fixed population, the city constructed on a line, a somewhat mechanical specification of the gain to a firm from agglomerating) and still ended up with a very challenging analysis to work out formally. They simplified the analysis further by solving their model numerically and restricting their attention to three possible symmetric outcomes—a monocentric city, a duocentric city (two clusters of firms) and a tricentric city (three clusters of firms). They provided a systematic treatment of land use for a city that was potentially monocentric but that could under certain conditions end up quite differently.

Lucas and Rossi-Hansberg (2002) revisited the Fujita–Ogawa analysis and relaxed some of the Fujita–Ogawa assumptions: they worked with symmetric cities on a plane rather than on a line and introduced explicit inter-firm distances and the related payoffs to proximity. They too were forced to solve their model numerically rather than in a more general qualitative fashion.

Commuting by a resident eats up some of her potential labor time in the Lucas–Rossi-Hansberg model (exponential in distance) and all residents are assumed to end up with the same utility. This latter is defined in terms of residential space and a composite consumption good. The city produces one good which is exported from the city and the city has a fixed amount of land to be built upon. Land rents accrue to land owners external to the city. Output per unit of land at distance x from the center is $q(x) = z(x)^{\gamma} An(x)^{\alpha}$ where $n(x)$ is labor per unit of land at x and $z(x)^{\gamma}$ is "the productivity function" reflecting the positive effect one firm has on its neighboring firms. The favorable impact of a nearby production activity on a producer is assumed to decay exponentially with distance from a point. Clustering is then good for production activity but clustering takes land away from potential residential activity. A worker must commute to her employing firm and more commuting involves less labor available for work at the firm. Hence strong clustering of producers implies "extra" commuting cost by workers. This is the fundamental trade-off in the Lucas–Rossi-Hansberg model. Clustering or dense arrangements of producers is good for aggregate production but costly to workers, who are obliged to live away from their places of work and incur "extra" commuting costs. Alternatively, spatial arrangements that are light on aggregate commuting activity leave production activity in spread-out or in low-density, low-productivity arrangements. A central conclusion of this very technical modelling effort is that relatively low costs of commuting per unit distance yield land-use arrangements that exhibit much clustering of production (a monocentric city) whereas more costly commuting costs per unit distance yield land-use arrangements of mixed firms and residences; some arrangements have residents living right at their places of work. The exporting of the city's product is assumed to be costless and thus independent of the location of the production activity within the city. There is then no port or airport for firms to cluster around.

Lucas and Rossi-Hansberg draw attention to the role of geometry in affecting the intensity of the production externality. Consider firms spread out in equal density for the moment. A firm at the edge of the city has neighbors on only three "sides" whereas a firm at the center has neighbors on all sides. Hence the firm at the center reaps a productivity advantage simply because of geometry and this force will itself induce clustering at the center. But in addition, Lucas and Rossi-Hansberg have a parameter for varying the strength of distance-decay of the positive neighboring-firm effect. "The more localized is the external effect (stronger distance decay) the higher is the value to a firm from locating near other producers and the more likely are firms to outbid residential users for land near production centers" (Lucas and Rossi-Hansberg 2002; p. 1471). Their claim is that if positive effect of firm j on firm i is weakened by an increase in distance decay then firm i will want to adjust by moving closer to firm j. Their key figure (Figure 12) "illustrates how a higher δ (more decay with distance) concentrates production in one or many business sectors and how mixed areas tend to disappear" (p. 1470).

Whenever externalities are present in economies, we wonder about Pigovian interventions that might mitigate their effects and improve the overall performance of the economy in question. Rossi-Hansberg (2004) reports that in his model the optimal land-use solution exhibits more concentration of production at the center than does the corresponding equilibrium city. This suggests that a firm fails to take account of its positive contribution to the productivity of its neighbors and intervention by a central authority can improve matters by essentially giving it "more neighboring firms."

Cities adjusting: short term and long term

We have emphasized in Chapters 2 and 3 that wage increments and transportation-cost decreases show up systematically in land rent (local cost of living) changes. We were obliged to work with relatively simple representations of "a city" in order to extract fairly uncomplicated expressions for land-rent changes. We inferred, in spite of the simplicity of our models, that the phenomena were empirically relevant. The high wages of larger cities translate into high local land rents. What else influences the local cost of living, given a fairly good employment market? Two things come to mind. The local attractiveness of the place matters, as in how much sunshine is there? And one might also reflect on the quality and cost of the local government and its services. Are local schools good? Are local government revenues well allocated? Are local taxes reasonable? Here we take up first the question of local amenities such as average temperature in January and how the amenities affect local land rents (house prices). In Chapter 9, we delve into local government "production" and revenue raising.

Later in this chapter we consider the stickiness of actual cities in responding to negative shocks. It turns out that the durability of housing prevents a city from down-sizing in an "orderly" fashion and we report on this pathology. We then turn to long-term "shocks" to cities and how a city has been evolving over periods of decades. Of particular interest is how the large decline in the cost of moving goods has impacted individual cities as well as on the system of US cities as a unit.

We start with two identical cities and then perturb one by having its local amenity larger. In a two-city world the better climate (and utility jump) will draw workers from the other city. The drizzly city will become smaller and have its rent function shift down somewhat and the larger city will become larger and have its rent function shift up somewhat. Migration will stop when the utility level of a worker in each city is restored to equality. In the end the city with the extra amenity will be larger, have land rents on average higher (higher local cost of living) and will have a bit of a wage premium due to a positive productivity effect of city size increase. This simple case is one with the amenity premium showing up mostly in local land rents. We say that the extra amenity gets capitalized primarily in local house prices (residential land rents). A wage rise should go along with a rise in the city's size but this we argue will in general be a secondary capitalization effect.

The less attractive city should experience a downward wage shift because it has become somewhat smaller and again we argue that this is a secondary capitalization effect of the differences in local climate amenities. Matters are then complicated for a city such as New York. It has high wages because it is big and thus is reaping the benefits of bigness in extra labor productivity. However, New York City does not have a particularly benign climate and a resident there faces the negative externalities of noise, congestion and perhaps "extra" crime. We have two forces keeping wages high: compensation for disamenities and a premium for the extra productivity of an average worker in a larger city. In a statistical study these two forces would be difficult to disentangle. This thinking leads us to be skeptical of making strong inferences from the early investigations of Sherwin Rosen (1979). He chose to emphasize the disamenities effect "driving up" local wages and neglected to consider the well-documented productivity effect of city bigness. Rosen was writing about disamenity effects in wages in US cities at a time that New York City was coping with economic decline and a local government budget crisis. Hence his concentration on local disamenities and their impact on wages rather than the effect of city bigness on wages. Glaeser (2011; p. 131) suggests that the current good record of the economy of New York City has shown up in some wage write-downs, an indirect "tax" being paid by some residents who see New York as a leading "consumer city." Such residents are willing to accept a wage somewhat lower than one might expect because they value the experience of living in New York so highly. The amenity being consumed in this case is New York City buzz, not fine weather.

New York City illustrates another difficulty in this analysis of high wages in large cities. We have contended that locally-anchored activities (many non-basic activities such as municipal administration) are candidates for wages with a local amenity effect. If we accept that such wages are indeed relatively high in New York City, can we reject the possibility that there is a strong spillover effect from wages kept high because of a productivity effect? Labor markets have freely flowing workers and niche activities with low productivity, such as municipal government, can have workers who benefit from being present in a labor market with on average "high" wages. The wages of municipal workers could, for example, contain a union mark-up component. The least a strong union could do would be to press hard for municipal workers to be paid the going local wage, the one that has been pushed "high" because of a strong big-city productivity premium in local wages. This ratcheting up of municipal wages, a free-riding phenomenon, is a variant of the so-called "levelling up" process that occurs in municipal wage-setting.

Consider a different abstract case. Think of New York City and Los Angeles in the 1940s, before air conditioning became widely adopted. We start then with a large NYC and a small LA. City size will feed back into wages via the size productivity effect. We suppose that worker-households are identical. The high wage in NYC must be associated with "export" firms which are active in the production of goods different from those associated with firms in LA. Each city specializes in distinct export activity. Utility levels for workers in each city are the same at the outset. The arrival of widespread air conditioning is like an amenity jump for LA. There is in-migration from NYC and LA becomes larger and land rents rise (the LA cost of living rises). Population shifts to the southwest until the utility level of a worker is once again the same in the two cities.

A large population shift will cause a significant decline in the wage in NYC and a significant jump in the wage in LA. Overall, LA will experience a relatively large population increase, a large wage increase and a large land-rent increase. The air conditioner (amenity) effect will show up in both land rents and in wages. Does history correspond to this narrative? History indicates that the large population increase in LA was drawn from all over the United States, not just NYC. This means of course that NYC did not experience a significant decline in population and wages. Its economic development ended up being simply somewhat slower than that of LA. And each city continued to expand with largely distinct "export" sectors. NYC's wage would have moved up gradually as its population increased gradually, whereas the wage in LA would have moved up faster. LA's growth was actually propelled by the growth in the movie industry, the oil industry and the aircraft production industry. Not far south of LA is Long Beach, a world-class port for ocean-going ships.

The growth of cities in the South-central United States was aided considerably by the spread of air conditioning after 1945. In the 1920s, department stores and movie theatres

Table 4.2 World cities and their climatic conditions

Annual averages: temperature and precipitation	*Average high °C*	*Average low °C*	*Snow cm*	*Precipitation mm*	*Wet days No.*
Major cities	...	...	...	...	...
Beijing, China	17	7	30	623	66
Cairo, Egypt	27	16	0	22	5
Capetown, South Africa	21	13	0	652	95
London, England	14	7	0	594	107
Los Angeles, USA	21	13	0	373	39
Mexico City	23	11	0	726	133
Montreal	11.1	1.4	217.5	978.9	163
Moscow, Russia	8	1	161	575	181
New Delhi, India	31	20	0	715	47
Paris, France	14	7	0	585	164
Rio de Janeiro, Brazil	30	20	0	1,093	131
Rome, Italy	20	11	0	749	76
Sydney, Australia	22	14	0	1,205	152
Tokyo, Japan	19	12	20	1,563	104
Toronto	12.5	2.5	115.4	792.7	145
Vancouver	13.7	6.5	48.2	1,199	166
Washington, DC	19	9	42	991	112

Source: Environment Canada, 2006; Climate Normals 1971 to 2000 (accessed August 23, 2007); Environment Canada; Canadian Meteorological Centre; Climate Information Branch; Climate Normals 1951 to 1980 (for international data).

introduced central air conditioning but it was after 1945 that there was large-scale adoption by offices and homes. By 1993, 68 percent of American homes were cooled with air conditioning and this rose to 90 percent in 2013. Worker productivity rises considerably when offices and factories are not hot and humid. Nordhaus (2006) mapped worker productivity across the globe and quantified the much higher outputs in temperate zones. Spikes in temperature in summers put strain on electricity systems. Capacity has to be built in to meet the peak demands. In the United States, just 8 percent of the average household's electricity budget goes towards air conditioning, compared with 41 percent for heating and 20 percent for providing hot water. Cooling buildings and vehicles generates some 500 million tons of carbon dioxide each year. Chinese homes are taking up air conditioning rapidly and 70 percent of that nation's electricity is produced in coal-fired plants. It is dehumidifying the air during the process of air conditioning that takes most of the power, and technical progress is moving forward to improve energy efficiency. Compressing key refrigerating gases has been the traditional approach, but innovators are developing processes based on evaporation.[12]

Table 4.2 contains some climate data for some large world cities.

These cities are large because they have experienced growth for one or more reasons. Hence we should not take them as "average" or ordinary cities of the world. One can still ruminate on the role of climate on their history of growth.

Wages and basic activities

We expect that workers in non-basic activities (municipal government workers, retail workers, restaurant workers, etc.) will have wages that are quite sensitive to the magnitudes of local amenities. We start with the proposition that city X needs a certain array of non-basic activities to function or to support the basic (export) activities. Some cite the multiplier 1.1 for the non-basic to basic employee ratio in an average city. However, the plausible claim is also made that a larger city will have a proportionately larger non-basic sector. "Larger cities have more internal trade" is a claim along these lines. Thus, given city X specializes in a certain line of basic activities, the non-basic activities are fairly tightly tied to the local population. Roughly speaking, the non-basic workers support the activities of the basic workers, those in the city's export sectors. An active city must have "support workers." When the export sectors are doing well there is in a sense an inelastic demand for workers in the non-basic sectors. This implies some wage-setting power by these workers in the non-basic sectors, and they can thus demand compensation for local disamenities such as congestion, pollution, crime and an adverse climate.

Wage-setting power is limited. The local wage premium must not climb so high that local suppliers get priced out of the local market by suppliers from other cities (reverse import substitution). And we recognize some substitution possibilities. Very costly workers in the non-basic sectors will be economized on in various ways, at the margin. Nevertheless, the somewhat inelastic demand by workers in the basic sectors for the services of workers in the non-basic sectors gives the latter some wage-setting power. This line of thinking leads us to conclude that larger cities will be subject to more wage adjustment for disamenities than smaller cities, other things being the same. (This is an important claim that of course merits being checked out with good quality data.) Once workers in the non-basic activities obtain compensation in wages for local disamenities, they will have created by indirection an essentially high-wage city. This becomes a burden for firms in the basic activities. They must draw workers to their firms who are acclimatized to a high-wage environment, so to speak. These firms become "high-cost" firms and must contend with competition from firms in similar lines of activity in other cities. The outcome is a lack of competitiveness of firms in cities with a significant array of disamenities. Relatively high wages for workers in the north-eastern United States may have contributed to the general shift in industrial activity away from the north-east since about 1950 and of course the north-east lacks the warm and sunny climate of the south and south-west United States.

Slavery and variants such as debt servitude tend to occur when demanders for workers are facing a relative scarcity of labor. The demanders see that in a free labor market they will be obliged to pay relatively high wages. The remote mining and industrial places in Siberia were unattractive and in a free labor market would have been places of high wages. Planners in Moscow responded with rigid restrictions on the movement of households. Workers were assigned to jobs in remote places in Siberia and were issued with identity cards. Migration was forbidden and wages were kept from rising to a free market level. Mining towns in remote places in Canada and Alaska tend to be places of relatively high wages. Voisey's Bay is a nickel mine on the coast of Labrador, above Newfoundland. The owners have decided not to develop a town for workers and families. The workers live in barracks and get frequent trips out for rest and recreation.

Analytical detail for amenity increase

We turn to the analysis of how natural amenities show up in a simple abstract city. We set out a city in equilibrium and "increase" its natural amenity and see how the city changes. Implicit here, then, are two cities, one with less natural amenity than the other. For two cities otherwise the same, we observe that the one with more amenity will be larger and denser. Its rent schedule will be shifted out relative to the city with less amenity.

Our city has $N(\overline{x})$ worker-households each with income w and utility $U(c, h, A)$ for c other consumption goods, h housing and A natural amenity[13] (e.g. hours of sunshine per year). We set $\overline{x}$ as the radial edge of our city. Each worker commutes radial distance x to the center to earn his wage. His income net of commuting is spent on other consumption, with price unity, and housing with price $r(x)$ at x:

$$w - tx = c(x) + r(x)h(x).$$

The edge of the city, $\overline{x}$ is defined by $r(\overline{x}) = r_A$. Under the open-city assumption, the utility level remains unchanged when our city gets a jolt of extra amenity. Hence, given utility, $U(c, h, A)$ of a household, we have

$$dU = U_c dc + U_h dh + U_A dA = 0.$$

Consumer efficiency implies $\frac{U_h}{U_c} = r$. Hence we have $dc = -rdh - \frac{U_A}{U_c}dA$. We also have

$$dw = tdx + dc + rdh + hdr = 0.$$

We substitute for dc from above to get $tdx - \frac{U_A}{U_c}dA + hdr = 0$. Hence we have

$$\frac{dr}{dA} = \frac{1}{h}\frac{U_A}{U_c} - \frac{t}{h}\frac{dx}{dA}.$$

We turn, then, to how rent in our city is impacted by an increase in A. That is, we have

$$\begin{aligned}\frac{dR}{dA} - 2\pi\overline{x}r_A\frac{d\overline{x}}{dA} &= \int_0^{\overline{x}} \frac{dr(x)}{dA}2\pi x dx \\ &= \int_0^{\overline{x}} \frac{U_A}{U_c}\frac{1}{h}2\pi x dx - t\int_0^{\overline{x}} \frac{dx}{dA}\frac{1}{h}2\pi x dx.\end{aligned}$$

Recall that the population of the city is $\int_0^{\overline{x}} \frac{1}{h}2\pi x dx$. Hence net land rent increase $(dR - 2\pi \overline{x}r_A d\overline{x})$ is

$$\Delta R_n(\overline{x}) = \left[\int_0^{\overline{x}} \frac{U_A}{U_c}\frac{1}{h}2\pi x dx\right]dA - \left[t\int_0^{\overline{x}} \frac{dx}{dA}\frac{1}{h}2\pi x dx\right]dA.$$

The term $\int_0^{\overline{x}} \frac{U_A}{U_c}\frac{1}{h}2\pi x dx$ is a straightforward benefit term from public goods theory, the sum of every resident's indirect "price," $\frac{U_A}{U_c}$, for a unit of the amenity. (In public goods theory, each household's marginal benefit is placed in a sum.) The term $t\int_0^{\overline{x}} \frac{dx}{dA}\frac{1}{h}2\pi x dx$ is now standard to us: it measures in dollars the change in aggregate commuting cost for the city because each resident shifts her location and house-size as a result of the increase in amenity showering down on the city. This latter term we have called an adjustment cost. Net rent increase does capture the marginal benefits over all residents of an increase in A. Hence to a first approximation net rent change is measuring what we expect it to measure. But as we have seen before, there is the adjustment cost term which breaks any simple relationship between the direct benefit measure and the net land rent change. With ordinary utility functions, the effect of the amenity increase will be to make the city larger and denser. Migrants "rush in" to take advantage of the sudden improvement in natural amenities.

Thus very similar residents in City A with a good climate and in City B with a less attractive climate can end up with similar wages and utility levels but quite different housing costs (local costs of living) and densities. Simply put, costless migration leads to each resident ending up on the same indifference curve, regardless of location,[14] but those "consuming" the good climate end up paying indirectly via higher housing costs (site costs). An important secondary effect, however, is that a resident of City A should end up with a wage premium because City A should end up somewhat larger and have a denser arrangement of residences. City largeness and increased density have been established as contributors to a productivity enhancement for a worker. Hence the wage premium. But this wage effect of better natural amenities should be viewed as secondary. Natural amenities are typically captured by higher local land rents.

Silicon Valley, south of San Francisco, represents something of an anomaly. It does have an attractive climate and it does have high housing costs, as well as average wages, but it does not have a high density like New York City. Glaeser and others attribute the low density to NIMBYism (NIMBY stands for "not in my back yard"). Residents of Silicon Valley oppose land-use changes that would lead to increased residential density. Thus someone moving into Silicon Valley must incur a regulatory "tax" as part of the price of their residence. Land use is regulated to prevent density rising to a more normal level. As Glaeser (2011; p. 210) puts it:

> The drive along Route 280 through the heart of Silicon Valley is like a drive through an open Eden. There are about 2 people living on each acre in Santa Clara County... By contrast, Montgomery County in Maryland has about 3 people per acre. Cook County Illinois has almost 9 people per acre. Manhattan has 111 people per acre, and that isn't counting the vast crowd of workers that comes and goes each day.

There are indirect regulations on land-use in California, not simply lot-size restrictions. "In 2008, California's regulations generated 583 environmental impact reviews, considerably more than the 522 impact reviews that occurred nationwide in response to federal guidelines" (Glaeser 2011; p. 212). Glaeser notes that even Manhattan suffers from land-use restrictions that prevent new construction that would occur in a freer market environment. Cheshire and Hilber (2008) suggest that the "regulatory tax" in the price of office buildings in Frankfurt, Paris and Milan is over 300 percent. Houston, Texas with very light land-use regulation has a "regulatory tax" on office buildings and homes of zero. A high regulatory tax on residences means that in-migrants will have to command above-average wages to be able to live in certain places. Paris has incomes some 59 percent above the average for Western Europe[15] Wealthy people who live on dividends from stocks and interest from other investments often choose to live in the central parts of cities such as Paris, London and New York. Demand for luxury accommodation by these folk can explain part of the very high costs for accommodation in general in these world-famous cities. *The Economist* returns intermittently to the theme that some large cities in Europe, India and China are not of an efficient (large) size. The argument is, of course, that some government intervention is preventing the free market from being allowed to function. Certainly in Europe there is in many places a culture of sticky land-use change. Local residents place a high value on how their neighborhoods, towns and cities have looked over decades and centuries. They resist clearing out very old structures and replacing them with modern ones. This taste for "the traditional" interferes with the reorganization of the geography of productive activity, including the distribution of residences relative to other sorts of activity. There can be a persistent tension between "occupants" and those wanting to move into a town at a reasonable cost of "entry." "Occupants" are indirectly imposing a tax on in-migration—and may also be indirectly taxing themselves by not allowing land use to become more efficient. But this indirect price "occupants" pay may be willingly incurred. They are willing to pay to have their local geography remain the way they have grown to like it. There is an element of NIMBYism in this since prospective entrants are discouraged from moving in by the high cost of accommodation.

Glaeser and Gyourko (2005) present a statistical test of the effect of local amenities on local house prices (local average land rents). They are careful to control for (net out the effect of) local wage differences on local house prices. They regress house price by city for 102 US cities (with populations in excess of 150,000) in 1980 on local median family income and local January temperature. This latter is a proxy for the local natural amenity. Their fitted equation is

$$p^H = -155{,}954 + 4.56w + 1{,}441T^J,$$

where p^H is median house price in a location, w is median family income and T^J is January temperature. All variables are statistically significant and the R^2 is 0.6. We would say here that the local wage and amenities are capitalized in local house prices (land rent beneath a standardized "house"). Glaeser and Gyourko comment that "a more thorough analysis would use exogenous sources of labor demand and allow for individual heterogeneity." For example it is known that larger cities have higher-quality labor in the sense that the local worker-resident is more likely to have a college degree in a larger city. So this regression is somewhat preliminary or broad-brush but serves nevertheless to "highlight the empirical power of the Rosen–Roback equilibrium concept."

Sherwin Rosen (1979) started the modern analysis of positive wage correlations with city size with his statistical investigation of how firms in large cities pushed local wages up because they were forced to compensate local workers for large-city disamenities such as crime, congestion, noise and pollution. He drew on the long-standing idea that a worker in a difficult job (e.g. a trash collector) would have to be compensated with a wage premium in order to take on his unpleasant job. Wage compensation is a doctrine that involves essentially distinct tasks for similar workers. Some expositors use the riskiness of the job as a disamenity that has to be compensated for.[16] Consider 40 identical workers available to work on constructing a skyscraper. Assume that a worker on a higher floor has more risk of serious injury. We divide the 120 storey building into say four risk categories (low risk for the first 30 storeys, more risk for storeys 31 to 60, more risk for storeys 61 to 90 and most risk for storeys 91 to 120). The builder is demanding ten workers for each of the four risk locations.

We can assign an index number for riskiness per level in the building and solve a simple problem[17] of allocating the 40 workers to the four levels. If we minimize the total expenditure by the builder for risk and require worker demands to be met by our 40 available in supply, we will obtain four "allocations" of ten workers each, each with a distinct wage: a base wage plus a wage premium based on the particular risk index associated with the place in the skyscraper a worker ends up at. Given a larger risk index for a higher level in the building, we will end up with workers in the top 30 storeys with highest wages. Workers in the bottom 30 storeys will earn the lowest wage and so on for the in-between two groups of 30 storeys. This is how it is, of course. Workers who erect the steel frames of skyscrapers and end up working very high up in the construction of the building get paid relatively high wages. We can complicate matters by having heterogeneous workers, say two sets of 20 workers, with a worker in each set having the same attitude to payment for risk in construction but each worker in a distinct set having a different attitude toward risk. We could proceed as above: minimize the total payment for risk compensation. There will be distinct base wages for the two groups and presumably a clean separation of workers to heights; that is, no mixing for the two types of workers in a particular level (30 storey zone) of the building. We might have four types of workers, ten in each group and end up with distinct types allocated to distinct levels in the building. In such a case, the type that was less sensitive to the riskiness associated with height would end up working in the 91 to 120 storey area and get a wage with a modest risk premium. Workers who could deal with height easily would end up working high up and would not demand a large premium for working high up. So much for distinct "tasks" and wage adjustment for task-type. We have a sketch of the theory of wage compensation for tasks with a disamenity.

With regard to essentially big city disamenities, Rosen performed a statistical analysis, regressing average city wage on local disamenities and found that indeed the high wages of a city, such as New York, could be explained by the compensation argument. Rosen was writing at a time that the government of New York City was experiencing a near bankruptcy and commentators were dwelling on the fact that local firms were leaving the city center for suburban locations. Large cities appeared to have bleak futures at the time and Rosen was capturing, somewhat indirectly, this negative opinion. Today, we contend that much of the big-city wage premium is in fact a reward for a productivity premium and that large-city disamenities count negatively in a particular city's wage premium. High local crime rates, for example, dilute the large-city productivity premium associated with a city, contrary to the classic Rosen argument.

Rosen realized the inadequacy of his approach and persuaded his graduate student, Jennifer Roback (1982), to investigate the positive correlation between city size and average wages more thoroughly. Hence the term, "Rosen–Roback equilibrium concept." With fairly homogeneous workers, we can argue that local house price differences (land rent differences) are caused by local differences in wages and amenities. We have argued this and presented good statistical evidence in support of this view. Matters become complicated, however, when we ask about cases in which local wage differences reflect primarily local geographic anomalies such as a mine, for example. The geographic stickiness of the location of employment means that the hiring firm must compensate workers for any disamenities of the location. Remote mining towns are often places of relatively high average wages. There is some self-selection here. Miners may enjoy hunting and fishing in their leisure time and some may not mind the absence in remote communities of a variety of "city" amenities. Hence heterogeneity of workers enters into the level of compensation needed by a mining firm in order to recruit workers. The problem the firm has is that the average worker dislikes working in a place with a poor climate and few urban amenities. Hence if the firm offers the prevailing wage, only a few workers will show up, presumably those who like living away from larger places and a benign climate. To get more workers to show up, the firm must raise the local wage. The premium can be looked on as compensation for the local "bads." The ultimate size of the premium will depend on the intensity of aversion to local bads by the average worker and on the size of the labor force that the firm needs. The simple statement that a firm compensates workers who choose to work in an unpleasant place is a bit simplistic. The lack of mobility of the employment site (a mine is stuck where the mineral is deposited) provides workers with some wage-setting power. In the absence of geographic stickiness, the firm would of course relocate if the local workers became aggressive with their wage demands.

There are different sorts of stickiness in labor mobility associated with particular places. Consider civil servants in local government in large cities. The local government needs a workforce and the "prevailing wage" in the large city is relatively high. Hence the local civil servants can be expected to demand the "prevailing wage" regardless of the relative productivity of those workers. (This an instance of the so-called levelling up of wages in the local public sector.) We have then a different example of the employer being stuck in one place and the workers being able to bring some wage-setting power to the bargaining table. One might be inclined to generalize and argue that every employer has some sunk capital at his current site and can be gamed by his workers into compensating them with a bit of a wage premium. We would say that geographic stickiness gives the current workforce a margin of wage-setting power and hence every job and its attendant wage reflects some local site capitalization. A firm's capacity for a low cost of relocation is the principal lever the firm has to prevent its workers from having their wage reflect some site-specific capitalization. Hence the more geographically trapped or sunk the current firm is, the more we can expect workers to capture some "rent" in their wages.

Recall how General Motors and Ford began to decentralize automobile assembly away from Detroit in the 1960s. There was an element of shifting to lower-wage places in these scenarios. In addition, the companies wanted to end up shipping completed vehicles shorter average distances to dealers. The decline in Detroit as a center of the automobile industry was surely in part a response by the producers to aggressive wage bargaining by the workers in Detroit. The producers began to focus on relocating activity to lower-cost areas and the city of Detroit experienced a notorious decline. In the end, decentralization of production did not solve the problems of high costs of production for General Motors. The company was forced to reorganize itself under bankruptcy proceedings in 2008 and to draw on federal government funds for a bail-out.

We conclude that the direct role of geography on wages is small, except for certain special cases. It is best to assume that local amenities are capitalized in local land rents (housing costs). The general rule is: when firms and workers can readily relocate at low cost, there will be almost no impact of geography on local wages. Climate amenities will, however, have a positive impact on local home prices.

Sticky adjustment to shocks to a city

Glaeser and Gyourko (2005) raised the question of the speed of adjustment of the labor market in a city to a negative shock to the demand for its exports. They made the case that the durability of housing creates a drag on the population adjustment that a city "needs" in order to reach a new equilibrium. They documented a basic disequilibrium in the housing market in many cities and they argue that this disequilibrium persists over many years, if not decades. Their point of departure is the fact that in 1980 some 42 percent of homes were selling below the cost of replacement for a sample of 123 cities in the United States. When a city is hit with a negative shock, many of the more mobile residents move out and the local housing stock is hit with its own negative demand shock. Houses are of course durable and remain in place even when demand for them declines. An analysis of durability of housing is important for two reasons. First, many arguments about the evolution of cities turn away from economics because the interlocutors contend that the durability of roads, infrastructure and structures means that textbook economics is not suitable for analyzing the problem in hand. Glaeser and Gyourko counter this argument with a systematic economic analysis, at least a very good first pass at one, of housing durability and city evolution. Second, Glaeser and Gyourko paint a picture of an endemic adjustment pathology. The durability of housing creates a sink of low-cost accommodation for poor people to gravitate to and this contributes to the impoverishment of the local municipal government. Local government revenues tend to decline with the decline in the average price of local homes. A hard-up local government then provides low-quality services and this makes the community relatively unattractive to prospective higher-skilled entrants.

Glaeser and Gyourko (2005) develop a disequilibrium Rosen–Roback model based on the durability of housing. A city receives a negative shock to the demand for its exports and this drives the local wage down. This is in line with our earlier analysis. Given utility unchanging "out" in the system of cities, this negative wage shock induces out-migration, a smaller local population and a land rent contraction (lower housing prices). The new elements that Glaeser and Gyourko add to this story are (1) the out-migration leaves a large "margin" of available, durable houses and the excess supply induces downward pressure on local house prices overall and (2) the out-migration is concentrated in workers with above-average skill. The argument is that the available "excess" housing attracts "outside" low-skilled and poor families to settle in the city. Glaeser and Gyourko (G&G) argue that the adjustment of the city to the initial negative shock to the demand for its exports gets worked out over many years, possibly decades, mainly because the durability of housing retards a prompt adjustment in the labor market. They refer to the stickiness of population adjustment for a declining city as "persistence." An outcome of this decline scenario is that cities experiencing negative demand shocks can end up with a pool of residents that are poorly skilled and living on very low incomes. "Skilled people particularly value a robust labor market and high amenities, so they leave even though durable housing keeps the overall size of the population roughly constant" (G&G 2005). Lower home prices leave such cities with a contracted tax base. Less revenue results in a public sector under-funded and deteriorating. This contributes to making the city even less hospitable for skilled, higher-wage households. In the absence of durability of housing, a city with a negative demand shock would simply contract (houses would evaporate and many workers would migrate away fairly quickly) and would not become a magnet for lower-income families in search of low-priced accommodation. Glaeser and Gyourko were careful to check that house prices were not low because the houses in question were significantly dilapidated. They remarked: "Even new housing is relatively inexpensive in Philadelphia and Detroit, and even old housing in San Francisco is quite expensive."

The phenomenon of decline and persistence applies to a sizable number of US cities. "There were 39 US cities with at least 100,000 people in 1950 that lost population during the 1950s. Of these, 33 declined in the 1960s, 37 declined in the 1970s, 22 declined in the 1980s, and 23 declined in the 1990s" (G&G 2005). One must keep in mind that a city in the analysis of Glaeser and Gyourko will generally be a central agglomeration of people, exclusive of distinct municipalities and towns at the edge. For example, various media outlets announced with some fanfare in February 2011 that Chicago had lost 200,000 people in the previous decade. But it was also noted that

> the suburban collar counties continued to grow, some spectacularly. The biggest gainers were Will County, growing by 34.9 percent in the last 10 years to 677,560 residents, Kane County, growing 27.5 percent to 515,269 and McHenry County, growing 18.7 percent to 308,760. Several suburban cities also experienced phenomenal growth, including

> Joliet, growing by 38.8 percent to 147,433 residents in 2010, Aurora by 38.4 percent to 197,899, Bolingbrook, by 30.3 percent to 73,366, Elgin, by 14.5 percent to 108,188, and Naperville by 10.5 percent to 141,853.[18]

Though Chicago as a legal entity may be losing households, the Chicago centered region is expanding. Decentralization of residential activity and jobs is taking place. While Detroit's population was declining dramatically, the counties surrounding Detroit were growing quite rapidly, both in size and in per capita income.

Urban decline is then quite different from urban growth. Glaeser and Gyourko argued that a city experiencing a positive shock for its exports would accommodate the increase in immigration with the construction of new housing. House prices, they contended, would not leap up as supply came on line to accommodate the new entrants to the expanded city. However, their data contained some outliers, cities experiencing rapid growth as well as rapidly rising house prices before 2001 (cities along the coast of California as well as Seattle and Boulder, Colorado). They contended that such places were facing "binding regulatory constraints on new construction." Authorities in some cities oppose zoning changes that might allow for a rise in density in their communities. Hence in-migration is often very costly for new households entering some communities that are growing rapidly.

Long term change for cities in the United States

The durability of housing constrains the smooth contraction of a city, a city hit with a negative demand or productivity shock. What about the hit on a city or system of cities from (a) declining costs of transport for goods over many decades and (b) the rise of commuting by one's own automobile in cities? Glaeser and Kohlhase (2004) paint an interesting picture of how these "shocks" have impacted and continue to impact cities in the United States. They suggest that economists should think about cities operating, to a first approximation, in a world of transportation costs at zero for goods and relatively high for people.

Glaeser and Kohlhase note that the cost of moving a ton a mile has declined by a factor of eight in the United States since 1850. The rail network was installed and then the development of the internal combustion engine brought us automobiles and trucks. Then the road systems within and between cities were much invested in. Much of the decline in shipping costs has come in the period 1960 to 1990. The development of the container for shipping goods is also a significant factor. In addition the interstate highway system dates from the later 1950s. In 1985 legislation to deregulate trucking was passed and cost by this mode declined (in 2001 dollars) from 38 cents to 28 cents per ton-mile. Of course, the market shapes what is transported and how long trips are. Only 18 percent of all shipments occur in industries where transport costs are more than 6 percent of total value. Some 80 percent of all shipments by value occur in industries in which transport costs are less than 4 percent of total value. If transport costs for a good rise by 10 percent, the average distance a shipper is willing to transport declines by 3.2 percent.

The classic link between a port, its rail links and manufacturing activity of the early twentieth century has gradually disappeared. Now much traditional activity is not tied to sites adjacent to port facilities. For example the Sparrows Point steel plant, on Chesapeake Bay near Baltimore, was the largest in the world in the 1950s. Today there remains just a small operation, albeit with up-to-date technology (the modern "L" blast furnace). Overall, however, "Sparrows Point is mostly a landscape of empty buildings and weed-filled lots."[19] Modern steel mills are not the monster operations tied to port facilities that they once were. Steel-making occurs today in compact plants in towns often remote from ocean shipping.

Durability of structures and transportation infrastructure means that changes in urban form evolve slowly. The evolution of a particular city is much constrained by the durability of its infrastructure—its roads, the pattern of its streets, its great buildings, its railroads and port facilities and possibly its subway. Davis and Weinstein (2002) examine the reconstruction of Japanese cities and their economies following severe bombing during World War II. Their theme is that reconstruction was relatively rapid and in some sense restored settlements to their pre-war forms. *The Economist* reported the more recent rapid restoration of the Kobe economy of 1997 following a strong earthquake.[20] Though 100,000 buildings were completely destroyed, in less than 15 months after the quake, manufacturing activity was at 98 percent of its pre-quake level. Port volumes were fully restored within a year, even though the port infrastructure was only half rebuilt.

Trucking and containerization have, over recent decades, induced manufacturing activity in North American cities to locate in middle-sized settlements, places with abundant and low-cost land. And manufacturing activity employs a much smaller fraction of available workers than it did even 40 years ago. Glaeser and Kohlhase (G&K) (2004; p. 128) see an "impressive increase in proportion of the population living in middle densities." Between 1920 and 2000 the share of US population in its densest counties declined from 9 percent to 4 percent. The "rise of sprawl" has brought far fewer apartments into annual new construction compared with single-family homes (G&K 2004; p. 220). They document a long-term trend of households to locate in coastal cities in the United States and, departing from "the hinterland" in the center of the continent. A 10 percent rise in share of workers in natural resource industries (farming, mining, etc.) in specific counties implies a 45 percent decline in the rate of growth between 1920 and 2000 (G&K 2004).

The benign climate amenity shows up clearly in the data on population shifts. Between 1980 and 2000 a 10 percent warmer January was estimated to yield an increase in the local growth rate of 5.4 percent. And between 1920 and 1950 a benign climate was already impacting county growth significantly: a ten degree increase in January temperature for a state increased county-level population growth by 8 percent. With a worker's productivity increasing with local density, one wonders about extreme outcomes. A 10 percent rise in county density implies a $206 increase in median household income. But the efficiency of density is countered by a household's desire for open space about the home. It turns out that people can now live at lower densities and commute to tall office buildings and still exploit advantages of proximity. Cities can now "sprawl without limit" because of the proliferation of sub-centers of employment. The so-called polycentric form of a city is now quite common, often a major center and a number of outlying sub-centers. "The main factors that stop convergence to a single area (a mega-city) are heterogeneity of tastes for weather, government policies and historically developed infrastructure." (G&K 2004; p. 200)

The proliferation of sub-centers in cities has been in part a response to congestion of city roads during the rush hour. There has been a large increase of automobile ownership and use since the 1920s. This increase was abetted by rising incomes for households and declining prices of cars. *The Consumer Expenditure Survey* for 2001 indicated that the average household allocated 18 percent of total expenditures to vehicle purchases, gasoline, maintenance and insurance. In 1960, 64 percent of the US population drove to work, 12 percent used public transportation and 10 percent walked. In 2000, 88 percent drove to work, 5 percent used public transportation and 2.5 percent walked (G&K 2004; p. 220). The growth in commuting by automobile has resulted in increased congestion, to be sure. For all 75 urbanized areas, annual delay from congestion went up 280 percent over the period 1975 to 2005. For the largest cities, it is up 450 percent. Between 1980 and 2000 commute times are up by 13 percent for the combined 75 urbanized areas. All of the top ten cities experienced increases. During one year a resident of Los Angeles experiences on average 47 hours of delay because of congestion.

Partly in response to the increase in congestion, we observe that employment has suburbanized steadily and the activity that remains in central business districts is more specialized. A doubling of county population density implies a 57 percent rise in employment in finance, insurance and real estate. These are the "industries" that we usually consider occur most efficiently with considerable face-to-face activity.

Glaeser and Kohlhase (2004) draw out strong conclusions from their investigation of the decline in the cost of goods transportation and the rise in congestion costs for commuters who choose to use their own vehicle to get to work. They also make interesting inferences based on population shifts and climatic differences. Curiously, they did not tie-in the general rise of service industries in western economies and the decline in traditional manufacturing industries to their analysis of urban change and population redistribution. In a world of low-cost transportation for goods, manufacturing should move to where workers and factory sites are inexpensive. Hence the move to the suburbs of large places and often out to distinct smaller cities. This trend of the twentieth century became noticeable after 1950. If the contemporary western world is dominated by service industries, we might expect people to favor residing in cities over rural places. And if service industries are weakly tied to a narrow range of geographic places, we can expect the cities that would grow as service industries multiplied will be those with benign climates. Hence the growth of populous corridors along the coasts of the United States, including those along the Gulf of Mexico. This leaves only the Chicago conurbation without an ocean location, but it has made do quite well as a port by being beside Lake Michigan, itself a part of the Great Lakes, themselves something of an inland ocean. The St. Lawrence Seaway, jointly developed by the United States and Canada in the 1950s, connects the Great Lakes to the Atlantic Ocean.

When it comes to changes in the structure of a typical city, we observe that port activity is no longer carried out with large crews of workers. People who work in services have less need to cluster near nodes such as ports. They can allocate part of their income to a large lot for their homes. Cities have become less dense in recent decades with employment more decentralized within cities. A smaller fraction of workers in any city in the United States are employed in a traditional CBD. Are CBDs dying? Becoming less dominant is of course quite different from fading away. The huge Boston to Washington conurbation can be viewed as a very large mega-city with many distinct CBDs. Each CBD has its own residential area and employment subcenters. We are moving into the age of the spread-out mega-city with multiple centers.

Harris–Todaro migration-unemployment model

We turn to a classic analysis of the migration of workers from rural to urban areas. Harris and Todaro (1970) were interested in the migration of workers in the third world from essentially subsistence rural employment to city activities. They suggested that such workers migrated in the hope of getting a position with a "high" wage in, say, the government sector but realized that there was a strong possibility that they would end up on the margin of the city, mostly unemployed. Harris and Todaro theorized that there should be an equality between the low rural wage and the high urban wage when the latter was multiplied by the probability of a migrant landing a job with the high urban wage. They argued that this probability would reflect the number of unemployed urban workers looking for a high-wage job. Hence if a worker migrated to the city, she could expect to earn w^H with probability π, where the latter reflected the number of job seekers at the margin of the city. So πw^H should end up equal to w, the implicit wage that a migrant could earn if she remained in the rural area, and π should reflect the number of applicants per year relative to the number of jobs offered per year. The number of applicants would of course be the number of unemployed at the margin of the city, say N^U. Let N^O be the number of new jobs offered per year in the city. Then the equilibrium number of unemployed at the edge of the city would be N^U in

$$w^H \frac{N^U}{N^O} = w.$$

It is pretty reasonable to think of the rural wage w and the urban wage w^H as values known to workers in an approximate way. The number of new jobs offered in the city per year would be harder for a rural worker or an urban unemployed worker to estimate. Thus the number of unemployed at the urban fringe trying to land an urban job could be wide of the precise value N^U that brings the two sides of our equation into equality. There are of course large numbers of mostly unemployed people living in poverty, generally in slum conditions, at the edge of large cities in the under-developed countries of the world. Each able-bodied person is presumably hoping to land a well-paying job in the city. There would also be turnover, with discouraged unemployed workers heading back to the rural area, while new rural workers migrate into the city in the hope of landing a job in the city at the high wage w^H. Some observers consider the interval a migrant spends in a slum as an important learning experience, a way-station on the route to an urban life with a reasonable income. Data suggest that many slum dwellers have in fact become trapped for long spells that in the end do not lead to a reasonable life after the slum interval. We comment more on this in Chapter 10.

In Delhi, India's capital city, some 100,000 ragpickers live by picking though garbage dumps each day in search of re-usable items. A ten-hour day yields under US$2 for an experienced picker. When current laborers are retrained for the formal economy, a horde of migrants emerges from the countryside to replace those who have moved on (according to Suneel Pandey of the Energy and Resources Institute, reported in *The Economist*[21]). Workers in the dumps face health issues as well as shakedowns from local by-law enforcement officers.

China continues to break records for numbers of rural folk migrating to cities in search of well-paying jobs. This has made much sense for the migrants since the number of people who have moved out of abject poverty has also broken historic records. And in fact recently some firms in cities have been obliged to raise wages due to labor market tightness. The average GDP per person in the interior of the country was 1/3 of the value in coastal cities in the late 1990s and rose to 1/2 by 2012. A migrant's life is complicated because each person in China is assigned a permit or *hukou* (local household registration identity) indicating his or her official place of residence. This registration system dates from the 1950s. To access important city services, one must possess an urban *hukou*, which is extremely difficult for a migrant from the countryside to "earn." About 54 percent of China's people are now urban residents but only 36 percent of the population has been assigned an urban *hukou*. An applicant needs a stable job and legal place of residence, this latter somewhat hard to obtain. This leaves millions of marginalized urban folk without legitimate access to urban services.

The term apartheid has been used to describe this situation.The *hukou* entitles the holder to full access to schools and hospitals in the cities at essentially subsidized costs. China's recent plan on urbanisation (*The Economist*, March 16, 2014) foresees 60 percent of the country's population living in cities by 2020, up from the current 54 percent, and this increase would bring China in line with other countries of the world with similar levels of per capita income. China's new urban policy (2014) calls for *hukou* barriers to be cancelled for migrants moving to cities of less than 500,000 people. This is part of a larger plan to have smaller cities expand faster than the largest places, places like Shanghai and Shenzhen that have of course been most attractive to migrants over the past few decades. Some observers argue for Tokyo, at 35 million people, being the current benchmark for a very large and well-functioning city. By this standard, many cities in China, including Beijing, can grow and develop significantly further. The new 2014 plan calls for 100 million migrants in cities to be granted the urban *hukou* by 2020. Many cities will be faced with large groups of residents that are suddenly certified as first-class members of their communities and officials are concerned about the extra spending on education, health care and housing that they will be obliged to deal with. There are some unregistered folk with no *hukou*, urban or rural. These people are referred to as *heihu* ("black *hukou*"). Such people cannot access state-run schools or get subsidized health care. These unfortunate individuals may have been "extra" children born to a family limited to one child, under the "one child" policy, in effect for many years.

In Indonesia about three million migrants move from the countryside to cities such as Jakarta each year. The World Bank estimates that a migrant doubles her productivity by working in the low-end activities, such as hawking food by roadsides or from handcarts, in cities compared with what she was producing back in the country. Unskilled workers in factories have productivities well above those in the low-end service sector. But of course such factory jobs are relatively scarce.[22]

We might amend the model above to incorporate a positive value to an exciting life in the city compared to the country. Let r and *urb* represent the rural and urban environment, respectively. We assume that *urb* is preferred to r. Then poor people are migrating not only in hope of landing a high-paying urban job but they are also attracted by the bright lights of the big city. The wage and environment then become part of a "package," with utility defined over both income and the "environment." The "package," valued in terms of utility, has a migration equilibrium defined by:

$$u(w, r) = \pi u(w^H, urb).$$

Here $u(w, r)$ is the base utility level of living in the rural area and $u(w^H, urb)$ is the anticipated utility level that a migrant will have when she moves to the city and lands an urban job. The probability π is defined as above but could have a quite different value from that in the earlier formulation.

"The Great Migration" in the United States was the movement of six million African Americans out of the rural southern areas to the urban northeast, midwest, and west. Historians differentiate between the first Great Migration (1910–30), numbering about 1.6 million migrants who left mostly rural areas to migrate to northern industrial cities, and a second Great Migration (1940–70), in which five million or more people moved from the South, many to California and other western cities. By the end of the second Great Migration, African Americans had become an urbanized population in the North and West. A majority of 53 percent remained in the South. A reverse flow of African Americans, the New Great Migration, has occurred since 1965. As early as 1975–80, seven southern states were net gainers of African Americans. African-American populations continue to drop throughout much of the Northeast, particularly out of the states of New York and New Jersey.

Table 4.3 contains estimates of upward mobility for a group of cities in the United States.

High-mobility areas in Table 4.3 have (1) less residential segregation, (2) less income inequality, (3) better primary schools, (4) greater social capital, and (5) greater family stability. There seems to be a rough correlation between a city being economically "successful" and good prospects for upward mobility.

Discrimination

It is fair to say that modern, industrial economies have a persistent pool of unemployed workers. On average these workers are less skilled and have records of irregular employment spells. The issue of discrimination in hiring can be posed as: why are certain distinctive groups, such as Hispanics, over-represented in this pool of above-average levels of unemployment? It is well known that hiring people have tastes for hirees. For example, when 20 applicants register for a position, many hirers invite for interviews those with surnames that they find congenial. The hirers discriminate against applicants with uncongenial names, even though all 20 applicants may appear equally qualified for the position in question (Oreopoulos 2009). Even more broadly, psychologists have found that on average a person is more comfortable with members of certain groups than others. Ordinary people have preferences for what types of people are around them. Hence those offering jobs are very unlikely to be neutral in who they hire. This phenomenon would not be a serious social problem if labor markets were tight and there were many openings relative to applicants but labor markets typically have slack built into them. We might say that if hiring people are fairly homogeneous then the rejectees for openings themselves may be fairly homogeneous. If all hiring people were born in Warsaw, then the group of people hired, even though each was taken on in isolation, would likely be fairly homogeneous.

Negative feelings by a hirer can be based on "racial profiling." It may well be that African Americans are less trained on average than a random group of "similar" workers. Thus a hiring person will discount the abilities of a particular African-American candidate for a position, even though the candidate's credentials on paper look adequate. The candidate is being stigmatized by the reputation of her racial group. The "average" work characteristics of her group are spilling over into the judgement of her individual work characteristics. This form of discrimination in hiring is pretty firmly rooted. A measured dimension of

Table 4.3 Odds of a young person reaching top fifth of the income distribution in a city (starting from bottom fifth for 50 biggest metro areas in the United States)

1	San Jose, CA	12.9%	41	Cleveland, OH	5.1%
2	San Francisco, CA	12.2%	42	St. Louis, MO	5.1%
3	Washington, DC	11.0%	43	Raleigh, NC	5.0%
4	Seattle, WA	10.9%	44	Jacksonville, FL	4.9%
5	Salt Lake City, UT	10.8%	45	Columbus, OH	4.9%
6	New York, NY	10.5%	46	Indianapolis, IN	4.9%
7	Boston, MA	10.5%	47	Dayton, OH	4.9%
8	San Diego, CA	10.4%	48	Atlanta, GA	4.5%
9	Newark, NJ	10.2%	49	Milwaukee, WI	4.5%
10	Manchester, NH	10.0%	50	Charlotte, NC	4.4%

Source: Chetty *et al.* (2014).

one's "group," an average of some kind, is being applied to oneself, regardless of one's personal measurable characteristics—and is being applied in a way that harms the individual candidate in question.

This process of the unemployed having many attributes in common is negatively reinforcing over time. When a hirer sees an application from a qualified job seeker and can identify the applicant as a member of the group with many unemployed, the hirer may discount the qualifications of the applicant. A group stigma "infects" almost all members of a group with a history of persistent unemployment. It becomes very difficult for certain persons linked to groups with members with poor work histories to break free of the stigma. We can summarize by saying that the presence of a persistent pool of unemployed workers, combined with hiring people that have a bias for congenial hirees can lead to homogenization of the pool of unemployed. This process requires that hiring people identify uncongenial prospective hirees by some simple trait and skin color often emerges as the default marker. There is a history in the United States of rates of unemployment being persistently higher for African Americans and Puerto Ricans, people with skin of black and brown pigmentation. See Table 4.4.

The discrimination problem can become exacerbated when members of groups that are discriminated against in the labor market become discouraged and in consequence, fail to invest in themselves.

> Beyond the unemployment rate, there are other indicators of growing economic distress for black and Latino households. It seems men are dropping out of the labor force faster than women, and more black and Latino men are without work than others. The twin phenomenon have pushed the male workforce participation rate to a new low unseen since the federal government began reporting this data in 1948.[23]

The push on one side comes from hiring people discriminating in hiring and the push on the other side comes from discouragement and negative reactions of people discriminated against: "Why should I work hard in school and practice pleasing social habits when these efforts will not pay off anyway?" To counter the discrimination syndrome, individuals in the negatively affected group must be superior in some way in a competition for an opening or must be favored formally, as in "affirmative action" programs. New problems can arise when

Table 4.4 Unemployment rates[a] by race, Hispanic or Latino ethnicity,[b] age

	Men		*Women*	
	2012	*2013*	*2012*	*2013*
Total, 16 years and over	8.2	7.6	7.9	7.1
Black or African-American, 16 years and over	15.0	14.2	12.8	12.1
Asian, 16 years and over	5.8	5.6	6.1	4.8
Hispanic or Latino ethnicity, 16 years and over	9.9	8.8	10.9	9.5

Note

a Annual averages; percentage figures.

b Estimates for the above race groups (white, black or African-American, and Asian) do not sum to totals because data are not presented for all races. Persons whose ethnicity is identified as Hispanic or Latino may be of any race. Updated population controls are introduced annually with the release of January data.

Source: Current Population Survey (US Bureau of Labor Statistics 2014; household data).

the person hired ends up in a position she is not suited for. She can be unhappy and the hirer can be unhappy with the outcome. More generally, there is the need to remove the "racial profiling" dimension associated with discrimination by getting large numbers of African Americans to occupy a variety of jobs and to perform well in those positions. As long as the average dark-skinned candidate with the same paper credentials as her light-skinned counterpart performs less well on the job, all dark-skinned applicants suffer, to varying degrees, from a "racial profiling" syndrome.

Not all members of visible minorities are treated unfairly. Asian-Americans are over-represented among university students and many have distinguished academic records. Unemployment rates for Asians are below average in the United States (see Table 4.4).

Summary

We have dealt with forces of agglomeration in this chapter. Agglomeration is generally linked to "scale economies" and we have attempted to be systematic in discussing what scale economies are. Marshall's three forces leading to clustering continue to frame much of the discussion: information interdependencies, similarities of workers in certain activities, and economizing on the transportation of goods. We have taken up these forces from a variety of perspectives. The contribution of Lucas and Rossi-Hansberg provides something of a climax: a formal model of land use involving firms needing workers, workers demanding residential space, and firms benefitting from proximity to each other as well as to their workers. The monocentric city becomes one of a variety of equilibrium land-use arrangements. One dimension of firms benefitting from proximity to each other is in allowing for lower-cost face-to-face activity by workers in different firms. We looked into this so-called face-to-face activity.

Amenities affect population distributions and the migrations that have been triggered by climate premiums in different places. The bottom line is that wage differences between places will be persistent when there are amenity differences between them and the wage differences will in general not be simple indicators of the amenity differences. Amenity differences end up, in dollar terms, mostly in the rent associated with a home. One pays for "consuming" a nice climate by having to pay a premium for one's home. In brief, other things being the same, sunnier places should be places of higher-density living and higher land rents associated with homes. We ended with a model in which utility differences between rural places and city places drove migration, but central to the migration equilibrium condition was uncertainty about actually landing a good job in the city. We observed the decline for a city is a quite different process than growth. The durability of structures tends to make a city in decline relatively more attractive to low-income households and tends to leave the local government in a perpetual revenue crisis. City services are often curtailed. It becomes difficult for a city losing its traditional employment centers in a large scale to attract new activities with highly skilled workers.

Main points of Chapter 4

1 A firm joins others when the local labor force is dominated by the right sort of workers. A firm often locates near good markets for its product or some key input to its production. Some firms prefer to locate where there are ideas "in the air" that are useful for its product development. (Alfred Marshall's three reasons for firms to agglomerate.)

2 A worker of average skills and training will prefer to be in a large city. When her employer is in a downturn, there will likely be other firms in a large city that are hiring. Larger cities can offer a worker insurance against prolonged spells of unemployment (the law of large numbers).
3 A worker with very deep and narrow skills will seldom find demanders for her services in a small place. A larger city is the place to head for (the Helsley–Strange analysis).
4 Highly skilled workers are often most productive when they "network" intensively. They benefit from "face-to-face activity." Such ways of working can economize on "transportation costs" when carried out in the denser parts of a city, such as the central business district.
5 Significant amenities that a city possesses will make some cities more attractive and larger than others. This tends to mean that attractive cities have a higher cost of living and they are often higher-wage places. A local amenity can be capitalized in an attractive city's expensive housing (site cost).
6 Workers can be expected to relocate over a lifetime and they tend to migrate to the most dynamic cities. The Harris–Todaro model is a good way to think about migration to cities by hopeful rural workers.

Questions and problems

1 List Alfred Marshall's three "mechanisms" that "cause" agglomeration.

  a Name a firm or industry that appears to be agglomerating in accord with Marshall's "process."
  b Can we identify the agglomerating mechanism in each of the following?

    i Clustering of computer firms and computer-components firms in Silicon Valley, south of San Francisco.
    ii Clustering of financial firms on "Wall Street" in New York City.
    iii Clustering of oil refineries along the coast of Louisiana.
    iv Clustering of condominium towers in the center of Vancouver, British Columbia.
    v The de-clustering of automobile production activity from Detroit.
    vi Clustering of Russian immigrants in certain areas of New York City.
    vii Why Tokyo is so large (about 35 million people).

2 Are Marshall's three "mechanisms" exhaustive or has he missed out on other "mechanisms"? Think of two additional "mechanisms" that "cause" agglomeration.
3 The geography of no nation is an unlimited featureless plain. How do irregularities in a nation's geography connect to agglomerated economic activity? Have some nations become especially prosperous because their geography endowment was better than the endowment for other nations?
4 Name three large cities of the world that grew up around nearby extraction or mining activity.
5 For metropolitan areas in the United States in 1977, the cities with 10 percent more small businesses (more firms per worker) than others, ended up by 2000 with 9 percent more employment growth. (Glaeser 2011; p. 58). Hence a great variety of small firms

in a city is a good indicator of future employment growth. Does this explain the lack of growth for Cleveland and/or Detroit?

6 "It is safer to settle in a large city because there will always be a demand for my skill and talent." Analyze this line of thinking carefully.

7 Agglomeration can be interpreted as the pull on households or firms to be close to "neighbors"—to essentially economize on distance gaps or on connecting distances. Explain.

8 Internal migration of households is hard to analyze because every household has its own reasons for relocating. Evaluate this contention.

9 "The shantytowns of Rio de Janeiro may look terrible, but poverty rates in Rio are far lower than in Brazil's rural northeast" (Glaeser 2011; p. 10). Is there an equilibrium flow of migrants into cities from the countryside in nations like Brazil?

10 Urban governments "must do what too many American cities have failed to do: break the isolation that can rob poor children of the advantages that most people get from living in a big city" (Glaeser 2011; p. 94). What is "the isolation"? What are the "advantages that most people get"?

Notes

1 Hartwick (2010) formalizes this line of thought: division of labor deepens (specialization increases) as community size increases.

2 In their earlier study of agglomeration of similar activities, Ellison and Glaeser (1999) found that "about 20 percent of observed concentration can be explained by a small set of (natural) advantages" (p. 315). The index of natural advantage was broadly defined.

3 This quotation is unchanged in the subsequent editions of the textbook, the fifth appearing in 1993 co-authored with Bruce Hamilton. See page 20 in that edition.

4 Krugman (1991a; p. 39) takes this approach to wage-setting in a model of labor pooling. "Imagine a wage bargaining process that sets the wage at an expected market-clearing level before the shocks to labor demand are revealed—not too unrealistic an assumption." His model is a "first cousin" to ours.

5 Since a firm owns arc 1/m and half its workers are in equal density on, say, the right half of its arc. The average distance such a worker is required to "commute" is $\frac{1}{2}[\frac{1}{2m}]$.

6 This is a version of the Henry George result: with an optimal population, land rent equals the cost of the public good. We take this up in detail in Chapter 9. Here as we vary $\overline{x}$ we are selecting a certain population level.

7 Obviously many of the large cities of the world are located at the edge of a navigable waterway, including London. Getting started as a port represented a natural economic advantage. Fujita and Mori (1996) take up this topic including the question of how a formerly great port can transform itself into a large modern city.

8 Arzaghi and Henderson (2008) investigated the productivity advantage of the spatial concentration of advertising firms in Manhattan. They found that the productivity premium declines rapidly with distance from the dense cluster of firms. They also found that the productivity premium shows up in site rents rather than in wage premia.

9 *Financial Times*, February 19, 2011, p. 3.

10 There remains a notable tendency of industries that use the same type of workers to locate in the same area and this provides some evidence on the "continuing importance of transport costs for people" compared with such costs for the shipment of goods (Glaeser and Kohlhase 2004).

11 Following work of Mills, and Hartwick (1976) considered a simple circular land-use problem with one final export good and one intermediate input good. For relatively high transportation costs for the intermediate good, the outcome was the location of the intermediate good activity "on top of" the final good activity and for relatively low transportation costs for the intermediate good, there

were two distinct areas, a circle in the center with the final good and an outer annulus with the intermediate good. Hartwick related these possibilities to some broad-brush history of city development over long periods.

12 *The Economist*, January 5, 2013, p. 46.

13 The Blomquist *et al.* (1988) analysis of capitalization of amenities in local land rents assumes that firms as well as households respond to local amenities. We favor the view that a firm is relatively footloose with regard to amenities, extractive firms and holiday resort firms being exceptions. We envisage persons or households adjusting their locations at the margin in response to amenities, rather than firms. This view leads to the conclusion that most of positive local amenities will show up in local house prices (land rents) and in marginal adjustments in the density of settlement in response to the higher local land rents. The central question is whether local wages can be affected by local amenities and our thinking is yes, but only indirectly via, say, a city size effect.

14 Head and Lloyd-Ellis (2012) report that finding a buyer for one's home in the United States can interfere with labor mobility and thus contribute to local unemployment, particularly in adverse conditions of the business cycle.

15 *The Economist*, October 13, 2012, p. 90.

16 A standard textbook exposition starts with a worker having utility defined over her wage and the disamenity, such as riskiness of the job; that is $U(w^i, B)$ for B the level of "bad." An analysis follows. The problem with this is that one's wage is part of one's income, which is generally defined in dollars. The researcher has a hard time working with income defined in utility terms. Our illustration gets around this difficulty, for the most part.

17 A "transportation problem" from linear programming. See Chapter 5 for details.

18 William Mullen, *Chicago Tribune*, February 15, 2011.

19 Mark Reutter, *Baltimore Sun*, 2006.

20 *The Economist*, March 19, 2011, p. 86.

21 *The Economist*, April 5, 2014, p. 34.

22 *The Economist*, May 3, 2014, p. 66.

23 US Bureau of Labor Statistics, Division of Labor Force Statistics, "Unemployment rate by major worker group," BLS Posting, March 14, 2013.

5 Basics of location economics

Competition for larger market areas. Basic analysis of firm location. Zero profit spatial arbitrage prevails. Land use by linear programming.

Introduction

We move away from an emphasis on cities and urban structure at this point and present some classic analyses of the economics of location. Three analyses come to mind straightaway: those of Losch on small service towns and their market areas, of Hotelling on duopolists competing for market areas on a line (two ice-cream vendors on a beach), and Weber on the location of a firm, given its suppliers and demanders at distinct points. We proceed to report on these analyses in some detail. In addition, we consider spatial arbitrage, the phenomenon of prices between demand points and supply points differing by transportation costs, when goods are flowing between the points. This topic is developed with the aid of "the transportation problem" in linear programming. And the topic of linear programming leads us to a consideration of models of land use in cities as linear programs.

The Loschian service town

August Losch (1906–45) was the first economist to formalize the trade-off between scale economies in production, the force tending to concentrate workers at one point, and distribution (transportation) costs, the force working against the tendency for all production to be a one point. His great monograph is *The Economics of Location* (1940). He asked us to imagine a homogeneous plain dotted in uniform density with farms. He mentioned Iowa in his formal work. These farmers demanded beer which Losch took to be produced with scale economies (declining average costs with quantity produced). But beer had transportation costs associated with it; the farther a farmer was from the beer place, the fewer trips he made for purchasing and the less on average he consumed relative to a farmer living closer to the beer place. The costliness of distribution meant that the whole market would be best served by having many beer producers, each sacrificing some potential scale economies in order to be closer on average to their customers. A "market area" defined the total demand that each beer producer ended up serving. If trips for beer distribution were radial (there was assumed to be no rectangular road system), Losch reasoned that market areas would probably be space-filling, leaving no farmer unserved by his "nearby" beer place. But in addition Losch conjectured that hexagonal market areas would probably be most efficient. He defined efficiency here as providing the highest density of beer producers on a huge plain compared with any other form of market area per seller. A maximum density of sellers, he argued, was analogous to a most competitive arrangement of sellers. Hence the Losch Theorem: hexagonal market areas will emerge and they provide a most efficient outcome. Losch provided a proof for his ideas.

We have each farmer purchasing beer in quantities that decline with distance from the seller. We take a farmer's demand as linear. Hence

$$q(x) = a - b(p + tx),$$

where p is "mill price" (price per unit at the supplier), t is transportation cost per unit per unit distance, x is distance from the supplier, and a and b are positive parameters of the demand function. Suppose for the moment that the market area we are interested in were circular. Then its area, given edge $\overline{x}$, could be expressed as

$$A^C(\overline{x}) = \int_0^{2\pi} \int_0^{\overline{x}} x dx d\theta = \int_0^{2\pi} \frac{\overline{x}^2}{2} d\theta = \pi \overline{x}^2,$$

and this area would define total demand in

$$D^C(\overline{x}) = \xi \int_0^{2\pi} \int_0^{\overline{x}} [a - b(p + tx)] x dx d\theta = \xi 2\pi \int_0^{\overline{x}} [a - b(p + tx)] x dx,$$

where ξ is the density of farmers on the plain. Integration here is pretty straightforward. So working with a market area that is a circle is not too difficult. Working with a market area that is a hexagon involves similar steps. However, our basic object is a 90:60:30 degree triangle, and we simply multiply by 12 to get results for a complete hexagon.

The area of a 90:60:30 degree (right-angle) triangle can be expressed as

$$A^T(\overline{x}) = \int_0^{\pi/6} \int_0^{\overline{x}/\cos\theta,} x dx d\theta$$

where the angle between "long-side," $\overline{x}$ and the hypotenuse is 30°. Think of $\overline{x}$ as the base of this triangle and the hypotenuse has been rotated up through 30°. Now the total demand for this triangle is

$$D^T(\overline{x}) = \xi \int_0^{\pi/6} \int_0^{\overline{x}/\cos\theta} [a - b(p + tx)] x dx d\theta$$

and the total demand for the corresponding hexagonal market area is simply $12 \times D^T(\overline{x}) = D^H(\overline{x})$. When we integrate the expression for $D^T(\overline{x})$, we get

$$D^T(\overline{x}) = \xi \overline{x}^2 \left[\frac{a}{2\sqrt{3}} - \frac{bp}{2\sqrt{3}} - 0.2027bt\overline{x} \right].$$

Each beer supplier was assumed to have a total cost function in $C = A + BQ$ for output level Q, where A is the fixed cost and B the marginal cost of production. This of course implies an average cost of $\frac{C}{Q} = \frac{A}{Q} + B$.

Losch was much inspired by monopolistic competition theory. Each seller could be viewed as having some control over his mill price within his market area. An equilibrium market area

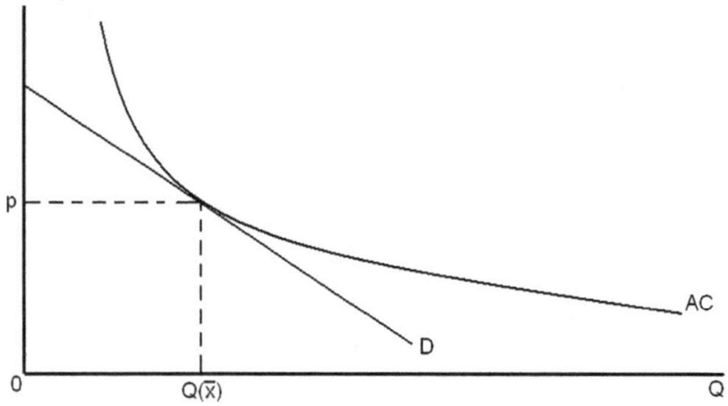

Figure 5.1 Zero profit and tangency define equilibrium (mill) price for Losch's beer seller and market size $\overline{x}$.

for a supplier was defined by a p and $\overline{x}$ such that the supplier was earning zero profits and the market demand schedule was tangent to the average cost schedule. See Figure 5.1.

To solve Losch's model we set $p = \frac{A}{Q} + B$ for zero profit and the slope of the demand schedule, namely $\frac{-2\sqrt{3}}{b}$ equal to $\frac{-A}{Q^2}$, the slope of the average cost curve, where $Q = 12\xi\overline{x}^2[\frac{a}{2\sqrt{3}} - \frac{bp}{2\sqrt{3}} - 0.2027bt\overline{x}]$ for a hexagonal market area. These are two equations in p and $\overline{x}$. If one solves for such equilibrium pairs (p and $\overline{x}$) for various market areas such as squares, equilateral triangles and even circles, one finds that the maximum density of beer sellers on a huge, finite, homogeneous agricultural plain is achieved when each seller has a hexagon for his market area.

Losch achieved two important things: he related scale economies in production to the countervailing "force" of distribution or transportation costs (using the theory of monopolistic competition) and he established that within the confines of his model, hexagons were the efficient shape for a seller's market area.[1] It seems he was also the first economist to put market area analysis on a solid analytical foundation. Krugman's work on trade and monopolistic competition (see Chapter 6) is in a linear descent from the pioneering work of Losch in the 1930s. Note that Losch's equilibrium is, like textbook cases of monopolistic competition, a competitive outcome that is not welfare-maximizing. One has to turn to some notion of maximizing social surplus to come up with Loschian outcomes that are welfare-maximizing. One might be inclined to say that we have arrived at a market failure for a central spatial model. However, the market failure derives from monopolistic competition as a phenomenon rather than from the force of geography or space.

Hotelling's excessive clustering argument

The Smithies (1941) version of the famous Hotelling (1929) spatial duopoly model has purchases by demanders decline with distance from a seller, as in Losch's model above. Thus if a seller is located on the line at x^1 then a customer at x' with $x' > x^1$ will buy amount $q(x') = a - b(p^1 + t(x' - x^1))$, an amount declining with distance from the seller. Here t is delivery or transportation cost per unit distance. The Hotelling spatial duopoly model can be envisaged as having two ice-cream sellers with mobile units on a beach with length Z. Each seller selects a "mill" price p^i and a location x^i to maximize her profit under the assumption that the other seller's price and location are fixed forever. We will assume all customers in density unity on the beach. Then for seller 1, closest to our coordinate 0, current profit over c the unit cost of providing the good (let c be positive and very small to avoid complications) is

$$\pi(x^1, p^1) = \int_0^{x^1} \{a - b[p^1 + t(x^1 - x)]\}[p^1 - c]dx$$
$$+ \int_{x^1}^{x^s} \{a - b[p^1 + t(x^s - x)]\}[p^1 - c]dx.$$

For seller 2, profit is

$$\pi(x^2, p^2) = \int_{x^s}^{x^2} \{a - b[p^2 + t(x^2 - x)]\}[p^2 - c]dx$$
$$+ \int_{x^2}^{Z} \{a - b[p^1 + t(x - x^s)]\}[p^2 - c]dx,$$

for x^s the point of market split, where each seller's delivered price is the same. Here x^s is defined by $p^1 + t[x^s - x^1] = p^2 + t[x^2 - x^s]$. This gives us

$$x^s = \frac{[p^2 - p^1]}{2t} + \frac{x^1 + x^2}{2}.$$

A purchaser at x^s is indifferent as to which seller she purchases from. Each seller maximizes her profit, assuming the price and location of her rival are fixed forever (an instance of Cournot competition). That is,

$$\frac{\partial \pi(x^1, p^1)}{\partial x^1} = \frac{\partial \pi(x^1, p^1)}{\partial p^1} = 0,$$

and

$$\frac{\partial \pi(x^2, p^2)}{\partial x^2} = \frac{\partial \pi(x^2, p^2)}{\partial p^2} = 0$$

gives us four equations to solve for x^1, x^2, p^1 and p^2. The first two of these equations, $\frac{\partial \pi(x^1,p^1)}{\partial x^1} = 0$ and $\frac{\partial \pi(x^2,p^2)}{\partial x^2} = 0$ give us, respectively,

$$\int_0^{x^1} -btdx + \int_{x^1}^{x^s} btdx + [A - b\{p^1 + t(x^s - x^1)\}]\frac{dx^s}{dx^1} = 0,$$

and

$$\int_{x^s}^{x^2} -btdx + \int_{x^2}^{Z} btdx - [A - b\{p^2 + t(x^2 - x^s)\}]\frac{dx^s}{dx^2} = 0.$$

Our x^s relation above gives us $\frac{dx^s}{dx^1} = \frac{dx^s}{dx^2} = \frac{1}{2}$.

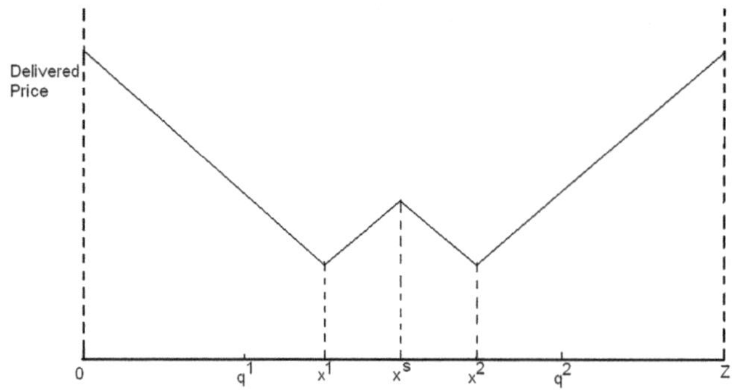

Figure 5.2 Competitive duopoly locations x^1 and x^2 are too close to the center of the linear market, relative to quartile locations at q^1 and q^2.

Let us introduce symmetry values $x^1 = Z - x^2$ and $x^s - x^1 = x^2 - x^s$ and $x^s = Z/2$. For reasonable values of A, b and t (we want parameter values such that at every location a buyer is buying a positive quantity of the commodity being sold by the two competitors), and $p^1 = p^2$, we will have $[A - b\{p^1 + t(x^s - x^1)\}]\frac{dx^s}{dx^1} = [A - b\{p^2 + t(x^2 - x^s)\}]\frac{dx^s}{dx^2} = \xi$ and $\xi > 0$. Thus our two first-order conditions can be written

$$\int_0^{x^1} btdx - \int_{x^1}^{x^s} btdx = \xi$$

and

$$\int_{x^2}^{Z} btdx - \int_{x^s}^{x^2} btdx = \xi.$$

Given some x^1 and x^2, with $x^1 = Z - x^2$ and $x^s - x^1 = x^2 - x^s$, the first-order conditions will be satisfied and the clustering result follows, namely

$$x^1 > x^s - x^1$$

and

$$Z - x^2 > x^2 - x^s.$$

More work would of course give us the result that $p^1 = p^2$ under a symmetric solution and give us the fact that the symmetric solution is the profit maximizing case, for each firm "playing" Cournot.

The central Hotelling result is that Cournot competition between the sellers results in a symmetric equilibrium with the two sellers excessively clustered close to the center. See Figure 5.2.

If the sellers were located at the quartile points q^1 and q^2 for our linear market, then total delivery costs for the market would be at a minimum, an "ideal" outcome for the customers. Instead free market competition yields excessive clustering, leaving extra delivery costs to be borne by customers.

Table 5.1 Transportation problem in matrix form

min	$t_{11}x_{11}$	$+t_{12}x_{12}$	$+t_{13}x_{13}$	$+t_{21}x_{21}$	$+t_{22}x_{22}$	$+t_{23}x_{23}$	
	x_{11}	0	0	$+x_{21}$	0	0	$\geqq D_1$
	0	x_{12}	0	0	$+x_{22}$	0	$\geqq D_2$
	0	0	x_{13}	0	0	$+x_{23}$	$\geqq D_3$
	x_{11}	$+x_{12}$	$+x_{13}$	0	0	0	$\leqq S_1$
	0	0	0	x_{21}	$+x_{22}$	$+x_{23}$	$\leqq S_2$

Zero profit spatial price arbitrage

Consider two sites each with a flow of refined oil, S_1 and S_2, that is to be allocated to three demand sites (say three cities) demanding flows D_1, D_2 and D_3. Let t_{ij} be the transportation cost per unit flow from supply point i to demand point j ($i = 1, 2$ and $j = 1, 2, 3$). We are interested in the allocation problem: find flows x_{ij} that satisfy demanders and minimize transportation costs per unit time. Clearly for this problem to be of interest, the sum at the supply points must at least equal the sum of demands at the three demand points. This problem, known as "the transportation problem" in linear programming, is an example of a generic problem with many suppliers and many demanders. It is useful to represent the problem in matrix form (Table 5.1).

The first line is the "objective function," namely minimized total transportation costs. The second line indicates that demands at demand place 1 must receive sufficient flow from the two suppliers. Similarly for lines three and four. The fifth line indicates that flows from supply point 1 must not exceed the amount available. And the sixth line indicates that the flows from supply point 2 must not exceed the amount available. The optimizer must of course come up with the correct $x_{ij}s$ (cost minimizing flows).

For example, suppose we have $S_1 = 4$ and $S_2 = 7$. The demands are $D_1 = 2$, $D_3 = 3$, and $D_3 = 5$. The transportation costs are $t_{11} = 1, t_{12} = 2, t_{13} = 3$, and $t_{21} = 2, t_{22} = 4, t_{23} = 6$. My students never fail to solve for the $x_{ij}s$ after a two-minute inspection. (Hint: The sum of transportation costs turns out to be US\$34. Transportation problems with integer quantities for demands and supplies always solve in integers. See Appendix 5.1 for the solution.)

Clearly the solution values must be non-negative. There are many software packages that will produce the solution values for such problems on a computer. What is of interest, however, is that our problem has a companion problem (the so-called dual problem), also a linear program, which is about solving for prices, p_j^D for each demand place as well as p_i^S for each supply place. The prices also must be non-negative and they turn out to satisfy the generic conditions

$$\left[p_j^D - p_i^S - t_{ij}\right] x_{ij} = 0,$$
$$\left[p_j^D - p_i^S - t_{ij}\right] \leqq 0,$$

which we call zero profit spatial arbitrage conditions. These equations indicate that if the solution to the original problem has $x_{ij} > 0$, then a shipper or transporter must be earning zero profits. That is, $x_{ij} > 0$ implies $p_j^D - p_i^S - t_{ij} = 0$. And if the shipper or transporter is earning negative profits, she is simply not doing any shipping on the link that is failing to

Table 5.2 Dual (pricing) problem in matrix form

max	$p_1^D D_1$	$+p_2^D D_2$	$+p_3^D D_3$	$-p_1^S S_1$	$-p_2^S S_2$	
	p_1^D	0	0	$-p_1^S$	0	$\leqq t_{11}$
	0	p_2^D	0	$-p_1^S$	0	$\leqq t_{12}$
	0	0	p_3^D	$-p_1^S$	0	$\leqq t_{13}$
	p_1^D	0	0	0	$-p_2^S$	$\leqq t_{21}$
	0	p_2^D	0	0	$-p_2^S$	$\leqq t_{22}$
	0	0	p_3^D	0	$-p_2^S$	$\leqq t_{23}$

satisfy the zero profit condition. That is, $p_j^D - p_i^S - t_{ij} < 0$ implies that $x_{ij} = 0$. In the jargon of linear programming, these conditions are known as "complementary slackness conditions."

We turn to the set-up for the dual or pricing problem. Roughly speaking, each row in the original problem becomes a column in the dual set-up (the linear program to be solved for prices at the demand points and at the supply points (Table 5.2)).

One is asking that a sort of surplus value be maximized in this pricing problem subject to the prices satisfying basic no "surplus" profit conditions. The related complementary slackness conditions state: if the solved shipments out of a supply point exceed the initial quantity available, the price at that supply point must solve in this dual problem as zero. That is, $x_{i1} + x_{i2} + x_{i3} - S_i \leqq 0$, and $[x_{i1} + x_{i2} + x_{i3} - S_i]p_i^S = 0$ for $i = 1, 2$. (For our example above, the solution has $p_2^S = 0$. See Appendix 5.1.) And if the total shipments going to a demand point exceed the quantity demanded, then the price at that demand point must be zero. That is $D_j - x_{1j} - x_{2j} \leqq 0$, and $[D_j - x_{1j} - x_{2j}]p_j^D = 0$ for $j = 1, 2, 3$. Clearly no solution makes sense that has more quantity shipped to a demand point than has been asked for. Such a situation would be an "excess shipping" solution.

The transportation problem has very instructive solution conditions in the complementary slackness conditions, particularly the "coincidence" of negative profits to a shipper on a link and a zero quantity shipped. Such a condition must characterize commodity flows throughout the geography of an economic system, say a system of cities. A positive flow between points can only exist if the profit to a shipper is not negative. And of course commodity prices at various places reflect this implication of transportation cost "wedges." But the transportation problem in linear programming is "artificial" economics because demands and supplies at points are fixed numbers rather than demand and supply schedules that involve local quantities varying with local prices. When we replace the scalars with demand and supply schedules we have what is called a "spatial price equilibrium" problem.

Since carrying out transportation cost minimization can be complicated and demanding of good quality data, a back-of-the-envelope approach is to appeal to the "gravity" formulation. This postulates that the flows between supply point i and demand point j can be approximated by the product of the "masses" at each point, divided by the costs of transporting the commodity in question between the two points. Mass at the supply point is taken as some representation of total quantity available and at the demand point is taken as some representation of total quantity demanded. These "masses" are readily available when one is solving a transportation problem in linear programming. Hartwick (1972) explored how well the gravity model was working relative to pure transportation cost minimization in some numerical simulations. The gravity model yielded very good approximations in that investigation. More recently, economists specialized in the analysis of international trade have explored its usefulness in predicting patterns of trade. See, for example, Feenstra *et al.* (2001).

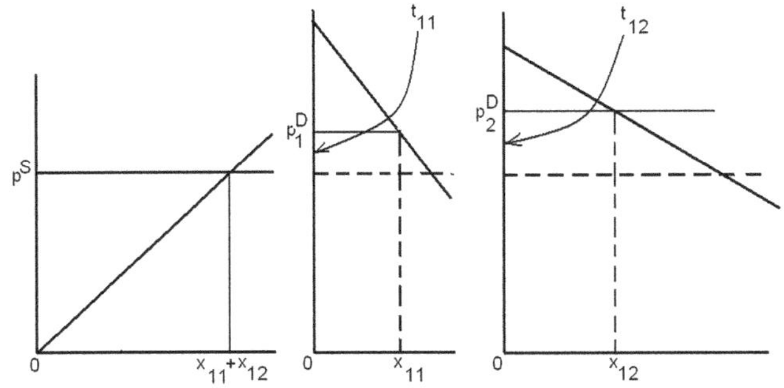

Figure 5.3 Our one supplier is shipping to two demand points with positive transportation costs per unit shipped.

Spatial price equilibrium

So-called spatial price equilibrium can be viewed as a generalized transportation problem. In place of quantities at supply and demand points, we start with supply schedules and demand schedules at the relevant points. By a supply schedule we of course mean quantity supplied at the point as a function of the price at that point. A positive flow between supply point i and demand point j will end up with a supply price at i and a demand price at j, differing by the unit cost of transport between the two points. We take up a simple case: one supplier separated from two demanders, also separated. At the supply point is a supply schedule, quantity supplied rising in the local price p^S and at each demand point there is a demand schedule, quantity demanded declining in the local price, p_j^D $(j = 1, 2)$. See Figure 5.3. Transportation cost per unit shipped is t_{ij}.

The solution to this problem simply involves solving for the p^S that has total quantity supplied, $x_{11} + x_{12}$, at price p^S equal to demand at point 1, x_{11} at price $p^S + t_{11}$ $(= p_1^D)$ and demand at point 2, x_{12} at price $p^S + t_{12}$ $(= p_2^D)$. If we rule out "perverse" demand and supply schedules, there will be a p^S that works.

One naturally begins to think of many supply points, each with its distinct supply schedule and many demand points, each with its distinct demand schedule and an optimizing solution. For these more complicated problems (optimization problems), one searches for a solution that maximizes aggregate net consumer surpluses and aggregate net producer surpluses, where transportation costs must be netted out of the surpluses achieved.

The analysis can be extended to the case of multiple commodities rather than our single commodity. The multi-commodity case involves demand and supply schedules that are functions of the many local prices for the many commodities specified. Such problems are again optimization problems and the objective function is aggregate net consumer and producer surpluses. There is a fairly large literature on how to solve such large optimization problems. One can of course consider such problems as representing equilibrium commodity flows for a complete system of cities, with each city's location fixed with respect to the others.

The Weber firm location problem

Imagine three demand points in the plane, each with a number or scalar for quantity demanded, and one "central" supplier at a distinct point, with her own scalar for quantity she is supplying, a number larger than the sum at the three demand points. The location point of the supplier is variable for the moment. The points of demanders are fixed. Let there be transportation costs per unit distance t_1, t_2 and t_3 for shipping from the supplier to each of the demanders. What is the best location for the supplier? We are dealing with an "optimal location" problem that involves some aspect of transportation cost minimization. This is an instance of the famous Weber problem in locating the supplying firm. Our problem in the section immediately above (one supplier with her supply schedule and two geographically separated demanders, each with their own demand schedules) is easily adjusted to become a Weber problem, one with demand and supply as schedules varying with local price.

Let us simplify somewhat. Suppose each of the demanders in the above problem were at the end of a line of length Z, demander 1 at the zero point and demander 2 at the point Z. We place the supplier at distance y from demander 1 and thus $Z - y$ from demander 2. Change transportation costs per unit to $t_{11}y$ for the supplier accessing demander 1 and to $t_{12}[y - Z]$ per unit shipped from the supplier to demander 2. For the supplier fixed at one interior point on the line, we have a problem exactly as the one in the previous section. There will be a supply price, $p^S(y)$, that solves the allocation from the supplier to the two demanders. We can say that $p^S(y)$ is the equilibrium price, given the supplier located at y. The Weber problem (on a line) involves varying the seller's location, y, so as to maximize net producer and consumer surpluses, net of transportation costs. This is an interesting problem in optimal location for the supplying firm.

To make this problem more closely related to the standard Weber problem, we would have to consider locating the supplier on the plane rather than on the line. Furthermore, we have introduced supply and demand schedules at the various points, whereas the true Weber problem would have only scalar quantities (just numbers rather than schedules varying with quantities varying with price) for supplies and demands. Mathematicians have worked on various versions of the Weber problem over recent decades.

Intermediate goods and urban structure

Think of a city as a vast array of square blocks or areas, each block a production unit importing inputs, including labor, from each of four neighbors and exporting other goods to these four neighbors, with the flows across each of the four boundaries being costly or incurring transportation costs in the form of capital and land. In addition, designate a few special squares as nodes through which the city is importing inputs from other cities and exporting a bill of "final" goods to other cities. Each square has access to the same production technology as every other square but flows produced and imported adjust so that the "final goods" vector for the city as a whole is satisfied at a minimum cost (comprising labor, capital and transportation costs). The cost of land gets solved for in the optimization as well as block-specific choices of techniques for production (essentially points on isoquants). The equilibrium structure for such a city can be posed as the solution to a large linear program, where each square becomes a tiny diverse production place with possible residences. Since each square represents a local land constraint, each square emerges in the solution with an equilibrium land rent. Land is in a sense rationing how much activity can take place in that sub-location and the "final goods" requirement becomes a constraint on what the city must do to rationalize its existence as a unit trading with other cities in a larger system.

Overall cost minimization for the city, including internal transportation costs, and subject to it meeting its outside demand requirements, involves the assigning of $\sum_{q=1}^{r+1}(q \times S_q)$

production activities to each square at non-negative levels of operation. Production of a commodity involves a choice of technique, determined in part by how much land is used by the technique. One aspect of a technique is the number of storeys of structure which a technique is associated with. At an aggregate level, one can think of the city bidding land away from agricultural use, this latter paying R_A per unit. The objective function being minimized comprises two transportation cost terms, one for internal cross-boundary flows for each square and another for export flows from the city, plus a primary input term comprising the use of land, labor and capital in production of commodities, including housing. The finiteness of land in each square in an abstract city translates, via demand for area by production and transportation activities, into a rent for land per square, a value that shows up in the dual problem.

Details of the linear program which "produces" such an equilibrium city were set out in Hartwick and Hartwick (1974; restated in Appendix 5.2). A special case with a single import-export node would end up as a spatially-detailed monocentric city. In Figure 5.4, we have the output from optimized linear program for a city with, by assumption, two import-export nodes (one at $i = 5$, $j = 3$ and another at $i = 5$, $j = 9$). Much land is used for transportation for these nodes since large flows of commodities are flowing in from the four neighbors for each and flowing out since the nodes are centers for importing into and exporting from the city. The blank squares are areas that remain in agriculture, in equilibrium. There are, aside from transportation, four goods potentially producible in each block.

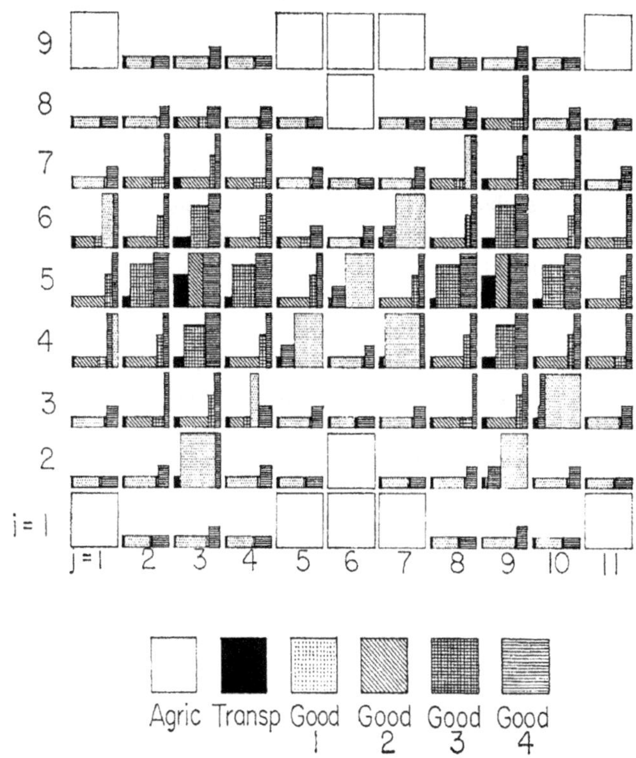

Figure 5.4 LP city with two nodes.

We allow activities in each square to choose their best techniques from an assumed array "available" to each square (the same for each square) and this includes substituting capital for land. In the diagram the vertical dimension can be interpreted as reflecting storeys of structures in that sub-area. And we see that taller buildings are located on average near the "trade" nodes, where in fact land prices will be relatively high. There is a dual linear program which, among other things, assigns a scarcity land rent to each block. Prices for a commodity flowing between two adjacent blocks will differ by the transportation costs. The land prices per block, emerging from the dual problem, are considerably higher near the two "trade" nodes. A household is represented by a vector of input flows and earns a wage exogenous to the city. The "household" is allowed to commute to its location of work. Consumer choice is being modelled somewhat crudely in this approach. In particular, wage gaps between squares direct the "redistribution" of labor throughout the city rather than gaps between utility levels achievable at different places for similar workers.

This formulation of a city "explains" the city size and structure as a response to its "trading requirements" and the location of its "trade" nodes. The city in a sense grows around the "trade" nodes and its size is roughly speaking determined by the vector of exports it is asked to meet at its "trade" nodes. A node could of course be a deep water port and we would then say that the city is where it is because of its "natural advantage." This model of a city descends from formalisms of Koopmans and Beckmann (1957) and Mills (1972b). Mills, who became the "dean" of urban economists, retained a lifelong commitment to addressing questions of urban structure and functioning as primarily matters for economic analysis. He became a restrained crusader against social or sociological approaches to thinking about urban structure. In 1969, Jay Forrester published his *Urban Dynamics* and the Forrester non-economic, differential equations, computer-simulation approach became a focus for economists to rally against. For Mills, a city should be viewed as an equilibrium economics system with many households, each maximizing its utility, and many firms, each maximizing its profit. Issues in transportation should, he felt, be addressed with the standard tools of cost–benefit analysis. Mills's approach represents an interesting "reference case" but slights the complicated issues of income distribution and externalities. A transportation system for a city not only moves goods and people around but also "dictates" relative accessibility of places of employment for people and relative values of homes. Few urban policies, particularly those involving school budgets, levels of police expenditure and investment in public transportation are free of an income distribution component. And perhaps too often the focus is on the income distribution aspect while the efficiency aspects, central to the Mills's agenda, are neglected. It is not obvious that the introduction of space into textbook economics implies that traditional welfare economic analysis remains unchanged. Geography affects the cost of a worker accessing her employment and introduces a special friction into a standard model of the labor market.

Our programming model of a city is a formulation that places a city close to a representation as a large, complicated firm. In the programming formulation key prices appear in the dual problem. In the real world, large firms usually have few prices operating within their structures to organize things. Workers respond to orders from above or directives, not local prices. A city, however, operates with very few direct orders to workers. The latter get their directives from the price system and it becomes very interesting to ask how well "the price system" functions in organizing activities in a real-world city "for the best."

The above programming model produces a complicated city. The city size and layout responds to the exogenous bill of goods which we present to the city. Agglomeration here is driven by the port effect—goods traded externally must pass through one of two particular sites. Many cities of the world developed around ports. Our model has no scale economies. We infer that cities can be complicated and realistic without the imposition of scale economies. It probably makes sense to think about city structure in two stages—what it looks like with only a port effect and how much more complicated it gets with scale economies grafted on in a second stage. The model of Lucas and Rossi-Hansberg (2002) has no port effect and no scale economies in the textbook sense. Firms agglomerate because proximity between firms raises the productivity of a worker. The product of the firms is carted away costlessly by helicopters, these latter visiting each firm. Workers also demand space for residential activity and this becomes a wedge which interferes with two firms exploiting proximity. A city spreads out to provide space for residential activity; otherwise the city would be one large blob of firms, each close to one another. Lucas and Rossi-Hansberg obtain land-use patterns that approximate some real-world cities and their route is rather different from the port approach or the scale-economy approach. The monocentric city can be viewed as a special case of the Lucas and Rossi-Hansberg city. Each worker can be viewed as a firm and these firms agglomerate together in the center of the city each day to exploit firm-to-firm proximity. (Each firm produces a net export which is helicoptered out to an external group of demanders.) Implicit here is the idea that if each worker worked at her residence and communicated with other firms, say by telephone, then per worker productivity would be lower. The classic monocentric city then becomes something of a corner solution to the Lucas and Rossi-Hansberg (2002) model. One can of course view the classic monocentric city circle model, half a disc at least from a circular form, as an entity growing up around a port. Worker concentration is then employment at the port, not a productivity-enhancement mechanism.

The model of a city in Hartwick and Hartwick (1974) minimizes the value of primary inputs needed for a city to meet an exogenous bill of final good exports. Novel is the fact that (a) the location of exporting is exogenous and (b) transportation costs are explicit and defined in terms of primary resource inputs, including land. Linear programming tells us that the equilibrium value of exports, at the site of exporting, equals the value of primary resources needed to generate the export vector, including the value of inputs into transportation. A city then exists because it has the capacity to generate exports to demanders and it takes the form it does in part because exports must exit through exogenously given channels. The city as trading unit in Chapter 1 took "world" prices as exogenous whereas the Hartwick–Hartwick city takes local and "world" quantities demanded as exogenous. The linear programming formulation allowed us to set out a very detailed internal structure for an abstract city. One might say that the model with the next most detailed internal structure is that of Lucas and Rossi-Hansberg.

We solved our example with each areal unit set at 1 distance unit to each side. Suppose we re-solved simply setting each areal unit at 0.95 distance to each side, other things being the same. We could end up with a more compact city satisfying its "bill of exports." A city is by definition an economic arrangement of production and residential activity that economizes on transportation costs. Urban land is expensive because it is close to important things such as businesses, theatres, jobs, etc. A piece of urban land has relatively low transportation costs connecting itself to important related economic "things." A city that is in some sense too congested will tend to have new activity locate away from places of persistent gridlock. A city subtly trades off clustering people and businesses together while allowing goods and people to move about in the city at reasonable cost.

Summary

This chapter has been devoted to classic analyses in location economics, certainly those pre-dating the work of Krugman on scale economies and the geographic concentration of economic activity. We considered Losch on scale economies, market area development and competition among service towns for market share. In this case, monopolistic competition was central. We considered Hotelling on competition between two sellers for market area, the so-called spatial duopoly problem. We set out the Weber problem on the location of a firm, using the geography of the Hotelling problem. In fact, applied mathematicians have worked hard on the Weber problem and variants of it. We then considered pricing and transportation costs between points in space, the so-called spatial arbitrage problem. Here the classic transportation problem in linear programming was helpful. And the topic of linear programming took us into the programming approach to the analysis of land use in a city. We observed a fairly detailed example of this "highly economic" approach to the analysis of urban structure.

Main points of Chapter 5

1. A (Loschian) service town has a commodity which it produces with scale economies and then "sends out" with positive delivery costs to customers spread out around the town. Getting the amount produced and the area of the producer's market around the town are the things to work out. The pattern of towns and market areas on a large plain matters.
2. Competition between two sellers in one linear market area involves a tricky choice of site choice (Hotelling duopoly). The free market solution is generally not best for consumers.
3. Where should a supplier to three towns locate her operation? We look at this Weber problem for just two towns making demands on the supplier.
4. "Spatial price arbitrage" bids away any profits above costs of transportation between places. The transportation problem in linear programming illustrates this principle well.
5. Linear programming has well-developed software that allows the construction of a numerical model of a quite intricate city.

Questions and problems

1. Iowa was the example of a featureless plain of similar farms which August Losch used to motivate his analysis of service towns for farmers. Sketch Losch's argument for the equilibrium size of a services town in the plain. Sketch his argument for the equilibrium number of services towns in the plain. Is Losch's equilibrium number of towns a welfare optimum?
2. Hotelling presented a market area analysis of duopoly with "too much concentration" in the location of firms. If one relaxes one of his key assumptions, does spreading out of location of firms follow directly? Evaluate the Hotelling spatial duopoly as a mechanism driving agglomeration of activity in cities.
3. A Weber equilibrium involves a seller locating "close to" multiple spread-out markets. Do vehicle tire makers in the United States appear to locate in accord with Weber's principles? Raw cement "manufacturers" tend to be spread in diverse locations. Does the location of a cement plant follow along the lines of a Weber equilibrium?
4. The linear programming model of a city has many dimensions that exhibit constant returns to scale. How is the size of the city determined?

Appendix 5.1: Solution to our transportation problem example

The cost-minimizing flows are $x_{11} = x_{12} = 0$, $x_{13} = 4$, $x_{21} = 2$, $x_{22} = 3$ and $x_{23} = 1$. For the dual problem in prices, $p_1^S = 3$, $p_2^S = 0$ and $p_1^D = 2$, $p_2^D = 4$ and $p_3^D = 6$. Observe that the value of the solved objective function for each problem is US$34.

Appendix 5.2: Urban land use in an activity analysis linear model

In the text we presented a picture of the solution to the linear model of Hartwick and Hartwick (1974). Here we fill in the details of equilibrium land use for such a model. One starts with farmland on a specific grid of squares. Certain squares are specified as transportation nodes for delivering a vector of commodities to "the outside world." The urban economy "grows up" around this bill of exports. Labor and produced capital are available at exogenously given rentals. Land is scarce, with each square typically having some goods production activity, some housing activity and some road-services or transportation activity.

Square (i, j) has four direct neighbors, referenced as $1, 2, 3$ and 4, located north, east, south and west of (i, j). The objective function to be minimized with respect to commodity flows moving over space and activity levels corresponding to output and input flows of commodities in production is

$$Z = \sum_{i,j} \left\{ \sum_{s=1}^{S_t} \sum_{d=1}^{4} (Ra_{r+2,t,s} + R_A a_{r+1,t,s}) x_{ts}^d(i, j) + \sum_{q}^{r} z_q(i, j)\delta(i, j) x_q(i, j) \right.$$
$$\left. \times \sum_{q}^{r} \sum_{q=1}^{S_q} (Ra_{r+2,q,s} + R_A a_{r+1,q,s} + wa_{r+3.q.s}) x_{qs}(i, j) \right\}$$

where s defines a technique ranging from 1 to S_q for producing commodity q,

d defines one of four possible boundaries for square (i, j),

R is the rental price of a unit of capital, capital freely available to a square at this rental,

$r + 1$ indicates capital,

R_A is the rental price of a unit of agricultural land (the undeveloped optional activity for a square),

$r + 2$ indicates land,

w is the wage rate per worker per week,

$r + 3$ indicates labor,

$a_{k,q,s}$ is the input of commodity k required to produce a unit of commodity q with technique s. k ranges from 1 to $r + 3$. Commodity r is housing. Hence $a_{r,q,s}$ is set equal to $a_{r+3,q,s}$ to identify 1 worker with 1 house. q ranges from 1 to r, plus the additional commodity, t for transportation.

$z_q(i, j)$ indicates how attractive (i, j) is as an export node and $\delta(i, j)$ is 1 when (i, j) is an export node and is 0 otherwise,

$x_{ts}^d(i, j)$ is the aggregated flow of commodities crossing boundary d of (i, j) using technique s for producing transportation service output,

$T_q^d(i, j)$ is the flow of commodity q flowing out of (i, j) across border d,

t_q is a coefficient on transportation; the amount of transportation required to move a unit of q from one square to its neighbor,

$x_q(i, j)$ is the export flow of commodity q from (i, j),

$x_{qs}(i, j)$ is the activity level s for producing commodity q in (i, j); also gross output flow of q with technique s.

We turn to details of flows across boundaries.

Each square, with some non-agricultural activity, is in a flow equilibrium with its four neighboring squares for each of the possible r goods producible in a square. We have the following cross border flow conditions for square (i, j):

$$\begin{aligned} &T_q^1(i-1, j) + T_q^2(i, j-1) + T_q^3(i+1, j) + T_q^4(i, j+1) + \sum_s x_{qs}(i, j) \\ &\quad - \sum\sum a_{qks}x_{ks}(i, j) - \sum_{d=1}^{4} T_q^d(i, j) - \delta(i, j)x_q(i, j) \\ &= 0 \qquad (q = 1, \ldots, r; i = 1, \ldots, M; j = 1, \ldots, N), \end{aligned}$$

where the first four terms indicate flows of commodity q to square (i, j) from each of the four neighbor squares, the fifth term is gross output of commodity q in square (i, j), the sixth term is total intermediate use of commodity q by other activities in (i, j), the seventh term is total flows of commodity q from square (i, j) to its neighboring squares, and the eighth term is export of commodity q from (i, j) for the case in which (i, j) is a transportation node (some squares are denoted with a $\delta(i, j)$ as special import or export nodes for the city at the outset).

Summing over nodes, we have

$$\sum_{i,j} \delta(i, j)x_q(i, j) \geqq x_q^* \qquad (q = 1, \ldots, r; i = 1, \ldots, M; j = 1, \ldots, N).$$

When the final demand for a commodity is zero, the commodity is a purely intermediate good. Commodity r is identified as housing and is treated as intermediate (not imported or exported) to the city. Each house is also linked to one worker. Hence labor supply is also "housing supply" for the city. Household equilibrium is defined in the dual problem as where land rent, a wage, and prices per square are "produced."

Transportation flow of commodities and workers across the borders of a square "equates" with inputs of land and capital. A more capital-using transportation production technique corresponds with, say, subways. Note $a_{r+1,t,s}$ and $a_{r=1,t,s}$ are inputs of land and capital, respectively, for producing one unit of transportation service with technique s.

The amount of transportation output required in square (i, j) to transport the flow of good q across the north boundary of square (i, j) is $t_q(T_q^1(i, j) + T_q^3(i+1, j)$. This leads to the following constraints which define the production of transportation services.

$$\sum_s x_{t,s}^1(i, j) - \sum_{q=1}^{r} t_q(T_q^1(i, j) + T_q^3(i+1, j)) \geqq 0$$

$$\sum_s x_{t,s}^2(i, j) - \sum_{q=1}^{r} t_q(T_q^2(i, j) + T_q^4(i+1, j)) \geqq 0$$

$$\sum_s x_{t,s}^3(i,j) - \sum_{q=1}^{r} t_q(T_q^3(i,j) + T_q^1(i+1,j)) \geqq 0$$

$$\sum_s x_{t,s}^4(i,j) - \sum_{q=1}^{r} t_q(T_q^4(i,j) + T_q^2(i+1,j)) \geqq 0 \quad (i=1,\ldots,M;\ j=1,\ldots,N).$$

Land in a square is fully occupied by production of either commodities 1 to 4, or transportation, or agriculture or a combination of these activities. Hence

$$\sum_{q=1}^{r}\sum_s a_{r+1,q,s}x_{q,s}(i,j) + \sum_d\sum_s a_{r+1,t,s}x_{t,s}^d(i,j) \leqq 1 \quad (i=1,\ldots,M;\ j=1,\ldots,N),$$

where the first term indicates land use in commodity production, other than agriculture, and the second term indicates land use in transportation. When the equation solves as an inequality, the understanding is that there is some agricultural activity remaining in the square.

The dual problem yields commodity price $p_q(i, j)$ for commodity q in square (i, j) as well as land rent, $R_A + p_{r+1}(i, j)$ per square. The central inequality is

$$p_q(i,j) - \sum p_k(i,j)a_{kqs} \leqq wa_{qrs} + R_A a_{r+1,q,s} + Ra_{r+2,q,s}$$
$$\text{for } s=1,\ldots,S_q,\ \text{for each } q;\ q=1,\ldots,r,t;$$
$$i=1,\ldots,M;\ \text{and } j=1,\ldots,N.$$

Labor is employed in varying intensities in various squares, corresponding to activities 1 to r. A worker is paid direct wage w plus 1 house. Two workers resident in square (i, j) will pay distinct amounts for their houses, depending how far from square (i, j) they work. Commuting costs are represented by "moving house" costs and the worker who works more distant from (i, j) will pay less for his house in square (i, j). The idea is to have each worker in the city live with the same real income. All workers are considered to be the same.

Note

1 Samuelson once commented that when he flew over Iowa and looked down he saw no hexagons. And Eaton and Lipsey (1976) attacked the notion that equilibrium market areas would turn out to be hexagonal. They defended squares. Actual market areas can of course be hexagons without the edges being obvious to the eye.

6 Growth of cities

Urban growth. The pre-industrial mode of horizontal growth (division of labor). The industrial mode of import substitution and the exploitation of scale economies. Local concentration of production. Hierarchies of cities.

A growing economy

Economic growth from the historical perspective is surprisingly controversial. There is, for example, much dispute over the forces that got the industrial revolution going in Britain around 1770 and why an industrial revolution did not get started earlier in, say, China in the Yangtze River valley or in north-central Italy or in France. Some economists emphasize that growth was essentially a capital accumulation process, one of more machines per worker; others emphasize the technical progress dimension of an economic take-off—better ways to produce cotton thread, more efficient ways to garner energy from a steam engine and so on. Then others emphasize the accumulation of new skills in workers, a process that seemed to be coincident with families ending up with fewer children. de Long and Schleifer (1993) emphasize the importance of the entrenchment of some variant of "the rule of law" as a precursor to economic take-off. Urbanization and reductions in family size are usually part of the growth process. In the United States, "total population grew twelvefold between 1800 and 1890 while those living in cities increased an astonishing eighty-seven times" (Appleby 2010; p. 197).

With regard to pre-industrial economic activity, historians emphasize the Malthusian nature of economic "growth"—an unexpected rise in per capita income is inevitably followed by a population increase, one that eats up the earlier gains that had been just realized. Hence the rate of pre-industrial economic growth (before 1770) in Europe is taken as minuscule but not negative. Members of the elite lived quite comfortably but the average person was turned out in rags and lived in a hovel, in the words of Robert Solow. Life expectancy would have been in the neighborhood of 30 years century after century and this figure was kept low because of high infant mortality and frequent deaths of young women in childbirth.The city of Rome had a population of about one million in the first century AD. The Empire had its impressive public works including remarkable aqueducts and massive sewer systems in many towns. But Rome faded to just a large town by about AD 6. The capital of the Roman Empire moved to Constantinople. Elsewhere, cities became large. By AD 1000 there was a very large city in present day Nigeria and another on the site of present day Shanghai. There was then economic "growth" and change but it was essentially horizontal in nature—more people grafted onto the edges of communities without a significant rise in per capita income. Some economic historians refer to this as Smithian growth—a society's exploitation of division of labor, different individuals largely specialized in different lines of activity, "taking in each other's wash" in a fairly dense community. A different dimension of Smithian growth is a society's exploitation by trade of regional comparative advantages rather than each person's comparative advantage. The Roman empire would have had some regions specialized in wheat-growing, others in grape-growing, others in mineral extraction and so on. Inter-regional trade would have been an important source of welfare improvement.[1] During its golden age (about AD 25 to AD 225) the core of the Roman Empire was five large Mediterranean cities engaged in considerable trade. Developing a sophisticated, large-volume trading system was simply one more stroke of genius of the Romans. Ades and Glaeser (1995) argue that the city of Rome grew large because the rulers offered subsidies to poor people for food (the *anona*) and amusement to buy their loyalty. They suggest that autocratic governments fear insurrections and offer "bread and circuses" to keep otherwise restive groups tranquil. These subsidies in turn make capital cities in many places unusually large. In 2007, of the 19 cities of the world with over ten million people, 11 were capitals of the nations they were in (United Nations Population Division 2008).

Though economic "growth" may have always left the huge lower class in basic poverty everywhere before the industrial revolution, there was some population growth, some growth in towns and cities, some technical progress in agricultural methods, military activities, the quality of ocean-going vessels, and in the production of various kinds of cloth. There was also noticeable advancement in business accounting methods, insurance and financial market structures and in government management of debts. These were conspicuous in Holland (mostly in Amsterdam) and England (mostly in London). England and Holland were locked over many decades in various sorts of competitions that may have accelerated modernization in both places. England ultimately leapt ahead. Central Italy had a "modern" and partially mechanized textile industry ahead of both Holland and England. Yet Italy's industrial revolution came later than it did for most other European countries.

The growth of a community placed demands on the surrounding areas for food and fuel. Advanced economies like that of Rome could exploit long distance trade but less advanced towns and cities had to rely on farms and forests nearby. The capacities of these local hinterlands constituted constraints on the growth of the central community. Eric Jones (2010) emphasizes that the Industrial Revolution in England was preceded by the decline of small-scale industrial activity south of London and the rise there of more modern agricultural activity. The growth of London would have abetted this process since a bigger London required more food and fuel, better production from nearby farms, and cheap food would in turn have abetted the growth of London at a crucial period of England's economic development. Ades and Glaeser note that around 1700 both Paris and London had become unusually large and that England had just emerged from a period of political instability. In the hundreds of years before Paris and London grew rapidly, Byzantium (later Constantinople) and Cordoba were the largest cities in Europe. Pomeranz and Topik (2006; pp. 51–55) reflect on social unrest in capital cities and the price of food during the eighteenth and nineteenth centuries: "London, surrounded by unusually productive and market-oriented farms, and with excellent water transport, was not that big a problem: but even there, various new laws were needed to direct enough grain to the city." Paris, they argue, drew on a thin cushion of surplus grain and the residents experienced fluctuations in the prices of basic foodstuffs of 300 or 400 percent: "And even Paris was not Europe's worst case: that was Madrid, swollen with silver from the Americas, but located in a very dry region that mostly raised sheep." Peking drew rice from fertile regions along its Grand Canal, completed in 1420. In addition there were both state-run and private charitable granaries that stockpiled rice in good times and kept prices from rising in bad times. Delhi, on a dry plain in India, benefitted from a policy of encouraging well-digging by prosperous families. The actual grain, however, flowed in by slow but numerous caravans, land transportation provided by the Banjara caste. Tokyo (Edo then) could import rice by coastal shipping but in addition organized massive road-building programs, and even so force was resorted to in order to get rice tribute from recalcitrant farmers. Tokyo was probably the world's largest city in the seventeenth century. It contains some 35 million people currently.

Malthusian stasis suggests no economic change. In fact there was some qualitative change before the industrial revolution, but relatively little change in average per capita income. The most significant change was simple population increase, a gradual filling in of interstices, so to speak. More farm land was taken under cultivation and some villages grew into towns. Urban growth before the Industrial Revolution was primarily of the horizontal sort, the addition of households at the spatial margin but with no significant rise in per capita income. A new head of household would bring his particular skills to the built-up place and division of labor would deepen very slightly on average because the new person's skills would in general differ from the average of those in the place he was joining. There would be urban growth and an infinitesimal growth in per capita income because of a new arrangement of division of labor and interpersonal trade but the big picture would still be one of Malthusian "development," though a "development" with more populous communities. This is an important dimension of economic change before the Industrial Revolution—gradual demographic change and the growth of villages, towns and some cities. One might go so far as to say that the growth of London's population was an important component of the constellation of forces that represent the start of the Industrial Revolution. After the Industrial Revolution the growth of towns and cities was much different. There were still gains from division of labor as new people arrived but there was now the noticeable accumulation of durable capital. Factories of various sorts appeared in various towns, first in the north of England, in places with water power. Vibrant industrial sectors in larger places were able to attract new activities that were intermediate to the leading sectors. This is the well-known process of import substitution, though here it is the urban place that is the "trading nation." Large cities can draw in activities that formerly were located in towns "down the road." There is generally a scale economy in this draw-in of intermediate goods activity. The intermediate goods firms provide a cost reduction to the primary goods firms when they move closer and better communication between the upstream and downstream firms may itself provide an additional payoff. The drawing in of intermediate goods can be referred to as the vertical growth of a city since the intermediate goods firms that migrate in, appear underneath, so to speak, the primary goods firms.

Large cities are typically more industrially diversified than are small cities. In other words, judging by the variety of goods, larger cities are more self-sufficient. This is a result of steady import substitution that coincides with the growth of a city. It simply pays firms exporting to city A to establish a branch in city A when city A has grown beyond a certain size. When the branch is set up in city A, the transportation costs that were being incurred in shipping to city A are eliminated. Firms do not, however, locate a branch in city A when city A is small because the market is not yet large enough to support a new stand-alone firm. Scale effects are generally central to this process of import substitution and city growth.

The so-called branch will often be a new firm in the same line of production. This is not to deny that each of ten large cities will generally appear to specialize in a distinct line of "export" activity. The top tier industries specialized in by a large city can differ, but lower down activities in large cities will be generally very similar in size. In a somewhat dated terminology, larger cities have proportionately more workers in non-basic activities (own-serving activities) than do smaller cities. Non-basic activities (retailing, municipal government, schools, churches, etc.) are those that provide output to residents of the city in question whereas basic activities (other-serving activities) are those that provide output to residents of other cities.

Krugman and Livas Elizondo (1996) argue that Mexico City grew unusually large because central government policy favored import substitution for the nation and Mexico City received most of the in-migrating firms. Mexico City became the de facto magnet for the new activities favored by the general policy of import substitution. Returns to scale were central to the super-agglomeration of economic activity in Mexico City. Krugman and Livas Elizondo contend that nations with open economy policies will not see one city become extremely large. They flesh out their argument with a formal model with scale economies and transportation costs, an agglomeration model with ingredients similar to those we report on below when we take up scale economies explicitly. Buenos Aires is another capital city which contains an unusually large fraction of the population of its nation, Argentina. And Argentina is a nation that explicitly favored import substitution from the 1930s to the 1970s. The fact that Buenos Aires emerged as a primate city in the same sense that Mexico City did appears to offer support to the Krugman–Livas Elizondo view. In fact, up to the mid-nineteenth century most "modern" nations pursued a policy of high tariffs in an effort to foster import substitution. This policy may well have been central to the emergence of London and Paris as the two largest cities in Europe in 1700.

The growth of cities after the Industrial Revolution was also driven by technical progress. Placing large groups of working people together in a dense setting often leads to the somewhat spontaneous spawning of productive ideas—lower-cost ways of producing things and the percolating up of ideas for useful new things. At a minimum it is very difficult for a business to remain active in a city when it fails to adopt the best practices on display in the city in question. This is a Darwinian force for efficiency gain—failure to adapt one's ways to the current best practice gets one left behind in the race for engaging the best suppliers and winning a good share of the market for one's output. Since about 1675, London has been one of the world's leading cities. It managed to innovate in governance; institutions were developed for controlling the sovereign's spending and meddling in the lives and businesses of citizens. In addition, the party system in politics was developed: the losing party in Parliament learned to avoid precipitating violence when thwarted. The power of religious leaders was held in check. A system of channelling the savings of individuals and groups into productive private investments emerged, an effective though undeniably *ad hoc* financial system. Much was learned about finance and insurance from the Dutch. A culture of tolerance took root. London emerged as the destination of choice for refugees of various sorts, some extremely talented. Recognition of tangible achievement, irrespective of the religion or national origin of the achiever, was institutionalized. Jews, for example, were able to prosper in England, while elsewhere they were discriminated against. The Huguenots were refugees from religious conflict in France. Many settled in the east of London and became active in the textile sector.

Certain cities grow faster than others and some end up very large indeed. We can associate winners in the race for dominance generally with a geographic advantage—the presence of a very good port for ships being a classic example. New York City was picked out for colonization by the Dutch presumably because it represented a good port, a good place for a settlement on the land and it was an attractive site relative to the Hudson River. By the first census in the United States in 1790, New York City was already larger than sophisticated Philadelphia, this latter lacking a natural route to the interior. In fact New York City was the largest city in the US by 1790 and found ways to protect its dominance over the next 220 years. When, then, we contemplate the growth of a city in history we do well to reflect first on whether the place in question had a head start in that it was taking advantage of a special geographic endowment—a transportation node, so to speak. In 1900 the 20 largest cities in the United States were all ports: Boston, Providence, New York, Jersey City, Newark, Baltimore and San Francisco on an ocean; Milwaukee, Chicago, Detroit, Cleveland and Buffalo were all places where a river meets one of the Great Lakes; Minneapolis, St. Louis, and New Orleans on the Mississippi River; and Louisville, Cincinnati and Pittsburgh on the Ohio River. The remaining two ports were Philadelphia and Washington, DC. The latter's claim to having been a port is clearly a stretch. Given something of a head start as a port city, many of these port-places became centers of manufacturing. "As late as 1950, seven of the eight largest American cities had a greater share of their workforce in manufacturing than the US average" (Glaeser 1998). But claims to local advantage shifted, presumably driven by the rise of highways and trucks for transporting goods. The central municipalities of Baltimore, Buffalo, Cleveland, Detroit, Pittsburgh, St. Louis and Philadelphia all lost population since 1950 in every decade. In 1947, 50 percent of the transportation bill for the United States was for rail. By 2000, 77.4 percent of the bill was for trucking, even though trucking in 2000 was still about ten times more expensive than rail per ton mile. Hence the large share measured in dollars for trucking. But in terms of tons of stuff shipped, rail still dominates in the United States and rail's share is still rising (Glaeser and Kohlhase 2004).

The medieval fortified village

Recall our report of the wealthy von Thunen in Chapter 2 with his sprawling estate in northern Germany and his tenant farmers supplying harvest to a small community at the center. This was a very common form of community in Europe in say 1400—a wealthy strongman in a large fortified home surrounded by tenant farmers who had to hand over some of their harvests as rent, a charge from the lord, the owner of a large estate. The lord of the manor would sell his produce in a market and buy consumer goods for himself, his family and his retainers. The tenants would be offered security by the lord in addition to the plots they would be allowed to work. Typically the lord's home would be some sort of fortified central place into which the tenants and their families would retreat when outside marauders threatened the community. The tenants would of course be expected to take up arms along with the lord's retainers to fend off attackers. This type of village would have been seen throughout much of medieval Europe as well as in many other parts of the settled world before the emergence of more modern nations with monarchs, armies and navies.

Observers such as North and Weingast (1989) and McGuire and Olson (1996) were interested in the tension created in the minds of the tenants by the size of the rent skimmed off by the lord. High rents tend to go along with relative impoverishment of the tenants and unhappy tenants can be a threat to the tranquility of the lord and his family. Is there such a thing as a fair rent? What about the lord just skimming off a rent equal to the contribution of his land to the output from the tenant farms? The lord can justify a large share since he is aware that he is providing security to his tenants. Here we reformulate the von Thunen model as a closed equilibrium system with a rent level chosen by the lord.

On a tenant's farm at distance x from the center, we have land rent $r(x)$ defined by

$$1 - tx = a_N w + a_L r(x),$$

where the price of output at the village is unity. A unit of, say, wheat evaporates on its way to the village at the center, losing tx of value. Hence $1 - tx$ are the dollars to spread over labor

a_N and land a_L at x, in amounts $a_N w$ and $a_L r(x)$. Then a_N is labor input per unit of wheat produced and a_L is land input per unit of wheat produced. The land rent $r(x)$ can be viewed as a residual in this calculation. Suppose fraction λ of land rent is the rent that the lord extracts from his tenants. Then in a circular economy we have the lord's "take," C defined by

$$\lambda \int_0^{\overline{x}} r(x) 2\pi x dx = C,$$

and total wheat produced is $Q = \int_0^{\overline{x}} \frac{1}{a_L} 2\pi x dx$, with total land cultivated given by $\int_0^{\overline{x}} 2\pi x dx = \pi \overline{x}^2$. The total number of tenant-workers is Qa_N. Then the all-important wage is defined by

$$wQa_N = Q - T - C,$$

where T is total output lost to transportation. That is, $T = \int_0^{\overline{x}} tx \frac{1}{a_L} 2\pi x dx$. We can solve for the value of $\overline{x}$ in the relation $r(\overline{x}) = 0$. In this simple economy, the more that the lord takes as his rent (the larger is λ) the lower is the equilibrium value of w. And the more likely there is to be a tenants' insurrection, the higher is λ. North and others were interested in this question of the lord buying local tranquility or absence of insurrection by selecting λ appropriately. In addition to his wage, the tenant would be interested in the security that the lord provides to himself and his family. The lord would press for a larger share (λ larger) with the argument the he needed more resources to provide better security to the community. The maintenance of fortifications around these centers could of course be costly. What about worker mobility? It is not fanciful to view the long sweep of modern history as one of upper class people striving to extract labor from less powerful people at a minimum cost. They strive to pay a subsistence wage. A starting point of this wage control is control of labor mobility. Slavery is the most egregious form of wage control. A worker is simply compensated with a subsistence bundle of food, shelter and clothing. The worker is left with no possibility of relocating him or herself, of moving to a better situation. Domar (1970) argued that slavery would most likely emerge in pre-industrial societies when the labor-land ratio was low. In such a situation, the wage of free labor would be relatively high and land-owners would strive to re-set the "wage" at a lower level. The direct route to a low local wage would be the elimination of labor mobility. A worker could not relocate to a place with a better wage. Clearly the creation of a setting of no labor mobility is not easy. Those with power must resort to draconian measures. There would be pressure for slavery to arise. In other words, in times of labor scarcity, the pressure for slavery to emerge would be high. Many situations from history can be brought forth to support the Domar thesis. But there are exceptions to Domar's idea—for example Britain after the Black Death. Though labor became scarce suddenly and upward pressure on the wage of working people emerged, pure slavery did not take root.[2] This raises the question of whether the ability of workers in many places in Europe to preserve their freedom after the Black Death marked a major fork in the road for the future economic development of Europe. The freedom of working people was perhaps at this time woven in subtle ways into the social and political fabric of European society. Tenants and other workers could claim rights as dignified members of the social order. Others might view this period differently. Though outright slavery did not arise, there may have been the emergence of certain medieval institutions that tied working people quite closely to their "masters," institutions that limited worker mobility in key regions of

Europe. One can think of tenant farmers tied to owners of large estates by various obligations, enforced in nasty ways. The tying of poor people to certain employers via debt obligations persists to this day in certain third world countries.

The Domar thesis can be interpreted as different for the case of a lengthy period of stable "high" wages and for one of noticeably rising wages. The pressure to enslave workers would seem to be most obvious when labor has recently become scarce and wages have been noticeably increasing rather than in a period of stable "high" wages. In this latter case, the enslaver would have to infer that there is an alternative subsistence wage that can be brought into being with harsh tactics. One tends to view the pre-industrial centuries as ones of relatively stable institutional arrangements. Large estates were farmed by poor people and surpluses were skimmed off by the owners of the land. We should not, however, discount the upsetting effects of wars and lesser social dislocations on seemingly stable social arrangements between those with power in the elite and those without who tilled the soil. Economic development would have been impossible in Britain without a mobile workforce, one with basic skills and productive habits. Innovation and investment die on the vine when there is no reliable labor force available to implement the new ideas, build the new structures and operate the new machines. It is not an exaggeration to claim that Britain had a very high quality labor force on the brink of the Industrial Revolution. A working person could readily up and relocate to a new sub-market for labor when he was unhappy with his current situation. People could communicate with fellow workers in almost any community. One could speak of "the wage" of a working person in Britain in 1800 whereas across the Channel there would be a variety of wages associated with a variety of labor markets for different regions of continental Europe. Britain was able to take advantage of a productive labor market at the onset of the Industrial Revolution. The Industrial Revolution was the grafting on of new investment and innovation to this resource. Though the wage of working people finally rose significantly around 1850 in Britain, it was really in America where working people finally emerged as high-wage individuals.

There are institutions designed to immobilize working people in the modern age. Some nations require citizens to carry identification cards and codes on these cards indicate where the holders are permitted to live. One often hears of restrictions of people moving to the large cities in various nations. The outcome is often a low-wage life for a worker forced to reside away from economically vibrant places. Quasi-slavery is too harsh a description of such situations but the motivation for restricting mobility is often the same as that which inspired outright slavery in an earlier age. When a worker cannot migrate away from a low-wage place, she is suffering a similar sort of impoverishment, though often on a lesser scale, that a slave was forced to endure. One hopes that low-wage regions would become magnets for mobile firms but the low-wage regions are often short of the infrastructure that a modern, mobile firm would seek out. The Soviet state restricted labor migration from Siberia in order to develop a labor force for its mining operations as well as for some of its "dirty" industries. Restrictions on out-migration meant that low wages could be maintained. Clearly very high wages would have been required to get sufficient workers to settle in some of the cold, isolated cities that were developed as industrial centers by Soviet planners.

Horizontal growth of villages

Consider two persons, both aged 20 years, each with particular skills. We could be considering a young male and female. With a bit of a stretch of the imagination, we could consider each living in isolation doing their two basic activities, hunting and gathering. This is a particular case of autarky. Some biologists speak of the survival of organisms as the coping with feeding, fear and procreation.

If our young male and female formed a unit, one could spend most of his time hunting, while the other could spend most of her time gathering and they could share their respective "harvests." It is not hard to see that each could be much better off (have more consumption of harvested hunted product and gathered product) than when each was in autarky. This is the fundamental result of the Ricardian model of trade. Forming a sharing unit (trading unit) allows each to specialize in the activity which each is somewhat better at and this specialization results in a larger combined harvest than they were getting when they were in autarky. The gains from each specializing and "trading" with one another is what Ricardo was explaining in his celebrated 1820 monograph: he had England specializing in cloth production and Portugal in wine production and had the two nations trading with each other. What is true for England and Portugal is true for a healthy young male and female. Relative specialization in the activity in which each has a "comparative advantage" yields a larger pool of product than what the pair would obtain when each "does everything" on his or her own (remains in autarky).

What is true for two persons remains true for a village of 150 persons. When each active person pursues the activity which she is relatively good at, the pool of products will be larger than the pool that would exist when 150 autarkic persons pooled their respective "harvests." The living in groups by early humans was not just for companionship and pleasure in procreation, it was also to reap the productive surpluses that were possible when each person spent proportionately more time doing the activity which he or she was good at. Group living, free of violence, allows Ricardian comparative advantage across persons to be exploited by members of the group and each person in the group can benefit significantly. This holds true for mutual defence as well. Defence by a group, each pursuing a "military" activity which he or she is good at, will generally be more effective than defence activity by one or two persons in isolation. Division of labor (relative specialization by persons) is good for organizing defence as well as for organizing hunting and gathering activities.

Before the development of farming in the Middle East some 10,000 to 12,000 years ago, humans lived in villages and survived by hunting game, gathering aquatic creatures and gathering fruit, tubers, etc. They practiced division of labor, each person spending most time doing what he or she was relatively good at doing. The gains from the practice of division of labor made living in groups a natural strategy. We might say that communities grew horizontally. Tools or productive capital more generally was primitive and scarce.

The development of farming (crop development and harvesting by an individual or household in one place) changed the social interaction among humans dramatically. Most of a person's life would be spent in one place. Towns developed when a region had productive farms that were able to trade away surplus harvest. The "surplus" agricultural product supported the people in towns. Leaders in communities had attractive homes constructed for themselves and their close associates. This was one form of capital accumulation. But farming led to the development of new tools and new capital accumulation more generally, including livestock. Towns developed around mineral deposits and around ports and nodes in trading systems. Regions became relatively specialized by 2000 BC and traders from various regions pursued commercial exchanges with one another (Smithian growth, in the words of some economic historians). However, with the exception of members of various elites, most people lived in hovels and were clothed in rags. Economic development was essentially horizontal, more regions developing like those which had developed. There was glacial technical progress and glacial population increase. Capital accumulation was mostly the construction of homes in towns and places for worship. Homes for ordinary persons were cramped and rudimentary. Horizontal economic development had no mechanism that could release ordinary persons from lives in rags and hovels. An individual's view of "the world" and her place in it would reflect an often short and physically demanding life. The earth was a stage on which people, mostly poor, lived out their days and had to respond to the bidding of some member of the elite, infrequently if they were fortunate.

The size of a town would be constrained by its ability to bring food and fuel in and this "ability" would depend on the quality of management in the town. Rome in the first century was able to have food flow in each day for about a million people. One can marvel at the effectiveness of the management behind this phenomenon... a steady stream of cargo boats sailing up from Egypt with wheat for Rome. "Market mechanisms" carry out this management task in a decentralized way today and no doubt Rome included skilled merchants working in the wheat trade. But the Roman Empire was not a large decentralized economy like many such economies today. There would have been a significant top-down way of having economic activity carried out and Roman culture developed and sustained an effective culture of getting many things organized effectively. The penchant for decision-makers to see aqueducts and roads built is well known, but in addition Roman decision-makers were wedded to the idea of building towns and cities with effective and durable sewers. In this regard they were some 1800 years ahead of their time.

Though the Romans, like the earlier Egyptians, were remarkable builders, the Roman culture was still one of moving forward with an elite wonderfully provided for and a proletariat turned out in rags and housed in hovels. Think about contemporary, so-called slums. The world's settlements were all slums until the Industrial Revolution, punctuated with the attractive places occupied by members of the tiny elites, those with power of one kind or another. Historians contend that about one-third of the population of the Roman Empire were actual slaves, most locked up each night to keep them from escaping. A free peasant, living in what we would refer to as poverty, could feel superior to these down-trodden people. A few bright slaves became managers of various sorts for their owners, some on rural estates.

Over this period of Smithian growth, though the well-being of the ordinary person was improving at an imperceptible rate, the stock of knowledge was evolving. Huygens in Holland, Leibnitz in Prussia and Newton in England emerged in the second half of the seventeenth century. Calculus was invented and this mathematics allowed members of the elite to adopt a radical new view of nature with the motion of planets, projectiles and perhaps tinier particles viewed as mechanistic, as behaving in accord with formulas. Double-entry bookkeeping emerged in Italy about 1494. If the books of a business could be set out and balanced rationally to the satisfaction of many observers, so too the motion of observable things could satisfy an "accounting" principle: a certain amount of motion of a particular body corresponds to a specific amount of energy "used up."

And political thinking was evolving. The rationalizing of the social order by an appeal to divine design was giving way to new theories of a good social order. The divine right of members of the elite to ride rough-shod over the claims to dignity of ordinary persons was eroding in many places. Martin Luther challenged the rights of the prevailing Christian Church in 1517 to charge heavily for its granting of expiation of sins for ordinary people. His revolt represented a successful challenge to the prevailing social order. Other challenges percolated underground. Locke, an empirically-thinking political theorist, provided a blueprint for a new social order in Britain. The Industrial Revolution did not develop in arid soil.

A larger town had an elite and numerous lesser folk. Elites lived in centers with many underlings who could show deference and gratitude. Less exalted places were nodes on trading routes or places where surpluses from farms could be marketed. Economic development was the phenomenon of making living standards (shelter, food, clothing) higher for the mass of people outside of the elites. Strangely enough, the roots of the revolution in economic outcomes for ordinary people are to be found in towns and hamlets of north-central England around 1740. In these places the mechanization of the production of cotton thread started. Suddenly cotton fabric became easily accessible to ordinary people in Britain. The price of cotton cloth declined by about 90 percent between 1795 and 1830. Then iron production became much more efficient. Output at the famous Darby works rose from 81 tons per year in 1709 to 4,632 tons in 1850. Energy-efficient steam engines began powering small factories all over England. A Newcomen engine (1705) burned 45 pounds of coal in order to generate 1 horse-power of energy. In the later nineteenth century, just one pound of coal could yield the same energy. For centuries factory owners had linked production to low-cost energy sources, typically rivers and streams with a good flow of water. The Romans harnessed water-flows with water-wheels. Thus the linking of production in a small factory to a steam engine was not a huge leap. Nevertheless historians have not documented a rapid revolution in the powering of factories by steam in England or elsewhere. To characterize the Industrial Revolution as one of steam-power adoption for production is overly simplistic. The adoption of new technologies is a complicated process. Steam engines were used for decades to pump water out of mines in England before they began to be used to power small factories. Considerable improvement in the reliability and efficiency of steam engines was required before they were taken up widely.

Railways and steam boats were developed in the 1840s, and cities grew rapidly; the sizes of families of working people were reduced and the incomes of ordinary people in England finally registered a significant improvement around 1850. Urbanization was a significant dimension of the Industrial Revolution and one might say that once the Industrial Revolution got started, urbanization became a significant supporting phenomenon, but oddly enough cities, either ancient or recently big, cannot claim to have spawned "the industrial revolution." Large cities existed in some places and no industrial revolution followed. For an industrial revolution to become rooted in a society, the evolution of some towns to relatively large cities was probably a necessary condition. One can probably assert with some high degree of confidence that without large-scale urbanization during the Industrial Revolution, the nascent revolution would have died out just as many previous mini industrial revolutions had in fact done. We noted above that in the United States "total population grew twelvefold between 1800 and 1890 while those living in cities increased an astonishing eighty-seven times" (Appleby 2010; p. 197).

Up to 1800, Paris and Naples were among the three largest cities in Europe. London went from being seventeenth in 1500 to second in 1650 and then almost tripled in size up to 1800.[3] Amsterdam moved from seventh place in terms of population in 1650 to fifth place in 1800. Venice fell from fourth place in 1500 to fifth place in 1650 and down to twelfth place in 1800. Remarkably, Manchester appears in the 30 largest cities in Europe by 1800, at twenty-second place (de Long and Schleifer 1993). This indicates how advanced the Industrial Revolution was in England by 1800. Manchester was the center of the new mechanized textile industry and large-scale mechanization would have taken hold sometime after 1800. Though the mechanization of producing cotton thread was a major breakthrough and is associated with the name of Richard Arkwright and 1768, mechanization of cotton cloth production (weaving of cotton thread) came well after 1800. When we think of Manchester and the Industrial Revolution, we usually think of huge rooms with loud clacking weaving machines.

London was clearly a special settlement by the later part of the eighteenth century, being almost twice the size of the next largest city in Europe. It was in 1798 that Robert Malthus wrote his famous treatise on population growth and general immiserization. He could easily have been dismayed at having to move about in the large, dense settlement that London had become by the late 1790s.

London in 1800

London became then the first very large city of the industrial age. How did this come about? London had many things going for it. It was the seat of government. Governments need civil servants, military chiefs and buildings for Parliament and the royals. London worked well as a port, in spite of the tricky manoeuvering required of sailing vessels to reach its docks up the Thames River. London grew rapidly because ordinary working people from other parts of Britain migrated into it because their prospects were seen by them to be better there. It would be wrong to argue that incomes of farming people in eighteenth-century England were in decline and excess labor was driven off the land. Considerable research indicates that British agriculture was commercially based and open to technical improvements during the eighteenth century. It must have been that prospects in London and Manchester looked good for village folk and they responded by relocating. Eric Jones (2010) has documented the hollowing out of small-scale industrial activity in villages south of London during the eighteenth century. Presumably London and Birmingham and Manchester could accommodate these industrial activities more effectively (at larger scales) and the enterprises in the growing cities out-competed the older, smaller-scale counterparts in the towns and villages.

We know from the books of Charles Dickens (1812–1870) and the movies and television shows based on them that living conditions in London for working people were most slum-like in the first half of the nineteenth century. Proper big-city sewers were not developed in London until 1858. Safe drinking water was not easy to come by. The Thames River was a scary, polluted watercourse until well into the twentieth century. Observers document the shorter lifespans of working people in London compared to their counterparts in smaller settlements. Working people may have planned to earn some money in the larger places and to return to their villages in later years. Following cholera outbreaks and "The Great Stink" of 1858, work on a proper sewer system got under way. Engineer Joseph Bazalgette got some 82 miles of large tunnel-pipes dug and these connect to more than 1,000 miles of street sewers. Security was improved with the introduction of police ("Bobbies" named for Sir Robert Peel) in 1829. Gas lighting for streets in the fancier parts of London arrived in 1807. Of course, London was blanketed in dense fogs until the 1950s. It was the burning of "dirty coal" in the fireplaces and stoves of homes that created the conditions for the famous fogs. The steady increase in population made London difficult for a working person to live in but at the same time as the place for a person to migrate to in the hope of a more prosperous living. By 1800 London was already huge by European standards and economically vibrant. And the Industrial Revolution was just getting under way.

Around 1740, an inquisitive traveller might well have selected Italy as the place where an industrial revolution was about to unfold. It had large cities (Naples, Milan, Venice) and factories, powered with water-wheels, producing silk yarn. Venice had been the center of a textile industry for more than 200 years. It had a deep culture of commerce and political openness. What was missing, or what did England have that Italy did not? de Long and Schleifer (1993) point to politico-social differences. They indicate that the rule of law prevailed in Britain while Italy had fallen into the hands of autocratic rulers. This line of reflection deserves much consideration. But we should add that England, particularly London–Newcastle, had a coal culture. London, down south, was a primary market for Newcastle's coal. Coal mining became linked to the development of steam engines and of iron smelting. The three distinguishing features of the early part of the Industrial Revolution were the factoryization of cotton production, the development of steam power for pumping water and powering mills, and the improving of the way iron was smelted. Italy may have been a world leader in the development of mechanized spinning mills, and England in fact borrowed some of Italy's cutting-edge technology, but the development of cotton spinning factories in England turned out to be just a piece of a larger jigsaw puzzle.

Cities in England (London, Birmingham, Manchester, Liverpool and Newcastle) grew rapidly as the Industrial Revolution took off. Birmingham became a center for metal working. Its population doubled to 147,000 between 1801 and 1831 and then doubled again over the next 30 years. There was an area, for example, with many tiny "factories" doing the manufacture of guns and parts of guns. Cities often had neighborhoods which housed small factories each specialized in a similar product. The textile industry was centered in Manchester. Its population doubled to 142,000 between 1801 and 1831. Liverpool became the dominant port for the upper industrial region. Newcastle had coal nearby and for centuries was a coal exporting port. London became both the central commercial center (finance and trade contracting) and the center of diversified industry. It is not an exaggeration to say that the booming cities of England sucked industrial activity from the cottages and villages into new factories. The expanding cities drew productive activity into themselves and were able to get along more with "own production" rather than imported goods. City bigness made this process of spawning "own production" easier because a bigger city meant a larger "own market" for a firm and supplying a larger market often went hand-in-hand with the exploitation of scale economies. There seems to be no doubt that the co-option of the activities of other towns and villages was significantly abetted by scale economies associated with those activities. Urban industrial expansion was a virtuous cycle of the drawing-in of an activity, followed by the drawing in of activities linked to that activity. Costs associated with transportation and organization could be economized on as related activities agglomerated in one place.

Import substitution by larger cities

Often, as a city grows, commodity j which was being imported gets to be produced locally or in that city. This saves on the transportation costs associated with importation. Hence there are always transportation cost savings waiting to be exploited. But the scale of production is crucial. For a small town to have a factory for commodity j, it must be able to compete on price with the importer of j and typically a small town lacks a market size to support a competitive production facility. Import substitution typically goes together with adequate local market size and market size is generally linked to city size itself. City growth both drives import substitution and is driven by import substitution. This process of a place taking on more production facilities with largeness implies that larger towns and cities will be more self-sufficient, will have a large variety of commodities produced within their boundaries. Some of these highly variegated commodities will be final, produced for households, and some will be intermediate, produced for local firms and governments. We turn to a model of a place with a larger population having a wider range of towns with different populations (a layering of towns, if you will) and larger towns housing producers specializing in a wider range of commodities. One might think of a series of snap-shots at different decades. The rural area starts with many farms and groups of farms with a small service town. A larger population is associated with larger service towns specialized in a new commodity which is sold down to the smaller towns as well as to the farmers. One of the reasons that the new larger town is larger is because it has within itself a small service town, as with a smaller doll inside a larger Russian doll. Our model involves adding a new layer of larger towns in a sequence, as the population of the "nation" is growing over decades. Of particular interest is the growing complexity of the industrial structure of the larger towns as they are added to a growing hierarchy. Growing complexity can be summarized in the phrase: more import substitution of activities has taken place in the larger towns. We start with a service town surrounded by s farms. This service town supplies, say, beer (commodity 1) to each of its own N_1 residents, plus the s farmers. It takes $\widehat{L}_1(N_1)$ workers to do the supplying. Hence $\widehat{L}_1(N_1)=\alpha_1[N_1+s]$. Larger towns have more commodities produced in them or have more layers of workers. Let us consider some possibilities, starting with small towns. The solution for the city sizes proceeds as follows. (An upward recursion is required for a city in a system of order greater than 1.)

For a hierarchy of order 1 (the town produces one commodity, say beer, and farmers are producing farm goods on the s farms), we have

$$\widehat{L}_1(N_1)=\alpha_1[N_1+s],$$

and the basic population-size equation is $N_1=\alpha_1[N_1+s]$, with s exogenous. Recall that $\widehat{L}_1(N_1)$ is the labor required to satisfy N_1+s demanders and commodity 1 is the only "higher order" commodity in our system. The solution gives us value N_1^*. See Figure 6.1.

We now consider a system with a larger population, a system with farms and small service towns plus a new larger town, producing a new commodity for its own population, the population of small service towns and the population of farmers. We call this new system a hierarchy of order 2. For a hierarchy of order 2, we have the labor required for producing commodity 2 in the new large town in

$$\widehat{L}_2(N_2)=\alpha_2[N_2+s+2(N_1^*+s)]$$

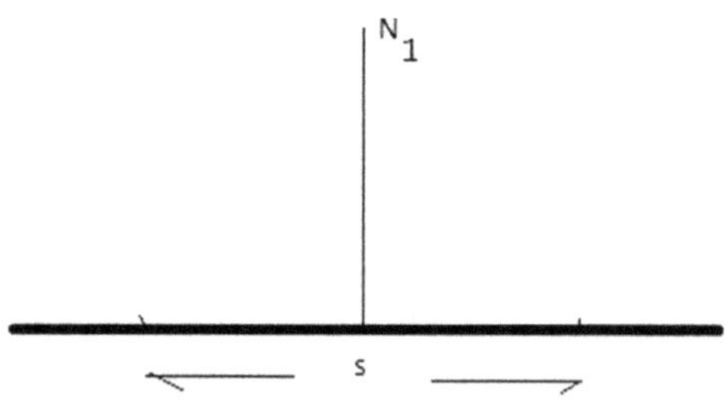

Figure 6.1 A service town with N_1 people serving an area with s farmers.

for all demanders in the hierarchy. This new large town is producing both its own new commodity to the system plus the "old" commodity 1, to its own subset of demanders. The population of N_2 will be

$$\begin{aligned} N_2 &= \widehat{L}_2(N_2) + \widehat{L}_1(N_2) \\ &= \alpha_2[N_2 + s + 2(N_1^* + s)] \\ &\quad + \alpha_1[N_2 + s], \end{aligned}$$

an equation in N_2 which once solved yields N_2^*. See Figure 6.2.

For a hierarchy of order three, we have

$$\widehat{L}_3(N_3) = \alpha_3[N_3 + s + 2(N_1^* + s) + 2\{N_2^* + s + 2(N_1^* + s)\}]$$

as the labor required to produce commodity 3 for the system. The population of N_3 will be

$$\begin{aligned} N_3 &= \widehat{L}_3(N_3) + \widehat{L}_2(N_3) + \widehat{L}_1(N_3) \\ &= \alpha_3[N_3 + s + 2(N_1^* + s) + 2\{N_2^* + s + 2(N_1^* + s)\}] \\ &\quad + \alpha_2[N_3 + s + 2(N_1^* + s)] \\ &\quad + \alpha_1[N_3 + s], \end{aligned}$$

an equation in N_3 which yields solution N_3^*. See Figure 6.3.

And so on for N_4 in a fourth-order hierarchy, N_5 in a fifth-order hierarchy, etc. For the total population of the hierarchy, we simply substitute the solved population values in the right side of L_1 above for a first-order hierarchy, of L_2 above for a second-order hierarchy, of L_3 above for a third-order hierarchy, etc.

A kth-order hierarchy has its populations defined by parameters $s, \alpha_1, \alpha_2, \ldots, \alpha_k$. We solve our system on a line with $k = 10$. Our parameter choice is $s = 1, \alpha_1 = 0.12, \alpha_2 = 0.11, \alpha_3 = 0.10, \alpha_4 = 0.08, \alpha_5 = 0.06, \alpha_6 = 0.04, \alpha_7 = 0.03, \alpha_8 = 0.02, \alpha_9 = 0.01$ and $\alpha_{10} = 0.005$. See Table 6.1 for the numbers of towns of various orders or types in our solved system.

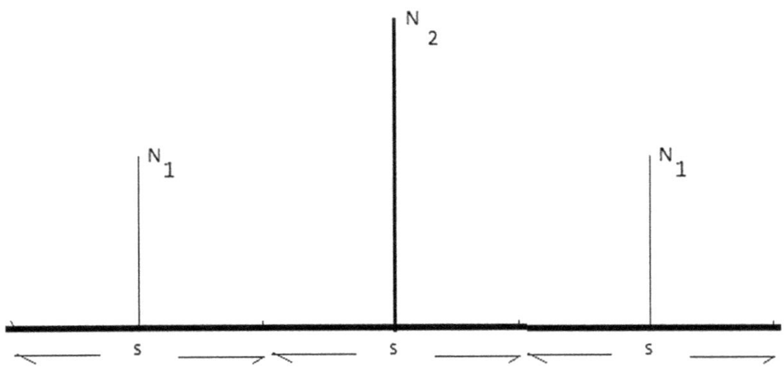

Figure 6.2 A hierarchy of two types of towns. The central service town (a) has a smaller service town nestled inside it serving the first-order commodity to s farmers plus the N_2 town residents and (b) is serving a second-order commodity to all residents of the system of towns and farms.

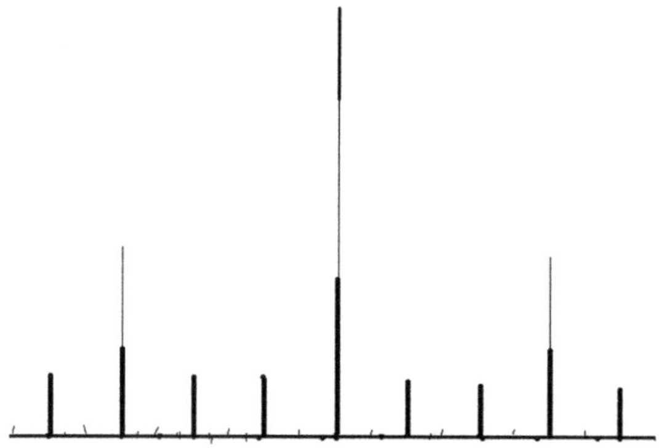

Figure 6.3 A hierarchy of three types of towns. The horizontal line comprises nine farming regions, each with *s* farmers. In the center of each farming region is a town. Vertical lines indicate population size. Second-order towns produce two commodities (workers indicated by heavy and then light lines). The central or third-order town produces three commodities. Produced commodities flow down to market specific "areas." Farm product flows up to town people.

Table 6.1 Number of towns in various hierarchies[a]

	N_1	N_2	N_3	N_4	N_5	N_6	N_7	N_8	N_9	N_{10}	*Population*
Size	0.136	0.623	2.37	7.83	20.96	60.4	156.4	370.2	713.4	1,246.2	
1st	1	0	0	0	0	0	0	0	0	0	1.1
2nd	2	1	0	0	0	0	0	0	0	0	3.9
3rd	6	2	1	0	0	0	0	0	0	0	13.4
4th	18	6	2	1	0	0	0	0	0	0	45.8
5th	54	18	6	2	1	0	0	0	0	0	150.4
6th	162	54	18	6	2	1	0	0	0	0	490.7
7th	486	162	54	18	6	2	1	0	0	0	1,568.1
8th	1,458	486	162	54	18	6	2	1	0	0	4,918.1
9th	4,374	1,458	486	162	54	18	6	2	1	0	15,097.3
10th	13,122	4,374	1,458	486	162	54	18	6	2	1	45,824.7

Note
a A program in the MAPLE software was used to solve the recursive system.

For each of these systems of cities there are a number of farming areas, this number corresponding to the total number of cities in the respective system. Thus a first-order system has one *s* area, a second-order system has three *s* areas, a third-order system has nine *s* areas and so on. The total population of a system or hierarchy includes all residents of cities in the system plus the respective number of farmers, residing on the *s* subareas. Observe that the population increases as a new layer is added, by a factor of about three. We "predicted" this earlier. The row "Size" contains the population of the largest city in the respective hierarchy. The population of any town lower down in a hierarchy corresponds to the population of the largest town in that lower-down system. Hence the largest city in the tenth-order hierarchy has a population of 1,246.2 residents and in this same hierarchy a fourth-order town has a population of 7.83 residents. The tenth-order hierarchy has 45,824.7 residents and 19,683 towns as well as 19,683 farm subareas. The fourth-order hierarchy has a total population of 45.8 residents and 27 towns.

Table 6.2 Town size and linked rank (from computation)

Size	1,246.2	713.4	370.2	156.4	60.4	20.9	7.8	2.4	0.62	0.14
"Rank"	1	3	9	27	81	243	729	2,187	6,561	19,683

The Pareto distribution asks for $x_i = \ln N_i$ on the x-axis, with N_i a population and $y_i = \ln Z_i$ on the y-axis (Z_i is the number of towns with N_i or more ("rank")) and relates these two variables as

$$y_i = a + bx_i \qquad (i = 1, \ldots, n).$$

The rank-size rule (Zipf's Law) asks for b to be approximately unity in value. The relevant schedule of points for our tenth-order hierarchy is shown in Table 6.2.

When we take logarithms of these values and regress y on x values we obtain $a = 8.404$ and $b = -1.0715$, with $r^2 = 0.9835$. The plot of these logged values is slightly concave. Clearly there is an "excess" of small towns in our system and this is preventing us from getting slope $-b$ closer to unity.[4]

One can of course get an exact fit with the Pareto distribution by pre-cooking our parameter values $\alpha_1, \alpha_2, \ldots, \alpha_{10}$. We selected our values so that (a) the sum was less than unity (since they are functioning as expenditure shares; see below) and (b) that $\alpha_j > \alpha_{j+1}$ (higher order goods have smaller expenditure shares or are in a sense less "essential" to the household; think of "symphony concerts" as the highest order commodity).

Incomes, prices and technology

We can introduce a wage, the same for all workers, and get

$$w\widehat{L}_k = \alpha_k w \Pi_k.$$

This implies that $w\widehat{L}_k$ is an expenditure value and α_k is measuring the share of total income $w\Pi_k$, being spent on commodity k. Here Π_k is total population in the system of towns. Hence the seemingly strange α_i coefficients introduced by Beckmann and McPherson (1970) have a standard interpretation. If we make a larger addition to the model (a technology of production), we have

$$\widehat{L}_k a_{kL} = Q_k$$

for Q_k the total production of commodity k, where a_{kL} is the amount of commodity k produced per unit of labor L. The a_{kL}'s are textbook Leontief coefficients. We take as exogenous the values of $a_{0L}, a_{1L}, a_{2L}, \ldots, a_{kL}$. Commodity 0 is the good produced on farms and in part exported to towns up the hierarchy. Then

$$\widehat{L}_k p_k a_{kL} = p_k Q_k$$
$$\text{and } w\widehat{L}_k = p_k Q_k,$$

with $w = p_k a_{kL}$. This is compatible with each person having a Cobb–Douglas utility function, $U = q_0^{\alpha_0} q_1^{\alpha_1} \ldots q_k^{\alpha_k}$, with $q_i = Q_i / \Pi_k$. It makes sense to assume, as we do, that

$\alpha_0+\alpha_1+\cdots+\alpha_k=1$. We can normalize with $p_0=1$ and solve for w in

$$\widehat{L}_0 a_{0L}=Q_0,$$
$$\widehat{L}_0=k\times s$$
$$\text{and } Q_0=\alpha_0 w\Pi_k.$$

Then prices, $p_1, p_2, \ldots, p_k$ follow from $w\widehat{L}_i = p_i Q_i$, $i = 1, 2, \ldots, k$. There is a complete fixed coefficient economics narrative for the Beckmann–McPherson model. This is interesting but the "inverse" is what economists are interested in. Given the decentralized decision-making of households and firms, when does a Christaller or Beckmann–McPherson hierarchy emerge as the equilibrium geography?

The clustering tendency (geometry and distribution costs)

It is pretty clear that some combination of scale economies in production (only large cities are able to produce certain goods (at low unit cost)) and transportation costs (service towns with a commodity essential to farmers are located near the farmers) is playing a central role in the causal chain that results in a Christaller hierarchy. It turns out that geometry is also playing a central role here. Consider a simple system, as in Figure 6.2, for example.

Let us assume that we have our three farming areas, each with a service town and a town's commodity 1 being produced to serve each "local" town and farm area. We assume that transportation costs are "high" and there are scale economies preventing each farmer from producing her own commodity 1. These farm areas and service towns are taken as essentially exogenous in our analysis here. Consider now the production of good 2. Given scale economies, we assume that only one town, of three possibilities, will produce this commodity. Clearly if either "end" service town is the production center and all citizens in the economy consume positive quantities of a similar magnitude, distribution costs (transportation or delivery costs) will be higher than if good 2 were produced by the central town. Geometry and distribution friction is dictating a central location for the production of good 2. This argument implies more "centering" of production as each new commodity with "large" scale economies is added to the system. The Christaller hierarchy has this agglomeration or additional centering mechanism underlying it. Roughly speaking, commodities with larger scale properties should be "more centered," geographically, in order to keep distribution costs in the system relatively low. The volume of distribution costs is a function of the geometrical arrangement of places of production.[5]

More complicated geographies

In place of the line as our geography, we can assume that our geography is two lines on the plane intersecting at right angles. The principal town will be at the point of intersection. Consider an earlier third-order system on each line (nine s subareas on each line). One can see that labor required is now

$$\widehat{L}_1(N_3)=\alpha_1[N_3+2s],$$
$$\widehat{L}_2(N_3)=\alpha_2[N_3+2s+4[N_1+s]],$$
$$\widehat{L}_3(N_3)=\alpha_3[N_3+2s+4(N_1^*+s)+4\{N_2^*+s+2(N_1^*+s)\}].$$

Though these labor requirements resemble those for the case of the line, they are different and would result in a rather different recursion of populations for the largest city, upward. This system would be more peaked, since the largest city has a much larger market area for the highest order good, as well as for its other export goods.

We could of course pursue a similar analysis for three intersecting straight lines on the plane. This would take us closer to a hexagonal hierarchical system. The nature of the geography is clearly relevant for the nature of the shape of the corresponding hierarchy of cities.

Simultaneous lateral and vertical growth

Observe in Table 6.1 that as a new layer is added to the system and the base of small service towns expands "laterally" at each end of the linear geography, the population of the system expands by a factor of about 2.2 (the growth rate declines uniformly from 2.545 to 2.033). This is approximately proportional growth in population in a relatively complicated system of cities going through both lateral expansion (the addition of new subsystems in each wing of the system) and vertical expansion (the addition of a new dominant central city with a new commodity). Early modern neoclassical growth theory (Solow 1956) was built up from an economy experiencing proportional exogenous growth in its population (labor force). These early models postulated an exogenous savings rate and derived a benchmark case, proportional growth in both the capital stock and labor force, as the one of interest. The fact that we have approximately proportional growth in our population as the system expands suggests that we could think about adding savings behavior and durable capital to our hierarchy model. The aim would be to develop a benchmark case with proportional growth in both population and the durable capital stock. Technical change in such a system would be reflected in a new commodity being produced at the center as the system expanded.

As we have observed, central to big city agglomeration in this Beckmann–McPherson model is the possession of a size or scale by a city that allows it to produce efficiently any commodity that a lower-order (smaller) city is "specialized" in, while the reverse does not obtain. Hence large cities have active production of all commodities except agriculture whereas smaller towns do more importing, generally from a larger city. This somewhat simplistic model of a system of cities (scale effects and transportation costs implicit) illustrates effectively the way in which larger cities have a larger fraction of their workers in non-basic activities than do smaller cities. In the words of one commentator, larger cities have more internal trade. Note that under constant returns to scale in the production of goods 1, 2 and 3 (no implicit scale economies) each farmer would be self-sufficient. There would be no goods shipped and there would be no towns. In this framework, the existence of cities, as distinct from just self-sufficient farmers, requires scale economies in production.

Glaeser and Kohlhase suggest that we view population distribution in the United States in terms of eight "great centers": the Boston–Washington corridor, the Los Angeles area, the San Francisco Bay area, the Portland–Seattle corridor, Chicago, Atlanta, Miami and southeastern Texas. "Each of these areas is relatively compact and it seems likely that altogether these areas will continue to attract an increasing share of the US population" (G&K 2004; p. 219). It is reasonable to view each of these conurbations as dominant, diversified top-tier places (first-order centers) essentially serving a large regional population with high-order "exports" such as finance, insurance, legal work, advertising, specialized medical care and entertainment. If one were to divide up the continental United States (excluding Alaska) into six approximately equal sized rectangles, one would have the

Boston–Washington corridor serving the northeast area, Chicago, the north-central area and the Portland–Seattle corridor, the northwest area. The San Francisco Bay area could be assisting in serving the northwest region. The southwest area would be served by Los Angeles, aided by the San Francisco Bay area; the south central would be served by southeast Texas; and the southeast area would be served by two "centers," namely Miami and Atlanta. Each of the six areas would of course be relatively self-sufficient in the sense that if a household wished to purchase something, the thing would be available within its "local" conurbation.

The Economist argues that the five English cities of Leeds, Manchester, Liverpool, Sheffield and Birmingham form a natural global metropolis with a population similar to that for Chicago alone and yet per capita GDP for Chicago is about twice the value of that in the five-city collection.[6] *The Economist* blames the poor economic performance of the five-city metropolis on poor transport links, including roads, and on a fragmented local government. Cities today, they argue, must prosper or stagnate, based on how well they foster connections between people and firms. It is the rapid flow of information within cities that is "the new dynamo." London turns out to have a per capita GDP close to Chicago's.

A two-city type hierarchy under Ricardian assumptions

The Ricardian model is amenable to yielding a hierarchy like that above. The basic Ricardian model assumes that the location of the trading entities is fixed. This might be referred to as immobile inputs. It turns out that this fairly natural assumption for the location of nations engaged in trade is more controversial for the case of towns and cities within a nation engaged in trade. However, if we are willing to assume the locations of towns and cities as given, we can generate a simple hierarchy of towns engaged in trade without invoking increasing returns to scale or transportation costs. The key ingredients of the model are the assumptions of towns existing at fixed locations and workers in these towns exhibiting distinct relative productive advantages.

We start then with a central town and two outlying towns which are about the same size, both producing two outputs, in a trading relationship. We will assume that the two outlying towns are identical. Hence both will be exporting the same good in the same amount to the central town. Both towns are relatively small and are specialized in production.

See Figure 6.4. Let us assume this equilibrium obtains. (We leave open the question of why "productivity" of a worker in each outlying town is different from the productivity of a worker in the central town.) We assume tastes (indifference curves) the same for every person in the economy.

We change things now by simply making the central town large (shift its production possibility in parallel, outwards from abc to ABc in Figure 6.4). There will be some size at which goods prices in the three-town economy become those prevailing in the new central, large town.

Hence the two small towns will continue to specialize and export their particular produced good, x_2, to the central, large town but in our Figure 6.4 the large town will now be diversified in production (producing both products) and will be exporting its non-import, x_1, to the two outlying towns. We have then created a hierarchy of two types of towns, a central one diversified in production and outliers specialized in production. Relative size-change alone led to the change from "ordinary" Ricardian trade among the towns to "hierarchical" trade, a central large town diversified and two outlying towns specialized. In this change, the smaller towns end up reaping the full gains from being in trade while the central town can be said to be indifferent between trade and no-trade.

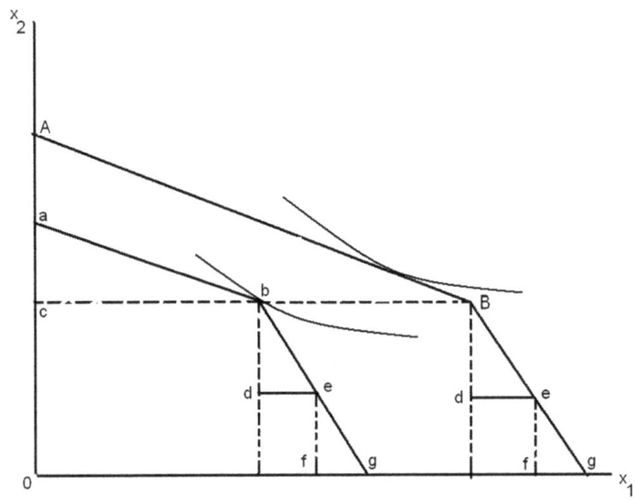

Figure 6.4 Three towns trading. Three small towns with production possibility schedules abc, bde and efg. Two commodities. "Tastes" at b imply each town specialized in production. We expand the population of the first town to have production possibilities schedule ABc. It becomes diversified, producing some of both commodities.

The size change can be said to have created "import substitution" in the large town. It was specialized in x_1 when it was "small" and it became diversified when it became relatively large. Bigness in this case led to diversification, a familiar phenomenon we see all about us for large cities. This easy construction of a hierarchy of cities in trade turned on the assumption of fixed location of active places. In a sense, fixed locations and differences in the "productivities" of workers have worked as substitutes for scale economies and transportation costs.

Intermediate goods, scale and transportation costs

Though the model underlying Figure 6.4 of a system of cities illustrates well the advantage of size in supporting diversity in productive activity, it is somewhat old-fashioned in the sense that all goods are final to consumers. A distinctive feature of large cities and their diverse productive structures is their "ability" to support the production of goods going into the production of final goods, namely intermediate goods. We consider this the salient feature of large, modern cities: the ability to economize on transportation costs on imports by importing (having the firms relocate) the activities themselves (import substitution). Krugman and Venables (1996) consider two cities, each with a final and an intermediate good. When intercity transportation costs are high, they are both self-sufficient (no trade). At lower transportation costs an agglomerated equilibrium can arise with one city doing both activities and exporting some product to the other. We would emphasize that once agglomeration gets underway in one place, scale economies "kick in" and suck in more economic activity to the larger city. Scale economies can trump transportation costs and contribute to agglomeration, via the economizing "by the city" on the transportation costs that have been eliminated. More on this below.

The Krugman–Venables model is a member of a class of models (center-periphery models) which emerged from Krugman's 1991 article "Increasing Returns and Economic Geography" (Krugman 1991b). We turn to a detailed analysis of one member of the class, the Forslid–Ottaviano model (Forslid and Ottaviano 2003) in which scale economies and transportation costs play essential roles.[7] We take up the Krugman–Venables model later.

In the Forslid–Ottaviano model of two cities, unskilled workers are immobile and are employed in both the production of a simple good (handcrafted item) under constant returns to scale and a higher-order good produced in diverse types under increasing returns to scale. Skilled workers are costlessly mobile between the cities and work only in the production of the higher-order good (a manufactured product). This latter good is shipped between cities with positive transportation costs. Under reasonable assumptions, this model admits of more than one solution, including the possibility of all manufacturing activity being "agglomerated" in one city. This agglomerated entity will still be producing some of the simple good and thus we can have a two-city system, with the larger city diversified and shipping the higher-order good to the smaller city, and the smaller city specialized in producing only the simple good and in turn shipping some of the latter to the larger city. Thus, this model allows us to generate a rudimentary version of our system of cities, set out above but now with explicit scale economies and transportation costs.

These "scale economies" models descend from Chamberlin's monopolistic competition model, fleshed out in a modern form by Dixit and Stiglitz (1977). Dixit and Stiglitz proposed a utility function for a representative consumer of the following form:

$$u = x_0^{1-\mu} V^{\mu}, \text{ for } V^{\rho} = \sum_{i=1}^{n} x_i^{\rho},$$

where x_0 is an ordinary good while V is a composite, comprising n varieties or close substitutes. A consumer need not consume every variety in equilibrium but there will be a well-defined demand of the consumer for a variety in

$$x_i = \mu \left(\frac{p_i}{P}\right)^{-\rho} \frac{Y}{P} \text{ for } P^{1-\sigma} = \sum_{j=1}^{n} p_j^{1-\sigma}.$$

Here P is a price index which figures centrally in any analysis deriving from the Dixit–Stiglitz set-up. These demand functions "work" like the classic Chamberlinian demands: in equilibrium they will be tangent to the average cost schedule for declining average costs of production of x_i.

Since scale economies are the Hamlet of this drama, Dixit and Stiglitz postulate total costs: $C = F + cx$, for F fixed costs and c marginal costs. The analysis generally takes costs as the same for each variety. We sketch an equilibrium in Figure 6.5 for one variety. The Dixit–Stiglitz assumptions are introduced so that closed form calculations can be carried out in an analysis deriving directly from classical Chamberlinian thinking.

We turn to a two-city trading model (Forslid and Ottaviano). There are now two places with Dixit–Stiglitz demand set-ups. The ordinary good, X_i, in place i is our lower-order good, and A_i is the composite of closely substitutable varieties. Following Forslid and Ottaviano, there is a continuum of varieties in each place instead of a discrete "bundle." The hypothesis of a continuum ends up having no bearing on the subsequent analysis, however.

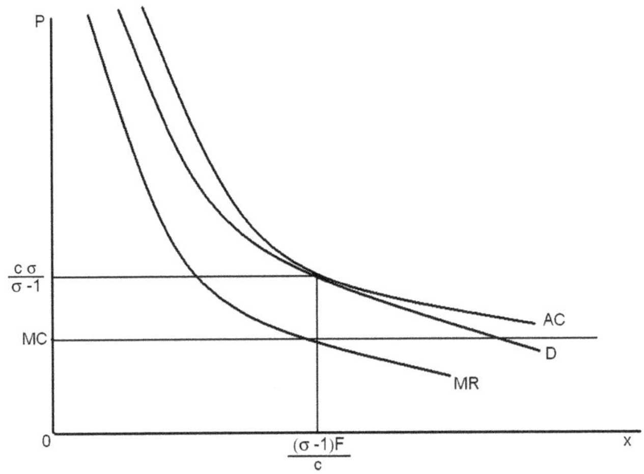

Figure 6.5 Chamberlin–Dixit–Stiglitz monopolistically competitive equilibrium.

We have

$$U_i = X_i^{\mu} A_i^{1-\mu}$$

$$\text{for } 0 < \mu < 1 \text{ and } X_i = \left(\int_{s \in N} d_i(s)^{(\sigma-1)/\sigma} ds \right)^{\sigma/(\sigma-1)},$$

where X_i is person i's consumption of manufactured goods (simultaneously many varieties) and A_i is her consumption of the lower-order, freely-traded good. N defines the number of varieties of the manufactured good and a type belongs to a continuum; n_i is the number of types (varieties) produced in city i, with $n_1 + n_2 = N$; and σ is both the elasticity of demand for any variety and the elasticity of substitution between any two varieties.

Returns to scale in the production of a variety appear in the total cost function for variety s in city i in

$$TC_i(s) = \alpha w_i + \beta x_i(s) w_i^L$$

for w_i the wage of a skilled worker in city i and w_i^L the wage of an unskilled worker. Since $x_i(s)$ is output of variety s in city i, we have unskilled workers tied up in the variable portion of the cost function while skilled workers are linked to the fixed part of the cost function.

Central to the analysis are transportation costs on a manufactured variety. Thus for $d_{ij}(s)$ shipped from i to j, $\tau d_{ij}(s)$ must be produced in i. Note that τ exceeds unity and this implies that a fraction of production melts away on the trip from i to j. Each region has L_i unskilled workers with $L = L_1 + L_2$ and H_i skilled workers with $H = H_1 + H_2$. These latter are mobile and are distributed by the equalization of real income for a representative in each city (costless relocation in response to a real-income gain). For the time being, we take the number of unskilled workers in each region as fixed and the same.

Utility maximization by workers and profit maximization by firms yields the following wage for skilled workers in city i, given H_1 and H_2 temporarily fixed:

$$w_i = \left[\frac{(\mu/\sigma)[L/2]}{1-(\mu/\sigma)}\right] \frac{2\phi H_i + [1-(\mu/\sigma)+(1+(\mu/\sigma))]\phi^2]H_j}{\phi(H_i^2+H_j^2)+[1-(\mu/\sigma)+(1+(\mu/\sigma))\phi^2]H_iH_j}.$$

Skilled worker relocation will cease when

$$W(h,\phi) \equiv \mu^\mu(1-\mu)^{1-\mu}\left[\frac{w_1}{P_1^\mu}-\frac{w_2}{P_2^\mu}\right]=0,$$

where $\frac{w_i}{P_i^\mu}$ is the "real wage" for a skilled worker in city i and P_i is a price index capturing the cost of living in city i. These two indexes are defined in

$$P_1 = \frac{\beta\sigma}{\sigma-1}\left(\frac{H}{\alpha}\right)^{1/(1-\sigma)}[h+\phi(1-h)]^{1/(1-\sigma)}$$

and

$$P_2 = \frac{\beta\sigma}{\sigma-1}\left(\frac{H}{\alpha}\right)^{1/(1-\sigma)}[1-h+\phi h]^{1/(1-\sigma)}.$$

for $\phi=\tau^{1-\sigma}$ and $h=H_1/H$. With these expressions available, we can obtain an expression for skilled worker indifference between cities, namely $W(h,\phi)=0$, for

$$W(h,\phi)=\frac{\Omega V(h,\phi)}{\phi(h^2+(1-h)^2)+(1-(\mu/\sigma)+(1+(\mu/\sigma))\phi^2)h(1-h)},$$

for $\Omega=[\eta\mu L\alpha^{\mu/(1-\sigma)}(\sigma-1)^\mu]/[2(\sigma-\mu)H^{(1+\mu-\sigma)/(1-\sigma)}(\alpha\beta)^\mu]$ and

$$V(h,\phi)=\frac{2\phi h+[1-(\mu/\sigma)+(1+(\mu/\sigma))\phi^2](1-h)}{[h+\phi(1-h)]^{\mu/(1-\sigma)}} - \frac{2\phi(1-h)+[1-(\mu/\sigma)+(1+(\mu/\sigma))\phi^2]h}{[(1-h)+\phi h]^{\mu/(1-\sigma)}}.$$

The equation $W(h,\phi)=0$ should admit multiple solutions for reasonable parameter values, with some stable solutions highly asymmetric (much of the skilled labor and higher-order goods production in one region) when transportation costs are not too high. The principal result here is that each city is autarkic when transportation costs are high and trade opens up when transportation costs are not so high. The opening of trade often leads to asymmetric solutions appearing as returns to scale are exploited in one of the cities. Of additional interest is the study of when these asymmetric solutions are dynamically stable (not departed from under perturbations). We omit consideration of dynamics here. One might argue, however, that Krugman's contribution was to graft some rudimentary dynamics on to a model that was standard in location theory, one of scale economies and geographic concentration.

Intermediate goods and scale advantage

The above analysis involves trade in two final goods, one simple and the other involving varieties, each of the latter produced with increasing returns to scale. In our view quintessential early urban growth involved the massing of intermediate goods in certain cities, with the massing being initiated by a scale advantage in a particular place. That is, if one city is a bit bigger than another, its size advantage represents a potential scale advantage in producing for the larger local market and this attracts firms which can exploit a scale aspect of their technology. But the process is cumulative, because the exploitation of the scale aspect often means that these larger producers can also export to other places with a bit of a cost advantage.[8] Once a community is large it becomes very difficult for a smaller community to catch up. To catch up the smaller place usually needs large markets in order to get its own costs down and the larger place can usually service any market which the smaller place tries for. It is not crazy to argue that a central focus of urban economics should be on why small cities are able to prosper and sometimes actually grow. This view considers large cities to be in some sense the top predators. Krugman and Venables (1996) developed a model of co-option of an intermediate good by a "country" that exploits scale economies. We are viewing the country as a city. Each of two places produces varieties of a differentiated product under increasing returns to scale. When transportation costs decline, in the words of Krugman and Venables (1996; p. 961) a producer:

> in a country with a strong initial position in some industry may find itself with an advantage that cumulates over time. Producers of final goods will find that the country with the larger industry supports a larger base of intermediate producers, which gives them low enough costs to export to other markets; producers of intermediate goods will find that it is to their advantage to concentrate their production near the large final good industry. Thus each industry will tend to concentrate in one of the countries... This is a simple and intuitively plausible story, but it is not easy to formalize.

The Krugman–Venables model has two places, two goods produced, each with multiple varieties and each under increasing returns to scale. Each composite becomes partly final in the production period and partly intermediate. Each good is subject to melting (transportation costs) during shipment between the two places. Labor is the only primary input and is in a fixed quantity in each place. We omit details of the derivations. Dynamics end up involving worker migration between sectors and the final equilibrium has wages the same in each sector in each place. The analysis of these labor re-allocations is done with numerical examples. The central result is that with "high" transportation costs, each place is autarkic and with lower transportation costs, trade becomes efficient. Scale economies "kick in" with trade and one place can become a large producer of one commodity and supply both places with its requirements. Each place can become the large supplier to the economy. The "American" outcome has "highly localized industries serving the whole continental market" (Krugman–Venables 1996; p. 964). Initial symmetry is compatible with a highly asymmetric stable "final" outcome. Each place trades in final goods but has most of its intermediate input located near its final goods production. This is a rendering of city growth by "co-option" of the production of intermediate goods.

Separation of high-level decision-making from direct production activity

A feature of the early industrial revolution in the United States was the concentration of economic activity in burgeoning small and a few not-so-small cities. The populations of the cities grew and they in turn became stronger magnets for traditional and newer activities. Transportation was by sailing vessels and horse-drawn wagons. Sites near docks became centers of factory development. Then rail transportation arrived and dockside sites became better linked to inland suppliers and inland markets. Spur lines (sidings) from main rail lines became new sites for factories. Production activity became separated from some "head-office activity" (finance, legal work and marketing activity) for larger firms. Smaller firms would continue to have their "head offices" on the same site as their production activity. The centers of larger places became concentrated with law firms, marketing firms and financial specialists plus head-office activities for some of the larger firms. The people working in these central firms came to reside in enclaves, nascent suburbs, separated from the firms themselves.

The modern urban form had evolved by 1910. Cities in Europe had become larger before railways arrived and many developed with cramped centers—isolated patches of open space connected to each other by twisting narrow alleyways. In many of these, head-office activity and its allied specialties did not come to dominate the centers of cities. These activities, clustered in the CBDs of most North American cities, were more decentralized for European cities.

The three new forces that came to accentuate the separation of head-office and allied activities from production activities were the telephone, the truck with its internal combustion engine and mechanized personal transit. Residential activity became even more separated from production and head-office and allied activities because personal transportation allowed people to move about faster and at reasonable cost. Buses, subways and personal automobiles arrived. Reliable trucks made spread-out sites for production the natural form for factories and factories no longer needed to be linked to rail lines with a private spur-line. Factories around 1780 relied on waterwheels for power and they tended to be vertical in order to connect various machines to conveyor belts, all connected to the power from the waterwheel. When power was derived from electric motors, factories tended to the horizontal form. Telephones allowed managers of production facilities well away from head offices to feed information up to key executives and allowed executives to send orders down to the on-the-spot managers. One thinks of New York City becoming a center for head-office activity when railways and then oil companies were consolidated into huge corporations after say 1880. Then the Mohawk valley and the Erie Canal (Albany to Buffalo) came to house a string of towns with large manufacturing plants. The Buffalo area benefitted from the hydroelectricity that was developed at Niagara Falls. Other plants were set up in suburban New York City itself.

Central New York City became the center of clothes-making in the United States. Immigrants chose New York City to settle in and provided a disciplined, readily trained labor force. Clothes-making was carried out with workers close together at their sewing machines, often in low-rent spaces above the ground floor. Dozens of so-called sweat shops with women at sewing machines remained active in Manhattan for over a 100 years. Raymond Vernon (1972) argues that dress-makers prospered when they located close to button-makers, both groups in lower Manhattan. He argues that successful dress-makers, as well as button producers, had to be abreast of style changes. The dress-makers and button-producers had to be "on the spot" as new styles emerged.

Modern cities such as Atlanta, Denver and Phoenix continued to evolve, with much of head-office and allied activities in a CBD and production activities in spread-out establishments in suburban places. Now the latter get inputs and send outputs on large transport trucks. Suburbs have high-quality roads that accommodate large trucks. The relatively cheap land in the suburbs allows the firms locating there to acquire "extra" land for parking and low-cost parking makes the prospect of working in the suburbs more attractive to prospective employees. Between 2003 and 2013 Toronto shed 46,000 jobs in manufacturing and "created" 155,000 jobs in office and service-sector activities.[9] Near Toronto's center and on the main rail line is a large meat processing plant and yard which the municipality owned until 1960. The current owners are seeking a re-zoning ruling so that the site becomes available for the development of condominiums. The separation of head-office and allied activities from production activities has become sharper over the years. Communication has of course become better. Conference calls are common and many large firms have "studios" that allow conferees to be seen live on screens by other parties involved in the calls. Duranton and Puga (2005) present data indicating the more voluminous "sloughing off" of production activities to surrounding towns by firms in France between 1950 and 1990. Key decisions for these firms are made in offices in the CBDs of larger settlements. The cities exhibit a greater concentration of head-office jobs (management jobs) in centers as time passes.

This is part of a general trend: decision-making for the evolution of large companies takes place in city centers in tall buildings and production activity is hived off to places with lower wages for production workers and lower land costs for "spread-out" facilities. And as we have observed in recent decades, "shop-floor" jobs for many large American corporations have been hived off beyond the shores of the United States. Key decisions on product design, marketing and finance continue to be made in tall buildings in the centers of large American cities. Hands-on production activity is often carried out in factories in China, Taiwan and Malaysia. With regard to software production, the same key high-level decisions are made in the United States and the "grunt-work" is often placed in locations such as India.

The industrial revolution brought production (shop-floor) jobs from cottages, villages and towns into cities, often around port facilities or at least around access to port facilities. Improvements in transportation and then communication led to the geographic separation of the shop-floor jobs from the higher-level management jobs, with the latter tending to concentrate in the centers of cities—and more improvements in transportation and communication have led to more geographic separation. One of the transforming transportation innovations was containerization. A great variety of materials and packages could be placed in a metal box of a standard size and transportation of goods became the transportation of standardized containers. Trucks, barges, ships and trains were engineered to carry containers in an orderly fashion. Early development dates to the later 1950s. The introduction of containers resulted in significant improvements in the efficiency of handling freight at nodes such as sea-ports and rail-yards. A crane-lift no longer was customized for each motion. Now each crane-lift involves a standardized package. Breakage and theft were major problems in freight handling before container "packaging" became standardized. These problems were much reduced since a steel container could be made reasonably secure and a steel container represented a "skin" that protected the contents fairly well against routine breakage. There is also a fairly seamless flow of material and commodities between trucks, trains and ships since containers are easily shifted from one mode to another. One might have conjectured that railways would suffer from competition with modern trucks but this has not been the case. Trucking and rail-hauling have become integrated modes of transport for commodities. In 2003, the six largest container ports were in Asia. Rotterdam and Los Angeles were seventh and eighth (Levinson 2008; p. 273). Logistics is the term for the processing of inputs and products in transit between firms and between producers and consumers. Warehousing, careful management and low-cost transshipping are central to efficient logistics in a nation. China spends about twice as much (18 percent of GDP) as developed nations on logistics: trucking and goods flow there is demonstrably inefficient. Government officials have drawn up plans to boost efficiency in its logistics sector.[10]

The spread of truck transport, good highways and containerization has led to the suburbanization of manufacturing jobs in cities in North America. As Mills (1999 ; p. 2) puts it:

> These innovations made it economical to produce in suburban locations—free from high land prices, congestion, strong unions, high taxes, and burdensome regulations—while shipping inputs directly from, and outputs directly to, distant areas. There can be no doubt that the result has been enormously beneficial. Manufacturing dispersal has been little influenced by, but probably has promoted, population suburbanization.

Technical progress and cities

The claim is long-standing that it is in cities where inventive activity occurs. There are well-known exceptions to this position but let us accept the claim as generally valid. Like molecules of a confined gas dancing out their Brownian motions, it is felt that bright people need to spark off other bright people in somewhat random interactions to come up with inventive ideas. As Glaeser (2010; p. 9) observes: "The interaction of smart people in urban areas both enhances the development of person-specific human capital and increases the rate at which new ideas are formed." Density is needed for the interaction and people live in denser arrangements in cities. The way people connect in networks also matters. The micro-structure of productive inventive activity is of course hard to delineate. If it were easy, we would presumably see much more inventive activity. But putting bright people in larger places seems to help. Some universities produce imaginative and useful new knowledge and some of these are not in large places. But patenting is done mostly by people in larger settlements. On a state by state basis, California, New York, Texas and Washington lead in patenting activity per capita (Moretti 2012; p. 83). The first three are large in terms of population alone. These four states generate about half the patents in the United States per year and this rate is higher now than it was in the 1980s. A dimension of interest here is that if technical progress is the ultimate engine of rising living standards and this engine works better in urban places, can we develop a theory of inventive activity that derives somehow from urban-ness?

And if indeed technical progress is the driver of rising living standards it must be showing up in urban areas since that is where most people live. This raises the issue of the sectoral impact of technical progress. Do service industries benefit most from current technical progress? Or are shop-floor production activities benefitting most? Is it product design or product invention that is registering most technical progress or techniques for producing existing products? Baumol (1967) argued that services were experiencing slow or no technical progress relative to sectors producing more tangible commodities. The unbalanced nature of technical progress could be pointed to as an explanation of why municipal costs were creeping ever upward while no corresponding gain in productivity was being experienced. It is not clear whether the computer revolution or IT revolution more generally has in fact resulted in good gains in productivity in the services sector since Baumol first wrote about "unbalanced growth." There is no evidence that municipal governments have experienced easy times in balancing their revenues with expenditures in the Western World.

Tesla and Westinghouse and Niagara Falls

Electric power was first produced in Niagara Falls in huge quantities on August 26, 1895. The power was in turn first transmitted to Buffalo in November, 1896. Tesla was the lead engineer for the modern production of electricity in Niagara Falls and Westinghouse was the businessman behind the project. Edison, with his General Electric Company centered in Schenectady, New York, had been keen on doing the project but he was wedded to generating electricity in its DC form rather the AC form, the form to which Tesla had made major development contributions. The Niagara Falls project was innovative in many ways but generating AC power was a distinctive feature. Power to Buffalo was purchased by the company operating the city trolley system.

Subsequent work was split between the two great manufacturers, General Electric and Westinghouse. All the power from the Canadian station was transmitted across the Niagara River on overhead lines to Buffalo. There was already a cluster of factories using the flow of the Niagara River to power their activities when the big project was started. However, the availability of abundant cheap electrical power spawned an entirely new industry in Niagara Falls—the electrochemical industry—whose power requirements right from the start accounted for virtually the entire supply. Aluminum smelting was pursued by the Pittsburgh Reduction Company, founded in 1886. This smelter was relocated within a few years and the company, renamed the Aluminum Company of America (Alcoa), became the dominant supplier of aluminum in the world.

The second electrochemical industry in Niagara Falls, the Carborundum Company, also transferred from the Pittsburgh area. Its contract of 1894 with the Niagara Falls Power Company was for 1,000 horsepower, with which it increased its output 20-fold and within a decade it was making use of 5,000 horsepower of electricity. Union Carbide Company, also a heavy user of electric power, became established in Niagara Falls. It produced acetylene gas and later merged with other local companies. Graphite production became a leading product. Graphite was used to make electrodes for the rapidly expanding electrical industry. Other users of electricity in Niagara Falls were involved in producing chemicals such as chlorine and caustic soda, and metals such as titanium, vanadium, tungsten and molybdenum that steel producers made use of. Down the road in Buffalo, electrical power was used in grain handling and processing, iron foundries and in machine shops. The biggest industries in Buffalo were grain milling, iron and steel production, and these spawned much manufacturing of products downstream. Buffalo hosted the Pan-American Exposition of 1901. Many observers argue that the completion of the St. Lawrence Seaway in 1958 spelled doom for Buffalo. Ships had no reason to stop off at the docks of the city. Grain storage and processing activity contracted severely.

Electricity provided the power for New York City's subway in 1900 and for the elevators in its new tall buildings. One can argue that New York City has more tall buildings than other American cities because its center, Manhattan,represents a tricky land constraint on the expansion of its CBD. Chicago grew up without such a constraint. Hong Kong is often singled out as the place with most tall buildings in the world and like New York, it has been faced with special constraints on horizontal expansion. The recent tilt of many households toward high-rise living near the centers of cities has been driven in part by the lower cost of personal security that one can find in such a lifestyle. Mansions, not too far from city centers, may be affordable to many high-income households but such residences often come with extremely costly security outlays. Being known as rich and famous has its downsides. One may attract fascinating friends but also harassers of various kinds, including thieves and even kidnappers.

Decomposition of aggregate growth into city-specific growth

Growth is regularly measured at the level of the nation. Given current national product, Q, with production function $e^{\xi t}F(K, N)$ for K the current capital stock (buildings and machines and roads, etc.) and N the current labor force, one has

$$\frac{\dot{Q}}{Q} = \xi + s_K \frac{\dot{K}}{K} + s_N \frac{\dot{N}}{N}$$

for s_K as the current share of capital value in Q and s_N as the current share of labor value in Q. Here ξ is the rate of exogenous technical progress. The expression $\frac{\dot{Q}}{Q}$ is the current growth rate for the economy. Current Q gets divided among $\dot{K}$, new capital, δK, replacement capital and C, aggregate current consumption. The large behavioral issue is how society chooses to divide current Q between current consumption, yielding current happiness, and $\dot{K} + \delta K$, providing for future happiness. A simple formulation has the current savings rate simply given as s, at say 12 percent. Then $(1 - s)Q = C$. Given a specification of population growth and ξ, we can trace out the future path of the economy. Capital is accumulated and the population grows and ξ showers down, raising output each year.

For the special case when the savings rate is constant, with no technical progress and no decay in capital, Solow (1956) observed that

$$\dot{k} = sf(k) - nk$$

for $k = \frac{K}{N}$, $n = \frac{\dot{N}}{N}$ and $f(k) = F(\frac{K}{N}, 1)$ for $F(K, N)$ the constant returns to scale production function. During growth, $\dot{k}$ tends to zero or the capital–labor ratio tends to a constant. An indirect message here is that for growth in per capita terms to be present, technical progress needs to be present. Simple accumulation of durable capital prevents decline in the economy but does not provide for expansion of key per capita magnitudes. If we thought that development was somehow generically about capital accumulation, this result is startling and sobering. In a sense the economy is just keeping up with population growth by accumulating capital.

When technical progress and capital decay are added we obtain the important variant of the above equation. Consider the case of technical progress, labor-augmenting.[11] Our production function is then $F(K, AN) = Q$ with A growing at, say, 2 percent per year. We define labor in efficiency units as $L = AN$, and $k_A = K/L$. Then the above Solow equation becomes

$$\dot{k}_A = sf(k_A) - (n + \delta + \gamma)k_A$$

where δ is the rate of capital stock decay or evaporation and $\gamma = \frac{\dot{A}}{A}$. In this new world of exogenous growth in labor force quality, the wage rate rises at rate γ. The interest rate remains constant at $F_K - \delta$ and k_A becomes the limiting capital–labor ratio. Now as time passes, workers not only become more productive, but also their wages keep rising and they can expand their consumption. This simple growth model serves as something of a modern benchmark for sketching development of a nation. The average person becomes richer because technical progress makes the average person more productive year after year. Recent estimates by McKinsey has productivity growth at about 8.5 percent between 1990 and 2012 for China and about 1.8 percent for the United States. Each nation had about the same contribution of input-growth to GDP growth over this period: just under 1 percent.[12] Toronto's productivity declined by 6 percent between 2000 and 2010 while Vancouver and Calgary posted gains. Causes include under-investment in transportation infrastructure (long commute times), an education system that is failing to produce young people with the skills in demand and new businesses constrained by start-up capital. Only nine of the 20 largest sectors in Toronto grew between 2001 and 2012.[13]

Two extensions of the above model involve (a) making the savings decision somewhat more "behavioral" and (b) making the technical progress endogenous. The modern variant of our model has technical progress "produced" as with R&D and universities. Such models are referred to as endogenous growth models. Certainly when one looks back on the Industrial Revolution in England, one observes many clever tinkerers and thinkers at work doing important R&D. Recall the excitement over improved cotton-spinning machines and steam engines in the later 1700s. There may well have been a jump up in such activity during the Industrial Revolution. Difficult to pin down, however, is whether a burst of tinkering and R&D, preceded the economic development of England or simply coincided with it. A formalization of endogenous R&D is

$$\dot{A} = \varpi A N_1,$$

where N_1 are workers in R&D and ϖ is a constant. This of course leaves $N - N_1$ workers in goods production. The solution of the model determines the efficient number for N_1.

So much for our brief tour of the basic theory of economic growth. Things are happening at the level of the nation in this narrative, not down at the level of creative individuals in social networks in various cities. Innovation tends to be individualistic—a person coming up with an idea and developing it. This individualistic process usually happens in built-up communities, in cities. Invention will then remarkably enough have "urban community" as one of the inputs to the process. The urban-ness input will of course only be showing up indirectly: more successful patents are filed by individuals and firms in larger communities. Smart immigrants have played a large part in the development of "tech" in its various forms in the United States, and "the clustering of ethnic inventors can explain a significant amount of the increased clustering of patents" (Kerr 2010; p. 10).

In principle, one should be able to decompose $\dot{K}$ into an urban component and a rural component and then decompose the urban component into the set of towns and cities (plus villages) in, say, the United States for the accounting year in question. We have never seen such an exercise attempted. Data are not collected to answer every question that a researcher might ask. In a year, however, one can contemplate, say, New York City doing replacement investment, both private and that associated with roads, ports, airports, etc., and new investment. In this latter, one hopes for a breakdown into infrastructure (roads, bridges, sewers, water supply, port facilities, fire protection services, airports, etc.) and private investment. This latter would comprise new residential structures, new office buildings, new factories and related production facilities and probably some new infrastructure associated with a new residential or business development. And there is labor force growth. The growth of a city is often summarized with a report on population growth over the period in question. In a comment in 2007 on some new census figures, Edward Glaeser noted that Atlanta, Houston, Dallas and Phoenix (the fastest growing cities in the United States) had each increased their populations by more than 750,000 between 2000 and 2006 whereas Boston had grown by only 63,000.[14] Boston's growth rate was 277th for cities in the United States. Glaeser attributed the relatively poor growth performance of cities in California to heavy-handed, NIMBY-like regulation by cities of the establishment of new residential developments. San Francisco worked for ten years on a plan to increase density. Then a developer came forward with a plan to put up a 16-unit apartment building in the Mission District. He followed the regulations carefully. Six years later his original proposal, with two mandated units for low-income tenants, was approved. There is no parking in the plan because the city is keen to move residents into the regular use of mass transit. Over the lengthy approval process planners had redesigned the plan as first submitted and then reversed their changes.[15]

Does population growth lead or lag employment growth? Glaeser hints at population expansion leading employment growth in his comment. The expansion of attractive residential areas will induce employment growth. This is of course not a general rule. There was a component of growth for the fast-growing cities that could be attributed to the unusual availability of funds for new residences (the so-called sub-prime mortgage episode). One would like to be able to identify ratios like infrastructure capital per person in an average city and business capital (buildings and factories) per person. One could contemplate capital expenditure that promotes growth and that which follows private sector growth. Another way to think about the economic health of a city is to consider the number of police stations per capita, the number of police personnel per capita, the number of fire stations per capita and the number of people assigned to deal with fires. One can then move on to contemplate bottlenecks in public investment constraining the growth of a city.

Long-term demographic reorganization

It is conventional to view colonial America as a high-wage place. There was an abundance of land and a worker with some basic knowledge of farming could set himself up and in due course earn a decent living relative to what he could earn in Europe, including Britain. Urban workers had the option of moving to a new farm and this kept the wages of urban workers relatively high. So the United States started as a somewhat high-wage place, certainly on the East coast and around the Mississippi delta. Mountains prevented the steady movement of settlement and farming westward but in due course routes through these geographic barriers opened up. The Eire Canal (1825) in up-state New York was very important for moving people and goods into the central part of the country. And then railways arrived. The completion of the railway across the continent to California in 1865 made virtually all of the territory of the United States accessible to ordinary people. Settlements could proliferate in the center of the nation. In short, the ready availability of accessible farmland, well beyond the colonial period, went along with relatively high wages for unskilled workers. Relatively high rural wages, directly or indirectly measured, meant that urban activities were obliged to contend with a relatively costly labor input. (Many economists argue that relatively high costs for labor induce business people to seek out labor-saving innovations.[16])

The end of the Civil War in 1865 freed up a large pool of unskilled workers, formerly enslaved mostly in the south, and African Americans began to migrate from their low-wage area in the south to higher-wage places in the north and later south-west. Hence there was a slow rise in wages in the southern United States after the Civil War and a lessening of an upward pressure on wages in the north and north-east. The Chicago area became a popular urban area for African Americans to settle in the 1940s. Presumably they were drawn to a labor-scarce locality. The broadbrush history of wages in the United States is one of disequilibrium adjustment toward a fairly uniform wage level for unskilled workers in the nation. Internal migration drove this process of wage convergence between two regions.

California is of particular interest. The popular take is one of migrants flowing in after World War II to take advantage of the benign climate and attractive beaches. It makes sense to abstract from climate in an analysis of the settlement of California. The Gold Rush of 1849 provided a boost to settlement and then came railroad construction, culminating in the joining of the east and west track-laying projects in 1865. Later came agriculture to the central valley which of course was made possible by large-scale irrigation and the development of refrigerated rail-freight cars. At the same time the oil extraction and refining industry and then aircraft manufacturing arrived, mostly during and after World War II. Overall, one would identify California as a labor-scarce, relatively high-wage place right up to recent years. And we conjecture that California would have been a high-wage place even if its climate was like that of, say, New York. California had much going for it besides beaches and a benign climate. It is reasonable to ask then: can we net out a climate component on the average wage in California? And what effect did climate have on the evolution of wages and economic activity more generally? This question is worth taking up but we leave it here with a restatement of our conjecture: the quantitative impact of California's climate was not large. One piece of evidence might be the pattern of out-migration of African Americans from the south. They appear to have moved to places of high wages (excess demand for labor) rather than places with especially benign climates. Most headed to the industrial cities in the north and center of the United States, rather than to California.

One is drawn to the conclusion that geography must play a large part in wage formation because regional differences in economic performance take so many years to disappear. Healthy people are very mobile and in theory they should move to places with better opportunities—as in higher wages or higher GDP per capita—or places that allow them to reach higher indifference curves. The migration effect on local wages seems, however, demonstrably sluggish. Geography appears to represent a large friction in wage adjustment via worker migration. *The Economist* reports that in 2000, the currently (2011) five poorest states by GNP per capita had a three times larger share of manufacturing in local GNP than the currently five riches states.[17] Declining activity in the manufacturing sector represented a strong drag on overall economic performance for the poorer states. The reporter for *The Economist* made some currency conversions and estimated that over 25 percent of the regions in Britain and Italy and 10 percent of those in Germany will have a lower GDP per capita than that for the municipalities of Shanghai and Beijing. Glaeser and Gyourko (2005) point out that the durability of housing is a principal component of migration stickiness. Unskilled people will remain, often close to subsistence, where houses have become very cheap. A place with low wages and low-cost housing can of course leave a person on a higher indifference curve than a place with higher wages and more expensive housing. There is more to migration than wage differences alone.

When we paint with a broad brush, we take the history of wages in the United States as one of a gradual convergence to a national norm via internal migration abetted by considerable migration from outside the country, which itself helped to speed up the internal migration. Is the more recent shift in population to the south and southwest a response principally to a climate premium in the utility function of workers? There seems to be little doubt that the arrival of large-scale air-conditioning (cooling in summertime) for homes, offices, stores and vehicles has greatly influenced the pace of recent expansion of city populations in the south and southwest of the United States. The arrival of ubiquitous air-conditioning is partly driven by advances in technology (making air-conditioning available at low-cost) and partly by rises in average incomes. The south and southwest of the United States became well supplied with air-conditioning when it did because the "amenity" became available at relatively low-cost and average incomes of citizens rose steadily to make air-conditioning affordable by ordinary households. Air-conditioning changed from a luxury item in the south and southwest to a "necessity," as did second cars for a family, spacious backyards and more recently cell phones and large-screen, digital television sets. The availability of low-cost air-conditioning changed the south and southwest United States from a low-wage (excess labor-supply) area to one of excess labor-demand. History should probably record that the recent growth of cities in the south and southwest has been industry-led. Firms were attracted to places with abundant low-cost land, low-cost container transportation and low-cost labor. The absence of strong labor unions should be considered a component of low-cost labor. The availability of low-cost air-conditioning made the south and southwest United States attractive places for new production facilities to be located. The fast-growing urban areas of the south and southwest are essentially sprawling, automobile-oriented places where families with modest incomes can afford a home with a backyard. As Mills emphasized, larger homes come with higher incomes and a central component of many larger homes is a large lot.

We are being a bit inconsistent when we argue here for a general wage convergence across cities in the United States, having emphasized utility-level convergence for similar workers earlier. Without doubt, wage convergence across urban areas and utility convergence move together when considered in broadbrush terms. Given a general trend toward wage convergence for similar workers across cities in the United States, we still have persistent measurable wage gaps that cry out for careful analysis. Much of our analysis in earlier chapters was devoted to explaining these persistent wage gaps.

Data for city sizes in a system

For some decades, it has been known that in nations with many cities, the second largest city is about half the size of the largest and the third largest city is about a third the size of the largest and so on down to towns of some 50,000 people. Clearly the product of our two pieces of data (rank × size) are constant, equal to the population of the largest city. This regularity is referred to as "the rank-size rule" or "Zipf's Law." The general representation of this law is the function (Pareto distribution), $\text{Rank}^i = A \times [\text{Size}^i]^B$ for $B = -1$, where A is the population of the largest city. When the value of B is not -1, one infers that the pure rank-size rule is not showing up in the data. With many cities in a nation, one selects a small population, size 1, and the rank is then the number of cities larger than size 1. Rank 2 becomes the number greater than size 2, etc. These two columns of data can be analyzed with a regression of rank "against" size in $y = a + bx$, where the y values are log of the rank values and the x values are the log of the size (population) values. When one does the regression analysis for the United States, the value of b comes out somewhat less than unity, not quite corresponding to a pure rank-size rule. This closeness of b to -1 for many systems of cities in nations of the world has of course captured the attention of many people. Science is about finding regularities in sets of observations and proposing simple explanations or "laws" for the regularities. The rank-size rule seems like a very attractive regularity. The most recent supportive empirical work comes from Rozenfeld *et al.* (2011), who work from a dataset constructed with detailed satellite information on spatial concentrations of populations for the United States and Great Britain. They find good support for Zipf's Law for populations of cities and towns of all sizes (down to 12,000 inhabitants for the United States and 5,000 for Great Britain).[18]

It turns out that there is another empirical regularity linking the populations of cities in a nation: larger cities do not grow faster or slower on average than do smaller cities. On average, the growth of cities in a system is proportional: they all grow at a distinct rate, with the rates for cities i and j clustered around the average growth rate. Proportional growth for a set of observations implies that the underlying distribution of the data is lognormal and the growth process is called Gibrat's Law. When the growth rates are stochastic and on average proportional, the underlying distribution is said to be asymptotically lognormal. This was the point of departure for Eeckhout (2004)[19]. He decided to work with a set of 25,000 villages, towns and cities in the United States for the year 2000, whose sizes ranged from single digits up to eight million. He found that the lognormal distribution fit quite well for ranks against sizes. He inferred that since the data fit the lognormal distribution reasonably well, the growth process underlying city size increase must be "proportional" or conform to Gibrat's Law. So he developed a theory of the growth of city i, based on intra-city externalities (larger cities have more efficient labor markets because of information sharing as well as more congestion) and inter-city migration of workers. The interested reader now must choose between Gibrat's Law defining city growth and Zipf's Law characterizing city rank and size.

One indicator of city size for a modern urban area is how brightly the place shines when viewed from a satellite at night. Henderson *et al.* (2012) have estimated the amount of economic activity taking place in various parts of the world with this yardstick and compared their results to familiar measures published by statistical agencies. The fit between the two measures is fairly good but for Africa they observed more economic activity away from the coast than was being recorded in the standard sources.

Great ratios for cities

Bettencourt and West (2010) present evidence for average wages in a city rising with city size for a sample of 360 US cities. They plot the ratio of a city's average income to the average for all 360 cities against the city's population expressed as a ratio to the average for all cities, in logs, and obtain a linear trend with observations clustered close to the trend line. They report (Bettencourt and West 2010; p. 913):

> On average, as city size increases, per capita socio-economic quantities such as wages, GDP, number of patents produced and number of educational and research institutions all increase by approximately 15% more than the expected linear growth. ...negative metrics including crime, traffic congestion and incidence of certain diseases all increase following the same 15% rule.[20]

Large city disamenities go along with large city productivity premia. For two similar workers, then, it is more expensive to buy a home in a larger city and the more expensive home is made affordable by the higher wage. Larger cities are "more productive" workplaces and larger cities are more expensive to own or rent a home in. Bettencourt and West also note that there are macro-scale economies of city bigness. "Doubling the population of any city requires only about an 85 percent increase in infrastructure, whether that be total road surface, length of electrical cables, water pipes or number of petrol stations" (Bettencourt and West 2010; p. 912). This implies that for two similar workers in two cities of different sizes, the one in the larger city can get by on a slightly lower wage. Or if the wages are the same, the worker in the larger city can spend more on "other consumption" and this could lead to the larger city being somewhat disproportionately large and thus a "high rent" city. As we emphasized in Chapter 4, it is overly simplistic to attribute wage levels to city size alone.[21] As we have argued earlier, there are systematic deviations from a linear relation between wages and city size that cry out for analysis. Industry composition is of course an obvious variable to consider to explain such deviations. We addressed some of these matters in earlier chapters.

Bettencourt and West argue quite generally that a city's infrastructure tends to expand at a slower rate than a city's population. We might pursue the following high-level abstraction in this regard. Think of a city's infrastructure as a length of pipe, with the flow-through per unit time as the city's aggregate production (proportional to population). The relevant measure of the pipe is $I = 2\pi r \times \lambda$ (λ is length of pipe) and the relevant measure of current production is $O = \pi r^2$. This implies that output grows faster than the pace at which input (infrastructure) expands. That is, $dI/dr = \lambda 2\pi$ and $dO/dr = 2\pi r$. Hence $dO/dI = r/\lambda$. This may be a rule of thumb of some use when thinking about cities as special entities that exploit scale or size effectively.

It is fairly natural to argue that X families comprising a city will require or sustain Y workers in retail activity, Z workers in police and municipal administration and so on to other own city-serving activities. One then aggregates up and argues for a city of X families sustaining (supporting) H workers overall in own city-serving activities. The remaining workers in the city end up working in the other city-serving or so-called basic activities. Basic sectors are then, roughly speaking, export industries. Clearly this approach is simplistic since it is easy to argue that a city with a high average income for its X families will sustain more own city-serving activity and exhibit more workers in that large own city-serving sector. Hence the fraction of workers in a city in own city-serving (non-basic) activities should rise with average family income. It should probably also rise somewhat faster than the population of a city. Consider a place needing a certain level of retailing activity. If the place were large it would likely also have an active wholesale sector that supports the retailing sector and if the place were small the wholesale sector would likely be located in a neighboring larger city. This line of thinking leads us to infer that the fraction of own city-serving activity that a city displays should increase faster than proportionately with a city's population, in addition to a city's average income. Large cities are more autarkic or self-sufficient in this view. Our formal model of a hierarchy above had this property.

We might try to be more precise by turning to formal analysis. Let us assume that a city has two types of workers, skilled in the other-city serving sector and unskilled in the own-serving sector. We have then two production activities in a city. We can assume that utility functions are the same for all workers. But let our economy comprise two cities, each with its unique export good (produced in the other-serving sector) and each with its own own-serving sector. We assume that every worker consumes three goods: a local non-traded good produced in the local own-serving sector of each city and some of each of the export goods produced by each city. We can assume that zero cost "migration" equalizes the utility levels of skilled and unskilled workers.

The central question becomes: in equilibrium, is the average number of unskilled workers (number of unskilled workers divided by total number of workers in each city) the same in each city? Or does the larger city have a higher average number of unskilled workers? And what determines which city is larger in equilibrium? Is there a tendency, as we add cities to our model, each with a distinct export good, for the average number of unskilled workers in a group of cities to cluster around a key value? Analysis along these lines could allow one to pin down arguments about city size and the sizes of basic and non-basic sectors.

Decline

Decline is experienced by many communities including very large cities such as ancient Rome and Vienna in the early twentieth century. The process is not mysterious. Think of a community having two sorts of activities: basic or export-oriented and non-basic or local activities. When demand for the output of the basic activity declines, local jobs are lost and often homes are put on the market as the laid-off workers frequently migrate away. Unoccupied homes are linked to less tax revenue for the local government and to less demand for non-basic activities, such as retail. Shops are closed and sometimes get boarded up. A new equilibrium of sorts can emerge with a smaller community surviving within the shell of a formerly larger place. Rome declined gradually from a city of a million residents in about AD 100 to a town of some tens of thousands in AD 700 after the seat of government of the Empire was moved to Constantinople. Vienna declined in size when the empire of the Hapsburgs was broken up after World War I. The new state of Austria needed a smaller scale of government.

Many "manufacturing cities" in the United States and the United Kingdom experienced noticeable declines in the demand for their basic goods. Shipbuilding declined in Glasgow in Scotland, for example. The steel industry gradually altered production methods: the large blast furnaces based on the Bessemer technology were replaced by smaller-scale entities operating with electric arc furnaces. Steel cities such as Pittsburgh, Baltimore, Gary,[22] Bethlehem and Lehigh were impacted negatively. The *Wall Street Journal* listed its Ten Dead Cities in the United States for 2010 and the decline in key product for each. See Table 6.3.

The three other cities on the list of ten, left out of Table 6.3, were Atlantic City, Allentown and Galveston. Of course major cities such as Philadelphia and Baltimore lost population and important employment centers as well.

Communities do suffer when demand for their basic activities shrinks. House prices decline, local government revenues decline, the public sector becomes shabby when municipal revenues become scarce, and non-basic or locally-focused activities such as retail are forced to decline. One dimension of Detroit's decline has been the withdrawal of name-brand supermarkets from much of the city. Residents end up with little choice of food for basic sustenance. The bulldozing of blighted neighborhoods is often turned to as a program of

Table 6.3 Decline of some cities in the United States (2010)

	Base population	*Population (2010)*	*Loss*
Albany	134,000 (1950)	95,000	Finished lumber and iron
Buffalo	510,000 (1955)	250,000	Steel
Cleveland	914,000 (1950)	475,000	Auto parts
Detroit	1,500,000 (1950)	760,000	Auto plants
Flint	200,000 (1960)	95,000	GM autos
Hartford	177,000 (1950)	124,000	Insurance
New Orleans	627,000 (1960)	250,000	Port jobs

Source: *Wall Street Journal*, available at http://247wallst.com/economy/2010/08/23/americas-ten-dead-cities-from-detroit-to-new-orleans/ (accessed January 2014).

"urban renewal." Funds are sought from state and federal government programs. A renewed neighborhood is presumed to be an attractive place for an outside investor to step into with profitable activities and new jobs. Renewal and economic revival have, however, turned out to be challenging routes for municipal leaders to move along. Tearing down old structures (slum dwellings) is the easy part. Getting investment to flow in subsequently has seldom been easy. The TIF (tax increment financing) program in the United States exempts firms of local tax increases for up to 25 years when they locate in designated areas of a city. This type of area development program was started in California in 1952 and has been implemented in many cities in the United States. Chicago, for example, has numerous TIF areas within its borders. Frequently the municipal government borrows against future tax revenues that will accrue to the city from new activity within a TIF area and the local government pursues infrastructure development in parallel with the arrival of new private sector investment.

The later 1950s saw the arrival of something of a perfect storm for many older cities in the United States and the United Kingdom. Technical change suggested smaller scales for new production entities for activities such as steel and auto production. Smaller steel mills and "remote" auto assembly plants were built where land was cheap and low-cost labor was available, usually away from the historic centers of activity. At the same time, lower prices for automobiles and higher incomes for mid-skilled workers allowed the workers to move their families to less crowded suburban neighborhoods. Many cities had freeways built which made commuting to city centers for suburban people easier. There was partly the suburban pull of newer homes and newer schools and more open space and partly a push as areas near the center experienced decay of various sorts. Large factories in large cities were shut down while ordinary folks were moving to suburbs. Central cities were left with poor people who were able to find low-cost accommodation in older homes, the latter broken up into multi-family units. Many older cities, mostly in the northeast of the United States were faced with a march of ordinary folks to the less dense suburbs and the simultaneous shutting of factories that were being replaced by newer entities, often far away. A host of cities were faced with this same problem... lower-income people stuck near the centers of cities in low-cost accommodation. Most of these cities were saddled with revenue problems because many properties were not delivering a steady flow of property tax. The lower quality of public services provided the push of middle-income families to the suburbs. A good neighborhood needs schools of reasonable quality as well as security for all, including children in the streets. Many cities were faced with the same problem of central city decline.

Glaeser tends to emphasize (a) the steep decline in the cost of moving commodities ("the death of distance") and (b) the high cost of moving people as key factors in the reorganization of relative sizes and prosperities of cities in the United States. "The importance of transport costs for people may explain why services have remained urbanized, even as manufacturing has fled to lower density settings" (Glaeser 2010; p. 8). He cites scale economies (large cost reductions in communication) in what are essentially face-to-face activities as the growth driver in cities that have prospered recently. The successful cities in recent times tend also to have been able to build up leads in the production of newer types of commodities. Glaeser and Ponzetto (2010, p. 303) indicate that of the 20 cities in the United States with populations above 450,000 in 1950, only Los Angeles, Houston and Seattle did not shed residents by 1980. They ask what caused Boston, New York and San Francisco to bounce back economically since 1980 and what caused the other cities to remain economically challenged. They investigate the broadly specified cause: large declines in the cost of transporting commodities and scale economies and cost reductions in communication. Boston, New York, Minneapolis and San Francisco expanded with "idea-intensive industries like finance, professional services and new technology." They were able to build up activities that turned on the scale economies of having many people concentrated in an area who needed to interact or communicate in order to produce their outputs. The Z/Yen Group places New York, Boston and San Francisco in the top ten of world financial centers.[23] (The top ten in order were New York, London, Hong Kong, Singapore, Zurich, Tokyo, Seoul, Boston, Geneva and San Francisco. Toronto, Montreal and Vancouver were 14, 16 and 17, respectively.) Even head-office activities could function in places well apart from their factories, given the low costs and new modes of communication. Older industries tended to resettle in new cities in the south and west of the United States, leaving Detroit, Cleveland and Buffalo in noticeable economic decline. Chicago is among the growing places.

Glaeser and Ponzetto (2010) present a formal model of how large declines in transportation costs, including those involved in communication, could result in declines for some cities and expansion of others, and they execute some empirical tests of the idea. "Urban density that once served to connect manufacturers with railroads and boats now serves to facilitate contact of smart people in idea-producing sectors" (Glaeser and Ponzetto 2010; p. 303). In modern America, "high human capital industries tend to be centralized within metropolitan areas, manufacturing is in medium density areas, and natural resource based industries are generally non-urban" (p. 304). Two phenomena of special interest to Glaeser and Ponzetto are the rise in heterogeneity in the growth of income and population in many older cities since 1980, and the concentration in some older cities of idea-intensive sectors, while all older cities were shedding manufacturing jobs. The nature of the labor force mattered in generating growth for a city. "A 1 percent increase in skilled occupations in 1980 is associated with an approximately 4 percent increase in income growth since then" (p. 322). And across cities, patenting intensity and skill intensity move together and both correlate with rising income levels. Something of a puzzle is the growth in wage variation for cities with more rapid growth in incomes (p. 328). LeDuff (2013; p. 80) cites the following factors in Detroit's decline.

> You might blame it on white racism and legal mortgage covenants that barred blacks from living anywhere but the most squalid ghettos.
>
> You might blame postwar industrial policies that sent the factories to the suburbs, the rural South and the western deserts.
>
> You might blame the city's collapse on the 1967 riot and the white flight that followed. You might blame it on Coleman Young—the city's first black mayor—and his culture of corruption and cronyism.
>
> You could blame it on the gas shocks of the seventies, which opened the door to foreign car competition.
>
> You might point to the trade agreements of the Clinton years that allowed American manufacturers to leave the country by the back door.
>
> You might blame the UAW, which demanded things like near-full pay for idle workers, or the myopic management, who instead of saying no took their piece and simply tacked the cost onto the price of the car.

We should ask whether these "causes" of Detroit's particular decline hit other cities in the northeast in the same way, or more heavily or less, or possibly not at all. Certainly Detroit was somewhat distinct. In 1925, British author Ramsay Muir, quoted in LeDuff

(2013; p. 170) described Detroit as "the home of mass production, very high wages and colossal profits, of reckless installment buying and shifting labour surplus." Detroit's factories employed more than 300,000 workers in 1925 and another 50,000 people were involved in the illicit trade in alcoholic beverages, distilled across the St. Clair River in Canada. Observers have suggested that Detroit's economy became overly concentrated on vehicle production and when the negative shocks to big-city industries and their governments arrived in the 1960s, Detroit was unable to turn to "med and ed" as Pittsburgh, Baltimore and Philadelphia were able to. Baltimore was also able to clean up its old port and establish a reasonable scale of residential activity there. Cleveland cleaned up its famously polluted river and developed a good reputation for high-tech medical activity. There is no doubt that vehicle manufacturing was hit hard by foreign competition in the late 1970s and Detroit was not able to adapt to the new competition quickly. "Unfair trade" became a familiar phrase in the United States in the early 1980s. Japan agreed to let the yen appreciate significantly in 1985 in response to pressure from the United States government. The automobile sector was only one of many sectors that shifted assembly activity toward the southern United States to be where workers were less unionized. Singling out the UAW for ratcheting wages up unreasonably for workers cannot be decisive in getting so much auto activity closed down in Detroit. The generous benefits for the workers agreed to by management are again not plausibly decisive in driving the auto manufacturers in and around Detroit toward bankruptcy. We should think of a constellation of "causes" of Detroit's economic collapse coming together to form a single storm.

Detroit's problems were in fact not hugely different from those of other older cities of the northeast United States in the 1960s. Urban freeways and lower-cost automobiles made suburban living more attractive to many families. Family incomes were rising for many. A suburban lifestyle became attractive and affordable for many. Somehow, however, Detroit ended up with more poor people stuck in low-cost accommodation near its center than did other "problem" cities. Detroit's public services declined well below the levels of other "problem" cities. The flight of middle-income families to the suburbs took place on a scale larger than elsewhere. LeDuff (2013; p. 45) points out that

> Detroit reached a peak population of nearly 1.9 million people in the 1950s and was 83 percent white. Now Detroit has fewer than 700,000 people, is 83 percent black and is the only American city that has surpassed a million people only to contract below that threshold.

LeDuff (2013) keeps the issue of numbers of African Americans and segregation central to his sketch of Detroit's decline:

During Detroit's great expansion between 1920 and 1960, nearly half a million blacks came north from the cotton fields of the South as part of what is known as the Great Migration.[24] Detroit was seen as the "Promised Land" and it "had plenty of jobs." (p. 43). "Then came the urban renewal and interstate highway projects that rammed a freeway down the middle of Paradise Valley, displacing thousands of blacks." (p. 44) "Predictably, the city exploded. And following the 1967 riots, whites would begin their rapid exodus to the suburbs, leaving behind their homes and taking their factories and their jobs and their tax dollars with them." "Five years after the riot, blacks seized political control of Detroit with the election of Coleman Young, the city's first black mayor." South Warren, where LeDuff's brother was living with only a part-time job, used to have "the Dodge factory and the General Motors plant and the cinder-block mom-and-pop too-and-die shops that supplied those factories"

(p. 40). "By the time I arrived back in Detroit in 2008, perhaps 75 percent of those shops had died" (p. 44).

Many large cities have areas with poor people, housed in poor-quality structures. Levels of unemployment are generally high in these areas. Many young people in these communities could do basic jobs such as stacking boxes or even carrying out check-out duties in retail establishments, but openings for unemployed workers are not in their neighborhoods. Many low-skilled workers are trapped in communities cut off from employment opportunities. Lawlessness is common since young people have time to get into trouble and a desire to get money, by almost any means. The degree of lawlessness can turn on the quality of policing of the neighborhoods. Many cities find it very expensive to have good-quality police devoting much time and resources to street supervision in poor and decayed areas. There are then these run-down areas with weak street security and few local employment prospects for the many unemployed, low-skilled residents. Investors do not move in with new enterprises because the quality of the workers is not good enough and security in the streets is not adequate. Why, for example, does a supermarket not open up to serve these residents? It must be that security is such that wholesalers refuse to stock a store in such a run-down area. Then the operators of potential retail establishments would have to contend with a high level of shop-lifting.

These low-income areas generally settle into some sort of equilibrium with respect to the rest of the city. The areas occupy about the same area year in and year out. The city's functioning becomes imperilled when these areas are persistent and become large, when their size "infects" other areas. Detroit is unusual because its decayed residential area has become most of the city itself. The "bad area" is not a large pocket in the city as is often the case in many modern cities in the United States, but has almost taken over the city. Less than one third of Detroit's 88,000 streetlights are in working order. The quality of policing and fire intervention are poor throughout the city, not just in one "bad area." Dan Gilbert, Detroit's central city developer-booster, has provided his own security force with 24/7 patrols and 300 surveillance cameras monitored at a command center. As part of a program to revive a strip of retail activity, Detroit beer-maker John W. Stroh III is paying for 3,500 hours of private security patrols of the area. Rather than stabilizing in size, as has been the case of most large cities in the United States, the "bad area" in Detroit, some 139 square miles in total, simply kept growing. Of Detroit's 380,000 properties, 114,000 have been bulldozed and as of 2014 some 80,000 more are in line for demolition. In 2013, the city declared bankruptcy. Detroit as a political entity lies within Wayne County and Dearborn is the city in Wayne County that Henry Ford made famous by siting there his huge integrated River Rouge production system. The Ford company produces pick-up trucks at the River Rouge site today but Ford's steel mill, next door, is now owned by a large Russian company. Steel producers have depended on vehicle production as part of their market for output and vehicle manufacturers are turning to aluminum sheet for body panels to make their products lighter and thereby use less fuel. Steel producers are in turn developing thinner, stronger sheet output to sell to vehicle producers. Is the mostly aluminum automobile the vehicle of the future?

Beyond Wayne County is Oakland County, an area about the size of Rhode Island, with a population of about 1.2 million people. The central community is Pontiac. There is a sense that the white flight from Detroit in the 1960s and 1970s recreated something like 1950s Detroit in a new suburban form as Oakland County. We can think of the Detroit-centered area as a huge city with a functioning CBD, a gigantic ring or annulus with mostly low-income residents in decayed dwellings (Wayne County) which in turn is abutted by sprawling Oakland County. Economic activity is robust and diversified in Oakland County. There are communities of lower-income families as well as affluent families. This view of Detroit-in-the-large suggests that it represents something of an extreme example of job and residential decentralization, a process that many older cities in Canada and the United States have had to live through. Younger cities such as Los Angeles, Atlanta, Houston, Dallas and Phoenix have grown up as decentralized, automobile-oriented entities. They have not had to experience the transformation from a downtown or CBD-focused place to a more modern community of decentralized workplaces. The durability of structures, plants and residences has made the transformation of a city from a CBD-focused place to a decentralized, very suburban place very difficult. Durable structures introduce a special sort of stickiness in large-scale urban restructuring.

Part of William Cronon's attention in his *Nature's Metropolis* (1991) was directed to how Chicago managed to out-compete St. Louis, on the Mississippi River, in becoming the dominant city in the mid-west of the United States. Chicago is currently the third largest city in the United States. St. Louis was well connected to New Orleans as an ocean terminal and Chicago became connected to New York City when the Erie Canal was completed in 1825. The trip from New York City to Albany on the Hudson River and to Buffalo on the Erie Canal is not a short hop. From Buffalo to Chicago, a ship must in turn traverse Lake Erie, Lake Huron and Lake Michigan, again not a short voyage. However, the pairing of St. Louis as a prairie metropole and New Orleans as its transshipment point for contact to Europe turned out to be a less formidable combination than the Chicago–New York City pairing. The arrival of the railroads appears to have favored Chicago as the metropole for the west in the central United States. Linking that city to New York City by rail was a bit easier than linking St. Louis to a major port on the Atlantic seaboard. The first New York–Chicago rail route was provided on January 24, 1853 with the completion of the Toledo, Norwalk and Cleveland Railroad to Grafton, Ohio on the Cleveland, Columbus and Cincinnati Railroad. The route later became part of the Lake Shore and Michigan Southern Railway, owned by the New York Central Railroad. East St. Louis was connected to the Baltimore and Ohio Railroad in 1857. However, the Mississippi River posed a barrier to a seamless rail link from west of St. Louis to the B&O railroad. It was 1874 that the Eads Bridge was completed at St. Louis and rail traffic could flow freely from the west of the river to the east at St. Louis. Basically St. Louis was about 20 years behind Chicago in becoming a good cental hub between the west of the United States and the eastern cities.

St. Louis did in fact prosper while Chicago expanded. The city reached its highest recorded census population in 1950, reaching 856,796, and its population peaked in the early 1950s with approximately 880,000 residents. From 1950 to 1960 the city declined by 13 percent to 750,026, and from 1960 to 1970 by another 17 percent to 622,236. In this decline, much of the white population ended up in the suburbs.

Summary

For most of human history there was no rise in the standard of living of humans. Populations rose at very slow rates and division of labor among individuals in a town implied infinitesimal growth in per capita "income." This form of horizontal economic growth was pervasive and qualitatively important. In about 1700 significant quantitative economic growth occurred in Europe when a larger town was able to attract industrial activity away from villages around the town. A form of vertical integration of economic activity took place as primary activities attracted secondary activities and larger-scale activities attracted related intermediate goods activities. Some gains from economizing on transportation costs were being reaped by the larger places. We considered some formal models of the mechanics of this agglomeration. Hierarchies of cities emerged. We examined a simple formal model of a hierarchy of cities. The empirical regularity associated with groups of cities of different sizes in a large nation is the rank-size rule. We reported on research associated with the rule, also known as Zipf's Law.

Mechanized transportation was developed following the refinement of the basic steam engine. The internal combustion engine followed some 100 years later. Within cities, residential activities became relatively separate from industrial and business activities. The income of the average urban household rose significantly. Commuting to places of work became commonplace and the average household demanded a home with some open space around it. The flight of the average household to lower density living started with the mechanization of urban transportation facilities and has not abated. Some businesses gradually migrated toward residents. Different lines of business became organized in different sorts of urban geography. Face-to-face activities clustered in arrangements that allowed for the direct interaction of the relevant workers. Large and efficient trucks allowed for businesses to locate away from ports and rail yards. Containerization reduced the cost of moving many sorts of goods significantly. The suburbanization of certain businesses became commonplace.

The "life-cycles" of many cities in the United States and elsewhere since 1900 have been noticeably varied. One tries to select cities with common "life-cycles" for distinct groups and then one attempts to understand the forces (laws?) of growth, change and sometimes decline. The analysis in this chapter has proceeded along such lines.

Main points of Chapter 6

1 Over most of human history, economic growth was horizontal, the addition of more people to "the edge" of a community, people with marginally different abilities and skills. Population increase went along with more division of labor and slight improvements in living standards.
2 Fortifications meant families gathered in centers. Farming provided food surpluses to support families in towns.
3 Modern economic growth is synonymous with the introduction of factories for the production of commodities, urbanization and infrastructure development, and family size limitation. Improvements in labor efficiency has meant rising wages to workers. Technical progress has been tied to capital accumulation and the formalization of education and training over the past 250 years.
4 When a city exploits a scale economy for producing commodity i, the cost of producing i becomes lower because production runs and markets are large. Since big cities are "large markets," big cities can out-compete smaller places in many lines of production. Then producers of inputs for making i are attracted to where i is being produced. Urban growth is cumulative since many producers and their input suppliers are doing better in larger places with large markets "at hand."
5 In many larger nations, the distribution of cities by size is very regular. Hence the "rank-size rule": multiply the rank of city in the national hierarchy by its population and one gets the size of the largest city.

Questions and problems

1 A larger city tends to suck industries located in nearby smaller places into itself. Evaluate this contention. Sketch a process that might cause this to occur.

2 A large city frequently sloughs off some low-tech activities to smaller places. Evaluate this contention. (Does moving the manufacture of computers to factories in China fit this argument?)

3 If the world's geography were a featureless plain, we would expect all activity to concentrate in one large urban area. Evaluate this contention.

4 Sketch economic processes that stop the agglomeration of all the world's economic activity in one large urban area.

5 Singapore is only 217 square miles in area and has well over a million residents. It has no natural resource deposits and no fresh water sources within the territory. In 1965 Singapore's per capita income was about one fifth of that in the United States. Today it is an advanced, high-income nation. What factors were important in Singapore's successful economic development?

6 Can Tokyo, with a population 35 million, serve as a useful role model for other large cities of the world? Is Tokyo's history "too unique" to be relevant as a model of a successful very large city?

Notes

1 In its heyday, Rome and its surroundings imported large quantities of wheat from Egypt. These inflows would have been financed by the revenues from taxation and the seigniorage from the mining of gold and silver in government mines. Ancient Italy did not prosper because it produced great stuff to export in return for food. China in contrast had products that Europe never ceased to desire to import.

2 Acemoglu *et al.* (2001) argue that the success of certain nations today, nations that were formerly colonies of European powers, reflects the type of institutions that the colonists laid down. In places where life expectancy was short, the argument goes, low-quality institutions were set out. There was an attitude of grab local material for quick profit and not bother with long-term "community building."

3 Given innovations in design, the number of vehicles in Paris grew from 320 in 1658 to 20,000 by 1765, all before significant industrialization. In England the number of carriages rose from 18,000 in 1775 to 106,000 in 1840 (Conover 2010; p. 218).

4 Gabaix (1999) and Eeckhout (2004) argue that the Pareto distribution captures data on cities of the United States only approximately. They present alternative distributions and related economic models with a stochastic base that fit with the data somewhat better.

5 "The image of Germanic geometry is that of eighteenth century mechanics the problem of location was represented directly as a matter of balancing several discrete forces of attraction" (Paul Krugman 1997; p. 42). This statement may be relevant for the Weber problem in the location of a firm, but fails to describe what the underlying economics is for the Christaller "problem."

6 *The Economist*, April 19, 2014, pp. 49–50.

7 The Forslid–Ottaviano model solves with a basic closed form polynomial, while the Krugman–Venables model does not. Hence our exposition of the former despite our particular interest in import substitution when intermediate goods are playing a central role.

8 A different sort of cumulative process of growth in cities is discussed by Rosenthal and Strange (2010): "the amount of new establishment formation in an area is tightly linked to the number of small firms" (p. 11).

9 *Globe and Mail*, May 31, 2014, p. M4.

10 *Economist*, July 12, 2014, p. 38.

11 Black and Henderson (1999) set out a growth model with many type 1 cities (producing and exporting an intermediate good) and many type 2 cities (producing and exporting some of a final good) that is driven by exogenous population increase and costly human capital accumulation. Land is in infinite supply and goods shipment is costless. New cities are born as growth ensues. They were in part inspired by the data that indicate that larger cities, certainly in the United States, have citizens

with somewhat more than average human capital. In their model each skilled worker invests directly in her own human capital.

12 *The Economist*, May 17, 2014, p. 64.

13 Study by Roger Martin, former Dean of the Business School at the University of Toronto, reported in *Globe and Mail*, March 29, 2014.

14 *Boston Globe*, April 23, 2007.

15 Michael Kimmelman, *New York Times*, June 1, 2014, Arts & Leisure, p. 18.

16 Ferguson (2011; p. 203) cites work by Robert Allen on Britain being an essentially high-wage economy on the eve of the Industrial Revolution, high-wage relative to France, Prussia, Italy and China. Many argue that when labor is dear, attentive entrepreneurs seek out innovations that economize on the labor input. In addition, Britain had abundant coal to be extracted around Newcastle. It was then in a sense a low-cost energy economy on the eve of the Industrial Revolution.

17 *The Economist*, March 12, 2011, p. 83–84.

18 Dissent comes from Holmes and Lee (2010). They use population concentrations instead of data on populations of cities from standard sources and they find "a coefficient of 2 among their high-density squares, which means that rank rises more quickly than population" (p. 7); and "political definitions of units seem to be driving the received wisdom about the size distribution of cities" (p. 8); and "some form of congestion sets in at ultra-high densities" (p. 8).

19 See also Gabaix (1999), n5.

20 Bettencourt and West (2010; p. 913) also report:

> We also find that quantities such as GDP are more variable for urban centers in developing countries, such as China and Brazil, than for older cities in developed areas such as North America or Japan. It is unclear whether this is a fundamental property of developing nations or an artefact of data collection.

21 Luis Bettencourt (2013) has developed a system of equations to capture some aspects of cities that grow faster than population (superlinear) and others that grow slower than population (sublinear). His model is based on the payoff individuals experience in interacting or being part of a network in a city. Space or geography means that meeting-up has costs associated with it but there are at the same time benefits from cross-fertilization. "When people brush up against each other, that's when the magic of the city happens—the social reactor begins to work," argues Bettencourt. The model is capped off with an indicator, G^*. For any city, the closer its G is to G^*, the more effective it is at generating productive interactions. One implication is that top-down interventions can be counter-productive for a city. Highly productive interactions must be preserved and fostered. Ultimately the productivity of a city is proportional to the number of social interactions and is thus not a simple function of population.

22 Gary's population declined to 80,000 today from 180,000 in 1960. Manufacturing jobs disappeared and "so did many white residents, who moved to the suburbs after the election of Richard G. Hatcher, one of the nation's first black mayors of a major city" (Steven Yaccino, *New York Times*, April 1, 2014, p. A12).

23 *Globe and Mail*, March 17, 2014, p. B3.

24 The (second) Great Migration (1940 to 1970), involved about five million African Americans moving from the South to northern US cities, many to California and other western cities. By the end of the Second Great Migration, African Americans had become an urbanized population. Some 53 percent remained in the South, while 40 percent lived in the North and 7 percent in the West (Wikipedia, February 2014).

7 Transportation

Urban transportation issues are in the face of many people who commute each day to jobs at some distance from their homes. Gridlock is a common term of frustration for urban dwellers. Tokyo is famous for having pushers at subway stops assigned to squeeze one or two more riders into each transit car. London has become famous for its congestion charge on a vehicle entering the city center. Our analysis of urban transportation starts with demand analysis—what factors determine which mode of travel a commuter chooses in her commute to work. In only five US cities in 2006 did 30 percent or more of commuters use the available mass transit (the five are New York, Jersey City, Washington, Boston and San Francisco). We map the areas of heaviest auto and transit use in Toronto, Chicago and Houston below. Demand analysis explains this phenomenon of the generally light use of mass transit. Users consider time costs, out-of-pocket costs and the quality of the experience of the trip when choosing a mode for their regular travel in their city. These dimensions of mode choice are measurable. We then take up the simple economics of charging road users a congestion tax in order to lighten use of a road—to speed the flow at rush hour. Economists have differing opinions about the merits of congestion charges. We also consider charging vehicles a tax for entering the center of a large city. And we turn to the issue of paying for the construction and maintenance of mass transit in different parts of the world.

Demand for alternative modes for commuting

Figure 7.1 is a map of, approximately, the actual "City of Toronto" with about two million residents, with the darkest areas indicating places with most commuters using their own automobiles. We have zoomed in on the "extensive" version of Toronto in order to get "activities" in central census tracts to show up well. The light lines are subways.The lighter shaded areas around the subway lines indicate that the subways do capture more commuters on average over all areas (census tracts).

The vertical spine of the subway is Yonge Street and just below its right-hand branch is Toronto's major east-west freeway, the 401. A newer east-west toll freeway exits above the map. Toronto has a freeway along its waterfront that brings in people from the west right up to the city of Hamilton, some 40 miles distant, as well as travellers funnelled in from the north-east via the Don Valley Parkway. Auto use in the map is largely suburban except for some areas near Yonge Street which are places with high-income residents. Figure 7.2 displays a map of relative mass transit use in Toronto for 2011.

The darkest areas indicate heaviest use and roughly speaking these heavy users of public transit live close to the subway lines. About 36.5 percent of residents in Toronto used public transit to commute to work in 2011. Some 42.8 percent of low-income (less than

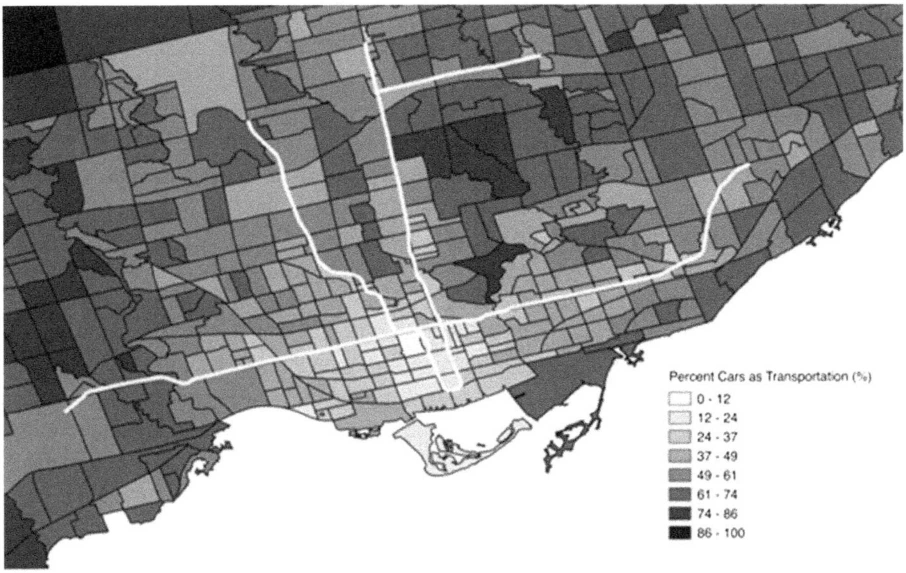

Figure 7.1 Auto use for commuting in Toronto, 2011.

Source: Based on Census Tract data.

Figure 7.2 Public transit use in Toronto, 2011.

Source: Based on Census Tract data.

US$20,000 annually) residents used mass transit compared with some 27.4 percent of higher-income (more than US$80,000 annually) residents.[1] A recent survey for Toronto finds that about 12 percent of commuters take an hour or more each way, 25 percent took less than 15 minutes each way and 56 percent took less than 30 minutes each way. A person's tolerance for daily travel, since the days of walled towns, has been estimated to be one hour per day (the so-called Marchetti Constant referred to by urban planners). One US study puts 16 minutes of commuting each way as a worker's ideal. Congestion makes commuting tiring because of the uncertain duration of the delays. Toronto has experienced substantial growth in ridership on its subways and commuters for this mode are also stressed getting to and from their places of work.[2] Toronto has ranked as one of the long-commute-time cities in recent surveys. A study by the Organization for Economic Co-operation and Development (OECD 2010) estimated that congestion in Toronto cost about US$3.3 billion per year in 2009 (the figure for Chicago was US$8.2 billion). The authors of this study censured Toronto for abetting commuting by automobile (currently around 70 percent of trips). A vigorous debate about how to expand the mass transit system for Toronto has been going on for some years. One group has been pressing for expanding the subway system, at huge expense, and another has pressed for much new LRT (above-ground rail systems[3]). A focus of conflict is, of course, where the needed funds should come from.

Two comparable maps for the movement of households in Chicago are shown in Figures 7.3 and 7.4. Chicago is both larger[4] than Toronto and possessed of a more extensive system of mass transit lines (the lighter lines on the map in Figure 7.3 represent core mass transit arteries).

The darkest areas in Figure 7.3 indicate Chicago's heaviest use of private autos for commuting. We contrast this map with Figure 7.4 indicating relatively most use of mass transit in commuting. (Now the mass transit lines are black.)

Heaviest users tend to live closer to the mass transit lines. Residents north and south of the CBD appear to be heavier users of mass transit. Houston has light use of mass transit. See the map in Figure 7.5.

The census tracts for Toronto and Chicago showing residents who are heavy users of mass transit give figures in the 60 and 70 percent range, whereas Houston's "heavy" users rise to only the 20 percent to 30 percent level. The map for auto-using commuters for Houston is mostly black, indicating large-scale commuting by automobile. We have not included this map.

Modern travel demand analysis deals with choice of mode by commuters. One might take neighborhood k and consider all N_k commuters from k to the CBD of a city. One then asks what fraction of these commuters takes mode i, given the observed characteristics of mode i (say vector y_i) and the observed characteristics of the commuters on this mode (say vector z_i) and the unobserved characteristics of the commuters of this mode (error term ε_i). One ends up with an equation to estimate of the form

$$\frac{N_{ki}}{N_k} = f(y_i, z_i, \varepsilon_i).$$

Some characteristics of the mode might be the elapsed time of trip, the dollars disbursed for the trip on the mode i, and some characteristics of the demanders might be wage and years of schooling. Richard Quandt became involved in demand estimation in the 1960s for inter-city travel by various modes and in place of our fractions $\frac{N_{ki}}{N_k}$ he used number of trips on mode i

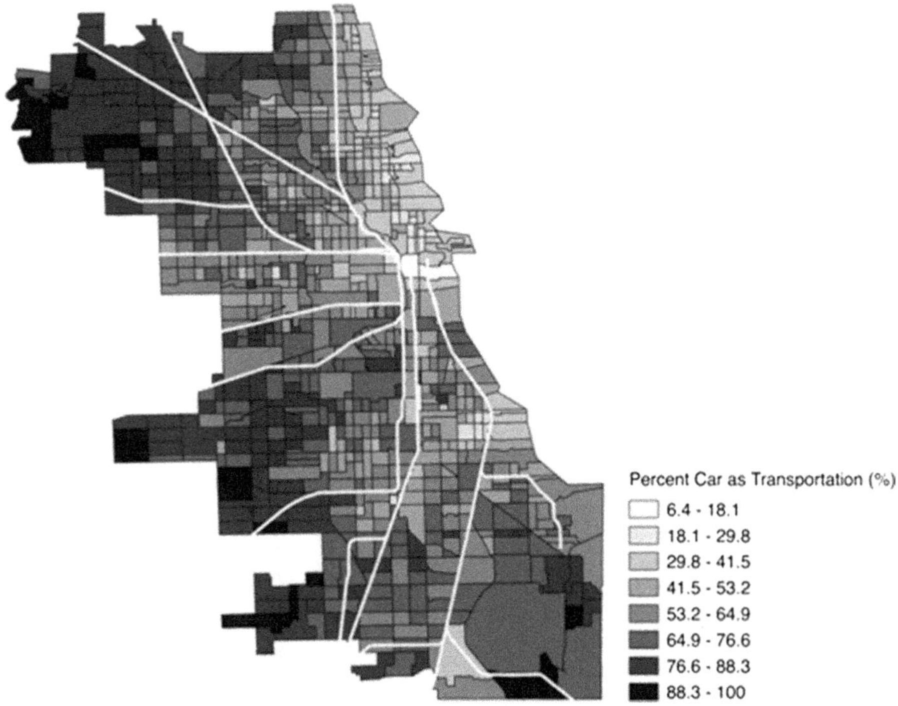

Figure 7.3 Auto use for commuting in Chicago, 2011.

Source: Based on Census Tract data.

between two cities. However, he and William Baumol, his collaborator, recognized that they were dealing with a special type of discrete choice problem and that estimation required innovations to econometric methods. They considered explicitly the introduction of a new mode of travel on a link and how one might estimate the demand for the new "product." They also introduced the axiom, "independence of irrelevant alternatives" which became central to McFadden's subsequent contributions, which we sketch below. Quandt collected his work and that with Baumol and others, including innovative estimations, in *The Demand For Travel: Theory and Measurement* (Quandt 1970).

Meanwhile, Tobin (1958) and others confronted the estimation problems associated with dependent variables that lie between zero and unity such as our fractions, $\frac{N_{ki}}{N_k}$. Tobin referred to such problems as those with limited dependent variables. In his pioneering analysis he estimated demand for durable goods by households with the dependent variable as the fraction of household expenditure on such items. His explanatory variables were age and the ratio of liquid assets to a household's disposable income. Daniel McFadden in about 1970 became interested in both discrete demand as a consumer theory problem (choice of travel mode, for example) and estimation of demand for alternative modes of urban transportation. He became a consultant to the team engaged in constructing a new mass transit system for the "Bay Area" (San Francisco, Oakland, Berkeley, etc.). There was much solid published material for him to build upon. His large contributions were a focus of the work for which he was awarded the Nobel Prize in economics in 2000.

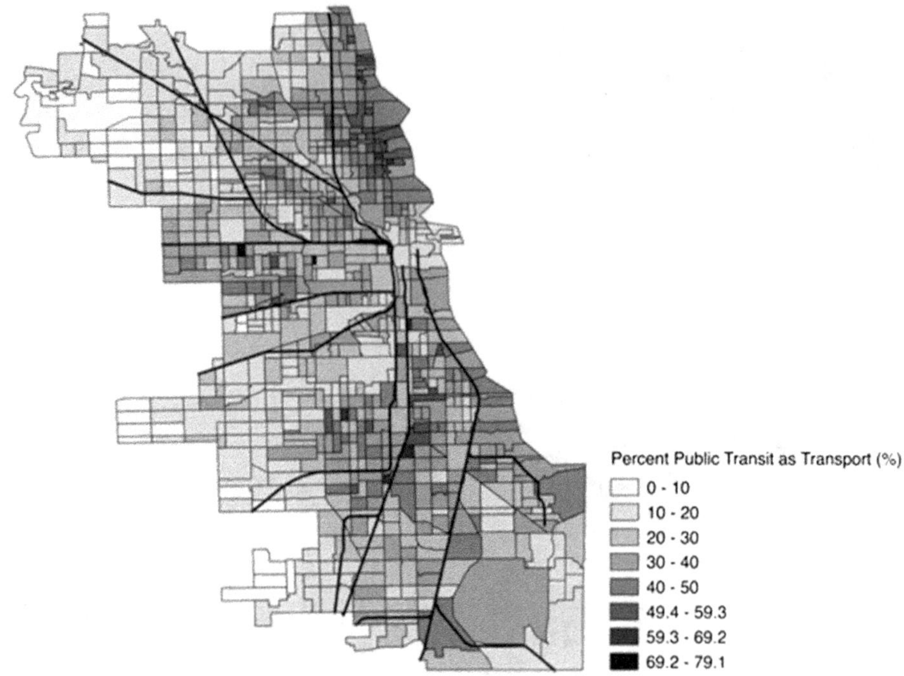

Figure 7.4 Public transit use in Chicago, 2011.

Source: Based on Census Tract data.

He proceeded to put choice by a consumer over discrete alternatives on an axiomatized basis (derive choice over discrete alternatives from utility theory or to provide a utility theory framework for choice by a rational consumer over discrete alternatives) and to provide an econometric framework (estimation methodology) for estimating our fractions, $\frac{N_{ki}}{N_k}$ (see Appendix 7.1) He recognized that in order to be able to carry out his estimations he had to make special assumptions about how the utility of a representative demander was structured. His (and others) subsequent work in 1989 allowed for estimations that were not restricted by some of the early maintained assumptions. Large-scale computation allowed for a lifting of some of the restrictions that were introduced into the early approaches to estimation.

In an early demand estimation study (McFadden 1974a) based on a sample of 160 commuters in the Bay Area of San Francisco, he regressed auto-bus choice (zero if bus is usual or frequent mode, one otherwise) on different groupings of the following dependent variables:

(i) Family income with ceiling of US$10,000, in US dollars per year.
(ii) Car-bus cost, in cents per round trip.
(iii) Car-bus on-vehicle time × post-tax wage, in minutes per 1-way × US dollars per hr.
(iv) Bus walk time × first wait time × wage, same units.
(v) Bus first wait time × wage, same units.
(vi) Bus transfer wait time × wage, same units.
(vii) Bus total wait time × wage, same units.
(viii) Bus total access time × wage, same units.

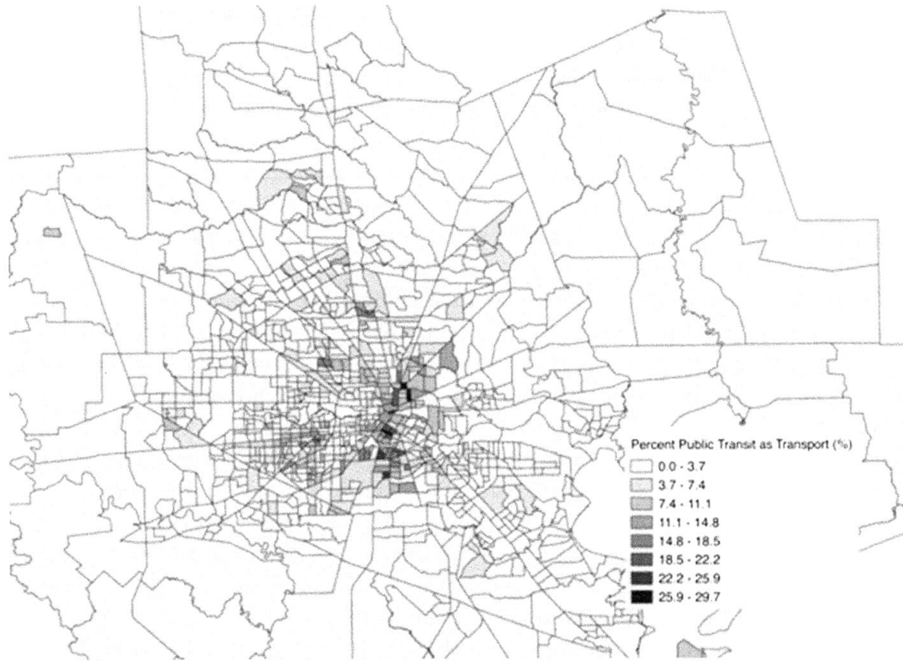

Figure 7.5 Public transit use in Houston, 2011.

Source: Based on Census Tract data.

(xi) Bus total travel time × wage, same units.
(x) Pure auto mode preference effect (constant).

His estimations yielded an equation which allowed him to predict car choice at about 85 percent success and bus choice with between 68 and 79 percent success. And the estimations allowed him to infer value of time to the commuter (in percent of after-tax wage) of between 28 and 43 for on-vehicle travel and between 56 and 60 for waiting for the bus to arrive at the stop. He warned the reader that the quality of his estimates was unclear because his sample size was relatively small. His results (McFadden 1974b; p. 324)

> suggest that the most effective way to increase bus patronage is to increase auto costs, say, by introducing parking fees[5] or gasoline taxes. A 10 percent reduction in bus fares or in running times would each yield a patronage increase of approximately five percent.

The Bay Area Rapid Transit (BART) was a third mode which was of primary concern to McFadden, and he used his conditional logit model to estimate ridership up-take to BART in response to "shocks." He reported that "the elasticity of BART demand with respect to auto cost is relatively high, suggesting that policy measures such as increasing tolls or parking taxes will have a substantial effect on BART patronage," and he also noted that ridership on BART showed up as sensitive to running times: "A ten percent increase in fares would increase revenue by only 1.4 percent" (McFadden 1974b; pp. 326–27).

McFadden ushered in a revolution in travel demand estimations. Textbooks today give examples of the cost of a commuter trip by mode, each trip broken into "access to mode costs," "line-haul costs," "distribution from mode to office costs," with costs broken down into value of time spent and dollars directly spent. Consider Table 7.1, illustrating the choice of commuting by car, from O'Sullivan's (2009; p. 287) textbook.

Automobile travel comes out with the lowest cost per trip because of the low time cost—less than half of the two mass transit alternatives. These data reflect the situation for a certain "demographic," namely those people with an automobile available for commuting each workday and who can access parking at the workplace at a reasonable cost. This way of framing the cost of commuting started with McFadden and helps to make clear why ridership on mass transit is relatively low throughout the United States. Commuting by automobile eliminates the "expensive" component: getting to the bus or subway stop and waiting, and getting from the bus or subway stop downtown to the place of work. Of 30 million vehicles added between 1990 and 2000, five million were acquired by households without a vehicle. Two-thirds of households without vehicles have incomes less than US$25,000 per year. African Americans use transit at four times the rate of whites. Only New York City and DC have significant transit use (24 and 33 percent). About 32 percent of commuting occurs in areas with over 4,000 persons per square mile and 80 percent of transit use occurs in such places. In 2000, New York State, New Jersey, Maryland and Illinois had 10 percent of workers commuting for 60 minutes or more. Driving alone exhibited lowest average travel time. Transit time was double on average that of driving alone.

Pisarski (2006) provides some more interesting data. About 18.5 percent of household spending goes to transportation outlays, "well beyond" that for commuting alone. In 2003, the average was US$7,781 per household. Vehicle costs have declined to about the value of 20 weeks of average pay, the "lowest in about 25 years." Multi-worker-households have a base expenditure of US$5,300 per year on transportation with an extra US$2,500 per year per additional worker. Only 1 percent of average spending per person (just above US$100) is spent on tolls, non-residential parking, transit and taxis.

Table 7.1 Personal cost per commute

	Auto	*Bus*	*BART*
Collection time cost			
Collection time (minutes)	0	10	15
Cost per minute (US$)	0.30	0.30	0.30
Collection time cost (US$)	0	3.00	4.50
Line-haul cost			
Line-haul time (minutes)	40	50	30
Cost-per-minute (US$)	0.10	0.10	0.10
Line-haul time cost (US$)	4.00	5.00	3.00
Distribution time cost			
Distribution time (minutes)	0	5	9
Cost per minute (US$)	0.30	0.30	0.30
Distribution time cost (US$)	0	1.50	2.70
Total time cost (US$)	4.00	9.50	10.20
Monetary cost			
Operating cost or fare (US$)	2.00	1.00	1.50
Parking (US$)	3.00	0	0
Total cost: Time + Monetary (US$)	9.00	10.50	11.70

Source: Adapted from O'Sullivan (2009; p. 287).

To increase ridership on mass transit in the United States, policy-makers have to make automobile travel considerably more expensive[6] and/or travel by bus and subway fast and convenient. McFadden provided early estimates of riders assigning a relatively low value of their time foregone while riding on, say, a subway but a relatively high value of time while getting to a transit stop and waiting for a bus or subway train. A fairly recent innovation in mass transit is the introduction of arrival time indicators at stops for the next bus or subway train. Such an aid may well reduce the time cost a person assigns to the unpleasant spell of waiting. Data for Toronto indicate that it is people with somewhat lower incomes, including students, who dominate riders of the public transit and we are used to the idea that lower-income people assign a lower value to the marginal hour of leisure time. The first-order measure of the value of an hour of leisure time is of course the hourly wage of the person in question.

Mass transit

The history of the evolution of the Los Angeles city form often emphasizes the elimination of the light rail system (street cars or trams) that had been active since about 1900. In the 1930s General Motors became a lead partner in a company, National City Lines, that bought up streetcar companies in L.A. and some 40 other cities in the United States. Other big companies in the consortium were Philips Petroleum, Standard Oil of California and Firestone Tire. National City Lines proceeded to retire the streetcar lines in various cities and to replace these mass transit systems with bus systems with the buses produced by GM. Though a seeming conspiracy against commuters, this revolution in mass transit was in fact a response to the steady decline in ridership on streetcars in most cities. The United States had entered the age of mass ownership of the automobile in the 1920s and cities that grew rapidly after the 1930s were destined to be places in which mass transit had a tough time competing with the private car for the commutes of many people. Mass transit became even less competitive with the spread of freeways funded under President Eisenhower's Federal Highway System legislation of 1956. Most of the modern nation-wide freeway system in the United States dates from the establishment of the Highway Trust Fund (HTF) in 1956, a pot of money, built up from fuel taxes, to be spent on highway construction and maintenance: 22 percent of all highway funding and 17 percent of mass-transit funding currently derives from fuel taxes. The remaining expenditures are covered by state and local governments.[7] Once automobiles became affordable by most Americans and beautifully engineered roads were laid down throughout the United States, the sprawling suburbanized form of a city superseded the dense form which, up to the 1930s, characterized New York and other historic US cites on the eastern seaboard. National City Lines was in fact fined US$5,000 for being in contravention of antitrust laws but it would be hard to argue that a conspiracy by General Motors executives and their partners was a key factor in diminishing the role of mass transit in the life of modern cities in the United States. When the time cost of accessing a subway car and then getting oneself off to the final destination is low, and safety is assured, ridership demand is robust. But low density residential arrangements are generally associated with onerous time costs for a trip by mass transit and such high costs keep demand for trips low.

People often remark that the expansion of a city's road system is met by an "equal" expansion in vehicle flows on the roads. Duranton and Turner (2011) report evidence for this view. Their econometric evidence is in line with the long-standing intuition that urban congestion cannot be mitigated by increased road-building. Road use expands to congest the new capacity. Road traffic flow can be reduced at the margin by raising the direct cost per user. The local authorities impose user fees or Pigovian taxes to raise the cost for each user of the facility. Alternatively, the introduction of a very high quality mass transit system can persuade some road-users to leave their cars at home. Here the idea is that when commuting by transit becomes the lower-cost alternative, some commuters will switch away from commuting by automobile. But when one considers a commuter's cost-per-trip, it is generally financially infeasible to provide a modern city with a high-quality mass transit system. Modern cities in most parts of the world have evolved in low-density arrangements, arrangements hugely influenced by the relatively low cost of owning and operating a car. High-quality mass transit cannot serve customers living and working in low-density arrangements at a reasonable cost per person. In 1961 Jane Jacobs (1916–2006) recorded her view of an effect of lower-cost commuting by automobile: "Increased city accessibility by cars is *always* accompanied by declines in the service of public transportation. The declines in transit passengers are always greater than increases in private automobile passengers" (Jacobs 1961; p. 352). Jacobs of course was a vocal advocate for a high-density, mass-transit lifestyle.

Jane Jacobs rose to prominence in the 1950s in New York city as an activist against the freeway development programs of Robert Moses, the energetic executive[8] in charge of urban development in New York. She combined her activism with articles and a book, *The Death and Life of Great American Cities*, in which she argued in favor of the preservation of established neighborhoods in Manhattan. She was a leader in the movement that led to the cancellation of the Lower Manhattan Expressway.[9] At the time she was living near Washington Square in lower Manhattan. She argued against allowing established neighborhoods to be fragmented by new urban thoroughfares and the razing of established neighborhoods to make way for new freeways. Her name has become synonymous with the movement to let central city neighborhoods evolve with the lightest of direct planning and to not be broken up by big boulevards and freeways. At the time of the Vietnam war she moved to Toronto with her husband and children and settled in an older neighborhood near the central campus of the University of Toronto. She became a leader in the movement to stop construction of a new freeway that would have sliced down from the northwest suburbs into her neighborhood. She followed up her book against the planning of neighborhoods with a book about cities more generally. In the new volume she argued that cities are hotbeds of creativity, the places where the technical progress of economies develops by the interaction of talented people in informal networks.[10] Her name continues to be iconic in the literature about cities, linked firmly with arguments against programs that fracture established neighborhoods and with the stream of thought that sees cities as the foci of inventive activity and innovation.

Greater Phoenix has about twice the population of Manhattan and takes up some 200 times as much land. Its public transit system has about 1 percent of the passenger miles that the system in New York City has.[11]

Of course the very spread-out nature of the city makes it uneconomic to cover the city with a mass transit system that is convenient for a large number of residents. Some people see a new subway or light rail line as devices to increase the density of settlement in some modern cities and Phoenix has invested in a new light rail link between the center of the city and the campus of the State University of Arizona. However, we see virtually no cases of large-scale density build-up following the installation of new higher-end mass transit systems. Automobiles are widely affordable and key decision-makers in modern cities are obliged to lay out the roads to allow the cars to get around and in particular to allow workers to access their places of employment. It would be a rather eccentric mayor of a rapidly growing small city who would commit the future of his town to high residential density and high-quality mass transit. Portland, Oregon has become famous for striving to create a community with less sprawl and less dependency on the automobile but it is a city that still is forced to contend with fairly familiar congestion problems.

Chicago has the second largest mass transit system in the United States but is not one of the five cities with over 30 percent ridership for commuting. Chicago is not a land-constrained place like San Francisco and its suburbs keep spreading far out in low-density patterns. One strategy to increase ridership on commuter trains is the provision of inexpensive parking at train stops. It is unclear that this strategy has been exploited effectively in many cities.

Congestion charges

A congestion charge is a tax on a vehicle entering a crowded road or a complex of roads, such as an area near the center of a city. The idea is that when the cost to the driver of a vehicle rises upon entering a congested roadway, she will alter her time of entry along with other drivers also charged or taxed and the bunching of vehicles will be smoothed out over an extended interval. Traffic will flow faster when fewer vehicles are moving past a point under the smoothed out flow. There will be a better flow of vehicles per unit time when appropriate congestion charges are in effect. This idea was developed with the idea of a roadway in mind and the drivers considering an entry at a particular time to a crowded roadway. But today the idea of charging for road use has been extended to the cores of large cities: the number of vehicles in the core can be regulated by imposing an entry fee to vehicle owners. When the charging scheme works, there are fewer vehicles in the core at certain times and vehicles can move about more rapidly. Gridlock is reduced by penalizing vehicles which approach the core at certain times. Though work trips in 2001 comprise only about 16 percent of all trips in the United States, they bunch up between 6 and 9 am in cities and thus constitute the main cause of congestion on roads. Some 91 percent of work trips occur in private vehicles in the United States while public transit bears 11.5 percent of work trips for cities with more than five million residents. In other cities public transit absorbs a smaller fraction of work trips. Some 26 percent of households with incomes below US$20,000 in 2001 did not own a car. In 2001 about 17 percent of work trips were from suburbs to central cities in the United States, 41 percent were between suburbs and 25 percent were within metropolitan areas (Pisarski 2006). These figures provide us with a different snapshot of the trend toward the suburbanization of jobs in cities in the United States.

Michael Bloomberg, then Mayor of New York City, drew up a plan for congestion pricing for travel in Manhattan south of 86th Avenue between six in the morning and six in the evening. The proposed levy was $8 per vehicle entering the restricted area. Experts indicated that US$400 million dollars of new revenue would flow in to the city each year and that traffic entering Manhattan would decline by 6.5 percent and flow would be some 11 percent less during rush hours. Time lost from congestion was estimated to decline by up to 40 percent. The experience of congestion-charging in London, England[12] was on the table for all to see. However, the Bloomberg proposal was voted down by the state government in Albany. Legislators were concerned about the burden the new charge would be for less affluent commuters. Political acceptability of congestion charging is indeed a vexing issue. Two reasons that the system in London was "accepted" was that the chief implementer, Mayor Ken Livingston, was a well-known maverick, somewhat unburdened of concern for being voted out of office and most of London's commuters were already used to patronizing the mass transit system before the congestion-charging system was introduced. There was a sense that those most severely impacted by the new system were in high-income brackets. Third, the area covered by the new system of charges left large areas of London's financial sector free of the "tax." He lost the next election. It is not obvious, however, that his congestion charging program was a central issue in his election loss. Singapore, which in 1975 was the first large city to implement congestion-charging,[13] had a somewhat autocratic government that was not concerned about a political backlash to its new congestion-control policy. The public transit system is in turn well funded. These policies have kept automobile ownership at under 30 percent of households in the city. In 2011 Beijing introduced a lottery system for awarding its 20,000 permits for new local licences for cars. The number of cars on Beijing's roads has nearly doubled in the past five years.[14] In addition to rationing permits in an attempt to control gridlock, it has a system of fines for owners of automobiles that show up on Beijing's roads at rush hour and are not properly registered in that city.

Consider a smooth flow of vehicles on a roadway. Think of a expressway, which can be accessed by various entry ramps, crowded with moving vehicles. When one more vehicle enters the expressway, the average speed of the flow of vehicles is reduced infinitesimally, say by Δt. Thus the marginal entrant imposes an extra cost of $w\Delta t$ on each vehicle on the roadway, where w is the average wage (the value of time) of people in the slowed-down vehicles. With N vehicles flowing, each vehicle is responsible for $(N-1)w\Delta t$ dollars of cost to all other vehicles on the roadway. This number becomes the social cost that any one vehicle imposes on all others on the roadway at a particular time. The marginal entrant ignores this external cost and enters when her private benefit is at or above her private cost of entry, say c^{priv}. Hence the doctrine of congestion charging is to increase each entrants private cost of entry to the roadway by her social cost or "damage." Hence the new full charge of entry becomes $c^{priv} + \tau$ for $\tau = (N-1)w\Delta t$. We illustrate this in Figure 7.6. The traffic flow (say number of vehicles passing a point) is N'' in the absence of a congestion charge. This flow is reduced to N^* when congestion charge τ is imposed on each vehicle on the roadway. The demand for trips is indicated by the demand curve, D. The reduced flow frees up the triangle with dots of extra costs that the sum of drivers were imposing on each other when congestion was unpriced.[15]

The congestion charge or tax per vehicle reduces the external costs that were being "passed around" by each vehicle onto others before the traffic flow was reduced by the tax.

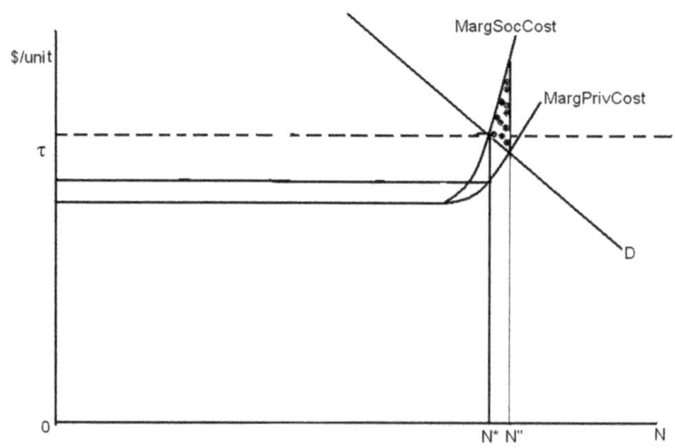

Figure 7.6 Effect of congestion charge. The congestion charge τ reduces traffic flow from N'' to N^* and yields welfare gain in dollars equal to the spotted area.

The spotted area is called the dollar welfare gain that would be reaped by the elimination of the congestion externality by the introduction of an appropriate congestion chargc. A better name for the charge would be congestion abatement charge.

The idea is to reduce flow at the time of congestion and spread it to nearby time periods. It only makes sense to consider using congestion charges when congestion is an issue—and of course congestion usually becomes an issue when a city has widespread ownership of vehicles. The idea of a congestion charge has been in the literature of economics for at least 100 years but it is only since Singapore's introduction in 1975 of an entry fee for a vehicle moving into the center of the city that serious policy interventions have been contemplated for various large cities. William Vickrey, a professor of economics at Columbia University in New York City, advocated back in the 1960s entry fees for vehicles entering Manhattan. His suggestions received no serious attention, perhaps because the cost of implementing a monitoring and charging scheme might have been quite high. There was the issue of wiring up vehicles with transponders in order to have them readily tracked. The reduction in the cost of monitoring and charging of vehicles no doubt brought a good idea, languishing in textbooks, to life.

A more detailed treatment of congestion charging would consider a group of connected time slots and consider spreading the flow from the most congested period over the adjacent periods. More on this below.

Tax revenue and the size of the roadway

An interesting notion is paying for the fixed cost of a roadway with congestion charges. Under constant returns to scale in production, with one factor being capital or the size of the road and the other being variable (fuel and wear and tear on the vehicle), we can derive this result. Consider Figure 7.7. The curves are taken as given and we have inserted an optimal congestion charge, τ and an optimal size of the road, K^*. Let us backtrack and see how this equilibrium works.

In the background we have a constant returns to scale production function, say $N = K^{\alpha} L^{1-\alpha}$ for K the capacity of the roadway and L the variable input to creating traffic flow,

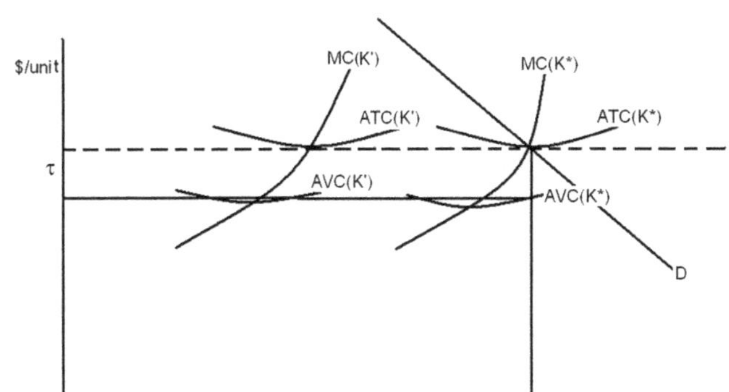

Figure 7.7 The constant returns to scale case. We can slide out cost curves sideways back and forth. Costs "fit" demand at N^*. Then τN^* equals total fixed cost.

N vehicles per minute. Total costs are $TC(N;\,K) = wL + rK$ where w is the price of a unit of the variable input and r is the rental rate for a unit of capital. From the production function we have $L = \left[\frac{N}{K^\alpha}\right]^{1/(1-\alpha)}$ and the variable cost is now $VC(N) = w\left[\frac{N}{K^\alpha}\right]^{1/(1-\alpha)}$.

These variable costs can be written as $VC(N) = wN[\frac{N}{K}]^{\alpha/(1-\alpha)}$. Then total costs are $rK + wN\left[\frac{N}{K}\right]^{\alpha/(1-\alpha)}$. This function is an instance of the one that Mohring and Harwitz (1962; pp. 59–90) start with in their demonstration that rK equals congestion tax revenue, given flow N, and K selected optimally.

Reverting to our production function, the fixed cost is then rK. Now average variable cost, AVC, is $VC(N)/N = \left[w\left[\frac{N}{K^\alpha}\right]^{1/(1-\alpha)}\right]/N$. Marginal cost is

$$MC(N;\,K) = \frac{dTC}{dN} = \left(\frac{1}{1-\alpha}\right) w \left[\frac{N}{K^\alpha}\right]^{[1/(1-\alpha)]-1} \frac{1}{K^\alpha}$$

$$= \left(\frac{1}{1-\alpha}\right) VC(N)/N$$

$$= \left(\frac{1}{1-\alpha}\right) AVC(N;\,K)$$

and the derivative of AVC works out[16] to be $\frac{MC}{N} - \frac{AVC}{N}$.

Given road size K, efficient traffic flow $N^*(K)$ corresponds to the minimum of the average total cost. The congestion tax[17] is then $\tau = MC(N^*;\,K) - AVC(N^*;\,K)$. Total revenue from the congestion tax is $N^* \times [MC(N^*;\,K) - AVC(N^*;\,K)] = N^*\tau$. Constant returns to scale implies that the average total cost schedule has the same minimum dollar value for each exogenous value of K. Hence if one chooses K correctly (where the demand schedule intersects the average total cost schedule at its minimum point), "residual" cost (total cost minus variable cost) must equal total congestion tax revenue. See Figure 7.7. And "residual" cost is of course rK, current fixed cost. Hence the attractive idea that "carrying costs," rK, for a road of the correct size can be covered by Pigovian road taxes.

Entry without tax has the marginal entrant equating her marginal benefit to the average variable cost, precisely as in free entry of a fisherperson to a common property resource stock. An appropriate entry tax to the fishery represents in aggregate a flow value for the fish stock. Without some form of entry restriction the value of the fish stock is dissipated, usually showing up as wages for the "excessive" entrants. The congestion tax for road use represents an entry charge which also in aggregate assigns a flow value to the road. Perhaps it is then not surprising that when the entry charge (congestion tax) for use of the road is set optimally, the aggregate revenue from the charge in fact equals the flow value of the road, namely rK. We are indebted to Mohring and Harwitz (1962) for making this intuition precise many years ago.

Winston (2013) estimates that congestion charges for US cities could raise about US\$40 billion. Trip delays would be reduced and urban sprawl curtailed and there would be new revenue for governments. Part of urban congestion results from exasperated people parking where they should not or simply cruising for a parking space. New cell phone apps have emerged that alert drivers to a parking spot about to be vacated. Some systems allow for the vacater to charge for alerting a driver in need of a space. A debate has broken out in San Francisco over the propriety of a person receiving payment for "using" part of the city infrastructure as a private income-earning asset.[18] Kohn estimates that New York City's 1,200 km^2 of land would sell piece by piece for about US\$600 billion (Kohn 2013). This exceeds the value of roads, bridges and structures in the city. Some argue that the city should be able to monetize the land value somehow and use the proceeds to cover the municipal budget. Hong Kong carries out a related procedure. The city buys up land around a new transit line before the line is built and then sells off the land after the transit development is completed. The gain in land value goes some way to defray the cost of the new line. This leads some observers to argue that the metro system of Hong Kong is in fact a property company. Hong Kong's approach was used in the United States and Canada to support the cost of constructing each nation's first railway to the Pacific. Much land was granted to the railway construction companies and they were able to sell off parcels for good prices, once the railway was up and running (Kohn 2013). In the United States the HTF has provided funds for highway construction and maintenance since the 1950s. The most recent adjustment in rates came in 1993: an 18.4 cent tax on gasoline and 24.4 cents on diesel. State taxes raise an additional 31.1 cents per gallon on average. These taxes are not providing enough revenue for current maintenance and new construction. The Congressional Budget Office estimated in October 2014 that the current revenues to the HTF would only cover US$33 billion of the US$45 billion currently committed over the next year. No new projects could be undertaken. Michael Webber of the Energy Institute at the University of Texas suggests that a new "ton mile" tax should replace the fuel tax. One merit of the "ton mile" tax is that it makes road-users who use natural gas and electricity as fuel carry their share of payment for use. He points out that the annual state check of a vehicle would be the point to assess "ton miles" traversed per year. The assessment per vehicle would be about US$50.

Winston (2013) estimates that about 17 percent of US GDP in 2007 was expenditure for transportation, broadly defined. This includes direct expenditure by households and firms on fuel and vehicles, and is related to some 175 billion person-hours in motion. Firms spent about US$1 trillion shipping inputs, and outputs and materials in transit "used up" about 25 billion ton-days. Local, state and federal expenditures on transportation system maintenance were about US$260 billion. Capital tied up in the transportation system was estimated to be worth about US$4 trillion. One is drawn to the inference that the building of the interstate highway system between 1956 and 1970 must have been a major contributor to the economic development of the United States over that period. Containerization was being developed at the same time. Somewhat later the air transportation system reached its mature form. Winston devotes most of the pages of his overview to advocating more efficient use of the transportation system in the United States, particularly urging for new policies that abate congestion in cities, on highways, on canals and at ports and airports. He presents many convincing examples of policies that could be implemented fairly directly and draws attention to various groups that have thwarted progress in promoting more increased efficiency in essentially transportation infrastructure. In some cases it may simply be bureaucratic inertia that has impeded improvement in the use of the existing transportation system.

Winston estimates that airport delays in 2007 cost passengers about US$8.7 billion. In addition, cancellations and missed connections cost about US$16.7 billion. Large costs are incurred by people in cities cruising to find a parking space; total cost estimate, US$1 billion. The gasoline tax faced by truckers provides no incentive to be "kind" to roads and bridges. An axle-weight charge in place of the simple fuel tax could induce truckers to shift to vehicles with more axles and save an estimated US$10 billion per year on road and bridge maintenance. Thicker layers of pavement in road construction might add about US$3.7 billion annually and save some US$14.4 billion in annual maintenance charges. Annual disbursements from the HTF do not get directed to places with the most intensive transportation taking place because there is a "state size" in the criteria for qualification.

Similarly the Airport Improvement Program has failed to allocate most of its disbursements to the largest, busiest airports. Within cities, Winston is critical of the allocation of vehicle capital to routes and busy times. He contends that use-intensity of buses and subway cars is poorly structured over daily cycles and a US$10.6 billion in savings could be obtained with betters use of vehicle capital. Winston is critical of regulations that developers must meet for parking space allocations. Careful analysis could yield savings, he contends.

This is not Winston's complete sketch of savings and welfare payoffs that could be achieved with better policy but it does provide an overview of how he sees matters in the United States. In a few places he asks for the use of sounder benefit–cost analysis for the development of new infrastructure. He endorses the view of various economists, namely that a high-speed passenger rail system cannot end up with benefits exceeding the high costs of such a system. He remains mostly silent on what investments in urban transportation make the most sense. He is keen to see an air traffic control system based on satellite and GPS technology (the NextGen system), rather than radar, brought on line. His agnosticism about a large-scale investment strategy for transportation in the United States leads him to conclude with a plea for more analysis of

> how transportation affects labor markets, urban and regional economies, international trade patterns, and industry competition... it is certainly reasonable that the field's ultimate ambition should be to explain how resources devoted to transportation contribute to an entire economy's performance and growth. A framework that could successfully address that question could then be exported to countries around the world to improve their transportation systems.
>
> (Winston 2013; p. 817)

A quite different topic that received considerable attention when the "new urban economics" emerged in the 1970s was the correct division of land between roads and, say, production activity. In principle one would adhere to the idea that competing uses for land should end up with an allocation that equalizes the value of the land between competing uses at the spatial margins. This seems somewhat counter-intuitive since roads are part of the transportation industry and other sites are part of goods production. One is not accustomed to thinking about these two activities competing for land. The allocation question becomes more complicated when in fact traffic flow on the road (the demanders faced by the transportation sector) has some congestion inherent in it. Solow and Vickrey (1971) constructed a model of the "optimal" allocation of land to roads in which the traffic flows were associated with production activity. They postulated a rectangular CBD and imposed certain rectangular flows between firms. The flows were land-using. They ended up with a rectangle divided lengthwise into three strips, the center strip being the land for "roads." Hochman and Pines (1972) commented that efficiency would be higher if the central strip devoted to "roads" were cigar-shaped.

Though the many essentially theoretical articles that were published on the allocation of land to roads seem of limited interest today, there remains the vexing policy question of keeping central cities economically vibrant by making access by residents fairly easy. One might refer to this as the Jacobs–Moses debate. Robert Moses was inclined to add more freeways to the New York City landscape in order to move more vehicles in and out of Manhattan faster. Perhaps he viewed Los Angeles as representative of the future, economically strong city and he wanted to try to restructure New York City's land use to make it more like that in LA. Jane Jacobs focused her attention on how more freeways would destroy stable, established residential enclaves. This debate about how land use should evolve in successful cities became sharp in Boston. There the Jacobs sympathizers argued that the elevated freeway that served tens of thousands of commuters who entered central Boston each morning had ruined established, downtown neighborhoods and had also cut the waterfront off from people who enjoyed perambulating about the historic district of central Boston. It was apparent that if the elevated freeway were removed gridlock would prevail each day in central Boston as commuters arrived for work. It was finally decided to put the elevated freeway underground for a few miles near the center of the city. Needless to say some participants in the debate about future land use were concerned about the high cost of putting the freeway underground. The final cost was in fact more than four times the original hefty price (US$12 billion over its initial allocated budget of US$2.6 billion). Once the project got going, the people of Boston were pretty well stuck with funding it to the end. The dreams of the advocates for dismantling the elevated freeway appear, however, to have been realized. Montreal pursued its own "big dig" for a freeway underground and Toronto continues to debate the merits and costs of getting rid of its elevated freeway separating the downtown from the waterfront.

Urban freeways do destroy downtown neighborhoods and do create barriers to flows of people and vehicles from certain sectors of a city to others, but urban freeways do allow vehicles, and the people and goods in those vehicles, to get in and out of dense sectors of a city more easily. The "stop the Spadina expressway" movement in Toronto in the 1960s allowed many neighborhoods along the route to evolve from their historic pasts in attractive ways but it also cut off a major access route for vehicles entering downtown Toronto from the north-west. The economic vitality of the business core of Toronto was clearly impacted by more difficult access. Toronto generates almost 20 percent of Canada's GDP and about 40 percent of Canada's business headquarters are based there. A 2006 study by the government of Canada (Transport Canada 2006) placed costs of congestion for large cities in Canada at US$2.3 to US$3.7 billion per year in 2002 dollars. Ninety percent of this figure was for value of time lost in slow traffic, seven percent was for excess fuel used up and three percent from excess emissions from vehicles. There was no accounting for a possible constriction in the growth of the center of the city. Do some firms choose to locate in other cities or in suburban places when they take account of high commuting costs a resident must deal with in a particular city? A marginal increase in congestion time for a commuter is like a marginal reduction in her wage. Other things being the same, a few workers would respond by migrating to jobs elsewhere, possibly in more suburbanized workplaces. These are subtle effects but should sum to the larger forces shaping the form our cities are evolving toward.

The Travel Time Index (TTI) provides an estimate of how much time congestion *per se* adds to basic trip time when no congestion is present. Vancouver is near the top of cities with the worst congestion at rush hour. Toronto also had a high rank. Many cities in the United States have relatively low rankings. For example Phoenix had a poor ranking when it was much smaller. Now that it is the 12th largest in area in the United States, its ranking for congestion at rush hour is a much better, 37. The relatively low ranking for many US cities turns on job distribution and residential density. Modern cities in the United States, such as Phoenix, have fairly widely dispersed job centers and relatively low residential density. Most people rely on automobiles for commuting and their commutes are not plagued by gridlock. Clearly there is not a simple relationship between city size and average commuting times. Portland, Oregon, a city bent on countering sprawl, ranks a surprising sixth worst in the United States for congestion at rush hour.

Vehicle emission controls

The OECD has presented estimates of annual air pollution costs to OECD countries of US$1.7 trillion. These costs take the form of health complications to people and premature deaths. About half the cost is attributed to emissions from cars and trucks. Diesel engines are responsible for some of the most damaging emissions and proposals are being made to make the costs of using such engines considerably higher.[19] Partly in response to the world oil price shock of 1973 and also in response to President Nixon's stated concern for preserving environmental quality, the US government implemented fuel consumption standards for automobiles and light trucks in 1975, the so-called CAFE (Corporate Average Fuel Economy) regulations. A vehicle manufacturer was required to have its fleet of vehicles being produced in a year meet a fuel consumption ceiling. The standard was averaged over the different types of cars and light trucks produced, leaving the manufacturer to decide how many of each type of vehicle to produce as long as the average standard was met across units being marketed. For many years pick-up trucks were exempted from fleet calculations. Vehicle producers began to tilt their production more and more toward pick-up trucks, which in many cases became primarily passenger movers. The market share of "light trucks" rose steadily from 9.7 percent in 1979 to about 50 percent in 2011. In 2011 the vehicle's "footprint" became a new measure of a vehicle's size for CAFE standards and in 2012 a simpler inverse-linear formula with cut-off values replaced a more complicated mathematical formula. The National Highway Safety Administration (NHTSA) regulates CAFE standards and the US Environmental Protection Agency (EPA) measures vehicle fuel efficiency. Critics of the US approach have pointed out that penalties for non-compliance have not been onerous. Mercedes-Benz paid penalties 21 times between 1983 and 2008. A dimension of the problem of getting less auto emissions is that, at the margin, a higher-cost vehicle, with a higher-tech engine, can shift many vehicle owners to hold on to their cars a bit longer than they otherwise would. Older vehicles are somewhat more polluting than are newer vehicles. Another margin to consider is the extra miles driven by a vehicle owner when her fuel costs per mile are lower. This is referred to as the "rebound effect," often attributed to the great English economist Stanley Jevons.

An economist wonders straightaway whether "engineering mandates" is the most cost effective way of implementing fuel-use economies for vehicles. This can be phrased as "standard setting versus 'price' setting." Why not let manufacturers offer vehicles with any type of fuel consumption they choose and ask purchasers to pay a penalty for buying a unit that uses relatively large quantities of fuel? A consumer can avoid a "guzzler" charge by buying a car or truck that is a light user of fuel. A producer of vehicles can avoid having her vehicles shunned because of a high fuel-use tax by producing vehicles that consumers find attractive for personal transport and are fuel-efficient. The bottom line in this sort of thinking is that innovation in engine and vehicle design will move faster along a track of fuel "conservation" when buyers end up dictating to manufacturers their preferences in vehicle design and fuel economy rather than when regulators and engineers are forced to come up with designs that achieve a regulated level of fuel economy. Competition among producers, bent on raising profit and market share, should lead to novel vehicle and engine designs when demanders "call the tune."

One can argue that the manufacturer can adjust her product mix to meet both fuel-efficiency standards and consumer preferences since the product mix is fully under her control. This argument has some validity. An element of additional flexibility could be introduced with tradable permits added on to the current program. A manufacturer that was exceeding the CAFE standard could sell permits to one whose fleet was currently in "violation." Overall fuel efficiency standards could be met but with a somewhat different mix of vehicles being offered by all manufacturers as a group. Fuel efficiency standards are at bottom an issue with the pace of innovation by producers. A good policy is one that results in good vehicles in the market place and that is linked to rapid increases in fuel-use "conservation." The "quantity controls" approach underlying the CAFE standards regulations is not one that an economist would identify as a "least cost" approach to getting to a high level of fuel use efficiency in the personal transportation sector. Crandall *et al.* (1986), among many observers, argued for a tax approach to constraining fuel-use and tailpipe emissions for vehicles.

Why was improved fuel efficiency in personal transportation approached via "quantity controls" (CAFE standards) rather than "price controls"? Quantity controls have an element of transparency about them. Engineers are asked to come up with vehicles and engines that meet fuel-use standards. Lawyers and engineers and automobile company executives sit around tables and debate at length what is doable and what will not damage the profitability of the industry. Consultants can benefit from producing reports on what is doable and of least damage to "the industry." Price controls are indirect. Vehicles are tested for fuel consumption, the data are pasted on the window of the vehicle in the showroom and a fuel-use tax is listed as part of the final price of the new vehicle. There is much room for policy-makers to debate over the level of the "excess" fuel-use tax but debate will be much more focused than it is when engineering issues are front and center, as they are when CAFE standards are adjusted as time passes. Quantity controls can be said to be regulator and regulatee intensive while price controls are regulator and regulatee "lite." The ultimate test of a policy intervention is: how can the goal be attained within timeframe X in the least cost manner? Economists favor price interventions or letting the market sort adjustments out via price signals, instead of nudging quantities in certain directions via interventions in production methods.

Congestion at a bottleneck

Vickrey (1969) constructed a simple model of the spreading of congested commuter flow over a time interval when the commuters in question all had to get past a bottleneck such as a bridge or possibly a single freeway accessing the CBD. The bottleneck allows only a certain number of vehicles, s, to flow per minute. There are N commuters, fixed in number, each trying to access the same workplace, with work starting at time T^*. Arnott *et al.* (1993) presented an instructive formal treatment of Vickrey's congestion problem.

At time t_0 A_E vehicles leave home per minute and arrive at the bottleneck (say a bridge). We assume that it takes zero time or zero cost to get from one's home to the bridge. The bridge has a starting queue of $B(t_0)$ vehicles waiting to cross. As the bridge has capacity s vehicles per minute, the queue builds up at rate $A_E - s$ per minute, for $A_E > s$. Given N commuters in total, the interval of commuting is $t_e - t_0$ satisfying

$$\frac{N + B(t_0)}{s} = t_e - t_0,$$

where t_e is the end of the morning commute time. It also takes zero time or cost for a commuter to move from the bridge to her place of work.

An "equilibrium commuting pattern" is defined here by each commuter (vehicle) facing the same total cost of her morning commute. Some fraction of our N commuters will arrive early for work and will be forced to kill time (say sacrifice "sleeping-in" time). Work at the office commences at T^*. Each worker who departs at t_0 thus incurs commute cost

$$\beta B(t_0)/s + \varepsilon[T^* - t_0 - B(t_0)/s],$$

where $B(t_0)/s$ is time waiting to cross the bridge, valued at β per minute and $[T^* - t_0 - B(t_0)/s]$ is time to kill at the office before work starts, valued at ε cost per minute. Recall that there is zero cost in getting from the bridge to the workplace.

The last commuters depart home at t_e and face an empty bridge at t_e. Hence they have no queueing cost. However, they have a late-for-work cost of $t_e - T^*$ minutes which is valued at λ per minute. The last person's commute cost is then simply

$$\lambda[t_e - T^*].$$

Given $B(t_0)$, t_0, N, β, ε and λ we can proceed to solve for T^* and t_e. Then we solve for time of peak queue $\tilde{t}$, $B(\tilde{t})$, A_E and flow of later arrivers, A_L. This derivation is given below, followed by a numerical example.

1 The first commuter at t_0 faces a queue wait of $B(t_0)/s$ and a workplace wait of $T^* - t_0 - B(t_0)/s$. Her cost is then $\beta B(t_0)/s + \varepsilon[T^* - t_0 - B(t_0)/s]$. This cost must be the same as the last commuter's cost (simply the cost of being late), namely $\lambda[t_e - T^*]$. The total time of commuting is total commuters divided by s. That is $t_e - t_0 = (N + B(t_0))/s$ for t_e defining the end of the interval of getting our $N + B(t_0)$ commuters to the workplace. The last commuter faces no queue at the bridge. Substitute for t_e and set the costs of the first and last commuters equal. Then we have

$$\beta B(t_0)/s + \varepsilon[T^* - t_0 - B(t_0)/s] = \lambda[t_0 + \{(N + B(t_0))/s\} - T^*], \tag{7.1}$$

which allows us to solve for T^*.

2 Given T^*, we can solve for t_e and the total cost, $C(T^*)$, each commuter faces. Recall the important assumption: equilibrium is defined by each commuter incurring the same cost of commuting, $C(T^*)$. $C(T^*) = \beta B(t_0)/s + \varepsilon[T^* - t_0 - B(t_0)/s]$ and drops out once we have obtained a value for T^*.

3 Some reflection tells us that the commuters that arrive on time at T^* must face the longest wait at the bridge. This follows from the fact that they do not incur any costs of being early or costs of being late. Their total cost must then be only a queueing cost at the bridge. Hence

$$\alpha B(\tilde{t})/s = C(T^*),$$

where $\tilde{t}$ is the time of leaving home of the commuters who arrive at the workplace at T^*. It also follows that

$$T^* - \tilde{t} = B(\tilde{t})/s.$$

We can then solve for $B(\tilde{t})$, maximum queue, and $\tilde{t}$.

4 The rate of queue build-up at the bottleneck is

$$\frac{B(\tilde{t}) - B(t_0)}{\tilde{t} - t_0} = A_E - s,$$

where A_E is the inflow of commuters, who are early to work, to the bridge per minute. The rate of the queue $B(\tilde{t})$ "melting" to zero is

$$\frac{B(\tilde{t})}{t_e - \tilde{t}} = s - A_L$$

for A_L the inflow of commuters to the queue at the bottleneck who will be late for work.[20]

Commuting costs: an example

There is initial backup, $B(t_0) = 60$. Bridge flow capacity is $s = 50$. There are $N = 10,000$ "new" commuters to cross the bridge in addition to the initial 60. The earliest group getting up and reaching the bridge "hits" the bridge at time, $t_0 = 400$. Time costs are $\lambda = 0.8$, $\varepsilon = 0.4$, and $\beta = 0.6$. We solve to get $T^* = 533.93$, queue-end time, $t_e = 601.2$, and queue-maximum time, $\tilde{t} = 444.24$. The flow of vehicles "hitting" the queue before $\tilde{t}$ is $A_E = 150$ vehicles per minute, and the flow after $\tilde{t}$ is $A_L = 21.43$ vehicles per minute. The queue starts then at 60 at t_0 and peaks at 4,484.5 vehicles 44.24 minutes after t_0. The complete commuting interval is 201.2 minutes. The cohort that departs home at $\tilde{t}$ and arrives at the workplace exactly on time is stuck in the bridge-queue for 89.68 minutes.

See Figure 7.8 for a sketch of this solution. Consider two checks on the numbers in Figure 7.8:

- Check 1—In phase 1, there are 100 vehicles above bridge capacity flowing in to the queue at each minute and hence 44.25 × 100 backed up plus the 60 initially backed up. This is approximately 4,485 vehicles backed up at time 444.24.
- Check 2—In phase 2, there are 50 – 21.43 vehicles being drawn down per minute from the back-up. We multiply this by total minutes for phase 2 and get $(50 - 21.43) \times (601.2 - 444.24) = 4,484.35$.

Observe that if the cost of being late, λ, rises then A_L is smaller. Fewer vehicles that involve their commuters being late leave home per minute. The peak $B(\tilde{t})$ "melts" somewhat faster: it shifts to the right and the right branch of $B(t)$ is steeper. When the cost of being early, ε, rises, the peak shifts to the left and the flow of early commuters per minute, A_E, is larger. This seems counter-intuitive. This might be capturing the notion of a "rush." A larger early-to-work cost ε means that bridge-wait cost β has declined in a relative sense and commuters are now willing to put up with a slightly longer wait-at-the-bridge interval. Average queue length $B(t)$ goes up slightly.

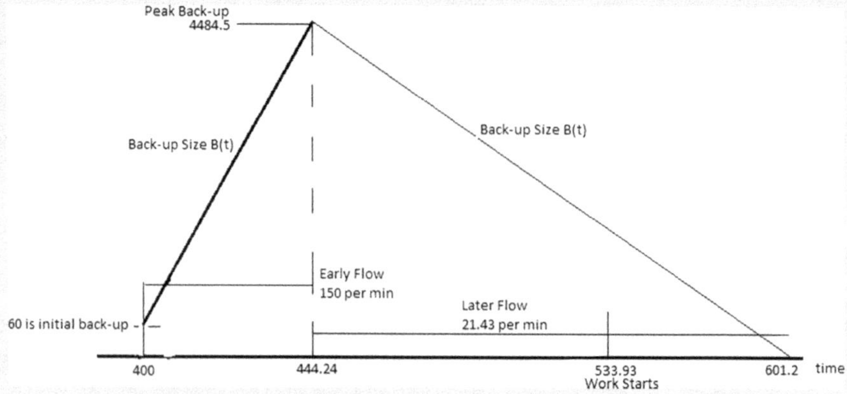

Figure 7.8 Bottleneck congestion: Early arrivals induce a gradual growth in a queue at a bottleneck. Arrivals abate and the queue melts down to zero, with some commuters late for the start of work.

The future of central city entry charges for vehicles

When one examines the welfare gains from the imposition of congestion charges, one is inclined to ask if these dollar values are relatively large. Recall the spotted area in Figure 7.6 representing the cost per road user of congestion. How much vehicle flow reduction does it take to yield a satisfactory equilibrium flow? How high is the required congestion charge? How costly is it to monitor entry flow to a restricted area and to collect congestion charges? And to enforce the collection of fees? Singapore, London and Stockholm have served as demonstration cases. The costs of operating a system are manageable and the gains in terms of improved traffic flow are significant. Is there a lower-cost way to achieving the same end? Arnott (2005), who has studied the congestion problem in cities for many years, has expressed reservations about the appropriateness of direct charging for congestion. Two obvious alternatives are (a) improved mass transit (dedicated lanes for buses and expansion of light rail and subways presumably) and (b) significant taxation of parking places in the centers of cities. Another strategy is the restriction of truck traffic over the interval of seven in the morning to seven in the evening. The loading and unloading of trucks in the centers of large cities contributes significantly to the creation of gridlock. Mills (1999) favors stiff taxes on gasoline and diesel fuel to alleviate congestion in cities:

> What would be the effect of a dramatic rise in fuel taxes? A few people would walk, cycle or take public transit. More people would gradually replace large cars with more fuel-efficient ones, as they did after the two fuel crises. A crude estimate is that my proposed fuel tax increase would reduce metropolitan driving by 15 to 25 percent.

Mills is attracted to this approach to congestion mitigation because, among other things, taxes on fuel are easy to collect at the pump.

It is important to distinguish between a charge for entering a crowded roadway (the traditional congestion tax) and a charge for entering the CBD such as has been developed in Singapore and London. A congestion charge for a roadway can be viewed as a device for unknotting clusters of vehicles on the road at certain times. The aggregate number of vehicles using the road may not change when the congestion charge is imposed but the timing of use of the road by various drivers is altered. One can think of congestion charges as smoothing out the flow of traffic over, say, an hour, perhaps between 8 and 9 in the morning. The volume of vehicles entering the center of the city is not changed but the timing of the flow entering is altered. The entry flow is smoothed out. In contrast a charge for entering the CBD between, say, 7am and 7pm will, if binding, actually reduce the number of vehicles moving about in the central area during the day. This was the intent of Mayor Livingston in London and Mayor Bloomberg in New York. The indirect effect of reduced vehicle entry is to make the CBD a more expensive place for a certain class of workers in which to do business. A stiff entry charge could cause firms at the margin to locate away from the city center. This could reduce the degree of clustering by certain firms in the center of a city and could create an efficiency loss for the city in question. The London scheme was cleverly designed to exclude most of London's financial district from the burden of the entry fee. Financial activity appears to work best in dense clusters of tall buildings. The imposition of an entry fee to such a cluster could drive marginal firms away from the cluster and make the cluster less efficient overall.

The central issue in mass transit economics is who pays for the fixed costs of a system. In Table 7.2 we see that only in a few cities in Asia do revenues from fares cover the costs of operating the mass transit system. The implicit large subsidies to transit users in cities in Europe and North America is a negative outcome in the eyes of Edwin Mills, who says (Mills 1999; p. 4), "I have seen no careful study concluding that any metropolitan fixed rail investment in the last 35 years had benefits anywhere near as great as costs (DC, Atlanta, Baltimore, Dallas and, worst of all, LA are examples)." Glaeser (1998, p. 155)[21] is equally distressed about the inefficiency of most modern subway construction. Clearly the density of settlement near stops is crucial to the volume of demand for mass transit. Tokyo, London and many cities in China have a high percentage of commuters who use the subway regularly.[22]

With a bus system, a new stop can be introduced and it does not take a high density of residents for enough of them to show up and have their fares cover the costs of the new stop. Bus systems are viable in relatively low density neighborhoods. Of course there is the negative network effect on others of a new stop. Each stop adds minutes to existing users of the system. If one adds a new subway stop to a system, there are large fixed costs. In low-density residential areas, the customers that show up for the new stop will each be required to pay a large fare to cover that customer's share of the fixed costs. Generally demand at any fare is insufficient to cover the cost of a new stop in a low-density area. See Figure 7.9.

In Figure 7.9 no single price cutting the demand curve will raise enough revenue to cover costs. However, if users with a high willingness to pay are charged a high price, while other users pay a medium price, there could be enough total revenue to cover costs. Truckers might be those hit with a high use-charge, for example.

One infers that land rents will be relatively high near transportation nodes (e.g. a subway stop) and this will induce developers to build in relatively high densities near these places. Two constraints are land-use regulations and a possibly high cost of assembling good-sized building sites, given the land already in use. It appears that owners of homes near a new node can bring much pressure to bear for not allowing current land-uses to change. A well-known hub in Vancouver where the light rail (Skytrain) meets many bus lines (Commercial and Broadway streets) has no high-density development and this has been attributed to the relatively high cost of assembling good-sized parcels of land on which to build upwards.[23]

Table 7.2 Ratio of fares to operating costs for public transport systems

	Ratio (%)	*Year*
Asia	...	...
Hong Kong (MTR)	149	2007
Osaka (Hankyu Railway)	123	1991
Osaka (OMTB)	137	1991
Taipei (MRT)	119	2006
Teito RTA (now Tokyo Metro)	170	1991
Europe	...	...
Brussels	28	1991
Copenhagen	52	1991
London Underground	~100	2004
Milan	28	1991
Munich	42	1991
Paris (RATP)	43	1991
Stockholm	44	1996
Vienna	50	1991
Zurich	66	1991
North America	...	...
Atlanta (MARTA)	31.8	2007
Austin (CMTA)	9	2007
Boston (MBTA)	43.7	2002
Chicago (CTA)	55.2	2010
Cleveland (GCRTA)	21.5	2002
Dallas (DART)	28.4	2008
Detroit (DDOT)	13.9	2002
Edmonton (ETS)	39.4	2007
Los Angeles (LACMTA)	30.6	2004
Miami	16.1	2002
Montreal (STM)	57.1	2006
New York City (MTA)	55.5	2009
New York/New Jersey (PATH)	41.0	2002
Ottawa (OC Transpo)	43.2	2007
Philadelphia (SEPTA)	58.6	2002
Philadelphia/New Jersey (PATCO)	61.4	2002
Puget Sound Region (King County Metro)	19.1	2006
San Francisco Bay Area (BART)	64.5	2008
San Francisco Bay Area (Caltrain)	41	2006
Toronto (TTC)	66.7	2009
Toronto, Hamilton and area (GO Transit)	88.4	2008
Vancouver (TransLink)	46.3	2009
Washington, DC (WMATA)	61.6	2002

Source: Wikipedia: "Farebox recovery ratio".

Many subways and elevated transit systems have been built in North America since the 1950s despite the consistent failure of revenues to cover costs. Routine calculations reveal that at any reasonable fare per trip, revenues fall well short of annual costs. Often not even annual operating costs are covered by revenues from fares and the renting out of advertising spaces. Municipal governments end up subsidizing their systems with funds from general revenues. Capital or construction costs are often subsidized by federal and state governments. Since, on average, a rider on a system such as a subway or elevated train is not in the high-income cohort, one can argue that large-scale income redistribution is taking place.

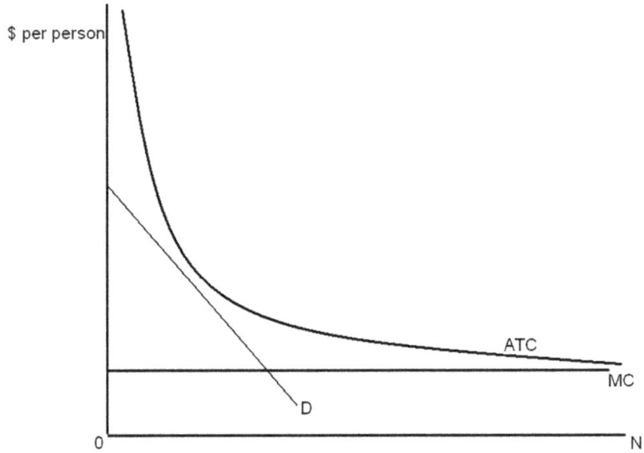

Figure 7.9 Revenue must be raised via price discrimination across users. There is no price (charge per person) that will cover the fixed cost "assessed" per person, given the "small" demand.

Riders are being subsidized in non-trivial amounts by the average tax-payer in a city. For Mills, the answer is: good quality bus systems should be promoted for urban transit. Subways fail a basic economics test. He seeks an approach to balance the fare paid with the cost per trip. He recommends much use of bus systems. Bus systems are much cheaper to develop and operate than are subways and elevated trains. They do of course usually leave the average commuter with a fairly long-duration commute. If subways do indeed represent large-scale subsidization of users by non-users these subsidies in turn represent a freebie that employers can draw upon when "setting" their wages. On average a worker subsidized on her commute can be offered a lower wage than she would otherwise need to be content to work where she does. Thus if there is large-scale subsidization of subway and elevated train use by non-users, there should be a built-in tilt in favor of more activity in the centers of cities, the focal point of most mass transit systems. Workers who rely on subway and elevated train use become marginally cheaper to employ in the centers of cities rather than in other locations. The subway construction boom in the United States in recent decades from this perspective represents a subsidization of central city economic activity.

Mills argues that because higher-tech mass transit systems, such as subways, do not pay their way in most cities in North America, the systems represent an indirect income transfer from higher-income people, who do not use the mass transit system very much, to lower-income people. He finds this route to income redistribution uncongenial. Is large-scale income redistribution taking place all over the world and is almost no one focusing attention on it? Or are subways a natural development for larger cities? For huge cities like Tokyo and Shanghai subways are heavily used each day and operating costs are easily covered with revenue from fares. In fact much of the capital costs are also probably covered by the revenue from fares. Hence there is really no redistribution of income going on when fares do cover costs. And it seems obvious that these subway systems are contributing heavily to the efficient functioning of each city. Commuters get around and automobile traffic is substituted for. It is not too difficult to make the case that a subway system generates indirect benefits for the city in question, in addition to the benefits accruing to the riders alone.

Consider a city without a subway system at time t_0. It will have a certain equilibrium size with much commuting being done by automobile and by buses. Now in time t_1 let us have the city build a subway system with a focus on the CBD. The new system should significantly reduce the out-of-pocket costs to citizens (we suppose that fares remain much under costs, given the familiar relatively low volumes of use in modern US cities). As we observed in Chapter 2, the edge of the city moves out and the city rent function becomes flatter. Typically the city is larger in population and area. To a first approximation the utility of the representative household will not change. However, we know that larger, denser cities have the representative worker's productivity increasing. That is, the average wage in the city rises. This rise represents an indirect positive externality that has emerged because the subway was built. The city has become a larger, lower commuting-cost city with a more productive labor force. The productivity boost per worker could be taxed to pay for part of the cost of the subway system. Casual empiricism supports the view that cities with new subways or skytrains do experience significant growth.

The question of new subway construction has become complicated because job-growth for many modern cities is taking place in suburban places rather than in CBDs. A fixed-rail mass transit network usually has a focal area to get riders to, a place such as a CBD with many office type jobs. A good quality bus system may make more sense for distributing residents to suburban places of work. Low-density residential arrangements make it very difficult for subway systems to ever pay a reasonable part of their costs. Where residential activity is densely built up, as in many large cities in Asia and Europe, subway systems can set reasonable fares which in total cover the costs of building and operating a subway system.

Hong Kong's subway is celebrated for its stellar record of keeping on schedule. The system is shut down every evening past midnight and has teams of workers attend to maintenance. The task assignment is coordinated with an artificial intelligence system, built up with so-called genetic algorithms. The transit system is owned and operated by the MTR Corporation which also runs systems in Beijing, London, Melbourne and Stockholm.[24] High-tech is also being harnessed to reduce congestion in San Francisco. A driver can consult an app that indicates when and where a parking space is available.

Efficient transportation for a city?

Suppose that on average the typical resident of a city in North America lived not too far from his or her job. We might say that for such a city, urban land-use was efficient. No? And of course relative efficiency could be inferred by the distance gap the average resident was from his or her place of employment. Hamilton (1982) measured this gap for a set of large US cities and came up with a large value for the distance gap. He estimated that the average commute for a resident would be about 8.7 miles if all jobs were in the CBD. He then determined that in fact the actual average commute was very close to this. (His model required each commuter to be working in the CBD only, whereas modern cities typically have a half or more jobs in areas away from the CBD.) He concluded that about 85 percent of commuting distances logged in aggregate were "wasteful." Critics responded that his methodology was flawed because he worked with distances radial from the CBD. Small and Song (1992) allowed for oblique-angle commuting in Los Angeles and arrived at the figure of 11 percent for wasteful commuting.

Summary

Large cities work best when goods and workers move about at low cost. "The market" seems to produce equilibria in which this low-cost flow is not the norm. Congestion is ubiquitous. Hence the attraction of congestion charges on vehicles contributing to significant congestion, and hence the attraction of more and better mass transit to some observers for large cities. Strangely enough it is not obvious that some cities have solved the goods-and-workers-flow problem and can be held up as models for others to follow. Mills argues that consumer sovereignty indicates that people desire more housing, including lot size, when their incomes rise and people desire rapid and comfortable commutes to places of employment. For him, relatively low residential densities and much commuting by automobile are not problems to be solved in modern cities but market outcomes that for the most part reflect a rich and happy society. This suggests that Houston and Los Angeles are models of the form of the modern city in a high-income nation. He does favor the rationing of automobile use by the imposition of high fuel taxes, however. On the other hand, the experiments with congestion charging in London and Stockholm have generated no significant backlash. Then again, the introduction of congestion charges for New York City was cancelled by state-level legislators who were in fact worried about a negative voter backlash. The world has both well-functioning high-density cities and well-functioning low-density cities. Solutions to the urban transportation problem are taking place in different forms.

Main points of Chapter 7

1. A commuter can take mass transit or a personal vehicle; she faces here a discrete choice, one or the other. Urban travel demand expands on the discrete choice issue and works toward sound expressions to estimate or to work one out with econometrics.
2. Travel demand analysis breaks the cost of a trip into components dealing with the cost of getting to the vehicle or tram, the cost of moving along on the mode and the cost of getting from the stop or garage to the workplace.
3. The high dollar value a typical commuter places on her time makes it difficult to persuade commuters to take up commuting by mass transit in larger numbers.
4. A congestion charge for a commuter represents an attempt to persuade the person to commute at a different time, or an attempt by authorities to smooth out demands on a crowded road.
5. Singapore and London are two large cities with significant charges to commuters who drive their personal vehicles into the centers of the respective cities.
6. Subway construction is very expensive and uptake by commuters has not been sufficient to pay for most newer installations. Low-density residential development means a typical subway rider has a problem in getting from home to a local stop.

Questions and problems

1. Land use in Washington, DC is heavily regulated. Its very good subway operates well below capacity. Would regulation mandating high-density residential development around suburban subway stops be a welfare-enhancing policy?
2. Strict regulation favoring dense residential development near subway stops could solve the sprawl problem in cities in North America. Evaluate this contention.
3. Why is mass transit so lightly used for commuting in most American cities?

4 "When countries move from having low gasoline taxes to high gas taxes, the density of development increases by more than 40 percent. Vehicle ownership falls as well" (Glaeser 2011; p. 178). How feasible is a high gasoline tax for solving the commuting congestion problems in North American cities?
5 Are cities such as Houston and Los Angeles prosperous because they are spread out and car-oriented or has prosperity caused the cities to evolve in a low-density fashion?
6 Must a "new city" have a low-density arrangement if it is to prosper today?
7 "Cities need radical new designs that offer affordable housing and quicker commutes" (Glaeser 2011; p. 180). Has Glaeser forgotten about Houston?

Appendix 7.1: Consumer theory and expressions for fraction of demanders

Travel demand commanded the attention of very good economists for a long time. The point of departure was estimating the fraction of a population of, say, a city using mode j to commute to work. This fraction would reflect the direct cost per trip, the income of the users, the value of time to them, the characteristics of the mode and additional characteristics of the demanders. In fact, regressing the fraction of a population selecting alternative j over other alternatives on a collection of explanatory variables was a standard statistical exercise outside of transportation analysis. There was recognition that the estimation procedure needed tightening up, from at least two directions: a demand theory to provide a route to the basic regression equation and econometric theory to provide a detailed route to the precise choice of regression equation being estimated. Daniel McFadden (1974a) provided a solution to the first problem in 1974 and he and others developed statistical analysis for appropriate regression-running.

With regard to the first issue, a consumer theory for choice over discrete alternatives, McFadden suggested starting with the utility of person n over J alternatives in

$$U_{jn} = V(z_{jn}, s_n; \beta) + \varepsilon_{jn} \quad (j = 1, \ldots, J)$$

where $V(.)$ is a function defined on the vector z_{jn} of attributes of alternative j as they pertain to person n, s_n is a vector of person $n's$ characteristics, β is a vector of parameters. Here $V(.)$ is referred to as the systematic utility, ε_{jn} is the unobservable part of utility capturing idiosyncratic characteristics of person n's preferences for alternative j.

Suppose that the functional form for V has been specified and denote $V(z_{jn}, s_n; \beta)$ by $V_{jn.}$ If person n favors alternative j, it must be true that

$$\begin{aligned}P_{jn} &= \Pr[U_{jn} > U_{in} \text{ for all } i \neq j] \\ &= \Pr[\varepsilon_{in} - \varepsilon_{jn} < V_{jn} - V_{in} \text{ for all } i \neq j] \\ &= \int_{-\infty}^{\infty} F_j(V_{jn} - V_{1n} + \varepsilon_{jn}, \ldots, V_{jn} - V_{in} + \varepsilon_{jn}) d\varepsilon_{jn},\end{aligned}$$

where $F(\varepsilon_{1n}, \ldots, \varepsilon_{Jn})$ is the cumulative distribution function for the random terms (the $\varepsilon'_{jn}s$). Here F_j is the probability density function of ε_{jn}, conditional on the inequalities above, and is the partial derivative of F with respect to the jth argument.

When $F(.)$ is specified as the multivariate normal, then the model is referred to as the multinomial probit with a general covariance structure.

When the J random terms are independently and identically distributed with the extreme-value distribution (Weibull distribution) defined by $\Pr[\varepsilon_{jn} < x] = \exp(-e^{-\mu x})$ where μ is a scale parameter, μ is usually set at unity. These assumptions on the random terms leads to the LOGIT form:

$$P_{jn} = \frac{\exp(V_{jn})}{\sum_{i=1}^{J} \exp(V_{in})}.$$

This "result" captures "the independence of irrelevant alternatives," i.e. the addition of a new alternative does not change the proportions in which the earlier alternatives were being used. This is clearly reflecting very specialized behavior and one is inclined to search for a less rigid model.

When $F(.)$ is specified as generalized extreme value, i.e.

$$F(\varepsilon_1, \varepsilon_2, \ldots, \varepsilon_J) = \exp[-G(e^{-\varepsilon_1}, \ldots, e^{-\varepsilon_J})]$$

and G is appropriately restricted, one obtains

$$P_j = \frac{e^{V_j} G_j(e^{-V_1}, \ldots, e^{-V_J})}{G(e^{-V_1}, \ldots, e^{-V_J})},$$

where G_j is the jth partial derivative of G.

So much for the consumer theory of discrete choice. From here one moves to the setting out of acceptable equations to estimate and to estimation. This in itself is a large topic. The reader can turn to a number of sources (e.g. Small and Verhoef 2007). In the text we report on an early estimation carried out by McFadden.

Notes

1 *Toronto Vital Signs Report, 2013.*
2 *Globe and Mail*, May 3, 2014, p. M4.
3 In Bolivia a cable car mass transit system has been constructed that runs seven miles near La Paz, has 11 stops and can carry 18,000 passengers per hour.
4 Our map of Chicago comprises 2011 Census Tracts and 8.3 million people for year 2011. The area is 17,381 km^2, exceeding twice the area of Toronto's GTA (7,124 km^2 and 6.05 million people). Settlement density for Chicago, defined by its large area concept, is light relative to Toronto, which for the concept of the GTA is itself lightly settled.
5 London, England has the world's highest price for parking by the month at US$1,083.59. New York comes in at US$589 per month and Calgary, Alberta at US$472.50 (*Globe and Mail*, July 13, 2011, p. B2).
6 In 2001, the average household in the United States had 2.58 people and 1.77 licensed drivers. Each person travelled 35,244 miles by car in 2001. See the *2001 National Household Travel Survey*, Federal Highway Administration, US Department of Transportation, 2004.
7 In 1982 a mass transit account was created within the HTF and of 18.4 cents per gallon of taxes, 2.86 cents funds mass transit work. Though the HTF is called a fund, dollars do not accumulate in it. Tax revenues flow in from fuel taxes and flow out that year. "Needs" have been exceeding funds, however. Between 2008 and 2010 Congress supplemented the revenue from fuel taxes for the first time with US$34.5 billion from general revenues. But there is no move to increase the rate of tax. Revenue shortfalls appear likely to be persistent in the near future. According to the American Society of Civil Engineers, US$78.2 billion is burned up in time and fuel costs due to congestion on major urban highways. Another group contends that a ninth of highway bridges in the United States are in need of major repairs (*The Economist*, November 19, 2011, pp. 35–36).

8 Robert Moses (1888–1981) was the "master builder" of mid-twentieth century New York City and its outer suburbs. He was also the planner for the development of a new hydro-power station at Lewiston, near Niagara Falls. His supporters believe he made New York City viable for the twenty-first century by building an infrastructure (freeways, bridges, etc.) that most people wanted and that has endured. His works remain extremely controversial. His critics claim that he preferred automobiles to people, that he displaced hundreds of thousands of residents in New York City, uprooted traditional neighborhoods by building expressways through them and precipitated the decline of public transport through disinvestment and neglect.

9 Her battles with Robert Moses and other authorities in New York City are recounted in Flint (2009).

10 Van Noorden (2010; pp. 906–908) reports on patenting rates and related indicators of scientific activity in various US cities as well as some other cities of the world. His data provide some evidence in support of Jane Jacob's contention.

11 New York City metro has 2.2 million households without vehicles. Of 50 metro areas with more than one million people, 30 experienced an increase in the number of households without a vehicle. Private vehicle trips account for more than 80 percent of all trips in 14 states, with Michigan exhibiting the highest value (83 percent). There has, however, been a 10 percent decline in auto use per household in metropolitan areas with over five million people. Car pooling has however declined. (Pisarski 2006).

12 The zone involving a charge was introduced in Central London on February 17, 2003, and extended into parts of west London on February 19, 2007. A payment of £11.50 is required each day for each vehicle which travels within the zone between 7 am and 6 pm (Monday–Friday only); a fine of between £65 and £195 is levied for non-payment. A charge increase was introduced in 2011.

13 Vehicles entering the city center were monitored and charged. In September 1998 the system was upgraded with electronic vehicle monitoring. Charges now vary by time of day. Authorities have kept car ownership to just 30 percent in Singapore with a variety of other policies, all directed to making ownership expensive for a resident. These measures have included high annual road tax, custom duties and vehicle registration fees. The flow of new motor vehicles has been regulated since 1990, when a Vehicle Quota System was introduced. Use-related charges, such as fuel taxes (50 percent of final sale price), congestion charges and high parking rates are utilized by public authorities to further constrain auto travel.

14 *New York Times*, January 9, 2011, p. 4 "Week in Review."

15 In fact, in addition to one vehicle's presence causing others to slow down marginally, considerable congestion is caused by vehicle breakdowns, "fender benders," construction and repair of roadways, weather and poor traffic signal timing (Pisarski 2006).

16 The derivative of AVC is worked out as follows.

$$\begin{aligned}\frac{d[AVC]}{dN} &= \frac{1}{N}\left(\frac{1}{1-\alpha}\right) w \left[\frac{N}{K^\alpha}\right]^{[1/(1-\alpha)]-1} \frac{1}{K^\alpha} - \left[\frac{N}{K^\alpha}\right]^{1/(1-\alpha)} \frac{w}{N^2} \\ &= \frac{MC}{N} - \frac{AVC}{N}.\end{aligned}$$

17 The marginal entrant to the crowded road is imposing an external cost of $\frac{d[AVC]}{dN}$ on each vehicle on the road and the sum of these external damages caused by each vehicle is $N\frac{d[AVC]}{dN}$.

18 *The Economist*, July 12, 2014, p. 62.

19 See *New Scientist*, May 31, 2014, p. 7. Comparable total costs of air pollution for China are US$1.4 trillion and for India are US$0.5 trillion. The net increase in car use in China and India yields air pollution that more than offsets the emissions reductions attributable to more efficient engines for vehicles.

20 We are assuming here that A_E and A_L are constants. One can verify that these constants solve the problem. A simple calculus analysis involving $dB(t)/dt$ also establishes that A_E and A_L are in fact constant for this problem. If being late was not a linear cost, but one increasing faster than the late-time interval a person incurred, then A_L would not be constant.

21 "...local governments still evince a strong predilection for building large (and preferably high-tech) subway systems, even when the best evidence continues to show that subway systems rarely, if ever, provide enough social surplus to pay for their construction" Glaeser (1998).

22 It currently costs US$7.34 to take a trip on London's subway (the tube) and revenue from fares and sales of advertising space only cover running costs. Capital costs must be met from other revenues. London's subway was opened in 1863 and including the above-ground rail parts is the largest in the world. Chicago was the second city to have a metro and it started its elevated system 29 years later. There are currently some 190 cities in the world with metros of various sorts, including Asuncion in Paraguay and Kathmandu in Nepal. Algiers recently completed its metro and behind Cairo becomes the second city in Africa to have such a mass transit system. Beijing plans to expand its network to 1,000 km by 2020. Spending on metro systems is expected to grow at 6 to 8 percent per year in the near future (*The Economist*, January 5, 2013, p. 50).

23 *Globe and Mail*, May 31, 2011, p. B13.

24 *New Scientist*, July 5, p. 17.

8 Housing

Supply and demand for housing. The annual cost-of-ownership equation (opportunity cost of funds). The impact of inflation and mortgage interest deductibility on the annual cost-of-ownership. Asset allocation neutrality and mortgage interest deductibility. Renting versus owning and housing price bubbles. Social housing and voucher mechanisms.

Introduction

A house is a complicated commodity because it is long-lived, each house is slightly different if only in terms of exposure to sunshine, and every house has a slightly different location. The long-lived nature of a house means that interest rates (discount factors), rates of depreciation and maintenance effort are crucial to current value. Housing comes with two payment schemes: renting versus owning. In addition, the business cycle in most countries appears sensitive to rates of production of new housing. Housing is a large component of the standard bundle in the consumer price index and has not proved easy to measure (Diewert *et al.* 2009).

Since a house typically comes with a resale price, say US$500,000, an economist wants to translate this into a number that represents the annual cost to the resident from living in her owner-occupied home. To a first approximation one would say that the annual cost was simply $i \times$ US$500,000 for current interest rate i. This represents the money that could be earned if the funds tied up in the house were placed in a good investment such as a long-term bond. This is the usual way to translate a capital value (here the house price) into a flow value or annual "cost." One then can say that the home-owner is paying "price," $i \times$ US$500,000 to live in her house for a year. This price is approximate or first order since in addition the resident must pay municipal taxes and maintenance and she also earns a capital gain (resale price appreciation) or capital loss over a year.

Housing economists refine this annual cost (the $i \times$ US$500,000 figure) for the flow of housing services to include "secondary" cost items, namely annual municipal tax ($\tau \times$ US$500,000), annual maintenance ($m \times$ US$500,000) and annual capital gains or losses ($g \times$ US$500,000). Hence the general representation that one assigns to the "price" of living in one's owned home for a year is

$$u^i = (i + \tau + m - g^i)V^i,$$

where V^i is the current selling price (value) of the house in question. This "price" u^i is referred to as "user cost" to the resident (u^i is not utility here). We use the superscript i to indicate a particular house. Hence the rate of capital gains g^i can be different for different homes. Just as the price of an apple, for example, is an underestimate of the dollar value of utility a person gets from the apple (recall the consumer surplus triangle above the price line) then u^i is also an underestimate of the dollar value of utility (consumer's surplus) that a person derives from living in her house for a year. User cost is thus working as a price, like the price of an apple, and not as the value or benefit to the resident of living in the home. The dollar benefit per year would be a consumer surplus concept whereas user cost is a concept of price of housing services per year.

One might try to make houses comparable by viewing the V^i as a price for say 1,600 square feet of "standard housing" with lot. Then when an individual experiences a reduction in her user cost, we might expect her to increase her quantity demanded of housing. At the margin, she might add to her house and have more square feet of housing. Or she might switch to a larger house. In any case we consider that a reduction in user cost leads to an expansion in quantity demanded for housing per resident. More quantity demanded per resident translates into more quantity demanded in the market as a whole.

When we move up to "the" market for housing, say nation-wide, we are pretty well obliged to think in terms of $Q(t)$ very similar owner-occupied units. We illustrate a reduction in user cost for the nation in Figure 8.1. A reduction can occur, for example, when the rate of interest declines (i declines) or the rate of capital gains for the market in question increases (g increases).

We expect a change in i or g to impact user cost directly. But there is a secondary effect on user cost via a change in house price V. The rudiments of a price bubble might be (1) a decline in interest rates (2) a jump in house prices (3) an increase in capital gains and thus a further reduction in user costs. This can be an open-ended spiral that has house prices rise well above trend values. Generally, as production accelerates to "meet" the high prices, the price bubble bursts and house prices ratchet downwards fairly rapidly. Of course, in a large nation like the United States, house price bubbles can have a regional basis rather than a national one. Capozza *et al.* (2004) treat house price dynamics with an explicit difference equation. Current price change ΔP_t reflects mean reversion, $\alpha \Delta P_{t-1}$, adjustment of current price to fundamental value, $\beta[P^*_{t-1} - P_{t-1}]$ and contemporaneous adjustment in the fundamental price, $\gamma \Delta P^*_t$. One presumes that α, β and γ will be less than unity. Their report on the dynamic properties of house prices abstracts from the stochastic nature of real

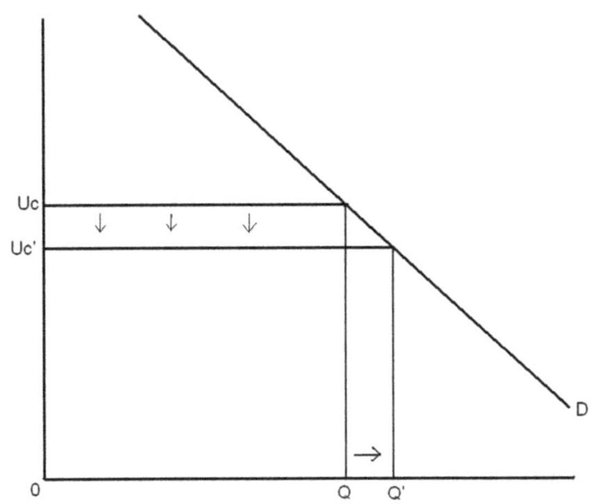

Figure 8.1 User-cost reduction. The decline in user cost (perhaps from a decline in interest rates) induces an expansion in quantity demanded of housing. Construction of new houses must accelerate. There is also upward pressure on house prices in the short run.

prices and thus provides us with just a preliminary guide. Using a sample of 62 metropolitan areas in the United States for the years 1979–95, Capozza *et al.* (2004) find that values of α and β differ significantly across cities. A larger value for α (more serial correlation) implies more overshooting in prices from the fundamental values. When real construction costs rise by 10 percent, they find that serial correlation increases by 15 percentage points. Higher construction costs can be associated with less elastic supply. Thus, as we expect, less elastic supply can be associated with more overshooting in current price from the fundamental price.[1] Head *et al.* (2014) explore new households entering a city in response to an exogenous income shock. They introduce an explicit costly home-search activity for the entrants. Entry congestion is cushioned somewhat by some "new" houses being placed on the rental market but ultimately new construction is the main response to the favorable shock to income for a city. Considerable attention is focused on home-price and construction dynamics and estimation is pursued for a set of 106 cities in the United States. "When calibrated to data on US cities the model accounts for 80 percent of the variance in house price movements driven by city-specific income shocks and nearly half of the observed autocorrelation of house price growth" (Head *et al.* 2014; p. 1172).

House prices according to the Case–Shiller repeat sales index, based on 20 cities in the United States, rose 70 percent from 2001 to a peak in April 2006. The less volatile Federal Housing Finance Agency index, with more cities, rose somewhat less. This defines the recent "boom" in house prices. Glaeser *et al.* (2010) find little evidence that low interest rates and lax lending standards were the direct cause of the boom in US housing prices up to 2008. They suggest that just 20 percent of the rise in prices between 1996 and 2006 could be attributed to the decline in interest rates. House prices rose on average in the United States some 30 percent. They also contend that lending practices loosened somewhat between 1998 and 2006, with loan values per home rising from 84 percent of the price to 88 percent in 2006. In the post-2008 period, loans came down to 80 percent of the price of a house. The most leveraged home buyers (top quarter of borrowers) borrowed some 96 percent of the house price in 1998 and 99 percent in 2006. Glaeser *et al.* (2010) conclude that the data do not support the view that loose lending practices caused the house price bubble that peaked in 2006 in the United States. Lending practices may have been loose, but only for borrowers at the margin of the market, and this margin was apparently small. Glaeser and Sinai (2012; p. 16) argue that "easy credit was necessary for the boom, but it seems unlikely to be a sufficient cause." They allude to "buyer over-optimism." Why, they ask, would a home buyer in Las Vegas not see that the price was way above construction costs and in addition that abundant sites for new homes stretched into the distance at the edge of the city. Glaeser and Sinai (G&S) point to "a wave of foreign lending" to the United States and note that the boom was "enabled by securitization." The easy credit turned on very low interest rates. Fannie Mae (Federal National Mortgage Association) and Freddie Mac (Federal Home Loan Mortgage Corporation) were able to borrow at rates very close to what the US Treasury could borrow at (G&S; p. 14). Shareholders in these private firms seemed to operate with the belief that the US Government would bail out the companies in a crisis and of course they were correct about this. "The eventual collapse of the companies seems almost inevitable" (G&S; p. 15), and

> The places that boomed in the 2000s also boomed during the previous run-up in housing prices during the late 1980s... [This is] compatible with the hypothesis that emphasizes a common national shock [such as a regime shift in credit availability] interacting with different local conditions.
>
> (G&S; p. 7)

The common shock then interacts with "large differences in [local] housing supply" (G&S; p. 6). Glaeser and Sinai reject novel supply conditions for new homes at the level of the nation or rapidly rising incomes of households as explanations for the boom in house prices (G&S; p. 3). Throughout the 1990s there had been "tight connection between overall state growth and the number of housing starts" but during 2000 to 2005 construction forged way ahead in many states, in particular in Arizona and Nevada (G&S; p. 10).

Glaeser and Sinai observe some decline in the quality of mortgages being placed. "Starting in 2002, there was a substantial increase in Alt-A and subprime mortgages originated through 2005 and 2006... exceeded GSE (government sponsored enterprises) originations by 2005" (G&S; p. 11). The new products called for risk certification by rating agencies such as Moody's Investor Services and Standard and Poor's, and many observers feel this work was not executed to sufficiently high standards. When confidence in the creditworthiness of some institutions declined and the credibility of the ratings on some products was questioned, the financial system of the United States and much of the world simply seized up. It was of course very unclear before 2007 how much of a threat that above-average housing prices posed for the economy of the United States. Ben Bernanke (testimony to Congress, October, 2005), for example, believed that the run-up in house prices was not a bubble that was about to burst but if it did, the bursting would not have negative consequences beyond the housing sector in the United States. He became Chairman of the Federal Reserve shortly after making this comment and played a central role in stitching the financial system of the United States back together after the collapse in September of 2008. A consequence of the financial crisis was a contraction in aggregate demand as many households cut back their consumption when they were forced to deal with their personal debts. Miran and Sufi (2014) emphasize that regions with the largest decline in consumption levels were those that had averages of household mortgage debt above the national average.

Glaeser and Sinai note that price increases were highest in cities along the coasts where restrictions on ready availability of new development tracts were more severe. Phoenix and Las Vegas were, on the other hand, two interior cities that experienced a large increase in house prices. Oddly enough, construction of new homes was moving rapidly forward in some places where price run-ups were large. And within cities price run-ups were somewhat higher for homes with good access to the city center. The communities with the large price increases were in turn those with the largest price declines after 2008. Dallas was different: it experienced almost no price rises between April 2000 and April 2006. The house-building industry was consolidating over this period. The ten largest builders carried out less than 10 percent of overall building in 1990 while in 2005 the ten largest were doing over 22 percent of building. Central to home construction was land assembly and the large firms were able to finance additions to their inventory of prospective sites. Housing starts per capita were high and short-lived in the 1960s, 1970s and 1980s and were followed by busts, but the price run-up to 2006 was preceded by a "building boom that had lasted for almost fifteen years" (G&S; p. 9). Glaeser dismisses a burst of family formation as a cause of the house-price run-up. However Figure I.2 of Glaeser and Sinai (2012; p. 9) has two intervals, and only two, of "New Households" above "New Housing Units": 1979–82 and 1999–2002. "Excess" family formation may have in fact been only a small force underlying the two house-price booms.

The local business cycle tends to contribute significantly to above normal rises in house prices. For example a boom in, say, the high-tech sector often creates an excess demand for high-skilled workers. The employment boom shows up in part as a shift in the demand schedule for local dwellings. Depending on how fast the local construction industry can respond to the new demand, there can be a large or less-large local house price bubble.

There remains the question of stickiness in the response of the construction industry to new demands for homes. Edward Glaeser and others contend that such local bubbles have been made severe by significant lags in the municipal and state approval process for new housing developments. Some even argue that foot-dragging in such approvals is deliberate—part of a policy to discourage the switch of large tracts of land from open-space and/or farming to housing development.[2] Thus lags in the response of the local construction industry to new demands for housing can develop in quite surprising ways. In any case, local business cycles do show up in local house price gyrations. In smaller places whose local economies are less subject to boom and bust (Kingston, Ontario, for example, where I have lived for 40 years), developers seem to build in advance of local "booms" and average house prices display few departures from trend. There has been a gradual relative rise in home prices nearer the downtown over the decades.

In keeping with his skepticism about the nature of the run-up in house prices in the United States early in the 2001 to 2010 period, Glaeser (2013) has examined the history of land price "bubbles" in the United States since 1800. His argument is that the price run-ups were motivated by rational bets by investors on future economic development in the relevant region. In Alabama the price of agricultural land boomed along with the boom in cotton exports from the United States to England in the early 1800s. The high land prices plummeted in 1819 when a general recession arrived and they failed to recover for decades. Glaeser resists identifying this episode of price rise as irrational herding behavior of speculators. Similarly Glaeser contends that land prices in Chicago shot up in the early 1830s because observers had solid reasons to believe that Chicago was emerging as a metropolis that would resemble New York City. Recall that the Erie Canal had opened, providing a water link between New York City and Chicago. Land transportation in 1816 per 30 miles could be about the same cost as moving the material across the Atlantic Ocean. Price per acre for a good property rose in Chicago by about 300 times between 1830 and 1837, when a crisis in international finance led to panic, a recession and a land value collapse. Glaeser argues that investors have a tendency to be myopic and fail to take account of supply responses to high prices. Building tall is one way to address high prices for usable space and investors in land may underestimate the impact of this avenue of supply. The option to default or "walk away" from a land purchase can contribute to price run-ups. Early in the 1800s, the law allowed some purchasers of public land to delay payment for two years. This left them the option to default when an anticipated run-up failed to materialize or when they realized they were stuck with land that they paid too much for. Securitization of mortgages started in the United States in the 1920s and investing in a bundle of securitized loans may have been riskier than an investor anticipated. This is a case where the securitizer probably understood the riskiness of the product better than the investor, an information asymmetry. Speculation is a tricky concept. From one perspective, a speculator is a business person who commits to buy up a farmer's crop at planting time. This frees up funds for the farmer and frees the farmer from the risk that prices will be very low when it comes time to harvest. The speculator may well end up with a delivered crop with units worth more than what she paid back at planting time. The speculator takes on the risk and on average expects to be paid for this service she provides to the farmer. This might be referred to as textbook speculation. Another kind of speculation is connected to herding behavior. If shares of company x are being bid up rapidly over a number of days, a speculator may jump in and buy some of the shares. The speculator is investing simply with the intention of selling when she senses that a peak in price is near. Such run-ups in price are usually identified as bubbles. The herd charges forward and each investor intends to sell or exit at the top of a price peak. Of course only a few end up exiting at the peak and often many other entrants make no profit at all. Glaeser is arguing that for many historic run-ups in land prices in the United States, the investors were judging that the properties in question were going to be very valuable within a few years. Most felt that values were climbing to a plateau, not a mountain top. History suggests that for many cases the plateau vision was correct but considerable over-shooting in price, due to herding behavior, was pretty standard as well.

A generic "house" or "home" can be thought of in terms of q square feet. We can have then $MC(q)$ for the marginal cost of a house of size q square feet. This cost deals with the capital value, say our US\$500,000, not the annual cost of living in the completed home. In a competitive market there will be a demand schedule for new homes with price equal to $MC(q)$. It is difficult to put down a supply schedule for new homes because the bundle of new units coming on the market at any date will be heterogeneous. The median new, single-family house in the United States went from 1,570 square feet in 1970 to 2,300 square feet in 2007.[3] Robert Frank contends that this increase is too large to be explained by income increases alone.[4] His view is that the average household tilted expenditure in favor of more housing in order to gain access to the neighborhoods with high-quality schools for the children.

Glaeser and Gyourko (2005) worked up estimates of construction costs in the United States for new houses, of different sizes, for 1980 and 1990. For 123 cities in the United States in 1980 they found that 42 percent were selling for less than construction costs. The equivalent figure for 1990 was 31 percent. For some older, manufacturing cities such as Flint, Michigan and Gary, Indiana some two-thirds were trading at values below replacement cost for both 1980 and 1990. Glaeser and Gyourko related these data to population growth or decline for US cities. Their interesting argument is that "excess housing" (prices below replacement cost) correlates positively with population decline and the durability of housing means that the impact of population decline could last for decades. The housing stock in a community that fits with population and income in one decade can be in excess supply for many years, once population decline sets in. "Excess" housing can attract families with few employment options and a very poor community can develop simply because older housing is available at low prices. Structures are durable and can often be lived in even when they are labelled as old.

User cost and asset equilibrium

The user-cost concept can be derived from the basic asset equilibrium condition for durable goods. The basic asset equilibrium condition says that the current price of an asset, V_t, should reflect the going rate of return, i, in the economy. Hence the asset's current income flow, I_t, plus the asset's current capital gains, $V_{t+1} - V_t$, should equal iV_t. For an owner-occupied house, the income term can be thought of as the dollar value of rent that the owner would have to pay to live in an identical house. Hence in brief, this approach implies a "user cost" equal to $iV_t - [V_{t+1} - V_t] = I_t$. This is close to what we had above for user cost. To flesh out the analysis we note that there are additional costs of living in one's own home so that net "income" is $I_t - \tau V_t - mV_t$ where τ is the property tax rate and m is the maintenance rate per year. Hence the more comprehensive user cost is

$$iV_t - [V_{t+1} - V_t] + \tau V_t + mV_t = I_t.$$

Recall our definition of user cost above as $u_t = [i + \tau + m - g]V_t$ with gV_t $(=V_{t+1} - V_t)$, the capital gain term. An estimate of current user cost depends on the estimate one inserts for capital gain, $[V_{t+1} - V_t]$. This has a future or next-period value in it and this makes it tricky to pin down. Hence the estimate of user cost depends on estimating capital gains fairly accurately. In practice, one would infer current capital gains from the recent trend up to the current date.

Renting

The owner of a rental property would have the same carrying costs as the owner-occupant. (We neglect business taxes and mortgage interest deductibility for the moment.) Thus to break even, the owner would have to charge a rent R_t equal to $i\,V_t(q) - g\,V_t(q) + m\,V_t(q) + \tau\,V_t(q)$. Breaking even implies that the market is competitive and every owner of rental property is making zero profits. In the United States home sector, the fraction of owners, as distinct from renters, rose from 48 percent in 1945 to 66 percent in 1980 and has remained near this figure since then. Rosen (1988; p. 411) reports on research that suggests the tax system in the United States caused about 25 percent of this increase (see also Glaeser and Shapiro 2003). We turn next to the tax status of home ownership. Some political leaders argue that home ownership correlates with good citizenship. This leads them to promote more ownership in place of renting. Sad to say there is clear evidence that neighborhoods dominated by renters in the United States do exhibit higher rates of violent crime and other indicators of a thinness of local social cohesion (see, for example, Sampson *et al.* 1997; Hoff and Sen 2005).

Figure 8.2 is a map for Toronto, 2011, showing areas of apartment dwellers. The downtown and waterfront has many apartment buildings and there has been much additional building of apartments in the downtown in recent years.

Toronto has many apartment buildings of 12 storeys and above, around the city. It is somewhat unusual in this regard. Figure 8.3 shows the dispersion of single, detached homes. They are somewhat dispersed from the center of the city.

Tax status of housing costs

Since the interest "cost" of a loan is tax deductible for a business, some nations have chosen to make interest "costs" of a mortgage (loan to buy a house) deductible from personal income before income tax is assessed on net income. If one considers one's house an investment like shares in General Electric and one can deduct interest on a loan to buy shares in General Electric from personal income, it seems reasonable to allow mortgage interest deductibility, at first glance. However, one is also living in one's house when it is viewed as an investment and of course one cannot use the shares of General Electric in a comparable way. Hence many observers look on mortgage interest deductability as simply a subsidy to those who own their own homes. Glaeser and Shapiro (2003) contend that mortgage interest deductibility (MID) has had no impact on the fraction of owners versus renters in the United States in recent decades. The distortion caused by MID is having a household with more "housing" in its portfolio of assets than it otherwise would have. In addition to the United States, the Netherlands and Switzerland each allows the deduction. In Belgium, Ireland and Sweden, only a minor part of mortgage interest is deductible. The debate over how to raise more revenue in the United States has in part involved the idea of allowing less than 100 percent mortgage interest deductibility.

In the United States, federal taxation allows mortgage interest deductibility and local (municipal) tax deductibility as well. Hence user cost in the United States, inclusive of deductions, is

$$(1-T)iV(q) - gV(q) + mV(q) + (1-T)\tau V(q),$$

where T is the rate of income tax. The Canadian tax system does not allow such deductions from gross income before tax but instead allows capital gains on one's principal residence to go untaxed. Hence in Canada if one moves from one's large house at, say age 70, to an apartment, the capital gains one realizes upon selling one's house are free of tax. This too appears to be a subsidy to those who can afford to own the place in which they live. This "subsidy" can only be cashed in or realized at the date of sale of one's house.

In the 1970s there were some years of high (double digit) inflation; prices of houses and farm land were not immune. Economists introduced the inflation rate to the user cost for the United States and observed that inflation created a small reduction-wedge in user cost for a homeowner. Some observers linked the high inflation and the apparent run-up in housing prices in the United States to this break in the prevailing user cost. Let us calculate this reduction-wedge. When the inflation rate is γ percent, the observed rate of interest is the real rate i plus γ. Also the rate of capital gains becomes $g+\gamma$. When we introduce these new rates to our user costs above, we have

$$(1-T)[i+\gamma]V(q) - [g+\gamma]V(q) + mV(q) + (1-T)\tau V(q).$$

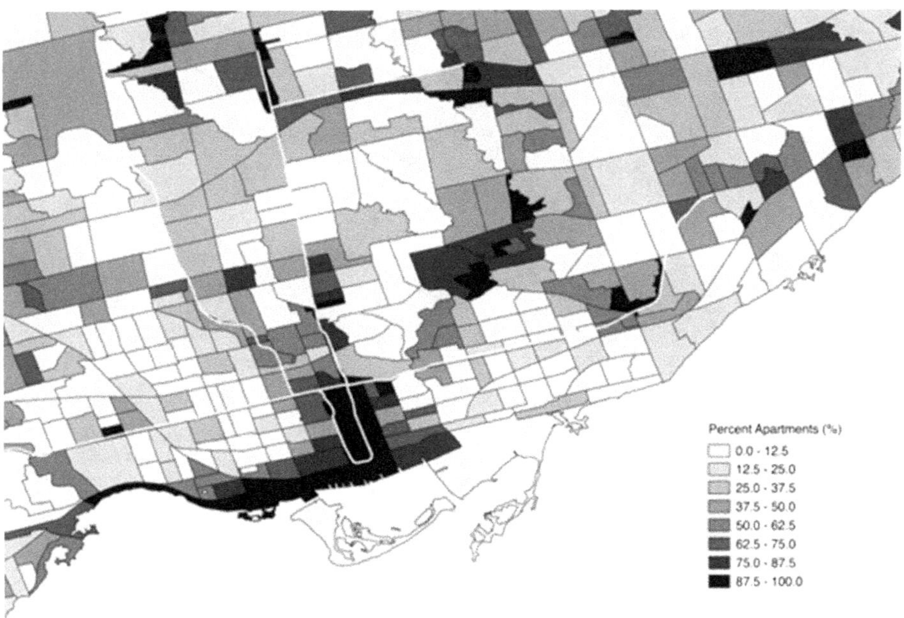

Figure 8.2 Apartment dwellers in Toronto, 2011.

Source: Based on Census Tract data.

Consider the difference between this user cost and the one with no inflation (subtract the user cost with no inflation from the user cost above with inflation; one gets $-T\gamma V(q)$). Hence user cost (the annual cost of living in one's own house) is lower during times of inflation and the higher the rate of inflation, γ, the larger the amount of cost reduction. As we noted above, some observers suggested that this annual cost reduction was driving up demand for "housing" and thus pushing up house prices in the United States during the 1970s. How much this cost reduction was driving a rise in house prices is unclear. Another contributing factor to excess demand for housing in the 1970s was an increase in family formation caused by the baby boomers reaching the age of family formation. (In Canada, and in many other countries, this inflation cost reduction is not operative since the Canadian tax system does not allow for mortgage interest deductibility.)

Housing in the measurement of inflation (change in CPI, the consumer price index) is labelled "shelter" and is a weighted average of annual changes in rent, mortgage interest, replacement cost, property taxes, home and mortgage insurance, maintenance and repairs, electricity, water, natural gas, and fuel oil. Over 2010, shelter rose 2.4 percent in Canada, and shelter was deemed to occupy 26 percent of the budget of the typical person. Changes in the annual cost of mortgage interest is difficult to measure since the bundle of all mortgages in Canada comprises those that have been taken on at many different dates in the past with distinct rates.[5]

A person renting out a home is a business and must consider business taxes on gross rental minus annual costs. There will be deduction from the gross revenue figure for interest payments on loans, municipal taxes, depreciation of capital and maintenance expenditures.

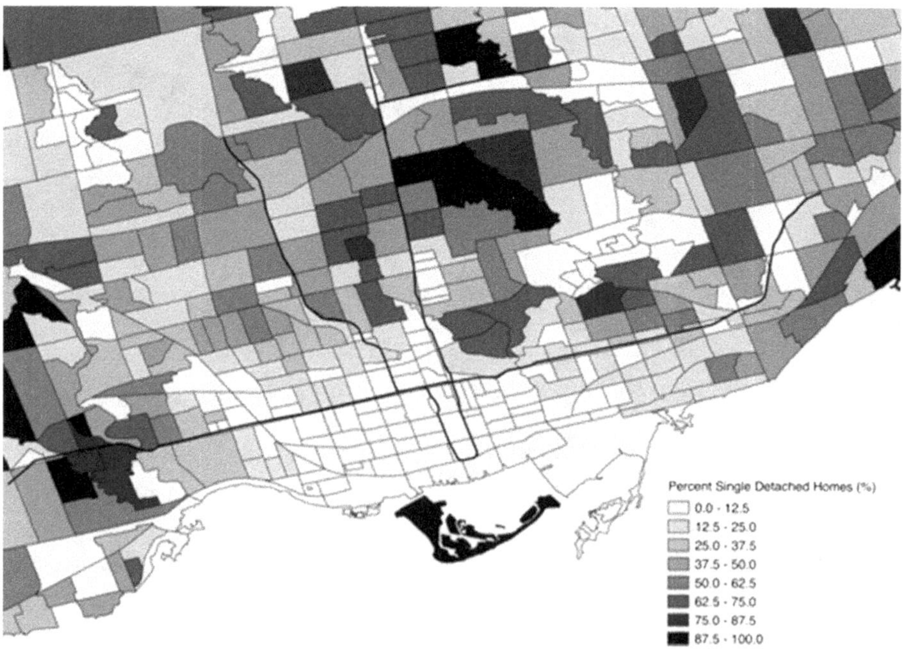

Figure 8.3 Single, detached homes in Toronto, 2011.

Source: Based on Census Tract data.

Hence tax payments will come to

$$T^{bus} \times [R^{gross} - D - [iV(q) + mV(q) + \tau V(q)]],$$

where D is legislated allowable deductions, mostly for "depreciation" and T^{bus} is the rate of business tax. This suggests that a rental business owner will likely end up with a very small net income on which he or she must pay the business tax. Hence rental charge on a generic house should not differ much from the user cost of a home owner. *The Economist* has focused on the difference between house rent charges and the value of $i \times$ current selling price (annual financial carrying cost) as an indicator of house price disequilibrium (prices above equilibrium values). It is unclear why rents do not jump up along with house prices in times of house price bubbles but apparently they do not. A simple definition of a house price bubble is when the opportunity cost of funds to the owner, $i \times V$, is far above the annual rent being charged for a very similar home.

The Economist gives a chart of the ratio of house prices ($i \times$ current selling price) to rents for Spain, Ireland, Britain and the United States for years 2000 to 2011.[6] The line for Spain rises to about 180 in 2007 from a benchmark of 100 for year 2000. Britain's peak, at about 160, occurs slightly later. The US peak is lowest at about 145 and this peak occurs just before 2006.[7] In the United States, the recent decline in the fraction of households where the home is owned is partly a result of the foreclosure crisis but also reflects risk-aversion of prospective home-owners. The recent declines in home prices has made owning one's home a less attractive place to tie up one's savings.[8] The market valuation of your home depends of course on its size, condition and location. Experts such as Robert Shiller point out that one's home as an investment can exhibit long-run returns below, say, the Dow-Jones market average:

> From 1890 to 1990 the appreciation in US housing was just about zero. That amazes people, but it shouldn't be so amazing because the cost of construction and labor has been going down. Housing takes maintenance, it depreciates, it goes out of style. All of those are problems. And there's technical progress in housing. So, the new ones are better.[9]

Shiller argued that rates of return to home ownership should be lower in Canada because land available for urban development is relatively abundant.[10]

In the United States one has to keep in mind the large tax break that MID provides to home owners. In any case, the city where one's home is and the location in that city can have large effects on the growth or lack of growth in the value of one's home. Obviously two identical houses, one on the edge of a city and one in an attractive neighborhood closer to the CBD are going to command very different prices when sold. Location matters in this sense. In addition some communities turn out to experience above average economic growth over the decades and such places fill in with more residents and homes as the years go by. Owning a home in such growth-places will have a strong influence on the long-run increase in the market value of one's home. Hoping for high returns on one's home is really hoping for large gains in the value of the lot one's house sits on. The idea that investing in one's home is the best way to save for retirement can be a delusion when one has spent decades in a slow-growth community. However, if one's community has grown substantially over the decades, one may well be in a position to receive a huge payoff when one sells one's home. Of course the gain can only be realized if one chooses to retire in a place with relatively low-cost residences.

User cost versus rent for estimating house service value

There are many reasons one would like a good estimate of the value of services a household is getting from living in its own home for a year. A primary one is to know what dollar value (current annual "price") we should enter in the CPI for consumption of housing. The problem arises immediately that survey data reveals a substantial gap between the annual charge for renting a particular home and the user cost for a very similar home. Some have suggested that rent is the better estimate of the annual value of services from living in the home. But the absence of a tight tracking of the two measures of value becomes a valuation problem demanding an explanation. *The Economist* observes that rent lags user cost and when user cost was well above local rent, then the wedge constituted evidence of a local house price bubble. Diewert *et al.* (2009) address the failure of the two measures of value to track each other and argue, for the purpose of national accounting, that the highest of the two measures should be used, at the level of the nation, year by year.

Rates of home ownership, relative to renting, differ around the world, with Switzerland having one of the lowest rates (around 37 percent), somewhat below the rate for Germany. See Table 8.1.

In New York City only one-third of residents own their homes. However, the high income subgroup (with incomes above 500,000 per year) has an ownership rate of 60 percent.[11] Many of these owners (25 percent) are in fact investors who rent their units out or occupy them irregularly.[12]

The rate of home ownership is occasionally a political issue. Many observers have argued that home ownership promotes family stability and civic mindedness in voters. Both the Clinton and George W. Bush administrations have been admonished recently for trying to significantly increase the percentage of home owners in the United States. The argument goes: to promote more ownership, easier lending standards had to be set and this led to excess borrowing and house building and a housing price bubble in many places. One of Mrs Thatcher's policies as Prime Minister of Britain was for the public sector to sell many social housing units that were being rented for many years to households at subsidized rates. She argued that the subsidized rent arrangement induced household immobility and this created ghettos of un- and under-employed workers. Economists have done some empirical work on how much the functioning of the labor market is affected by rates of home ownership. The hypothesis is that ownership, as distinct from rentalship, will build an element of labor immobility into markets. The evidence is not strong on this point.

Fannie Mae was set up as a quasi-government institution in 1938 to buy mortgages from commercial banks and thus remove mortgage risk from the primary lenders (mostly

Table 8.1 Home ownership rates

Singapore	84%
Spain	82%
China	80%
Ireland	72%
Britain	67%
United States	65%
Japan	62%
Germany	47%
Switzerland	37%

Source: *The Economist*, March 5, 2011, p. 5.

smaller banks), who were in many cases severely stressed with low-quality home loans. Fannie Mae could diversify more than smaller lenders and have risky mortgages placed in large pools of mortgages. At the same time, funds from Fannie Mae flowed into the commercial banks and thus allowed the banks to lend more, often to other purchasers of homes. Home ownership was greatly expanded in this securitization of mortgages. Fannie Mae was privatized by President Johnson and became a very large player in financial markets.

Freddie Mac was established in 1970 by the government to provide some competition for Fannie Mae. It became a private company owned by shareholders in 1989. Severe financial distress at these two huge institutions in 2008 induced the US government to take over these firms. The bailouts were of the order of US$187 billion and were in fact fully repaid in March 2014. Both firms are very active in buying up mortgages and at the same time providing "new" funds to lenders, who in turn churn out credit, generally for the housing sector. As of March 2014 legislators in Congress were trying to find a route to removing government from any ownership stake in these two huge financial firms.

Another "progam" that emerged in the 1930s was mortgage insurance. Companies were willing to sell coverage for a certain fraction of a loan. If the borrower defaulted, the insurance company would pay a certain fraction of the loan to the lender. A lender would then require a borrower to purchase a certain amount of mortgage insurance when the loan was given. This meant that the borrower would be granted better terms on the loan (namely a lower rate of interest). Mortgage insurance is now very common.

Investing in a home or in a mutual fund

When a person rents a home, there is a transaction each month as rent is transferred from the renter to the owner. This means that consumption of housing by the renter gets entered into her consumption expenditure and ultimately into aggregate consumption, capital C, in a nation's GDP. An owner has an annual bill for interest payments, maintenance, local taxes, etc. which ends up as income on the income side of the national account. This accounting breaks down when a person lives in the house which she owns. The owner of a home, which she lives in, possesses a durable asset, which from an accounting perspective should be throwing off interest income each period. Hence the need to complete the accounting by introducing an "imputation" for interest income flow from the durable asset. Once an income flow is introduced (imputed as some income), it becomes an item in one's tax liability in addition to being imputed income directly. From a consumption perspective, a home owner is living in one of the assets in her portfolio or is reaping consumption services from the asset (the home). This flow of consumption services must be imputed also in a complete accounting for a person living in the home which they own. This payment-adjustment imputation functions quite distinctly from the imputation for the return on capital noted above.

Imputations

A way to see these imputations in action is to first take up two benchmark cases for reference. First, consider a renter, with salary Y and no other income.

Renting option

Her annual income is Y dollars and her income tax rate is τ. Then her income after tax and after housing expenditure is

$$Y - \tau Y - R,$$

where R is the annual rent she pays for the house she is living in.

Consider now the same person, still renting but also borrowing V dollars to invest in an asset (say V dollars of a fund with good quality dividend stocks). When one borrows to buy income-generating investments such as mutual funds of dividend stocks, one is granted a deduction before taxes for the annual interest cost on the funds borrowed for buying the "investment." Consider then our renting person with income of Y dollars per year. She borrows V dollars and invests in a portfolio of dividend stocks, earning rV per year. Her annual borrowing cost is iV dollars per year. She rents her home for R dollars per year.

Investing option

In this situation her income after borrowing, tax and housing expenditure will be

$$Y + rV - \tau[Y + rV - iV] - iV - R.$$

Term $Y + rV$ is total income. The third term is income tax. The fourth term is interest payment to the lender (bank) and R is her annual rent for her home. We have drawn on 100 percent loan-interest deductibility in the tax term. For the somewhat contrived case of $r = i$, her net income is

$$Y - \tau Y - R = (1 - \tau)Y - R,$$

essentially the same as the case of a renter with no investments.

We say then that the agent is indifferent between our first two cases. She is neutral between the two possibilities. Her income, net of investing and paying for accommodation, is the same in both cases. We turn now to buying a home and living in it. One expects the owner-occupancy option to be another neutral possibility, no?

Owner-occupying option

We assume here full borrowing and 100 percent mortgage interest deductibility.

Let the price of the house be V dollars. We take M (instead of rV) to be the imputation for a dollar return, flow of "dividends" per year, from the home worth V dollars. Now iV is the annual interest payment on the mortgage. Hence after imputing for asset earnings, after tax and after housing expenditure, the owner's income is

$$Y + M - \tau[Y + M - iV] - iV - E,$$

where E is remaining housing expenditure per year after interest payments have been made. We want E to reflect the full cost of living in a home for a year. Hence we need to "replace" the iV netted out from E with imputation $\widehat{M}$. Then $E + \widehat{M} = U$, user cost, with $\widehat{M} = iV$. The home owner's new net income after imputations, taxes, interest payments and annual disbursements for housing becomes

$$\begin{aligned} &Y + M - \tau[Y + M - iV] - iV - (E + \widehat{M}) \\ &= Y + M - \tau[Y + M - iV] - iV - U. \end{aligned}$$

When imputation M is equal to iV, this net income reduces to $(1 - \tau)Y - U$. And when annual user cost equals market rent (i.e. $R = U$), a not extreme assumption for competitive housing markets, we have net income after renting or owning (with a 100 percent mortgage) the same. Hence neutrality to a household between renting and owning.

To obtain this latter neutrality, we (a) imputed a dollar income for a return to the durable asset ($M = iV$), the home; (b) imputed a dollar consumption benefit from living in one's home ($\widehat{M} = iV$); and (c) maintained the assumption of 100 percent mortgage interest deductibility. In fact both Canada and the United States do impute a net annual flow for owner-occupied housing on both the income side, for M, and expenditure side, for $\widehat{M}$, of the national accounts in each country. National accountants use our reasoning for a representative household when they move on to do imputations for all relevant households in the nation in question. We have looked at the reason for such imputations, one on the income side and one on the consumption side, starting down at the level of the accounts for a household.

The principle associated with these two imputations is: arrange the accounts for the household so that the home as durable asset has an account similar to that for any other income-yielding asset owned by a household and arrange the accounts so that the household is treating the cost of living in the home (with a 100 percent mortgage) the same way she would be accounting for her cost of renting an identical home. In the United States, the dollar value of the sum of all the individual imputations for owner-occupied housing is exceeded only by the dollar value of the imputation for "free" banking services, services supplied to customers of banks in the United States. Though imputations are made at the level of the national accounts in Canada and the United States, these imputations are in fact not implemented in the income tax laws governing filing by individual households. Thus the allowance for mortgage interest deductibility in the United States can still be argued as distorting the decision of a household toward consuming "excess" housing.

Lower rate of mortgage interest deductibility?

Would, say, a 50 percent mortgage interest deduction be an improvement in the United States? The tax break for owners of their homes would be reduced, of course. Neutrality would have a household account as

$$Y + M - \tau[Y + 0.5M - 0.5iV] - iV - [E + \widehat{M}],$$

for imputation $M = iV$ and imputation $\widehat{M} = iV$. These are the same imputations as we say immediately above. However, the complication here is that only half of income to capital, iV, (home value, V) should be imputed to household income for taxation, i.e. $0.5M$. This adjustment to imputing for taxation is necessary because only 50 *percent* of mortgage interest is allowed to be deducted from income for taxation. With this imputation, $0.5M$, we observe investment neutrality. In the absence of these imputations, a reduction in the mortgage interest allowance would indeed dampen the motivation of a household to hold a very large mortgage and as such should blunt the tendency to arrange housing ownership to maximize the tax break. If a policy-maker is committed to mortgage interest deductibility, she should also be committed to assessing appropriate imputations at the level of the household. This latter is obviously a large requirement. To avoid a household's rush to take advantage of tax breaks, given no imputations at the level of the household, it is better to simply have no mortgage interest deductibility.

In Canada there is a zero allowance for mortgage interest deductibility. Given a fully mortgaged, owner-occupied home, neutrality obtains in this case with a household account

$$Y + M - \tau[Y] - \{iV\} - [E + \widehat{M}],$$

for imputation $M = iV$ and imputation $\widehat{M} = iV$. It follows of course that $E + \widehat{M}$ equals user cost, including a term for the opportunity cost of funds tied up in the home, namely iV. Statistics Canada makes the two imputations above, namely $M = \widehat{M} = iV$ in its national accounts. However, when a household has paid off its mortgage, the term $\{iV\}$ is zero and neutrality across investment options is no longer present. There is a bias in Canada for a household to pay down its mortgage completely before allocating savings to other income-earning options. Hence, the combination of a "rush" by a household to pay off its mortgage and the imputing equally in the national accounts for iV on the income and expenditure sides of the national accounts is resulting in a wrong accounting outcome.

Imputations perform two functions. At the national level they "correct for" asset income flows that owner-occupied housing generates and separately for the consumption value of households living in owner-occupied homes. At the household level, correct imputations make investing in one's owner-occupied home neutral with respect to investing in other assets, such as mutual funds. At the level of the household, imputing should not be treated separately from an allowance for mortgage interest deductibility.

Housing supply by trickle-down

In cities that grow fairly steadily, upper-end houses built for higher-income residents often end up divided up into apartments some decades down the road. This phenomenon, passing down, has been labelled "filtering." Certainly the housing stock in a typical large city in Canada and the United States is far from homogeneous. Lower-income families live in older places with lower-quality fixtures and windows, places often "handed down" from higher-income families. Sweeney (1974)[13] developed a formal model of the handing-down or filtering of durables and interesting analyses addressing this topic followed.

We turn to the details of a filtering model, one with the decay of a structure endogenously generated. (We report on two related analyses and problems with them in Appendix 8.1.) We assume that income w^H is for a high-income household and w^L is for a low-income household. These incomes are both assumed to be rising linearly with time. That is

$$w^H + \gamma^H t = c^H(t) + r^H(t)q^H(t) \text{ for } 0 < \beta < 1 \text{ and } \gamma > 0$$

and

$$w^L + \gamma^L t = c^L(t) + r^L(t)q^L(t),$$

where $c(t)$ is the consumption of other goods, $q(t)$ the consumption of housing and $r(t)$ is the rent on a unit of housing. The utility function for both high-income and low-income households has the form $U(c, q) \equiv c + q^\beta$. Hence, given the price of a unit of c at unity, we have

$$\frac{U_c}{U_q} = \frac{1}{\beta q^{\beta-1}} = \frac{1}{r}.$$

Cross-multiplying gives us: $rq = \beta q^\beta$ and $c(t) = w + \gamma t - \beta q^\beta$. We substitute in our utility function to get $U = w + \gamma t + [1 - \beta]q^\beta$. For utility unchanging over time, we have

$$q(t) = \left[\frac{U - w}{1 - \beta} + \frac{\gamma}{1 - \beta}t\right]^{1/\beta}, \text{ neglecting superscripts.}$$

Clearly, $q(t)$ declines with time, since $1 - \beta < 0$, and $U - w$ must be negative in order for $q(t)$ to be positive. In a sense $q(t)$ becoming smaller is like the structure evaporating, as with deterioration.

We solve for the rent function in:

$$r(t) = \beta\left[\frac{U - w}{1 - \beta} + \frac{\gamma}{1 - \beta}t\right]^{(\beta-1)/\beta}, \text{ neglecting superscripts,}$$

which will increase in time since $\beta - 1 < 0$. The increasing "scarcity" of $q(t)$ is associated with the rising $r(t)$. There will be a rent function corresponding to a high-income and low-income household in

$$r^H(t) = \beta\left[\frac{U^H - w^H}{1 - \beta} + \frac{\gamma^H}{1 - \beta}t\right]^{(\beta-1)/\beta}$$

$$\text{and } r^L(t) = \beta\left[\frac{U^L - w^L}{1 - \beta} + \frac{\gamma^L}{1 - \beta}t\right]^{(\beta-1)/\beta}.$$

We introduce the assumption of a terminal amount of housing at time T when the unit is scrapped (abandoned): $q^L(T) = \overline{q}$. Hence abandonment date T is endogenous. We treat scrap value as zero, for convenience. Hence we have

$$\overline{q} = \left[\frac{U^L - w^L}{1 - \beta} + \frac{\gamma^L}{1 - \beta}T\right]^{1/\beta},$$

an equation in T and U^L.

The high-income household moves out of the home at date T^s and moves elsewhere to a new home. The low-income household moves into the deteriorated or shrunken home at date T^s. At the date T^s, each household values a unit of the house the same. We must have $r^H(T^s) = r^L(T^s)$ and this equation leads to

$$\frac{U^H - w^H - [U^L - w^L]}{\gamma^H - \gamma^L} = T^s.$$

This is an equation in unknowns U^H, U^L and T^s. It follows directly that if $r^H(T^s) = r^L(T^s)$ at T^s then $q^H(T^s) = q^L(T^s)$ also. Note also that at the switch we have $U^H - U^L = c^H - c^L$.

There is the switch in occupancy from the high-income to the low-income household and q is unchanging over the switch date. Hence c must decline for the low-income household in order that it move to a lower utility level. Now $c(t) = w + \gamma t - \beta q^\beta$ and q is unchanging over the switch and w declines from w^H to w^L. Hence c does indeed jump down over the switch to allow the new lower value of $\overline{U}^L$ to obtain. Note that the value of the decline in c must correspond with the "equilibrium" decline in $\overline{U}$. Hence there will be an equilibrium date, T^s, that allows for the simultaneous equilibrium jump down in $\overline{U}$ and c as time moves forward. When we substitute for q in $c(t)$ we get $c(t) = \frac{-\beta\overline{U}}{1-\beta} + \left(\frac{1-2\beta}{1-\beta}\right)[w + \gamma t]$. Since $c(t)$ must rise with time, we get the new restriction $\frac{1}{2} < \beta < 1$.

So far we have two equations in four unknowns, namely U^H, U^L, T^s and T. A third equation is the present value of the bid-rents, under occupancy, that between 0 and T must equal the cost of a new unit of q, namely K. That is,

$$\int_0^{T^S} r^H(z)e^{-iz}dz + e^{-iT^S}\int_{T^S}^{T} r^L(z)e^{-i[z-T^S]}dz = K.$$

This is a third equation in our four unknowns.

We require one more equation in U^H, U^L, T^s and T in order to have a complete model. A simple relationship is that the duration of occupancy for a high-income household is the same as the one for a low-income household. Behind this assumption is a simple notion of occupancy over a life-cycle. This gives us a fourth equation:

$$T^s = \frac{1}{2}T.$$

This completes our simple model of endogenous house decay and switch from occupancy by a high-income household to a low-income household, a simple model of filtering in the supply of housing. Figure 8.4 depicts the switch at date T^s from the high-income owner to the lower-income owner.

We have to verify that indeed the high-income resident will outbid the low-income resident early on and the opposite will occur beyond T^s. See Appendix 8.2.

It is undeniable that the restructuring of older single family homes so that more families can be accommodated, albeit often in cramped spaces, is a standard way of supplying housing for lower-income families. Even apartments for higher-income "families" are occasionally constructed from older single family homes. Housing supply by a process of filtering down is then an important way of getting roofs over residents of cities.

Some structures move through a cycle of quality decline with use and a subsequent rehabilitation later. This phenomenon has been labelled "gentrification." Location is a crucial

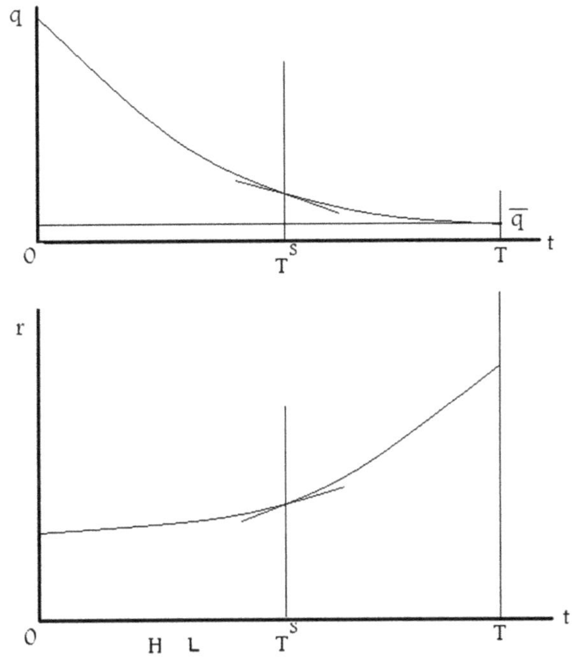

Figure 8.4 Switch date. $\gamma^H < \gamma^L$ assures correct intersection of q and r schedules.

dimension in this phenomenon. Often a good home is constructed fairly close to the center of a city and later is divided into apartment units, with lower rents. The land value under such a property can keep rising over the decades. Sometimes gentrification (rehabilitation of the structure) occurs. The owner-upgrader or developer is aware that the location is attractive to residents unhappy with commuting from far away. We might even say that the capital to land ratio has become out of line with prevailing prices and gentrification is a correction: more capital being added to a site, which has become higher priced. Guerrieri *et al.* (2010) examine home prices for cities in the United States that have experienced a positive demand shock for their exports. They find that areas with the largest jump in relative prices of homes are those neighboring the areas with high home prices. In this view gentrification is a spreading out of accommodation to higher quality from locations currently with high-quality homes. This analysis is capturing the process of gentrification, albeit indirectly.

A seeming speeding up in the pace of gentrification has been taking place in a number of large cities in the United States: Boston, Philadelphia, Washington, Pittsburgh, Atlanta, Seattle and San Francisco to name a few. This creates problems for long-term residents who find their neighborhoods changing rapidly and their municipal tax bills rising steeply as well. The values of their homes jump as developers move in, often to build condominiums nearby. The cause of this speeding up of gentrification can be blamed in part on the high wages commanded by young, well-educated workers moving into jobs in finance, medicine and medical research and computer-related activities. But there is also the problem of the centers of older cities lacking new areas for development. Developers head to the older neighborhoods and assemble plots of land for their projects. The lowest-cost plots are found in the older neighborhoods that are still without high-rise offices and residences. In addition, one asks why these young, urban professionals are asking for residential spaces downtown rather than farther out. Have tastes been shifting in favor of downtown living? Casual observing suggests "yes." Toronto's downtown population increased 18 percent between 2006 and 2011 and office jobs in the CBD rose by 43,000. Leaders in local government feel an obligation to the long-term residents who see gentrification taking place and an attempt is being made in many places to keep the property taxes of these people low enough so that they are not squeezed out of their homes. Even Detroit is enacting property tax rate reductions and is willing to proceed with the US$15 million of lost revenues. In Boston there is legislation to allow long-term residents to defer property tax payments until the owners sell their homes. Philadelphia has a similar law. The redevelopment of a neighborhood represents a loss of local character and nostalgia can weigh large in planning decisions in older cities.[14]

Clayton Patterson, bohemian avant-garde artist of New York City's Lower East Side, left his neighborhood because the atmosphere changed too much for his taste.[15] He was 65 and had lived and worked, with his companion, also an artist, in the same neighborhood since 1979. He moved to the Austrian Alps. Daniel Levin, a friend of Patterson's puts it this way: "Sadly, ironically, New York is displacing the people that made it what it was. The entire city has become a playground for money, wealth and sterilized housing, and that's not what's traditionally made it interesting." Patterson had actually been involved with a festival for 15 years in the village in Austria that he moved to. "They love me over there (Bad Ischl). They think of me as America's No. 1 underground photographer," Patterson explained.

Patterson was able to sell the building he had been living in and move to Austria with a nest egg. Gentrification is hardest on long-term renters who are forced to move out of the homes they are used to and are essentially forced to settle in new neighborhoods, distant from their familiar residences. Renters often lose their roots, their familiar surroundings, as gentrification takes over their old neighborhoods and they are squeezed out.

A related cost of gentrification is the squeezing out of small businesses, renters, who must make way for new developments in a commercial district. The business owners can face difficulties in finding a new premises at reasonable cost near their old one. They can face the loss of a client base when they are forced to relocate. Customers also can feel uprooted when they find their favorite shops and whole commercial strips repurposed or redeveloped. Kelley Anderson, a long-time resident of Brooklyn, New York, worked up a film, *My Brooklyn*, documenting local gentrification, the redevelopment of Fulton Mall at the center of the Borough. She argues that long-term residents, including owners of small businesses, received no reasonable consideration as plans for the redevelopment were worked out. The voices and interests of a community of shopkeepers and clients were ignored as new chain stores, brand-name hotels and large, up-scale condominium projects moved into Fulton Square. A committee of Mayor Michael Bloomberg's office is blamed for orchestrating the one-sided redevelopment process. We noted in Chapter 3 that zoning can prevent the highest bidder for a site from winning the site and imposing his or her use for the site on the neighborhood. Residents frequently strive to preserve the "atmosphere" of their neighborhood by lobbying for strict land-use regulation. The indirect cost of this "atmosphere preservation" is the "rationing" of sites for redevelopment for new apartment and condominium projects, projects that assist in preventing prices for residences from rising to very high levels.

The issue of the affordability of New York living has been playing out in the huge (11,200 apartments) Stuyvesant Town and Peter Cooper Village complex just north of the East Village. The complex was bought for US$5.4 billion in 2006 and great efforts were then made by the new owners to get regulated rents raised. About half of the apartments now have rents above the "middle class" levels. The 2006 purchaser was foreclosed upon. The remaining residents are fighting hard to find a route that will allow them to stay in their apartments and face affordable rents or mortgage payments. Turning the apartments into condominiums is one avenue being investigated by current residents.

Not far away, some well-connected residents of lower Manhattan fought successfully to keep their neighborhood free of radical change. In 1967 about 20 acres of decayed homes at Delancey Street in south-east Manhattan, occupied by some 1,800 mostly Puerto Rican families, were cleared for redevelopment by the city of New York. The displaced folk were promised places in new apartments to be built on the site. However, development of the site was blocked by nearby residents. Sheldon Silver and his protégé William Rapfogel grew up in "Cooperative Village" in the neighborhood, a largely Jewish enclave, and blocked moves over the years to have low-income housing placed on the acreage (the Seward Park Urban Renewal Area). Silver rose to be speaker of the Assembly of New York State and Rapfogel became a leader in the Metropolitan Council on Jewish Poverty, a large, publicly financed charity. They were motivated in part by the desire to preserve the character of their neighborhood and also by concern about how voting proportions of various groups might be altered with an influx of new families, many with low incomes. Cooperative Village was surrounded on the north, east and west by 14,000 units of public housing. Chinatown was encroaching from the south and west. Over the years Silver and Rapfogel supported various plans for the cleared area that did not involve residences, and supported prospective developers that were allies of Mr. Silver. Russ Buettner, a reporter, delved deeply into the records of various bodies and has documented the persistent blocking by Mr. Silver, with the help of Mr. Rapfogel, of any move by the city to place housing for any low-income families on the site.[16] Ironically, the character of the neighborhood has in fact changed in recent years, becoming more young, urban-professional rather than Jewish and traditional. In the last days of the Bloomberg mayoralty, a plan for the development of the site was approved, with some housing integrated into the project for low-income people. Some offspring of the Puerto Ricans, displaced back in 1967, are hoping to be able to move into new apartments on the site.

Unpacking the price of a house

Hedonic econometric estimation involves separating out the contribution of various dimensions of a home to its price: for example, one more bedroom will add x dollars to the price of a typical home. Among other things, people have been interested in how much proximity to an airport, with its considerable noise, detracts from the price of a typical home. To investigate this issue, one might collect prices for a set of very similar homes (same number of bedrooms, bathrooms, garages, lot sizes, house square footage, etc.) and see how the prices differ by location alone. Then one could back-out the price penalty on the home that comes from being close to an airport. In fact, econometrics allows one to do this exercise without having to tease out a set of various similar homes, at the start. Instead, one can collect a set of prices for relatively heterogeneous homes and their respective characteristics, including proximity to an airport, and run a regression of house price on characteristics for the set collected. In doing so one is "controlling for" contributions to price of characteristics other than the proximity to an airport. After running this so-called regression on a computer, one has estimates of the contribution of various characteristics to the price of a representative or "average" home, and one can then subtract out the contribution to a home's price of each characteristic, made by its number of bedrooms, number of bathrooms, lot size, square footage and so on. One is left with the contribution to the price of an average type of home of proximity to an airport. In the jargon of econometrics, one has controlled for contributions to the home's price of all things except proximity to an airport. One senior undergraduate in one of my courses estimated the loss in value of a home in Vancouver for being located on the "wrong" side of a bridge that thousands of commuters must navigate each rush hour. She worked up a hedonic regression estimation along the lines we have described above and came up with a premium of about 20 percent for an average home to be on the "right" side of the bridge. Living on the good side of the bridge means avoiding the back-up at the bridge each morning and the estimated house price wedge is measuring the implicit price of living on the good side.

Of interest to us in this book is the contribution to a home's price of proximity to the CBD. This has been investigated by Osland (2010) for Haugesund, a middle-sized city on the coast of Norway, and its surroundings. He collected selling prices and characteristics for 1,691 homes for the late 1990s and controlled for the precise year of sale. Key characteristics of the house controlled for were lot size, age of structure, year of upgrading, presence of a garage, floor-space area of the house, number of toilets, distance to the CBD and distance to a nearby cluster of employers. Except for dummy variables for year of sale and the "garage" variable, all other variables were entered into the estimation in logarithms, including the price of the house. The distance to the CBD was measured in minutes for a car travelling at the allowable speed limit. His variables were all statistically significant (i.e. they contributed non-trivially to the price of the house) and the value for distance to the CBD was −0.105. Thus an additional minute of distance from the CBD made the price of an "average" house decline by about 10 percent. For smoothly moving traffic doing 30 miles per hour, about a half mile would be covered in a minute. For a small city, a decline of about 10 percent in home price for a half mile of "less accessibility" to the CBD seems not unreasonable.

It is clear that the same house in a neighborhood of similar houses will be valued somewhat differently than if it were in a neighborhood of vacant, boarded-up houses. Hence one should break house price into characteristics not only of the structure and location but also of the neighborhood. That the value of a house and lot often varies with the characteristics of neighboring houses and lots complicates the simple decomposing of price on structure and location characteristics considerably.[17] In doing regression analysis, one hopes that the structure of the error terms in one's "equation" being estimated is standard and thus one can avoid complicated estimation procedures. However, once one argues that neighborhood effects play an essential role in house prices, one is pretty well stuck with "non-standard" structures for the error terms in one's abstract equation being estimated. Relatively complicated statistical estimation procedures are called for. In the 1990s, tricky estimation procedures were discussed by Can (1992) among others and empirical tests were performed. Can asks us to consider "neighborhood effects" on house price, such as the presence of a park nearby and "adjacency effects," the value of nearby homes. He ends up testing for spatial dependence and spatial heterogeneity in his estimated residuals (error values, ex-post), turning to heteroskedasticity-robust significance tests on the estimated coefficients of his equation, and employing a bootstrap estimation procedure to take account of auto-regressiveness in his error terms.

Can's exploration of the components of house price was carried out with 563 transactions in Columbus, Ohio for single family homes in 1980. The components of price were brick, stone or cedar exterior (EXT); the number of bathrooms (BATH); the lot size (LOT); the presence of a fireplace (FIRE); the presence of a two-car garage (GRG); the presence of central air conditioning (AC); and the presence of a basement (BASE). Unfortunately the square footage of the house and the number of bedrooms were not included in the characteristics of structure. A neighborhood quality index (NQ) was constructed via principal component analysis. The index comprised percentage non-white population in the census block, the median household income, the percentage of unemployed persons of 16 years or older, the percentage of families below the poverty level, the ratio of owner-occupied units to renter-occupied units, the percentage of units built in 1939 or before and the percentage of vacant units. The equation and its variants that Can estimates is

$$PRICE = a + b_1 \times BATH + b_2 \times EXT + b_3 \times LOT + b_4 \times FIRE + b_5 \times BASE + b_6 \times AC + b_7 \times GRG + b_8 \times NQ + \varepsilon.$$

The estimation produces numerical values for a and $b_1, \ldots, b_8$. One can plug actual values for *PRICE, BATH, EXT* etc. for a particular house sale into the equation and obtain a numerical "residual" value. The pattern formed by the 563 residuals contains information about the quality of the estimation. One uses the numerical values of $b_1, \ldots, b_8$ to infer values of the characteristics of a representative home in the sample. Can finds that in 1980 in Columbus, an additional bathroom contributed US$7,706 to the selling price of a house, a fireplace contributed US$5,024 to house-price and a double garage contributed US$4,070. An additional unit of neighborhood quality, captured by the NQ index, contributed US$5,750 to the price of a house.

Rent control

Rent control is intervention by the government in the adjustment of the rent a tenant typically pays for her apartment. Such controls usually arrive in a city in times of economic upheaval, wartime for example, when prices are changing rapidly. Since payment for accommodation often slices off a large fraction of the income of a household, a small increase in the level of rent can result in severe financial stress for a household. Households demand relief when their rents appear to be rising significantly and governments often respond with controls over the pace of rent increases. There are parallels with food price controls. Since food comprises a large fraction of the regular expenditure of a low-income household, governments often intervene in the pricing of basic foods to protect the consumption capacity of lower-income households. A food stamp program is an indirect program of subsidies for the purchase of many foods, generally by lower-income households. The downside of limiting price rises for certain commodities is that the suppliers can turn away from providing the good in question, or turn away from providing the good in question at a reasonable quality. Suppliers can argue that the revenue associated with their price-controlled asset (an apartment) is below a fair "market value." This can lead the owners to cut back on maintenance and the updating of their rental apartment and can also discourage new suppliers from entering a rent-controlled market. For rent control to function reasonably well, the government controllers have to make provision for owners to have sufficient revenue to do routine maintenance and possibly timely upgrading. The control of the rents must be fine-tuned so that apartments do not become so deteriorated from under-maintenance that units are uninhabitable.

Wijkander (2003), a resident of Stockholm where rent control is pervasive, looks to Belgium as a good model for organizing rent control. A new tenant in Belgium faces a so-called market rent when she moves in and her rent remains fixed for two years. Thereafter, the rent is adjusted each year, under public supervision, in accordance with an index number capturing rental changes in the locality in question. After nine years, the contract between landlord and renter is terminated and the tenant can quit the apartment or start a new nine-year contract. As in France and New York State, rent regulation in Belgium is carried out by the central government, not at the level of the municipality.

The phenomenon of "lock-in" is often publicized. A tenant in these circumstances is currently paying a rent far below the market rate for her unit in her neighborhood. Edmund Phelps, Nobel prize winner for economics, has rented the same rent-controlled, three-bedroom apartment in New York City, overlooking Central Park, for more than 30 years. His wife assured reporters at the time of the announcement of his winning the prize that they could never afford to purchase such an attractive and conveniently located unit. New York City has had various forms of rent control for over 80 years and currently more than one million apartments are covered by the state statute. One might ask why contracts have not evolved to cover the areas of landlord-tenant conflict without the need for a government agency, other than the courts. The answer seems to be that considerable legal expertise would be called for on the part of the tenant in such an environment and thus the government agency that supervises rent control and related landlord-tenant issues is delivering legal services that would otherwise be sought out and purchased in the private market. This perspective leads one to infer that considerable savings can be achieved by having a central, government housing authority dealing with tenant-landlord issues. The central authority delivers the services that might otherwise be delivered as contracts in the thousands between each tenant and landlord, negotiated with the aid of a lawyer in the "private sector."

One can envisage an equilibrium under rent control. The owner of the apartment wants some revenue and so he maintains the unit at a reasonable level and the tenant does not want to vacate the unit and so does not complain too vociferously and may even do some maintenance herself. Thus in many cities of Europe and the United States, there are rent controls and an equilibrium develops. The largest cost may be in stifling entry to the market. Rent controls can discourage developers from providing new apartments and can cause a city to have a shortage of reasonably priced accommodation. This in turn upsets apartment seekers, particularly those with modest incomes. Demands arise for government to provide more units via some sort of public or social housing program. Rent control will then tend to benefit the fortunate "incumbents" and generally discriminate against a newcomer who is seeking affordable accommodation. Policy design for cities is plagued by such "redistribution" trade-offs.

Public housing

New York City contains about 50,000 homeless people who make use of shelters at night (Barber 2013; p. 185) while Canada has 30,000 in total. The Mental Health Commission of Canada undertook research in five Canadian cities (Vancouver, Winnipeg, Toronto, Montreal and Moncton) in 2008 to investigate the effects of getting homeless people into their own small apartments. The subjects followed in the study were identified as the chronically homeless, many with mental health issues. A subject was typically homeless for more than five years, living on C$685 per month and this in his or her forties. Ninety-three percent were unemployed. The outcome of this C$110 million study was that for each dollar spent on getting a home for a homeless and possibly mentally ill person, some C$2.17 is saved in keeping an otherwise homeless person out of the hospital or jail or a shelter. By the end of the study, 72 percent of people in the study and 34 percent of those who were not were in their own home. Estimates of current outlays for maintaining a homeless and mentally ill person on his or her own are C$225,000 per year, on average. The Canadian government responded to the study by shifting funds in its budget of the Homeless Partnering Secretariat to a "Housing First" program, some C$600 million over a five-year period. Researchers argue that once a person has a stable place of his or her own, he or she can tackle addiction issues more easily as well as possibly moving into a job-training program. The Housing First idea is being extended from the original five cities to 18 cities across Canada.[18]

In the United States, programs to offer publicly owned housing to low-income families started in the 1930s. The motivation for such subsidized living arrangements was to assist low-income families in obtaining reasonable quality accommodation at a reasonable cost and also to clear away very poor quality structures in certain areas of cities: slum clearance. Increases in supply of social or public housing have occurred in diverse places since the 1930s but frequently such "projects" have become places of vandalism, violence and drug dealing. Many have been razed relatively quickly because of the rapid deterioration in hallways, stairways, etc. The modern substitute is the housing voucher for a low-income family. This is really a subsidy to the rent that the family will pay for a certain size and quality of dwelling in the community in question. The goal is usually to have a family end up paying no more than 30 percent of their income for shelter. In the United States in 2000, there were some 7.3 million renting households in poverty. Federal programs of rental assistance provided subsidies to 5.1 million households (Quigley and Raphael 2004). In the 1970s and 1980s the US government supported much research into the possibility of a universal housing allowance program for the nation (the Experimental Housing Assistance Program). In part the goal was to demonstrate that a carefully crafted program would not cause rents in general to be driven up. Observers expressed the view that this goal among others was attainable, but the program has never been implemented.

In 2001 in the United States there were about 34.4 million renting households. Of these, 1.2 million were deemed to be living in severely inadequate housing, 7.1 million were actually paying more than 50 percent of their incomes for accommodation and 5.05 million were subsidized. For the United States as a whole, some 6.8 million households were deemed to be living on incomes below the poverty line (Quigley and Raphael 2004). The Housing and Urban Development (HUD) Department runs a large subsidy program for low-income people known as Section 8. Vouchers are given to families to assist with rent payments or alternatively to landlords to assist with rental payments of low-income tenants. There is a provision for using the subsidy to pay for a home for a low-income household. The legal case of *Gautreaux v. Chicago Housing Authority (1969)* required HUD to diversify the design and location of public housing projects.

HOPE VI (1992) is a program aimed at the quality of accommodation for poor people. Over 15 years this program has led to the demolition of 96,200 substandard houses and apartments and brought on line 107,800 new or renovated units, many for low-income households. The *New York Times* reported in an editorial in 2010 that 2.3 million people were living in significantly dilapidated homes. Wait times for public housing can be up to ten years. Low-income families have gained access to mortgage funds through the Community Reinvestment Act (CRA, 1977). Developers are subsidized to create homes for low-income households under a tax credit program (Low Income Tax Credit, 1986). Some 2.4 million affordable homes have been built or renovated between 1986 and 2011. The HOME Investment Partnership (IPP, 1990) Program gives funds to state and local governments to support private sector developers willing to build affordable housing, and US$32 billion has been spent under this program.

The Tax Increment Financing (TIF) Program allocates funds for preparing derelict sites for redevelopment. There is an anticipated payback when the site becomes valuable for new development. Chicago has had 136 TIF sites developed, comprising a substantial fraction of the area of the city. Philadelphia has created a "land bank" that will consolidate some 40,000 vacant properties in both public and private hands. The hope is to attract developers and reduce the blight associated with vacant homes and lots. In addition it is repairing its 9,000 vacant city-owned properties, partly with federal government funds tied to eligible tax breaks.[19] At the household level, a neighborhood can organize as a Community Development Corporation and be granted funds for affordable housing and community service development.

Some 46.2 million working households in the United States paid more than half their incomes on housing in 2009, either as owner or renters. This was an increase of 600,000 households over 2008 (Platt 2014; p. 165). New York City Mayor Bill de Blasio proposes, in a new report, a US$41 billion effort to build or preserve 200,000 affordable apartments in five boroughs of New York City over ten years. Half a million people will benefit; 120,000 apartments are to be preserved and 80,000 new units built. Somewhat novel is the suggestion of relaxing height and density requirements in neighborhoods outside of Manhattan. The report considers new strains on schools and subways. A voluntary plan has yielded about 4,500 affordable units over the past 25 years. Builders set aside, for the long term, some affordable units in new projects. The Bloomberg administration was able to preserve or build 165,000 affordable units over 12 years. Rents in New York City have risen nearly 40 percent in the past 20 years while the wages of renters have risen less than 15 percent. An estimated 33 percent of New York's households pay more than 50 percent of their income on rent and utilities.[20] More than 400,000 people live in public housing apartments in New York City, most built over 50 years ago. The waiting list for a unit in one of the 334 developments operated by the New York City Housing Authority has over 250,000 households on it.[21]

Is there a crisis in the availability of affordable rental units in many cities in the United States? In the United States, 30 percent of gross income for a family is deemed the maximum that should be allocated to housing for a family. When the actual figure is higher, then a family is assumed to be having difficulty meeting its need for food, clothing and other things. One can work out the average income for a family in a city in the United States and the average rent for a home in that city and it turns out that in 90 cities, an average family is spending above the 30 percent maximum.[22] Chicago has recently seen a household's average rent payment rise to 31 percent of the city's average income. The figure for New Orleans is 35 percent, up from 14 percent about 20 years ago. One recent estimate puts fully 50 percent of renters in the United States as a whole spending at above the 30 percent level. The Low Income Housing Coalition estimates that families stuck with an outlay of 50 percent of their incomes for rent spend 33 percent less on food on average, 50 percent less on clothing and 80 percent less on medical care. Such shifts in expenditure can show up as a shortfall in demand for many struggling businesses in the United States. The relatively high rents can be attributed to a bump up in demand recently: 6.2 million new tenants between 2007 and 2013 compared with only 208,000 new owners. New affordable units are simply not coming on line fast enough. Some municipalities have changed zoning regulations to allow more building of micro-apartments. Land prices are usually high near city centers and many families are forced to live farther out from CBDs and incur substantial costs in terms of time and money for transportation. Federal subsidies for rent under the HOME program have been cut by half in the past decade. A Harvard University study reports that families receiving subsidies have declined to 24 percent from 27.4 percent recently. At the luxurious end of the supply spectrum there has been robust production of new rental units and in fact there has been downward pressure on rents for such accommodation. Part of the "backup" in demand for affordable rental accommodation is due to recent stringency in the granting of mortgages to the buyers of homes. In addition, many potential home buyers are apparently working off sizable student loans and are unable to take on the new debt associated with the purchase of a home.

Glaeser (2011; pp. 150–152) expresses exasperation with tight regulations which end up limiting the supply of new accommodation, particularly in new tall apartment buildings. He points out that current residents in New York City are inclined to promote regulations that prevent new tall apartment buildings from being constructed. "The elevator and the steel-framed skyscraper made it possible to get vast amounts of living space out of tiny amounts of land, but New York's building rules were stopping that process" (Glaeser 2011; p. 151), certainly up to the start of the administration of Mayor Michael Bloomberg. Glaeser argues that it costs about US$500,000 to essentially add one more 1,200 square foot apartment to a tall, but not ultra-tall, building and yet such an apartment was selling for twice this price. Suppliers were simply overly hemmed in by regulations from constructing more high-rise apartment buildings. "Zoning rules, air rights, height restrictions, and landmarks boards together form a web of regulation that has made it more and more difficult to build" (Glaeser 2011; p. 151). Glaeser's informal inquiry found that 80 percent of structures in the 1970s were 20 or more storeys high whereas in the 1990s, less than 40 percent were above 20 storeys. Glaeser appears to be making light of the negative aspects of a neighborhood dense with, say, 50-storey apartment buildings. Residents of a city do like to live with sunlight on streets, sidewalks and the windows of their apartments. A livable city has to balance an affordable price for a functional, reasonable-cost dwelling with the negatives of high-density, tall apartment buildings. New York City may have "room" for the introduction of many new, tall apartment buildings but some regulation is needed in order to get sunlight down to the streets, sidewalks and apartment windows as much as possible. Los Angeles has taken an opposite sort of route, having zoned more than 75 percent of residential land for single family dwellings. For New York City and San Francisco, in contrast, this figure is about 24 percent.[23]

"Inclusionary zoning" is a policy that mandates that an apartment builder set aside a certain number of units to be rented out at relatively low rents. The low-rent units are distributed to households with low incomes. One recent project in New York City, Abington House, has market rents about ten times more than the rents being charged to the low-income tenants.[24] Inclusionary zoning has been voluntary in New York. The developer is allowed to build 33 percent more square feet if he sets asides the correct number and type of low-rent units in his project. The uptake has been weak with only 3000 new affordable units coming to market between 2005 and 2013. Obviously the tenants paying market rents are subsidizing the tenants with the rent ceilings and this may be a stigma on a project. Mayor de Blasio is proposing to make inclusionary zoning mandatory for New York City. California's appeal court rejected inclusionary zoning in 2009 on the grounds that it violated the state's ban on new rent controls. One housing activist in New York City suggests simply charging a developer for the right to build more floor space than the local zoning mandates and using the funds to develop more social housing for low-income households.

A persistent concern about the accommodation poor people are stuck with is its proximity to food stores. So-called food deserts are areas devoid of food supermarkets. Residents of a food desert end up shopping in convenience stores, places without fresh vegetables and meat. Customers thus generally consume fatty, sugary processed foods and this routine contributes to obesity, among other health problems. In the United States, of the census tracts with more than 20 percent of residents below the poverty line, a third of households in these tracts live more than a mile from a supermarket. This implies an estimated 23 million people residing in food deserts in the United States. At the other end of the income spectrum are families in the suburbs who end up relying on their automobiles for shopping trips and much of their commuting. Here the case has been made that if these suburbs were more pedestrian-friendly, obesity could be checked. Eid *et al.* (2008) investigated, with careful econometric tests, whether the structure of modern residential suburbs was contributing to obesity and concluded that causality was more likely the other way around: people with a tendency to being overweight favored living in places that were especially automobile-friendly, namely contemporary pedestrian-unfriendly suburbs.

About 12 million people in the United States live in trailer parks. The 2013 US Census Bureau indicates that there are 8.6 million mobile homes in the United States. All park residents pay a rent of US$250 to US$300 for their lot and many pay an additional US$200 to US$300 to rent their trailer. A used three-bedroom unit costs between US$10,000 and US$20,000 in 2013. Water supply turns out to be the park owner's largest expense. Demand for accommodation in trailer parks is up because, between 1995 and 2012, the number of units of public housing in the United States declined by 211,000. Federal spending for rent assistance has not risen in the past decade, according to the Center on Budget and Policy Priorities. Twenty-five percent of working people are spending more than half their income on accommodation. "Worst case" households rose by 43 percent between 2007 and 2011, according to HUD. Trailer park residents in Texas tend to get behind in their rents more often than those in Wisconsin, North Dakota or Minnesota. The Rolfe-Reynolds trailer park company, with about 10,000 lots in the Midwest and Central Plains, estimates that their tenants are paying about 20 percent of their incomes for accommodation. A mid-size city in the United States would have about the same number of public housing units with tenants paying a maximum of 30 percent of their incomes on accommodation (*New York Times Magazine*, March 16, 2014, pp. 37–42).

A so-called mobile home is a form of factory-produced housing. *The Economist* reports on some large companies producing houses in factories in England, Germany and India.[25] The feeling is that there are significant economies to be reaped from expanding home production in some of these alternative modes.

African Americans and housing

African Americans lacked basic reading, writing and arithmetic skills at the end of the Civil War. The need for schools and education was apparent. Discrimination remained, however, and in 1896 (*Plessy v. Ferguson*) and 1899 (*Cummings v. Board of Education*) the principle of separate but equal was applied to the education of black children. The effect was severe underfunding (one-third of expenditure per student in white schools) of schools and teachers for African Americans over much of the first half of the twentieth century in the South, a violation in fact of the principle set out in *Plessy v. Ferguson*.

In the 1930s the National Association for the Advancement of Colored People (NAACP) launched law suits to get spending brought up for African Americans, starting with the salaries of teachers. In a seemingly defensive posture, Louisiana increased expenditure from US$16 to US$116 per black child between 1940 and 1955 (an increase of between 24 and 73 percent of expenditure per white child). In 1954 The Legal Defense Fund of the NAACP won in the Supreme Court the principle of no racial segregation in schools (*Brown v. Board of Education*). The NAACP pressed in fact for integration in schools or the abolition of a racial dimension in the make-up of schools in the United States. After the 1964 Civil Rights Act and President Johnson's Great Society program, busing, an instrument for integration, was mandated by the Court in *Swann v. Mecklenburg (1971)*. The Court's ruling was only partially implemented. In fact the courts followed up with decisions (*Milliken v. Bradley (1974)*) that resulted in limited actions for integration within pre-existing school districts and this often left white and black students in largely separate schools. Even when integration of a school did occur researchers generally found that black children did not perform better once they attended a school free of overt segregation. Such results probably contributed to a general cessation of moves toward large-scale integration of schools.

Since public schooling is a state function in the United States, local schools end up funded mostly by local taxes of which the property tax looms large. However, the decayed state of housing in ghettoes in many cities in the United States generally translates into a low level of support per student for local schools. The large disparity in per pupil spending in Texas was challenged by the Legal Defense Fund (*San Antonio School District v Rodriguez (1973)*) as violating the Constitution's Equal Protection Clause. Students in poor areas were funded at US$356 per head while those in wealthy areas were funded at US$594 per head. The Supreme Court ruled against the Defense Fund's challenge. Schools in poor districts and in the ghettoes occupied by many African Americans have ended up with significantly less financial support than schools in areas with higher-income residents. Black students score lower than their white counterparts in a variety of examinations and parental income does not seem to be crucial in many of these tests. Smith (2003; p. 309) says that:

> Explanations for this crisis in black eduction include poverty and racism; inadequate and poorly financed schools: lower expectations of teachers of the capacity of blacks to learn; biases in tests; and a climate of anti-intellectualism in the culture of the black community as reflected in the popularity of athletics and RAP music.

Even when the school system of a city is dominated by African Americans (as in Newark, Atlanta, Detroit, Gary and the District of Columbia) the test scores of black children are below those of comparable white children in school districts controlled by white parents.

In many cities in the United States the low-income people are not only in fairly clearly defined areas but many of these areas are dominated by African-American households. This suggests some element of discrimination in the sale and renting of housing. However, households with very low incomes tend to be ghettoized in most cities of the world and if African-American households are overly represented among households with very low incomes, then we should not be surprised that they are dominant in certain areas of most cities in the United States. It may well be a phenomenon of the ghettoization of poor households that we are seeing rather than ghettoization of African Americans *per se*. However, it turns out that African Americans are not the dominant fraction of poor households in cities with much segregation. There are many poor households that are not African American. Low-income households may indeed end up highly clustered but only some of the clusters are mostly African-American households in many cities in the United States. New census data indicate that more than one half of school-age children in the United States fall into the classification of "living in poverty." Such kids qualify for free lunches at school.[26] It is clear that explicit actions have been taken over the years to keep dark-skinned families from moving on to streets with white residents. Discrimination has taken the form of lenders not providing mortgages for African-American borrowers under certain circumstances.

An economist would like to know the extent of ghettoization of low-income African-American households that is attributable to policies based on explicit discrimination and the extent that is attributable to the general phenomenon of low-income households ending up in certain neighborhoods. History plays a role. A neighborhood can become dominated by African-American households due to a certain policy that discriminates and when discrimination abates the neighborhood can remain African-American simply because of inertia. When LeDuff (2013) reports that Detroit has switched from 83 percent white in the 1950s to 83 percent black in 2010, it must be that many white households moved out while a good many African-American households moved in. It was not only long-term low-income African-American households that came to make up contemporary Detroit but many households that kept migrating in while so-called "white flight" was taking place. Somewhat unusual then is Detroit's experience with a significant inflow of African-American households, even as the economy of the city was declining. Glaeser and Gyourko (2005) have linked this inflow to the attraction posed by the abundance of the low-cost housing, housing that became available to low-income families as the white families essentially abandoned city life in Detroit. African-American families flowed into the somewhat beaten-down housing stock in part because such accommodation was inexpensive. However, they were still faced with the general trend of job-shedding and outright flight by firms in Detroit.

Discrimination against certain households by groups of neighbors is of course well known. The roots are probably deep. A person usually defines who he or she is by "what" she presents to "the world," and one's home is a large part of that presentation. The presentation of one's home involves the street and the homes close by. It is unsurprising that a homeowner is significantly emotionally connected to the appearance of his or her home and street. At a minimum, the homeowner wants his or her immediate neighbors to keep their homes in good repair and possibly attractive to look at. In addition to the emotional pull, there is the basic economic consideration: one wants the value of one's home to "do well" and part of "doing well" is of course having homes near one's own well maintained. It is not surprising that current owners are motivated to screen prospective in-movers to their street and neighborhood. Zoning regulations protect current owners somewhat. There can be rules against parking vehicles on the lawn or recreation vehicles near the street; rules against letting weeds take over the ground around one's home; in some neighborhoods, strict rules on what changes can be made in the appearance of a current structure (as with historically designated neighborhoods); and in many neighborhoods the types of sheds that one can erect on one's property. Thus when current owners create barriers to certain types of in-movers, they may simply be thinking that they are keeping out new households that will almost surely "damage" the appearance of a home nearby in some fashion that they are buying. These attitudes may or may not be based on solid historical evidence but they are attitudes that are easily comprehended. When these attitudes are whims or emotional reflexes and are not based on evidence, a community has a genuine social problem. Most pernicious is that attitude: "I am not prejudiced against dark-skinned neighbors but most other people are. Thus I must keep dark-skinned entrants out of my neighborhood if I am to preserve the value of my home." When most people have this attitude we have discrimination built into neighborhood evolution.

Maintaining a home can be costly. If, say, family x that is in-migrating is African-American one might infer that they are a low-income family and will probably not be able to direct adequate funds to maintain their home. Whether this is a valid inference is of course beside the point. When current owners have these beliefs, racial segregation by streets or even neighborhoods can take root. There is much evidence of current home owners in the United States arranging to keep African-American families from moving onto their streets or into their school districts. The cost of this discrimination was borne in a first pass by African-American children who were forced to attend schools with few white children, schools that were funded at lower levels than those for most white children. Neighborhood segregation made for school segregation and different schools were funded at quite different levels. This largely reflected the size of the local tax base. Schools in neighborhoods with mostly low-income households tended to be funded at a lower level than schools with higher-income neighborhoods. Large-scale busing was of course introduced in the United States in 1964 as part of the Civil Rights Act. The goal was to not have schools that were mostly black or mostly white. However, the Supreme Court ruled that the Act required busing only for schools within city boundaries and thus the suburban schools could and mostly did end up with mostly white children. Segregated neighborhoods are typically found in older, large cities of the north in the United States. The first "Great Migration" (1910 to the early 1920s) brought between 300,000 and 1,000,000 African Americans from the south to the dynamic northern cities such as Detroit, Chicago, Cleveland, New York City, Boston, Philadelphia and Baltimore. The adjustment of established residential neighborhoods to newcomers was difficult. There were bombings of the homes of African Americans in some northern cities. Covenants were developed to keep black migrants from the south out of established neighborhoods. Dyja (2013; p. 6) writes of Chicago in 1945 having "more restrictive covenants in place than anywhere else in the nation." Up until 1910 the local African-American population was dispersed widely throughout Chicago's various census tracts, Dyja observes. But after 1910, "the vast black ghetto of the South Side" developed "a wide gash of slums down State Street and Michigan south of the Loop" (p. xxvi). Dyja goes on to say, "Panicking whites formalized the trend through use of restrictive covenants that kept blacks within a three-block-wide strip starting at 26th Street, swelling east at 31, and ending at 55th" (p. 6), and also "Between 1944 and 1946, there were forty-six racial incidents in the city, nearly all connected to housing" (p. 81).

Segregation in most cities in the United States was then the norm. Most job openings were near the centers of cities and ultimately this was the area where lower-income African Americans formed their own neighborhoods. The second Great Migration, largely post 1945, added large numbers of African American families to the established black neighborhoods. There appears to have been a substantial pull dimension to the two great migrations. There was a robust demand for unskilled workers in the buoyant cities of the northern United States. Of course the push dimension was the difficult life of a black family in the rural south. The emergence of what we might refer to as Black Pride was abetted by the experiences of African-American men in the military. Once many of them had seen the world outside of the rural south, they were prepared to take their lives and those of their families in new directions. Ordinary clannishness plus active discrimination led to a great deal of segregation by neighborhoods in the northern cities. Typically the large black neighborhoods were located near the centers of cities. Here older residences of white people could be subdivided and added onto to form functional homes of limited floor space. Though these homes were near employment centers clustered near the centers of cities, it was not long before many of the jobs were shifted from city centers to suburban areas. Hence by the late 1950s a spatial mismatch was becoming apparent. The new unskilled job openings were more prevalent in the suburbs and many unskilled workers were living in older neighborhoods near the centers of cities. By the 1970s, the typical black worker had a longer commute than his or her white counterpart.

Table 8.2 Largest metros (population of 500,000 or more): black-white segregation indices sorted by 2010 segregation

	1990	*2000*	*2010*	*1990–2010*	*Population*	*Share NH Black (%)*
Milwaukee–Waukesha–West Allis, WI	82.8	83.3	81.5	−1.2	1,555,908	16.4
New York–Northern New Jersey–Long Island	80.9	80.2	78.0	−2.9	18,897,109	16.1
Chicago–Naperville–Joliet, IL–IN–WI	84.4	81.2	76.4	−8.0	9,461,105	17.1
Detroit–Warren–Livonia, MI	87.6	85.7	75.3	−12.3	4,296,250	22.6
Cleveland–Elyria–Mentor, OH	82.8	78.2	74.1	−8.7	2,077,240	19.7
Buffalo–Niagara Falls, NY	80.1	78.0	73.2	−6.9	1,135,509	11.8
St. Louis, MO-IL	77.2	74.1	72.3	−4.9	2,812,896	18.3
Cincinnati–Middletown, OH-KY-IN	75.9	73.7	69.4	−6.5	2,130,151	11.9
Philadelphia–Camden–Wilmington	75.2	71.0	68.4	−6.8	5,965,343	20.2
Los Angeles–Long Beach–Santa Ana, CA	72.7	70.0	67.8	−4.9	12,828,837	6.7
Syracuse, NY	73.0	71.4	67.8	−5.2	662,577	7.7
Bridgeport–Stamford–Norwalk, CT	69.2	69.6	67.5	−1.6	916,829	10.1

Source: Compiled by John Paul DeWitt of CensusScope.org and the University of Michigan's Social Science Data Analysis Network.

Table 8.2 reports on a measure of segregation by area called the dissimilarity index for a city. We have listed the 12 most segregated cities. The index reflects the number of people from one race—in this case black or white—who would have to move for races to be evenly distributed across a certain area. A score of 1 indicates perfect integration while 100 signals complete segregation.

The average person is disturbed by large groups of households of different skin color set apart in some way from the mainstream of the larger society. Large-scale segregation of the homes of African Americans in many cities has an undeniable aura of discrimination against a minority. Can we calculate a meaningful cost of having African Americans segregated into ghettos? It may be unfair and socially reprehensible but is the unfairness quantifiable? It turns out that there are numerous costs. A study of test scores for children in Texas found that performance of children, other things being equal, was poorer in schools with a high proportion of black children (Hanushek *et al.* 2002). Cutler and Glaeser (1997) used census data to investigate the impact of segregation on the probability of a young person finishing school, finishing college, being idle (not employed, or in school, or in college, or in the military) and being an unmarried mother. They found large effects of what is essentially segregation on these outcomes. The elimination of segregation would, they found, eliminate differences between graduation rates for blacks and whites and also reduce the probability of being an unwed mother by two-thirds. When a ghetto young person can find a job, he or she tends to have a longer commute than a comparable white young person. Typically the availability of jobs in segregated communities is not as good as it is elsewhere in cities. Winston (2013; p. 805) reports that people earning less than US$15,000 per year use transit for only 10 percent of work trips. Mass transit allows poor people to access only one-third of metro jobs in under 90 minutes. Automobile commuting allows poor people to reach all jobs in the 51 largest metropolitan areas in under 60 minutes. Poor people are of course typically less likely to own an automobile.

The largest cost may have been that ghettoization allowed for the under supply of municipal public goods such as police protection, fire protection and particularly quality education for children of almost all ages. Evidence has been adduced in recent years to show a connection between stress and poor mental states. In particular, the ability of children to learn has been found to be impaired by stress (Mottowildo *et al.* 1986). Brain scans indicate that stressed children show evidence of PTSD (post-traumatic stress disorder). In East Palo Alto, a neighborhood of low-income families, researchers from Stanford University have been experimenting with yoga sessions in an effort of reduce the stress of school children. In controlled experiments the test scores of children in de-stressing sessions have improved significantly. One can easily make the case that in general children in low-income neighborhoods live with measurable excess stress. The stress can derive from insecurity on the street, sexual violence and frequent spells of food shortages. It could be that stress spills over from parents to children. Ellen (2000) found that African-American mothers from more segregated places are more likely to give birth to low birth-weight babies that mothers in less segregated places. Low birth weight is known to be associated with a higher probability of the occurrence of a variety of childhood illnesses.

Different research has demonstrated that babies who have been talked to a lot by their mothers at very early ages do better on tests of ability as early as three years old and when the talking-to involves a broader range of words, the children perform even better on tests, not too many years on. Anne Fernald of Stanford University has found that at 18 months children from disadvantaged families are several months behind more favored children.[27] This leads to the inference that better-educated mothers who talk much to their babies will have on average smarter toddlers. A schooling "deficit" of the mother can thus actually hinder the mental development of her children. Early childhood "education" of a variety of sorts is being recognized as very important for the mental development of children.

Clearly, the best way to reduce segregation is to have more job openings in heavily segregated cities and no discrimination in hiring. Families will migrate to less dense and probably less segregated neighborhoods when they have the means to do so. Education opportunities are very important for young African Americans. Poorly educated young people will occupy most of the low-paying jobs and a low-paying job will not allow a person to support a family in an attractive neighborhood. A long-term strategy to lift people out of decayed neighborhoods is to provide the children with high-quality education. One could envisage a series of high-quality schools near the edges of ghettos that could attract children from white homes as well as providing good educational opportunities for children from the ghetto. Providing especially good-quality schools in segregated areas would be an indirect form of affirmative action. Johns Hopkins University has in fact collaborated in the construction of a showcase school in a neighborhood of poor families near its famous hospital in East Baltimore. The school will be the center of a larger US$1.8 billion renewal project that includes a park, retail outlets and mixed-income housing. "Putting a cutting-edge school run by a great university in a historically troubled neighborhood flips the usual urban imbalance of power and changes the status quo of public education steeped in blight."[28]

Central to saving a neighborhood is then maintaining security on the streets and quality in the local schools. This is a pivotal point. Once security on the streets and quality in the schools tips below a threshold, one generally observes neighborhood flight. Flight frequently speeds up decline in local school quality. The MOP (Moving to Opportunity) program tested the idea of subsidizing a minority family in a city in the United States to move out of the segregated area, in fact mostly out of public housing projects. Most of the families involved were headed by a woman. Five cities (Baltimore, Boston, Chicago, Los Angeles and New York) were selected and the families were tracked over a ten-year period. Adult mental health improved after five years but being located to a low-poverty neighborhood did not result in less unemployment for the adults or more family income. Children did not register improved cognitive performance and teenage boys actually became more lawless. DeLuca and Darrah (2014) report much more success with a similar program in Baltimore alone. Counseling was central to this other case study in relocation of families to a higher-income, more integrated neighborhood. DeLuca and Darrah emphasize that "how people make choices is a function of their experiences and our experiences come as a function of structural opportunities and barriers."

Neighborhoods of mostly poor households are not only deficient because they lack schools of high quality. "In Los Angeles, for example, areas with predominantly African-American populations have 1.7 park acres per 1000, while white-dominated areas have 31.8 park acres per 1000" (Barber 2013; p. 206). By some measures, segregation by neighborhood is declining. Census figures indicate that in 1960 there were 4,700 all-white neighborhoods in the United States. In 2011, there were 170 (Barber 2013; p. 190). Low-income working people live also with higher than average rates of unemployment. Dickerson (2007) found, with some careful econometric work, that cities with more segregation had higher rates of unemployment.

Summary

Central to the analysis of the consumption of housing by a household is the translation of the selling price of a home into an appropriate annual cost of living in a home. The key step here is to express the selling price, a capital value, as an annual "cost," namely the annual interest that the selling price would fetch if it were in a bank account. Given this transformation from capital value to annual flow ("interest" on capital value) one comes up with "user cost," an expression for the annual cost of living in the home one owns inclusive of annual municipal taxes, maintenance and capital gains (change in selling price of the home, over a year). Changes in demand for housing can be related to changes in user cost. We also observe that user cost should be similar in value to the rent one would pay to live in a comparable home, under a rental arrangement. We considered how inflation impacts the level of user cost.

We inquired about the famous tax break for home ownership in the United States, mortgage interest deductibility (MID). This break has been linked to households selecting large homes with large bank loans attached in order to reap as much of the tax break as possible. Our interest is in how MID might invite less "excess" borrowing and we dwell on this question. The phenomenon of imputing in the national accounts for accounting for possible "excess" services from a home that is owned by the occupant is investigated. We link imputing to mortgage interest deductibility.

We also considered the supply side of the housing market, including filtering or "trickle-down" supply, and finished with a discussion of social or public housing.

Main points of Chapter 8

1. "User cost" is defined as the annual cost, dollars per year, of living in the home one owns. In addition to municipal taxes, and an allowance for maintenance, this cost includes an estimate of current yearly capital gains on the house value plus an estimate of the annual value of funds represented by the current selling price of the house (market rate of interest multiplied by the current price the house would fetch, if sold).
2. Mortgage interest deductibility is a break on one's income tax represented by the government allowing one to subtract one's annual mortgage payments from one's gross

income before working out how much income tax one owes to the government for a year.

3 Owning one's home rather than renting resembles owning an investment like shares in Microsoft, to a limited extent. Part of the annual return is the value of "free" housing services one is getting, without putting out rental dollars to oneself or a landlord. Another imputation is the interest one could be earning if the value of the house were turned into money sitting in a savings account.

4 The percentage of households that own their homes instead of renting varies from under 40 percent in Switzerland to about 65 percent for Canada and the United States.

5 To keep the cost of financing a home reasonable, governments introduced the purchasing of home loans from banks (securitization) in the 1930s, as well as government organized loan or mortgage insurance. More funds ended up in banks for lending and banks ended up with lower costs when borrowers defaulted.

6 A rule of thumb to estimate a local bubble in home prices is when the estimate of the user cost for local homes is well above the actual cost of renting similar properties. Excess "animal spirits" or "herding behavior" has been blamed for housing price bubbles in an area. New "adequate" supply eventually brings prices down to a normal range.

7 The hedonic home price equation allows one to break the price of a home into its principal components such as site value, value per unit floor space, value per unit bedroom, value per unit bathroom, etc. and value per unit distance from the city center.

8 Filtering in the housing market involves older larger homes becoming small apartment buildings for households with lower incomes. Gentrification involves dilapidated buildings in a neighborhood being upgraded for higher-income households.

9 Low-income households are sometimes supplied with government or social housing and are sometimes provided with allowances that permit them to reduce their out-of-pocket rent payment to 30 percent of their incomes. Inclusive zoning is when the builder of an apartment project gets a zoning break in return for setting aside units in her building that rent out for under-market rates.

10 Rent controls are government programs to "lessen" payments for housing for households in high-rent communities. They can discourage owners from maintaining their rental units to a good standard.

Questions and problems

1 "User cost" defines the dollar estimate of the direct annual cost to a home owner of living in her home over a year. Of the four standard components, "the opportunity cost of funds" sunk in the home is generally the largest.

   a For a house with a current market price of US$525,000 and an interest rate of 4 percent, what is "the opportunity cost of funds"?
   b What are the other three standard components of user cost?

2 Some economists prefer plotting a representative user cost over time, with capital gains left out of the calculation. Is this net user cost a better indicator of the financial burden of home ownership to a household?

3 The national accounts of Canada and the United States include two imputations (side calculations inserted when direct data are missing), one estimating the dollar value an owner-household is receiving for "housing services" being supplied to them by their

home, and another estimating the annual income from capital represented by their home as an asset, rather as if the household owned shares in, say, the Microsoft Corporation. One way to explain why these large imputations are made in the national accounts is to analyze the role of owner-occupied housing in the account of a typical household. Set out this account and highlight the two imputations.

4 Is zoning the mechanism that results in low-income households generally living in areas apart from high-income households?

5 Large cities typically have many schools, some identified as good and others as not of good quality. Is there an obvious route for making school quality quite uniform across a city?

6 When journalists write of an "affordability crisis" for housing in a city, what measures or metrics should they be considering? Is there an obvious solution to a city's "affordability problem" with housing?

7 "Death rates are 5.5 percent higher nationwide than in New York City for people 55 to 64 years old, 17 percent higher for those 65 to 74 and more than 24 percent higher for those 75 to 84" (Glaeser 2011; p. 115). Is this good evidence that dense residential arrangements lead to superior health outcomes?

Appendix 8.1: Two filtering models and difficulties

We turn to a two-class model in which new houses deteriorate with the passage of time alone and are passed from higher-income residents to lower-income residents at some "equilibrium date."

Central to the analysis is the splicing together of the two phases of occupancy: in the first phase the house is occupied by a high-income family and in the second phase the house is occupied by a low-income family. A resident has utility $U(c,q) \equiv c[q_0 - q]^{-\beta}$ for q the current quality (even floor space works here for quality) and c other goods. We have $q = q_0 - t$ for q_0 the quality when first built and c other goods consumed, and we also have two budget constraints:

$$w^i = c^i(t) + r(t)q^i(t), \quad i = H, L$$

where the superscript indicates high or low income, $r(t)$ is annual rental cost for the resident-owner and w^i is annual income. Each income group experiences an unchanging utility over its occupancy interval. The ratio of marginal utilities equal to the price ratio gives us

$$\frac{U_c}{U_q} = \frac{[q_0 - q]^{-\beta}}{\beta c[q_0 - q]^{-\beta-1}} = \frac{1}{r(t)},$$

or $r(t) = \beta c[q_0 - q]^{-1}$ and $r(t)q(t) = q\beta c[q_0 - q]^{-1}$. The rent function is declining since $q_0 - q = t$. The budget constraint becomes

$$w = c[1 + q\beta[q_0 - q]^{-1}],$$

which implies a value for c in the utility function. Then

$$\overline{U} = \frac{w}{[1 + q\beta[q_0 - q]^{-1}]}[q_0 - q]^{-\beta}.$$

This implies that q is unchanging since $\frac{\overline{U}}{w}$ is constant. Hence the model has broken down, given the above specification.

However, when we insert our expression for $r(t)$ we see that an unchanging value for $\overline{U}$ implies an unchanging value for $q(t)$. Hence this specification of the quasi-linear function for utility has "broken down." One reaches a similar impasse when one starts with the utility function $c + q^{\beta}$.

Neither Robson's utility function $c[q_0 - q]^{\beta}$ (Robson 1982) nor the quasi-linear function, $c + g(q)$, allow us to generate a meaningful filtering phenomenon. Braid (1986) presents an interesting analysis of filtering for the two-class case but leaves the specification under the assumption of $q(t) = q_0 e^{-\delta t}$. He leaves the details of his utility function unspecified. Hence we are left to assume that there is a utility function that works for his model, but what the function is, is left open. We are skeptical that there is a familiar form for the utility function that works. Hence the quite different approach in the text above.

Appendix 8.2: Checks on rent and quantity schedules for the filtering model

We have to verify that the high-income resident will indeed outbid the low-income resident early on and the opposite will occur beyond T^s. First, we observe that at the switch date, we have

$$\frac{dr}{dt} = (\beta - 1)\beta q^{\beta-2}\frac{dq}{dt}$$

and $$\frac{dr^H}{dt} - \frac{dr^L}{dt} = (\beta - 1)\beta q^{\beta-2}\left[\frac{dq^H}{dt} - \frac{dq^L}{dt}\right].$$

Hence we have to establish that $\left[\frac{dq^H}{dt} - \frac{dq^L}{dt}\right] < 0$. From above we see that

$$\frac{dq}{dt} = \left[\frac{U - w}{1 - \beta} - \frac{\gamma}{1 - \beta}t\right]^{\frac{1}{\beta}-1}\left(\frac{-\gamma}{1 - \beta}\right)$$

and it follows that

$$\frac{dq^H}{dt} - \frac{dq^L}{dt} = \frac{1}{1 - \beta}\left[\frac{U - w}{1 - \beta} - \frac{\gamma}{1 - \beta}T^s\right]^{\frac{1}{\beta}-1}\left[-\gamma^H + \gamma^L\right].$$

Hence $\frac{dq^H}{dt} - \frac{dq^L}{dt} < 0$ when $-\gamma^H + \gamma^L < 0$. Hence the rent functions intersect correctly when $-\gamma^H + \gamma^L < 0$. And this condition is easy to accept, namely that the high-wage resident's net income is rising more steeply than is the low-wage resident's net income. The schedules for rent and $q(t)$ are drawn in Figure 8.2 in the chapter text under the assumption that indeed $-\gamma^H + \gamma^L < 0$.

Notes

1 Leamer (2007) shows that a downturn in housing starts has preceded most modern downturns at the beginning of the business cycle in the United States.

2 See, for example, Glaeser (2011; pp. 188–90) where he discusses the very low density of residences south of San Francisco.

3 For the year 2000, there were more households living in mobile homes in the United States than in apartments, the latter in buildings with 50 or more units.
4 *New York Times*, April 3, 2011, p. B7.
5 *Globe and Mail*, April 20, 2011, p. B8.
6 *The Economist*, March 5, 2011, p. 9.
7 "Yield" for an office building is defined as Rent/Price. Yield would then be compared with going rates of return or the market rate of interest. One can be said to be comparing Rent > or < Price*i for i the current interest rate.
8 *New York Times*, May 31, p. 1.
9 Robert Farzad, *BloombergBusinessweek*, February 13, 2014, quoting Robert Shiller.
10 *Globe and Mail*, January 1, 2015, p. B1.
11 *New York Times*, July 27, 2014, p. 22.
12 *New York Times*, January 11, 2015, p. 8.
13 Sweeney worked with demand and supply schedules and did not confront the problems associated with a workable specification of the resident's utility function.
14 *New York Times*, March 14, 2014, p. 11.
15 *New York Times*, April 6, 2014, pp. 26–27.
16 Russ Buettner, "A Partnership that Kept a City Lot Vacant for 47 Years," *New York Times*, March 23, 2014; p. 26.
17 Sherwin Rosen (1974) is generally cited as the modern developer of the idea of hedonic estimation of house price characteristics.
18 Andre Picard, *Globe and Mail*, April 8, 2014, p. A4.
19 *New York Times*, March 18, 2014, p. A11.
20 *New York Times*, May 6, 2014, Editorial.
21 *New York Times*, August 12, 2014, p. A17.
22 *New York Times*, April 15, 2014.
23 *The Economist*, August 24, 2014, p. 24.
24 Josh Barro, "Affordable housing that's very costly," *New York Times*, June 7, 2014, Business Section.
25 *The Economist*, January 10, 2015, p. 61.
26 *The Washington Post*, January 16, 2015.
27 *The Economist*, February 22, 2014, p. 67.
28 *New York Times*, March 18, 2014, pp. 1 and A11.

9 The public sector

Service provision by local governments. Scale economies. Local public goods and voting equilibrium. Alternative routes to revenue raising. Migration and clustering induced by a household's fiscal "surplus." Zoning to mitigate free-riding. Henry George theory. Revenues and responsibilities. Crime in cities.

Introduction

We set out various economic "forces" or "mechanisms" that make a person happier and/or more productive when she is living with a group rather than alone or with multiple families rather than with a single family. One of the strongest such "mechanisms" for hunter-gatherer people is mutual defense. It is safe for a family to live with other families of able-bodied people if mutual defense is a standard problem. More "soldiers" can repel an attack better than fewer "soldiers" and effective strategy is better sorted out by a group of "interested" people than by only one or two defenders. I have division of labor in mind here. Mutual defense is a service mutually "consumed" by a group of people. The group shares in the production of "defense services." When one person in the group is effectively protected from outside violence, the other members of the group are generally equally protected. Defense services are shared in a somewhat roundabout fashion. From the dawn of human history, defense of members of groups has been an issue and the standard course of action was to live close to one's fellow members of the group and learn to help in defensive activity. Defense in a modern state has changed little except for scale. "National defense" is a flow of defense services provided by the state and one person's security generally means that everyone else is getting protection as well. National defense is said to be a public good. Much of this chapter is about public goods. There is a sense in which public good analysis is about a form of sharing in consumption. Thus a large dimension of life is about shared consumption. Self-interest may be the behavior ground-rock of modern economics but there is another large branch of economics that focuses on sharing. Curious, no?

Typically, a high level of government in a nation sets tax rates on personal incomes, including income from investments and on businesses, and directly or indirectly sets money supply growth, credit conditions and financial policy. Immigration and income support programs are also generally set out by the high level of government. Often the same high level of government decides on expenditure for infrastructure in a nation including urban highways, subways and light rail facilities. Yet in most modern economies a majority of the households reside in cities, the latter administered by governments with fairly demanding agendas for making the lives of households agreeable. These local governments are often significantly constrained in their abilities to raise revenue and frequently are required by higher levels of government to undertake a range of activities. There appears to be a persistent misfitting between accepted activities of local governments and the abilities of these governments to fund the activities that end up on their agendas. Officials in local government spend much of their time scrambling for more revenue and trying to expand their tax bases, and so are often in a begging position with regard to higher levels of government. Each city operating independently is not the answer. Higher levels of government have an important coordination function for the activities of what we might call lower-order economies. Exactly why local governments seem so often starved for revenue and authority for their economies should be kept in mind as we work through issues in urban public finance in this chapter.

In the abstract, government is a provider of "public goods." Such goods as law and order benefit all people simultaneously, once produced. A public good is roughly speaking "jointly consumed" by citizens. Municipal governments are expected to produce a range of goods and services, a plurality of public goods. We consider these demands. Households can register their unhappiness with "service" by voting against the incumbents or in more extreme cases by relocating—"voting with their feet," as the saying goes. And we have quite a bit to say about the revenues that a municipal government has to work with. We are generally sympathetic with the generic misfit line of thinking: cities are in charge of important services and are generally squeezed by revenue tightness in their efforts to deliver the services expected of them.

In the 1960s in the United States, the functioning of local governments came under scrutiny. There was the sentiment that the cores of many large cities were being hollowed out with the economic decline. Central city governments were facing a flight of businesses and middle- to high-income residents to the suburbs. Automobiles had become relatively inexpensive. Central cities were left with shrinking tax bases and many low-income residents in need of income support for food and shelter. Observers pondered consolidation of municipalities into larger units as a solution to the problems of the central cities. One view was that many suburban residents commuted to office buildings in the center of cities each weekday and yet did not pay fully for the services being provided by the governments of the centers of cities. Consolidation of local governments could then balance matters out: suburban residents could be made to pay for some of the services provided in city centers. And the centers of cities might stop deteriorating if they had more revenue to improve infrastructure.

A second argument was that the services of government often displayed scale economies—declining average costs with larger quantities of services being provided. Hence consolidation of central city governments with suburban units could provide the scale to lower the cost of provision of certain municipal services. Which services? And how much cost lowering? These questions became a focus of research for many economists in the 1960s. The evidence it seems is not unambiguous. Larger cities have not been able to provide, say, police services, or fire protection services, or tax collection services at lower cost per resident than medium-sized cities. What about public transit? Clearly when the center of a city has one government and the suburbs have their separate governments there is a need for the governments to cooperate and coordinate activities with regard to public transit. Does this line of thinking lead to the conclusion that consolidation of central-city with suburban governments is the appropriate course? One approach is for the governments to remain separate and concede authority over matters of public transit to a committee with members from all local governments in the region in question. But since capital expenditures for public transit are often very large, each government can feel its control of expenditure is being usurped by members of the public transit committee, often by representatives of the "other governments." Often it seems that today lower-income residents are settling on the edges of cities and they are in need of good public transportation. For a city to function well, lower-income residents must have access to a means of commuting to places with jobs. Getting mass transit functioning effectively has become central to the mission of a local government providing good services to residents. Local governments often turn to higher levels of government for assistance with the provision of mass transit, particularly with regard to capital expenditures. Large problems in coordination of needs with funding sources ensue. Still, we suggest that the provision of good-quality mass transit is not the defining argument for the consolidation of local governments in contiguous municipalities.

Opponents of consolidation often cite the "levelling up" argument. In this view, local government employees can readily argue for jumps in salary when the jurisdiction in which they work becomes larger. The argument is made: "if workers doing task X in "distant" city Y are earning Z dollars per year and the size of our municipality has become Y after consolidation, we people doing X should be receiving the same pay." This could be something of a reverse "scale economy" but it may also be true that doing task X merits more pay when its scope has increased. In the valuable survey of "municipal government consolidation"[1] the question of a deterioration in the quality of government services with local government bigness recurs. A citizen may well have more difficulty contacting the person in the local government responsible for task X when the local government grows large. Having services provided to the satisfaction of all local residents is obviously not easy. The "devolution movement" argues for having government services provided by government agencies that are as "close to the citizen-client as possible." Thus "subsidiarity" is an organizing principle that contends that matters ought to be handled by the smallest, lowest or least centralized competent authority. The term became part of the governing philosophy of the Roman Catholic Church and was adopted by framers of the "constitution" of the modern European Union. There may be certain scale economies in providing certain services in large quantities and this bigness may suggest that a "senior" level of government should do the providing, and yet some sacrifice in scale may mean that providers of services are more in touch with or more sensitive to the desires of the citizen-clients. The capital cities of many countries often have the highest level of government administering functions that one would expect to see handled by a lower level of government. The "high-level" civil servants may seem unresponsive to the wishes of ordinary citizens.

The provinces of both Ontario and Quebec in Canada embarked on consolidation of municipal governments early in the twenty-first century. In Montreal, the central city government was dealing with considerable debt that had been accumulated earlier and the Provincial Government may have pushed for consolidation of governments in 2000 in order to spread responsibility for debt payments over more citizens. But considerable push-back developed from the "outer" municipalities and the opposition party in the provincial legislature took up the cause of residents in these "outer" municipalities. When the opposition party came to power in 2003, it reversed the consolidations in both Montreal and Quebec City. In Ontario, consolidations proceeded in numerous locations and opponents were not strong enough to get any reversed.

Pure public goods

A pure public good, like national defence, is produced by the government and is consumed equally by all citizens. My consumption of, say, q_G is the same as your consumption of q_G and my consumption does not interfere with or diminish your level of consumption. In addition there is no way to exclude any citizen from consuming the level q_G, whether a person has paid her taxes or not. In this case, q_G is said to be a pure public good. (An impure public good may have a geographic dimension, for example, and arrive at two households in different places in different amounts.) Central to public goods analysis is the assumption that though each consumer will generally be receiving the same flow of services q_G, each consumer may be registering quite distinct desires or tastes for q_G. Hence the need, in the abstract, for personal charges or "prices" for a unit of q_G. Samuelson (1954) investigated, in the abstract, how much public good, q_G, the government should produce.

We set out an illustrative example, an economy with two people with different tastes for one private good, q_C, and one public good, q_G. There are fixed amounts of inputs K and N used to produce each of outputs q_C and q_G. Each person has her own utility function, namely $U^A(q_C^A, q_G)$ and $U^B(q_C - q_C^A, q_G)$. Static maximization of the utility sum $(U^A(q_C^A, q_G) + U^B(q_C - q_C^A, q_G))$ for two persons yields the five equilibrium conditions (9.1) to (9.3) plus the two commodity balance relations below. Current production of the private good is $f(K^C, N^C)$, with input levels K^C and N^C. Current production of the government good is $h(K - K^C, N - N^C)$, with input levels $K - K^C$ and $N - N^C$. We assume that our production functions $f(.)$ and $g(.)$ exhibit constant returns to scale. Maximization requires

$$U^A_{q_C^A} - U^B_{q_C^B} = 0, \tag{9.1}$$

$$U^A_{q_G} \times h_{KG} + U^B_{q_G} \times h_{KG} = U^A_{q_C^A} f_{KC} \text{ or } U^B_{q_C^B} f_{KC} \text{ using (9.1)}, \tag{9.2}$$

$$U^A_{q_G} \times h_{NG} + U^B_{q_G} \times h_{NG} = U^A_{q_C^A} f_{NC} \text{ or } U^B_{q_C^B} f_{NC} \text{ using (9.1)}, \tag{9.3}$$

$$q_C = f(K^C, N^C),$$

$$q_G = h(K - K^C, N - N^C).$$

Here $U^A_{q_C^A}$ is A's marginal utility for her private good and f_{KC} is the marginal product of K in the production of the private good. The above system is five equations in q_C^A, K^C, N^C, q_C, and q_G. When one combines equations (9.2) and (9.3) one obtains a familiar efficiency condition for the use of K and N by the consumption and government goods sectors.

Equations (9.2) and (9.3) can be written as

$$[U^A_{q_G}/U^A_{q_C^A}] \times h_{KG} + [U^B_{q_G}/U^B_{q_C^B}] \times h_{KG} = f_{KC},$$

$$[U^A_{q_G}/U^A_{q_C^A}] \times h_{NG} + [U^B_{q_G}/U^B_{q_C^B}] \times h_{NG} = f_{NC}.$$

The expressions $[U^A_{q_G}/U^A_{q_C^A}]$ and $[U^B_{q_G}/U^B_{q_C^B}]$ are referred to as the personalized prices that each person is required to pay for a unit of the public good. Here h_{KG} is a marginal amount of the public or government good. Similarly with h_{NG}.

We proceed under the assumption that the price of a unit of the consumption good is unity. We endogenize prices p_G, r, and w with the following relations (three equations):

$$r = w\frac{f_{KC}}{f_{NC}},$$

$$q_C = rK^C + wN^C,$$

$$p_G q_G = r[K - K^C] + w[N - N^C].$$

Equations (9.2) and (9.3) can now be written as

$$[U^A_{q_G}/U^A_{q^A_C}] + [U^B_{q_G}/U^B_{q^B_C}] = f_{KC}/h_{KG} = r/h_{KG} = p_G,$$

$$[U^A_{q_G}/U^A_{q^A_C}] + [U^B_{q_G}/U^B_{q^B_C}] = f_{NC}/h_{NG} = w/h_{NG} = p_G.$$

We use the fact that the price of a unit of q_C is unity here. This captures the original Samuelson statement: the sum of the marginal benefit charges, summed over persons, should equal the marginal cost of producing a unit of the public good. Note that $[U^A_{q_G}/U^A_{q^A_C}]$ and $[U^B_{q_G}/U^B_{q^B_C}]$ are personal "prices," charges or tax rates. Each person must pay $[U^A_{q_G}/U^A_{q^A_C}]q_G$ and $[U^B_{q_G}/U^B_{q^B_C}]q_G$, respectively, in order that the cost of the public good is covered. Note that $p_G q_G$ is the cost of producing level q_G of the public or government good.

We illustrate the equilibrium in Figure 9.1.

Each person ends up consuming level q_G of the public good and their own level of the private good, q_C. Here $[U^A_{q_G}/U^A_{q^A_C}]$ and $[U^B_{q_G}/U^B_{q^B_C}]$ are personal "prices," charges or tax rates and these two "prices" must sum to p_G, the cost of a unit of the public good. With private goods, "the market" slices up current quantity produced and allocates a certain quantity to each demander whereas with public goods, "the government" slices up the current cost or price of producing the public good and allocates a certain fraction to each "consumer." A person's tax ends up as q_G multiplied by her own fraction of the price.

In Figure 9.2, we have a different diagrammatic sketch, one with three distinct demanders of a public good. We sum the demands of each person vertically to get the total demand for quantity G. Here 13 emerges as the equilibrium amount of G to produce. At $G = 13$, total demand equals supply, this latter being produced at constant unit cost, 6.6. Note that each person is charged her own personal amount for the G she is consuming. The dashed lines demarcate rectangular areas defining a person's tax charge for the 13 units of G that she is consuming.

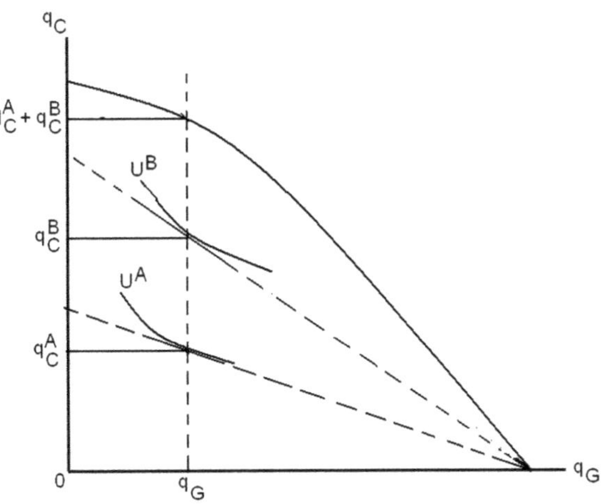

Figure 9.1 Equilibrium for two-person economy with public good q_G. Persons A and B each receive the same consumption flows of the public good but each receives her own distinct flow of the private good.

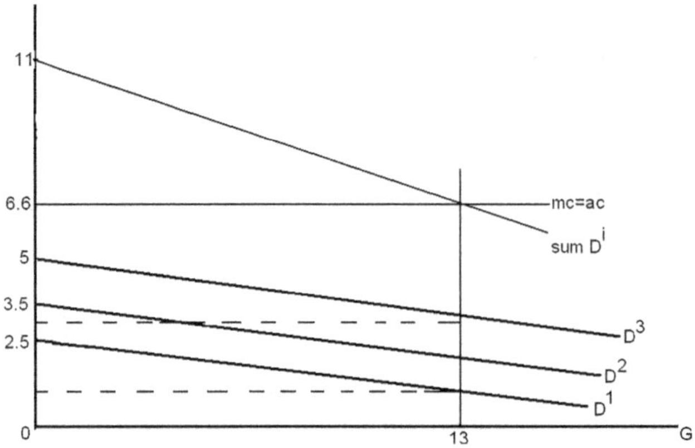

Figure 9.2 Equilibrium for three-person economy with public good. Each of three persons has a distinct demand for public good G. We sum the demands vertically to get the "market" demand. Each person is consuming amount 13 but paying an "own" amount tax. Dashed lines define three horizontal areas defining "tax" payments per person. The sum of the payments is dollar amount 6.6×13.

Samuelson was well aware of the fact that though he could determine the correct level of G in the abstract, he needed data on marginal utilities of citizens if he were to determine the correct level of G in reality. And these marginal utilities would translate directly into tax charges, person by person. The problem he noted was that each person would tend to understate their preferences when asked, to avoid having to contribute a "large" tax payment. Each person hopes that her neighbor will not understate. Inevitably, however, one ends up with everyone trying to free-ride somewhat on the payments of everyone else. The result will be the under-production of G, under-production relative to the ideal or efficient (Samuelson) level. At the ideal level, each consumer is paying her true marginal benefit per unit of G consumed.

Two approaches to the under-stating problem come to mind. First, one can assume that the level of G and the correct mix of various public sector outputs are determined by party politics and voting (allocation by "the political mechanism") or alternatively, one can strive to design a mechanism of "true preference revelation" by the citizens (consumers of G). Samuelson in fact hinted at a procedure to elicit true preference revelation. Ask the citizen to maximize not her own utility directly but indirectly in an optimization which turns out to incorporate the social or group "utility." When each citizen is asked to maximize a special form of the group "utility," each citizen ends up inserting their true preferences into their calculation. Put rather differently one might interpret the preference revelation mechanism (known as the Clarke–Groves mechanism) as one in which each citizen ends up being paid or "bribed" indirectly to reveal his or her true preferences.

Preference revelation

Suppose the government announces level G of public goods. It then asks each citizen to state a "bid" (willingness to pay) for G. Each person submits dollar value b_i. The government explains that G will be the production of the public good if the sum of the bids is positive, i.e. if $\sum_i^N b_i > 0$. In addition, the government says that not only will G be produced or carried out, but also each person will receive a bonus comprising the sum of every other person's bid. That is, person i ends up with benefit

$$v_i + \sum_{j(j \neq i)}^{N-1} b_j \text{ for the case of } \sum_{i}^{N} b_i > 0$$

$$\text{and 0 for the case of } \sum_{i}^{N} b_i < 0,$$

where v_i is person i's true private valuation of her benefit from G. Given these rules of the game, person i has no reason not to enter "bid" $b_i = v_i$ into the decision mechanism. Each citizen participates with her true valuation in the process.

Clearly there is a lot of extra money moving about in this process, seemingly paying each person to act individually like a social planner, i.e. to take all N citizens into account when a decision is being made. Can one make this Clarke–Groves mechanism operate with less "bribing" taking place? The answer is "yes." One invokes "the Clarke Tax" which is levied on essentially one person, she who is "pivotal" to the process. Other people do not have to be incentivized with extra payments. Suppose i is pivotal. Then:

> The amount of tax that i must pay is the amount by which agent i's bid damages the other agents (according to their stated bids). The price that agent i must pay to change the amount of the public good is equal to the harm that he imposes on the other agents.[2]

The median voter and a size for G

When one reflects on how expenditure and tax decisions are made in the real world, one is driven fairly directly to a consideration of parties, platforms and elections. One is then driven to ask how well each person's preference is registered in a system of decision-making "by politics" or more narrowly, decision-making by voting. A simplistic version of determining the level of G by voting is the theory of the median voter equilibrium.

Consider Figure 9.3. We assume that there is a vote organizer. She starts with a level of G, say $G = 13$, multiplies it by 6.6 and divides by 3. She then says to our three citizens, we are going to have a vote for $G = 13$, with payment 13×2.2 dollars each. (The 2.2 is of course our 6.6/3.) Person 3 says my valuation of the marginal unit, from my demand schedule, is above 2.2, given $G = 13$, while persons 1 and 2 each observe that their valuation of the marginal unit is below 2.2. Hence there are two votes against $G = 13$ and one vote in favor. So the vote organizer realizes that she is offering too much at unit charge 2.2 and so makes a new proposition, namely $G = 12$. Once again voter 1 finds her valuation of the marginal unit above 2.2 and voters 1 and 2 find theirs below 2.2. In a vote 1 and 2 reject the proposal (vote "no").

The vote organizer tries $G = 11$ at charge per person of 11×2.2 dollars. Now citizens 1 and 2 find their valuations of the marginal unit less than 2.2 and they vote "no." Quantities are repeatedly voted on until the quantity of G "offered" corresponds with person 2's valuation of the marginal unit (dollar value 2.2), namely 11.8 in Figure 9.3. At this offering, person 2 is indifferent, person 1 votes "no" (the unit charge is too much) and person 3 votes "yes" (the unit charge is attractively low). This "outcome" is the median voter equilibrium with $G = 11.8$. The median or middle voter ends up paying a per unit charge corresponding

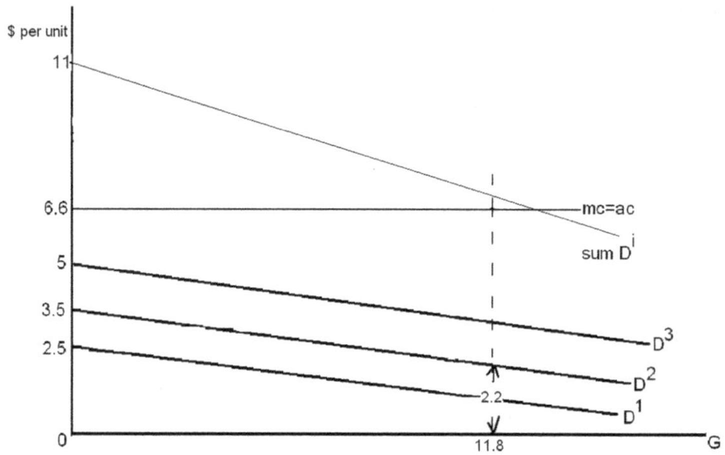

Figure 9.3 Under a median voter equilibrium, person 2's demand "prevails." The equilibrium amount of G is 11.8 and each person pays the same 11.8×2.2 dollars. The sum of the three payments is 6.6×11.8 dollars. Each person is consuming 11.8 of G.

exactly to her marginal valuation. Each person ends up paying the same amount. Approximately half the voters are happy and approximately half are unhappy with this outcome. The key aspect of this median voter equilibrium is that the equilibrium allocation corresponds precisely with the preferences of the median voter. Note that casting one's vote ends up "registering" a rough approximation of one's true marginal valuation. In a Samuelson world, the marginal valuation of each citizen gets sent to the organizer of the public sector whereas in a voting equilibrium, only a "yes" or "no" to essentially the current "price" is registered.

Though our voting procedure for achieving a median voter equilibrium seems convoluted and unrealistic, one can argue that it captures reality in the following sense. Party leaders in a municipal election are aware that they must offer a vote-winning level of G if they are to be elected. They do a mental calculation and arrive at the conclusion: "I must cater to the marginal voter 'in the middle' if I am to avoid outright rejection. Hence I will propose what the 'central' voter favors." This reasoning should lead the competing candidates to each try to discern the preferences of the median voter and to build a platform of proposals around the preference of the median voter.

The obvious problem with the median voter theory is that it only works well for single dimension "platforms" as in G in larger or smaller quantities. Real-world political platforms involve "more police persons, less funding for after-school programs, more funds for snow clearing, etc." Hence G in the real world is a vector or basket of items to be voted on. Median voter theory does not generalize in a simple way to the case of G comprising a variety of public goods bundled into a package to be voted on.

Public good in the utility function and city structure

We take our basic monocentric city model from Chapter 2 and add a city-wide public good to the utility function of each household-worker. We simplify somewhat by assuming that the city geography is a line, with the CBD at the center. The government produces a pure public good at constant unit cost. If G is the current level of production of the public good, then G is the amount currently consumed by each household. We explore two cases: marginal benefit charging (Samuelson (1954) type payment) and payment by taxation of property values at a uniform rate over the city. Under marginal benefit charging, each household pays $\frac{U_G}{U_c}$ for each unit of G. Under property taxation, the sum of property taxes paid equals the cost of the government producing flow G in the current period. In this case we continue to assume that G is the amount consumed by each household but the charge, the property tax "hitting" each household, is independent of the value of G to each household. Property tax can be said to be an *ad hoc* form of revenue raising whereas charging by marginal benefits is a precise first-best approach.

Each household-worker has utility function $U = c(x)^{\alpha} h(x)^{\beta} G^{1-\alpha-\beta}$ and the edge of the city is defined by $\overline{x}$ in $r(\overline{x}) = r_A$. We will assume that G is produced with constant marginal cost per unit, m. Budget balance for the production of G by the local government implies an endogenously determined city size, given an exogenous utility level, $\overline{U}$. We select parameters ($\alpha = 0.4$, $\beta = 0.2$, $w = 5.0$, (commuting cost) $t = 0.05$) for the households and $m = 1.1$ as the cost per unit of G. Edge rent is $r_A = 0.02$. The level of $\overline{U}$ is selected in a cluster of parameters: $[\frac{\alpha^{\alpha/\beta}\beta}{\overline{U}^{1/\beta}}] = J = 100$ for the case of no structures in the city. For the case of structures, we have production function $h = L^{\gamma} K^{1-\gamma}$ with $\gamma = 0.25$ and $\overline{U}$ set in

$$M = \frac{\overline{U}^{1/(\alpha+\beta)} \alpha^{\beta/(\alpha+\beta)} \left[\Omega i^{1-\gamma}\right]^{\beta/(\alpha+\beta)}}{\alpha \beta^{\beta/(\alpha+\beta)}} = 100.$$

First, we will obtain the rent function for the case of charging being based on marginal benefits. In this case, the level of G and edge $\overline{x}$ are determined in

$$2 \int_0^{\overline{x}} \frac{U_G(x)}{U_c(x)} \frac{1}{h(x)} dx = m,$$
$$\text{and } r(\overline{x}) = r_A,$$

which is a variant of the Samuelson (1954) condition for efficient production of public goods.[3]

Note that U_c and U_G are marginal utilities. Each household-worker ends up with the same utility level, $\overline{U} = c(x)^{\alpha} h(x)^{\beta} G^{1-\alpha-\beta}$. Recall that our city is on a line, symmetric about a center at 0. Workers live on their lots and commute each day from x to the center at cost tx, round-trip. For each household-worker's budget constraint, we have

$$w - tx = c(x) + r(x)h(x) + \frac{U_G(x)}{U_c(x)} G.$$

Thus $\frac{U_G(x)}{U_c(x)}$ becomes the price per unit of G and households at different radial distances x pay in general different amounts for the same G. Consumption efficiency here is

$$\frac{\alpha h(x)}{\beta c(x)} = \frac{1}{r(x)}.$$

Combine this with constant utility, $\overline{U}$, and we obtain

$$c = \frac{\overline{U}^{1/\alpha}}{G^{(1-\alpha-\beta)/\alpha} h^{\beta/\alpha}},$$

and since $h = \frac{\beta c}{\alpha r}$, we obtain

$$h(x) = \frac{\beta^{\alpha/(\alpha+\beta)}\overline{U}^{1/(\alpha+\beta)}}{\alpha^{\alpha/(\alpha+\beta)}G^{(1-\alpha-\beta)/(\alpha+\beta)}}\frac{1}{r(x)^{\alpha/(\alpha+\beta)}}.$$

This takes us pretty close to our solving for $r(x)$ for our city with charges for G set in accord with marginal benefits. See Appendix 9.1. The rent function becomes

$$r(x) = \left[\frac{\alpha^{\alpha/\beta}\beta G^{(1-\alpha-\beta)/\beta}}{\overline{U}^{1/\beta}}\right][w - tx]^{(\alpha+\beta)/\beta}.$$

We turn now to an equilibrium city, operating with payment by property taxes. Under the property tax, each household takes account of the property tax at rate τ and the budget constraint is

$$w - tx = c(x) + (1+\tau)r(x)h(x),$$

and consumption efficiency is

$$\frac{\alpha h}{\beta c} = \frac{1}{(1+\tau)r(x)}.$$

Tax revenue must cover the cost of G. Hence the condition

$$2\int_0^{\overline{x}} \tau\,[h(x)r(x)]\frac{1}{h(x)}dx = mG.$$

In this case the rent function comes out as

$$r(x) = \left[\frac{1}{(\alpha+\beta)^{(\alpha+\beta)/\beta}(1+\tau)}\right]\left[\frac{\alpha^{\alpha/\beta}\beta G^{(1-\alpha-\beta)/\beta}}{\overline{U}^{1/\beta}}\right][w - tx]^{(\alpha+\beta)/\beta},$$

very similar to that for the city with marginal benefit charging. See Appendix 9.1 for details.

We proceed to solve for $(G, \overline{x})$ first for the case of no structures in the city. Under charging in accord with marginal benefits, $G = 88.49$ and $w - t\overline{x} = 1.367$. Under property taxation at rate 0.02, $G = 1{,}938.82$ and $w - t\overline{x} = 0.105$. With the tax rate at 0.99, $G = 76.62$ and $w - t\overline{x} = 1.136$. Hence the spatial footprint of the city is always larger under a property tax charging system. The rent function $r(x)$ under property taxation is everywhere above the comparable rent function for the case of charging in accord with marginal benefits.

Public good cost incidence

Suppose the cost of the public good, m, were slightly higher, under property taxation. The city should shrink, no? And G should be somewhat smaller, no? We still anticipate that total tax revenue must be slightly larger. It turns out that our perturbation framework from Chapter 2 can be applied to this problem, without much complication. We follow those steps used in Chapter 2 where we considered the impact of a small wage increase on the equilibrium monocentric city.

We have utility unchanging in

$$dU = U_c dc + U_h dh + U_G dG = 0,$$

giving us $dc = -\frac{U_h}{U_c}dh - \frac{U_G}{U_c}dG = -(1+\tau)rdh - \frac{U_G}{U_c}dG$. Recall that consumer efficiency implies that $\frac{U_h}{U_c} = (1+\tau)r$. And we have the wage unchanging in

$$dw = tdx + dc + (1+\tau)rdh + (1+\tau)hdr = 0.$$

We substitute for dc here to get

$$tdx - \frac{U_G}{U_c}dG + (1+\tau)hdr = 0.$$

Now the revenue-expenditure balance for the city under property taxation is $\tau R = mG$ for R total land rent in the city. This gives us $dG = -\frac{G}{m}[1 - \frac{dR}{dm}\frac{m}{R}]dm$. Hence

$$t\frac{dx}{dm} - \frac{U_G}{U_c}\left\{-\frac{G}{M}\left[1 - \frac{dr}{dm}\frac{m}{R}\right]\right\} = -(1+\tau)h\frac{dr}{dm}.$$

We insert this in

$$\frac{dR(\overline{x})}{dm} - 2\pi\overline{x}r_A\frac{d\overline{x}}{dm} = \int_0^{\overline{x}} \frac{dr(x)}{dm}2\pi x dx$$

to get

$$\frac{dR_n(\overline{x})}{dm} = \int_0^{\overline{x}} \frac{U_G}{U_c}\left\{-\frac{G}{M}\left[1 - \frac{dr}{dm}\frac{m}{R}\right]\right\}\frac{1}{h}2\pi x dx - t\int_0^{\overline{x}} \frac{dx}{dm}\frac{1}{h}2\pi x dx - \tau\frac{dR_n(\overline{x})}{dm}.$$

Recall that $\int_0^{\overline{x}} \frac{1}{h}2\pi x dx = N(\overline{x})$ and $-\frac{G}{M}\left[1 - \frac{dr}{dm}\frac{m}{R}\right] = \frac{dG}{dm}$. The term $\tau\frac{dR_n(\overline{x})}{dm}$ represents the changed cost of the public good. It was being financed by property taxes which here turn out to be land rent taxes. The expression $t\int_0^{\overline{x}} \frac{dx}{dm}\frac{1}{h}2\pi x dx$ is the city-size adjustment cost. Households relocate and re-optimize in the face of having to pay more for G which has had its cost of production changed. This leaves the term $\int_0^{\overline{x}} \frac{U_G}{U_c}\left\{-\frac{G}{M}\left[1 - \frac{dr}{dm}\frac{m}{R}\right]\right\}\frac{1}{h}2\pi x dx$ as the measure of aggregate benefit-change, for G, as a result of m changing. With a different notation, we have

$$\Delta R_n = \Delta B dm - \tau\Delta R_n dm - \Delta T dm,$$

where ΔR_n is net land rent change, $\Delta B dm - \tau\Delta R_n dm$ is net benefit change and $\Delta T dm$ is aggregate city-size adjustment cost. The increase in m in this analysis implies that ΔR_n and $\Delta B dm - \tau\Delta R_n dm$ should be negative. The city shrinks somewhat, G declines and households must in aggregate produce more revenue to pay for the new level of G.[4]

Taxation with houses with structures (capital)

The good news is that the analysis is very similar to that reported above. Now under payment in accord with marginal benefits, the city satisfies

$$2\int_0^{\overline{x}} \frac{U_G(x)}{U_c(x)}\frac{1}{L(x)}dx = m$$

and

$$r(\overline{x}) = r_A,$$

where m is the unit cost of producing a unit of the government good, G. A house has production function, $L^{\gamma}K^{(1-\gamma)} = h$, where L is land per dwelling and K is capital per dwelling. The budget constraint for a household is

$$w - tx = c + q(x)h(x) + G\frac{U_G(x)}{U_c(x)},$$

where $q(x)$ is annual rental per unit of dwelling, $h(x)$. We require a pair $(G, \overline{x})$ that satisfies the two equations above.

Under property taxation, the household's budget constraint is

$$w - tx = c + (1+\tau)q(x)h(x)$$

and the government budget constraint is

$$2\int_0^{\overline{x}} \tau q(x)h(x)\frac{1}{L(x)}dx = mG.$$

We require a pair $(G, \overline{x})$ that satisfies the government budget constraint and $r(\overline{x}) = r_A$. Of interest is that city size is determined by the equilibrium $(G, \overline{x})$.

In Appendix 9.2 we obtain the rent functions for our τ-city (city with property tax) with structures and the B-city (city with benefit tax) counterpart. For each city we must solve for $(G, \overline{x})$. We have that

$$w - tx = \frac{\overline{U}^{1/(\alpha+\beta)}\alpha^{\beta/(\alpha+\beta)}\left[\Omega i^{1-\gamma}\right]^{\beta/(\alpha+\beta)}}{\alpha\beta^{\beta/(\alpha+\beta)}G^{(1-\alpha-\beta)/(\alpha+\beta)}}r^{\gamma\beta/(\alpha+\beta)}$$

defines the rent function for the B-city and

$$w - tx = \frac{\{(\alpha+\beta)(1+\tau)^{\beta/(\alpha+\beta)}\}\overline{U}^{1/(\alpha+\beta)}\alpha^{\beta/(\alpha+\beta)}\left[\Omega i^{1-\gamma}\right]^{\beta/(\alpha+\beta)}}{\alpha\beta^{\beta/(\alpha+\beta)}G^{(1-\alpha-\beta)/(\alpha+\beta)}}r^{\gamma\beta/(\alpha+\beta)}$$

defines the rent function for the τ-city. They differ only with respect to the term in braces. Think of each of these equations defining $\overline{x}$ in the edge equation $r(\overline{x}) = r_A$. Then the equation defining G for the τ-city is

$$\tau\left[\frac{2}{\gamma}\right]\int_0^{\overline{x}} r(x)dx = mG$$

and that for the B-city is

$$\frac{1-\alpha-\beta}{\beta}\left[\frac{2}{\gamma}\right]\int_0^{\overline{x}} r(x)dx = mG.$$

The same selection of parameters as above will generate a pair $(G, \overline{x})$ for the τ-city with values each larger than those for the B-city.

Under charging in accord with marginal benefits, $G = 86.86$ and $w - t\overline{x} = 3.68$. Under property taxation at rate 0.02, $G = 85.90$ and $w - t\overline{x} = 2.24$. With the tax rate at 0.99, $G = 72.07$ and $w - t\overline{x} = 3.145$. Hence the spatial footprint of the city is always larger under a property tax charging system.

The presence of structures ($\gamma = 0.25$) leaves unchanged the fact that the τ-city will occupy more space than the B-city. Of interest is the fact that the capital to land ratio declines with an increase in the tax rate, τ. The capital to land ratio is equal to $\frac{(1-\gamma)r(x)}{\gamma i}$ and the rent function is everywhere lower for an increase in τ. Higher-taxed cities will be less capital intensive cities in this view. See Appendix 9.2 for details.

Relocating to find a better public sector "outcome"

Samuelson showed how the size of government service flow and charges per household should be structured in a perfect world and emphasized that the attainment of his conditions in practice would pretty well never come about. For his conditions to obtain, the precise valuations of each consumer of government services are needed in order for the correct charges to be set. It is in no person's interest to announce their true valuation or valuations since they would likely get stuck with above average payments as their neighbors gamed the system with false valuations. This is the public goods allocation problem: how to elicit true valuations of consumers of government services in order to set fair charges or user-fees (taxes) and in turn to set the expenditure agenda for diverse services appropriately.

Tiebout (1956) responded to Samuelson's "dilemma" with what he considered an obvious solution. With regard to local government services, households would choose to live where benefit flows and charges suited their tastes. Older people would avoid neighborhoods with high charges for schools since they were mostly without children and so on. When one looks around, one seems to find fairly distinct neighborhoods; for example some with similar very expensive homes with large lots, some with mostly apartments for rent, some with plain family homes with back yards full of kids playthings and so on. There is, then, casual evidence supporting Tiebout's line of thought. Clearly if households come in not too many varieties, say three or four distinct types, and "supplies"of neighborhoods have some variety as well, then the case for Tiebout's equilibrium is stronger. If in contrast neighborhoods appear as messy collections of many quite different households, it becomes difficult to believe that the Tiebout mechanism is helping to solve the public goods allocation problem at the local government level.

Consider a stylized Tiebout equilibrium. Suppose that somehow a city is three separate jurisdictions, one with low-priced homes (at US\$200,000), one with medium-priced homes (at US\$400,000) and one with high-priced homes (at US\$800,000). Each district has the same number of residences and has to support similar schools, police and roads. The property tax ends up at 0.04 in the place with low-priced homes: each home pays about US\$8,000 per year. The high-priced area supports similar schools, etc. and only needs a tax rate of 0.01.

The mid-priced neighborhood ends up with a rate of 0.02. We summarize these facts in Table 9.1.

Each household is paying the same dollar amount for local government services but property tax rates are very different. A US$200,000 homeowner will try hard to move into the low-tax neighborhood and erect a US$200,000 home there. She would get the same government services for just US$2,000 per year. In fact there should be a mass relocation of households into the low-rate area. To prevent this shift, home-owners in the low-rate area impose zoning barriers. Any entrant to their area must end up with a home valued at about US$800,000. Building restrictions, such a lot-size requirements, will be legislated that require a new home to end up costing about US$800,000. Such zoning regulations typically work and one observes no relocations of households from the basic equilibrium set out above. Zoning regulations prevent a low tax-rate neighborhood, one with expensive homes, ending up with low-priced homes mixed in. Hence zoning regulations must be part of a stylized Tiebout equilibrium.

Our example has neighborhoods with similar offerings of government services but very different property tax rates. A more complicated Tiebout equilibrium would have distinct neighborhoods differing by rates (prices for government services) and quantities of things such as policing, school quality (classroom size), etc. One then conjures up many distinct neighborhoods (say in the tens) that are accommodating both distinct quantities of various government services and levels of willingness to pay for government services. For example, retired folk may gravitate to areas with low property tax rates and low expenditures on schools since they typically have no children of school age to find places for. One might say, however, the bad news is that it is difficult to imagine the right number of homogeneous neighborhoods for the many households in a city, each with distinct demands for government services and different levels of willingness to pay. Real-world cities only offer menus of government services and rates that satisfy the hundreds of thousands of households in an approximate sense. On the other hand, large cities do typically have distinct neighborhoods, each with their own rates and suites of services. There is some range of choice of distinct neighborhoods in most cities in the United States. One can argue that households do shop for the one that fits their taste for public services and their budget constraint. Tiebout was correct: location-choice for distinct households in cities does solve the Samuelson problem of fitting prices and offerings of government services to different tastes of different households, but only approximately.

In addition to neighborhood homogeneity and a variety of neighborhoods for a household to select from, there is the matter of the autonomy of the taxing authority. A Tiebout equilibrium requires a variety of homogeneous neighborhoods with a variety of tax rates and government service bundles. This all works best when the neighborhoods are distinct legal entities or distinct municipalities with distinct tax schemes. It turns out that many large cities in the United States are indeed amalgams of many independent municipalities. There is then a core Boston municipality, for example, and many surrounding independent municipalities.

Table 9.1 Stylized homogeneous distinct neighborhoods

	US$2.. Rate	*US$4.. Rate*	*US$8.. Rate*
US$200,000 homes	0.04		
US$400,000 homes		0.02	
US$800,000 homes			0.01

Such a situation is of course supportive of the possible realization of a Tiebout equilibrium. But different neighborhoods in the same legal municipality can be subject to different property rates as well. For example, condominiums in large buildings may have different rates relative to detached single-family homes. A resident faced with the wrong basket of local government goods, relative to her local taxes, is presumed to move to another neighborhood. However, moving can be costly. Hence one takes for granted that adjustment to change in a Tiebout world will be sticky and be seldom complete.

Consider the case of the local government messing things up somewhat and setting the property rate on condominiums at, say, 0.03. Each condominium costs US$300,000 to complete and is priced accordingly. Then each condominium owner pays US$9,000 per year in local taxes for what we will assume is still a US$10,000 dollar stream of government services. The present value of an annual "gift" of US$1,000 in perpetuity to a condominium-owner at an interest rate of 4 percent is US$25,000. Hence condominiums will end up selling for US$325,000 in the market place because they come with US$1,000 of free government services per year. The value of the free government services is being capitalized in the market price of a condominium.

We must be careful here. Each condominium owner who bought at US$300,000 can reap the US$25,000 premium when she sells but the next owner will generally pay the 0.03 rate on a "new" market price, US$325,000. The tax charge is then US$325,000 × 0.03 = US$9,750. This annual "price" of government services is now close to the value of the flow of services, namely US$10,000. Market processes can be said to be "arbitraging away" almost all "free" government services.

Worker "relocation" and local public goods

An organizing principle of our study of economics and cities is "the open-city" assumption. Similar workers (same education, work experience and family characteristics) will be on the same indifference curve in equilibrium, regardless of location. This means that a worker can be getting a fiscal surplus in some location, when her local taxes paid are less than the value of the local public goods she is getting in her chosen location. So-called rents, such as a fiscal surplus, can influence location decisions but free migration will not necessarily drive such surpluses or rents to zero. The example of the sneaky household above is a good example. The household is delighted to have its "tax" payment from the local property tax levy below is valuation of its flow G. So-called fiscal surpluses can persist. In the above case the positive gap gets capitalized in the value of the property, and when the property is sold the capitalized amount is realized. Hence when we see obvious local payment–benefit gaps we cannot infer that there is a disequilibrium. The gap will be capitalized in wages, in home value or in utility. We consider an explicit model of free migration between places with own levels of public goods.

Flatters *et al.* (1974) set out a simple model of distinct regions, each with its own Samuelson level of public goods being offered. Identical workers were assumed to equalize utility levels by free migration. Flatters *et al.* then observed that every worker's utility could be higher if unilateral transfers were introduced from workers in one region to workers in another region. Local public goods and free migration were leading to a sub-optimal outcome, in the absence of transfers.

Let us see how this works. We start with analysis for a single region. There are N identical workers and an amount L of land. Hence the economy is producing "output," $Q = F(N, L)$ and $F(.)$ is our constant returns to scale production function. We have to divide this Q among our N workers, equally. Each worker has a standard utility function $U(c, G)$ for c, the private level of consumption of the ordinary consumer good and G, the level of consumption of the public good. We assume that Q is allocated to maximize the utility of a representative worker in the economy, where $Q = Nc + G$. Hence we maximize $U(c, G)$:

$$U\left(\frac{F(N, L) - G}{N}, G\right)$$

with respect to G. This gives us

$$N\frac{U_G}{U_c} = 1,$$

which is the celebrated Samuelson efficiency condition for determining the correct level of G.

See Figure 9.4. The left-hand side is essentially the sum of N demands for G. The marginal cost of one more unit of G here is unity. With Q, N and L fixed we solve for G and c with two equations, namely $Q = Nc + G$ and $N\frac{U_G}{U_c} = 1$.

Before considering two distinct regions with a total of N identical workers, we observe that when we let N be chosen in the above single equation model, while the Samuelson conditions remains in force, we find that land rents, LF_L, equal the cost of the public good, G. Let us maximize $U(\frac{F(N,L)-G}{N}, G)$ with respect to N. Our first-order condition for maximization is

$$\left[-\frac{U_c}{N} + U_G\right]\frac{dG}{dN} + \frac{dc}{dN} = 0.$$

The term in square brackets is zero because it is the Samuelson efficiency condition which we assume is in effect. Since $c = \frac{F(N,L)-G}{N}$, we have $\frac{dc}{dN} = 0$ implies $Nc = NF_N$. Since

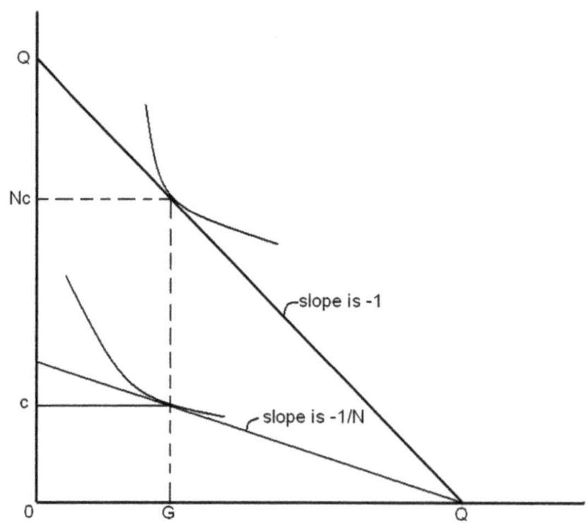

Figure 9.4 The single region case. A fixed amount of Q gets divided up into N equal bits of private consumption, c, and level G of public good. The Samuelson condition for public goods provision holds.

$Q = NF_N + LF_L$ for our constant returns to scale production function, is follows that G must equal LF_L which here is total land rent in the single region economy. See Figure 9.5. This result has been labelled "the Henry George result." Henry George was a nineteenth-century economist from Pennsylvania who preached in favor of paying for the public sector with taxes on land rents. This was a major part of his platform when he ran for mayor of New York City in 1886. He did very well in this one election but failed to win in a three-way contest.

For the two-region case, we have two production functions, $Q^A = F(N^A, L^A)$ and $Q^B = F(N^B, L^B)$ with labor mobile so that $N^B = N - N^A$ for N fixed. A worker in region A ends up with $U(c^A, G^A) = U(c^B, G^B)$ where c_i^A is worker i's private good and G^A is the level of the public good being provided in region A. Equal utility level across regions is assumed to follow from costless migration. Workers earn income from their own labor plus income from the land, as well as from transfers that end up in the region where the worker resides. There turn out to be transfers, between regions, to contribute to the achieving of the highest level of utility for an individual. An intuition behind the transfer is that one region will have more land initially than the other and transfers effect a sort of land sharing across regions. Hence $Q^A - N^A T = N^A c^A + G^A$ and $Q^B + N^A T = N^B c^B + G^B$ for T the per capita transfer from region A to region B. The Samuelson condition is presumed to hold in each region in isolation. Given utility functions the same for all workers, the equilibrium should end up with perfect "equalization": workers with identical consumption bundles in each region. Transfers and labor mobility cause each region to become a clone of the other from a consumption standpoint. This model, from Flatters *et al.* (1974) provides a simple framework for rationalizing inter-regional transfers by governments in federal states. One might say that the transfers are needed to equalize utilities in a world of regions with different natural endowments, here land. The analysis also yields the fundamental insight that free migration with distinct local public goods "in the world" will not bring about a welfare maximizing solution.

There is another instructive aspect of this model. Once workers become costlessly mobile, the equilibrium that obtains will be very sensitive to who owns what in the model. Land is usually privately owned and when one moves one does not necessarily sell one's land.

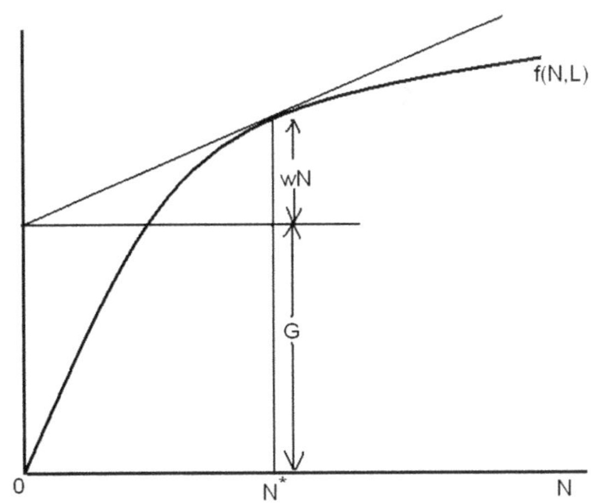

Figure 9.5 The Henry George result. With the optimal population, land rents equal the value of the public good. The amount of the public good is defined by the Samuelson condition.

Hence personal income becomes very difficult to keep track of when land ownership is fairly arbitrarily set out initially. When Wildasin (1986; pp. 66–69) does his interesting analysis of equilibrium with public goods, he assumes that the people that are migrating about in his multi-city world are working with wage income alone.

Public sector bundles

The agenda for municipal governments is quite variable. A local government is expected to keep streets and roads clear and surfaces suitable for vehicles to move about. It is involved in arranging for household waste to be carted away from residences and is often involved in seeing that local public transit is being offered. There is often a large input from the local government into arranging for local schools to be built and staffed. Local security is a central issue in cities. Many Canadian municipalities have experienced large increases in the sizes of their allocations for local policing. London, west of Toronto, Edmonton and Calgary saw their per capita expenditure on policing rise about 40 percent between 2001 and 2010. York region, on the edge of Toronto, and Surrey, on the edge of Vancouver saw their's rise by almost 60 percent. These places also experienced large increases in population. Toronto saw a 33 percent rise while Montreal and Vancouver contended with a 23 percent increase in their per capita expenditures for policing. Some of these increases were due to more constables on the forces and some due to significant pay rises. Data, imprecise as they are, suggest that crime rates in fact declined over the decade in question. Criminals are able to judge when risks of police intervention in certain places change and many will relocate their activities in response to increased police activity in a specific area.

The percentage of the municipal budget devoted to policing was about 23 percent for Vancouver and Calgary in 2010 and about 14 percent for Montreal and Edmonton. Toronto and Ottawa allocate about 10 percent of their municipal budgets to policing. On the edge of Toronto, the Peel region spends about 29 percent of its funds on policing.[5] Some municipalities are considering hiving off some of the services currently carried out by police personnel to non-police, skilled workers. These programs have been opposed by some police unions in some cities. We should keep in mind the famous Baumol argument ("Baumol disease") that the wages of municipal workers get pushed up by rises in the wages of workers in other sectors, these latter enjoying measurable increases in productivity, while the workers in local government may not be providing any increase in productivity. Estimates in Britain for 2013 indicate zero productivity growth for the public sector since the 1980s. Meanwhile wages of public servants rise. The private sector did experience significant productivity growth over this same time span. Some observers suggest that the consolidation of municipalities into larger governmental units drives union leaders to demand wages for municipal workers to be on a par with comparable large cities (levelling up). Municipal consolidation can then contribute to large increases in the wages of some municipal government workers. Careful empirical work is required to tease out the contribution of various forces to the rises in the wages of municipal workers in various sectors.

Brueckner and Neumark (2011) probe the question of whether public sector employees in the United States receive high wages relative to similar workers in the private sector. They argue that unionization and/or political clout gives public sector workers in state and local governments some nominal power in setting their own wages. This power, they argue, is countered by prospective out-moving of some local tax-paying households. Excessively high wages gleaned by local public sector workers will induce a margin of local households to relocate to areas free of the high wages for local public sector employees. Such a tendency to relocate, Brueckner and Neumark argue, will be countered by the draw of abundant local amenities such as higher than average sunshine, exciting downtowns, attractive local beaches, etc. Hence Brueckner and Neumark hypothesize that local public sector wages will only get relatively high and stay relatively high for places with abundant amenities. Statistical investigation yields strong support for this view; namely that wages of local public sector workers are only relatively high in places with abundant local amenities.

Anderson (2007, Table 9) indicates that in the United States, education is the largest expenditure category (38.25 percent) with sewer and water supply expenditures a distant second (6.31 percent). Fourth and fifth were police and highways, respectively (4.97 and 3.70 percent). Sedlak (2014) remarks:

- The East Bay Municipal Utility District in California provides water for about 1.3 million people and waste water treatment for about 650,000 people. It employs some 2,000 people (about 1 in 500), making it one of the largest employers in the area. The largest categories of expenditure allocation are daily operations, system maintenance and new infrastructure construction (pp. 170–71).
- Drinking water and sewer treatments consume about 4 percent of US electricity output (p. 175). In California much water is pumped over various mountain systems making electricity usage in this regard unusually high. Tucson in Arizona pumps its water up higher than some energy-using systems in California. The Central Arizona Project (costing US$5 billion) was developed when electricity for pumping was relatively low-cost. Projections for getting water up are coming in at much higher costs. New York City, in contrast, has gravity "pump" most of its water to the city. Adelaide in southern Australia pumps its water from deep aquifers at considerable cost for lifting. Between 10 and 20 percent of drinking water is lost to leaks in the typical distribution system (p. 172).
- Projections for a drier California suggest that expenditures for accessing clean water will be onerous. The San Diego area is projected to get some 20 percent to 30 percent less precipitation over the next 30 to 50 years. Traditional metal or concrete pipes fail after 75 to 120 years and overburden causes collapse (p. 173). Treatment systems built during the boom following the Clean Water Act (1972) in the United States are requiring replacement currently. Engineers refer to this period as "the Replacement Era" (p. 174). Between 1975 and 2006 an estimated US$90 billion was spent for better treatment systems for drinking water (p. 184). The OECD reports that most member countries in Europe are already paying about double what the average American pays for drinking water and sewer service, and costs in the United States are due to rise because of new requirements promulgated by the Environmental Protection Agency. Water quality concerns today are focused on newly discovered chemical contaminants, some with health risks despite being present only in trace amounts (p. 185).

Desalination costs about US$1.30 to US$2.50 per liter for recent developments in Tampa Bay and Perth, Australia. This is in line with assigned values per liter per day for water saved in Las Vegas. More than 2,000 desalination plants operated in the United States as of 2005, with about half dealing with brackish or river water. Rockland County on the lower Hudson River in New York State is turning to desalination to get some of its municipal water. The Hudson River is subject to ocean tides at Rockland County: the flows contain mercury from upstream power plants and pollution from upstream sewage treatment installations. Ocean water is more costly to desalinate because it has a higher concentration of salts. Still, desalinated water continues to be a minuscule fraction of total supply in the United States. The reverse osmosis process for desalination starts with removing particles with sedimentation and then flows the improved water through charcoal filters. Last comes pushing the water through membranes at a pressure of 350 pounds per square inch. Pressure comes of course from powerful pumps which consume abundant energy and getting this final filtering right is also costly because the delicate membranes are subject to tearing. So-called water-rich New England (Massachusetts, Vermont, Rhode Island and Connecticut) all suffer from "flow impairment" of streams and rivers (Glennon 2009; p. 83). Glennon is outspoken about "the tragedy" of sprawl and argues for "those proposing new development to purchase and retire existing water rights... to break the cycle of overuse... If developers must purchase water rights, at least some of them would shelve their plans" (p. 312).

A different cost burden to cities is the move to require local governments to only let contracts to firms which pay their workers a "living wage." This is part of a strategy to improve the situation for local low-income households. Some 120 cities and counties in the United States have enacted "living wage" rules. This imposes a floor that contractors with the local government in question have to pay their workers if they are doing contract work with the city or county. While minimum wage levels may be in the US$10 range, the level of the "living wage" is often in the US$12 to US$15 range. It makes good economic sense to have these floors on wages at different levels in different places since labor markets and local costs of living vary considerably across the nation. New York City's cost of living is about 25 percent higher than that in Utica, another place in New York State. Albuquerque's minimum wage is US$8.60 while the one in San Francisco is US$10.74 and many such standards have inflation adjustments built in. In Tokyo and Osaka, two of Japan's large cities, the minimum wage is 30 percent above that in places with lower costs of living. A benchmark of how a minimum wage is keeping up with the cost of living is the ratio of the minimum wage to the local median wage. For the United States, this ratio varied between 41 and 55 percent in the 1960s and early 1970s. The ratio has declined in recent decades to between 33 and 39 percent. For San Francisco, the ratio is currently at 40 percent.[6]

Economists have focused much attention on the effects of local minimum wage increases on local unemployment. The impact has been found to be relatively small, partly because the lowest paid workers are concentrated in some narrowly defined sectors such as the restaurant trade. Economists emphasize that a higher minimum wage can reduce worker turnover and increase worker efficiency. Often the higher labor cost can be passed along in a small increase in the price of the products. Economists emphasize that it is in getting levels of minimum wages locally defined that allows for the most effective use of this anti-inequality instrument.

We have argued that local amenity abundance should show up in a local high-cost of living (land rents bid up by in-migration) and marginally more density, this latter an outcome of locally relatively high land rents. High average land rents could be a convenient base for relatively high revenues for local governments. And a local high cost of living could be an argument for local union leaders to bargain for some sort of wage premium. This provides a narrative that could explain relatively high wages of local public sector employees. Will this translate inevitably into relatively high wages for local public sector workers? It depends on whether local tax-payers out-migrate because they are put off by the high wages. There is clearly an elasticity here to pin down. How much out-migration is induced by each extra dollar of relatively high wages for the local public sector employees? The Brueckner–Neumark argument raises a number of interesting avenues for further investigation.

Dachis (2010) has investigated costs of garbage collection for cities in Canada and contends that those cities that contract out can achieve substantial savings in average cost per household. It is not simply contracting out, however, that matters in achieving the savings. In addition the contracts must be clear on the specific targets to be met. Contracting can also be used to attain increased recycling rates if municipalities provide incentive payments for contractors who meet their targets.

The role of municipal government

Mills and Glaeser raise the question of what a local government should be doing. Both indicate concerns for mispricing of land resulting from local government policies and—expressed directly or indirectly—against activities of local governments that have significant dimensions of income redistribution. Mills (1999; p. 1) states: "I have presumed ... that any suburban land misallocation is the result of a mispricing of resources. This mispricing, in turn, results from ineffective regulation of externalities, or from other failed government policies." And on the next page (p. 2), he remarks:

> Chicago's Mayor Daley, and other large city mayors (and their planning organizations), have been loath to shed the fantasy that they can attract manufacturing back to central cities.... [Manufacturing] will certainly not be a source of job growth in central cities during the careers of people currently serving as government officials.[7]

Glaeser (1998) contends that local governments often favor "large, permanent structures or systems that are highly visible and tend to be extreme monuments to their builders" (he cites subway construction here). Glaeser (2011; pp. 58–64) is very critical of policies intended to help struggling cities that favor structures over schools and safety. He writes of the "edifice error" with regard to Detroit:

> Successful cities typically do build, because economic vitality makes people willing to pay for space and builders are happy to accommodate. But building is the result, not the cause, of success. Overbuilding a declining city that already has more structures than it needs is nothing but folly.

The Renaissance Center (1970) in downtown Detroit was Henry Ford II's disaster. It ended up being sold to General Motors in 1996 for a fraction of its cost. The "People Mover" is a three-mile monorail system in the center of Detroit that opened in 1987 and costs US$8.5 million in subsidies each year. It carries only about 6,500 people each day. The causes of the economic collapse of Detroit are numerous but large-scale renewal projects contributed almost nothing positive to counter the city's downward slide.

Municipal leaders in modern times have been drawn to stadiums and team franchises as routes to "upgrading" their cities. However, cost–benefit calculations rarely indicate that heavy expenditure by the local authorities, essentially subsidizing stadiums and new sports franchises, yields positive payoffs to the local taxpayers (Siegfried and Zimbalist 2000). A central problem is that the promoters of the local expenditure can usually get the ears of the local authorities easily and those picking up much of the tab, the local taxpayers, form a widely dispersed group that is costly to organize as a counter-force. Reporter Catherine Rampell tried to determine how the published estimates of the local benefits of "sponsoring" the Super Bowl to East Rutherford, New Jersey (US$550 to US$600 million) were arrived at.[8] She was ultimately unsuccessful, having slogged down a number of blind alleys, and wrote: "There is the possibility that politicians and their constituents aren't being hoodwinked at all: They know deep down that they will lose money, and they don't care. They just want to have a party." Local politicians are presumably attracted to the publicity they can garner by being associated with teams and large sports edifices. A subset of taxpayers, the sports enthusiasts, must reap a very large dollar-denominated benefit if the subsidies for new facilities and franchises can be justified in a careful analysis, although of course only a fraction of the local taxpayers are in fact sports enthusiasts.

Quite often a new sports facility is built, with much taxpayer funding, as part of an urban renewal strategy. Developers remain aloof about building new structures in a run-down area and the municipal politicians fall back on a stadium or arena as a good second-best course of action. Here again careful cost–benefit analysis suggests that this approach to urban renewal is costly for taxpayers. Rarely are complementary new activities drawn into the area of the new facility in numbers that were hoped for.

Urban renewal more generally involves clearing of older structures and the building of new roads and structures directed "from above" as distinct from "rebuilt" in a decentralized manner "from below." Nero famously let the slums of Rome burn and organized the building of the Forum and other showy edifices, including government buildings, apparently in an effort to compete in splendor with the center of Alexandria at the mouth of the Nile River. The redevelopment of the center of Paris is another famous case of urban renewal. Napolean III engaged Baron Haussmann to redevelop the center of Paris in 1851. Wide, straight boulevards were introduced to accommodate omnibuses and allowance was made to get steam trains into the city center. The renewal pre-dated the elevator and regulation of the heights of new buildings was central to the plan. "Paris was transformed from an ancient and somewhat dilapidated city of immense poverty into an urban resort for the growing haute bourgeoisie" (Glaeser 2011; p. 154). London already had its Hyde Park and Kensington Gardens (625 acres combined; by comparison Central Park (NYC) is 840 acres) and did not feel the need to keep up with Paris in a redevelopment race. There is always a pressure of sorts on municipal leaders to clear out the dilapidated dwellings of low-income people and introduce new streets and structures. Poorer neighborhoods are assumed to be havens for criminals and places very likely to catch fire. Robert Moses pressed forward with slum clearance in New York City in the 1930s. Rockefeller Center (22 acres with 19 commercial buildings) became world-famous for replacing dilapidated structures with art deco skyscrapers. The project got underway in 1930 and reached completion in 1939. This redevelopment was unusual because it was largely private, a renewal project organized and substantially financed by John D. Rockefeller, Jr. London got an injection of urban renewal in the 1980s as the decaying docks along the Thames River were replaced with attractive houses, apartments and restaurants. Redevelopment was initiated in a plan "from above." The large Canary Wharf project in the dilapidated Docklands of London's East End was started by the Reichman family. They were forced to depart in the early 1990s when ongoing debts associated with the project became unsustainable. Canary Wharf emerged as a notable success in due course when it was connected to the city with the Docklands Light Railway. The London City Airport opened nearby in 1987.

Of course, the notion that renewal will be followed by local prosperity does not hold reliably. Often a local redevelopment is a policy of desperation. The local tax base has shrunk where the structures are dilapidated and neighbors to the run-down area express concern about dilapidation spreading. Decay of neighborhoods may be a result of persistent low incomes of residents, a phenomenon associated with a city's economy as a whole. Sectors that once contributed to the growth of the city can begin to decline. For example, textiles sustained the growth of many towns and even in New York, "the garment district" was central to the prosperity of that metropolis not long ago. Low wages of workers in new places drew the textile industry away from its traditional locations in the northeast of the United States. Levelling structures in older neighborhoods will not generally bring in new businesses to employ people displaced by the departures of older businesses. Urban renewal, doing away with older structures, becomes a tricky strategy for promoting local economic renewal. The centers of many cities in the United States failed to attract developers in the late 1950s and municipal leaders turned to top-down strategies. The term "urban renewal" was not introduced in the United States until the Housing Act (1949) was amended again in 1954. That was also the year in which the US Supreme Court upheld the general validity of urban redevelopment statutes. Mortgage guarantees were introduced to induce developers to get started.

Pittsburgh, in 1950, became the first large US city to pursue renewal. The Mellon family were influential backers of the policy. The steel industry had made the city dirty and the air rather polluted. A large section of the downtown was converted to parks, office buildings and the Civic Arena (8,000 low-income residents were displaced for the arena to be built). The economy of the city was not kick-started by this large-scale redevelopment. In fact it took decades for the city to grow out of its reliance on the steel industry and is now considered prosperous because of its strengths in higher education and medical research ("ed and med"). Baltimore also suffered from the slow decline in its steel industry and its renewal has been led by the gentrification of the areas around its outmoded docks. Baltimore also has great strength in "ed and med," given the presence of Johns Hopkins University and Hospital and the medical school of the University of Maryland. Glaeser is critical of local governments for using quantity controls such as zoning ordinances and rent controls when they should be using transfers and explicit taxes to deal with externalities and redistribution. He is also unhappy with local governments that "often favor redistributive activities rather than productive efficiency... Redistribution at the local level causes major distortions to locational choices of both the rich and the poor" (Glaeser 2011; pp. 155–56). Let us reflect on the "hands-on" responsibilities of local governments.

Mayor Naheed Nenshi of Calgary remarks that

> every city in the world has the same issues. We have to take out the trash, we need to make sure the road networks are in good shape, we need police and fire responders... So our key is how we share best practices, because we all have to deliver the same services at the end of the day, and we are all looking for better ways of delivering those services.
>
> (Barber 2013; p. 170)

Let us turn to the familiar activities of local government and try to draw out some of the efficiency and redistributive dimensions of the activity in question.

1 *Local transportation policy*. Subways, bus systems, etc. are usually operated as municipal corporations. They tend to be used more by lower-income groups. Thus any subsidy to these systems represents a transfer from middle- and upper-income taxpayers to lower-income taxpayers. Can a city operate effectively without any public input into local transportation? Seemingly not. But the level of subsidy is a vexing issue. Local governments could pursue policies to allow municipal bus companies to operate very close to the break-even point while charging reasonable fares. Perhaps this is the role for local

government in local transportation. However, local governments are also involved in constructing urban roads and freeways and the activities of governments here can have a strong efficiency effect. Local governments are often on the front line of designating HOV lanes and express bus lanes, and good management here can be a positive input to the efficient functioning of a city. Local governments may become involved in congestion pricing like the systems in Singapore and London. Modern cities in North America tend to be not very densely settled and this makes it difficult for mass transit to capture large volumes of riders. Both Mills and Glaeser appear to view subway construction as useful for the functioning of a city, but also to involve a large income redistribution activity that benefits mostly low-income residents.

President Eisenhower's massive freeway construction activity surely had a substantial impact on the land-use policies of cities in the United States. The freeways were intended to be paid for with a dedicated tax on gasoline. We infer then that there was not a great deal of income redistribution associated with this policy. People who drove more paid more tax because it was bound up in the price of fuel. One might still argue that it was a policy that may not have contributed to the efficient operation of cities. The policy may have discriminated against the efficient functioning of central cities which were doing reasonably well in the early 1950s relative to the efficient functioning of suburban municipal entities. Almost every government policy carries some direct or indirect income redistribution dimension with it and economists often ask that somehow or other the losers are compensated, even if only partially. Central cities were forced to play catch-up over many decades for various policies that left them with shrinking tax bases and employment.

2 *Police and crime control.* An efficient city would have a small amount of crime and a not-large per capita expenditure on policing and crime control. Glaeser and Sacerdote (1999) report that the probability of being victimized by crime within a six-month period in the United States is 21.7 percent for a resident of a city of over one million people compared with 9.4 percent for a town of less than 10,000 people. And many people who migrate out of large cities cite crime as the main motivation. Clearly central cities with pressing revenue problems are less able to provide lavish policing than those without such problems. Thus there is a potential cyclical downward spiral associated with central city decay.

There is an element of redistribution associated with property crime—those with little are generally robbing those with more. However, much crime involves young men from poor homes stealing from the homes and businesses of lower-income people. And the street-level drugs trade would be mostly low-income youth selling to other lower-income younger people. Crime can lead to segregation of neighborhoods by income and lower-income families can become stuck in communities with poor schools and poor security. This would seem at first glance to be indirect redistribution rather than an efficiency loss for the city. However, if increased segregation by income leads to poorer schooling outcomes for children in the poorer areas, we are then confronting an efficiency cost, a cost deriving ultimately from the "excessive" level of crime in certain areas of cities. Robert Fairbanks (2014) finds that about two-thirds of the 35,000 prisoners released from prisons in Illinois each year end up in just seven areas (defined by zip code) on the West and South sides of Chicago, where unemployment for African Americans is over 40 percent. In Milwaukee two-thirds of men with criminal records come from the six poorest areas (defined by zip code). If a significant factor in "making a criminal" is a dysfunctional home in which the perpetrators were raised, then more policing will not have a large effect on lowering the current level of crime in various places. A pessimist might argue then that as long as the largest cities house the largest fraction of very poor families then the largest cities will be saddled with the highest rates of crime and the rate of police activity will have only a marginal impact on these rates. The inference that more police activity will not always result in less local crime may indeed be true. Much more complicated is the design of social policy, including policing activity, which leads to a significant reduction in local criminal activity for the long run. We will return to the incidence of crime in cities.

3 *Schooling.* There is a long tradition of schools policy being set locally. The parents of kids are most interested in outcomes in their local schools and do what they can to obtain the best results for their children. But superficial aspects of schools are highly resource dependent. Communities with robust revenues can equip schools better and maintain them to a higher standard. Some of these extra expenditures no doubt affect the outcomes for the average student. The issue of teacher-pupil ratios has been a concern to parents over many decades. There is an efficiency dimension to school quality. Better educated children should be in stronger positions to contribute to the economy as workers. The long-term decline in manufacturing jobs in the United States has led to more attention on a "knowledged based" economy as well as to increased attention on the quality of workers in the United States compared with those in other strong economies. Schooling outcomes for young people appear to be important in a world of many innovative economies in the world competing with one another. Observers worry about the long-term competitiveness of the economy of the United States and how effective its school system is in keeping its graduates highly effective workers.

Education also has an income distribution dimension to it. Better educated individuals earn more over their lifetimes and enjoy somewhat better life expectancies. Thus when poor schooling outcomes correlate with the location of schools, one is dealing in part with an income redistribution issue. Educational attainment depends both on nurture (schools and student effort) as well as nature (the genetic endowment of the person). The development of social skills will also affect a person's lifetime earnings. First-class schooling can only take a child so far in terms of educational attainment. Social policy should be designed then to squeeze out as much attainment as possible, given what nature has endowed children to start with. The federal government in the United States has been trying to improve schooling outcomes with head-start programs and the introduction of school performance indicators. This probably reflects more of a concern for the efficiency of the schooling system in the United States than for its redistributive consequences. In any case, new federal government regulations create more mandates on local governments. One wonders if one is looking at a weak delivery system that is being asked to carry a heavier load. One hopes for better outcomes but one may be hoping for more than one should be expecting, realistically. If so much of current prosperity can be attributed to technical progress, one might expect that schooling would be a very high priority for parents, local government officials and other government officials higher up. We seem to be seeing schooling get much more attention in recent decades but clearly more emphasis on effective schooling and successful educational outcomes is needed. And ultimately it is the neighborhood school that is the ultimate deliverer of effective schooling. Leaving it to experts and officials in higher levels of government is not going to fix current deficiencies. Interested parties must engage in the local government process.

4 *Zoning and land-use regulation.* Zoning was developed to protect activity X from the negative impact of activity Y if the latter were close by. There is an efficiency aspect of keeping a noisy, smelly activity at some distance from, say, a physician's office. But there is a substantial income redistribution dimension to zoning. By legislating an offensive activity from locating next to my residence, the value of my property is protected. Municipal zoning is supposed to function that way… to protect one another's property from the bad outcomes that could arise from the "poor" location of a new activity or an old activity reorganized. Zoning is often used to keep lower-value homes out of the neighborhoods with high-value homes. Part of the motivation here is to prevent the owner of a low-value home from free-riding on the government services in the neighborhood with the high-value homes. Neighborhoods with many large attractive homes can get by with low tax rates when they have a particular revenue target to meet. Thus there is always an incentive to try to sneak a low-value home into the high-price neighborhood and in so doing "buy into" a low tax bill tied to the smaller home. Large lot zoning is one instrument used to forestall such free-riding. Thus zoning can have this indirect income redistribution dimension. More generally zoning can work to promote neighborhood segregation by income. This has an obvious income redistribution aspect and maybe an efficiency dimension as well.

5 *Welfare activity.* Local governments are often mandated to administer direct transfers to poor individuals and families as well as to supply some public housing and some health services. These responsibilities can be costly to the local governments and often come with specific quantitative mandates from higher levels of government. Ultimately the local governments become the final administrators of a major component of society's income redistribution system. One can talk in generalities about income redistribution in a society but "outcomes" are largely the responsibility of our local governments. Local governments must guard against becoming major centers that disabled and unemployed people migrate to. Barber (2013; p. 329) contends that "potential clients of welfare flocked to cities like New York that offered attractive welfare benefits." It has become more common for the housing of poor people to be handled by the use of rent supplements rather than with government supplied units. One wonders why any housing is owned by local governments when the system of rent supplements (Section 8 vouchers in the United States) is used very widely.

The responsibilities of local governments are complicated: they have both income redistribution dimensions as well as efficiency dimensions. From the standpoint of political science, one wonders if local government is the important level and the federal government is more about talk than action. Local governments are faced with major issues in delivery and in discretion in program administration. They pretty well rule supreme in policy formulation for land use and for roads and transit. The seemingly easy activities left for local government would be the provision of fire protection for the community and garbage collection. Chicago recently leased out its parking structures and related activities for 99 years. This provided a large infusion of up-front funds which one hopes would be allocated to capital projects and/or debt pay-down. Parking administration seems like a reasonable activity to move into the private sector. Policy with respect to future parking capacity should be kept with the local government. Neither fire protection nor garbage collection is in fact easy to deal with but relative to the five activities listed above, these two are certainly in the class of "straightforward." Garbage collection can be contracted out. Fire protection used to be carried out by private firms but is now done everywhere by the local government. The reason for this must involve the public-goods nature of fire protection. It is most efficient to assess a modest annual levy on each household and have the hardware and personnel be supplied by a central body.

People live their lives in neighborhoods with local governments not too distant. Many policies such as tax levels, employment insurance, rules on immigration and expenditure bundles are designed by state and federal governments and end up being delivered by the local governments. To a considerable extent, then, local governments are agents of more senior governments. It is natural to ask how well the local governments are equipped to be on the delivery end of often complicated policies set out by legislators, far away. Can one disentangle the amount of security a household is receiving from, say, the national intelligence (spy) agencies compared with the services of, say, local constables? Security for an individual or household becomes complicated to measure. And education is tricky. Schooling happens for most children in the local school and this place will be administered ultimately by the local government. We should probably infer that the quality of education being delivered might be very sensitive to the quality of local government. More recently, the federal government in the United States has been attempting to "end run" around local governments and to set country-wide standards for school performance. This is a departure from past practice and represents an innovation that cannot be easily evaluated at this early date. One will be confronted with the question of how much a student's schooling outcome depends on federal government regulations and on the quality of the local government, its schools policies and the quality of the local school and its teachers. There remains that long-standing claim that educational outcomes for a child depend hugely on her home environment and, of course, it is difficult to design policies that can improve the home environment or can neutralize the negative impact of a poor home environment on a child's educational attainment.

Local government revenue sharing

Traditionally, local government revenue was derived from property taxes—taxes on buildings and lots. More recently fees for certain services have provided an additional source of revenue. And in the United States some cities collect revenues from local sales taxes and even income taxes.

The property tax comes in three forms. There is the rate multiplied by the value of a residence (structure and lot); there is usually a distinct rate for a business firm's structure and lot; and lastly there are often special assessments for, say, sidewalk replacement or sewage main upgrading. A good property tax will of course require a good and fair assessment of the value of the property being taxed. A high-quality assessment can involve a large number of trained assessors. In addition, assessments have to be updated regularly as property values change. Total revenue for a municipality can be steady from the property tax but the stream will not be sensitive to the business cycle unless assessments are redone quite frequently. In boom times, when a city might be expected to be investing heavily in new infrastructure, the revenue from the property tax can lag because the assessment underlying current revenue is outdated. In 2003, Canadian cities got 45 percent of their operating revenue from the property tax while the equivalent figure for US cities was only 18 percent.

Toronto experienced two sorts of problems with its property tax around 2001. Rates on businesses had drifted up well beyond those for residences and the municipal government was obliged to launch a rebalancing initiative. Second, the Toronto municipality was levying rates well above those for municipalities in the outer suburbs. This reflects the perennial problem of suburban folk so-called free-riding on the services of the central city. The costs per capita of running the central city were well above those for running a suburban municipality. A municipal sales tax could address in part the issue of collecting revenues from outsiders who were users of central city services. Many large cities in the United States earn revenues from local sales taxes. The Canadian constitution disallows such levies for municipal governments.

A residential property tax can be viewed as a special levy on part of the home-owner's portfolio of assets. A homeowner with US$100,000 of equities will pay an annual tax on her dividends and often a tax on the capital gains she gets when she sells the equities. A home worth, say, US$400,000 is another asset in a hypothetical portfolio. It gets taxed at the local municipal rate, quite distinct from the taxes on the US$100,000 of equities. Observers worry about whether the different tax treatment of these two assets will lead to a misallocation of capital, at the margin. In Canada, with no allowance for mortgage interest deductability, the municipal tax becomes a levy on the equity (home value minus dollars remaining to pay on the mortgage) that the owner has in her home. This can be a high rate of tax and provides a strong incentive for the home-owner to pay off her mortgage as quickly as possible. User fees are another source of municipal revenue. Such fees include charges for library use, use of municipal parking, use of municipal recreation facilities, etc. These fees typically yield less than 25 percent of a city's annual revenue. Complicated here is the allocation of such fees to capital cost amortization. A new municipal swimming pool needs to be paid for and often the user fees just cover annual operating costs, leaving the capital costs to be covered by some other revenue stream. Cities will usually have distinct budgets for capital expenditures (new libraries, swimming pools, etc.) and operating expenditures (salaries for civil servants, police and fire personnel, etc.)

Transfers from higher levels of government are the second largest stream of revenues for municipalities in Canada and the United States. In 2003, transfers accounted for 23 percent of revenues for Canadian municipal governments and 29 percent for those in the United States. Donor governments generally specify the target recipients of transfers, as with, say, so many dollars transferred specifically for special education. Sometimes the grants have a matching provision. The municipal government is asked to provide one dollar from its revenue for every dollar transferred down from the donor government. In this case there is an incentive for the municipal government to expand the activity being supported by the donor government in order to gain, at the margin, more outside revenue. Social assistance for disabled and indigent people generally involves large transfers from a senior government to the municipal government. In 2008, Canada's central government agreed to provide a transfer of C$30 million to 16 agencies that support new immigrants, some 10,000 per year, in Toronto.

Local public transportation is a complicated case. Higher levels of government often fund part of the capital cost of new subways and light rail lines. Local governments often end up funding much of the operating cost deficit that local public transportation leaves each year. In 2007, Toronto's municipal government introduced a new tax on vehicle registration and on the sale of property, to augment its annual revenue. This created a controversy which was exploited by those running in the subsequent election in Toronto. Mayor Miller, who introduced the new taxes, chose not to run for office again. Toronto did persuade the federal government to allocate a portion of its gasoline tax for general revenues for municipalities.

There is the general perspective, however, that locally-raised revenues are not large enough to provide sufficient revenue at reasonable rates to fund the activities that have been deemed local responsibilities. Local governments receive considerable revenue from grants from state and even federal governments. Rationalization here is straightforward. For example, education standards are set by legislators at the state level and the social compact requires that parents have input into the education of their children. Hence one ends up with two levels of government dealing with the education of children. Grants from the state and provincial governments to local school authorities emerge naturally. Similarly with urban expressways. Such roads are often part of the state or federal system and their construction and maintenance becomes a shared responsibility of local governments and those more senior. Again such shared responsibility goes along with revenue sharing with the local government and the governments higher up. Immigration is an interesting case. The rules are set by the federal government for the most part and local governments often end up delivering services to the immigrants to help them settle in a new country. Language training is an example of such services provided to immigrants. But there can be more costly support provided as well. Local governments often are asked to administer these immigrant assistance programs while the funding comes from a level of government higher up. Barber (2013)favors local governments having more control over their revenues and expenditure policies. He expresses the frustration of many over "the fiscal noose with which provincial and national governments can strangle urban aspirations" (p. 133), and

> Long term, cities pay out on average (if not in every case) far more than they receive from higher authorities and thus, in theory, possess the means of their own solvency. But in practice they are often in the thrall to the provinces and nations under whose legal and fiscal authority they live.
>
> (p. 339)

Local governments in China receive half of all government revenues and are responsible for 80 percent of spending. Local governments are obliged to resort to gray-market activities in order to find funding for their activities. The grabbing of plots at the edge of cities from peasant farmers is a frequent occurrence. The land is sold to developers and the local government ends up with the "profit."[9]

The revenue that flows down in shared programs is called grants-in-aid. The complicated matter for the economist to assess is the degree of displacement in the local government budget induced by such grants. Given a grant of x dollars from above, the local government can argue that it can reduce revenue raising from traditional sources at the margin. This displacement complicates the analysis of the funding of local governments. Economists are always searching for the ideal revenue stream for certain activities being undertaken by the public sector. The displacement effect of grants-in-aid has to be factored into the design of a good local tax system.

The financial crisis of 2008–09 left most of Canada's provincial governments in a deficit position. The federal government in Ottawa also faced large deficits. There is an echo here of the 1990s. From 1970 to 1995 the central government's debt and deficits grew steadily. In fact many governments in Western nations experienced something similar. In Canada, a program of downloading activities from the central government to the provincial governments was initiated. The provincial governments in turn downloaded activities to their municipal governments. For large cities with extensive mass transit systems, cut-backs to services were the only way to balance the books. Canada has been praised for getting its fiscal house in order in the late 1990s but the good news at the level of the central government has not been matched with good news at lower levels of government. Some observers argue that if households could link tax payments closer to services, there would be less reluctance on the part of households to pay their local taxes. If most of the payments go to the high level of government and then are fought over by governments at different levels, a household loses sight of tax disbursements relative to services from various governments. This is a principle different from subsidiarity but one with merit.

Detroit is perhaps the best-known case of a city entering the legal process of declaring itself bankrupt. Once in a legal state of bankruptcy the city gains flexibility in unburdening itself of some debts and heavy expenditure obligations. In 2012 Stockton, California, with 800,000 residents, filed for bankruptcy. Syracuse, New York has appealed to the State government for what amounts to a bailout to avoid declaring bankruptcy. Governor Andrew Cuomo was unsympathetic of "aging cities with aging populations and aging infrastructures that are consuming greater percentages of their revenues while their tax bases are declining."[10]

New York City faced bankruptcy in the spring of 1975. It had run deficits since the 1960s and was having difficulty selling new bonds. The Municipal Assistance Corporation for the City of New York (MAC) was established through State legislation on June 10, 1975 to address the New York City severe fiscal crisis. Governor Hugh L. Carey created the corporation on the recommendation of a special panel comprising Simon H. Rifkind, Felix G. Rohatyn, Richard M. Shinn and Donald B. Smiley. MAC had a Board of Directors consisting of nine private citizens and was endowed with the authority to borrow billions backed by some State revenues. The state passed legislation that converted the city's sales and stock transfer taxes into state taxes. In September the Emergency Financial Control Board (EFCB) was set up by the state to oversee day-to-day management of the city. The city continued to have difficulty selling its bonds. In November the federal government extended up to US$2.3 billion of short-term loans to New York City. The interest charge was 1 percent above the cost of funds to the federal government. Banks, employees and state taxpayers were brought into the process of assisting the city. City debt was sold to pension funds. The city raised US$200 million in additional taxes. City employment fell by 20 percent and wages were reduced. Raises were held at a rate below inflation. The city stumbled forward and by 1985 was able to operate without the assistance of the MAC, which was dissolved in 2008: it had helped to raise almost US$10 billion from new sales up to 2008 when it voted itself out of existence. The city ended up solvent after its severe fiscal crisis. Did the economy of New York City bounce back because MAC worked particularly well in raising funds and the EFCB did well in supervising the city's budgets, or because New York City's economy experienced a renaissance, led by Wall Street? Did the world economy develop a strong demand after 1975 for products that New York City was good at creating and supplying?

Parts of the fabric of a good city are attractive parks and interesting libraries, as well as vibrant theatres and related cultural activities. Local orchestras in cities in the United States have been hit with severe revenue problems. In June 2013, the Nashville Symphony Orchestra came within days of foreclosure on its concert hall, an imposing neoclassical structure, costing US$123 million, which had opened in 2006. Since the economic crisis of 2008, bankruptcies have afflicted orchestras around the country, leading to the closure of the Honolulu, Syracuse and Albuquerque symphony orchestras, and in April 2011 came the stunning news that the world-renowned Philadelphia Orchestra had filed for bankruptcy protection. The reorganization of the Philadelphia Orchestra involved cutting ten players and reducing the pay of the remaining members by 15 percent (Kennecott 2013). The New York City Opera was forced to close in 2013 after operating for 70 years.

One of the persistent issues linked to Detroit's bankruptcy (declared July 18, 2013) was how to deal with the city's very valuable collection of paintings at the Detroit Art Institute.

Estimates for the core collection range from US$454 to US$867 million. Some very wealthy Americans (including the Ford, Kresge and Kellogg Foundations) came forward with a US$330 million rescue plan for the art. Ownership of the museum would shift from the city to a nonprofit organization, protecting it from future municipal financial threats. The city in turn would guarantee pensions of many retirees. On June 10, 2014 Detroit's big three auto companies pledged US$26 million more to preserve the art collection and move the pension issue forward. In fact, on December 11, 2014, Detroit became the largest US city to date to successfully exit bankruptcy. Earlier, Robert Frank, a columnist with the *New York Times, Sunday Business* section mused in his March 30, 2014 essay about the possibility of the city selling some holdings. He starts with the estimate of US$200 million for Bruegel's "The Wedding Dance." If the city auctioned this painting off for the US$200 million, it would have some US$10 million of revenue each year, given a 5 percent interest rate. With the painting left on the wall, its display would cost about US$6,000 per hour, given the gallery open 2,000 hours per year. If five visitors lingered for an hour at the painting each day when the gallery was open, the city would be spending approximately US$1,200 per person per hour for having this famous painting in its gallery. To columnist Frank, this seems like an unsatisfactory way for a revenue-strapped municipality to be "spending" its money. If Detroiters are really committed to art, he suggests selling off "The Wedding Dance" and maybe more famous works and replacing them with works of young contemporary artists, whose paintings and sculptures sell for much less. These low-cost works could in turn rise in price, he argues, since much of the market value of a work of art lies in the fact that pieces are held by world-class galleries and collectors. "Yes," he comments, "communities benefit from famous paintings, but they also benefit from safer roads and better schools."

Criminal behavior

Becker's (1968) thinking about crime has the criminal compare the costs of her action with the benefits, B. Costs comprise the direct cost D of getting tools and information, going out and taking up time and returning with booty plus the indirect cost of being caught, with probability P and serving time with cost C. The person then does crime when $B > D + P \times C$. She continues to do criminal acts until she reaches an equilibrium with $B = D + P \times C$, with B yielding diminishing returns to aggregate booty taken. The rational thief considers the value of her take and the cost of being apprehended, convicted and jailed. Being caught is uncertain and thus the thief has a complicated problem of risk assessment. Complicating this way of thinking is the fact that the average IQ of those in jail is below that of law-abiding citizens. Hence much criminal activity is perpetrated by those who are in fact poor at evaluating the risks of apprehension. Moreover much criminal activity is undertaken when the perpetrator is high on alcohol or drugs. Levitt (1996, 1997) estimates the elasticity of crime with respect to different measures of deterrence (probability of arrest, number of police officers and size of prison population), as between -0.1 and -0.4. That is, a 10 percent increase in expenditure on deterrence results in about two percent less crime. There is much debate then about having more policing and/or the government legislating stiffer sentences for crimes. A recent report (2014) done for Houston found that 15,000 burglaries and thefts, 3000 assaults and about 3000 hit-and-runs went uninvestigated in 2013. Though burglaries have been declining recently, the report recommends that 45 new investigators be hired to address the problem of under-investigating of crimes.[11] The prison population in the United States is in absolute and relative terms about the highest in the world (716 incarcerations per 100,000 population in the United States versus, for example, 148 in England and Wales).[12]

Criminal activity in an equilibrium in a community would involve the same rates year after year. For example, one can think of a community with an unchanging population size. One can think of a steady state with a steady number of police, a steady number criminals and a steady size of the courts and jail system. Data on criminal activity could be approximately steady over time for such a community. In many cities in the United States, the rate of crime has in fact declined noticeably since the 1980s. This might be explained by (a) fewer young males in urban populations, (b) more policing of streets (more frisking of young males on streets for weapons and drugs), (c) more deterrence resulting from harsher sentences, and/or (d) more rapid jailing ("locking up") of first-time offenders. Josh Barro observes that automobile theft has declined sharply in the past 20 years in New York City, in part because new security mechanisms have made vehicles difficult to steal but also because the crime rate overall has declined significantly.[13]

Donohue and Levitt (2001) tested the hypothesis that more liberal abortion regulations in the United States in the early 1970s resulted in fewer unwanted pregnancies and fewer young men who were potential criminals some 20 years later. The idea was that fewer "unwanted children" were born after *Roe v. Wade (1973)* and thus fewer "lost young men" were on the streets as teenagers. The idea that there is a link between unwanted babies and more young criminals later on goes back many decades. Donohue and Levitt decided to try to find the link in data for the United States. Many observers had noted the curious decline in crime in the United States in the 1990s. Donohue and Levitt found pretty sound evidence for the connection between more liberal abortion (fewer "unwanted" babies) and later decline in crime.

Britain has recently recorded large declines in crime rates in the cities of London, Manchester and the region of West Midlands. The number of murders in these three large places declined by 34 percent between 2008 and 2013. In addition school performance by children in low-income districts of large cities is well up. These good results do not hold up for smaller communities. There is no simple explanation for these developments. Improved police activity seems to be a contributing factor in the decline in the crime rate in certain places.[14]

Stephen Levitt is also famous for research into the lifestyle of young drug dealers. He found that few individuals in the drug supply trade had large incomes; many were living in the homes of their parents or their single moms. Young pushers would mostly be working for a crime "company" or syndicate and would thus be employees rather than independent entrepreneurs. Unskilled young people typically earn low wages, regardless of their line of work. The media have probably developed the image of a drug dealer as a flashy high-roller, when in fact—as Levitt discovered—a drug supply organization has mostly lowly poorly-paid workers. Only a few "CEOs" in the trade would be getting high incomes.

The United States remains a place where guns, including those that one can conceal on one's person, are abundant. This may put something of a floor under the level to which violent crime can fall. As long as a certain density of concealed weapons remains, a certain flow of violent crimes will take place. Many guns end up being used in suicides and domestic disputes. This is a different sort of social disfunction from that associated with drug selling, prostitution and "protection." The criminalization of drug use in the United States contributes significantly to the high rate of incarceration in the country. Property crime (excluding arson) involved losses to victims of some US$15.5 billion in 2012 in the United States. Murder is considered to be the least under-reported crime in the United States. Rates by city vary from 54.6 per 100,000 population for Detroit to 19 for Atlanta. Chicago, with a population of 2.7 million, had a rate of 18.5.[15]

Urban crime

In cities, violent crime is usually perpetrated by young males. Cities offer a high density of targets for a criminal and more of a chance to remain "anonymous" when, say, the target is out of one's residential area. Property crime in rural areas is less intensive. Targets are less attractive and chance of detection is higher. Much violent crime in fact involves relatives and friends; strife among family members and incidents at social gatherings when alcohol and other disorienting substances are being used by participants.

For an urban or densely populated area to support more crime per capita, one should start with the premise that net gains per criminal act are higher in a larger than in a smaller city. For net gains to be higher, one looks for a higher dollar gain per act or a lower cost per act in a larger place. Higher gains can arise from richer, more densely arrayed "prey," as for example more homes with valuable items to snatch, and lower costs can arise from simply a lower probability of being apprehended in a larger city. These factors explain some 50 percent of the higher rate of crime in larger cities (Glaeser and Sacerdote 1999; p. S228). Glaeser and Sacerdote draw attention to a third consideration: there are more criminally inclined individuals in a larger city. This turns on larger cities having more dysfunctional families; for example, more households headed by single mothers with low incomes. About one third of extra crime in larger cities is accounted for by the larger number of "more criminally inclined" people.

Consider two nominally identical criminals, one operating in a small community and one in a city; we expect to observe quite different narratives. Glaeser and Sacerdote note that a burglar does not want to steal large, heavy objects since "getting away" quickly and unobtrusively is valuable. Low cost of transport can be achieved in places with a high density of prospective burglary sites. Similarly a mugger prefers a high density of passersby than a thin stream and of course cities are better at providing the sought-after ample prey. It is also easier to sell stolen property in a city with no questions asked than it is in a small town. Hence cities appear to have obvious advantages for a criminal to pursue property crime. And if his or her activity tilts into violence, it is easier to get away with murder and "disappear" in a large place. The rate of solved murders is of course well below 100 percent. Glaeser and Sacerdote (1999; p. S225) say that

> higher pecuniary benefits for crime in large cities can explain at most one-quarter of the connection between city size and crime rates. Lower probabilities of arrest and a lower probability of recognition are features of urban life, but these factors seem to explain at most one-fifth of the urban crime effect.

Tables 9.2 and 9.3 provide data on community size and rates of crime.

Cities typically are plagued by "organized crime." One might consider various forms of organized crime (drug selling, prostitution, "protection," illegal gambling) as industries,

Table 9.2 Crime rate (per 100,000 population) by type—selected large cities, 2009

	Average population	*Average murder rate*
Ten largest cities	2.59 million	236.9
Ten smallest large cities	0.204 million	16.6

Source: Table 309, United States Census Bureau, November 14, 2013.

Table 9.3 Crimes and crime rates (per 100,000 population) by type and geographic community, 2009

	Metropolitan statistical area	*Cities outside metropolitan areas*	*Non-metropolitan counties*
Murder	5.2	4.0	3.4
Aggravated assault	273.2	288.2	157.6
Burglery	727.2	822.6	552.8
Motor vehicle theft	286.0	142.6	105.3

Source: Table 309, United States Census Bureau, November 14, 2013.

often comprising competing "firms," not too different from, say, competition among newspapers produced in a large city. A city provides a sufficiently large market to support one or more "crime firms." The difference between a firm in organized crime and a regular, legally constituted company in a city is that the workers for the crime company use stealth and threats of violence in going about their tasks. In addition, the senior people in the company must resort to violence and sometimes murder to prevent defections and "cheating" by the workers. Violence and murder are also standard instruments used by a crime "company" to protect an established market area from entry by competitors or newcomers. "Market" size for a criminal organization must be reasonably large in order for costs of operation to be spread over "output." Hence we expect "serious" criminal organizations to operate where "markets" are large and other conditions are "supportive," most often in cities rather than small towns. On these grounds alone we should expect crime rates to be higher in cities compared with smaller communities. For a criminal organization to actually carry out violence is probably a sign of failure. A smoothly running crime firm or company does best when threats of violence and murder are enough to maintain discipline within the firm and to keep outsiders out of its established market area. In a sense it is a disequilibrium such as a war for turf or new market area that tends to correlate positively with violence and murder.

Consider the counterfactual argument. Suppose some "entrepreneurs" decide to pursue organized crime in a small town. The "market" for criminal services, say "protection," is small and the ability of the organization to operate in "the shadows" in the community is difficult. One might make the additional argument that some collaboration with law enforcement is part of the modus operandi of organized crime and this is more difficult when the police and local judges themselves have difficulty collaborating with criminals "in the shadows" when the community is small. Not only does everyone know everyone else in smaller communities, but everyone knows what everyone else is up to. Glaeser and Sacerdote take very seriously the idea that more crime-prone individuals tend to live in cities. They explore the idea that weak family structure correlates strongly with a larger number of crime-prone individuals. Families headed by a single parent becomes the indicator of weak family structure: "the percentage of female-headed households … has an extremely positive effect on the crime rate" in cities (Glaeser and Sacerdote 1999; p. S247). Between one-third and one-half of the urban effect on crime can be explained by the presence of more female-headed households in cities.

There is of course much threatened violence involved in the collection of payments by drug sellers or those owed funds more generally. Gamblers sometimes end up owing large sums, for example. For some reason, there are proportionately more regular gamblers and consumers of drugs in larger rather than smaller communities. Dysfunctional families and unhappy individuals may find cities a more congenial place to be than a town or village.

The average level of dysfunctionality for families and individuals may be lower in smaller communities. "Social capital" is the term used to characterize the social bonds between individuals and families in communities. Glaeser *et al.* (2002) report on why and how an individual invests in social capital and one might argue that it is easier to build up social capital in a small town when interpersonal interactions are more frequent and intense. When people relocate less, it is easier for them to build up social capital. Every individual may not do so, but it may be easier for an individual in a smaller town. Given then a larger "market" in cities for activities that are not legal, one ends up with more criminal "firms" in larger places and more crimes perpetrated in keeping the "firms" in the markets going. Glaeser and Sacerdote (1999; p. S241) conclude: "It is ironic that the same urban advantages, lower transport costs, faster urban information flows, and the same scale economies that help to make cities more productive also increase the level of crime in the city."

Summary

In earlier chapters, we emphasized that people agglomerated in villages thousands of years ago essentially to trade with one another, to take advantage of division of labor and in doing so, avoid transportation costs. We neglected the public goods dimension of clustering. Defense for a family was paramount since the dawn of primate communities. Defense of course is better done by groups of families rather than by a family alone. Defense is consumed equally by all the families in the village. Defense is a public good. In later times, defense involved walls and trenches and presumably some organization at a center. Defense needed to be funded as well. Hence from the earliest times, communities existed as clusters of families for reasons of defense or for reasons of public goods. Nations emerged and the defense function was taken over for the most part by the national government. But cities continue to rise up and generally expand. The modern public-finance argument for a city's existence is different, but has basic parallels.

The central anomaly of modern cities is that they are the places where most of the modern jobs are, where most of the modern economy is operating (for cities in developed countries, at least), where most of political activity is centered, generally where most of a nation's people are, and yet cities are generally severely constrained by higher levels of government in revenue raising, expenditure organizing and in political participation by voters. The turnout at elections is usually much higher for state and central government offices than for local government offices. As a writer for *The Economist* put it:

> Mayors think of municipalities as cradles of democracy where citizens meet government close up. They build and maintain schools, repair streets and help the jobless and the elderly. They account for almost two-thirds of public investment... Yet though a mayor may matter more to citizens than a state premier, voter turnout is higher in state elections. Towns have financial and political autonomy but no "state quality".... They are like branches of a head office that dictates most spending and provides or regulates most revenue.... Federal, state and local authorities tap the same sources of revenue, which makes tax reform harder. Citizens see no connection between local services and tax bills.[16]

More broadly, cities tend to be the centers of a nation's economic dynamism and their local government officials have relatively little authority in directing local economic development. Central to local economic development are good infrastructure, reasonable tax rates and fiscal prudence.

One can argue that the "branch office" arrangement is necessary for national political stability. If local governments in large cities had considerable authority over their revenues and expenditures, at the "expense" of the higher levels of government, the nation could unravel into competing and possibly warring city-states. Cities would compete to offload expenditures for income supports and social (subsidized) housing and strive to outbid rivals for investments by firms. Higher levels of government are valuable because these governments act as arbiters between the powerful governments of larger cities. This view derives from the general claim that the largest tension in a nation of reasonable size is between regions. It may not be surprising then that capital cities in many nations have grown disproportionately large. The capital and its local hinterland becomes the head office, with the task of mediating among the other regions (branch offices) in the nation, other regions distinguished each by the presence of a large city.

What issues might need mediating? The location of marginal investments would be one. The organization of migrants would be another. For example the generosity of welfare handouts for the disabled and indigent will affect the distribution of such households among cities. In the absence of a central authority, one can envisage a race among cities to shift the numbers of disabled and indigent to other cities. When a higher level of government sets the rules for income-support for residents in a group of cities, and has the means to support the general rules, such a race can be avoided. Regions are sometimes distinguished by special natural resource endowments such as oil fields. Then a nation must work out an amicable way to distribute the extra income between regions. The Flatters *et al.* (1974) model of local public goods, costless migration of households and distinct regional land endowments illustrates how the free market ends up with a suboptimal distribution of people and economic activity across regions. A higher level of government is required to implement Pigovian tax intervention on the mobility of households to improve the welfare of the average household in the abstract economy.

A sizable and important literature has developed on tax competition by various local governments. Each city strives to attract the marginal footloose investment by a firm by making itself somewhat more "business friendly" than its neighbors. There may even be tax competition to attract new residents at the margin. The power of local politicians is enhanced by an increase in the size of their constituency. Tax competition is an instance of competition among local governments and is not necessarily welfare enhancing. The intervention of a mediating government, one level higher up, can be socially beneficial (see, for example, Parry 2003).

Main points of Chapter 9

1 Government "bundle" offerings are difficult to arrive at because "consumers" strive to keep their taxes low by misrepresenting their true preferences. A pure public good for a city has each household receive exactly the same quantity of service. "Consumer" preferences are usually assumed to be in line with true marginal benefits.

2 Governments usually end up having a "dialogue" with "consumers," with parties offering an agenda of government goods and services at election time. Median voter outcomes are special cases, difficult to connect with actual elections for local officials.

3 Some argue that households tend to cluster with other households with similar tastes for public services (the Tiebout hypothesis). Different "offerings" by government in different places has a variety of effects on a household's choice of location. Certain kinds of exclusionary zoning encourage clustering of similar households.

4 Costs of running local governments are subject to wage increases for civil servants that may not be easily linked to efficiency improvements of workers.
5 Property taxes cover a major part of local government revenues. Some tests and other arguments suggest that property taxes tilt urban land use toward sprawl.
6 Municipal governments have relatively little flexibility in reorganizing their sources of revenue and are generally subject to the "tight reins" of higher levels of government.

Questions and problems

1 It is easy to argue that a municipal election is a very blunt instrument for getting the views of all of a city's residents "fairly registered" in the minds of elected officials.

  a Evaluate this contention.
  b Are the wishes of low-income residents of a city consistently not taken seriously? Do low-income households generally end up with lower qualities of municipal services and lower quantities of public goods?

2 The idea that urban residents in distinct neighborhoods tend to get the basket of municipal services that they are content to pay for with their taxes and fees is attractive, but is there much evidence for this point of view being valid?
3 "The fight against disease, crime and congestion in cities has never been won by passively accepting the way things are or by mindlessly relying on the free market" (Glaeser 2011; p. 10). Is there a boundary separating activities in cities between what the free market does well and what must be done by local government?
4 "Urban scale makes it possible to support the fixed costs of theatres, museums, and restaurants" (Glaeser 2011; p. 10). Sketch the cost schedule and revenue function for a large museum in, say, Chicago or New York City.
5 Is a big push (a surge) required to move a community with much crime and many (or few) police personnel to an equilibrium with little crime and few police personnel? Or can crime reduction move forward smoothly with many small improvements in policing and related interventions?

Appendix 9.1: Cobb–Douglas utility (no structures)

Charges based on marginal benefits

We need to compare outcomes under benefit taxation for public good G and house-value taxation for covering the cost of G. Our city's geography is a line with the CBD in the center. We will assume that G is produced with constant marginal cost per unit, m. First, we will obtain the rent function for the case of charging being based on marginal benefits. In this case, the level of G is determined in (a variant of the Samuelson (1954) condition for efficient production of public goods):

$$2\int_0^{\overline{x}} \frac{U_G(x)}{U_c(x)}\frac{1}{h(x)}dx = m,$$

where each household-worker has utility function $U = c(x)^{\alpha}h(x)^{\beta}G^{1-\alpha-\beta}$ and the edge of the city is defined by $\overline{x}$ in $r(\overline{x}) = r_A$. Here U_c and U_G are marginal utilities. Each household-worker ends up with the same utility level, $\overline{U} = c(x)^{\alpha}h(x)^{\beta}G^{1-\alpha-\beta}$. Workers live on their lots and commute each day to the center at cost tx, round-trip. For each household-worker's budget constraint, we have

$$w - tx = c(x) + r(x)h(x) + \frac{U_G(x)}{U_c(x)}G.$$

Thus $\frac{U_G(x)}{U_c(x)}$ becomes the price per unit of G and households at different radial distances x pay, in general, different amounts for the same G. Consumption efficiency here is

$$\frac{\alpha h(x)}{\beta c(x)} = \frac{1}{r(x)}.$$

Combine this with constant utility, $\overline{U}$, and we obtain

$$c = \frac{\overline{U}^{1/\alpha}}{G^{(1-\alpha-\beta)/\alpha} h^{\beta/\alpha}},$$

and since $h = \frac{\beta c}{\alpha r}$, we obtain

$$h(x) = \frac{\beta^{\alpha/(\alpha+\beta)}\overline{U}^{1/(\alpha+\beta)}}{\alpha^{\alpha/(\alpha+\beta)} G^{(1-\alpha-\beta)/(\alpha+\beta)}} \frac{1}{r(x)^{\alpha/(\alpha+\beta)}}.$$

Now $hr = \frac{\beta c}{\alpha}$ and $G\frac{U_G(x)}{U_c(x)} = \frac{(1-\alpha-\beta)c}{\alpha}$. Hence the budget constraint becomes

$$\begin{aligned} w - tx &= \frac{c}{\alpha} = \frac{h(x)r(x)}{\beta} \\ &= \frac{1}{\beta}\left[\frac{\beta^{\alpha/(\alpha+\beta)}\overline{U}^{1/(\alpha+\beta)}}{\alpha^{\alpha/(\alpha+\beta)} G^{(1-\alpha-\beta)/(\alpha+\beta)}}\right] r(x)^{\beta/(\alpha+\beta)}, \end{aligned}$$

and

$$r(x) = \left[\frac{\alpha^{\alpha/\beta}\beta G^{(1-\alpha-\beta)/\beta}}{\overline{U}^{1/\beta}}\right][w - tx]^{(\alpha+\beta)/\beta}.$$

Given $\frac{c}{h} = \alpha r/\beta$, the efficient level of G in $2\int_0^{\overline{x}} \frac{U_G(x)}{U_c(x)} \frac{1}{h(x)} dx = m$, reduces to

$$2\left(\frac{(1-\alpha-\beta)}{\beta}\right)\int_0^{\overline{x}} r(x)dx = mG,$$

or

$$2\left(\frac{(1-\alpha-\beta)}{\beta}\right)\int_0^{\overline{x}} \left[\frac{\alpha^{\alpha/\beta}\beta G^{(1-\alpha-\beta)/\beta}}{G\overline{U}^{1/\beta}}\right][w - tx]^{(\alpha+\beta)/\beta}\, dx = m.$$

Less clutter remains if we assume that $\left[\frac{\alpha^{\alpha/\beta}\beta}{\overline{U}^{1/\beta}}\right] = J$.

Upon integrating we get

$$2\left[\frac{(1-\alpha-\beta)}{\beta J^{(\alpha+\beta)/\beta}}\right]\frac{G^{(1-\alpha-2\beta)/\beta}}{t\left[\frac{\alpha+\beta}{\beta}+1\right]}\left[w^{\frac{\alpha+\beta}{\beta}+1}-[w-t\overline{x}]^{\frac{\alpha+\beta}{\beta}+1}\right]=m.$$

Our other equation is:

$$w-t\overline{x}=\left[\frac{J}{G^{(1-\alpha-\beta)/(\alpha+\beta)}}\right]r_A^{\beta/(\alpha+\beta)}.$$

We can insert this expression for $w-t\overline{x}$ into the previous equation and obtain an equation in G alone. It remains to determine when the solution, G, is larger or smaller than its counterpart for the case of a city with a property tax.

Charges based on a tax on home value

We proceed to the city with property tax at level τ. Hence a household-worker at x pays tax $\tau h(x)r(x)$ and receives government services G. There is constant utility in $\overline{U}=c(x)^{\alpha}h(x)^{\beta}G^{(1-\alpha-\beta)}$ and a worker's budget constraint is now $w-tx=c(x)+h(x)r(x)+\tau h(x)r(x)$. We thus identify the cost of housing at x in $(1+\tau)h(x)r(x)$ and the budget constraint is now

$$w-tx=c(x)+(1+\tau)h(x)r(x).$$

The level of G is determined in

$$2\int_0^{\overline{x}}\frac{\tau\,[h(x)r(x)]}{h(x)}dx=2\int_0^{\overline{x}}\tau r(x)dx=mG.$$

Efficiency in consumption is then

$$\frac{\alpha h(x)}{\beta c(x)}=\frac{1}{(1+\tau)r(x)},$$

and combined with the expression for $\overline{U}$ yields

$$c=\frac{\overline{U}^{1/\alpha}}{G^{(1-\alpha-\beta)/\alpha}h^{\beta/\alpha}}.$$

Since $h=\frac{\beta c}{\alpha(1+\tau)r}$, we get

$$h=\frac{\beta^{\alpha/(\alpha+\beta)}\overline{U}^{1/(\alpha+\beta)}}{\alpha^{\alpha/(\alpha+\beta)}G^{(1-\alpha-\beta)/(\alpha+\beta)}}\frac{1}{r(x)^{\alpha/(\alpha+\beta)}}\frac{1}{(1+\tau)^{\alpha/(\alpha+\beta)}}.$$

The budget constraint is $w-tx=c+(1+\tau)hr=\frac{\alpha+\beta}{\alpha}c=\frac{\alpha+\beta}{\beta}(1+\tau)h(x)r(x)$. Hence we have

$$w-tx=(\alpha+\beta)(1+\tau)^{\beta/(\alpha+\beta)}\left[\frac{J}{G^{(1-\alpha-\beta)/(\alpha+\beta)}}\right]r(x)^{\beta/(\alpha+\beta)}$$

which implies that

$$r(x) = \left[\frac{G^{(1-\alpha-\beta)/\beta}}{(\alpha+\beta)^{(\alpha+\beta)/\beta}(1+\tau)J^{(\alpha+\beta)/\beta}} \right] [w - tx]^{(\alpha+\beta)/\beta}.$$

We have the following integral to consider:

$$2\tau \left[\frac{G^{(1-\alpha-\beta)/\beta}}{(\alpha+\beta)^{(\alpha+\beta)/\beta}(1+\tau)J^{(\alpha+\beta)/\beta}} \right] \int_0^{\overline{x}} [w - tx]^{(\alpha+\beta)/\beta}\, dx = mG.$$

Integrating yields:

$$2\tau \left[\frac{G^{(1-\alpha-2\beta)/\beta}}{(\alpha+\beta)^{(\alpha+\beta)/\beta}(1+\tau)J^{(\alpha+\beta)/\beta)}} \right] \frac{1}{t\left[\frac{\alpha+\beta}{\beta}+1\right]} \left[w^{\frac{\alpha+\beta}{\beta}+1} - [w - t\overline{x}]^{\frac{\alpha+\beta}{\beta}+1} \right] = m.$$

Our other equation is

$$w - t\overline{x} = (\alpha+\beta)(1+\tau)^{\beta/(\alpha+\beta)} \left[\frac{J}{G^{(1-\alpha-\beta)/(\alpha+\beta)}} \right] r_A^{\beta/(\alpha+\beta)}.$$

We substitute this equation in the previous one to get a polynomial in G alone. Numerical solving with $\alpha = 0.4$, $\beta = 0.2$, $m = 1.1$, $t = 0.05$, $w = 5$, $J = 100$ and $r_A = 0.02$ yields a city under property tax larger for any positive value of τ between 0.01 and 1. One might say then that the property tax induces a form of sprawl with the benchmark being taxation in accord with marginal benefits. The equilibrium value for G rises with a decline in τ. A more sprawling city has more households to share the cost of G.

Appendix 9.2: Property taxation versus marginal benefit taxation with structures in the cities

We still have the utility of each household-worker as $c^\alpha h^\beta G^{(1-\alpha-\beta)}$ and utilities are constrained to be at level $\overline{U}$. Now a house has production function $h = L^\gamma K^{1-\gamma}$ for amount of land and structure on the lot of L and K, respectively. There is a prevailing rental of i per unit of K and land has its rental, $r(x)$, for x distance from the center. The budget constraint for a household is $w - tx = c(x) + h(x)r(x) + G\frac{U_G}{U_c}$ where $\frac{U_G}{U_c}$ is the marginal benefit charge. Here U_G and U_c are first derivatives of the utility function. Under marginal benefit "taxation," G satisfies the Samuelson public goods condition:

$$2\int_0^{\overline{x}} \frac{U_G(x)}{U_c(x)} \frac{1}{L(x)} dx = m,$$

for m the marginal cost of producing G. Note m is constant here. Also, $\overline{x}$ is the edge of the city and satisfies $r(\overline{x}) = r_A$. Observe that $\frac{U_G(x)}{U_C(x)} = \frac{(1-\alpha-\beta)c}{\alpha G}$. Hence our public goods efficiency condition becomes $2\frac{(1-\alpha-\beta)}{\alpha}\int_0^{\overline{x}} \frac{c(x)}{L(x)} dx = mG$ and $c(x) = \frac{\alpha hq}{\beta}$. Hence our integral becomes $2\frac{(1-\alpha-\beta)}{\beta}\int_0^{\overline{x}} \frac{h(x)q(x)}{L(x)} dx = mG$. Hence $\frac{h(x)q(x)}{L(x)}$ is of particular interest.

Under consumption efficiency we have $\frac{\alpha h}{\beta c} = \frac{1}{q}$ for q the rental price per unit of h. This price takes the form $q = \Omega r(x)^{\gamma} i^{1-\gamma}$ for $\Omega = \gamma^{-\gamma}(1-\gamma)^{-(1-\gamma)}$. Production efficiency takes the form $\frac{\gamma K}{(1-\gamma)L} = \frac{r(x)}{i}$. From the production function, we have

$$h = L\left[\frac{(1-\gamma)r}{\gamma i}\right]^{1-\gamma}.$$

Hence $\frac{hq}{L} = \left[\frac{(1-\gamma)r}{\gamma i}\right]^{1-\gamma} \Omega r(x)^{\gamma} i^{1-\gamma} = \frac{1}{\gamma} r(x)$. Once again we require the $r(x)$ function in order to do our analysis.

The familiar route is to consider the budget constraint:

$$\begin{aligned} w - tx &= c + rh + \frac{U_G(x)}{U_c(x)}G \\ &= c + \frac{\beta c}{\alpha} + \frac{(1-\alpha-\beta)}{\alpha}c \\ &= \frac{c}{\alpha}. \end{aligned}$$

To obtain c, we use the utility function and the expression for h, above, to get

$$c = \frac{\overline{U}^{1/\alpha}}{G^{(1-\alpha-\beta)/\alpha} L^{\beta/\alpha} \left[\frac{(1-\gamma)r}{\gamma i}\right]^{\beta(1-\gamma)/\alpha}},$$

and the consumption efficiency condition allows us to extract L, (we want $L^{\beta/\alpha}$) upon substituting for c and h:

$$L^{\beta/\alpha} = \frac{\beta^{\beta/(\alpha+\beta)} \overline{U}^{(\beta/\alpha)/(\alpha+\beta)}}{\alpha^{\beta/(\alpha+\beta)} G^{((1-\alpha-\beta)\beta)/((\alpha+\beta)\alpha)} \left[\frac{(1-\gamma)r}{\gamma i}\right]^{\beta(1-\gamma)/\alpha} \left[\Omega r(x)^{\gamma} i^{1-\gamma}\right]^{\beta/(\alpha+\beta)}}.$$

This is inserted in the expression for c to get

$$\frac{c}{\alpha} = \frac{\overline{U}^{1/(\alpha+\beta)} \alpha^{\beta/(\alpha+\beta)} \left[\Omega i^{1-\gamma}\right]^{\beta/(\alpha+\beta)} r^{\gamma\beta/(\alpha+\beta)}}{\alpha \beta^{\beta/(\alpha+\beta)} G^{(1-\alpha-\beta)/(\alpha+\beta)}}.$$

Since $w - tx = \frac{c}{\alpha}$, we have $r(x)$ in

$$w - tx = \frac{M}{G^{(1-\alpha-\beta)/(\alpha+\beta)}} r(x)^{\gamma\beta/(\alpha+\beta)}$$

for $M = \frac{\overline{U}^{1/(\alpha+\beta)} \alpha^{\beta/(\alpha+\beta)} \left[\Omega i^{1-\gamma}\right]^{\beta/(\alpha+\beta)}}{\alpha \beta^{\beta/(\alpha+\beta)}}$. Hence

$$w - t\overline{x} = \frac{M}{G^{(1-\alpha-\beta)/(\alpha+\beta)}} r_A^{\gamma\beta/(\alpha+\beta)}.$$

(i) We have then

$$r(x) = \frac{G^{(1-\alpha-\beta)/\beta\gamma}}{M^{(\alpha+\beta)/\beta\gamma}}(w - tx)^{(\alpha+\beta)/\beta\gamma}$$

and must integrate (the Samuelson condition)

$$\frac{2}{\gamma}\left[\frac{1-\alpha-\beta}{\beta}\right]\frac{G^{(1-\alpha-\beta)/\beta\gamma}}{GM^{(\alpha+\beta)/\beta\gamma}}\int_0^{\overline{x}}(w - tx)^{(\alpha+\beta)/\beta\gamma}\,dx = mG.$$

After integrating, we get

$$\frac{2}{\gamma}\left[\frac{1-\alpha-\beta}{\beta}\right]\frac{G^{(1-\alpha-\beta)/\beta\gamma}}{GM^{(\alpha+\beta)/\beta\gamma}}\frac{1}{t\left[\frac{\alpha+\beta}{\beta\gamma}+1\right]}\left[w^{\frac{\alpha+\beta}{\beta\gamma}+1} - [w - t\overline{x}]^{\frac{\alpha+\beta}{\beta\gamma}+1}\right] = m.$$

We substitute for $w - t\overline{x}$ and obtain an equation in G alone.
(ii) We require $r(x)$ for the case of property tax at rate τ.

For this case consumption efficiency is

$$\frac{\alpha h}{\beta c} = \frac{1}{(1+\tau)q}$$

and the condition defining G is $2\int_0^{\overline{x}}\frac{\tau q h}{L}dx = mG$. Again $\overline{x}$ is defined in $r(\overline{x}) = r_A$. The steps follow those above. From production efficiency and the production function, we have $h = L\left[\frac{(1-\gamma)r}{\gamma i}\right]^{1-\gamma}$. Constant utility gives us

$$c = \frac{\overline{U}^{1/\alpha}}{G^{(1-\alpha-\beta)/\alpha}L^{\beta/\alpha}\left[\frac{(1-\gamma)r}{\gamma i}\right]^{\beta(1-\gamma)/\alpha}}.$$

Consumption efficiency and substitution for h and c allows us to get

$$L^{\beta/\alpha} = \frac{\beta^{\beta/(\alpha+\beta)}\overline{U}^{(\beta/\alpha)/(\alpha+\beta)}}{\alpha^{\beta/(\alpha+\beta)}G^{((1-\alpha-\beta)\beta)/((\alpha+\beta)\alpha)}(1+\tau)^{\beta/(\alpha+\beta)}\left[\frac{(1-\gamma)r}{\gamma i}\right]^{\beta(1-\gamma)/\alpha}\left[\Omega r(x)^{\gamma}i^{1-\gamma}\right]^{\beta/(\alpha+\beta)}}.$$

Since $w - tx = c + (1+\tau)qh = \left[\frac{\alpha+\beta}{\alpha}\right]c$, we obtain $r(x)$ in

$$w - tx = (\alpha+\beta)\frac{M(1+\tau)^{\beta/(\alpha+\beta)}}{G^{(1-\alpha-\beta)/(\alpha+\beta)}}r(x)^{\gamma\beta/(\alpha+\beta)}$$

for $M = \frac{\overline{U}^{1/(\alpha+\beta)}\alpha^{\beta/(\alpha+\beta)}\left[\Omega i^{1-\gamma}\right]^{\beta/(\alpha+\beta)}}{\alpha\beta^{\beta/(\alpha+\beta)}}$. Hence

$$w - t\overline{x} = (\alpha+\beta)\frac{(1+\tau)^{\beta/(\alpha+\beta)}M}{G^{(1-\alpha-\beta)/(\alpha+\beta)}}r_A^{\gamma\beta/(\alpha+\beta)}.$$

We have then

$$r(x)=\frac{G^{(1-\alpha-\beta)/\beta\gamma}}{M^{(\alpha+\beta)/\beta\gamma}}\frac{1}{(\alpha+\beta)^{(\alpha+\beta)/\beta\gamma}}\frac{1}{(1+\tau)^{1/\gamma}}(w-tx)^{(\alpha+\beta)/\beta\gamma}$$

and must integrate

$$2\tau\frac{G^{(1-\alpha-\beta)/\beta\gamma}}{M^{(\alpha+\beta)/\beta\gamma}}\frac{1}{(\alpha+\beta)^{(\alpha+\beta)/\beta\gamma}}\frac{1}{(1+\tau)^{1/\gamma}}\int_0^{\overline{x}}(w-tx)^{(\alpha+\beta)/\beta\gamma}dx=mG.$$

Then, after integrating the efficiency condition for the supply of G, we get

$$2\tau\frac{G^{(1-\alpha-\beta)/\beta\gamma}}{GM^{(\alpha+\beta)/\beta\gamma}}\frac{1}{(\alpha+\beta)^{(\alpha+\beta)/\beta\gamma}}\frac{1}{(1+\tau)^{1/\gamma}}\frac{1}{t\left[\frac{\alpha+\beta}{\beta\gamma}+1\right]}\left[w^{\frac{\alpha+\beta}{\beta\gamma}+1}-[w-t\overline{x}]^{\frac{\alpha+\beta}{\beta\gamma}+1}\right]=m.$$

We substitute for $w-t\overline{x}$ and obtain an equation in G alone.

As for the case with no structures, we observe that for the same parameters of utility and $\gamma=0.25$, any value of τ between zero and unity implies a city with a larger footprint than is the case for the same city with taxation in accord with marginal benefits. And since the capital-land ratio is $\frac{K(x)}{L(x)}=\frac{(1-\gamma)r(x)}{\gamma i}$, we see from the rent function that this ratio is everywhere smaller when τ increases (and G must decline at the same time). Hence a higher-tax city is a less capital-intensive city.

From above, we have

$$L^{\beta/\alpha}=\frac{\beta^{\beta/(\alpha+\beta)}\overline{U}^{(\beta/\alpha)/(\alpha+\beta)}r(x)^{-\beta(\alpha+\beta-\beta\gamma)/(\alpha+\beta)}}{\alpha^{\beta/(\alpha+\beta)}G^{((1-\alpha-\beta)\beta)/((\alpha+\beta)\alpha)}(1+\tau)^{\beta/(\alpha+\beta)}\left[\frac{(1-\gamma)}{\gamma i}\right]^{\beta(1-\gamma)/\alpha}\left[\Omega i^{1-\gamma}\right]^{\beta/(\alpha+\beta)}}.$$

The exponent on $r(x)$ is negative and less than unity. Hence a larger $r(x)$ implies a smaller $L(x)$, land per household, or a larger $r(x)$ implies a larger density of households at distance x. But G responds endogenously to a change in a parameter impacting $r(x)$. Hence we cannot say from the expression for $L(x)$ alone whether density increases or decreases with an increase in τ.

Notes

1 "Literature Review and Analysis Related to Municipal Government Consolidation," available at www.stat.nj.us/dca/affiliates/luarcc/pdf/final_consolidation_report.pdf. This report contains a valuable list of sources with comments at the end.
2 Varian (1992; pp. 427–28). Varian's 1992 textbook has a good exposition of the "Clarke Tax."
3 The Samuelson condition is that the sum of the normalized marginal utilities of all "consumers" of the government good should equal the marginal cost of producing the government good.
4 Wildasin (1986; pp. 66–69) carries out a comparative statics exercise in a model like the one above. He inquires about a small increase in the unit cost, m, of producing our G, under the assumption that utility of our households is unchanging (the open-city assumption). He obtains a result similar to ours above. His model has no commuting and no agricultural land rent. Hence he has no adjustment term like ours and does not deal with net of differential land rent change.
5 These data are reported in *The Globe and Mail*, January 8, 2011, p. A4 and are drawn from data published by Statistics Canada.
6 Michael Reich and Miranda Dietz, "All Economics is Local," *New York Times*, March 23, 2014, p. 4.

7 For 2009, manufacturing's share of gross domestic product in the United States was down to about 10.5 percent. This compares to 14.2 percent a decade earlier and to about 30 percent for the 1950s when almost all products consumed in the United States were produced there. (*New York Times*, Sunday, February 13, 2011, p. B5.)
8 *New York Times*, January 26, 2014.
9 *The Economist*, April 19, 2014, p. 10 of the Special Report.
10 *New York Times*, January 24, 2013.
11 *New York Times*, June 3, 2014, p. A15.
12 Wikipedia, November 12, 2013, "Incarceration Rates for a Selection of Nations."
13 *New York Times*, August 12, 2014, p. A3.
14 *The Economist*, May 17, 2014, pp. 54–55.
15 Wikipedia, November 12, 2013, "US Cities with High Murder Rate (2012)."
16 *The Economist*, April 23, 2011, p. 54.

10 Populations, slums and planning

Population projections and the proliferation of large cities. Slums come in different forms. Planning evolving cities. Planning new cities.

Introduction

It is easy to forget that economics is about people, people and markets, and the outcomes people receive from interacting with others in markets, and in society more broadly. Is there a particular urban dimension that economics takes account of or should be taking account of or has been neglected? There is a sense in which a city can alert us to poverty because groups of poor congregate in the centers of cities and can be seen begging quite regularly where pedestrian traffic is dense. But the urban setting may conceal the poor because we grow accustomed to seeing people begging and we develop routines that allow us to ignore them. The Fabians in England were presumably upset by the throngs of poor people on the streets of London around 1900 and developed a socialist approach to economics and government activity. The Fabian agenda became a political platform of various parties in various countries and socialist policies such as unemployment insurance, welfare for the impoverished and pensions for the aged were enacted in the legislature in London. It is difficult to believe that such policies would have been pursued if poor people had not been seen in many places in many large cities, once the industrial revolution was well underway. These "socialist" policies are part of a critique of "the free market system." Modern social theory takes it for granted that a free market system leaves many behind and governments, acting for "the public," must be the carer of last resort.

Do cities make people, at the margin, poor? Do poor people end up poorer because they are living in cities? Are cities special settings for lifting poor people up to a decent living? When observers praise post-1979 Chinese reforms for raising 100 million people out of poverty, are they glossing over an urban dimension to this process? It does seem that people who were rural and poor and remained in the country have been bypassed by the prosperity in China that has lifted so many out of poverty. In this sense, improving one's standard of living turned on getting away from rural stagnation.

The United Nations researchers in the Population Division provide interesting projections for the populations of cities in various parts of the world over the next decades. However, they do not project the number of people living under two dollars a day or the number of people living in slums. They indicate that in 2007 the world had 19 "urban agglomerations," cities with more than 10 million people. Eleven of these are capitals. By 2025, the world is projected to have eight more urban agglomerations: Asia is expected to get five, Africa two and Europe one. These very large places contained about 8 percent of the world's urban population in 2005 and will have about 10 percent in 2025. Next down are the "large cities" with populations of between five and ten million. There were 31 of these in 2005 and there are expected to be 48 in 2025. These places account for 7 percent of the world's urban population in both years. Three-quarters of these cities are in the developing world. "Medium cities" have between one million and five million people. There were 361 of these in 2005 and there are projected to be 526 in 2025. In 2005 they accounted for 22 percent of the world's urban population. "Small cities" with populations between one half and one million were 448 in number in 2005,[1] and are projected to number 551 in 2025. These two smaller classes have about 32 percent of the urban population and will have a slightly smaller proportion in 2025. This leaves about half the world's urban population in places that contain under a half million people. We see that though the growth of "large agglomerations" receives much attention in the press, the future urbanization of the people of the world will take place in cities of a wide variety of sizes, most under ten million people.

Perhaps unsurprisingly, much city growth derives from natural increase. China is something of an outlier with much urbanization occurring because of rural-urban migration. Slums do not take root only because rural people are flocking to the edges of large cities. Natural increase in a large city can throw off new groups of poor people that need low-cost accommodation. And it turns out that there has been more city-to-city migration and rural-rural migration and urban-rural migration in recent times than rural-urban migration. Policies must take account of the net increase regardless of which forces are responsible for the increase. Decision-makers in countries around the world have expressed concern for their "population distribution" over many recent decades and often the response is to attempt to control in-migration, often to cities. Chinese officials have been attempting to force "illegal" residents of Beijing to return to their home towns. They are closing down so-called shelter dwellings and basement accommodation that house some one million people. Traffic congestion in Beijing is also a concern and the conditions for obtaining a vehicle permit have become very strict.[2] A new report (March 2014, World Bank and Development Research Center of China) recommends that China curb sprawl by reforming land acquisition at city peripheries, easing up on granting migrants urban residency permits, and allowing local governments to borrow directly within central government guidelines. More stable local government revenue streams are needed. "Ensuring that cities are livable and environmentally sustainable [in China] will require strong government action to provide sufficient public transport, public schools, public hospitals, parks, and effective zoning, among other public goods" (Stiglitz 2014). Researchers at the UN's population division oppose interventions to limit rural-urban migration. India's 31 percent of population that is urban makes it a notable outlier among developing nations, an under-urbanized large country.

In 1950, about 50 percent of the world's population was in places with more than 10,000 persons. By 2050 this figure is estimated to be up to 70 percent. For China the comparable figures are 35 and 75 percent. Hence the very rapid urbanization of China. By 2025, estimates put Beijing and Guangzhou in the top 25 of the world's richest cities, by city GNP. Today Shanghai and Hong Kong are already in that exclusive group. The top five are Tokyo, New York, Los Angeles, Chicago and London and they are expected to remain as leaders. Tokyo is in a class by itself, being the largest, richest and most "primate" because it is the business, financial, cultural and political capital of Japan. Mumbai, Delhi and Rio de Janeiro are expected to move into the group of richest world cities by 2025. Currently Rio and Sao Paulo in Brazil have about 16 percent of the nation's population and 30 percent of the nation's GDP. Meanwhile, Mexico City has become a dominant place for foreign firms to base their Latin American operations.[3]

Slums

Charles Booth became wealthy in the shipping business in the late part of the nineteenth century and, still in his forties, began with his wife Mary a large study of the very poor in London, England. His voluminous study is today famous for his use of maps. He was able to draw attention to the areas of London populated with the poorest residents. Some 30 percent of families were found to be living just above starvation. And of course the British economy had grown greatly during the nineteenth century; we can infer that a high fraction of families were living on the edge of starvation around 1810. Large cities appear to have been magnets for many poor families in earlier centuries and remain so today, both in many first-world nations as well as in many third-world nations. Recall photographs of streets of tenements in New York City around 1910. Most residents were probably not on the edge of starvation. People were living in high densities in depressing apartment buildings. The lower east side of Manhattan had about 400,000 residents in 1910, about 300,000 residents in 1920 and about 150,000 in 1940. Of primary interest today is how slum-intensive cities in the future will be. This should correlate closely with the projection of the number of very low-income families in these cities in 2025.

Casual observations suggest that urbanization and a local increase in the number of families in poverty go together, the so-called "urbanization of poverty." There is some truth in this view.

- In 2002, 75 percent of the world's poor lived in rural areas.[4] In urban areas, the proportion of poor (living at under one dollar per day) declined from 14 percent to 13 percent between 1993 and 2002. In rural areas the proportion also declined, from 37 percent to 30 percent. Obviously prosperity in cities draws migrants from the countryside and this phenomenon alone can account for an improvement in the standard of living of many rural people.
- About 100 million rural poor rose out of poverty in China over this period. "Simulations indicate that, at current trends, it would take many decades for the majority of the poor to be living in urban areas."[5] As of 2011, some 78 percent of residents of cities in poor countries live in slums. China has 38 percent of its urban population living in slums; India 55 percent; Brazil 37 percent. Poorer nations such as Pakistan has 74 percent of its urban residents living in slums; Nigeria has 79 percent; Bangladesh has 85 percent; Tanzania has 92 percent and Ethiopia has 99 percent.[6] In developed nations less than 10 percent of urban residents live in slums.
- In addition to low incomes, family size can contribute to impoverishment. The rural areas of Africa, Latin America and the Caribbean have high dependency ratios, ranging from 74 to 100 dependents per 100 adults of working age. The urban areas of Africa also have high dependency ratios (around 70) while those elsewhere are in the 54 to 59 range. Asia's dependency ratio is low, at 49, because China's rate is something of a low outlier.
- In 1954 British life expectancy was 70 years and 0.03 died in infancy. For Egypt, the figures were 44 and 0.35. When we move up to 2009, the British figures are 80 years and 0.0055 and the Egyptian figures are 70 and 0.021. Children per woman fell in Britain from 2.3 to 1.8 between 1954 and 2009 and in Egypt from 7.0 to 1.8. The consequences

> of these life expectancy and mortality rates is that in 2011 fully one half of Egypt's population will be under 25 while about 31 percent are now under 25 in the UK. There remains the vexing problem of finding adequate employment for all the young people entering the working age in various lower-income nations, like Egypt. However, by 2040, the US census bureau argues that the Egyptian population distribution will be much like that of the UK today.[7]

There is no strong evidence that there will not be millions of poor needing accommodation of some sort in cities in the future. Is there a formula that can be applied that will lead to the poor in cities being reasonably well housed and being reasonably smoothly integrated into their local economy? For a slum to be vibrant economically, it must be well connected to job centers with buses and commuter trains, must have clean water and some form of waste removal, residents must have a longer term interest in their homes (some recognition of some form of rudimentary "ownership") and the community must not be plagued with violence and theft. Given these matters as settled, small-scale local "industrial" activity can take root in various homes, and community action can develop to make sure that some basic level of sanitation and drinkable water is available. Schools and clinics come next. Clearly placing families in bare-bones, high-rise buildings at the edge of large cities is likely to not work well. Local "industrial" activity is generally very difficult to pursue in a high-rise apartment and being located far from the center of a large city generally makes access to employment difficult. Many new homes made available to low-income residents in Mexico under a government-run mortgage program are in difficult-to-access places.[8]

The United Nations Population Division reports[9] that in 2005 37 percent of the urban population in developing countries were living in slums, some 840 million people. A slum is defined by these researchers as a residence lacking one or more of: durability of the basic structure; sufficient living area; access to clean water; access to improved sanitation; or secure tenure. In most areas, it is the lack of adequate sanitation and living space that are the most common types of deficiency. Clearly both of these deficiencies would be less of a problem for residents of a rural area. Observers single out the lavatory deficit in urban India as a major social problem.[10] However, rural folk have poorer access to basic health care and education. In developing countries 15 percent of urban residents were not connected to electricity sources compared with 44 percent of rural residents. UN researchers estimate that rural residents are twice as likely to be lacking proper sanitation compared with urban residents. It is unclear whether a poor person living in a city in developing nations or in the country is more threatened with starvation. Life expectancy is generally lower for the rural poor and there is of course a net migration from country to city for low-income people. The "more mobile" of the rural poor become the builders for the most part of the new slums, often on the edges of the cities of the developing world.

We may view being poor but adequately nourished in a rural area as not a bad way to live out one's life. Many rural poor are, however, getting by at near starvation living standards. The "more mobile" do not head to cities for the bright lights but rather because their life prospects "on the farm" are generally very poor. And depending on what sort of a shack one ends up occupying in the city, life in an urban slum can in fact be an improvement over life back "on the farm." The basic services in slums are often steadily improved and the shacks are often rebuilt to a higher standard of construction. Ideally the first resident of a slum-dwelling ends up living in a better place later in life and sees her children ascend as adults to lives in homes outside of the slums. Saunders (2010; Chapter 6) recounts the history of a family settling in a shack on the edge of Istanbul and observing their slum,

Harem, evolve into an adequate town, a place in which the squatters acquired rights to their plots of land. The "modernization" view considers slums as transitory communities that shrink away as the economy of the larger community develops. Marx *et al.* (2013) take issue with this view. They dug up evidence that shows that many slums are "poverty traps" that show no sign of contracting. The slums have many families stuck inside the communities for multiple generations. In addition to inadequate sanitation and inadequate access to safe water, they see many slums as inadequately connected to the surrounding city in the sense that governance is left to local "lords" of one kind or another. The political class of the larger community leaves the slum in a governance limbo and of course this contributes to inadequate policing and an under-investment in basic infrastructure. Marx *et al.* urge the outside world to collect reasonable quality data on slum communities so that effective policies can be developed with a view to addressing the most egregious problems besetting these places.

Janice Perlman, a graduate student in anthropology, spent six month intervals in three locations in Rio de Janeiro in 1969. She lived with and interviewed residents of her three *favelas* (slum areas). She came away with a portrait of relatively cohesive communities with parents anxious for good schooling for their children and reasonable urban services such as running water, reasonable sanitation infrastructure and electricity. She returned in 2003 and was able to locate 41 percent of her original interviewees (Perlman 2005). She interviewed them once again and where possible also interviewed their children and grandchildren. Of the original interviewees she located, 37 percent were still in *favelas*, 25 percent were in public housing and 34 percent were in neighborhoods, mostly in the periphery of the city. One original interviewee she reconnected with reported: "We must not be passive. We must always strive for a better life. But at least we have our little shacks to sleep in, our TV sets to watch and our daily meals. We are neither beggars nor *marginais*." Urban services had arrived in some of her communities, houses were much sturdier, but other communities had been razed by the local government and the residents moved to public housing projects farther from the center of the city. The communities had acquired stable political leadership. Early, in response to a question on what were their rights and duties, some responded: "to obey the law and the authorities." The *favelas* were not, it seems, occupied by people seething with resentment. In 1969, 56 percent regarded their community as "very tightly united" whereas in 2003, this figure was down to 12 percent. New is the fact that considerable fear has taken root in the *favelas* because members of ubiquitous drug gangs resort to violence and killing quite regularly. "The relentless threat of violence is part of the core subtext of their lives... like grief the thing we cannot see may be the deepest part of their day."[11] Though the incomes of many residents were reasonable, these same people felt discriminated against when they had to present their addresses to someone.

Perlman reports that there were at least 752 *favelas* in Rio de Janeiro in 2003, with some 1.65 million inhabitants. The overall population of Rio is about 12 million. Of her later interviewees, 37 percent considered the state government helpful and 25 percent felt the same about the municipal government. They almost all reported that central to their aspirations was "decent work for decent pay." Such important matters as good health, education, housing, land tenure, good governance and personal security were all secondary. Rio has been noticeably impacted by the decline of the steel and shipbuilding industries and the loss of many thousands of traditional jobs. In 1969, 31 percent of her interviewees had been unemployed for more than one month in twelve while in 2003, 65 percent of interviewees of the same age had been unemployed for more than one month. Even openings in domestic service have not been buoyant, as middle-class employers had been taking on fewer servants.

The poor job situation related in part to the fraught security situation in the numerous *favelas* in Rio: young men get out of prison and have very little chance of starting a life in regular employment. Most end up as foot-soldiers for the drug lords who control the streets in many of the *favelas*. In fact considerable control of these organizations is centered in the prisons.

The World Cup took place in Rio in the summer of 2014 and the Olympics arrive in 2016. Consequently, authorities in various levels of government have recently been making large-scale attempts to gain control of the streets, in 250 *favelas*, with 36 pacification units. Police (and occasionally troops) roll in to an area with tanks and other armored vehicles, and set up permanent police stations. The city also now installs better lighting and basic public services. However, the young thugs employed by the drug lords are striking back. The killing of police officers has been a fairly regular occurrence. The costs of maintaining the new services are high and often active interest by the local government wanes. Alemao is a complex of 15 different *favelas* near the center of Rio with about 100,000 people in high density. Local authorities attempted to root out the Red Command drug organization, with limited success. Vidigal, an ocean-front *favela* was successfully brought under municipal authority and now boasts art galleries and small hotels catering to tourists. Rocinha, a *favela* near Ipanema with 170,000 residents, has had its streets made secure and now has health clinics, libraries and public transit access.[12]

Dharavi, a famous slum in Mumbai, India, is a thriving community of about one million people, with commuter rail lines on either side. Some residents are second generation. Besides having homes of people who commute to jobs elsewhere in Mumbai, many residences pursue handicraft industrial activity in small spaces. The product is often packed up and sold outside of the community. The value of annual product from the community itself is estimated to be more than US$650 million a year. It is a town or enclave of narrow dirty lanes, open sewers and cramped huts. Its virtue is of course that it is an affordable place for low-income people to live in and it exhibits solid productive activity. Mumbai, the financial center of India, is a very expensive place to be housed. Dharavi has become the center of a controversy because the land occupied by the rudimentary structures has become immensely valuable for the potential development of high-rise condominiums. The local government has a plan to clear away existing structures and create a new town with hospitals, schools, shopping complexes and high-rise apartments. Clearly Dharavi works today as a thriving place of homes and small scale "factories." Once transformed by the local government, the "town" will work very differently. Dharavi is a place today that sustains low-income families and after redevelopment will presumably offer much less for the average low-income family. Members of displaced families often have to rebuild their lives in a new place far out from, and generally poorly connected to, the center of the city.

Katherine Boo documented life in a different slum in Mumbai. She was an experienced American journalist with an interest in very poor communities. She happened to marry an Indian man, and this led her to study "the inhabitants of a single unexceptional slum over the course of several years (November 2007 to March 2011) to see who got ahead and who didn't and why, as India prospered" (Boo 2012; p. 349). Her report takes the form of a first-hand narrative-documentary. For Annawadi, her place for scrutiny in Mumbai, she "was struck by commonalities with other poor communities" in which she had spent time. She said (Boo; p. 63):

> As every slumdweller knew, there were three main ways out of poverty: finding an entrepreneurial niche, as the Husains in Annawadi had found in garbage; politics and

> corruption, in which Asha placed her hopes; and eduction. Several dozen parents were getting by on roti and salt in order to pay private school tuition.

She goes on to add: "Too often weak government intensifies instability and proves better at nourishing corruption than human capability" (Boo 2012; p. 253), and she contended that poverty "sabotaged the innate capacity of slumdwellers for moral action… In undercities governed by corruption,… it is blisteringly hard to be good. The astonishment is that some people are good and many people try to be" (Boo 2012; p. 254).

Another famous (or perhaps infamous) slum is located in East Africa in southwest Nairobi. Kibera is located roughly 5 km from the city centre. Much of its southern border is bounded by the Nairobi river and the Nairobi Dam, an artificial lake that provides drinking water to the residents of the city. UN-Habitat has released several estimations of Kibera's population, ranging between 350,000 and 1 million people.[13] It is divided into 13 villages, including Kianda, Soweto, Gatwekera, Kisumu Ndogo, Lindi, Laini Saba, Siranga/Undugu, Makina and Mashimoni. The multi-ethnic nature of Kibera has led to the community hosting a number of small ethnic conflicts throughout its century-long history. The Kenyan government owns all the land upon which Kibera stands but supplies no clinics, running water or sanitation infrastructure. One of the leading government schools in the country turns out to be located in the "town." There is a community radio station and a local railway station, but most residents use buses to access the city centre. Crime is a persistent problem in the "town."

In September 2009 the Kenyan government initiated a scheme which will end up placing the slum people in new apartments nearby. The new communities will have schools, markets and playgrounds. The first group of around 1,500 people to leave the slum were taken away by truck to 300 newly constructed apartments with a monthly rent of around US$10. The razing of the old Kibera is expected to take between two and five years to complete and is expected to cost US$1.2 billion.

Poor people and the future

A slum dwelling reflects "inadequate" income. To reduce the number of families living in slums, lower-income families need more income. More income per family requires more jobs with a basic wage. Poor rural people migrating to cities in search of a better life, higher lifetime income, is a phenomenon as old as history. It probably accelerated with the arrival of the Industrial Revolution around 1800 in England. There was a push from labor-saving technical progress in the agricultural sector and a pull from basic economic expansion in the nation, centered mostly in towns and cities. Cities almost everywhere need dwellings for low-income people. A central problem with slums as a "solution" to the housing problem is that the houses often end up on plots in which the occupants have no ownership. This means that the resident has almost no incentive to construct a durable house and the resident remains forever anxious about the possibility of "eviction." In addition the residents have almost no leverage with the local government for gaining urban services. De Soto (2000) became well known when he argued for governments to develop policies to assure low-income residents that they had complete ownership in their plots and houses. These low-income people could then use their homes as collateral for loans to start up their own businesses. Ownership could then create the possibility of unleashing considerable entrepreneurship among low-income folk. Ownership would also galvanize community action which in turn could work toward the acquisition of basic services for a low-income community (schools, sanitation, clean water, policing, etc.).

Glaeser (1998; p. 154) sketches a depressing scenario concerning poor families in contemporary cities of the United States:

> Perhaps the right view is that new cities initially attract all income groups, possibly because of their economic opportunities or because higher migration costs for the poor slow their coming to new cities. Eventually, the poor do come to the city, create social problems which stem the city's growth, and induce the wealthier members of the city to move. These wealthier members then start a new urban area which will eventually follow the same pattern. If this view is correct, we will always observe declining older cities which are mired in poverty, even though cities on the whole are still strong. . . even though the extreme concentration of the poor may doom certain cities (East St. Louis may be an example), many cities are basically unaffected by this problem.

Glaeser argues that poor people are attracted to larger cities because they can get by in such places without a car. Public transit solves their personal transportation problems. They can join social networks, perhaps of people of their own ethnic group, and benefit from such ready-made social groupings. They can take advantage of social assistance and perhaps local public housing. Glaeser notes that cities with over a million in population spend about six percent of their local government budgets on social welfare whereas cities under 100,000 in size spend just 0.3 percent. We must be careful not to infer that it is the generosity of the residents of the large cities that is attracting poor people to settle; large cities simply have disproportionate numbers of poor people to provide for. As of 1998 some 10 percent of all families in the United States were below the poverty line whereas in cities of over one million the poverty rate for families was almost 17 percent. Glaeser is also quite certain that the data support the view that cities are attracting their poor households rather than taking regular urban folks and making them poor.

In 2011 Toronto had more than one million residents living in low-income neighborhoods (places with an average income 20 percent or more below the city-wide average).[14] No low-income area would be referred to as a slum, however. Between 1970 and 2010 very high-income neighborhoods (average income 40 percent or more above the city-wide average) rose from 9 percent to 16 percent of all Toronto neighborhoods. Toronto does have a reputation as a city with a high proportion of immigrant residents as well as being a place to which immigrants choose to move to when they arrive in Canada. Recall the maps for the distribution of immigrants in Toronto and Chicago in Chapter 3 (Figures 3.5 and 3.6).

Sustainable cities

Two large threats to urban life today are pollution, including CO_2 emissions and prospective sea-level rise. Pollution problems are somewhat distinct for cities in poorer nations compared to those in high-income nations. In high-income nations, pollution is one of a number of problems to manage more aggressively, whereas in low-income countries officials in large cities must intervene urgently to raise the standard of basic public health. Recall the concern about the quality of air in Beijing for the 2009 Olympic Games.

One way to think about how well a city is coping with livability and sustainability is to develop indicators for (1) carbon emissions; (2) land-use intensification (countering sprawl); (3) nitrogen and sulphur oxide emissions; (4) waste recycling; (5) habitat preservation for small animals; and (6) water quality including rain water run-off. If a city can register improvements in these indicators over, say, a decade, the citizens can claim to be living in a more sustainable community. Mexico City is famous for its huge population (about 19.5 million) and its air pollution. Vehicles in Mexico City are responsible for 82 percent of nitrous oxide emissions, 50 percent of sulphur dioxide emissions and 31 percent of VOCs (volatile organic compounds), some of which are the result of burning diesel fuel in the engines of vehicles. The search for vehicle engines that burn clean, those with minimal emissions, is clearly a high priority around the world. Perhaps novel, however, is that the high densities of very big cities has a carbon economizing dimension. Bettencourt and West (2010; p. 912) note that

> most large, developed cities are "greener" than their national average in terms of per capita carbon emissions. It is as yet unclear whether this is also true for cities undergoing extremely rapid development, as in China or India, where data are poor or lacking.

Glaeser also notes that Hong Kong, a very high-income settlement has per capita emissions of CO_2 of about one third the level of those in the United States; Singapore's come in at about one half those in the United States. Glaeser notes that it is the high density form of these places that contributes much to the low use of energy and carbon-based fuels in particular.

The heating and cooling of buildings, including residences, involves much energy use. Of interest here is that Canada's housing stock comprises 25 percent of dwellings constructed before 1960 and 43 percent after 1980.[15] More recently built residences are more energy efficient in large part because of the arrival of new technologies for heating, cooling and insulating. Building codes get updated as new technologies come on stream. As Barber (2013; p. 319) puts it:

> In New York City, it is estimated that a startling 80 percent of carbon emissions come from buildings rather than vehicles, so programs such as LEED (Leadership in Energy and Environmental Design) can have significant impact regardless of what happens in Albany or Washington, DC.

Southern Alberta hosts a pilot project in geothermal community heating. The Government of Canada (Natural Resources Canada) partnered with other governmental organizations and private firms to construct a 52-home community at Drake Landing, in Okotoks, with large solar collectors on double garages, which supplied heat to a specially engineered, underground heat-storage system—a BTES (Borehole Thermal Energy Storage). The stored heat is accessed by the homes in the winter and the whole project economizes on hydrocarbon fuel that might otherwise be needed to heat the homes during the cold months. The system has 144 boreholes drilled 37 m into the earth. There are two 125,000-litre steel tanks underground involved in the storage system. An estimated 260 tonnes of greenhouse gas releases are avoided by deriving heat from the sun. Including the solar heating system, the homes ended up costing under US$500,000 each. Communities in Europe pioneered the use of large-scale solar heat storage.

"Smart growth" is a term used to characterize a certain pattern of urban growth and economic development. In part it is a view of development that is counter to "sprawl" (Platt 2014; pp. 162–63). Smart growth is, however, also concerned with sustainability of a community quite generally. One is drawn to comparing such a development with, say, edge development in Houston or even some older cities such as Boston, Baltimore or Detroit. How might a smart-growth community look compared to one governed by older zoning and building covenants? Smart-growth people envisage more park space, more energy efficiency in new homes and smaller lot sizes. They are also partial to mass transit over automobile commuting. It is not difficult to applaud the message of these advocates. However, there are the basic ingredients of choice in the background: communities have to be linked to employment centers wherever they are; the residents need incomes of various levels to live on and the families that move into homes in edge communities have preferences, shaped by their upbringing with their parents and siblings, and the larger society, including mass media. Homes in smart-growth projects must sell for prices that cover their costs.

A sprawl development at the edge of, say, Houston may violate the tenets of smart growth but may have homes with the large yards that families like and can afford. Houston has, roughly speaking, grown up with mostly automobile commuting and highly decentralized places of employment. We do not suggest that sprawl, low-density development and much automobile travel is the benchmark case. Many hundreds of thousands of families with high incomes compete to live in apartments in the downtowns of New York City and London and Paris. Families are consumption units, with tastes, incomes and preferences. The smart-growth enthusiasts can offer their settlement options to households and hope to attract buyers with good incomes and compatible aspirations. A large lot is, however, a "commodity" that many families hope to have with their home and many ordinary families choose such living arrangements when they can afford them. Sprawl, the four-letter word of the smart-growth advocates, is a byproduct of families desiring a particular housing package. Smart-growth promoters must not just preach and offer a few show projects; they must make families want suburbs with small lots, much pedestrian activity and much mass transit. Smart-growth advocates must convert many people to an alternative way of living. This is difficult to successfully engineer. It has, however, happened quite often before. A campaign against smoking, for example, has succeeded in turning the activity into an activity of a minority.

Part of Platt's campaign is blunt criticism of those with rather different views of society and cities:

> *Aerotropolis: The Way we'll Live Next*, by John D. Kasarda and Greg Lindsay, and Edward Glaeser's *Triumph of the City: How Our Greatest Invention makes us Richer, Smarter, Greener, Healthier and Happier* view cities first and foremost as the domain of the plutocracy, namely those who are or hope to be among the top few percent of Americans... who earn and own as much as everyone else combined.... It is rather stark to write off everyone outside the magic circle of the wealthy and privileged as "losers".... "Winning" also may be defined in terms of family, friendships, spirituality, public service, artistic pursuits, sports and outdoor recreation, and other life interests.
>
> (Platt 2014; p. 8)

Nicholas Lemann says:"Most people are looking for something pretty mundane: a neighborhood, a patch of ground, a measure of peace and security, a family, status, dignity."[16] Platt's is a historical take on how views of the good city have evolved. He contrasts top-down and bottom-up development of urban priorities and initiatives. He believes that "urban policies of the past century have been dominated by confidence in the infallibility of expert-driven solutions – architects in the earlier decades, developers and public officials in the postwar decades, and assorted policy wonks to the present time" (Platt 2014; p. 5). He chooses not to concentrate on green buildings, low-impact development (LID), transit-oriented development (TOD), urban farming and forestry, and ecological restoration. He advocates "Humane Urbanism," an effort to make cities and suburbs greener, healthier and safer, more equitable and multi-cultural, more efficient in the use of energy and water, and more people-friendly and fun. He considers that the Smart Growth/New Urbanist movement has helped to foster Human Urbanism.

The Congress for the New Urbanism founded in 1993 advocates revising zoning codes to allow for higher densities, diversity in building styles, mixed-use neighborhoods, front porches, sidewalks and protection of green spaces. Smart growth as envisaged by the National Association of Home Builders includes open space conservation, compact mixed-use development, revitalization of older downtowns, viable public transit, coordination of regional planning authorities and equitable sharing of fiscal resources across metropolitan regions. New Urbanists acknowledge that private profit and public interest may be incompatible in some cases. This is an argument for regulatory intervention to protect households.

The US Green Building Council (USGBC) has established its LEED system for certifying environmentally supportive and health-promoting building practices. Five qualities are highlighted: sustainable sites; water efficiency; energy and atmosphere; materials and resources; and indoor environmental quality. The LEED system also pays attention to locations and linkages, awareness and education, innovation in design, and regional impacts. LEED certification at one of four levels of merit is made by the Green Building Certification Institute (GBCI), established in 2008. Some 1.6 billion square feet of buildings, new and renovated, have been certified as of 2014. A new category of LEED certification is Green Neighborhood Development. Urban reforestation has been espoused in many places. Half a million trees were planted over a 15-year period in Chicago. Chicago city hall has a substantial green space growing on its roof. Los Angeles is on a planting crusade for a second million trees. New York City has launched its million tree campaign, part of Mayor Bloomberg's PlaNYC program. Smaller cities in the United States are involved in their own tree-planting programs. Olmstead's Central Park in a sense compensated for the under-supply of open space in New York City as it grew rapidly. London and Paris led in developing large open spaces for their urban residents.

China has joined the nations who are striving to create functioning, sustainable cities. *The Economist* reports:

> Few countries could dream of building a large city from scratch, let alone an eco one, but China has the advantage of an autocratic approach to urban planning (and to governance in general)... The 30 square kilometres of inhospitable terrain near the northern port city of Tianjin became a test bed [for new eco urbanization].[17]

A significant rise in sea levels around the world leaves many cities with immensely costly interventions, foremost being large-scale diking.[18] Some argue that when Florida's coasts are noticeably impacted by sea-level rise, the voting public in the United States will become seriously engaged in actions to control CO_2 emissions. It took an air pollution crisis in London in the early 1950s to get policies in place to roll back the use of dirty coal in heating homes and it took a different sort of air pollution crisis in Los Angeles in the early 1960s to get policies in place to have vehicles emit less NO_x, SO_2 and carbon monoxide. With regard to the future, India and Japan laid out plans, in November, 2010, for building 24 green cities with clean energy supplies and advanced waste recycling systems. Leading firms in the development are Hitachi and Mitsubishi. Saudi Arabia has hired Cisco to assist with planning four new cities there and IBM has set up a Smarter Cities Challenge with a prize of US$50 million of free development technology for the winning city. Technology companies are competing to gain much revenue from software and hardware sales to be used for improving the design and functioning of cities in the future. Barcelona has installed sensors in its parks that measure soil moisture: US$60 million has been saved by doing sprinkling in parks more parsimoniously. Early in 2014 Barber (2013; p. 261) describes some of the tech activity:

> Smart sensors of every kind are being used in cities across the world, including Cairo, Dubai, Kochi, Malaga, Malta, Yokohama, Songdo and Southampton. Santander, Spain, may have the world's most extensive sensor network, with the company Libelium having installed 400 devices to locate parking spots and 700 more to measure and control ambient parameters for noise and carbon monoxide as well as temperature and sunlight.

Regulation of urban development

Most cities in the modern parts of the world have planners in their municipal governments. This reflects a view that without central direction a city will evolve and grow in ways that are clearly undesirable. This is a bit paradoxical. Economists often contend that leaving economic development "to the market" will lead to better results than having specialists direct or plan economic development. To be sure, economists recognize the danger in advanced economies of natural monopolies, unregulated externalities and markets with clear informational asymmetries, such as banking for example. The recognition leads to the introduction of agencies to eliminate or at least mitigate these well-known "market failures." But why pervasive planning for cities? What is the market failure that direct intervention is addressing? Zoning is a standard instrument of government regulation in cities. Here one argues that the free market might lead to a noisy auto-body shop in a residential area and zoning or land-use restrictions can pre-empt such a problem. In fact the noisy shop is really only a problem when it gets sited after residences have been established in the area. The "late" arrival of the noisy shop will lower the values of properties nearby and this is deemed unfair. If the noisy shop were sited first, then presumably the price of the building lots nearby would reflect the irksome noise of the shop and residents entering would take account of the problem as well as the low price for the lots. Zoning in this case makes sense only when the noisy shop arrives in a residential area later in a sequence of arrivals.

Zoning has also been used to stratify neighborhoods. Thus when zoning dictates relatively large lots for an area as well as restrictions favoring expensive dwellings on those lots, zoning is being used indirectly to exclude lower-income residents from the area in question. Implicitly higher-income residents want to live in an area with other higher-income residents. This sort of zoning generally implies that each household ends up paying a similar amount of municipal taxes and this is deemed desirable by many observers. If someone can insert a small home into a neighborhood of large homes, the owner of the small home will generally end up paying a relatively low dollar amount of municipal tax each year and this is deemed undesirable by many observers. The small-dwelling household gets the same local public services including schooling for children as does the large-dwelling household, while the former pays less because its municipal tax burden is lighter. Zoning can rule out such potential free-riding for local services by the late entrant with the small home.

Basic economics tells us that land-use regulation in cities involves the allocation of land for roads, parks and subway stops. Cities function well when the movement of vehicles and people is not too congested. Cities function poorly when the local "transportation system" fails to provide for a reasonable flow of vehicles and people. "The market" cannot be relied on to provide for an adequate "transportation system" for a city. There can be adaptation, of course. A city that is growing and has a very congested center will likely see economic activity develop most rapidly away from the center. Still, it takes a "planner" to dictate that certain bits of land are for streets, parks and subway entrances. Houston, Texas is famous for being a large modern city without zoning. Nevertheless it resembles other so-called large sunbelt cities of the United States. There are restrictions on lot sizes for new homes as well as regulations governing the provision of parking for tenants and customers of shops, lawyers and physicians. The city has been criticized for being somewhat more sprawling than other cities and less pedestrian-friendly. Though Houston has an identifiable downtown it also has subcenters including Uptown, Texas Medical Center, Midtown, Greenway Plaza, Energy Corridor, Westchase and Greenspoint. Its economy is robust and its growth is conspicuous. Even during the financial crisis of 2008–09, the market for new housing was very active. There are two modern freeways around the city (Interstate 610 Loop and Beltway 8) and these clearly exert an influence on the evolution of large-scale land use. Though Houston voted down the introduction of zoning in 1948, 1962 and 1993, it still is in fact a city evolving with land-use direction from above, though not heavy-handed direction.

From economics to policy design

Economics is a body of quite standard "doctrine" and models. The so-called Walrasian model of an economy is a reasonable benchmark. There are dynamic versions involving standard formulations of assets for capital goods in equilibrium and households in a savings-consumption equilibrium. The theory of international trade has departed by either making technologies distinct across places (Ricardo) or endowments distinct across places (Hechscher–Ohlin–Samuelson). Krugman has focused on transportation cost frictions and local scale economies in trade. His approach takes standard economics far along into quite distinctive "urban economics." If one were to descend from "textbook economics" to urban economics, a few of Krugman's research papers on trade and geography would be a reasonable place to start. But many urban problems turn on externalities, particularly congestion on transportation links. Hence relative to "standard economics," urban economics seldom strays far from standard models with scale economies of various sorts and externalities of various sorts, added in. This makes urban economics both complicated economics and messy, which suggests a problem by problem approach to studying urban phenomena.

Though this makes obvious sense, one is hard-pressed to move from the problem via problem analyses to policy formulation. Policy change for an economy is like tossing a rock into a pond: there is the initial wave when the rock hits and then the ripples travel away. Policy works best when all the impacts are anticipated; but this is difficult to get right consistently. Since urban economics is dealing with essentially messy versions of standard models, the design of good policies, policies that do what is expected and not do "collateral damage" are hard to come up with. A posture of "do no harm" when intervening in a specific urban planning problem probably makes a great deal of sense. But such a posture is not easy to maintain. The world has many experts and an expert generally has strong convictions of the merits of his or her views. Incrementalism in policy intervention seems to be the best course of action in order to avoid doing large-scale harm, but economists know well that an improvement in the performance of a market by direct regulation, even a small improvement, can ricochet into other markets and yield a negative welfare gain overall. (This follows from "the theory of the second best.")

Urban economics is then difficult economics because it deals frontally with scale economies and externalities, and policy design based on good economics is freighted with complexities. Recall our discussion in Chapter 1 of the complexity of an adaptive equilibrium and later of path dependency in the development of an economy that has scale economies. Even cost–benefit analysis can be used poorly. Edward Glaeser[19] argues that "environmental reviews are only focused on the local environmental impact of building the project, but not the global environmental impact of NOT building the project." A severe scarcity of affordable housing can result when cities zone for landmark districts, height restrictions for new apartment buildings, and sidewalk set-backs. "Efforts to permit more land to be developed or to allow more development on a given piece of land often meet resistance from neighbors, who worry that noise will increase, light will be blocked and parking will become more difficult."[20] Dewan's short article focuses on what appears to be a crisis in the availability of rental accommodation in many cities in the United States.

Another dimension of policy design is the identification of winners and losers. No policy change is perfectly neutral with respect to the distribution of costs and benefits across individuals or similar groups of individuals. Economics contends that a good policy intervention will be one in which the winners can compensate the losers and still come out ahead. Compensation is, however, carried out infrequently. At the macro level, such interventions as tax changes can often be implemented with the winners and losers left largely uninformed. Intervene, move forward and losers will with luck be compensated later with a subsequent policy intervention. At the city and neighborhood level, however, a policy intervention can yield gains and losses to various individuals or groups that are easily discerned. Prospective losers seldom remain passive. Compensation becomes a central issue. Really good policy interventions can be difficult to implement. "Do no harm" does not mean do nothing to make cities work well for the current and future residents, but it suggests: maintain skepticism when policy activism appears to be the prevailing mode of "urban planning." Governments are essential for the task of restraining competition among lower units of government or even regulating government lower down. For example, a few state governments might get into regular bidding wars in an effort to attract new firms and end up subsidizing an entering firm at a very high rate to pre-empt what other state governments are doing to attract the new firm. Such situations are sometimes referred to as "races to the bottom," competition that leads to poor outcomes. If the process of attracting the new firm could be coordinated by the competing state governments, it is easy to envisage better outcomes emerging. The natural coordinator is a higher level of government. There is a principle here: higher levels of government have an important coordination role that can eliminate the adverse effects of some kinds of competition among lower levels of government. Government at every level has a role as arbiter of last resort, the distributor of costs and benefits of the actions of agents over various individuals and groups being impinged upon. Local governments and their boards do this and government one layer up can be called in under appeal. Distributing or redistributing the costs and benefits of actions of agents over those impinged upon is not a function that can be finessed away by any government of a high quality. The distributing function is there in every society, large and small. It gets done, sometimes with little rancour and recrimination, and often with hard feelings by those who see themselves as losers in the redistribution.

In the Province of Ontario zoning decisions are left to each local or municipal government. Many zoning decisions represent large financial redistributions. If ten residential properties can be re-zoned to make way for a high-rise apartment building, it is generally the case that the basic parcel of land becomes more valuable in the new or non-conforming use (with an apartment building rather than with ten single family homes). Many municipal government decisions have such "redistributions" associated with them. However, if an applicant for a building permit in a city in Ontario feels that his or her case is not being handled properly, the applicant can go to the Ontario Municipal Board (the OMB) to appeal. The OMB becomes an arbiter that settles differences. Without the OMB, an applicant would presumably head to the court system for a judgment and, on average, higher costs would be incurred by all. The OMB is essentially a dedicated court, specializing in municipal law. The efficiency argument would be that a specialist court for municipal government disputes is less costly for decision-making overall than what one could get in a general purpose court. Opinions differ on this matter. Some argue that pleaders with deep pockets can generally get the decision they want by heading out to the OMB.

Richard Florida, well known for his views about good cities, has set out ten rules for good "quality of place." It is fair to say that he favors cities with safe streets and downtowns that are interesting for being out in both day and night. He feels that a city must nurture its "creative class" to be a prosperous place and a city that attracts new entrants in a process of growth. Before we turn to his ten rules, it is useful to keep in mind places in the United States that have been successful in recent years. Near the top in many lists would be Atlanta, Houston, Phoenix and San Jose, a center of Silicon Valley, south of San Francisco. These are places that have exhibited rapid growth over the past 20 years and they tend to be low-density communities oriented to commuting on freeways by private automobile. One might refer to them as decentralized in the location of centers of employment. Houston is flat and sprawling. The downtowns of these dynamic cities do not draw people in at all times of the day and on weekends. In this sense they are different from older cities like Boston, New York and San Francisco. One should resist referring to these places as lacking in people-friendly places other than suburban malls but they do lack vibrant downtowns compared to New York, Boston and San Francisco. Would Richard Florida say such communities were inadequate in certain respects? There is then a tension here between cities that are centers of income and population growth and others that are famous for their people-friendly spaces. Here are Florida's desiderata.[21]

1 Good cities like "Toronto, Vancouver, New York and San Francisco" must get more affordable housing built near their centers since living in these cities has become so expensive. The logical route is the development of such accommodation in tall buildings. Low-rise near downtown is too expensive.
2 Downtowns must not be taken over by "the skyscraper canyons of Asia." The centers of good cities needs a mix of tall buildings and low-rise structures. "Creativity thrives in places like New York and San Francisco amid a downtown mix of towers and older, low-rise industrial buildings and denser suburbs."
3 "A new round of spending on urban transit can spark denser development and greater human connectivity." Such programs of "build-it and the city will prosper" have not worked out well in many cities in the United States. Attractive mass transit systems are very costly and ridership has never expanded sufficiently to cover variable costs, let alone fixed costs.
4 "It is time for people to pay for the roads they use." Florida supports congestion charges, preferably those that vary with time of day. Our view is that in principle congestion charges make good sense but they are difficult to introduce and operate. A supportive factor is a city with already a high intensity of mass transit use. In addition, a place like Manhattan, an island with not too many "entrances," is easier to "engineer" than a place like Toronto, with many roads and streets entering the downtown area.
5 An equitable city "requires upgrading millions of precarious jobs in the service sector." The redistribution of income in any modern society is a complicated activity that

authorities in a single city should probably leave to a higher level of government. For example if City A manages to set a high minimum wage within its boundaries, certain activities will leave the city for City B. We take for granted that considerable poverty in a city makes that city unattractive.

6 "Diversity can make a city a cauldron of creativity... but great cities are becoming so expensive that creative people are being edged out." Immigrants tend to migrate to cities with good employment prospects. Thus diversity is tied closely to current prosperity in a city. Decision-makers should do all they can to make their city attractive to newcomers in a variety of ways. It will be difficult to create islands of low-cost living for artists and "musical innovators."

7 "Many cities have improved their environmental records but they can do better." In addition they must foster resilience given recent "ice storms and hurricanes." No city can on its own protect itself from the flooding caused by a hurricane, of course.

8 Safety for all. "In Newark, Detroit, Chicago's South Side and Oakland, there are still killing fields, and not nearly enough is being done to halt the violence." Safety for all including poor people should be a higher priority.

9 "Favoring the automobile promotes obesity, high blood pressure, heart disease and diabetes... we can design cities for better health, lowering the cost of care in the process." Cities in the United States most committed to commuting by automobile have been some of the most prosperous and dynamic.

10 "Great cities have decent schools, safe streets, good jobs and affordable housing, all of which should make them friendly to families." Not so easy to accomplish but well worth striving for.

Some of Richard Florida's ideas seem to be at odds with how prosperous cities have been developing in the United States. Houston, Phoenix and Atlanta are sprawling entities with automobile commuting the dominant mode. Economic activity is itself decentralized compared with, say, older cities in the northeast. It makes little sense to try to make these new cities compact and oriented to, say, subway commuting. It does of course make much sense to zone for and invest in attractive places like Times Square in New York for pedestrians to congregate and interact. Oddly enough, New Yorkers make do with much walking since owning and operating an automobile is so expensive. Mayor de Blasio has a target of zero traffic fatalities as part of his agenda for New York City. He is looking at the successes of Stockholm in this regard for guidance.[22] The mixing of attractive apartment buildings and condominiums in downtowns with office and retail activity is a reasonable strategy. It is very important for residents in these buildings to feel safe and be enthusiastic to be out at night in clubs, pubs and theatres in the high-density areas. High-quality policing is necessary. Good schools are needed to keep young families interested in downtown living. Reasonable zoning and provision of public services, and solid economic growth for a city goes a considerable distance towards creating a "good city." The cities that struggle along many dimensions are those that are experiencing, or have experienced, economic decline.

New York City is an interesting case. It was near bankruptcy in 1975 and got its finances reorganized and its public sector restructured, a process that included lay-offs of police and fire people. Attention was focused on a seeming net migration of businesses out to distant suburbs, many in Connecticut. But the economy reversed its downward trend and has seen much new building and rising rents and home prices. One can think of three specific policies that have had a large influence. First, policing on the streets became a priority in recent years. The crime rate is well down, as it has been in other large American cities. Mayor

Giuliani's "zero-tolerance" roll-out was part of a wider set of reforms, parts of which had been underway since 1985. Police were required to more strictly enforce the law against subway fare evasion, public drinking, public urination, graffiti artists and the "squeegee men" (who had been wiping windshields of stopped cars and aggressively demanding payment). According to a 2001 study (by George Kelling and William Sousa) of crime trends in New York, rates of both petty and serious crime fell suddenly and significantly, and continued to drop for the following ten years. While crime was declining the rate of unemployment in New York City also declined considerably. "Street life" in most public spaces is now vibrant, including at night. Between 2006 and 2013 tourist visits rose from 43.8 to 54 million. Second, the subway was cleaned up in a policy of "zero tolerance" for graffiti. The last graffitied train was removed from service in 1989. And third, the municipal government found funds to implement the clean-up of the streets and the subway system. The city's economy "was made to grow."

This last factor in New York City's boom is the most subtle, of course. To revive the economy, one needed in part to clean up the city and make streets safe, and this is costly. When a city's economy is down, the public sector is usually squeezed for funds to boost activity in the public sector. The most plausible explanation for New York City's revival is that key sparks burned brightly in the private sector and the economy demonstrated signs of growth. About the same time, aggressive activities in the public sector got the subway cleaned and the streets safer. The better the economy performed, the more funds there were for more productive interventions by the public sector. When we reflect on the years of Michael Bloomberg as Mayor (2001–13), we see many innovations that appear to have taken New York City to a new plane of livability and prosperity. An economist would pause and ask: how much of the recent success New York City has enjoyed can be ascribed to the presence of Michael Bloomberg as mayor and how much can be ascribed to an exogenously driven boom in the city's economy, that any mayor might have placed him or herself in the midst of? Bloomberg was interventionist and innovative in many ways. He has become renowned for his so-called data-driven approach to analysis and policy development, the main features of which are listed below.[23]

1 He became famous or notorious for his anti-smoking regulations for restaurants and parks. He targeted public health with his initiative for smaller soda bottles being marketed in the city.
2 He introduced "smart" signals to keep traffic flowing more freely in congested parts of the city. He introduced legislation for congestion charges for vehicles entering Manhattan. These proposals were rejected by the state government in Albany. A ferry service was reintroduced successfully for the East River.
3 He developed new parks (about 300 hectares) and related public spaces (e.g. the new Flatiron Building plaza). He arranged for new pedestrian areas such as the one in Times Square. He got the High Line Park, on an abandoned rail line, started and funded.
4 Zoning adjustments led to the construction of new homes, many taken up by some 300,000 new entrants to the city over 2001–13.
5 He pressed for greener construction codes. The updated Empire State Building is 38 percent more energy efficient.
5 165,000 new public housing units were built. New York City has a massive public housing sector.
6 He saw the Freedom Tower completed and got the US$15 billion Hudson Yards project underway.

7 He pressed for the development of new activity in bio-tech and computer-tech in the city and got the new graduate research campus of Cornell started on Roosevelt Island in the city. Test scores in the public schools were raised slightly.

Bloomberg has been criticized by some observers who see much of the city becoming too expensive for ordinary residents to live in. His successor Bill de Blasio ran on a platform which highlighted the need to reintegrate ordinary residents into the fabric of the city. This may be very difficult to effect. Rent controls are costly to administer and have unsatisfactory side-effects. Manhattan as a playground for high-income residents may be the natural state for central New York City. Great "consumer cities" of the world offer a "New York City lifestyle" as an amenity in itself. People who service the areas lived in by high-income people will for the most part be obliged to commute from outer parts of the city to their jobs. Mayor Bloomberg could be characterized as pro-development. He strove to get more apartments and condominiums built, perhaps while offending current residents who liked things the way they were. Recent data suggest that Bloomberg may have abetted new demographic shifts. For the year ending June 30, 2013, Census Bureau surveys indicate that the city experienced a net population increase for white non-Hispanic folks. This is part of a three-year trend and a trend like this was last recorded in the 1960s. Obviously the availability and affordability of accommodation is necessary for an expansion of households in New York City's five boroughs. There has also been a rise in the numbers of children in the city, with those under 5 increasing by 7 percent, while at the same time, there was a decline of 14 percent for residents under 5 in the suburbs of the city.

Slum clearance and rebuilding cities

Throughout the nineteenth century as the Industrial Revolution spread out from Britain, worries about poverty and disease in the high-density areas of European cities became a concern. London emerged as something of a leader in opening up space in its center for parks and squares and then in launching a huge sewer construction project (1858). Officials in the government of France decided to restructure Paris, with its basically medieval layout of streets and very high-density neighborhoods housing the families of working people. Baron Hausmann was put in charge (leading the redevelopment between 1853 and 1870) and with the support of Napolean III (arriving in office in 1852) embarked on the famous clearing of slums and the construction of a series of long, straight boulevards. Strict codes for new urban residences were set out and the current beautiful five-storey apartment structures were put up along the new streets and boulevards. The reconstruction of Paris dragged on for some 20 years and really slowed down only when budget problems became vexing. But redevelopment continued right to the end of the nineteenth century. A popular take on the redevelopment has Napolean III introducing long flat boulevards to Paris so that the government was in a position to move soldiers and equipment around easily in the event of unrest in the streets.

Liverpool and Glasgow cleared their slums in the late nineteenth century and a Scottish planner, Patrick Geddes, was called out to India in 1914 to plan slum clearance for cities there. A plague which took some 10 million people to early deaths was waning

> when he arrived. He came up with a novel alternative to the policies pursued in Europe. He rejected neighborhood clearance in favor of "conservative surgery." He recommended simply cleaning and fixing up homes in the slums and collecting human waste regularly and spreading it on gardens and farms. He achieved small-scale successes in Lucknow, Baroda and Indore (Davis 2013).

Ken Greenberg, an urban planner with training in architecture has summed up his career in *Walking Home: The Life and Lessons of a City Builder* (2011). His idea of a good neighborhood is one with a variety of housing options, shops that can be accessed on foot and close-by daycare facilities, schools and parks. "The idea is being able to age in place, to go from one stage to another in the same neighborhood, so you can put down roots."[24] "Walkability" sums up his description of the good neighborhood. These views are close to those of Jane Jacobs, the late, celebrated activist from lower Manhattan. Jacobs and her husband did up a run-down townhouse on a street of run-down places in Greenwich Village shortly after they were married. Decades later the area had been revitalized and Jacobs' home had become affordable only to high-income people. Recall that Edward Glaeser criticized the Jacobs' view as being unrealistic; her ideal neighborhood had residences that were essentially townhouses, easily accessible to the street. Neighbors could "look out for one another" and also keep an eye on children at play near their homes. Glaeser remarks that such living near the centers of large cities was most often well beyond the budget of the average household. Glaeser envisages high-rise living as the practical alternative. He returns in his *Triumph* book to the view that six-storey apartment buildings are a good benchmark for urban densities. This was the size that downtown Paris was laid out with. Glaeser saw thousands of "neighborhoods" in the big Asian cities he visited. Chongqing is one of the most striking of China's dense cities, with dozens of new tall apartment buildings. High-rise living leaves a small ecological burden from each household on the planet and high-density cities have proved, of course, to be high productivity places quite generally. Planners and economists must recognize high-density living as the future for very large cities and come up with good designs for the apartment buildings and the neighborhoods they are erected in.

Regulation of land use

In most modern cities, the owner of a site must get approval of the local government's officials before changing things. Recently, for example, the restaurant WD-50 in lower Manhattan is being closed down so that the site can be cleared for a new apartment building. Local residents will now have to travel farther to access a "good restaurant." Some residents have patronized the eatery very irregularly but still value WD-50 because they have an option demand for its services. They value the possibility of dining there, even though they seldom patronize the establishment. Consider the possibility of a local food market being closed down so that the site can be used for a new apartment building. Then also the local residents would be forced to travel farther for routine shopping. There are obviously measurable costs to the current residents when they lose easy access to a local good restaurant or food market. Underlying these issues is one type of activity being able to outbid another activity for the site in question. There is a cliché among restaurant operators that they fear imminent rent increases in the same way that farmers live in anxiety about adverse future weather events. The restaurant operator can only afford to pay a certain level of rent to the owner of the site before their profits go negative. Matters can be set right if local authorities dictate that the site in question must be used for "retail" rather than residences. Then an apartment developer cannot bid the site away from the current use in, say, food vending.

Underlying this decision is that the activity on the site will generate a maximum of land rent for the site—given the activity allowed by regulation. Hence there are many, many cases in which sites are not occupied by the highest bidder, among all bidders. Rather the site becomes occupied by the highest bidder among bidders who are allowed by regulation to bid for the site. The idea is that regulators "know best" about the needs of the neighborhood and that retail for a site is in the best interests of the local residents, relative to those who will benefit from a new apartment building. As Edward Glaeser has argued, decisions that favor the current residents often hurt incoming residents who desire affordable accommodation. This is a major problem and it turns in part on NIMBYism or the power of the local existing residents to get land use decisions that favor themselves relative to outsiders. However, we want to emphasize a different point here. Many land-use decisions have a large component of regulation-by-planners embodied in them rather than the playing out of "market forces." The criteria that regulators bring to these decisions vary widely. They often include aesthetic considerations, as with the favoring of "conforming land-use" activity. Seldom is land allocated to new activities without the legally mandated input of planning authorities. Hence much of land allocation is a joint outcome of a planner's ruling and a developer's reach for profit. There is an interesting analogy to Ronald Coase's point about a distinction in firms between allocation by a manager within a firm and allocation by the market activities "outside" the firm. Firms are to a considerable extent a hierarchy of workers making allocation decisions within the entity while at the same time working through an agenda of allocation decisions for their firm relative to other firms, these latter essentially market decisions. Within-firm decisions resemble those of urban planners employed by municipal governments while between-firm decisions resemble those of developers of sites seeking to maximize profit. Hence with cities, many decisions about land use are made by planners or regulators while others are made by agents "in the marketplace." The type and volume of decisions made by regulators or planners is very difficult to arrive at with confidence. This question merits much consideration and debate. First off, one must decide the nature of the failure of the free market to allocate sites on its own. Then one must try to pin down the volume and type of decisions best left for planners.

Consider the case of a developer laying out a new suburb with a view to maximizing her return on the large parcel of land she owns. Other things being the same, she knows that she will get more per residential lot if she allows for a shopping center in the project. She may be somewhat agnostic about the area to leave for the shopping center. It is probably in her interest to try to get as many residential sites in her plan as possible. A planner can step in and specify the area required and the number of parking places that are efficient for the type of shopping center that the project supports, once completed. It often makes much economic sense for such land-use decisions to have serious input from planners and engineers acting in the interests of "the public." Suppose the developer allowed for a shopping center which ended up being extremely crowded. Another developer might enter, buy up some nearby homes and expand the parking area for the shopping center. This type of costly rebuild can be avoided if good land-use decisions are made at the outset.

When the free market fails to make good allocations, economists search for causes, usually generic causes called market failures. What is the generic market failure in urban land allocation? It is difficult to imagine an efficient grid of streets, land for streets, being laid out by the market. Then there is the quality of information-asymmetry issue. A developer may not install the state-of-the-art sewer system for her project or make provision for the state-of-the-art distribution of clean water to homes. Planners can oversee sewer and water distribution systems for new projects. Aesthetics have loomed large in many projects, such as the rebuilding of central Paris in the nineteenth century. "Conforming land-use" is a central principle in planning. This is largely an aesthetic consideration. "Preservation of neighborhood quality" is another aesthetic desideratum. This is also a tricky notion since preservation for the incumbents can be costly for those who want to move into the city in an affordable mode. "What works" for the largest number of people may be a better principle. Planners should probably act like the planner of textbook economics: she should act to maximize welfare—not always a simple task, of course.

O'Flaherty (2005; Chapter 7) compares the densities of settlement in Tokyo and New York and asks "Is Tokyo Better?" He is in fact somewhat obliquely addressing the question of whether many cities in the United States exhibit too much sprawl. New York City has a lower density. After listing policies that promote decentralized lower-density living, he sets out the basic economics textbook argument: "Cities are a way of helping people live their lives better; they're not an end in themselves." We have argued that "high" incomes per household have nudged residents of cities to opt for relatively large lots to live on and relatively many autos to get around in. Roughly speaking, planners went along with these trends and attempted to supply roads, bridges and parking lots that could accommodate the lifestyle associated with relatively low-density residential arrangements. Decision-makers could have levied very high taxes on the use of downtown parking places and they could also have levied very high taxes on the fuel for cars. Some combination of such policies would have induced residents to live closer to workplaces and to have sacrificed some space around their houses. Mass transit was never given as high a priority in the development of cities in North America as it was in cities in Europe and Asia. There is truth in the claim that planners became aware explicitly or implicitly that residents liked and were able to pay for relatively large lots in the suburbs and as well they could afford one or two cars. The planners responded by nudging the laying-out of roads and mass transit to accommodate these revealed preferences of residents. Roughly speaking, planning decisions followed the dictates of consumer sovereignty. O'Flaherty emphasizes that there is not a right or wrong layout for a city. Cities reflect the technologies that were dominant at crucial stages in their development. O'Flaherty (2005; p. 148) says:

> Lagos shouldn't end up looking like either New York or Tokyo or Phoenix.... Whether or the policies of Robert Moses in the 1930s in New York were the right ones or the wrong ones depends in large measure on the technologies that were available then—how people drove, shopped, worked, communicated with each other, and played. People in Lagos in decades to come won't be doing any of these things like 1930s New Yorkers did, and so figuring out how New York would look if Moses had followed better policies is not going to help policy-makers in Lagos today.[25]

O'Flaherty is implicitly buying into a variant of the doctrine of "path dependency." Roughly speaking certain technologies allow certain activities to get locked into certain configurations for long intervals. For example, many European cities reflect street layouts that were right for the days of horse-carts. Horse-cart dimensions of streets got locked in. Such places have become convenient for twenty-first-century pedestrians but horrible for twenty-first-century cars and trucks to move around on. Tourists like to visit many towns and cities in Europe because they are quaint and pedestrian-friendly. Economists have no special talent for predicting which new technologies will emerge and might restructure the economies of a nation, region or city decades or centuries down the road. Cities are places where the deficient foresight of the market system shows up conspicuously. The attractive high-rises of the 1960s turn out to house concentrations of dysfunctional folk, often with very low incomes, some 40 years later. Bullying and criminal activity become knitted into the social environment. Wide arteries with rapidly moving commuters become gridlocked freeways decades on. Economies adapt to new technologies and related challenges in various ways and cities as economies often have the most difficult time adapting because roads and structures are durable. Planning decisions often look wrong after an interval because adaptation "around various decisions" that were made and ended up as durable structures is very costly. Bangkok has few arterial roads and only partial systems for piped sewage and fresh water. It is known far and wide for its epic traffic jams and polluted groundwater. New York's Manhattan, on the other hand, had its rectangular grid of streets set out in 1811, well in advance of the planting of its many tall buildings.

Shlomo Angel (2011) emphasizes that a growing city needs to set aside land for roads and other infrastructure in advance of the influx of new residents. He opposes top-down policies set out to block the expansion of the footprint of a city. Greenbelts, for example, cannot effectively curtail sprawl and in fact often end up driving up residential land prices excessively. His view is based in part on satellite data for 120 cities taken between 1990 and 2000. He and colleagues at New York University discovered that a pattern, quite independent of local policies, was evident in local population increase and city land-use expansion. Boston built a wonderful freeway through its center in the 1950s and decided some decades later that the installation was a mistake. The authorities decided to tear it down and run the roadway underground. The resulting "big dig" was a hugely costly public works project. The lives of Bostonians would have been quite different had the freeway been built underground in the first place. Halifax, the port city in Nova Scotia, got caught up in energizing its downtown in the 1960s with a new freeway, entering from the suburbs and running along its dilapidated waterfront. Some access roads were built and then protesters managed to get the project halted before the waterfront area was bulldozed. Planners are now working to have the lightly used interchange of the freeway torn down to make way for a park, development sites and new roads.

Economists are proud of the subtlety of Ricardo's doctrine of "comparative advantage" or "relative cost advantages" of different places. The idea underlies trade and specialization of different people, regions, cities and nations. However, the doctrine lacks flexibility. One nation's comparative advantage in 1850 is generally quite different from its comparative advantage in 1925. The industrial structure of a nation has to adapt to new demanders with different tastes and incomes as well as to new ways of producing things and new products. Comparative advantage shifts over the decades. The best economics can contribute is to recommend that a place be adaptable to hard-to-predict new conditions—to have a somewhat flexible view of its current comparative advantage. The transportation infrastructure of a city requires continual adaptation to new arrangements of residential activity and job distribution. Good planning is difficult to carry out. Bad planning has direct costs in the form of excessive congestion at various times around various bottlenecks as well as indirect costs that take the form of driving certain activities away from their most productive locations in a particular city.

Competition between cities should be reflected on. The recent rise of large cities in Asia could be said to draw from a template of a successful modern city. A city needs a center for getting organization done (legal work, marketing, advertising, financing, direction of branch plants) and it needs roads or transit to be able to get "high-end" people to the center or centers as well as working people from adequate homes to the sites of trade and manufacturing. Some sort of freeway system has become a component of a modern large city and the largest all have extensive mass transit systems, including subways or light rail systems. There is clearly more to getting a dynamic city growing rapidly than simply providing a business-friendly legal and tax system.

The construction of a large airport is a new form of leading local development with abundant infrastructure. Busy airports attract businesses and jobs to nearby sites. The area around Toronto's major international airport, well away from the city center, has been a hub for businesses for at least two decades. Clearly certain types of activity oriented to huge flat warehouses are attracted to airports. Fedex has driven the whole economy of Memphis in Tennessee to prosperity and UPS has done the same for Louisville, Kentucky. Amazon and Zappos have contracted to locate near these airports as well, in return for being able to assemble huge areas for their warehouses. Amsterdam's Schipol airport is a hub for the world flower trade, with flows inbound from farms in East Africa. In addition the government of the Netherlands has developed the district of Zuidas near the airport to be a center for financial firms. Two of the showiest "airport cities" are Dubai in the Persian Gulf and Songdo International Business District near Seoul, South Korea. The latter is being developed almost from scratch on an island with a 20 minute link to the airport. Dubai's huge airport has been developed as a "state capitalism" initiative to capture flight traffic between Europe and Asia. Each of these initiatives is essentially an infrastructure-led approach to growth. Chongquing has developed large areas around its airport to get firms on the coast to relocate in its region. The plan includes producing half the world's laptop computers by 2015 and having the products flown out to world markets. GMR, a big conglomerate in India, has developed a new airport for Hyderabad and a new terminal for Delhi in exchange for land for development around both installations (Kasarda and Lindsay 2011). This has echoes of companies building railroads in the nineteenth century in return for land for development around those installations. Both India and China have less than half their populations in cities and observers anticipate that each of these places will move along the path of cities in Europe and North America and become predominately urbanized over the next decades.[26]

It would not be unexpected, then, to see a large part of forthcoming urbanization occur around busy, modern airports. The way a modern airport connects to its principal city is crucial for the good development of the area. Ten years ago New York finally got a rail link to Kennedy International Airport and Los Angeles is struggling with different proposals for effectively connecting its Green Line to LAX (Los Angeles International Airport). Chicago, Philadelphia, Boston, Atlanta and Washington have had good mass transit links for many years. More recently Portland, Minneapolis, Seattle, Newark, Phoenix, Miami and San Francisco have constructed rail links to their airports. Infrastructure-led development is a part of a government policy favoring a certain location, part of which is referred to as place-based economic policy. Moretti (2014) reflects at length on when such policies might be successful and why they often fail to yield the outcomes that people expected of them.

Paul Romer, a famous academic economist, decided to get practical and turn himself into a "city-planter." An airport is central to his current project, building a city in Honduras from scratch. Some place in central America will be a hub airport in the near future, he contends, and he would like his new city to be the place that wins the race. Romer's thinking has been framed by the experience of Hong Kong. This place became an economic powerhouse, he argues, because it had few regulations constraining commercial activity and was overseen by foreigners (the British) who by luck or design fostered the best rules and institutions for economic success. He is attempting to replicate the Hong Kong model and the Government of Honduras has bought into his scheme. It is still too early to tell how this ambitious experiment will work out. Romer's view of history is that good rules and technical progress yield economic development. Somehow the British provided the correct rules for both Hong Kong and Singapore, and they flourished. The popular view is that both of these city states have been low-tax, low-regulation entities and the rule of law has remained prominent. One might add that when a foreign power is in charge of a colony, the colony is mostly free of the bother of foreign policy organization and the maintenance of a self-defence structure. Local government can in a sense focus on economic development without the distractions that governments of most nations must face. Romer's ideal new city-state would be governed by a foreign power with good rules, free markets and an up-to-date technology.

Planned capital cities and other places

We turn to the question of planning for the development of a new city. Christopher Wren drew up a design for a new London following the great fire of 1666. Various planners set out a plan for St. Petersburg in the early eighteenth century. Baron Hausmann created his design for a new Paris in the early 1850s. Canberra, Australia, Brasília, Brazil, and Islamabad, Pakistan are cities laid out almost from scratch by designer-planners. Can economics provide guidance to the design process for a new city? Lucio Costa had strong views about traffic flow and his plan for Brasília reflects this eccentricity. Hausmann dictated the height and style of residences for his planned streets. Washington, DC has evolved in distinct ways because decision-makers demanded that new buildings not be tall and not slight the "profile" of the Capitol (the legislature building) on the horizon. Were any of the well-known planned cities obvious failures? Could these planned capital cities have been better in some sense if instead they had been built up in existing settlements, as for example Ottawa, Canada's capital, was? There is always the risk that places planned from scratch lack the dense interaction associated with economic prosperity and social vitality.

Washington, DC

Washington, DC became the capital of the United States in 1790. Madison, Hamilton and Jefferson agreed to a site in the South as part of a compromise on the assumption of war debts of the various states. The village of Georgetown existed at the time the new capital was laid out, ten miles square, on the bank of the Potomac River. The burning of Washington in 1812 resulted in the Capitol, the well-known legislative building, not being completed to its current form until 1868.

Brasília

Brasília, the capital of Brazil, was planned by Lúcio Costa, who won the competition in 1957 for its design. Costa's friend, Oscar Niemeyer, became the chief architect of most of the public buildings. Roberto Burle Marx was the landscape designer. The city was built between 1956 and April 1960. By relocating the capital city from Rio de Janeiro to the interior, the Brazilian government hoped to populate that remote area. Many of the workers engaged to build the new city were from the northeast region of Brazil.

Brasília was planned to have an especially smooth traffic flow. Cars and buses were to use thoroughfares to travel longer distances, and then use one of several loops for access to local streets to reach specific destinations. A six-lane freeway bisects the city. Costa planned a road system, free of traffic signals. He failed to foresee the rapid growth of the city, nor the growth of satellite cities around it. Brasília today has traffic signals and locating a parking space is difficult during the day. Traffic jams occur regularly at peak hours. Although the present situation is not as planned by Costa, traffic flow in Brasília is better than in other major Brazilian cities.

Canberra

Canberra is another capital carved out of uninhabited territory; its construction began in 1913 and was largely finished in the late 1920s. It contains large green spaces and the planning was influenced by the garden city movement in Britain. Some refer to it as "the bush capital." It is sited between Melbourne and Sydney, Australia's two largest cities. Following an international contest for the city's design, a blueprint by the Chicago architects Walter Burley Griffin and Marion Mahony Griffin was selected. The city began to thrive after World War II, when Prime Minister Robert Menzies championed its development and the National Capital Development Commission was formed with executive powers. In addition to "Parliament House" and the High Court, the city hosts the Australian National University, the National Gallery, the National Museum and the National Library. Canberra's population is under 400,000.

Islamabad

Islamabad was designed by the Greek firm Konstantinos Apostolos Doxiadis, and construction started in 1960. The site was selected to be more geographically central to Pakistan than was the traditional capital, Karachi. Islamabad is also close to Rawalpindi, the headquarters of the army. The city was planned as a grid of streets and triangular overall. Islamabad's population today exceeds four million.

Levittown, Long Island, New York

William Levitt was an experienced house-builder by the time he decided to innovate in house-building on Long Island after World War II. He assembled 20 square miles of land near Hampstead with his father and brother, and launched a suburb of his design between 1947 and 1951 with houses mass produced—similar to the way Henry Ford produced automobiles on his assembly lines. The homes cost less than US$65,000 in 2009 dollars and came with television sets and kitchen appliances installed. There were parks and open spaces and a train station nearby that gave residents of Levittown ready access to Manhattan and points in between. In a sense, Levitt invented a new type of suburb, quality homes with yards for families of modest means. A car was pretty much a necessity for getting groceries and moving children about. Philosophically inclined urbanists disdained Levittown and its residents, but the houses sold quickly and residents were content. "Home buyers tend to put more weight on floor-space, lot size, modern conveniences, good schools, and access to jobs" (Glaeser 2011; p. 175). Glaeser also makes the point that the suburbanization of residences was fostered by the indirect subsidy of mortgage interest deductibility: "Owner-occupied houses are overwhelmingly single-family houses, and they tend to be in the suburbs. When public policy promotes home ownership, it also pushes people to leave cities" (Glaeser 2011; p. 176).

Stapleton, Colorado

Stapleton, at the edge of Denver, is a "promising Smart Growth/New Urbanist project" being developed on 7.5 square miles of the old airport and its surroundings. An edge town with a prospective light rail connection to the downtown is being developed as a planned entity from the start. Some 8,000 people in 3,000 residences have already moved into the project, which envisions ultimately 8,000 energy efficient homes and 4,000 apartments, six public schools, many hundreds of acres of parks, several shopping complexes and ten million square feet of office space (Platt 2014; pp. 162–63).

La Defense, Paris, France

Paris developed an office building district in 1958 in an area of older factories and shanties and farms at the edge of the city. The development, named for an iconic statue, acquired a rail line to the city center in 1970 and the Metro linked up in 1992. The first tall building, the Nobel Tower, was opened in 1966. A height limitation of 330 ft (100 m) was in place. A second generation of office buildings arrived in the early 1970s. The tallest skyscraper in the district, the Tour First, went up in 1974 and has 50 storeys in its 758 ft. A large commercial center opened in 1981. Many of France's very large companies, including Société Générale, Total, Aventis, Areva and Arcelor have head offices in a building in La Defense. The area has been taking on apartment buildings and becoming a bit of a residential area.

There are a number of remarkable aspects to this development. First, of course, it preserved Paris as the dominant business and government city in France and allowed the historic center to remain a must-live-in and must-see area for Parisians and tourists. La Defense is bustling and has noticeable traffic congestion. Second, the area has worked economically from the start. Developers did not endure years of struggle as businesses slowly migrated out to the district. And third, it served as a template for other major cities which strove to maintain an economic dominance while at the same time preserving their historic districts. London's Dockyard Project appears to have been inspired by the success of La Defense. Frankfurt in Germany is somewhat different. It also distinguishes between its city center and its central business district, the latter dominated by tall office buildings occupied mostly by banks (the area is the Bankenviertel). This CBD has no legislated borders and in fact spills over into three districts, formally defined. It is very well served by mass transit. The Central Bank of the European Union is in the Bankenviertel. Frankfurt has evolved like Paris and London in a way that allows "the center" to develop at a pace different from that of the central business district. London and Frankfurt are world financial centers.

We turn to approaching urban issues from a problems perspective. We raise what we consider to be the main problems needing attention in a typical city or system of cities and ask how economics can shed light on solutions. We have in mind that urban problems are often posed as requiring the attention of an urban planner. We are inquiring about the possibility of putting urban planning on a more of an economics basis; and we will divide our inquiry into three parts for convenience:

- macro-level issues;
- city reform issues; and
- city design issues.

Macro-level issues

The two important topics to consider here are population distribution and migration policy.

1 *Population distribution.* Central governments generally have views about "excessive" growth of regions. The rapid growth of cities in the coastal area of China is a case in point. Economics should be able to offer guidance on this topic. Governments worry about employment prospects for migrants to cities and the development of neighborhoods with poor people in dangerous living arrangements. The *Economist* suggested that Chinese policy was contributing to too many medium-large cities in an efficient system, relative to the development of a few very large cities and fewer medium-large cities: "only 27m Chinese live in cities of more than 10m, compared with 58m Indians and 32m Brazilians. . . . China's big cities are still surprisingly small."[27] Some observers consider Tokyo, at a population of 36 million, to be a benchmark of a very large, well-functioning city. There is a large literature on the evolution of population distributions for cities in various nations, under relatively free-market conditions. We reported on some of this literature in Chapter 6.

2 *Migration policy.* This issue is related to the preceding one. There have been many episodes in history in which a central government has regulated internal migration in a nation by issuing permits to allow a person to reside in a certain area. See, for example, "Population Control in Beijing."[28]

Such policies are amenable to economic analysis. In addition, governments usually have quite explicit policies about the in-migration of people from other nations to their territories. The design of such policies in the future will become more controversial as the movement of poor people becomes easier. Migration of people from Mexico to the United States and from Turkey to Germany, for example, illustrates how this topic complicates political discourse in the nations involved.

City-reform issues

We can conveniently discuss these issue under eight distinct headings.

1 *Urban highways.* Since the 1950s, cities in North America have wrestled with the issue of moving workers to the centers of cities from farther out residential areas. Freeway construction was often resorted to, in part because capital funding was made available for such new roads. In the United States such funding came out of the special highway trust funds. Critics argued that the automobile mode of commuting was being heavily

subsidized relative to forms of mass transit. When is a highway into a city a good new capital project? We might reflect on the problems which Boston confronted with its elevated road into the city and its subsequent shifting of the road to below ground (the so-called "big dig"). There are presumably many lessons to take from highway construction around and in New York City under Robert Moses. Toronto experienced its own stop-the-northwest-expressway action in the early 1970s. The construction of an urban highway must be planned with full account taken of current mass transit "supply" and plans as well as policies for congestion controls, like those in London, England.

2 *Mass transit policy.* Economic analysis here has progressed considerably following the careful and extensive work of Daniel McFadden. We are probably in a position to develop a handbook that can be used by city officials in guiding policy on mass transit, including the installation of subways and/or light rail. One might be inclined to separate the topic into "new infrastructure" and "extensions to existing infrastructure." Mass transit for a city cannot be developed separately from the development of urban highways or from the introduction of congestion taxes like those in London, England.

3 *Congestion tax policy.* Such controls can include dedicated bus lanes and HOV (high occupancy vehicle) lanes as well as the direct levying of "entry fees" like those in London, England.

4 *Parking pricing policy.* A planner can in principle select the number of automobiles entering the center of a city each day by setting an appropriate price per space. This could involve a tax to bring the market rate up to the "planner's rate." Urban planners do of course require builders to provide a certain number of parking spaces when they build their new structures. This is a blunter method for controlling the flow of vehicles into an area of a city. We are unaware of a place that has attempted to deal with congestion in an area of a city with a precisely designed pricing policy for parking spaces. Senior people in businesses and government agencies in the center of cities are often given rights to a parking space as a perquisite of their position. The value of such perks should be correctly assessed and assigned as imputed income to the beneficiaries. The beneficiaries would then have to pay income tax on the value of the perk. Obviously a parking pricing policy would be related to actions on mass transit "supply" as well as actions on urban highway "supply."

(Two versions of city growth and evolution come to mind. In one version, policy in one of our four mandates above is done somewhat in isolation, the city responds via market processes and lobbying of government, and there is a policy response. This might be referred to as the *ad hoc* policy evolution model of planning. In the other version, much effort is made to coordinate current policy positions on our four mandates with the intention of creating a smooth process of city growth. The striking lesson here is that agents such as firms and households can respond reasonably well to the current actions of policy-makers and in most cases the city can grow and evolve reasonably well. It is difficult for intelligent decision-makers at the center, in various levels of government, to kill a city. Agents in the private sector can retreat to a stationary mode awaiting new, sounder policy at the center.)

5 *Revenue raising policy.* Cities have demanders of municipal services: from pools for kids to quality bus services. The quantity and quality of the services provided will be revenue-dependent. Property values have been the natural tax bases for cities but such bases have well-known problems associated with them. There is great scope for rethinking the service provision of cities as distinct from other levels of government and for rethinking revenue-raising programs. The idea of having higher levels of government

involved in policy-design here makes sense since one wants to minimize the use of tax and expenditure policy by one city to compete for the "capture" of new businesses and/or high-income residents. Economics does not have a theory of socially desirable tax competition between cities, in contrast with, say, price competition between firms with similar products.

6 *Infrastructure development policy.* Infrastructure is generally durable capital as in roads, bridges, libraries, social housing, etc. A city needs funds or revenue-raising mechanisms in order to implement policies of infrastructure development. There are often large, one-off expenditures involved and higher levels of government get involved in, say, bond issues. An orderly infrastructure development policy rather than an *ad hoc* approach is ideal. Rules of thumb would be helpful here, as in capital requirements per 100,000 of population, but obviously some cities need more bridges than others, given their geographical endowments. We alluded to the fact that in recent history some cities appear to have benefited from infrastructure-led growth as when lumpy investments such as subway systems get built before a city's population and economy expand rapidly. There is a literature in economics on the so-called capacity expansion of a growing firm when set-up costs are central, but this work is at best marginally relevant to the phenomenon of infrastructure-led growth of a city. A natural port is like a piece of durable infrastructure, as with, say, an airport and the growth of a city around a port can be viewed as a case of infrastructure-led growth. This is clearly a special case.

7 *Census tract redevelopment policy (urban renewal).* Since at least the period of Rome flourishing, urban renewal has been pursued by policy-makers. There is the reflex to raze the neighborhoods of deteriorated homes and shops and to replace them with new residences or public works such as sports venues. Robert Moses was enthusiastic about razing older structures to make way for urban highways. London got something of a head-start in urban renewal after it was struck with a gigantic fire in 1666. And in a sense, modern urban renewal was set in motion in Paris after 1850 by the collaboration of planner, Hausmann, and government leader, Napoleon III. In the 1960s many cities in the United States rebuilt their centers in an attempt to get central-city growth restarted. As with all government initiatives there are people who gain and those who lose. An ideal policy has the sum of gains exceeding the sum of losses and some form of compensation gets implemented. Urban renewal is one of those tricky policy initiatives that tends to leave the losers conspicuous and compensation less than total. Scale matters since successful renewal usually involves clearing fairly large spaces to make way for something different. Small-scale renewal can involve razing old residences and replacing them with new structures. The city of Toronto is part way through razing a social housing development (Regent Park) built in the 1940s and replacing it with new residential structures, some for households with very low incomes.

8 *Density policy in census tracts.* Urban planners are regularly faced with decisions about densities: densities of residential places and those of businesses. Implicit is the notion that there are significant negative externalities involved with the "wrong" densities. Planners are intervening in order to mitigate the impact of potential externalities, such as the noisy, smelly auto-body shop located in an area of residences. If land uses are specified before development takes place, one assumes that the negative impacts from the "wrong" location of activities can be pre-empted. This makes much sense. One can worry perhaps about planners wedded to a certain view of a "correct" residential density and have them direct development toward excessive sprawl or possibly excessive density. These

may be small costs associated with policies of land-use design to minimize the negative impacts of externalities. There is of course a connection between urban renewal and density policy. One wonders whether narrow views of land-use planners can lead to a static or slow-growth city when different views of planners may have allowed for a better growth trajectory for a city.

The eight points above summarise the city-reform issues faced by city planners. New thinking about city planning, broadly defined, is being motivated by new "planning" technologies (the so-called "smart city movement"). The idea here is to push research and actual city planning with the use of modern sensors, computing and data-sifting technologies. More precise knowledge is supposed to lead to more precise resource use. Some observers estimate savings from better knowledge of 30 to 50 percent in the use of electricity and water in a modern city. Already in effect in New York City, for example, is intelligent traffic control, where controllers at a command center vary the times of green and red for traffic lights with the observed flows of vehicles. New York University has plans to be a research center with a focus on the smart-city approach.

The allocation of inputs and products of a city depends directly on the city's transportation system. This means that there must be interactions between private agents and transportation planners. Allocation mechanisms for such situations become complicated interactions of privately motivated agents and design agents. Economics does not offer a standard analysis of such allocation problems. There is probably a reflex action for these problems: let the planners sort things out. We argue for changing this "procedure." Bring more profit-and-loss thinking into these allocation problems. Transportation system design needs much benefit–cost analysis. There is room for more careful transportation design and at the same time better allocation of sites to activities.

City design issues

The key issues to consider here are the transportation system and the land-use plan.

1 *The transportation system.* Does economics provide guidance for the laying out of a good intra-city and intercity transportation system? A committee of urban economists (transportation specialists) and transportation engineers (civil engineers specializing in transportation) could presumably provide a good design for a new city's transportation system. In our view, leaving the design to architects is not a good way to proceed.
2 *Land-use plan.* The initial allocation of land to various activities cannot be separated from the arrangement of streets and mass transit "supplies." Economists would presumably suggest allocating land in such a way that the allocation resembles that of other prosperous, well-growing cities. Again, civil engineers and economists would probably make a better plan than would designers coming from a background in architecture.

UN-Habitat

UN-Habitat is the division of the United Nations focused on urban issues. Its offices are centered in Nairobi, Kenya. Its vision of "urbanization" encompasses all levels of human settlements, including small rural communities, villages, market towns, intermediate cities and large cities and metropolises, i.e. "wherever a stable community is continuously located and there are housing units together with permanent social and economic activities, common public spaces, urban basic services, and a local governance structure."[29] Current priorities for research and outreach are (1) Urban legislation, land and governance, (2) Urban planning and design, (3) Urban economy, (4) Urban basic services, (5) Housing and slum upgrading, (6) Risk reduction and rehabilitation and (7) Urban research and capacity development.

A parliament of mayors

Barber (2013) observes that cities in the developed world have about 80 percent of the population and about 80 percent of the GDP of the world. This should make mayors important political leaders who could usefully exercise more power in a parliament of mayors. Mayors are pragmatic political leaders, he argues—"problem-solvers first of all." Higher levels of government in a nation may shut down for a spell, without too much dislocation to the nation, while the shut-down of a municipal government could have a disastrous impact—no transit, no police, no fire protection, no schools, no sanitation workers and so on. The solving of a city's pollution problem would become a model to get global pollution under control. Barber (2013; p. 349) says:

> The start-up process calls for the leadership of cities on the forefront of cooperation and cross-border networking, and it might include such developed Western world cities as New York, Los Angeles, Hamburg, Amsterdam, Vienna and London... as well as cities such as Seoul, Singapore, Hong Kong, Buenos Aires, Kinshasa and Mumbai, whose size and influence make their participation vital and whose role in the developing world, where inequality is so prevalent, makes their participation mandatory.

Global intercity networks currently include United Cities and Local Governments (UCLG), the International Council for Local Environmental Initiatives (ICLEI), Metropolis, CityNet and City Protocol. Such organizations have influenced urban carbon emissions abatements, the campaign against nuclear proliferation, sharing of best management practices, the campaign against gun violence, sound budgeting and cultural and arts promotion. Mayor Sheila Dikshit of Delhi suggests that big Indian cities such a Delhi, Mumbai, Kolkata, and Chennai be treated as "city-states" (Barber, p. 239). Ms Dikshit is a mayor singled out by Barber for her distinguished work in office. She got the first phase of the Delhi Metro completed on time and within the budget; she privatized power distribution, reduced pollution, improved school performance of students and expanded green areas within the city. She also introduced "town halls" (Bhagidari) for communicating with residents.

A problem with the parliament idea is that, in many nations, cities are in fact administered by committees or agents from a higher level of government. A collection of big-city mayors from many countries could include people with considerably different powers and spending authorities. Only in some countries are municipal leaders elected as decision-makers with considerable local power and large budgets. In Europe local governments are often completely funded by transfers and grants from the national government. Intercity associations exist now in many countries and cross-border discussions and collaborations can be very useful. The parliament idea, however, seems some decades ahead of its time.

Economic policy

Conventional wisdom asks that a nation sets a good monetary policy, a good tax system, a good infrastructure program and a good legal and regulatory system—and prosperity will follow.

A small contribution to an economy's success is attributed to a good urban policy. There are at least two ironies here. Often when a person is able to get some leisure time, she jets off to one of the world's great cities (New York, London, Paris, Prague, Budapest, St. Petersburg, Shanghai, Sydney, Rio de Janeiro, etc.). There is a clear sense that the complete life includes visiting the world's large interesting cities. One might argue then that a nation should be coddling its cities in an effort to bring them up to world-class status. The other irony is that observers are pretty well unanimous in the view that invention and innovation occur mostly in cities and of course it is technical progress that ultimately drives living standards. Again one might expect cities to be especially coddled in order for them to keep technical progress going. Cities in these senses are especially important economic entities and at the same time "urban policy" is placed well down the list of policies central to a nation's economic well-being. As far as I know, no one ever dissected the growth of a nation's economy and quantified the contribution of "urban policy" to the growth rate. We are left with the interesting question: how much might a nation do better if its urban policy were improved, where doing better gets reflected in a higher per capita income and/or a more rapid rate of growth?

Summary

We reflected on some population projections and whether the many slums of the world will multiply and expand. Most slums are functioning residential areas or even productive localized nodes. They generally need better security and sanitation. We turned to urban development and urban planning and asked about inserting ideas and principles from economics into these topics. Some key players and places were introduced.

Main points of Chapter 10

1. Slums are essentially urban phenomena and are more prevalent in low-income nations. A fraction of residents are stuck in the slum and others "view it" as a place of transition to a better urban life. Some slums are beehives of small-scale economic activity.
2. Slum clearance can push residents to places separated from job centers and new places with poor mass transit.
3. Infrastructure deficits are common in cities in low-income nations. Airport development has become a route to city development in many communities in lower-income nations.
4. Sustainable urban growth has many dimensions and has become a priority for many cities in the world.
5. Urban planning, a formal discipline related to architecture, needs to develop more links with basic economics. A careful benefit–cost approach to many urban problems requires development.
6. The specification of the role of local government is useful and complicated. Higher levels of government have considerable authority over local governments.
7. Mayors of large cities of the world are developing codes of best practice and other useful forms of dialogue.

Questions and problems

1. "There is no free market solution for the urban problems facing slums like Dharavi, in Mumbai. Cities need forceful, capable governments to provide clean water, safe neighborhoods, and fast-moving streets" (Glaeser 2011; p. 95). How forceful and capable

were the governments in charge of London and Paris in assisting with the growth of their cities in the nineteenth century?

2 Janice Perlman's two visits to the slums of Rio de Janeiro in Brazil some 35 years apart revealed large changes in the lives of people she was able to reconnect with. Unemployment and street-level security has worsened considerably.

   a Analyze the causes of the decline in the livability for residents in the slums (*favelas*) that Perlman visited.
   b Are there parallels between the decline in the livability for residents of Perlman's slums and the apparent decline in the quality of living for low-income people in Detroit over 35 years?

3 (Glaeser 2011; p. 101) remarks:

> There is a lot to dislike in political systems that lodge too little power in local hands, but the right answer isn't complete autonomy, either. When things work right, multiple layers of government—federal, state, and city—can check each other, especially when different parties hold power at different layers.

Is there a natural way to allocate responsibilities to different levels of government? How is the allocation biased by the need for different levels to collect sufficient revenue for their programs and tasks?

4 Suppose the government of each state (province) was a committee comprising the mayors of the five largest cities in each state (province). This committee would collect the taxes in each state (province) and allocate funds to programs and projects as well as to smaller municipal governments.

   a Is there an obvious problem with this sort of combined mid- and low-level of government?
   b Would the average household in the state or province be better off (end up on a higher indifference curve) under this system of government (a five-mayor council)?

5 Many people express negative views about low-density residential development ("too much sprawl") and others express negative views about high-density living arrangements in, say, Hong Kong ("concrete canyons"). Is there a desirable path for future residential development for, say, New York? for Los Angeles? for Calgary, Alberta?

6 Regulations set up to preserve the appearance of areas of cities can stifle redevelopment (e.g. the tearing down of warehouses to make space for the building up of new apartment buildings). Choked-off redevelopment often goes hand-in-hand with a slow growth in the supply of new accommodation and price increases for existing accommodation. How serious are these circumstances for New York City? for Atlanta? for Paris? for London?

7 Glaeser (2011; p. 260) remarks:

> There are roughly three times as many people in their thirties, forties and fifties in the United States as there are in their twenties, so it would be a mistake for cities to think that they can survive solely as magnets for the young and the hip.

Have a flood of "the young and the hip" into certain US cities created obvious new prosperity? Name a few such cities.

Notes

1 We ran a regression of the log of the number of cities on the log of average size of the cities for this hierarchy of cities and obtained a statistically significant value of -1.2 for the underlying Pareto statistical distribution. This hierarchy of cities thus has small cities "too large" (or small cities "too numerous") relative to the "ideal" rank-size rule with the key parameter then having value -1.
2 *The Economist*, February 19, 2011, p. 41.
3 "Metropolis Now," *Financial Times*, February 19, 2011, p. 14.
4 United Nations Human Settlement Programme (UN-Habitat), p. 21.
5 United Nations Human Settlement Programme (UN-Habitat), p. 23.
6 United Nations Human Settlement Programme (UN-Habitat), p. 24.
7 Martin Wolf, *Financial Times*, February 19, 2011, p. 7.
8 *New York Times*, September 9, 2014, p. A5.
9 United Nations Population Division (2008) "An Overview of Urbanization, Internal Migration, Population Distribution and Development in the World," New York: United Nations Secretariat, Department of Economic and Social Affairs, UN/POP/EGM-URB/2008/01.
10 "The Final Frontier," *The Economist*, July 19, 2014, p. 35.
11 Haugen and Boutros (2014) cited by David Brooks in the *New York Times*, March 25, 2014. Haugen and Boutros observe that the federal government in Washington, DC spends about US$850 per person per year on police while the government in Bangladesh spends less than US$1.50 per person per year. In the United States, there is a prosecutor for every 12,000 citizens while in Malawi the ratio is 1 to 1.5 million. Foreign aid in the form of police training rather than infrastructure development might have a much higher social payoff, they point out.
12 *The Globe and Mail*, April 19, 2014, pp. A10–A11.
13 Wikipedia, February 28, 2011.
14 *Toronto Vital Signs Report 2013*.
15 *The Globe and Mail*, July 4, 2011, p. B7.
16 Nicholas Lemann, *The New Yorker*, June 27, 2011, p. 9.
17 *The Economist*, April 19, 2014, p. 12 of the Special Report.
18 See, for example, Bicknell *et al.* (2009).
19 Quoted in Shaila Dewan,"Rent Asunder," *New York Times*, May 4, 2014, pp. 16–19.
20 Josh Barro, "Affordable Housing that's very Costly," *New York Times*, Business Section, June 7, 2014.
21 *Globe and Mail*, March 15, p. F7.
22 *New York Times*, May 13, 2014, p. A17.
23 *Globe and Mail*, March 15, 2014, pp. F6–F7.
24 *The Globe and Mail*, July 5, 2011, p. B8.
25 The Lagos–Ibadan–Cotonou region extends from Lagos in Nigeria into Cotonou in neighboring Benin. Lagos itself is projected to reach a population of 25 million by 2025, putting it with Mumbai and Tokyo as one of the world's largest three cities. Nigeria has six additional cities with over 1 million residents and 12 with between 500,000 and a million residents. A recent reworking of Nigeria's national accounts in 2014 places the nation well ahead of South Africa in terms of GNP, though not ahead in terms of GNP per capita. Nigeria is densely settled with over 150 million people.
26 Tata Steel corporation in India has developed a prototype of a house that will be sold in shops in India for about US$500 (*The Economist*, March 5, 2011, p. 78). See also "Providing better and more affordable housing could be the next 'capitalist achievement'," (*The Economist*, January 10, 2015, p. 61).
27 *The Economist*, "Economics focus," September 16, 2010.
28 "Population Control in Beijing," *The Economist*, February 17, 2011:

> During meetings of Beijing's district and city-level legislatures in January, a frenzy of calls by party-picked delegates demanded tighter population controls. An old slogan was dusted off about using housing, employment and identity papers to keep numbers in check. Closing down underground accommodation, officially on health and safety grounds, was touted as one useful technique. Another was a crackdown on partitioning flats for rent. On February 16th the

government announced that homebuyers would be subject to similar restrictions as people buying cars. For the first time in years, says *Century Weekly*, another magazine, officials are talking about making the *hukou*, a proof of domicile that is hard to obtain when not inherited and that confers all sorts of health and welfare rights, even more difficult to get.

29 "Time to Think Urban," UN-Habitat, April, 2013, p. 5.

References

Acemoglu, Daron, Simon Johnson and James A. Robinson, (2001). "The Colonial Origins of Comparative Development," *American Economic Review*, 91, 5: 1369–1401.

Ades, A. and E. Glaeser, (1995). "Trade and Circuses: Explaining Urban Giants," *Quarterly Journal of Economics*, 110: 195–228.

Albouy, David, (2008). "Are Big Cities Really Bad Places To Live? Improving Quality of Life Estimates across Cities," NBER Working Paper No. 14472.

Alonso, William, (1960). "A Theory of the Urban Land Market," *Regional Science Association, Papers and Proceedings*, 6: 149–157.

Anderson, Rich, (2007). "Local Government Expenditure for Sewer and Water: 1991–2005," The United States Conference of Mayors.

Angel, Shlomo, with Jason Parent, Daniel L. Civco and Alejandro M. Blei, (2011). *Making Room for a Planet of Cities*, Cambridge, MA: Lincoln Institute of Land Policy.

Appleby, Joyce, (2010). *The Restless Revolution: A History of Capitalism*, New York: Norton.

Arnott, Richard, (2005). "City Tolls – One Element of an Effective Policy Cocktail," *Cesifo Dice Report, Journal for Institutional Comparisons*, 3, 4: 5–11.

Arnott, Richard, Andre de Palma and Robin Lindsey, (1993). "A Structural Model of Peak-Period Congestion: A Traffic Bottleneck with Elastic Demand," *American Economic Review*, 83, 1, March: 161–79.

Arzaghi, M. and J.V. Henderson, (2008). "Networking off Madison Avenue," *Review of Economic Studies*, 75: 1011–1038.

Barber, Benjamin R., (2013). *If Mayors Ruled the World: Dysfunctional Nations, Rising Cities*, New Haven: Yale University Press.

Baumol, William J., (1967). "Macroeconomics of Unbalanced Growth: The Anatomy of Urban Crisis," *American Economic Review*, 57, 3, June: 415–426.

Bazhanov, Andrei and John Hartwick, (2006). "Dispersed Interactions of Urban Residents," MPRA Paper 766, University Library of Munich, Germany.

Becker, Gary S., (1965). "A Theory of the Allocation of Time," *The Economic Journal*, 75, 299, September: 493–511.

Becker, Gary S., (1968). "Crime and Punishment: An Economic Approach," *Journal of Political Economy*, 76, March/April: 169–217.

Beckmann, Martin J., (1976). "Spatial Equilibrium in the Dispersed City," in *Mathematical Land Use Theory*, edited by G.J. Papageorgiou, Lexington MA: Lexington Books, Chapter 8.

Beckmann, Martin J. and John C. McPherson, (1970). "City Size Distribution in a Central Place Hierarchy: An Alternative Approach," *Journal of Regional Science* 10, 1, April: 25–33.

Bettencourt, Luis M. A., (2013). "The Origins of Scaling in Cities," *Science*, 340, June 21: 1438–1441.

Bettencourt, Luis and Geoffrey West, (2010). "A Unified Theory of Urban Living," *Nature*, 467, October 21: 912–913.

Bicknell, Jane, David Dodman and David Satterthwaite, editors, (2009). *Adapting Cities to Climate Change: Understanding and Addressing the Development Challenges*, London: Earthscan.

Black, Duncan and Vernon Henderson, (1999). "A Theory of Urban Growth," *Journal of Political Economy*, 107, 2: 252–284.

Blomquist, Glenn, Mark C. Berger and John P. Hohen, (1988). "New Estimates of Quality of Life in Urban Areas," *American Economic Review*, 78, 1: 89–107.

Boo, Katherine, (2012). *Behind the Beautiful Forevers*, New York: Random House.

Boustan, Leah Platt, Devin Buntan and Owen Hearey, (2013). "Urbanization in the United States, 1800–2000," NBER Working Paper No. 19041.

Braid, Ralph M., (1986). "The Comparative Statics of a Filtering Model of Housing with Two Income Groups," *Journal of Urban Economics*, 16: 437–448.

Brueckner, Jan K., (2000). "Urban Sprawl: Diagnosis and Remedies," *International Regional Science Review*, 23, 2: 160–71.

Brueckner, Jan K. and David A. Fansler, (1983). "The Economics of Urban Sprawl: Theory and Evidence," *Review of Economics and Statistics*, 65, 3, August: 479–82.

Brueckner, Jan K. and David Neumark, (2011). "Beaches, Sunshine, and Public-Sector Pay: Theory and Evidence on Amenities and Rent Extraction by Government Workers," NBER Working Paper No. 16797.

Burchfield, Marcy, Henry G. Overman, Diego Puga and Matthew A. Turner, (2006). "Causes of Sprawl: A Portrait from Space," *The Quarterly Journal of Economics*, 121, 2: 587–633.

Can, Ayse, (1992). "Specification and Estimation of Hedonic House Price Models," *Regional Science and Urban Economics*, 22: 453–74.

Capozza, D.R., P.H. Hendershott and C. Mack, (2004). "An Anatomy of Price Dynamics in Illiquid Markets: Analysis and Evidence from Local Housing Markets," *Real Estate Economics* 32, 1: 1–32.

Cheshire, Paul and Christian A.L. Hilber, (2008). "Office Space Supply Restrictions in Britain: the Political Economy of Market Revenge," *Economic Journal*, 118, 529: F185–F221.

Chetty, Raj, Nathaniel Hendren, Patrick Kline and Emmanuel Saez, (2014). "Where is the Land of Opportunity? The Geography of Intergenerational Mobility in the United States," NBER Working Paper No. 19843.

Ciccone, A. and Robert Hall, (1996). "Productivity and the Density of Economic Activity," *American Economic Review*, 86, March: 54–70.

Combes, Pierre-Philippe, Gilles Duranton, Laurent Gobillon and Sebastien Roux, (2010). "Estimating Agglomeration Economies with History, Geology, and Worker Effects," in *Agglomeration Economics*, edited by Edward L. Glaeser, Chicago: University of Chicago Press, Chapter 1.

Conover, Ted, (2010). *The Routes of Man*, New York: Alfred A. Knopf.

Crandall, Robert W., Howard K. Gruenspecht, Theodore E. Keeler and Lester B. Lave, (1986). *Regulating the Automobile*, Washington, DC: Brookings Institution.

Cronon, William, (1991). *Nature's Metropolis: Chicago and the Great West*, New York: Norton.

Cutler, David and Edward Glaeser, (1997). "Are Ghettoes Good or Bad?" *Quarterly Journal of Economics*, 112, 3: 827–871.

Dachis, Benjamin, (2010). "Picking Up Savings: the Benefits of Competition in Municipal Waste Services." Available at www.cdhowe.org (last accessed February 1, 2015).

Davis, Donald R. and David E. Weinstein, (2002). "Bones, Bombs, and Break Points: The Geography of Economic Activity," *American Economic Review*, 92, 5: 1269–89.

Davis, Michael, (2013). "Monumental Knock-offs," *Nature*, 494, February 28: 427–28.

Davis, M.A. and J. Heathcote, (2007). "The Price and Quantity of Residential Land in the United States," *Journal of Monetary Economics*, 54: 2595–2620.

de Long, J. Bradford and Andrei Schleifer, (1993). "Princes and Merchants: European City Growth before the Industrial Revolution," *Journal of Law and Economics*, 36, 2, October: 671–702.

DeLuca, Stefanie and Jennifer Darrah, (2014). "Living Here Has Changed My Whole Perspective: How Escaping Inner-City Poverty Shapes Neighborhood and Housing Choice," *Journal of Policy Analysis and Management*, 33, 2, Spring: 350–384.

de Soto, Hernando, (2000). *The Mystery of Capital: Why Capitalism Triumphs in the West and Fails Everywhere Else*, London: Black Swan.

Devine, Theresa J., (2004). "Supply and Demand: City and State May be Planning too Much Office Space," New York City Independent Budget Office Background Paper, August.

Dickerson, N.T., (2007). "Black Employment, Segregation, and the Social Organization of Metropolitan Labor Markets," *Economic Geography*, 83, 3: 283–307.

Diewert, W. Erwin, Alice O. Nakamura and Leonard I. Nakamura, (2009). "The Housing Bubble and a New Approach to Accounting for Housing in a CPI," *Journal of Housing Economics*, 18: 156–171.

Dixit, Avinash K. and Joseph E. Stiglitz, (1977). "Monopolistic Competition and Optimum Product Diversity," *American Economic Review*, 67, 3: 297–308.

Domar, Evsey D., (1970). "The Causes of Slavery or Serfdom: A Hypothesis," *Journal of Economic History*, March: 18–32.

Donohue, John J. III and Steven D. Levitt, (2001). "The Impact of Legalized Abortion on Crime," *The Quarterly Journal of Economics*, 116, 2: 379–420.

Dougherty, Conor, (2014). "Rentals Reach for the Skies," *Wall Street Journal*, April 26: A3.

Duranton, Gilles and Diego Puga, (2001). "Nursery Cities: Urban Diversity, Process Innovation, and the Life Cycle of Products," *American Economics Review*, 91, 5: 1454–77.

Duranton, Gilles and Diego Puga, (2005). "From Sectoral to Functional Specialization," *Journal of Urban Economics*, 57: 343–370.

Duranton, Gilles and Matthew Turner, (2011). "The Fundamental Law of Highway Construction: Evidence for the US," *American Economic Review*, 101, 6, October: 2616–2652.

Dyja, Thomas, (2013). *The Third Coast: When Chicago Built the American Dream*, New York: Penguin.

Eaton, J., B. Curtis and Richard G. Lipsey, (1976). "The Non-Uniqueness of Equilibrium in the Loschian Location Model," *American Economic Review*, 66: 77–93.

Eaton, Jonathan and Zvi Eckstein, (1997). "Cities And Growth: Theory And Evidence From France And Japan," *Regional Science and Urban Economics*, 27, 4–5, August: 443–474.

Eeckhout, Jan, (2004). "Gibrat's Law for (All) Cities," *American Economic Review*, 94, 5: 1429–1451.

Eid, Jean, Henry G. Overman, Diego Puga and Matthew A. Turner, (2008). "Fat City: The Relationship Between Urban Sprawl and Obesity," *Journal of Urban Economics*, 63, 2, March: 385–404.

Ellen, Ingrid Gould, (2000). "Is Segregation Bad for Your Health? The Case of Low Birth Weight," *Brookings-Wharton Papers on Urban Affairs*, 1: 203–238.

Ellison, Glenn and Edward L. Glaeser, (1999). "The Geographic Concentration of Industry: Does Natural Advantage Explain Agglomeration?" *American Economic Review*, 89, 2: 311–16.

Ellison, Glenn, Edward L. Glaeser and William R. Kerr, (2010). "What Causes Industry Agglomeration? Evidence from Coagglomeration Patterns," *American Economic Review*, 100, 3, June: 1195–1213.

Fairbanks, Robert, (2014). "The Illinois Reentry Imperative: Sheriden Correctional Center as National Model." Available at www.ssa.uchicago.edu/end-mass-incarceration (last accessed February 1, 2015).

Feenstra, Robert C., James R. Markusen and Andrew K. Rose, (2001). "Using the Gravity Equation to Differentiate among Alternative Theories of Trade," *The Canadian Journal of Economics*, 34, 2, May: 430–447.

Ferguson, Niall, (2011). *The West and the Rest*, London: Penguin.

Flatters, Frank, Vernon Henderson and Peter Mieszkowski, (1974). "Public Goods, Efficiency, and Regional Fiscal Equalization," *Journal of Public Economics*, 3, 2, May: 99–112.

Flint, Anthony, (2009). *Wrestling with Moses: How Jane Jacobs Took on New York's Master Builder and Transformed the American City*, New York: Random House.

Forrester, Jay Wright, (1969). *Urban Dynamics*, Cambridge: MIT Press.

Forslid, Rikard and Gianmarco I.P. Ottaviano, (2003). "An Analytically Solvable Core-periphery Model," *Journal of Economic Geography*, 3: 229–240.

Fujita, Masahisa and Tomoya Mori, (1996). "The Role of Ports in the Making of Major Cities: Self-Agglomeration and Hub-Effect," *Journal of Development Economics*, 49, 1, April: 93–120.

Fujita, M. and H. Ogawa, (1982). "Multiple Equilibria and Structural Transition of Non-monocentric Urban Configurations," *Regional Science and Urban Economics*, 12: 161–96.

Gabaix, Xavier, (1999). "Zipf's Law for Cities: An Explanation," *Quarterly Journal of Economics*, 114, 3: 739–767.

Gabriel, Stuart A. and Stuart S. Rosenthal, (2004). "Quality of the Business Environment Versus Quality of Life: Do Firms and Households Like the Same Cities?" *Review of Economics and Statistics*, 86, 1, February: 438–444.

Gan, Li and Qinghua Zhang, (2006). "The Thick Market Effect of Local Unemployment Rate Fluctuations," *Journal of Econometrics*, 133: 127–152.

Gilmore, Jason, (2009). "The 2008 Canadian Immigrant Labour Market: Analysis of Quality of Employment," Ottawa: Statistics Canada.

Glaeser, Edward L., (1998). "Are Cities Dying?" *Journal of Economic Perspectives*, 12, 2, Spring: 139–60.

Glaeser, Edward L., editor, (2010). *Agglomeration Economics*, Chicago: University of Chicago Press.

Glaeser, Edward L., (2011). *Triumph of the City: How Our Greatest Invention Makes Us Richer, Smarter, Greener, Healthier and Happier*, New York: Penguin Books.

Glaeser, Edward L., (2013). "A Nation of Gamblers: Real Estate Speculation and American History," *American Economic Review*, 103, 3: 1–42.

Glaeser, Edward L. and Bruce Sacerdote, (1999). "Why is There More Crime in Cities?" *Journal of Political Economy*, 107, S6, December: S225–S258.

Glaeser, Edward L. and David Mare, (2001). "Cities and Skills," *Journal of Labor Economics*, 19: 316–342.

Glaeser, Edward L. and Jesse M. Shapiro, (2003). "The Benefits of the Home Mortgage Interest Deduction," in *Tax Policy and the Economy*, edited by James M. Poterba, NBER, Cambridge: MIT Press, 37–82.

Glaeser, Edward L. and Janet E. Kohlhase, (2004). "Cities, Regions and the Decline of Transport Costs," *Papers in Regional Science*, 83: 197–228.

Glaeser, Edward L. and Matthew E. Kahn, (2004). "Sprawl and Urban Growth," in *Handbook of Regional and Urban Economics*, edited by J. V. Henderson and J. F. Thisse, New York: Elsevier, Volume 4, Chapter 56, pp. 2481–2527.

Glaeser, Edward L. and Joseph Gyourko, (2005). "Urban Decline and Durable Housing," *Journal of Political Economy*, 113, 2, April: 345–375.

Glaeser, Edward L. and Giacomo A.M. Ponzetto, (2010). "Did the Death of Distance Hurt Detroit and Help New York?" in *Agglomeration Economics*, edited by Edward L. Glaeser, Chicago: University of Chicago Press, Chapter 10.

Glaeser, Edward L. and Todd Sinai, editors, (2012). *Housing and the Financial Crisis*, Chicago: University of Chicago Press.

Glaeser, E. L., D. Laibson and B. Sacerdote, (2002). "An Economic Approach To Social Capital," *Economic Journal*, 112, 483, November: 437–458.

Glaeser, Edward L., J. Gyourko and R.E. Saks, (2007). "Why Have House Prices Gone Up?" *American Economic Review, Paper and Proceedings*, 95, 2: 329–333.

Glaeser, Edward L., Joshua Gottlieb and Joseph Gyourko, (2010). "Can Easy Credit Explain the Housing Price Bubble?" NBER Working Paper No. 16230.

Glaeser, Edward L., Joshua D. Gottlieb and Oren Ziv, (2014). "Unhappy Cities," NBER Working Paper 20291.

Glennon, Robert, (2009). *Unquenchable: America's Water Crisis and What To Do About It*, Washington: Island Press/Shearwater Books.

Greenberg, Ken, (2011). *Walking Home*, Toronto: Random House Canada.

Guerrieri, Veronica, Daniel Hartley and Erik Hurst, (2010). "Endogenous Gentrification and Housing Price Dynamics," Working Paper No. 10-08, July, 2010, Cleveland Federal Reserve.

Hamilton, Bruce W., (1982). "Wasteful Commuting," *Journal of Political Economy*, 90: 1035–1058.

Hanushek, Eric, John Kain and Steven Rivkin, (2002). "New Evidence about Brown vs Board of Education: The Complex Effects of School Racial Composition on Achievement," NBER Working Paper No. 8741.

Harris, John R. and Michael P. Todaro, (1970). "Migration, Unemployment and Development: A Two-Sector Analysis," *American Economic Review*, 60, 1: 126–142.

Hartwick, John M., (1972). "The Gravity Hypothesis and Transportation Cost Minimization," *Regional and Urban Economics*, 2, 3, October: 297–308.

Hartwick, John M., (1976). "Intermediate Goods and the Spatial Integration of Land Uses," *Regional Science and Urban Economics*, 6, 2, May: 127–145.

Hartwick, John M., (2010). "Encephalization and Division of Labor By Early Humans," *Journal of Bioeconomics*, 12, 2: 77–100.

Hartwick, John M. and Philip G. Hartwick, (1974). "Efficient Resource Allocation in Multinucleated City with Intermediate Goods," *Quarterly Journal of Economics*, 87, May: 340–352.

Haugen, Gary A. and Victor Boutros, (2014). *The Locust Effect: Why the End of Poverty Requires the End of Violence*, New York: Oxford University Press.

Haurin, Donald R., (1980). "The Regional Distribution of Population, Migration, and Climate," *The Quarterly Journal of Economics*, 95, 2: 293–308.

Head, Allen and Huw Lloyd-Ellis, (2012). "Housing Liquidity, Mobility, and the Labour Market," *Review of Economic Studies*, 79, 4: 1271–1307.

Head, Allen, Huw Lloyd-Ellis and Hongfei Sun, (2014). "Search, Liquidity, and the Dynamics of Home Prices and Construction," *American Economic Review*, 104, 4, April: 1172–1210.

Helsley, R. and W. Strange, (1990). "Matching and Agglomeration Economies in a System of Cities," *Regional Science and Urban Economics*, 20, September: 189–212.

Henderson, J. Vernon, Adam Storeygard and David N. Weil, (2012). "Measuring Economic Growth from Outer Space," *American Economic Review*, 102, 2, April: 994–1028.

Hochman, Oded and David Pines, (1972). "Note on Land Use in a Long Narrow City," *Journal of Economic Theory*, 5, 3: 540–541.

Hoff, K. and A. Sen, (2005). "Homeownership, Community Interactions and Segregation," *American Economic Review*, 95, 4: 1167–89.

Hofmeister, Heather, (2005). "Geographic Mobility of Couples in the United States: Relocation and Commuting," *Zeitschrift-fuer-Familienforschung*, 17 Heft 2, 2005–2: 115–128.

Holmes, Thomas J. and Sanghoon Lee, (2010). "Cities as Six-by-six Mile Squares: Zipf's Law?" in *Agglomeration Economics*, edited by Edward L. Glaeser, Chicago: University of Chicago Press, Chapter 3.

Hotelling, Harold, (1929). "Stability in Competition," *Economic Journal*, 39: 41–57.

Hulchanski, David, (2007). "The Three Cities Within Toronto: Income Polarization Among Toronto's Neighbourhoods, 1970–2005," University of Toronto: Cities Center.

Jacobs, Jane, (1992) [1961]. *The Death and Life of Great American Cities*, New York: Vintage Books.

Jones, Eric L., (2010). *Locating the Industrial Revolution: Inducement and Response*, Singapore: World Scientific.

Kahn, Matthew E., (1993). "A Revealed Preference Approach for Ranking City Quality of Life," Discussion Paper No. 669, Columbia University, Department of Economics, October.

Kahn, Matthew E., (2010). "New Evidence on Trends in the Cost of Urban Agglomeration," in *Agglomeration Economics*, edited by Edward L. Glaeser, Chicago: University of Chicago Press, Chapter 11.

Kasarda, John and Greg Lindsay, (2011). *Aerotropolis: The Way We'll Live Next*, New York: Farrar, Straus & Giroux.

Kelling, George L. and William H. Sousa, (2002). "Policing Does Matter," *City Journal*, Winter.

Kennecott, Philip, (2013). "America's Orchestras are in Crisis." Available at www.newrepublic.com/article/114221/orchestras-crisis-outreach-ruining-them (last accessed August 25, 2014).

Kerr, William R., (2010). "The Agglomeration of US Ethnic Inventors," in *Agglomeration Economics*, edited by Edward L. Glaeser, Chicago: University of Chicago Press, Chapter 8.

Kohn, Kari, (2013). "Financing Infrastructure and Services through Land Value Capture," Urbanization Project, New York University.

Kolko, Jed, (2010). "Urbanization, Agglomeration and Coagglomeration of Service Industries," in *Agglomeration Economics*, edited by Edward L. Glaeser, Chicago: University of Chicago Press, Chapter 5.

Koopmans, Tjalling C. and Martin Beckmann, (1957). "Assignment Problems and the Location of Economic Activities," *Econometrica*, 25, 1: 53–76.

Krugman, Paul, (1991a). *Geography and Trade*, Cambridge, Massachusetts: MIT Press.

Krugman, Paul, (1991b). "Increasing Returns and Economic Geography," *Journal of Political Economy*, 99: 483–499.

Krugman, Paul, (1997). *Development, Geography and Economic Theory*, Cambridge, Massachusetts: MIT Press.

Krugman, Paul and R. Livas Elizondo, (1996). "Trade Policy and the Third World Metropolis," *Journal of Development Economics*, 49: 137–150.

Krugman, Paul and Anthony J. Venables, (1996). "Integration, Specialization and Adjustment," *European Economic Review*, 40: 959–967.

Landa, Janet T., (1981). "A Theory of the Ethnically Homogeneous Middleman," *The Journal of Legal Studies*, 10, June: 348–62.

Leamer, Edward E., (2007). "Housing IS the Business Cycle," NBER Working Paper No. 13428.

LeDuff, Charlie, (2013). *Detroit, An American Autopsy*, New York: Penguin Press.

Levinson, Marc, (2008). *The Box: How the Shipping Container Made the World Smaller and the World Economy Bigger*, Princeton, NJ: Princeton University Press.

Levitt, Steven D., (1996). "The Effect of Prison Population Size on Crime Rates: Evidence from Prison Overcrowding Litigation," *Quarterly Journal of Economics*, 111, May: 319–52.

Levitt, Steven D., (1997). "Using Electoral Cycles in Police Hiring to Estimate the Effect of Police on Crime," *American Economic Review*, 87, June: 270–290.

Losch, August, (1954) [1940]. *The Economics of Location*, translated by William. H. Woglom, New Haven: Yale University Press.

Lowrey, Annie, (2014). "Bluegrass-State Blues," *The New York Times Magazine*, June 29: 13–15.

Lucas, Robert E. Jr, (2004). "Life Earnings and Rural-Urban Migration," *Journal of Political Economy*, 112, 1: S29–S59.

Lucas, Robert E. Jr and Esteban Rossi-Hansberg, (2002). "On the Internal Structure of Cities," *Econometrica*, 70, 4, July: 1445–1475.

McFadden, Daniel, (1974a). "Conditional Logit Analysis of Qualitative Choice Behavior," in *Frontiers in Econometrics*, edited by Paul Zarembka, New York: Academic Press: 105–42.

McFadden, Daniel, (1974b). "Measurement of Urban Travel Demand," *Journal of Public Economics*, 3: 303–328.

McGuire, Martin C. and Mancur L. Olson, Jr, (1996). "The Economics of Autocracy and Majority Rule," *Journal of Economic Literature*, 34: 72–96.

Marshall, Alfred, (1920). *Principles of Economics*, London: Macmillan.

Marx, Benjamin, Thomas Stoker and Tavneet Suri, (2013). "The Economics of Slums in the Developing World," *Journal of Economic Perspectives*, 27, 4: 187–210.

Miezkowski, Peter and Mahlon R. Straszheim, editors, (1979). *Current Issues in Urban Economics*, Baltimore: The Johns Hopkins University Press.

Mills, Edwin S., (1972a). *Urban Economics*, Glenview, Illinois: Scott Foresman.

Mills, Edwin S., (1972b). "Markets and Efficient Resource Allocation in Urban Areas," *Swedish Journal of Economics*, 74: 100–113.

Mills, Edwin S., (1999). "Truly Smart 'Smart Growth'," *Illinois Real Estate Letter*, University of Illinois at Urbana-Champaign, Summer: 1–7.

Mills, Edwin S. and Bruce Hamilton, (1994) *Urban Economics*, 5th edition, New York: Harper-Collins.

Miran, Atif and Amir Sufi, (2014). *House of Debt*, Chicago: University of Chicago Press.

Mohring, H. and M. Harwitz, (1962). *Highway Benefits: An Analytical Framework*, Evanston: Northwestern University Press.

Moretti, Enrico, (2012). *The New Geography of Jobs*, Boston: Houghton Mifflin Harcourt.

Moretti, Enrico, (2014). "Are Cities the New Growth Escalator?" World Bank Policy Research Paper No. WPS 6881.

Mottowildo, S.J., J.S. Packard and M.R. Manning, (1986). "Occupational Stress: Its Causes and Consequences for Job Performance," *Journal of Applied Psychology*, 71: 618–29.

Murdie, Robert A., (2008). "Diversity and Concentration in Canadian Immigration Trends in Toronto, Montreal and Vancouver, 1971–2006," University of Toronto, Centre for Urban and Community Studies.

Nordhaus, William D., (2006). "Geography and Macroeconomics: New Data and New Findings," *PNAS*, 103, 10, March: 3510–3517.

North, Douglass C. and Barry R. Weingast, (1989). "The Evolution of Institutions Governing Public Choice in 17th Century England," *Journal of Economic History*, 5, November: 172–200.

OECD, (2010). *OECD Territorial Reviews: Toronto, Canada*, Paris: OECD.

O'Flaherty, Brendan, (2005). *City Economics*, Cambridge, Massachusetts: Harvard University Press.

Oreopoulos, Philip, (2009). "Why Do Skilled Immigrants Struggle in the Labor Market? A Field Experiment with Six Thousand Resumes," NBER Working Paper No. 15036.

Osland, Liv, (2010). "An Application of Spatial Econometrics in Relation to Hedonic House Price Modelling." Available at https://www.google.ca/search?q=liv+osland+2010&ie=utf-8&oe=utf-8&gws_rd=cr&ei=8Iu2VNSWHIWkyQSV0oLwCA (last accessed January 2015).

O'Sullivan, Arthur, (2009). *Urban Economics*, 7th edition, New York: McGraw-Hill.

Overman, Henry G. and Diego Puga, (2010). "Labor Pooling as a Source of Agglomeration: An Empirical Investigation," in *Agglomeration Economics*, edited by Edward L. Glaeser, Chicago: University of Chicago Press, Chapter 4.

Parry, Ian W.H., (2003). "How Large are the Welfare Losses from Tax Competition?" *Journal of Urban Economics*, 54: 39–60.

Perlman, Janice E., (2005). "The Myth of Marginality Revisited: The Case of Favelas in Rio de Janeiro, 1969–2003," in *Becoming Global and the New Poverty of Cities*, edited by Lisa M. Hanley, Ruble A. Blair and Joseph S. Tulchin, Washington, DC: Comparative Urban Studies Project, Woodrow Wilson School, Chapter 1.

Petty, William, (1686). *An Essay Concerning the Multiplication of Mankind*, reproduced by EEBO Editions, ProQuest, January 17, 2011.

Pisarski, Alan E., (2006). *Commuting in America III: The Third National Report on Commuting Patterns and Trends*, Washington, DC: Transportation Research Board, TCRP-NCHRP.

Platt, Rutherford H., (2014). *Reclaiming American Cities: The Struggle for People, Place and Nature since 1900*, Boston: University of Massachusetts Press.

Pomeranz, Kenneth and Steven Topik, (2006). *The World that Trade Created: Society, Culture, and the World Economy, 1400 to the Present*, Armonk: M.E. Sharpe.

Quandt, Richard E., (1970). *The Demand For Travel: Theory and Measurement*, Lexington, MA: Heath Lexington Books.

Quigley, John M. and Steven Raphael, (2004). "Is Housing Unaffordable? Why Isn't It More Affordable?" *The Journal of Economic Perspectives*, 18, 1, Winter: 191–214.

Roback, Jennifer, (1982). "Wages, Rents, and the Quality of Life," *Journal of Political Economy*, 90, 6, December: 1257–78.

Robson, Arthur J., (1982). "Comparative Statics of the Market for a Consumer Durable with an Age/Quality Structure: A Reprise of Models of Urban Structure," *Journal of Urban Economics*, 11: 169–79.

Rosen, Harvey S., (1988). *Public Finance*, 2nd edition, Homewood, Illinois: Irwin.

Rosen, Sherwin, (1974). "Hedonic Prices and Implicit Markets: Product Differentiation in Pure Competition," *Journal of Political Economy*, 72: 34–55.

Rosen, Sherwin, (1979). "Wage-based Indexes of Urban Quality of Life," in *Issues in Urban Economics*, edited by Peter Mieszkowski and Mahlon Straszheim, Baltimore: Johns Hopkins University Press.

Rosenthal, Stuart S. and William C. Strange, (2007). "The Micro-Empirics of Agglomeration Economies," in *A Companion to Urban Economics*, edited by Richard J. Arnott and Daniel P. McMillen, New York: Blackwell, Chapter 1.

Rosenthal, Stuart S. and William C. Strange, (2010). "Small Establishments/Big Effects: Agglomeration, Industrial Organization and Entrepreneurship," in *Agglomeration Economics*, edited by Edward L. Glaeser, Chicago: University of Chicago Press, Chapter 9.

Rossi-Hansberg, Esteban, (2004). "Optimal Urban Land Use and Zoning," *Review of Economic Dynamics*, 7, 69–106.

Rozenfeld, Hernán D., Diego Rybski, Xavier Gabaix and Hernán A. Makse, (2011). "The Area and Population of Cities: New Insights from a Different Perspective on Cities," *American Economic Review*, 101, 5: 2205–25.

Sampson, Robert J., Stephen W. Raudenbush and Earls Felton, (1997). "Neighborhoods and Violent Crime: A Multilevel Study of Collective Efficacy," *Science*, 227, August 15: 918–24.

Samuelson, Paul A., (1954). "The Pure Theory of Public Expenditure," *The Review of Economics and Statistics*, 36, 4, November: 387–389.

Saunders, Doug, (2010). *Arrival City: How the Largest Migration in History is Shaping our World*, London: William Heinemann.

Schweizer, Urs, Pravin Varaiya and John Hartwick, (1976). "General Equilibrium and Location Theory," *Journal of Urban Economics*, 3: 285–303.

Sedlak, David, (2014). *Water 4.0: The Past, Present and Future of the World's Most Vital Resource*, New Haven: Yale University Press.

Shoag, Daniel and Stan Veuger, (2014). "Uncertainty and the Geography of the Great Recession." Available at http://web.stanford.edu/group/sssl/cgi-bin/wordpress/wp-content/uploads/2014/03/MasterDraft.pdf (last accessed January 2015).

Siegfried, John J. and Andrew Zimbalist, (2000). "The Economics of Sports Facilities and Their Communities," *Journal of Economic Perspectives*, 14, 3, Summer: 95–114.

Small, Kenneth A. and Shunfeng Song, (1992). "'Wasteful' Commuting: A Resolution," *Journal of Political Economy*, 100: 888–898.

Small, Kenneth A. and Erik T. Verhoef, (2007). *The Economics of Urban Transportation*, Abingdon: Routledge.

Smith, Robert C., (2003). *Encyclopedia of African American Politics*, New York: Facts on File: 308–310.

Smithies, Arthur, (1941). "Optimum Location in Spatial Competiton," *Journal of Political Economy*, 41: 423–39.

Solow, Robert M., (1956). "A Contribution to the Theory of Economic Growth," *The Quarterly Journal of Economics*, 70, 1, February: 65–94.

Solow, Robert M. and William S. Vickrey, (1971). "Land Use in a Long Narrow City," *Journal of Economic Theory*, 3, 4: 430–447.

Stiglitz, Joseph E., (2014). "Reforming China's State-Market Balance," *Project Syndicate*, April 2.

Sweeney, James L., (1974). "A Commodity Hierarchy Model of the Rental Housing Market," *Journal of Urban Economics*, 1, 3, 288–323.

Tiebout, Charles M., (1956). "A Pure Theory of Local Expenditures," *The Journal of Political Economy*, 64, April: 160–164.

Tobin, James, (1958). "Estimation of Relationships for Limited Dependent Variables," *Econometrica*, 26, 1, January: 24–36.

Tomer, Adie, Robert Puentes and Joseph Kane, (2013). "Metro-to-Metro: Global and Domestic Goods Trade in Metropolitan America," Metropolitan Policy Program at Brookings: Washington, DC.

Transport Canada, (2006). *Cost of Urban Congestion in Canada.*

United Nations Population Division, (2008). "An Overview of Urbanization, Internal Migration, Population Distribution and Development in the World," New York: United Nations Secretariat, Department of Economic and Social Affairs, UN/POP/EGM-URB/2008/01.

Van Nieuwerburgh, Stijn and Pierre-Olivier Weill, (2010). "Why Has House Price Dispersion Gone Up?" *Review of Economic Studies*, 77: 1567–1606.

Van Noorden, Richard, (2010). "Building the Best Cities for Science," *Nature*, 469, October 21: 906–908.

Varian, Hal R., (1992). *Microeconomic Analysis*, 3rd edition, New York: Norton.

Vernon, Raymond, (1972). "External Economies," in *Readings in Urban Economics*, by M. Edel and J. Rothenberg, New York: Macmillan.

Vickrey, William S., (1969). "Congestion Theory and Transport Investment," *American Economic Review*, 59, 2, May: 251–60.

von Thunen, Johann Heinrich, (1826). *Der isolierte Staat* [The Isolated State].

Wheaton, William, (1977). "Income and Urban Residence: An Analysis of Consumer Demand for Location," *American Economic Review*, 67, 4: 620–31.

Wijkander, Hans, (2003). "Comment on Richard Arnott: Tenancy Rent Control," *Swedish Economic Policy Review*, 10: 127–133.

Wildasin, David E., (1986). *Urban Public Finance*, Chur, Switzerland: Harwood.

Wilson, John Douglas, (1999). "Tax Competition," *National Tax Journal*, June: 269–394.

Winston, Clifford, (2013). "On the Performance of the US Transportation System," *Journal of Economic Literature*, LI, September: 771–824.

Index

For Product Safety Concerns and Information please contact our EU representative GPSR@taylorandfrancis.com
Taylor & Francis Verlag GmbH, Kaufingerstraße 24, 80331 München, Germany

www.ingramcontent.com/pod-product-compliance
Lightning Source LLC
LaVergne TN
LVHW080806011026
849160LV00015B/1548

* 9 7 8 1 1 3 8 8 8 5 6 4 6 *